MASTERPIECES
OF
AMERICAN
INDIAN
LITERATURE

MASTERPIECES

OF

AMERICAN INDIAN LITERATURE

EDITED AND
WITH AN INTRODUCTION BY

Willis G. Regier

MJF Books
NEW YORK

Published by MJF Books
Fine Communications
POB 0930
Planetarium Station
New York, NY 10024-0540

Library of Congress Catalog Card Number 93-79556
ISBN 1-56731-035-4

Manufactured in the United States of America

MJF Books and the MJF colophon are trademarks of Fine Creative Media, Inc.

10 9 8 7 6 5 4 3 2 1

Contents

v

Preface

The five works collected here are parts of a long and passionate testimony about American Indian cultures as related by Indians themselves. For too long, images of American Indians have been formed by white authors—James Fenimore Cooper's *Last of the Mohicans*, for example, or Henry Wadsworth Longfellow's *Song of Hiawatha*—or by TV and movies. This anthology seeks to restore balance and perspective. It is meant to begin a library, not complete one.

In the 1980s a "Native American Renaissance" was proclaimed. An outpouring of superb new Indian writing attracted readers from coast to coast. More than a rediscovered sentiment or point of view, this renaissance renewed a long literary tradition. It returned America's attention to primary questions, to beginnings, to first Americans.

It is with some misgivings that this anthology uses the word "Indian." The term has provoked protests; it's a swarm of confusions. It mixes up the peoples of India (or Bharat, to use India's name for India) and America (or Turtle Island). It is an imposed term, never the name of any Indian tribe. The term blurs differences between tribes and encourages stereotypes. But "Indian" is used anyway. It is the term used in the works collected here; these authors enrich it. The Blackfoot author Long Standing Bear Chief takes up the term in his *Ni-Kso-Ko-wa*: "The word *Indian* . . . is an anglicized version of *Indios* . . . *Indios* means with God. . . . I cannot be insulted by someone calling me an Indian, because he is saying I am with God."

George Copway was an Ojibway missionary, one of the first authors from a tribe that can also boast Louise Erdrich, Basil Johnston, and Gerald Vizenor. Mourning Dove, an Okanogan, is the author of *Cogewea*, one of the first novels to be written by an American Indian woman. Charles Eastman was Santee, Zitkala-Sa was Yankton, and Black Elk was Oglala, three different divisions of the Sioux. Other Sioux authors have sustained and built on their heritage: Luther Standing Bear, Ella Deloria, Vine Deloria, Jr., Elizabeth Cook-Lynn.

We are fortunate to have them. Mayan libraries and Aztec codices were incinerated in the name of Christianity; in the name of civilization, Indian children were taken from their parents and punished if they tried to be Indian. Loss gapes like a canyon through American

Indian literature. Yet no sooner were there gaps than Indian literature crossed them.

All the works collected here are complete and unabridged. All are in English, which is but one language of Indian literature; other works are written in Arikara, Hopi, Cherokee, Lakota, Nahuatl, Spanish, and French. Indian literature once belonged only to Indians; now the world wants it. Every human topic converges in its pages: identity, family, community, caste, gender, nature, the future, the past, solitude, duty, treaty, betrayal, leadership, war, apocalypse.

These five authors have much to say and many to teach.

—WILLIS G. REGIER
University of Nebraska-Lincoln

Introduction

"Thank heaven, I am an Indian," George Copway told the Pennsylvania legislature in 1849. Though he placed his thanks in heaven, he put his hopes in the good people of Harrisburg, Boston, Charleston, Philadelphia, New York, Norfolk, Washington, D.C., and other centers of influence. He took his sermons to church, saloon, drawing room, and legislative chamber. Indians could tell the nation much, he said, if only the nation would listen. Instead, "the white men have been like the greedy lion, pouncing upon and devouring its prey. They have driven us from our nation, our homes, and possessions; compelled us to seek a refuge in Missouri, among strangers and wild beasts; and will, perhaps, soon compel us to scale the Rocky Mountains; and, for aught I can tell, we may be driven to the Pacific Ocean, there to find our graves. My only trust is, that there is a just God."

"Thank heaven, I am an Indian," Copway said. Soon, perhaps, heaven would be the only place left for Indians.

Copway sought to stir the nation's conscience about one catastrophe at a time when another seethed. The scandal of slavery and threats of civil war eclipsed everything else. Indians were outnumbered, overpowered, cheated, disenfranchised, excluded, insulted, bullied, and infected by the advance of civilization, but Copway could still thank heaven for being Indian. He was free to travel, free to speak, and free to publish his speeches and autobiography.

The heaven he thanked was a Christian heaven. Copway first learned the traditions of the Ojibways, then the traditions of the Methodist Church. He asked the ministers of North and South to "preach and practise a pure Christianity." He was one of a long line of Indian authors—Peter Jones, Black Elk, Fool's Crow, Joseph Dudley—who took long looks at religion.

Copway's *Kah-ge-ga-gah-bowh* appeals to heaven. Its concerns keep close to the land. In his lectures up and down the Atlantic Coast, Copway asked the United States for land—one hundred and fifty miles square. No preacher of assimilation, he proposed that a reservation be set aside, "one hundred miles north of Council Bluffs," with a governor "who shall be a white man." The Indians of the South had

been removed to Indian Territory; he proposed another for the Indians of the Old Northwest.

Indian reservations continue to change size and character. Fights over their fishing, hunting, and water rights still make headlines. Hardly quaint tourist sites or weekend casinos, reservations are specifically Indian places. From them has come great literature. Now readers in great numbers come, too. Let the authors collected here attract more readers still.

George Copway
Kah-ge-ga-gah-bowh
(1818–1869)

When first published in 1847, Copway's *The Life, History, and Travels of Kah-ge-ga-gah-bowh* was so successful that he published an enlarged edition as *The Life, Letters and Speeches of Kah-ge-ga-gah-bowh* in 1850. Superficially an account of his conversion to Christianity and of his wish to convert more "degraded and benighted Indians," Copway's book is a record of internal conflict and divided hope. Copway makes the usual confession of humility, claiming to be "a mere worm of the dust," but he is obviously proud of Ojibway history. He reminds readers that the Ojibways were undefeated in war, victors over Hurons, Iroquois, and Sioux. Prior to citing standard Biblical verses he reverently relays traditional wisdom learned from his father. Although seeking to convert other Indians to Christianity, he wants to spend more time with elder Ojibways to learn the ancient ways. With as much sorrow as piety, he relates that the world of the Indian has been confiscated and ruined by white conquest, leaving Indians only the other world promised by Christianity.

Copway saw clearly that most Americans wanted Indian lands, not Indians. He saw the multiple dangers before Indians—warfare, of course, and also alcohol, poverty, and disease. He was aware of Indian wars against other Indians and saw how they could be manipulated by whites. His book was part of a widespread effort by some Indians and certain Christian churches to save not only Indian souls, but also Indian lands and freedoms.

For a few years heaven blessed Copway with fame and famous friends, including (briefly) Washington Irving and Henry Wadsworth

Longfellow. Copway enjoyed celebrity and used his autobiography to promote it. According to Donald Smith, Copway's biographer, Copway was an early example of an Indian who collapsed under the stress of trying to represent all Indians. He falsely claimed to be an Ojibway chief. He had barely won acceptance before he fell into steep decline, struck by tragedy and failure. Three of his four children died in the few months between August 1849 and January 1850. His novelty wore off, his enterprises failed, his friends defected, and he moved from place to place and job to job. He died in 1869, shortly after converting to the Roman Catholic Church.

Charles Eastman
Ohiyesa
(1858–1939)

Copway worked to save Indians with Christianity. Charles Eastman sought to demonstrate that Indian souls were already well attuned to the sacred. *The Soul of the Indian*, first published in 1911, was addressed to a country that had forced most Indians onto reservations. Barely four years earlier, the last hopes for a distinct Indian state vanished when Oklahoma entered the Union. As usual, the federal government stupidly wondered whether Indians could take care of themselves.

Eastman was one of the last generation of Santee Sioux to grow up in the traditional manner, but those traditions were under siege. Provoked by broken promises, the 1862 Sioux Uprising sought to expel settlers from Minnesota, but the poorly armed Sioux were no match against federal troops. In retribution for the revolt, the federal government deprived the Santees of their Minnesota reservation and removed them to Dakota Territory. Thirty-eight Santees were executed by hanging; Many Lightnings, Eastman's father, was said to be among them.

Called Ohiyesa ("the Winner") since childhood, Eastman earned the name many times throughout his long life. At fifteen, he was astonished by the return of his father, who had been imprisoned rather than executed. Many Lightnings had changed his name to Jacob Eastman and had converted to Presbyterianism. Ohiyesa joined his father on a 160-acre farm near Flandreau, South Dakota, and began to

attend school. At home his father pushed him to adapt to the white world and his grandmother encouraged him to resist. He became adept at moving between the two worlds.

Showing ever-increasing academic ability, Eastman attended Beloit College, Knox College, then Dartmouth College, where he graduated with honors in 1887. Determined to become a physician, he studied medicine and surgery at Boston University. In 1890 he accepted a commission as a physician for the Pine Ridge Agency. He arrived there in November. Within weeks bliss and tragedy were his. On Christmas day he announced his engagement to Elaine Goodale, Supervisor of Education for the Dakotas. On December 29, 153 Indian men, women, and children were massacred at Wounded Knee Creek, South Dakota, a few miles from Pine Ridge. Eastman cared as he could for the wounded and dying, reminded again of the terrifying risks of being an Indian surrounded by armed whites.

For the rest of his life he worked to protect the Sioux from further attacks, cheating schemes, legal maneuvers, and popular misunderstandings. With the help of Elaine he wrote a sequence of books that describe the acculturation of the Sioux to white ways and defend the culture of the Sioux themselves.

Eastman died of a heart attack on January 8, 1939.

Gertrude Bonnin
Zitkala-Ša
(1876–1938)

White perceptions have squeezed Indian men into crude clichés: warrior, chief, and medicine man. American Indian women have been even further underestimated and misunderstood. A generation younger than Eastman, Zitkala-Ša was among the first American Indian women to write for the American public and correct misconceptions. No mere entertainment, her work shows the power, intelligence, and courage of Indian women.

Despite the simplicity of its title, *American Indian Stories* (1921) is much more than a collection of tales. The stories are knit by accounts from Zitkala-Ša's own life. Unified by her perspective as a Yankton Dakota, they are rooted in her affection for her people and especially for her mother. "These were my mother's pride,—my wild freedom

and overflowing spirits. She taught me no fear save that of intruding myself upon others."

Zitkala-Ša was a prodigy in two arts: violin and oratory. Music and speech combine in *American Indian Stories*. In a book full of emotion, anger and unhappiness have their turn. The book begins with mother's tears. A keen observer, Zitkala-Ša saw both the sweeping changes occurring among the Sioux and the sharp details that pierced the heart. Seeing what whites had done to the Dakota people and to themselves she wrote, "few there are who have paused to question whether real life or long-lasting death lies beneath this semblance of civilization." She was one of those few.

Christine Quintasket
Mourning Dove, Humishuma
(1885?-1936)

Wily and resilient, the coyote has long been a favorite character in American Indian literature. His tricks and his fatal mistakes, his repeated resurrections and incorrigible vanity, his appetites and resourcefulness have made him an ideal symbol of all that is ambiguous in power or desire. Mourning Dove's collection includes delightful retellings of the coyote stories told by the Salish Indians of North-central Washington.

Mourning Dove's own Foreword should not be skipped: it reminds all readers that these stories were first told, not written, and were told by great storytellers. Her comments emphasize that what is now enjoyed as Indian literature was once performed with wonderful art.

Mourning Dove's works also illustrate a problem that has been widely discussed: the role of white collaborators in the publication of Indian works. Copway probably relied on an anonymous assistant to polish his English. Mourning Dove's works were heavily edited by Lucullus V. McWhorter and Heister Dean Guie. Mourning Dove angrily objected, but the editors had their way, condensing the tales by cutting out details that might offend white readers.

Charles and Elaine Goodale Eastman collaborated successfully on several books. Mourning Dove and McWhorter published only two: these stories and her novel, *Cogewea* (1927). One of the most successful of all collaborations soon followed when Black Elk met John G. Neihardt.

Black Elk
Hehaka Sapa
(1863–1950)

For a multitude of reasons *Black Elk Speaks* has become a touchstone of American Indian literature. Black Elk matured in the last years of Lakota independence, felt their glory and tribulation, participated in numerous key events, and left his biography as a testament to all that had been stolen, ruined, or lost—or narrowly saved by the grasp of memory.

Barely a teenager, Black Elk took part in the Battle of the Rosebud and the Battle of Little Big Horn (June 17 and 25, 1876). For the next four years, Black Elk and other Lakota groups continued to flee army pursuit, eventually escaping to Canada. In 1881, Black Elk returned to American territory, joining other Lakotas at Pine Ridge Reservation. In 1886 he accompanied Buffalo Bill's Wild West Show in time to travel with it for its performances in England. He returned to Pine Ridge in 1889. The next year was crowded with events. The Ghost Dance began at Pine Ridge, prompting the U. S. Army to fear another Indian war. On December 15, 1890, Sitting Bull was murdered by Indian policemen. Two weeks later, Black Elk witnessed the massacre at Wounded Knee.

The narrative of *Black Elk Speaks* concludes with Wounded Knee, but Black Elk lived much longer. He married twice, fathered four children, and joined the Catholic church, adjusting as he could to reservation life. One other great event awaited him. In 1930, he met John G. Neihardt.

While working on his epic poem of the American West, Neihardt wanted to check the facts about the Sioux wars and the Ghost Dance of 1890. In 1930 Neihardt drove from his home in Missouri to Pine Ridge Reservation in South Dakota to meet Black Elk and other Lakotas. Black Elk and Neihardt quickly became close friends. In May, 1931, Neihardt returned to the reservation with his two daughters, Enid and Hilda, to interview Black Elk at length.

They talked for two weeks, with Benjamin Black Elk, Black Elk's son, as interpreter. Enid served as Neihardt's stenographer. Every word was carefully chosen. Black Elk spoke, his son interpreted as closely as he could, Neihardt suggested wordings for accuracy, Ben Black Elk translated Neihardt's questions into Lakota, and Black Elk

approved or clarified. At some sessions, other Lakota elders also participated in the interviews.

In the middle of the interviews Neihardt was made a member of the tribe. A ceremony and feast were held on May 15, 1931, during which the old men of the tribe gave Neihardt the name Peta Wigmunke, or Flaming Rainbow.

The following year, *Black Elk Speaks* was published. Black Elk's account of events were also woven into *The Song of the Indian Wars* (1935) and *The Song of the Messiah* (1941), the fourth and fifth books of Neihardt's *A Cycle of the West*.

Black Elk Speaks represents another precious portion of the American Indian literary heritage: an Indian narration written down by someone else. Unable to transmit their accounts in English, some Indians had to rely on other men and women to record and translate for them. These collaborations added much to the national literature: stories and legends, songs, herbaria, adages, prayers and ceremonies, tribal histories, ethnographies, and autobiographies. For better or worse the Indians' accounts depended upon the skill, industry, and honesty of their confidantes.

As *Black Elk Speaks* gradually won worldwide attention—it has been translated into Bulgarian, Danish, Dutch, German, Italian, Thai, and other languages—Neihardt was often asked about how the book came to be. In an April 1971 interview with Sally McCluskey, Neihardt responded, *"Black Elk Speaks* is a work of art with two collaborators, the chief one being Black Elk. My function was both creative and editorial. I think he knew the kind of person I was when I came to see him—I am referring to the mystical strain in me and all my work. He said, 'You have been sent so that I may teach you and you receive what I know. It was given to me for men and it is true and it is beautiful and soon I will be under the grass.' And I think he knew I was the tool—no, the medium—he needed for what he wanted to get said. And my attitude toward what he said to me is one of religious obligation. But it is absurd to suppose that the use of the first person singular is not a literary device, by which I mean that Black Elk did not sit and tell his story in chronological order. At times considerable editing was necessary, but it was always worth the editing."

In 1944 Neihardt again interviewed Black Elk about Lakota culture. These interviews became part of Neihardt's 1951 book, *When the Tree Flowered*. Their friendship continued until Black Elk's death on August 19, 1950, at age of 87. Neihardt passed away on November 3, 1973.

The Life of
Kah-ge-ga-gah-bowh

George Copway
(Kah-ge-ga-gah-bowh)

To
The Clergy and Laity
of the
American and British Dominions,
This Brief
History of a Child of The Forest,
and of
His Nation
Is Most Respectfully and Affectionately
Inscribed
by
The Author.

Contents

5

Preface

In presenting my life to the public, I do so with the greatest diffidence, and at the earnest solicitation of numerous friends. I am an Indian, and am well aware of the difficulties I have to encounter to win the favorable notice of the white man. Yet one great object prompts me to persevere, and that is, that I may, in connection with my life, present the *present state* and *prospects* of my poor countrymen—feeling that the friends of humanity may still labor and direct their benevolence to those who were once the lords of the land on which the white man lives—and assist in rescuing them from an untimely and unchristian grave.

I have noticed some of our prominent chiefs now living; the missionaries laboring amongst my people; the extent of the missionary field; and an appeal to all who feel interested in the welfare of the Indian race.

If ever I see the day when my people shall become happy and prosperous, I shall then feel great and lasting pleasure, which will more than repay me for the pain, both of body and mind, which I have endured for the last twelve years. My motto is—"*My poor People.*"

In all my crooked paths, I have endeavored to mean well. I thank my friends for their kind gifts and wishes. Yet still as much, and more, remains to be accomplished.

Pray for us—that *religion* and *science* may lead us on to intelligence and virtue; that we may imitate the good white man, who, like the eagle, builds its nest on the top of some high rock—*science;* that we may educate our children, and turn their minds to God. Help us, O help us to live—and teach us to die a Christian's death, that our spirits may mingle with the blessed above.

<div align="right">KAH-GE-GA-GAH-BOWH</div>

A Word to the Reader

It would be presumptuous in one, who has but recently been brought out of a wild and savage state; and who has since received but three years' schooling, to undertake, without any assistance, to publish to the world a work of any kind. It is but a few years since I began to speak the English language. An unexpected opportunity occurred of submitting my manuscript to a friend, who has kindly corrected all *serious* grammatical errors, leaving the unimportant ones wholly untouched, that my own style may be exhibited as truly as possible. The public and myself are indebted to him for his kind aid, and he has my most sincere thanks. The language, (except in a few short sentences,) the plan, and the arrangement are all my own; and I am wholly responsible for all the statements, and the remaining defects. My work is now accomplished; and I am too well aware of the many faults which are still to be found therein. Little could I imagine, that I should have to contend with so many obstacles. All along, have I felt my great deficiency; and my inadequacy for such an undertaking. I would fain hope, however, that the kind Reader will throw the mantle of charity over errors of every kind. I am a stranger in a strange land! And often, when the sun is sinking in the western sky, I think of my former home; my heart yearns for the loved of other days, and tears flow like the summer rain. How the heart of the wanderer and pilgrim, after long years of absence, beats, and his eyes fill, as he catches a glance at the hills of his nativity, and reflects upon the time when he pressed the lips of a mother, or sister, now cold in death. Should I live, this painful pleasure will yet be mine. *"Blessed be the Lord, who hath helped me hitherto."*

KAH-GE-GA-GAH-BOWH
alias George Copway

July 1847

I

The Christian will no doubt feel for my poor people, when he hears the story of one brought from that unfortunate race called the Indians. The lover of humanity will be glad to see that that once powerful race can be made to enjoy the blessings of life.

What was once impossible—or rather thought to be—is made possible through my experience. I have made many close observations of men, and things around me; but, I regret to say, that I do not think I have made as good use of my opportunities as I might have done. It will be seen that I know but little—yet O how precious *that little!*—I would rather lose my right hand than be deprived of it.

I loved the woods, and the chase. I had the nature for it, and gloried in nothing else. The mind for letters was in me, *but was asleep*, till the dawn of Christianity arose, and awoke the slumbers of the soul into energy and action.

You will see that I served the imaginary gods of my poor blind father. I was out early and late in quest of the favors of the *Mon-e-doos* (spirits,) who, it was said, were numerous—who filled the air! At early dawn I watched the rising of the *palace* of the Great Spirit—*the sun*—who, it was said, made the world!

Early as I can recollect, I was taught that it was the gift of the many spirits to be a good hunter and warrior; and much of my time I devoted in search of their favors. On the mountain top, or along the valley, or the water brook, I searched for some kind intimation from the spirits who made their residence in the noise of the waterfalls.

I dreaded to hear the voice of the angry spirit in the gathering clouds. I looked with anxiety to catch a glimpse of the wings of the Great Spirit, who shrouded himself in rolling white and dark clouds— who, with his wings, fanned the earth, and laid low the tall pines and hemlock in his course—who rode in whirlwinds and tornadoes, and plucked the trees from their woven roots—who chased other gods from his course—who drove the Bad Spirit from the surface of the earth, down to the dark caverns of the deep. Yet he was a kind spirit. My father taught me to call that spirit Ke-sha-mon-e-doo—*Benevolent spirit*—for his ancestors taught him no other name to give to that spirit

11

who made the earth, with all its variety and smiling beauty. His benevolence I saw in the running of the streams, for the animals to quench their thirst and the fishes to live; the fruit of the earth teemed wherever I looked. Every thing I saw smilingly said Ke-sha-mon-e-doo nin-ge-oo-she-ig—*the Benevolent spirit made me.*

Where is he? My father pointed to the sun. What is his will concerning me, and the rest of the Indian race? This was a question that I found no one could answer, until a beam from heaven shone on my pathway, which was very dark, when first I saw that there was a true heaven—not in the far-setting sun, where the Indian anticipated a rest, a home for his spirit—but in the bosom of the Highest.

I view my life like the mariner on the wide ocean, without a compass, in the dark night, as he watches the heavens for the north star, which his eye having discovered, he makes his way amidst surging seas, and tossed by angry billows into the very jaws of death, till he arrives safely anchored at port. I have been tossed with hope and fear in this life; no star-light shone on my way, until the men of God pointed me to a Star in the East, as it rose with all its splendor and glory. It was the Star of Bethlehem. I could now say in the language of the poet—

> "Once on the raging seas I rode,
> The storm was loud, the night was dark;
> The ocean yawned, and rudely blowed
> The wind that tossed my foundering bark."

Yes, I hope to sing some day in the realms of bliss—

> "It was my guide, my light, my all!
> It bade my dark foreboding cease;
> And through the storm and danger's thrall,
> It led me to the port of peace."

I have not the happiness of being able to refer to written records in narrating the history of my forefathers; but I can reveal to the world what has long been laid up in my memory; so that when "I go the way of all the earth," the crooked and singular paths which I have made in the world, may not only be a warning to others, but may inspire them with a trust in God. And not only a warning and a trust, but also that the world may learn that there once lived such a man as Kah-ge-ga-gah-bowh, when they read his griefs and his joys.

My parents were of the Ojebwa nation, who lived on the lake back of Cobourg, on the shores of Lake Ontario, Canada West. The lake was called Rice Lake, where there was a quantity of wild rice, and much game of different kinds, before the whites cleared away the woods, where the deer and the bear then resorted.

My father and mother were taught the religion of their nation. My father became a medicine man in the early part of his life, and always had by him the implements of war, which generally distinguish our head men. He was a good hunter as any in the tribe. Very few brought more furs than he did in the spring. Every spring they returned from their hunting grounds. The Ojebwas each claimed, and claim to this day, hunting grounds, rivers, lakes, and whole districts of country. No one hunted on each other's ground. My father had the northern fork of the river Trent, above Bellmont lake.

My great-grandfather was the first who ventured to settle at Rice Lake, after the Ojebwa nation defeated the Hurons, who once inhabited all the lakes in Western Canada, and who had a large village just on the top of the hill of the Anderson farm, (which was afterwards occupied by the Ojebwas,) and which furnished a magnificent view of the lakes and surrounding country. He was of the *Crane tribe*, i.e., had a crane for totem—*coat of arms*—which now forms the totem of the villagers, excepting those who have since come amongst us from other villages by intermarriage, for there was a law that no one was to marry one of the same totem, for all considered each other as being related. He must have been a daring adventurer—*a warrior*—for no one would have ventured to go and settle down on the land from which they had just driven the Hurons, whom the Ojebwas conquered and reduced, unless he was a great hero. It is said that he lived about the islands of Rice Lake, secreting himself from the enemy for several years, until some others came and joined him, when they formed a settlement on one of the islands. He must have been a great hunter, for this was one of the principal inducements that made him venture there, for there must have been abundance of game of every kind. The Ojebwas are called, here and all around, Massissuagays, because they came from Me-sey Sah-gieng, at the head of Lake Huron, as you go up to Sault St. Marie falls.

Here he lived in jeopardy—with his life in his hand—enduring the unpleasant idea that he lived in the land of bones—*amidst the gloom*, which shrouded the once happy and populous village of the Hurons; here their bones lay broad-cast around his wigwam; where, among

these woods once rang the war cry of the Hurons, echoing along the valley of the river Trent, but whose sinewed arms now laid low, with their badges and arms of war, in one common grave, near the residence of Peter Anderson, Esq. Their graves, forming a hillock, are now all that remain of this once powerful nation. Their bones, gun barrels, tomahawks, war spears, large scalping knives, are yet to be found there. This must have taken place soon after the formation of the settlement in Quebec.

The *Crane tribe* became the sole proprietors of this part of the Ojebwa land; the descendants of this tribe will continue to wear the distinguishing sign; except in a few instances, the chiefs are of this tribe.

My grandfather lived here about this time, and held some friendly intercourse with the whites. My father here learned the manners, customs, and worship of the nation. He, and others, became acquainted with the early settlers, and have ever been friendly with the whites. And I know the day when he used to shake the hand of the white man, and, *very friendly,* the white man would say, *"take some whiskey."* When he saw any hungering for venison, he gave them to eat; and some, in return for his kindness, have repaid him after they became good and great farmers.

My mother was of the *Eagle tribe;* she was a sensible woman; she was as good a hunter as any of the Indians; she could shoot the deer, and the ducks flying, as well as they. Nature had done a great deal for her, for she was active; and she was much more cleanly than the majority of our women in those days. She lived to see the day when most of her children were given up to the Lord in Christian baptism; while she experienced a change of heart, and the fulness of God in man, for she lived daily in the enjoyment of God's favors. I will speak more of her at a proper time, respecting her life and happy death.

My father still lives; he is from sixty-five to seventy years old, and is one of the chiefs of Rice Lake Indian Village. He used to love firewater before he was converted to God, but now lives in the enjoyment of religion, and he is happy without the devil's spittal—*whiskey.* If Christianity had not come, and the grace of God had not taken possession of his heart, his head would soon have been laid low beneath the fallen leaves of the forest, and I, left, in my youthful days, an orphan. But to God be all the praise for his timely deliverance.

The reader will see that I cannot boast of an exalted parentage, nor trace the past history to some renowned warrior in days of yore; but

let the above suffice. My fathers were those who endured much; who first took possession of the conquered lands of the Hurons.

I was born in *nature's wide domain!* The trees were all that sheltered my infant limbs—the blue heavens all that covered me. I am one of Nature's children; I have always admired her; she shall be my glory; her features—her robes, and the wreath about her brow—the seasons—her stately oaks, and the evergreen—her hair—ringlets over the earth, all contribute to my enduring love of her; and wherever I see her, emotions of pleasure roll in my breast, and swell and burst like waves on the shores of the ocean, in prayer and praise to Him who has placed me in her hand. It is thought great to be born in palaces, surrounded with wealth—but to be born in nature's wide domain is greater still!

I was born sometime in the fall of 1818, near the mouth of the river Trent, called in our language, Sah-ge-dah-we-ge-wah-noong, while my father and mother were attending the annual distribution of the presents from the government to the Indians. I was the third of our family; a brother and sister being older, both of whom died. My brother died without the knowledge of the Saviour, but my sister experienced the power of the loving grace of God. One brother, and two step-brothers, are still alive.

I remember the tall trees, and the dark woods—the swamp just by, where the little wren sang so melodiously after the going down of the sun in the west—the current of the broad river Trent—the skipping of the fish, and the noise of the rapids a little above. It was here I first saw the light; a little fallen down shelter, made of evergreens, and a few dead embers, the remains of the last fire that shed its genial warmth around, were all that marked the spot. When I last visited it, nothing but fur poles stuck in the ground, and they were leaning on account of decay. Is this dear spot, made green by the tears of memory, any less enticing and hallowed than the palaces where princes are born? I would much more glory in this birth-place, with the broad canopy of heaven above me, and the giant arms of the forest trees for my shelter, than to be born in palaces of marble, studded with pillars of gold! Nature will be nature still, while palaces shall decay and fall in ruins. Yes, Niagara will be Niagara a thousand years hence! The rainbow, a wreath over her brow, shall continue as long as the sun, and the flowing of the river! While the work of art, however impregnable, shall in atoms fall.

Our wigwam we always carried with us wherever we went. It was

made in the following manner: Poles were cut about fifteen feet long; three with crotches at the end, which were stuck in the ground some distance apart, the upper ends meeting, and fastened with bark; and then other poles were cut in circular form and bound round the first, and then covered with plaited reeds, or sewed birch bark, leaving an opening on top for the smoke to escape. The skins of animals formed a covering for a gap, which answered for a door. The family all seated tailor-fashion on mats. In the fall and winter they were generally made more secure, for the purpose of keeping out the rain and cold. The covering of our wigwam was always carried by my mother, whenever we went through the woods. In the summer it was easier and pleasanter to move about from place to place, than in the winter. In the summer we had birch bark canoes, and with these we travelled very rapidly and easily. In the winter every thing was carried upon the back. I have known some Indians to carry a whole deer—not a small one, but a buck. If an Indian could lift up his pack off the ground my means of his arms, it was a good load, not too light nor too heavy. I once carried one hundred and ninety-six weight of flour, twelve pounds of shot, five pounds of coffee, and some sugar, about a quarter of a mile, without resting—the flour was in two bags. It felt very heavy. This was since I travelled with the missionaries, in going over one of the portages in the west.

Our summer houses were made like those in gardens among the whites, except that the skeleton is covered with bark.

The hunting grounds of the Indians were secured by right, a law and custom among themselves. No one was allowed to hunt on another's land, without invitation or permission. If any person was found trespassing on the ground of another, all his things were taken from him, except a handful of shot, powder sufficient to serve him in going *straight* home, a gun, a tomahawk, and a knife; all the fur, and other things, were taken from him. If he were found a second time trespassing, all his things were taken away from him, except food sufficient to subsist on while going home. And should he still come a third time to trespass on the same, or another man's hunting grounds, his nation, or tribe, are then informed of it, who take up his case. If still he disobey, he is banished from his tribe.

My father's hunting ground was at the head of Crow River, a branch of the River Trent, north of the Prince Edward District, Canada West. There are two branches to this river—one belongs to George Poudash, one of the principal chiefs of our nation; the other to my father; and

the Crow River belongs to another chief by the name of John Crow. During the last war the Indians did not hunt or fish much for nearly six years, and at the end of that time there were large quantities of beaver, otter, minks, lynx, fishes, &c.

These hunting grounds abound with rivers and lakes; the face of the country is swampy and rocky; the deer and the bear abound in these woods; part of the surrendered territory is included in it. In the year 1818, 1,800,000 acres of it were surrendered to the British government. For how much, do you ask? For $2,960 per annum! What a *great sum* for British generosity!

Much of the back country still remains unsold, and I hope the scales will be removed from the eyes of my poor countrymen, that they may see the robberies perpetrated upon them, before they surrender another foot of territory.

From these lakes and rivers come the best furs that are caught in Western Canada. Buyers of fur get large quantities from here. They are then shipped to New York city, or to England. Whenever fruit is plenty, bears are also plenty, and there is much bear hunting. Before the whites came amongst us, the skins of these animals served for clothing; they are now sold from three to eight dollars apiece.

My father generally took one or two families with him when he went to hunt; all were to hunt, and place their gains into one common stock till spring, (for they were often out all winter,) when a division took place.

II

In the fall we gathered the wild rice, and in the winter we were in the interior. Some winters we suffered most severely, on account of the depth of snow, and the cold; our wigwams were often buried in snow. We not only suffered from the snow and the cold, but from hunger. Our party would be unable to hunt, and being far from the white settlements, we were often in want of food. I will narrate a circum-

stance of our sufferings, when I come to speak of the actual condition of our people, before Christianity was introduced among us, which, when I think of it, I cannot but bless God for his preserving kindness to us, in sparing us to hear his blessed word.

Soon after being Christianized, my father and another Indian, by the name of Big John, and myself, went out hunting, my father left his family near the mission station, living in the wigwam. While we were out on the hunting grounds, we found out that some Indians had gone before us on the route up the river, and every day we gained upon them: their tracks were fresh. The river and the lakes were frozen, and we had to walk on the ice. For some days together we did not fire a gun, for fear they would hear it and go from us, where we could not find them. At length we found them by the banks of the river, they were Nah-doo-ways or Mohawks, from Bay Quinty; they were seven of them, tall fellows. We shook hands with them: they received us kindly. My father had determined to take all they had, if we should overtake them. After they gave us a good dinner of boiled beaver, my father stepped across the fire and ripped open two packs of beaver furs, that were just by him. He said to them, "We have only one custom among us, and that is well known to all; this river, and all that is in it are mine: I have come up the river behind you, and you appear to have killed all before you. This is mine, and this is mine," he said, as he touched the handle of his tomahawk each of the packs of beaver, otter, and muskrat skins. I expected every moment to see my father knocked down with a tomahawk, but none dared touch him; he counted the skins and then threw them across the fire-place to us. After this was done, the same thing took place with the guns; only one was left them to use on their way home. He talked to them by signs, and bade them, as the sailors say, "weigh anchor and soon be under way;" they left, and we took possession of the temporary wigwam they had built. We never saw them afterwards on our hunting grounds, though some of them have been there since.

My father was ever kind and affectionate to me, particularly after the death of my brother, which was occasioned by the going off of a gun, the load passing through the arm, and so fractured it that it soon mortified and caused his death. He believed in persuasion; I know not that he never used harsh means, but would talk to me for hours together. As soon as it was dark he would call me to his side and begin to talk, and tell me that the Great Spirit would bless me with a long life if I should love my friends, and particularly the aged. He would

always take me with him when going any where near, and I learned his movements, for I watched him going through the woods. Often would he tell me that when I should be a man that I must do so, and so, and do as he did, while fording the rivers, shooting the deer, trapping the beaver, etc., etc. I always imitated him while I was a hunter.

My mother was also kind and affectionate; she seemed to be happy when she saw us enjoying ourselves by her; often she would not eat much for days together; she would leave all for us! She was an industrious woman; in the spring she made more sugar than any one else; she was never idle while the season for gathering wild rice lasted.

I was taught early to hunt the deer. It was a part of our father's duty to teach us how to handle the gun as well as the bow and arrow. I was early reminded to hunt for myself; a thirst to excel in hunting began to increase; no pains were spared, no fatigue was too great, and at all seasons I found something to stimulate me to exertion, that I might become a good hunter. For years I followed my father, observed how he approached the deer, the manner of getting it upon his shoulders to carry it home. The appearance of the sky, the sound of the distant water-falls in the morning, the appearance of the clouds and the winds, were to be noticed. The step, and the gesture, in travelling in search of the deer, were to be observed.

Many a lecture I received when the deer lay bleeding at the feet of my father; he would give me an account of the nobleness of the hunter's deeds, and said that I should never be in want whenever there was any game, and that many a poor aged man could be assisted by me. *"If you reverence the aged, many will be glad to hear of your name,"* were the words of my father. "The poor man will say to his children, 'my children, let us go to him, for he is a great hunter, and is kind to the poor, he will not turn us away empty.' The Great Spirit, who has given the aged a long life, will bless you. You must never laugh at any suffering object, for you know not how soon you may be in the same condition: never kill any game needlessly." Such was his language when we were alone in the woods. Ah! they were lessons directed from heaven.

In the spring, but few deer were killed, because they were not in good order, the venison being poor, and the skin so thin, that it was no object to kill them. To hunt deer in the summer was my great delight, which I did in the following manner:—During the day I looked for their tracks, as they came on the shore of the lake or river

during the night; they came there to feed. If they came on the bank of the river, I lighted pitch pine, and the current of the river took the canoe along the shore. My lantern was so constructed that the light could not fall on one spot, but sweep along the shore. The deer could see the light, but were not alarmed by it, and continued feeding on the weeds. In this way, I have approached so close that I could have reached them with my paddle. In this manner our forefathers shot them, not with a gun, as I did, but with the bow and arrow. Bows were made strong enough, so that the arrows might pierce through them.

Another mode of hunting on the lakes, preferred by some, is shooting without a light. Many were so expert, and possessed such accuracy in hearing, that they could shoot successfully in the dark, with no other guide than the noise of the deer in the water; the position of the deer being well known in this way on the darkest night. I will here relate an occurrence which took place in 1834. My father and I were hunting on the river Trent, in the night; after we had shot two deer, and while returning homewards, we heard the noise of a deer's footsteps. The night was dark as pitch. We approached the deer. I asked my father at what part of the animal I should aim. He replied, "at the head or neck." I poised my gun and fired; hearing, no noise, I concluded that my game was sure. I lighted some pitch pine, and walked towards the spot from which the noise had come. The deer lay dead and bleeding. On examination, I found that I had shot it just below the ear. In the fall of the year, also, I was accustomed to hunt; the meat was very fine, and the skins (from which our moccasins were made) and much thicker at this season. Those that could track the deer on fallen leaves, and shoot one each day, were considered first-rate hunters. The fall is the best time to determine the skill of the huntsman.

Of all animals the bear is the most dangerous to hunt. I had heard so many stories about its cunning that I dreaded to meet one. One day a party of us were going out to hunt the bear, just below Crooke's rapids. After we had made a temporary place to stay for several days, we marched in file; after a while we halted, each took a different direction. My father said, "My son, you had better loiter behind the rest. Do not go far, for you may lose yourself." We parted—I took my course, and the rest theirs. I trembled for fear I should see what I was hunting for! I went only where I least expected to see a bear, and every noise I heard in the woods, I thought must be one. As I stood

on an old mossy log, there was such a crack on the side of the hill, that my heart leaped within me. As I turned and looked, there was a large bear running towards me! I hid myself behind a tree—but on he came; I watched him; he came like a hogshead rolling down hill; there were no signs of stopping; when a few feet from me, I jumped aside, and cried *Yah!* (an exclamation of fear.) I fired my gun without taking sight; in turning suddenly to avoid me, he threw up the earth and leaves; for an instant I was led to believe that the bear was upon me. I dropped my gun and fell backwards, while the bear lay sprawling just by me. Having recovered, I took up my gun, and went a few feet from where I fell, and loaded my gun in a hurry. I then sought for a long pole, and with it I poked it on its side, to see if it was really dead. It did not move—it was dead; but even then I had not courage to go and touch it with my hands. When all was over, and I had told my father I had killed a bear, I felt as though my little leggings could hardly contain me. In examining it, I found the ball had gone through its heart.

Bear meat is like pork. It can be kept a long time when cured. For some weeks together this was the only kind of food we used to eat.

The oil of the bear is used for various purposes. One use is, to prevent the falling out of hair. The apothecaries buy it from the Indians for about five dollars a gallon.

The skins of bears are what our forefathers wore, before the white people came amongst us, as blankets; but now *land-sharks*, called by traders, buy them from the Indians for a mere trifle.

I loved to hunt the bear, the beaver, and the deer; but now, the occupation has no charms for me. I will now take the goose quill for my *bow*, and its point for my *arrow*. If, perchance, I may yet speak, when my poor aching head lies low in the grave; when the hand that wrote these recollections shall have crumbled into dust; then these pages will not have been written in vain.

> "O! land of rest, for thee I sigh—
> When will the season come,
> When I shall lay my armour by,
> And dwell in peace at home?"

The beaver was hunted in the spring and fall. They were either trapped or shot. Among all the animals that live in the water, the beaver is of the kindest disposition, when tamed; it is a very cleanly animal; sits on its broad tail on the ground while feeding; feeds all

night, and sleeps most of the day. Beaver skins were once worth from eight to ten dollars apiece, or four dollars per pound.

The otter, too, is much valued. The whites buy the skins, and make caps of them. They are mostly caught in traps. In the fall and spring they are always on the move.

The otter is a greedy animal; it can be tamed, but when hungry becomes cross, and often bites. It if be half a mile off, it will scent any food preparing in the wigwam.

When about five years old, I commenced shooting birds, with a small bow and arrow. I have shot many a bird, but am no more a marksman. I used to feel proud when I carried home my own game. The first thing that any of the hunters shot, was cooked by the grandfather and grandmother, and there was great rejoicing, to inspire the youthful hunter with fresh ardour. Day after day I searched for the grey squirrel, the woodpecker, the snipe, and the snow bird, for this was all my employment.

The gun was another instrument put into my hands, which I was taught to use both carefully and skillfully. Seldom do accidents occur from the use of fire-arms among our people. I delighted in running after the deer, in order to head and shoot them. It was a well known fact that I ranked high among the hunters. I remember the first deer I ever shot,—it was about one mile north of the village of Keene. The Indians, as has just been said, once had a custom, which is now done away, of making a great feast of the first deer that a young hunter caught: the young hunter, however, was not to partake of any of it, but wait upon the others. All the satisfaction he could realise, was to thump his heels on the ground, while he and others were singing the following hunter's song:—

> "Ah yah ba wah, ne gah me koo nah vah!
> Ah yah wa seeh, ne gah me koo nah nah."*
>
> The fattest of the bucks I'll take,
> The choicest of all animals I'll take.

In the days of our ignorance we used to dance around the fire. I shudder when I think of those days of our darkness. I thought the Spirit would be kind to me if I danced before the old men; and day after day, or night after night, I have been employed with others in this way. I thank God that those days will never return.

*These lines are sung over and over again, for about half an hour.

III

—————————What are these,
So withered and so wild in their attire,
That look not like the inhabitants o' the earth,
And yet are on't?—*S*

However absurd may have been our notions of the multiplied deities of the earth, yet, as a general thing, the Ojibways, as well as many others, believed that there was but one Great Spirit, who made the world; they gave him the name of good or benevolent; *kesha* is benevolent, *monedoo* is spirit; Ke-sha-mon-e-doo. They supposed he lived in the heavens; but the most of the time he was in the *sun*. They said it was from him they received all that was good through life, and that he seldom needs the offering of his red children, for he was seldom angry.

They also said he could hear all his children, and see them. He was the author of all things that they saw, and made the other spirits that were acknowledged by the Ojibways. It was said that these other spirits took special care of the various departments of nature. The god of the *hunter* was one who presided over the animals; the god of *war* was one who controlled the destinies of men; the god of *medicine* was one who presided over the herbs of the earth. The fishes had their god, and there was another over the moon and stars!

"Millions of spiritual creatures walk the earth
Unseen, both when we sleep and when we wake."

There was one unappeasable spirit, called the Bad Spirit, Mah-je-mah-ne-doo. He, it was thought, lived under the earth; and to him

was attributed all that was not good, bad luck, sickness, even death. To him they offered sacrifices more than to any other spirit, of things most dear to them. There were three things that were generally offered to the Bad Spirit, viz., a dog, whiskey, and tobacco,—fit offerings, with the exception of the poor dog. The poor dog was painted red on its paws, with a large stone and five plugs of tobacco tied about its neck; it was then sunk in the water; while the beating of the drum took place upon the shore, and words were chanted to the Bad Spirit.

The whiskey was thus offered to the Bad Spirit:—When the Indians were seated around the wigwam, or on the grass, and the person who dealt out the whiskey had given all the Indians a dram, then the devil was to have his share; it was poured on the ground, and if it went down quickly, it was thought he accepted the offering.

Fire-water was sometimes poured out near the head of the graves of the deceased, that their spirits might drink with their former friends. I have often seen them sit around the grave, and, as they drank, make mention of the name of their dead, and pour some whiskey on the ground.

Our religion consisted in observing certain ceremonies every spring. Most of the Ojibways around us used to come and worship the Great Spirit with us at Rice Lake. At this festival a great many of the youth were initiated into the medical mysteries of the nation. We were taught the virtues of herbs, and the various kinds of minerals used in our medicine. I will here describe the Me-tae-we-gah-mig, or Grand Medicine Lodge. It was a wigwam 150 feet long and 15 feet wide. The clan of medicine men and women alone were allowed to be inside, at each sitting, with their medicine badge, on each side of the wigwam. Then there were four old men who took the lead in singing, and beating the drum, as they stood near the centre. Before them were a company who were to take degrees. There were four grades in the institution. A medicine man is the most important personage in the worship of the Indians. He is the high priest of the ceremony, and keeps all the records of traditions and emblems. He is also the keeper of the great bag which is full of herbs, which is opened only when lectures are given for to illustrate them.

He is supposed to possess a great power over man and beast, and, therefore, to court his favour was an object worthy the consideration of young men.

After the singing commenced, the whole company arose and danced, as they moved from one end of the wigwam to the other. As

they go round, one-half of them cast their heads down upon their bosoms, as if affected by the medicine, which was kept in small skins, and which they pretended to thrust at each other: this was done to deceive the ignorant. These forms were continued several days. The party to be made medicine men and women looked on in the meantime, to see what they would have to do themselves. Then they are taken to another place with our medicine men, and are taught the science of medicine. After receiving instructions, another day was allotted to give them instruction on morality. They were advised on various subjects. All were to keep silence, and endeavour to retain what they were taught. I will here give some of the sayings of our medicine men:—

"If you are a good hunter, warrior, and a medicine man, when you die you will have no difficulty in getting to the far west in the spirit land."

"Listen to the words of your parents, never be impatient, then the Great Spirit will give you a long life."

"Never pass by any indigent person without giving him something to eat. Owh wah-yah-bak-mek ke-gah-shah-w a-ne-mig—the Spirit that sees you will bless you."

"If you see an orphan in want, help him; for you will be rewarded by his friends here, or thanked by his parents in the land of spirits."

"If you own a good hunting dog, give it to the first poor man who really needs it."

"When you kill a deer, or bear, never appropriate it to yourself alone, if others are in want; never withhold from them what the Great Spirit has blessed you with."

"When you eat, share with the poor children who are near you, for when you are old they will administer to your wants."

"Never use improper medicine to the injury of another, lest you yourself receive the same treatment."

"When an opportunity offers, call the aged together, and provide for them venison properly cooked, and give them a hearty welcome; then the gods that have favoured them will be your friends."

These are a few specimens of the advice given by our fathers, and by adhering to their counsels the lives, peace, and happiness of the Indian race were secured; for then there was no whiskey among them. O! that accursed thing. O! why did the white man give it to my poor fathers? None but fiends in human shape could have introduced it among us.

I recollect the day when my people in Canada were both numerous and happy; and since then, to my sorrow, they have faded away like frost before the heat of the sun! Where are now that once numerous and happy people? The voice of but few is heard.

When I think of them, I feel pained to know that many have fallen a prey to its soul and body-destroying influence. I could adopt the language of the poet:—

> "I will go to my tent and lie down in despair,
> I will paint me with black, and sever my hair,
> I will sit on the shore where the hurricane blows,
> And relate to the God of the tempest my woes;
> I will for a season on bitterness feed,
> For my kindred are gone to the mounds of the dead,
> But they died not of hunger, nor wasting decay,
> For the drink of the white man hath swept them away."

The Ojibway nation, that nation unconquered in war, has fallen a prey to the withering influence of intemperance. Their buoyant spirits could once mount the air as on the wings of a bird. Now they have no spirits. They are hedged in, bound, and maltreated, by both the American and British governments. They have no other hope than that some day they will be relieved from their privations and trials by death. The fire-water has rolled towards them like the waves of the sea. Alas, alas! my poor people! The tribe became dissipated, and consequently improvident, and often suffered intensely.

It was in visiting the interior that we always suffered most. I will here narrate a single circumstance which will convey a correct idea of the sufferings to which the Indians were often exposed. To collect furs of different kinds for the traders, we had to travel far into the woods and remain there the whole winter. Once we left Rice Lake in the fall, and ascended the river in canoes, above Belmont Lake. There were five families about to hunt with my father, on his grounds. The winter began to set in, and the river having frozen over, we left the canoes, the dried venison, the beaver, and some flour and pork; and when we had gone farther north, say about sixty miles from the whites, for the purpose of hunting, the snow fell for five days in succession to such a depth that it was impossible to shoot or trap anything. Our provisions were exhausted, and we had no means to procure any more. Here we were. The snow about five feet deep; our wigwam buried; the branches

of the trees falling around us, and cracking from the weight of the snow.

Our mother boiled birch bark for my sister and myself, that we might not starve. On the seventh day, some of them were so weak that they could not raise themselves, and others could not stand alone. They could only crawl in and out of the wigwam. We parched beaver skins and old moccasins for food. On the ninth day, none of the men were able to go abroad, except my father and uncle. On the tenth day, being still without food, those only who were able to walk about the wigwam were my father, my grandmother, my sister, and myself. O how distressing to see the starving Indians lying about the wigwam with hungry and eager looks! The children would cry for something to eat. My poor mother would heave *bitter sighs of despair,* the tears falling from her cheeks profusely as she kissed us. Wood, though plenty, could not be obtained, on account of the feebleness of our limbs.

My father, at times, would draw near the fire, and rehearse some prayer to the gods. It appeared to him that there was no way of escape; the men, women, and children dying; some of them were speechless. The wigwam was cold and dark, and covered with snow. On the eleventh day, just before daylight, my father fell into a sleep; he soon awoke and said to me, "My son, the Great Spirit is about to bless us; this night, in my dream, I saw a person coming from the east, walking on the tops of the trees. He told me that we should obtain two beavers this morning about nine o'clock. Put on your moccasins and go along with me to the river, and we will hunt the beaver, perhaps for the last time." I saw that his countenance beamed with delight; he was full of confidence. I put on my moccasins and carried my snow shoes, staggering along behind him, about half a mile. Having made a fire near the river, where there was an air-hole, through which the beaver had come up during the night, my father tied a gun to a stump, with the muzzle towards the air-hole; he also tied a string to the trigger, and said, "should you see the beaver rise, pull the string and you will kill it." I stood by the fire with the string in my hand. I soon heard a noise occasioned by the blow of his tomahawk; he had killed a beaver, and he brought it to me. As he laid it down, he said, "then the Great Spirit will not let us die here;" adding, as before, "if you see the beaver rise, pull the string." He left me; I soon saw the nose of one, but I did not shoot. Presently another came up; I pulled the trigger, and off the gun went. I could not see for some time for the smoke.

My father ran towards me, took the two beavers and laid them side by side; then pointing to the sun, said, "Do you see the sun? The Great Spirit informed me that we should kill these two about this time this morning. We will yet see our relatives at Rice Lake; now let us go home and see if they are still alive." We hastened home, and arrived just in time to save them from death. Since which, we visited the same spot, the year after the missionaries came among us. My father, with feelings of gratitude, knelt down on the spot where we had nearly perished. Glory to God! But what have I done for him since? Comparatively nothing. We were just at death's door, when Christianity rescued us. I have heard of many who have perished in this way, far in the woods. In the travels to the west, I have met many whose families had perished, and who had themselves merely escaped starvation. May God forgive me, for my ingratitude and indolence in his blessed cause!

I will here introduce a favourite war song of the Ojibway nation. It was accompanied by dancing, and an occasional war-whoop. At the end of each stanza, a warrior rehearsed some former victories, which inspired them with ardour for war. Unchristianised Indians are often like greedy lions after their prey; yes, at times, they are indeed cruel and blood-thirsty. I have met with warriors who, when they had killed their enemies, cut open their breasts, took out their hearts, and drank their blood; and all this was out of mere *revenge*. But to the *War Song*, which was first translated for Col. McKinney, *"the Indian's friend,"* on the shore of Lake Superior.

> "On that day when our heroes lay low—lay low—
> On that day when our heroes lay low,
> I fought by their side, and thought, ere I died,
> Just vengeance to take on the foe—the foe—
> Just vengeance to take on the foe.

> "On that day when our chieftains lay dead—lay dead—
> On that day when our chieftains lay dead,
> I fought hand to hand, at the head of my band,
> And *here, on my breast,* have I bled—have I bled—
> And here, on my breast, have I bled.

> "Our chiefs shall return no more—no more—
> Our chiefs shall return no more—
> And their brothers in war, who can't show scar for scar,
> Like women their fates shall deplore—shall deplore—
> Like women their fates shall deplore.

"Five winters in hunting we'll spend—we'll spend—
Five winters in hunting we'll spend—
Then, our youths grown to men, to the war lead again,
And our days like our fathers we'll end—we'll end—
And our days like our fathers we'll end."

IV

There are more things in heaven and earth, Horatio,
Than are dreamt of in your philosophy.—*S.*

Superstition raises and nurses children from the cradle—through the wide world. Laugh as we may at another's simplicity and folly, the civilised and uncivilised have always had their notions of ghost-spirits.

Our people believed much in omens. The barking of foxes and of wolves, the bleating of the deer, the screeching of owls, bad luck in hunting, the flight of uncommon birds, the moaning noise of a partridge, the noise of a *chuck chuck ske sey*,* were ominous of ill; the two last were certain omens of death. But the sailing of an eagle to and fro, and the noise of a raven, were omens of good.

Dreams, too, were much relied on by our nation. They thought the spirits revealed to them what they were to do, and what they should be,—viz., good hunters, warriors, and medicine men. I would fast sometimes two, and sometimes even four days. When fasting, we were to leave the wigwam early in the morning, and travel all day from one place to another, in search of the favour of the gods. I was taught to

*To this bird I have given its *Indian* name, because I have not been able to discover it among the collections of the various birds in the books and in the museums. It is about the size of the smaller kind of parrot. The colour of its feathers is like that of a jay, having short wings, small and broad beak, with an upper and lower row of teeth, like a human being. In this last respect, it is different from any other bird. It takes its name from the sound it utters,—viz., *chuck, chuck*.

believe that the gods would communicate with me, in the shape of birds, animals, &c., &c. When I fell asleep in the woods, and dreamed some strange dream, I felt confident that it was from the spirits. I will now relate what I dreamed when I was but twelve years old, and also my father's interpretation of my dream.

Myself and others were sleeping far from the wigwam, near a large pine. I saw, in my dream, a person coming from the east; he approached, walking on the air: he looked down upon me, and said, "Is this where you are?" I said, "Yes." "Do you see this pine?" "Yes, I see it." "It is a great and high tree." I observed that the tree was lofty, reaching towards the heavens—its branches extended over land and water, and its roots were very deep. "Look on it while I sing; yes, gaze upon the tree." He sang, and pointed to the tree; it commenced waving its top; the earth about its roots was heaved up, and the waters roared and tossed from one side of their beds to the other. As soon as he stopped singing, and let fall his hands, everything became perfectly still and quiet. "Now," said he, "sing the words which I have sung." I commenced as follows:—

> "It is I who travel in the winds,
> It is I who whisper in the breeze;
> I shake the trees,
> I shake the earth,
> I trouble the waters on every land."

While singing, I heard the winds whistle, saw the tree waving its top, the earth heaving, heard the waters roaring, because they were all troubled and agitated. Then said he, "I am from the rising of the sun; I will come and see you again. You will not see me often: but you will hear me speak." Thus spoke the spirit, and then turned away towards the road from which he had come. I told my father of my dream, and, after hearing all, he said, "My son, *the god of the winds* is kind to you; the aged tree, I hope, may indicate long life; the wind may indicate that you will travel much; the water which you saw, and the winds, will carry your canoe safely through the waves."

I relied much on my dream, for then I knew no better. But, however, little reliance can be placed in dreams; yet may not the Great Spirit take this method, sometimes to bring about some good result?

There was no such thing known among our people as swearing, or profaning the name of the Great Spirit. The whites first taught them to swear. I often swore, when I knew not what I said. I have seen

some *white faces* with *black hearts,* who took delight in teaching them to profane the name of God. O merciless, heartless, and wicked white men, may a merciful God forgive you your enormous turpitude and recklessness!

There was a custom among us, before Christianity visited us, that when the Ojibways intended to take a general whiskey "spree," several young men were appointed by the head chief to collect all the fire-arms, knives, war-clubs and other weapons, and keep them in a secret place, till the Indians had completed their frolic. This was done to prevent them from murdering each other when intoxicated. By this means many lives have been saved; although many have been killed during their drunken fights. They would walk very far for a dram of liquor. I once heard of an individual, whom I had seen many times, who would travel all day for a single drink of fire water. When he arrived at the trading post, he obtained and guzzled down a cup full of whiskey. When the poison had operated, he said that he felt as if his head was going down his throat; and added, "Whah ! I wish my neck was a mile long, so that I might feel and hear the whiskey running all the way down!"

A certain Indian once teased a Mrs. F. for whiskey, which he said was to cure his *"big toe,"* that had been badly bruised the preceding night. Mrs. F. said, "I am afraid you will drink it." He declared he would not drink it; and after much pleading, she handed him some; he took it, and looking first at his toe, and then at the liquor, alternately, all of a sudden he slipped the whiskey down his throat, at the same time exclaiming, as he pointed to his toe, "There, *whiskey,* go-down to my poor big toe."

One of our people, who had much resolution, and was determined to seek religion, when he heard that the Methodist Indians were not to drink any more fire-water, remarked as follows:—

"Well, if that is the case, I'll go to-night, and bid my old friend whiskey a final farewell." He went, and drank and caroused with his rum-companions all night. On the following day, about noon, he came staggering towards his wigwam, singing out to all whom he met, *"Me goes to Methodist; me no drink little more; me am Methodist."* He was true to his word, for he drank no more, and the Lord blessed him in the forgiveness of all his sins. For eighteen years he was a consistent Christian, and died last June, with the brightest hopes of immortal bliss. Oh! the heights and depths of the goodness and mercy of God!

In view of these things, I have often exclaimed from the bottom of my heart, in the language of "The Indian's Regret," and which is the language of all who have been brought from darkness to the marvellous light of the Gospel:—

> "O had our Indian fathers known
> What prophets told of Christ and heaven!
> For them we drop a tear and mourn,
> But weep for joy our sins forgiven."

V

Rash, fruitless war, from wanton glory waged,
Is only splendid murder.—*T.*

The *traditions* handed down from father to son were held very sacred; one half of these are not known by the white people, however far their researches may have extended. There is an unwillingness, on the part of the Indians, to communicate many of their traditions. The only way to come at these is to educate the Indians, so that they may be able to write out what they have heard, or may hear, and publish it. Should I be spared till next summer, I design to visit my people in the far west, and abide with them long enough to learn the rest of their traditions, with an account of their migration to this country.* My own belief is, that they came to this country, and fought with the original inhabitants; and having overpowered them, became the owners of the soil. I will not give my reasons for this belief, as I expect at some future day to collect all the necessary information for this purpose, from histories and discoveries, corroborated by these tradi-

*This tradition history of the Ojibways will soon be given to the public, and each may judge for himself with reference to the former history of our Indians. [Editor's note: Copway kept his promise. See Further Reading.]

tions. My readers will then be able to judge whether we are to be identified with the dispersed and "lost tribes of Israel." Can it be possible that, had we sprung from any of the Hebrew tribes, we should be so completely ignorant of a Messiah, a Sabbath, or a single vestige of the Levitical law? But enough of this for the present.

As far as I am able to learn, our nation has never been conquered; and have maintained their ground wherever they have conquered. The *Saxe* tribe have tried their ingenuity, power and bravery, to drive them from the south shore of Lake Superior. The *Hurons* mustered their warriors against the aggressions made by the Ojibway nation. Their war canoes were once directed against the Ojibway nation, but they were obliged to turn back, and flee for protection to the Shawnee nation. The sound of the war-whoop, which once rang all around the shores of Lake Huron, receded, and died away on the waters of Sandusky. The arms that once wielded the war-club were strewed about their grounds, on account of broken treaties made in former days, and massacres at the mouth of French River. The *Iraquois,* who struck terror wherever their mere names were mentioned, also tried to check our progress, after we had conquered the Hurons. Their war-whoops resounded over the dismal regions of the conquered land; but they, too, shared the same fate. They went, as spies, as far as Le Pointe, on the south shore of Lake Superior; but not with their armies any farther than Ke-wa-o-non, in the copper regions. Here they were massacred by hundreds, and fell in their canoes at one of the narrow passes, on their way to the portage, about fourteen miles from the Bay of Aunce. After these fruitless attempts to drive the Ojibways from their land, they fought many battles with them in the regions now called Canada West; but in these they suffered much, and were defeated. It was then, probably that the Hurons and Iraquois leagued together, hoping by their combined forces to conquer us. This accounts for the confederacy that existed when the whites came among them.

The migration of the Ojibways has been traced from the upper part of Lake Superior, and even several hundred miles above its head, along the shore of Lake Superior, down to Lake Huron, St. Clair, the foot of Lake Michigan, north of Lakes Erie and Ontario, and some distance down the St. Lawrence.

They now inhabit a portion of land extending about 2000 miles east and west, and from 250 to 300 miles from north to south. They have in each village a chief who governs them, besides a great number of

war chiefs. Each village has a council of its own, made up of the different tribes. A tribe is a band of Indians whose sign or mark is the same; for example, such as wear the sign of the *crane,* recognise each other as relatives; and although each village may be composed of different tribes, yet they must be of the same nation.

Councils of peace must be held by two nations. These councils are held in high esteem. When two nations are at war, if either sues for peace, they hand to each other some token, such as a belt of wampum (or beads), or a calumet (a long pipe.)

There was once a general council held between the Hurons and the Ojibways; it was conducted in the following manner:—They came together near Sault St. Marie, and agreed upon a peace for five years. After the pipe of peace was prepared, the Ojibway and Huron warriors arranged themselves in two lines, on each side of their chiefs, and said that they must ascertain whether the Great Spirit would approve of their proceedings. Two from each nation were chosen: the Hurons held the pipe filled with tobacco; the Ojibways, the steel, flint, and spunk. The steel was then struck against the flint, and if, on the first stroke, the spunk was ignited, so as to fire the tobacco, and thus enable the warrior to draw in and to emit a volume of smoke, then the evidence was complete that the Great spirit approved of their plans and proceedings; and the whole assembly now would set up the most tremendous shout of joy. The two nations were successful in this. The shout was given, peace was secured, and these two powerful nations separated for their own homes. For three years, no dark cloud hung over the two nations.

The Ojibways began to trade with the whites at Quebec. It usually required all the summer to journey from the shore of Lake Superior to that place and back again. These were tedious and perilous journeys; but they were determined to obtain *"the snake which spit fire, smoke and death;"* this was their description of *a gun* to their brethren.

It was during these journeys that forty of them were massacred by the Hurons, at the mouth of French River, without the least provocation; plunder alone was their object. This, in connection with similar acts, occasioned that war which resulted in their complete extermination from Canada by our nation.

The *future state* of the Ojibways was in the *Far West.* They described that state or country *as being full of game,* and with *trees loaded with fruit of every description.*

When an Indian warrior died on the field of 'battle, his soul, it was

said, took its immediate flight to this paradise. The souls of those, however, who died in other circumstances, it was believed, departed from the grave, and journeyed in the ordinary way, although unseen by mortals, to this same land.

There was a difficult bridge near this land, over which the soul was to cross. A warrior, hunter, or medicine man, would have no difficulty in crossing this bridge. Under this bridge was a rapid stream, and he who was not a good warrior, hunter, or medicine man, would either fall into the water, or lose his way, after having crossed, in some barren country, where there was no game or fruit, although there might be, occasionally, a deer, or the like. O, how barren! How dismal! A place where distress, want, and despair would continue! On the other hand, the favoured warrior entered the fields of paradise, amidst the shouts and welcome of his fellow-warriors, who had preceded him to this land of plenty. The deer, the moose, the elk, and all kinds of animals, fruits, flowers, and the singing of birds fill and charm the land; while the ever rolling valleys are visited with delightful and refreshing winds. To kill, eat, and shoot, are their only employments. No sickness, no fatigue, no death, will ever visit them. The valleys and the mountains are to be clothed with evergreens. No winter to chill the earth. A carnal heaven indeed! A sensual paradise. Oh! the credulous and misguided Indians!

> "Lo! the poor indian, whose untutored mind
> Sees God in clouds, or hears him in the wind;
> Whose soul proud science never taught to stray
> Beyond the solar walk or milky way.
> Yet simple nature to his hopes has given,
> Beyond the cloud-topped hill, a humble heaven,
> Some safer world in depths of woods embraced,
> Some distant island in the watery waste.
> Where slaves once more their native land behold,
> Nor fiends torment, nor Christian thirsts for gold."
>
> *Pope.*

My father often spoke of that country, while I was young. He informed me, that if I should become a great warrior, a hunter, or a medicine man, I would have no difficulty in reaching that happy spot. Little then did he know of a *heaven revealed in the Gospel.* That heaven, where angels and pure spirits dwell, and where we shall see the blessed Jesus as he is, and, what is a still greater honour, be like him.

"O for a thousand tongues to sing
 My great Redeemer's praise!
The glories of my God and King,
 The triumphs of his grave!

"My gracious Master, and my God,
 Assist me to proclaim,
To spread thro' all the earth abroad
 The honours of thy Name.

"Jesus! the name that charms our
 fears,
 That bids our sorrows cease;
'Tis music in the sinner's ears,
 'Tis life, and health, and peace."

"Oh uh pa-gish ke che ingo' dwok,
 Neej uh ne she ag baig,
Che nuh nuh guh mo tuh wah wod
 Niug e zha Mun e-doom.

"Ning e che Noo sa weej e shin,
 Che ween duh mah ga yon,
O mah a ne gook kuh me gog
 A zhe wa be ze yun.

"Jesus! kah be 'non duh we 'nung
 Kah gah see beeng wa 'nung;
Ka gait 'che me no ne kah zo,
 Kah noo je mo e nung"

When our warriors were dying, they told their children that they would soon reach the happy country. Their eyeballs, rolling in death, were turned towards the setting sun. O white man! why did you not tell us before, that there was a better heaven than that of the Indian's? Did not the blessed Saviour command, "Go yet into *all* the world and preach the Gospel to every creature?" Reader, almost by the door of your churches, my forefathers perished for the lack of the bread of life, while you have reached out your arms, and extended your means for the relief of those in *distant lands!* O what a thought! Thousands have already perished, and thousands more will yet perish, unless converted to God. The thought of *perishing!* how *insufferable!* O how *intolerable!*

"O mercy, O mercy, look down from above,
 Great Creator, on us, thy sad children, with love;
When beneath to their darkness the wicked are driven,
 May our justified souls find a welcome in heaven."

VI

So blue yon winding river flows,
It seems an outlet from the sky,
Where, waiting till the west wind blows,
The freighted clouds at anchor lie.—*H. W. S.*

Rice Lake, that beautiful lake, extends about twenty-five miles. On each side of the lake are high hills, which soon rise from the edge of the water to the top. This lake beautifully winds along a mountainous region, and is from two to three miles in breadth, running from northeast to south-west. It contains about twenty islands. Large quantities of wild rice abound in almost every part of the lake; it resembles fields of wheat. As ducks of all kinds resort here in great abundance, to feed upon the rice, there is consequently much good game in the fall of the year. They fly in large flocks, and often appear like clouds. Some of the islands just referred to are beautiful; for example, *Sugar Island*, with its beautiful edge of evergreens near the water; *Spoke Island*, a place of fashionable summer resort. One of the largest of these islands contains about three hundred acres.

In 1818, our people surrendered to the British Government a large part of their territory, for the sum of £750; reserving, as they had good reason to believe, all the islands. As they could neither read nor write, they were ignorant of the fact that these islands were *included* in the sale. They were repeatedly told, by those who purchased for the Government, that the islands were *not* included in the articles of agreement. But, since that time, some of us have learned to read, and to our utter astonishment, and to the everlasting disgrace of that *pseudo* Christian nation, we find that we have been most grossly abused, deceived, and cheated. Appeals have been frequently made, but all in vain.

Rice Lake contains quantities of the finest fish. In the summer great numbers of boats may be seen trowling for *mascalounge*, a species of pike, some of which weight about thirty pounds. Bass, eels, &c., are also found in this lake. Since locks have been made on the canal down to Crooke's rapids, much fur can be procured all around the lake, especially *muskrats*—Shah-won-dase O dah me koo mun.

This is the spot on which I roamed during my early days. Often have I gone with my birch-bark canoe, from island to island, in quest of ducks and fish. The plain on the south shore is called Whortleberry Plain. A steamboat runs from Gore's Landing to Peterboro once a day.

The village of the Ojibways is on the north; the land gradually slopes toward the water. Its farms, church, school-house, and council-house, can be seen at a considerable distance. It was here where the Rev. James Evans, whose obituary was noticed in the following manner in the "Albany Evening Journal," December 22, 1846, first taught an Indian school.

"Suddenly, on the 23rd of November, at Keelby, England, Rev. James Evans, for many years a Wesleyan Missionary in Canada, and the territory of the Hudson Bay Company. On Sunday, the 22nd, he preached twice, and on Monday evening, 23rd, spoke at a missionary meeting with great fervency. He had complained of a slight indisposition previous to the meeting; but, after he had finished his address, he said that 'his indisposition had been completely removed.' Soon after his head fell back and life was gone."

He was a missionary in every sense of the word. From Rice Lake he went to Lake Superior, and afterwards to the Hudson Bay territory, where he laboured with much success. His precious life was spent in rescuing the Ojibway nation from misery and degradation. Fatigue and hunger were often his companions; but the power of living faith was that on which his soul feasted. O thou man of God, enviable are thy labours, thy rest, and thy glory! I, myself, still hold in sweet remembrance the sacred truths which thou didst teach me, even the commands of the Most High! *Memory*, like an angel, will still hover over the sacred spot, where first you taught me the letters of the alphabet.

There are numerous lakes near Rice Lake, about some of which the Ojibways reside, particularly Mud, Schoogaug, and Balsam Lakes. The country, in this vicinity, is rapidly increasing in population; the whites are continually settling among us. The deer was plenty a few

years ago, but now only a few can be found. The Ojibways are, at present, employed in farming instead of hunting; many of them have good and well cultivated farms. They not only raise grain enough for their own use, but often sell much to the whites.

The Canadian Commissioners on Indian affairs, in their report to Parliament, in 1845, remarked, in relation to the Rice Lake Indians, as follows:—"These Indians are Methodists, and have either a resident missionary, or have been regularly visited by the missionary belonging to the Alnwick settlement. They have a school, and a school-master is supported by the Methodist Missionary Society."

VII

He patient showed us the wise course to steer,
A candid censor, and a friend sincere;
He taught us how to live; and (O! too high
The price of knowledge) taught us how to die.—*A.*

Several years we had been with the English people after the war, and learned to drink the *fire-water* of the Paleface. The day at last arrived when we were to learn something better from them.

The missionaries first visited us on the island called *Be-quah-qua-yong*, in 1827, under the following circumstances. My father and I went to Port Hope, to see our principal trader, John D. Smith, in order to obtain goods and whiskey, about twelve miles from Rice Lake. After my father had obtained the goods, he asked for whiskey. Mr. Smith said, "John, do you know that whiskey will yet kill you, if you do not stop drinking? Why, all the Indians at Credit River, and at Grape Island, have abandoned drinking, and are now Methodists. I cannot give you any whiskey."

"*Tah yah!* (an exclamation of surprise,) *it cannot be; I must* have

whiskey to carry home; my people expect it," said my father. He wished to buy a barrel, but only obtained, after much pleading, about five gallons. My father *promised* to drink no more when the missionaries should have come to Rice Lake. We reached home the same day, about one o'clock, and the Indians were awaiting our arrival, that they might have some fire-water. They assembled themselves together and began to drink and to smoke. Many of them were sitting on the grass when the whiskey began to steal away their brains. One of our number suddenly ran into the crowd, and said, *"The black coats* (missionaries) are coming, and are on the other side of the point." Each looked at the other with perfect astonishment. My father said to our informer, "Invite them to come over to us;" and to the one who was dealing out whiskey, "cover the keg with your blanket, and don't let the black coats see it." The whiskey was concealed, and then came the messengers of glad tidings of great joy. They were converted Indians, saved by grace, and had been sent to preach to us, and to invite us to attend a camp meeting near Cobourg. After shaking hands all around, one of them delivered a speech to the half-drunken Indians. He referred to the day when they were without the good news of *salvation*. He spoke with great earnestness, and the tears fell from his eyes. He said, *"Jesus Christ, Ke-sha-mon-e-doo O-gwe-son,* (i.e., the Benevolent Spirit's Son,) came down to the world, and died to save the people; all the Indians at the Credit River and Grape Island are now on their road to the place where the Saviour has gone. Jesus has left a book containing his commands and sayings to all the world; you *will see it, and hear it read*, when you go to Cobourg, for the black coats have it. They wish you to come and hear it. To-morrow is the *Sabbath,* and on that day we do not hunt, or work, for it is the day which the Great Spirit made for himself." He described the way that the Son of God was crucified. I observed some of them crying; my mother heaved deep sighs; the half-drunken Indians were struck dumb, and hung their heads. Not a word was uttered. The missionaries said, "We will *sing,* and then we will *kneel down* and *pray* to the Great Spirit." He gave out the following hymn:—

> "Jesus ish pe ming kah e zhod."
> "Jesus, my all, to heaven is gone."

They stood up and sang. O what sweet melody was in their voices! The echo was so great that there appeared to be a great many more

singers than we could see. After the hymn, they prayed with the same fervency as they sang.

Peter Wason prayed, and in his prayer said, "O Great Spirit! here are some of my own relatives; open their eyes and save them!" After the prayer, they said they were going to Cobourg that evening; and if any desired to go with them, they would have them do so.

My father arose and took the keg of whiskey, stepped into one of the small canoes, and paddled some thirty feet from the shore; here he poured out the whiskey into the lake, and threw the keg away. He then returned and addressed us in the following manner:—"You have all heard what our brothers said to us; I am going with them this evening; if any of you will go, do so this evening; the children can attend the great meeting some other time." Every one ran at once to the paddles and canoes, and in a few minutes we were on the water. The missionaries had a skiff, in which they went from the island to the opposite side. They sang again, and their very oars seemed to keep time on the still water. O how charming! The scenery of the water; the canoes moving in files, crossing the lake to visit their first camp meeting. When we arrived on the other side, it was about dusk, and we bought five candles for a *dollar (!)*, and obtained an old lantern. We marched on a new road the whole of Saturday night, in order to reach the camp ground. During the journey, we had to wade through deep creeks. Just before the dawn, we were about half a mile from the camp ground; here we tarried until daylight, and then approached the camp.

When the Indians beheld the fence and the gate, and a great number of whites, they began to feel rather timid and suspicious, for the trader had told my father at Rice Lake, that *it was for the purpose of killing all the Indians* that the blackcoats had invited them to the meeting. My father told me to keep away from the ground, and hunt birds and squirrels with my bow and arrow; his object was to save my life, in the event of the Indians being killed. After remaining on the camp ground awhile, I departed; but while there, I saw a large number of converted Indians who belonged to Credit River and Grape Island. Some of them were singing, some praying, and others lying about the ground as if dead. There were a great many preachers present.

On the third day many of our company were converted; among this number was my dear father!

As I entered the ground in the afternoon, I heard many voices, and among them my father's voice. I thought my father was dying; I ran to him, and found him lying partly on one of the seats. "My father,"

said I, "what is the matter with you? Are you sick?" "Come here, my son; I am not sick, but I am happy." He placed his hand upon his breast while he spoke. "I told you, you must keep away from the ground, that your life might be spared; but I find that these are good, and not bad people; kneel down and I will pray for you." I knelt, while he prayed. This was *my father's first prayer!* The people were all around me kneeling, and most of them praying. The feeling was so general and powerful, that the influence was felt throughout the camp, both by the Indians and the whites. This was one of the happiest seasons I ever witnessed, except the season of my conversion. Many of my relatives were converted on this occasion. Many of them have since gone to the world of spirits, and are now singing the praises of redeeming love. This *heavenly fire* began to spread from the camp to Mud, Schoogaug, and Balsam Lakes, the homes of the Ojibways; also to the shores of Lake Simeco and Lake Huron, and to the vicinity of Lake Superior.

> "Waft, waft, ye winds his story,
> And you, ye waters, roll,
> Till like a sea of glory
> It spreads from pole to pole."

On the camp ground, the Ojibways sat in squads, giving and receiving instruction in singing, learning and teaching the Lord's prayer, and other things. Some were singing,

"Jesus, kuh ba ke zhig
 Ning ee e nuh uh moz,
 Uh pa gish kuh ke nuh wahb' dum
 'wod
 Ning ee 'nuh da moosh
 A zhe o ne zhe shing,
 O ge che o duh nuh me ah win."

"Jesus, all the day long,
 Was my joy and my song;
 O that all his salvation might see!
 He hath loved me, I cried;
 He hath suffered and died
 To redeem such a rebel as me."

The *conversion of my mother* took place during the summer, on Poutash Island, where the Indians had erected a bark chapel. For two years she lived in the enjoyment of religion. Before this chapel was ready she would call us together in the wigwam, and pray with and for us, several times a day, whether our father was at home or not. I remember well, at this moment, the language of her prayers.

She was taken sick in the winter of 1829, and was confined to her bed, most of the time, for three months; her disease was consumption.

During these three months she enjoyed much religion; there was not a day in which she did not speak of Jesus and his promises with the greatest confidence and delight.

When she grew worse, she called for the class leaders to pray with her. She said to her mother, whom she supposed would die first, because her hair was *white,* "You will still live, but I am going to die, and will see Jesus first; soon, however, you will follow me."

The spirit of my dear mother took its flight on the 27th day of February, 1830. Just before her death, she prayed with her children; and advised us to be good Christians, to love Jesus, and meet her in heaven. She then sang her favourite hymn—

> "Jesus ish pe ming kah e zhod."
> "Jesus, my all, to heaven is gone."

This was the first hymn she had ever heard or learned; and it is on this account that I introduce and sing this sweet hymn, whenever I lecture "On the origin, history, traditions, migration, and customs of the Ojibway nation." We all knelt again by her bed-side, and while clapping her hands, and endeavouring to shout for joy, she swooned away in death. The last words, which she feebly uttered, were, *"Jesus, Jesus."* Her spirit then fled, her lips were cold, and those warm hands that had so often and so faithfully administered comfort and relief, were now stiff. I looked around the wigwam; my father, sister, and brother sat near me, wringing their hands; they were filled with bitter grief, and appeared inconsolable. I then began to understand and appreciate fully her kindness and love. Who, who can, or will, take the place of a *mother?* Who will pray for us when we are sick or in distress? Her body was consigned to the grave without any parade. No church bell was tolled; but the whistling wind sounded through the woods. I have often knelt down, at the head of her grave, and wished that the time would soon arrive when it might please God to relieve me from my troubles and cares, and conduct me to the abode of my beloved parent. My sister Sarah, too, who has since died, is doubtless with my mother. O how glorious the thought, *that both are now in heaven!* There is one spot where none will sigh for home. The flowers that blossom there, will never fade; the crystal waters that wind along those verdant vales, will never cease to send up their heavenly music! The clusters hanging from the trees over-shadowing

its banks will be immortal clusters; and the friends that meet will meet for ever!

Little then did I think that I should have to pass through so many afflictions, and so many hardships. O my mother, I am still in a *cold, uncharitable, miserable world!* But the thought that thou art happy and blessed, is truly sweet and encouraging! It is this fact, and my own hopes of future bliss, that buoy me up, and sustain me in the hours of conflict and despondency. Although many years have elapsed since her death, still I often weep with mingled joy and grief when I think of my dear mother. "Blessed are the dead who die in the Lord." "I am not ashamed of the Gospel of Christ, for it is the power of God unto salvation to every one that believeth." The Gospel is the only remedy for the miseries and sins of the world.

My mother and sister's cases are not the only ones that I could relate concerning the happy lives and deaths of those once degraded and benighted Indians. Many have already reached heaven, and many more are now rejoicing on their road thither. Who will now say that the poor Indians cannot be converted? The least that Christians could have done, was to send the Gospel among them, after having dispossessed them of their lands; thus preparing them for usefulness here, and happiness hereafter. Let no one say that I am ungrateful in speaking thus. It was the *duty* of Christians to send us missionaries; and it is *now* their duty to send *more* of them. There are still 25,000 of my poor brethren in darkness, and without the Gospel. Let the prayers of all the churches ascend to the Most High in their behalf, that He who has power to deliver may save the poor Indian from misery, ignorance, and perdition.

VIII

———————

_____ While he lives,
To know no bliss but that which virtue gives;
And when he dies to leave a lofty name,
A light, a land-mark on the cliffs of fame.—*M.*

Here comes the sunshine of my life. The first ray of light flashed in my soul, and, strange as it may appear, it remained. In the summer following my mother's death (1830), I felt that *I was converted.* The following are the circumstances connected with my conversion:—My father and I attended a camp meeting near the town of Colbourne. On our way from Rice Lake to the meeting, my father held me by the hand, as I accompanied him through the woods. Several times he prayed with me, and encouraged me to seek religion at this camp meeting. We had to walk thirty miles under a hot sun, in order to reach the place of destination. Multitudes of Indians, and a large concourse of whites from various places, were on the ground when we arrived. In the evening, one of the white preachers (Wright, I believe, was his name) spoke; his text was, "For the great day of His wrath is come, and who shall be able to stand?" He spoke in English, and as he closed each sentence, an Indian preacher gave its interpretation. He spoke of the plain and good road to heaven; of the characters that were walking in it; he then spoke of the bad place, the judgment, and the coming of a Saviour. I now began to feel as if I was a sinner before God. Never had I felt so before; I was deeply distressed, and knew not the cause. I resolved to go and prostrate myself at the mourner's bench, as soon as an opportunity offered. We were now invited to approach. I went to the bench and knelt down by the roots of a large tree. But how could I pray? I did not understand how to pray; and

besides, I thought that the Great Spirit was *too great* to listen to the words of a poor Indian boy. What added to my misery was, that it had rained in torrents about three quarters of an hour, and I was soaking wet. The thunder was appalling, and the lightning terrific. I then tried again to pray, but I was not able. I did not know what words to use. My father then prayed with and for me. Many were praising God, all around me. The storm now ceased, but nearly all the lights had been extinguished by the rain. I still groaned and agonised over my sins. I was so agitated and alarmed that I knew not which way to turn in order to get relief, and while kneeling down with the rest I found relief, as though a stream had been let loose from the skies to my heart. Joy succeeded this knowledge, and, were I to live long, I never can forget the feelings with which I rose and spoke the following first. English words—*"Glory to Jesus."* I looked around for my father, and saw him. I told him that I had found "Jesus." He embraced me and kissed me; I threw myself into his arms. I felt as strong and happy, yet as humble as a poor Indian boy saved by grace. During that night I did not sleep. The next morning, my cousin George Shawney, and myself, went out into the woods to sing and pray. As I looked at the trees, the hills, and the valleys, O how beautiful they all appeared! I looked upon them, as it were, with new eyes and new thoughts. Amidst the smiles of creation, the birds sang sweetly, as they flew from tree to tree. We sang

"Jesus, the name that charms our fears."

O how sweet the recollections of that day! "Jesus, all the day long, was my joy and my song." Several hundreds were converted during this meeting. Many of the Indians were reluctant to leave the camp ground when the meeting was broken up. When we reached our homes at Rice Lake, everything seemed to me as if it wore a different aspect; everything was clothed with beauty. Before this, I had only begun to spell and read. I now resumed my studies with a new and different relish. Often, when along, I prayed that God would help me to qualify myself to teach others how to read the word of God; this circumstance I had not told to any one. On Sabbath mornings I read a chapter in the New Testament, which had been translated for my father, before we went to meeting.

During this summer, one of our chiefs, John Sunday, with several others, departed from Rice Lake for the west, with a design to preach

to the Ojibways. When they returned, they told us that the Indians were very eager to hear the word of God, and that many had been converted. John Sunday informed us of a certain Indian, who was so much opposed to the meetings that he confined his wife and children to one of the islands, to prevent her attending them. But this poor woman was so anxious to obey God in attendance on worship, that she was in the habit of fording the river every night, and carrying her children on her back. Her husband was afterwards converted. He mentioned also an instance of an Indian who brought his medicine sack with him to the meeting, but on being converted, he scattered its contents to the four winds of heaven. These sacks were held very sacred among the Indians. He spoke likewise of the conversion of many chiefs, and of the flocks of children anxious to hear the word of God. He left such an impression on my mind, that often, while alone, I prayed that God might send me to instruct the children in the truths of religion.

I joined my father's class meeting, and as often as possible I attended school during the period of two years. In June, 1834, our white missionary, Daniel McMullen, received a letter from the Rev. Wm. Case, in which it was stated that a letter had been sent to him by the Rev. John Clark, who was then the superintendent of the mission on Lake Superior. The superintendent requested that two native preachers and two native teachers should be sent to him. John Johnson and I were told that we were to accompany Brothers John Taunchey and Caubage to Lake Superior, to aid Brother Clark.

Brother Caubage and my cousin Johnson took their departure. John Taunchey hesitated about going, because I was undecided, and my father felt unwilling at first to let me go.

One day I determined to leave the village so as to avoid going to Lake Superior; I hunted along the river Trent, hoping that John Taunchey would be gone before my return; I felt very unwilling to go. I was absent over two weeks; they were the longest two weeks I had ever experienced. Yet the whole time I felt dissatisfied; something seemed to whisper to me, "George, go home, and go to Lake Superior with your uncle John Taunchey." I returned to the village. The first person I saw informed me that my uncle was waiting for me, and that my father had left it to me to decide whether to go or stay. Here I was; the missionaries came, and said, "George, your father has left it with you to go or stay. It is your duty to go; John is waiting, and to-day you must conclude." Our school-mistress, Miss Pinney, came

and reasoned with me. I recollected, too, that I had prayed that God might prepare me to be useful to my brethren; and now, that I had some good reason to think that my prayers had been heard, and still to refuse to go, would perhaps be acting in opposition to the indications of God. I wept and prayed; but O! that night of struggle! I could not sleep. In the morning, I said to my father, "I have concluded to go; prepare me for my journey." That morning we were prepared; and on the 16th of July 1834, about noon, we were on the shore. The canoe was ready; many of the Indians prayed with us on the beach. After shaking hands with my father and the rest, we bid farewell to all we loved so tenderly. We went on board the steam-boat "Great Britain," at Cobourg, and arrived at Toronto the next day. On the 20th July, we left in the stage for Holland Landing; here we remained two days, for the want of a conveyance to the Snake Island mission. At this island we tarried the whole of the Sabbath with the Indians, and had some glorious meetings. They conveyed us to the Narrows mission. In crossing from Narrows to Cold Water mission, we were obliged to carry our trunks on our backs. About 11 o'clock we met two runaway horses on the road to Narrows. We caught them, tied our trunks on their backs, and led them back to Cold Water. Thus we were relieved of our heavy loads.

On Wednesday, the 26th July, we went from Cold Water mission to Pane-ta-wa-go-shene, where we saw a great number of Ojibways from Lake Superior, Ottowas, Menomenese, &c. Here we fell in with John Sunday, Frazer, and others, who were engaged in instructing the Indians in this vicinity.

An opportunity occurred now to go to Sault St. Marie, where the Rev. John Clark resided. We were out of provisions several times. By fishing and shooting gulls on our way, we were enabled to reach Sault, where we met brother Clark, John Caubage, and cousin Johnson; this took place, I believe, on the 24th of August. We stayed here about two weeks, preparing to go to the Aunce, the Ke-wa-we-non mission. During our delay in this place, the Rev. Messrs. Chandler and Bourne (the latter a member of the Illinois Conference) arrived. Brother Chandler has since died. My cousin, H. P. Chase, was Brother Clarks' interpreter. The Indians were comfortable in their new houses. We held meetings with them several nights.

IX

The clouds may drop down titles and estates,
Wealth may seek us, but wisdom must be sought.—*Y.*

I now began to feel the responsibility resting upon me. The thought of assuming the station of a teacher of the Indians, with so few capabilities, was enough to discourage more gifted men than myself. Frequently did I enter the woods and pour out my soul to God, in agony and tears. I trembled at what was before me, and said, "who is able for these things?" But a still small voice would answer, "My grace is sufficient for thee." Soothing words indeed, especially to an unlearned and feeble Red man—a mere worm of the dust.

Having provided everything necessary for our journey, and a residence of eight months at the Ke-wa-we-non mission, we started in company with Rev. Mr. Chandler, uncle John Taunchey, and the traders who intended to winter on the shores of Lake Superior and do business with the Ojibways. We were more than three weeks on our journey—three hundred and fifty miles. At one place, we were weather-bound for one week. Our French companions were the most wicked of men. They would gnash their teeth at each other, curse, swear, and fight among themselves. The boat, oars, the winds, water, the teachers, &c., did not escape their execrations. I thought now that I understood what *hell* was, in a very clear manner. My very hairs would seem to stand, while I would be obliged to listen to their oaths, when they gave vent to their malevolence and passions. They would fight like beasts over their cooking utensils, and even while their food was in their mouths. I will just say here that I have often seen them eat boiled corn, with tallow for butter.

On our road, we saw the celebrated Pictured Rocks, Sand Banks,

and Grand Island. On a point of the latter place we encamped. Every Sabbath I devoted about an hour in sighing and crying after *home*. "What good can *I do*, when I reach the place of labour?" was a question that often occurred to my mind. Still we were going farther and farther from home. We were obliged, too, to do our own cooking, washing, and mending.

At last, in September, we arrived at the Aunce Bay. Here, our house was no better than a wigwam; and yet we had to occupy it as a dwelling, a school-house, a meeting-house, and a council-room.

We commenced labouring among our poor people, and those that had been Christianised were exceedingly glad to see us. Brothers Sunday and Frazer had already been among them more than a year. We began to build quite late in the fall, and although we removed a house from the other side of the bay, yet we experienced much inconvenience. We visited the Indians daily, for the purpose of conversing and praying with them. There were about thirty, who had, for more than a year, professed to experience a change of heart. As my uncle was experienced in conversing with the unconverted, I endeavoured to pursue his course in this respect. Each day we took a different direction in visiting the unconverted. We would sing, read the Scriptures, and then pray with them. Sometimes they would be impudent, and even abusive, but this did not discourage us, or deter us from our duty. By persevering, we soon discovered that the Lord was about to bless our efforts. While my uncle was visiting some four or five wigwams, I was visiting as many others—their wigwams being near us. Our influence, with God's blessing, was now felt among them. Singing and praying were their constant employments; and some of them seemed to know nothing else but the enjoyment of the truth of the Gospel, and that God can and does "forgive sin." They became the happiest of beings; their very souls were like an escaped bird, whose glad wings had saved it from danger and death. Brother Chandler preached twice every Sabbath, and taught school every other week. One Sabbath, in January, 1835, Brother Chandler preached from these words, *"And they were all filled with the Holy Ghost."* He spoke with unusual liberty; I caught some of the *same fire* with which the sermon was delivered, and interpreted it with much ardour. O what a melting season it was! The anxious and expressive looks of the Indians—the tears streaming down their cheeks, all tended to add to the occasion. My readers, here was comfort! here was one bright spot, at least, in my chequered life, that I never can forget! My poor

brethren appeared to swallow every word of the sermon as I inter-
preted it. One John Southwind, who had been notoriously cruel and
revengeful, was among the humblest and the happiest. He had been a
great *conjuror*.

On Sabbath evenings, every converted Indian would try to induce
his relatives to embrace religion, and pray in the wigwams of their
unconverted relatives. These happy scenes often made me forget home.

Many of the unconverted were very revengeful; but we let them
expend their vengeance on the air. One of them, *Kah-be-wah-be-ko-
kay,—i.e.* Spear Maker,—threatened to tomahawk us, if we should
come to his wigwam "with the white man's religion;" for, said he,
"already some of my family are very sick and crazy." Notwithstanding
this threat, we commenced our visits, and with no other weapon than
a little calico bag containing our Testament and Hymn Book. When-
ever he saw us near his wigwam (we were obliged to pass near his, in
visiting other wigwams), he would run out, and grumble and growl
like a bear escaping from its den for life. In this way we continued our
visits, and had opportunities to converse with the family, which
resulted in the conversion of all his children. In the month of Febru-
ary, he himself came to us, and pleaded earnestly for our forgiveness.
He had gone out to hunt the marten, with his youngest daughter, who
was about ten years old. While her father was preparing a marten trap,
or dead-fall, as it is sometimes called, the daughter slipped behind a
tree, knelt in the snow, and prayed for her father. The Lord heard her
prayer. The old man "felt sick in his heart," and everything he looked
at appeared to frown upon him, and to bid him "go to the missionar
ies, and they will tell you how you can be cured." He returned home
three days earlier than he had intended. Just after day dawn, we heard
a number of Indians praying. John Southwind came in and said to us,
"Ke-ge-ke-wa-ye-wah, Kak-be-wah-be-koo-bay ke-che-ah-koo-sey,"
i.c. "Your friend *Spear Maker* is very sick; he wishes you to call at his
wigwam and pray with him." This was good news indeed! We went at
once, and prayed with him. He could not speak, but sat sobbing and
sighing over the fire. We conversed with him, and then left him; but
before breakfast he entered our house with his large medicine sack,
containing little gods of almost every description. He stood before us,
and said, *"Ah bay, ah was ah yak mook,"*—"Here, take this." He cast
the bag, or sack, down upon the floor, and wept and sobbed bitterly,
saying, "I have done all I could against you, but you have been my
friends. I want you to pray for me, and to burn these gods, or throw

them where I can never see them." Shortly after his interview, he obtained religion, and became truly happy in the Lord.

There were many equally interesting conversions about this time. I must here mention what was often very amusing to the missionaries, and would often create a smile, if nothing more. When some of the Indians were under *conviction,* they would take some of their own medicines (herbs) to cure their "sickness,"—for so they termed *conviction.* An old medicine man once sent a message to us, stating that his daughter was dying, and that it was caused by our singing and praying before her so much; he also added, that in the event of her death, he would have his revenge by killing us, and insisted upon it that we must come immediately, and endeavour to relieve her. We went, and after having prayed with her for some time, she revived, and expressed her confidence that the Holy Spirit had operated upon her heart. The old man soon became convinced that his daughter was not dying, except unto *sin;* he, therefore, at once, became reconciled and delighted too.

We now commenced travelling on snow shoes within fifteen or twenty miles around where the Indians were hunting, praying and preaching to them. The Lord owned and blessed our labours wherever we went. We held prayer meetings in the woods. All this time the *Mah-jee Mon-e-doo* (Bad Spirit) was not asleep. In the spring the heathen party started in a body to visit their old friend *Spear Maker,* for the purpose of uniting with him in dancing, and in their medicine worship; but the old man had too much religion in him to gratify them. As soon as they discovered that they could not prevail upon the old man, they sent word to all, that they could excel us in worshipping the Great Spirit, and that they intended to hold their regular spring Grand Medicine Worship. Every night we held meetings. They commenced with their *paw-wahs* (singing), and beating of the drums, on the other side of the bay, and continued it for a whole week. We kept up our usual meetings, and at the end of the week their drumming, singing, and dancing ceased. We continued our meetings for two months. The chief of this place was yet unconverted.

During this spring, Brother Clark, our superintendent, arrived from Sault St. Marie, with Brother William Herkimer and family, and my cousin Johnson. These were to take our places in the mission. We had now an excellent quarterly meeting. Brother Clark preached a sensible and warm sermon; my cousin interpreted it. It was a blessed time; over twenty were baptised before the services began. There was a

circumstance which rendered the occasion peculiarly interesting; an old Indian woman of about eighty years came crawling to the meeting, for she was unable to walk; her name was Anna. The year before, she had travelled three hundred and fifty miles in a canoe, to be baptised by Brother Clark. She now lived about two miles from our mission, and on the Sabbath was brought to meeting in a canoe. But on this Sabbath the wind was so high that no canoe could be launched. In the morning, after the others had left, she started for meeting, and crawled over logs, through creeks, and other difficult places near the edges of rocks. Old Anna made her appearance in the house, to the astonishment as well as to the delight of all. She seated herself in front of the preacher, and listened attentively to the words of eternal life. She united with others in praising God for his mercy and goodness, especially to herself. She spoke of the day in which she was in darkness; but now she knew, by experience, that the Lord had forgiven her sins. She cared not for the *water, mud,* or *precipices,* if she could only crawl or creep to meeting, for she felt well rewarded, because the Lord blessed her. She did not, like some, fear to soil her clothes, neither was she a *fair-day visitor* of meeting. Before her conversion she was a celebrated conjuror, and a dread to the nation; every one was afraid to incur her displeasure. The last time I saw her was in 1842, and she was still confiding in the Lord.

We were now to accompany Brother Clark to St. Marie. We started on Tuesday afternoon, at about three o'clock, in our large bark canoe, which was about thirty-six feet long, five feet wide in the centre, and three feet high. We paddled about nine miles. On the next morning, we hoisted our sail before a fresh breeze, and sailed at the rate of nine knots an hour. We reached the point on the Sand Banks in the evening, having previously tarried three hours with the Indians at Grand Island. The next day we sailed about six miles from the shore; it was quite boisterous, and when in the trough of the wave, it was impossible for us to see the land. We now came within a few miles of White-fish Point. On the following day we hoisted our sail again, and had a favourable wind; we went down the falls of St. Marie in handsome style. About twelve o'clock, *Waub-ke-newh** (White Eagle) walked about Sault St. Marie, attending to the interests of the missions. He

*This was the name given by my poor brethren to Brother Clark, and a more appropriate one could not have been given—*The King of Birds.* They knew that he had come to be instrumental in saving their never-dying souls.

was the theme of conversation in every circle, for none had ever travelled the distance in so short a time. The traders were much surprised. The Indians could hardly think it possible for any person to travel the distance in so short a time.

NOTE.—On our way to St. Marie, we saw that one of the points of Grand Island had sunk. It was formed of quicksand. It was told to the trader, Charles Holiday, by the Indians, that the Great Spirit had removed from under that point to some other point, because the Methodist missionaries had encamped there the previous fall, and had, by their *prayers*, driven the Spirit from under the point. They did not wish the missionaries to encamp any where on their island again, fearing that the island would sink.

X

And he who's doomed o'er waves to roam,
Or wander on a foreign strand,
Will sigh whene'er he thinks of home,
And better love his native land.—*W. S.*

We spent a few weeks at the Sault with the brethren, with whom we had some previous seasons. We were soon informed by our beloved superintendent that three of us would have to go to Ottawa Lake:— Taunchey, Marksman, and myself. We had, as was supposed, provisions enough to last till we reached La Pointe, where we were to obtain a fresh supply for seven months. Brothers *Tay-yash* and *Ma-mah-skah-wash*, i.e., *Fast-sailer*, accompanied us. We had a new canoe, good oars, and a new sail. After leaving, the first place which we arrived at was about six miles above the Sault St. Marie. We here saw a porcupine on the beach; and having beaten it to death, we cooked and ate it for supper. After this we were wind-bound for several days,

which delayed our arrival at the Ke-wa-we-non mission, on our way to La Pointe. On entering Aunce Bay, we were in much danger. The wind rose, with a dense fog accompanying it, and we were without a compass. We steered our course by the wind. We were very near being dashed to pieces against a large rock, a few feet from us, which we espied just in time to avoid. I had been on Lake Superior, but never saw the waves run so high as on the present occasion. It was truly wonderful that our bark canoe stood the sea so well. Nor could we see any prospect of landing. Still the spray of the gigantic waves continued to roll after us in terrific fury. The canoe still struggled between the mountain waves, and then would rise on the top. The sail spread itself like a duck just ready to fly. It appeared at times that we must all perish. But God was with us. O how kind and merciful is that Being who has the winds and waves in his hands! "O Lord, *I will* praise thee," &c. It is religion alone that can support in the time of danger. Faith lays hold on God. Yes, let *distress, sickness, trials, perils,* and even *death* come, yet if in thy hands, O Lord, we are secure.

Through a kind Providence we arrived at last at Brother Herkimer's, about ten o'clock, A.M. How we surprised them when they were told that we sailed all the morning through the fog. They at once saw the danger; but we could take no other course. We remained here but a few days. On Tuesday we left for La Pointe, 160 miles. Here was another tedious journey, for we were again wind-bound for three days; in consequence of this misfortune our provisions were exhausted. We went to Ah-too-nah-kun River on Friday evening, and travelled all night to reach Porcupine Mountains, where we arrived at daylight. We stepped out of the canoe, took our blankets, wrapped them around us, and lay on the solid rocks, where we slept about an hour and a half. Saturday morning arrived, and found us with nothing but half a pound of tea; we were now eighty-eight miles from La Pointe. We rowed all the morning, when a favourable breeze sprang up, which enabled us to gain fifty miles during that day. After nightfall we toiled to reach La Pointe by twelve o'clock on Saturday night; but we were so fatigued, sleepy, and hungry, that it was impossible to continue rowing. Now and then a little land-breeze would help us along slowly, without rowing. At last we were obliged to give up rowing, as the oars were dragging in the water. I steered the boat as well as I could. We laboured hard to keep awake. I thought of the tea; I chewed a mouthful of it and swallowed the juice; but in a few minutes I suffered so much from a griping pain that I was alarmed. Oh, I was

miserable, sick, and hungry. I could not wake any of the company; and when my pain ceased, I could scarcely keep myself awake. I now steered for the shore; it was about twelve o'clock. I threw my blanket around me, and left all hands sleeping in the boat. I threw up a little bank of sand for a pillow, and the soft wet sand was my bed.

Sabbath morning came. I had dreamed that we were just about sitting down to a warm breakfast, when Peter Marksman woke me, and said, "George, come, get up, *blackfast*," (breakfast, he meant— he could speak but little English.) If it had not been the Sabbath, I might have been induced to retaliate. It was, indeed, a *black fast*— dark enough; nothing to eat, and only tea to drink for breakfast, dinner and supper; and yet, only about fifteen miles from La Pointe; indeed, we could *see* the place; and had it not been that it was the Sabbath, feeble as we were, we would have proceeded. Here, then, we spent the Sabbath. I walked into the woods, and all that I could think of while reading my Bible, was *home*. I looked towards *home*, and wept at the thought of it. I said to myself, "O my father, if you knew my situation to-day, you would feel for me, and fly, if possible, to assist me! I feel that your prayers ascend for me; and then descend, like gentle rains, into my soul. *Home! home!* however humble, it is still *home*. This day, however, is a glorious day for my soul; but how insupportable for the body!" We had a prayer-meeting in the evening, which is still as fresh in my grateful memory as if it had but just taken place.

Monday morning, before the sun arose, we were on our way to La Pointe, where we arrived about ten o'clock. Mr. Warren, the trader at this place, supplied us with some necessaries. We breakfasted with him, and never did fish and potatoes taste half so sweet as now.

We called on the Rev. Mr. Hall, and others of the Presbyterian mission. How kindly they received and entertained us! they compelled us to live in their families, while we remained in that place. We had now to prepare to depart for Ottawa Lake, where we had been appointed by Brother Clark to spend the winter, in teaching the Indians. O what a field of labour in all these regions! Indians, from every direction, congregate here every summer; those, too, who have never heard of a Saviour!

When will all my poor people "sit together in heavenly places in Christ Jesus?" When will they cease to offer up to the Bad Spirit all they possess? Shall these also perish as did the Indians on the eastern coast? The red men of the forest were then unconscious that the white

man would at some future day spread his white sails on these waters, and claim their native woods; that a steamboat would make its appearance, like a monster from the deep, snorting *fire* and *smoke* near their shores. God of mercy, save, save my poor people!

We started for the Ottawa Lake about the eighth of October, 1835. We had to carry our canoes, with the rest of our articles, over eight portages, or carrying places, one of which was nine, and another five miles long. No language can convey an idea of the hardships and toil to which we were exposed, before we reached there; for we had to carry all our things over the carrying places; and as it was too late in the fall, and on account of the disagreeableness of the weather, we were obliged to return to La Point. The winter set in, and we travelled 170 miles by land. It was on one of these carrying places that I carried the heavy load mentioned on p. 16.

When we arrived at Ottawa Lake, the Indians were glad to see us. The chief, Moose Ogeed, *Moose tail*, was particularly kind. Here we laboured with success, though at the time many of them were absent hunting. I commenced a dayschool with few scholars. During the winter our provisions gave out; for seven weeks we had nothing, except what we caught by spearing and shooting; but in the latter part of the winter we could neither shoot rabbits, nor spear fish. What now was to be done, except to go to La Pointe, 170 miles, and obtain some flour? We ran nearly all day through the woods, and the next day my feet were blistered, occasioned by the strap of my snow shoes. The young man who accompanied me suffered still more, for the blood was oozing out through his moccasins. At the expiration of two days, at about ten o'clock in the morning, we were at Rev. Mr. Hall's, at La Pointe. Brother Hall could hardly credit the fact that we had walked 170 miles in *less* than two days.

On returning to the mission, we were one week on our journey. I had over seventy lbs. of provisions to carry when I left, and my friend and companion, whom I hired, had eighty-five lbs. The Indians, too, were almost starving, but the spring opened just in time to save them. In their journey down the river we accompanied them, and had an opportunity to converse with them about religion. On our way, the Indians pointed to the battle-grounds of the Ojibways and the Sioux. How dreadful and awful was their description! The chief, pointing to a certain spot, observed, "There I killed two Sioux, about thirteen winters ago; I cut open one of them; and when I reflected that the Sioux had cut up my own cousin, but a year before, I took out his

heart, cut a piece from it, and swallowed it whole." As he spoke, the fierceness of the Indian gleamed from his countenance. Every half mile, trees were blazed (barked), and notches made according to the number that had been killed.

The Sioux and the Ojibways have been at war from time immemorial. The neutral ground of these two nations is full of game, such as deer, bears, elks, &c. We went down to the Me-ho-me-nee Mills, on the Chippewa River, where the whites were cutting down pine trees. We then returned to Ottawa Lake, and afterwards to La Pointe.

During this winter I was with the Rev. Mr. Hall, at La Pointe, and assisted him in translating the Gospel of St. Luke and the Acts of the Apostles into the Ojibway tongue. Although I have sat hour after hour in assisting him in his good work in the west, yet I can never, never repay him for the kindness and affection shown to me. May God reward him for his labours of love, and for his Christian benevolence. He is like a pure and limpid stream which is ever running, and which never dries up. He is like a high rock on the seashore, when the storms and waves have passed by, unchanging and unchanged. He is in all respects the most suitable man for this work, being devoted, humble, kind, affectionate, and benevolent, and is master of our language. I hope to see him once, if not many times more, that I may thank him again and again for his Christian goodness. May his holy and arduous life and health be precious in God's sight.

Here I must make a remark. In that country, we ought not to know each other as Presbyterians, Methodists, or Baptists, but only as missionaries of the cross. We should labour with and for each other, and do all the good we can. Our language should always be, "Come, brethren, let us labour side by side, hold up each other's hands in the work, share each other's trials and privations, and spread the Gospel of the blessed God." May many Brother Halls be raised up for these stations, so that the poor outcast red man may soon take his station among Christians of every civilised clime. Should these observations fall under the eye of dear Brother Hall, he will, I am sure, forgive me for the warm and candid confessions of a sincere heart.

XI

The melancholy days are o'er,
 The sadness of the year,
Of wailing winds, and noded woods,
 And meadows brown and scar.—W. C. B.

We spent part of the summer at La Pointe, waiting for our superintendent, Rev. John Clark, who intended to go by the way of Ottawa Lake, down the Mississippi. He arrived in the latter part of June, with his companions. We went in two canoes up *Bad River,* and thence over the portages already named. We divided our provisions, bedding, &c., &c., so that each should carry an equal weight. In ascending Bad River we were nearly half of the time in the water, dragging the canoe up the stream. One day, Brother Clark stepped on a rock above the water, in the centre of the river, for the purpose of holding the canoe, while those that were exceedingly tired might rest. As soon as he had put his foot on the rock, the canoe wheeled around with the current, which drew him into it, and carried him down the river. We were alarmed for some time, and it was with the greatest effort that we could save him. At times, we could only see his white hat above the water. At first, we could not render him the least assistance. The stream conveyed him near the shore, where he seized the limb of a tree, which enabled him to reach land. We hurried to the spot where he landed, jumped out of the canoe, and ran after him; but before we could see him, we heard him cry out *"whoop,"* and in a few moments saw him coming through the leaves, soaking wet. We were all thankful, indeed, to see him alive, and so cheerful too. On that day we would not permit him to carry but two loads, or packs, the others carried three. Our wish was, that he should not, *at any time, carry anything;* but he

insisted upon helping us, and to this we had to submit. This was one of those kind traits which endeared him so much to all his fellow labourers. He has also shared the last morsel of bread with us. Often has he carried the canoe on his back; and when we were discouraged and faint, he would encourage us by his cheerful countenance, and words of consolation. Our sinking hearts have often been made to beat with emotions of joy; for during these journeys we had ample reasons and time for desponding. But according to our trials did we enjoy the smiles of heaven.

We were three days going over the Nine Mile Portage, where we spent the Sabbath. We had three loads each; and the two canoes had also to be carried, each one taking his turn every half mile. We were now completely jaded out; our bones ached. This was the hardest journey that I ever made, with the exception of the one which will hereafter be related.

After severe toil and privations, we arrived at Ottawa Lake, where Brother Clark met the chief and some of his warriors in council. He explained the object of our visit,—viz., to live among them and teach them; to which the chief assented.

Brother Clark now left Johnson, Marksman, and myself here, to do all the good we could. On departing, we accompanied him down the river for two days; and on the first of August we bade each other farewell.

That day, Peter and John were inconsolable because Brother Clark and the rest had left us for a whole year. I felt so "choked up" and deserted, that I talked but little during the day. After praying, as Brother Clark was parting with us, and our heads were resting on the canoe, he said, "Brethren, take courage; do all the good you can. Pray much; trust in God; tell the Indians how the Saviour died; we will pray for you; good bye; and may the Lord bless you and your labours."

We returned to Ottawa Lake, and built a house, where we resided during the year. Quite late in the fall, Johnson and Marksman left me, and went to La Pointe, where they remained all the winter. It is true, there were but few Indians here, but yet, too many for one teacher. They wished me to go with them, but I preferred, from a sense of duty, to spend the winter and spring in teaching, singing, and praying among the people here. In the spring, an interesting conversion took place; the convert committed to memory the fourteenth chapter of St. John, before he had learned the alphabet. This young man had been

remarkably kind and humane, before his conversion; he was more like a Christian than any unconverted man I ever saw. I never heard anything proceed from his mouth that was censurable. One Sabbath morning, while we were in the woods, I was reading to him, "God so loved the world, that he gave his only begotten Son, that whosoever believeth on him might not perish, but have everlasting life." This was like an arrow in his heart; he prayed and wrestled with God, until the Lord spoke peace to his soul.

In the summer, when Johnson and Marksman arrived, John and I went down to Prairie Du Chien, on the Mississippi. On our way, we had to pass through the land of the Sioux, the enemies of the Ojibways, and we knew not what would be our fate. However, we pursued our course and ventured to their village. As soon as we approached, they raised the war-whoop and fired some guns over our heads, and the bullets either splashed in front of our canoe, or whizzed about our heads. Still, we kept on our course, and as soon as we stepped from our canoe, they seized us, and kept us prisoners for nearly three days. When we told them (through an interpreter) that we were missionaries, they released us, and treated us kindly. On the third day we were on the water again, on our way to Prairie Du Chien, which place we reached, and there saw Brother Brunson, the superintendent for that year. We accompanied him to St. Peter's near the falls of St. Anthony; and the same summer, through the kindness of Brother Clark, we were sent to school near Jacksonville, Illinois. To Brother Clark, under God, I owe all the education (little as it is) which I now possess. Before this, I could neither speak nor read five words correctly. Brothers Johnson, Marksman, and myself, were placed under the car of the Rev. John Mitchell, now an assistant at the Book Concern, in Cincinnati. For two years we attended school at the Ebenezer Seminary, about two miles north of Jacksonville. At this institution I passed some of the happiest seasons of my life. Many who were with me at this school are now ministers of the Gospel, both among the whites and the Indians. The groves seemed vocal with the praises of God. The camp meeting and the quarterly meetings which I then attended, are still fresh in my memory. The remembrance of the many delightful acquaintances formed, the appointments filled, the interesting meetings I attended in different parts, about Jacksonville, at Lynville, Manchester, Rushville, and Versailles, will always hold a seat in my heart. It was here that I learned to read the word of God, and often, for hours together, upon my knees, in the groves,

have I been thus engaged. O the sweet communion I then had with God!

Among the many letters which I have since received from my schoolmates, I will trouble the reader only with the following:—

> "Mt. Sterling, *Brown Co., Ill.*
> *February 8th, 1845.*

"Dear Brother Copway,

"With pleasure I improve this privilege of answering your kind epistle, and taking a 'paper talk' with you. By the blessings of the good Lord, we are well. But I hear you say, 'What does he mean by *we?*'—Only myself, my wife, and boy! Now, if you will pardon me this time for marrying young, I will promise never to do so again. But I think you will not be severe in your censure, inasmuch as I have a worthy precedent in you. Brother Troy travelled three years, and married Brother Stratten's daughter, of Pike county; and I, who commenced three years after him, preached two years, and married another; so we, who had long been brothers, became brothers-in-law. Brother Wm. Piper was married, since Conference, to Squire Baynes' daughter, near Columbus; Harden Wallace married Miss Bronson, of Athens, one year since. Brother S. Spates is on a visit to his friends, and has the ague; neither he nor Reason is married, but have a 'good desires.' I visited Brother George two weeks since.

"We have glorious times in religion. O it would have done you good to have heard Dr. Akers tell his experience, in our last quarterly meeting. In speaking of his sanctification he said, with a peculiar emphasis, while his lips trembled and tears filled his eyes, '*It was the revelation of the Son of God in me.*' But time would fail to tell of these 'Ebenezer' boys, who, through faith, preach 'big sermons,' exhort thousands, 'who are valiant in fight,' who slaughter many a sinner, and wear the marks of many a well-fought field, although death has done his work among us! Our faithful teacher, and a beloved schoolmate, Brothers Troy and Piper, are no more; they fell victims to fever just after conference; but they fell like martyrs,—they died at their post. Brother Troy and I attended Brother Piper's funeral, (the sermon was preached by Brother Berryman,) at Barry. It was a solemn time. While I stood by his coffin, I thought of you all, and of Brother *Huddlestun,* who had gone before him. The day before I left, Father Stratten, Brother Troy, and I, walked out on the Mississippi bluffs, while the bright surface of the river reflected upon us the last rays of the setting sun. We talked of the happy days of other years, spent with kindred spirits now scattered over the world. His breast seemed warmed at the recollection. The flame of his zeal mounted high, and pointing to the bright waters that rolled in the distance, he said, 'I feel like preaching till the last sinner on the last tributary of that stream is converted to God.' Alas! he had even then preached his last sermon. Peace to their memory.

> 'They taught us how to *live,* and, O how high
> The price of knowledge, taught us how to *die.*'

Sister Piper, and her two children, live at her own home in Barry; Sister Troy, with one child, lives with her father. You have, perhaps, read the obituaries of Brothers Benson, Otwell, Corey, Edmunson, and Hale—gone home. Brother N. W. Allen married down south, and John Mathers to Miss Julia Tucker. Brother Hedenburg is in Springfield. I believe M. has concluded not to marry, but to keep house for her father. Moses C. lives and prospers in Petersburg circuit.

"*March 13th.* I commence again, not having time to finish when I commenced. I record with sorrow the death of our child, aged eight months. The affliction of one short week carried him beyond the sorrows incident to mortality, to rest with God. O it was a trial to see him sink in death, and bear him to the grave. But now, thank God,

> 'The storm that wrecks the winter sky,
> No more disturbs his sweet repose,
> Than summer evening's latest sigh,
> That shuts the rose.'

"The Lord has given us some tokens for good; we have some glorious prayer and class meetings. Thirteen joined on my last round. I expect Brother Wallace with me at a protracted meeting next week; can you not come too?"

"Well, Brother George, how do you get along in religion? This is the subject *all important.* Time, in its rapid roll, still bears us on. The sun stood still in Gibeon, but time did not stand still. The sun went back ten degrees on the dial of Ahaz, but time rolled on with unremitting speed. *Mutation* is written all around us. The little flower, so bright, is nipped by the untimely frost of winter. The rainbow is beautiful, but it passes away with the weeping cloud. And O how soon the fleeting years of time will be lost amid the mighty cycles of eternity. And yet, my brother, we know that on this inch of time hang everlasting things. Lord, help us to stamp every moment with improvement. Now, if God has entrusted to us the care of souls immortal, how should we pray and labour, lest we should lose a prize so dear!

"Brother George, I shall never forget our band society and 'young men's' prayer meeting; these were precious seasons. Though I view my brethren falling round me, the hope of immortality makes the 'valley of the shadow' flame with the glory of God. Thank God for religion—that can conquer death, and view the grave but as a subterranean passage to the skies. Go on— I expect to hail you in a better clime. Brother, I think I have *experienced* that the *blood of Christ cleanseth from all sin.* O glorious truth! Have you not found it too? It is by simple *Faith.*

> '*Faith* has an eye no tears can dim,
> A heart no griefs can stir;
> She bears the cross, and looks to Him
> Who bore the cross for her.'

"Go on, brother; the land of rest lies just across the rolling tide of Jordan. Methinks I see a Troy, a Huddlestun, and Piper, put forth their hands from

the banks of glory, to beckon us onward. They look out for us; O let us not disappoint them! You know the north and south talk of division; thank God they can't divide me, nor break those ties that bind me to good brethren everywhere, from whom 'joy, nor grief, nor time, nor place, nor life, nor death, can part.'

"I must close my scattering letter, though not half done. Brother, come down, and I'll try and tell you the rest. We can go over to Ebenezer, and have a meeting. Pitner is there now. He says that the Lord has the best market in the universe; Christian duties are always good sale there, and then we are sure to get a 'back load' of grace. He says, 'the Lord has a great big two-story *warehouse:* the promise of the life that now is, that's the *lower* story; and of that which is to come, this is the *upper* story. There,' says he, 'brethren, I'll not tell you any more; you'll have to die to know the rest.'

"My very best respects to your lady, and the little Copways.

<div align="right">

"Yours fraternally,
"WILLIAM J. RUTLEDGE."

</div>

"N. B.—Dr. Vandevanter, Brother Bond, and many others, still speak of your preaching at Versailles. We have some good times there now. Brothers Billy and Cabble Patterson are married; yes, and Aquilla, too. He preaches and teaches school. Brother Saxon still goes it with a rush. The 'first year' class of boys in this Conference are now first-rate; some of them could almost stride a mountain. Q Sir, it would do you good to see Brother Billy Piper throw his searing thunderbolts and river the forest oak, or bury them in the smoking earth. See him rise in the fulness of his strength, and exclaim, 'Man fell; Heaven was robed in silence, earth in sorrow, and Hell alone was glad.' Farewell.

<div align="right">

"W. J. R."

</div>

I attended several of the Conferences; the last of which was in Bloomfield, in 1839, where I parted with some of my dearest friends and companions, for nine months. Still it was pleasant to reflect that the Conference had appointed Brothers Spates, Huddleston, Johnson, and Peter Marksman, to labour at the head of the Mississippi. Brother Kavanaugh was appointed superintendent of the missions for that year. I was allowed to visit home in the fall, to see my friends. I travelled to Chicago free of expense; I drove a pair of fine grey horses for an individual who was on his road to that place. We slept in our waggons every night. At Chicago* I embarked in a schooner for Buffalo; but getting tired of this, left it at Detroit, and took steamboat for Buffalo, where I arrived just about daylight. I had lost my cap; the wind blew it into the lake, with my pocket book, containing 27 dollars

*Chicago signifies *the place of skunks.*

in bills, and 2.50 dollars in silver, with a silk handkerchief, in which my all was wrapped. Here I was—moneyless, friendless, and hatless, and in a strange land! I had, however, a little change left. I had made up my mind to visit the East before my return to Canada. But this must now be abandoned. I walked about Buffalo quite disheartened. At last I saw on a sign, "Temperance Hotel." I concluded to put up at this house, and, to my surprise and joy, the landlord was a warm-hearted Methodist—James Madison. At night, I accompanied him to the prayer meeting, where he told a Brother Copeland my circumstances. They made up the whole amount of my loss, and gave me a dollar over. I could now visit the East, as I had purposed before my loss. The next day I started for Rochester, where I spent the Sabbath. I was very anxious to see the great cities, of which I had read so much at school. I resolved to go through thick and thin for the sake of seeing New York. At Rochester I stopped with Brother Colby; Miss Colby, perceiving that I was not warmly clad, gave me a cloak, which she obtained from Brother S. Richardson. Should either, or both, of these dear friends see these remarks concerning their kindness, I hope they will excuse me for thus mentioning their names. I must thank them again for their goodness; I often remember them in my closet and by the wayside. May God reward them and all other friends.

On Monday I left for Albany. When I reached Syracuse, I took the long-looked-for railroad. We were soon on our way, moving along like a streak of lightning. In the morning I arrived in Albany in time for the morning boat for New York. I walked around this Dutch city, and as everything appeared to be somewhat new, I was interested, especially with the vessels, &c. As I wished to be economical, I left without any breakfast. I was charmed with the steamboat. We passed down the Hudson; the towns, villages, and the splendid scenery enchanted me. I had seen but very few such magnificent scenes before.

About noon, a plain looking man approached me; I discovered at once that he was of that class of men called Quakers. He spoke of what they were doing for the Indians in New York. I was very much interested with his conversation. I felt glad and proud to have the honour and pleasure of seeing and conversing with one of Penn's descendants—the friend of the poor Indians. While conversing with him, the bell was rung for dinner; he wished me to go down and eat; I told him I was obliged to be saving, as I had but little money, and was not accustomed to travelling. Upon saying this, he pulled out a dinner ticket from his pocket and said, *"Friend,* thou must take this

and come down to dinner." I had an exalted opinion of the Quakers before, but this kind act increased my feelings, and confirmed all that I had ever heard of their generosity to my poor people. "God bless the Quakers," said I, silently, as I descended to dinner. After dinner we finished our conversation. He said he was on his way to Philadelphia. God bless him, wherever he is. He has my kindest wishes.

In the evening I arrived at New York, and went immediately to see Brother Mason, who directed me to go to Sister Luckey's, in Broome-street, where I tarried during my stay.

On the 25th of October, came that great jubilee of Methodism. In the morning I went with Dr. Bangs to meeting. He preached the centenary sermon, which was afterwards printed. In the evening I attended the Allen-street Station. Oh, what a happy meeting this was. Here I saw some of the greatest among them weep for joy. "Amen," "Hallelujah," "Glory to God," and similar ejaculations, rang through, and filled the house. In this vast assembly was a solitary Indian— George Copway! Never can I forget that evening! Whatever may be my future lot in this life, I will always thank God for the privilege of attending these services. May the Lord pour out his Spirit on all his churches.

The next day I visited Newark, N.J., to see Brother Abraham Hedenburg, with whom I had become acquainted in Illinois, at the house of his brother James. Here I met with a great deal of kindness. Brother Bartine, of the Franklin Station, requested me to preach for him in the morning; and Brother Ayres, of the Northern Station, invited me to preach for him in the evening. Brother Ayres gave me about $8.00 worth of books, which I had the pleasure of perusing during the winter. This was a favour—a distinguished favour indeed. I have seen that dear brother but once since. May the Lord be gracious to him.

My visit to Brother Hedenburg was delightful. I met many friends here, to whom I can never be thankful enough. May God visit them in great mercy. I saw them again last summer, and partook of their kind hospitalities. I feel more and more indebted to them; especially to Brother Hedenburg.*

My next journey was to Boston. Dr. Bangs gave me a letter of

*My English friends will, I hope, excuse me for calling all good people that I have met "Brother" (though this apology may not be required by many, yet it is necessary with some), for God is my father, and every man a brother.

introduction to a brother in that city. I remained about two weeks, looking at the Yankees and their city. Boston is much overrated; there are a few, very few, pretty spots; the rest is crooked and narrow. It is far behind New York, Philadelphia, and, perhaps, Baltimore and New Orleans. I met with a few choice spirits—Brothers Kind, Rand, Wise, and Smith; and on the Sabbath I addressed the Sabbath school in Russell-street. In the evening we had a delightful meeting. I remained with Brother H. Merrell's family during my sojourn, and I shall always recollect them with feelings of sincere gratitude. I visited several noted places while in that vicinage,—the monument on Bunker's (or rather Breed's) Hill, &c.; I went also on the top of the State House when the sky was clear. It was from this point that I saw the works of the white man. The steeples, vessels arriving, and others spreading their sails for distant lands. The wharves were filled with merchandise. A few steamboats were running here and there, breathing out fire and smoke. On my left I noticed several towns. The steam cars from Worcester rolled on from the west; others were starting for Providence, and whizzed along the flats like a troop of runaway horses. Here were factories in different directions. As I saw the prosperity of the white man, I said, while tears filled my eyes, "Happy art thou, O Israel; who is like unto thee, O *people saved by the Lord!*" When I thought of the noble race of red men who once lived and roamed in all the land, and upon the waters as far as my eye could reach, the following thoughts arose in my mind, which I have since penned.

> Once more I see my fathers' land
> Upon the beach, where oceans roar;
> Where whitened bones bestrew the sand,
> Of some brave warrior of yore.
> The *groves*, where once my fathers roamed—
> The *rivers*, where the beaver dwelt—
> The *lakes*, where angry waters foamed—
> Their *charms*, with my fathers, had fled.
>
> O! tell me, ye "Palefaces," tell,
> Where have my proud ancestors gone?
> Whose smoke curled up from every dale,
> To what land have their free spirits flown?
> Whose wigwam stood where cities rise;
> On whose war-paths the steam-horse flies;
> And ships, like mon-e-doos in disguise,
> Approach the shore in endless files.

I now visited the Missionary Rooms of the American Board, whose invaluable labours are felt throughout the globe. I saw some articles wrought by our people in the west, such as bead work, porcupine quills, moccasins, war clubs, &c. I thought, that if Brother Green had seen as much of war clubs as I had (for I have seen them stained with blood, and notched according to the number of individuals they had slain), he would conceal them from every eye.

XII

See, winter comes, to rule the varied year,
Sullen and sad, with all his rising train—
Vapours, and clouds, and storm.—*T.*

About the 4th of November, I took my leave of Boston, for the great commercial emporium, on my route homewards. My travelling companion was the Rev. E. Taylor, the sailor's friend. He was on his way to Philadelphia to preach. I should suppose that a better sailor's preacher cannot be found in the Union. I was much pleased with his conversation. In one of his public addresses I was told that he said, "When I die, smother me not under the dust; but bury me in the sea, where the sea-weed will be my winding sheet, the coral my coffin, and the sea-shell my tombstone." I heard an individual say of him, "start him where you will, he will go to sea."

I was now, once more, in the magnificent city of New York. I bought a few books at the Book Rooms. After surveying the beauties and curiosities of the city, I left in the steamboat "Rochester" for Albany. I spent one day in Albany, and attended a Methodist prayer meeting. The Rev. Mr. Seymour, the preacher in charge at the Division-street Station, introduced me to Brother Page, who had the charge of the South Ferry-street Church. At the latter church I was present at a delightful and soul-stirring meeting.

The following day I took the canal for Syracuse and Oswego. On my way from Schenectady to Utica I preached twice on board the boat; and even here I found some pious souls. I observed the tears falling from several eyes. "The Lord be praised," was the language of my heart. When shall this poor heart feel fully and wholly alive to the unsurpassed favours of heaven?

I took a steamboat at Oswego, and arrived at Kingston, C. W., on the evening of Nov. 11. Here I had to pay duties on the books which I had obtained in New York. The amount to be paid was $32.50, and I had but $27. I went to Charles Oliver, deputy collector; and as soon as I laid my circumstances before him, he said, "pay the $27, and I will advance you the balance; and as soon as you reach home, write to Mr. McCaulay, the inspector-general, who lives in Toronto, and inform him who you are; he will, doubtless, authorise me to refund you the money." I did so, and shortly afterwards received the whole amount. In this public way I would express my most hearty thanks to these gentlemen for their acts of kindness towards an Indian stranger.

I arrived at Rice Lake on the 12th day of November, 1839, having been absent from home five years and four months. Never did I feel so rejoiced as when I stood on the top of a hill, and saw my village, seven miles across the lake. I gazed upon it with pure delight; and as I took a retrospective view of all the scenes which I had passed through, I wondered at myself, and at the great goodness of God. I knelt down and "blessed and thanked Him who liveth for ever," for his unspeakable goodness to a child of sin: While crossing the lake, I was in perfect ecstasies; my heart leaped with joy; and my thoughts and emotions were at my home long before my person. O how tedious and tardy the boat seemed to be; I wished for wings several times. But, at last, I planted my foot upon the spot on which I had been reared from my infancy, and where some of the sweetest and happiest recollections of my life were centered. But "every sweet has its bitter." On inquiring for some of my relatives, I was informed that they had left this, for a better life. Many of my old friends and acquaintances had gone to try the realities of another world. Numbers were bathed in tears, and the wounds of their hearts were re-opened. My own heart seemed to bleed at every pore. What a painful interview! I now requested to be shown the graves of my dear relatives and friends. I wended my way to these consecrated spots, and sighed and wept over them. My reflections were solemn indeed! I followed many of them, in my thoughts, to heaven, where they doubtless now are, celebrating

the praises of God around the throne of the blessed Redeemer. This was great consolation amidst my griefs; and I felt now determined, with God's assistance, to follow them, so far as they followed Christ, and thus be prepared to unite with them in the songs of the upper world, whenever God shall see fit to call me hence.

Brother John Sunday was at this time stationed in our village. The Lord soon visited this mission with a glorious revival; many were converted, and others reclaimed. The tracts that I had received at the Book Rooms, and the books from the American Tract Society (N.Y.) I distributed among those that could read, and they were duly appreciated. I believe that these were the means which prepared their minds to relinquish the world, and place their hopes in God.

I will now speak of Christmas and New Year. When Christmas arrived, we were invited to a centenary tea party, in company with the Rev. William Case, a well-known friend of the Indians. The party met at Alderville, eight miles from the mission. This was a season of much joy and happiness. The chiefs referred to the time when they were without the Gospel. One of them said, "Before I heard the Gospel, when Christmas came, I began to thank the Great Spirit for the day on which I could get plenty of *whiskey*. Brothers, you know how often I was dragged through the snow to my wigwam, where my wife and children were cold and hungry. Now, I drink *tea* instead of *whiskey*, and have religion with it; now my house is comfortable, and my children are pious and happy. I expect to pursue a Christian course till I arrive in heaven. My fond hope is to meet these good missionaries in the land of bliss; and not only these, but also the good John Wesley, with whom I expect to shake hands there." John Sunday's brother (Big Jacob) said, "When the Methodists were preaching to our people, I heard that the chiefs and warriors were frequently in tears. I then said, I would not shed tears were I to hear them. Still, I wished to understand for myself. I went, with a full determination not to behave myself like a *woman*—I mean, by crying. I sat near the door. The preacher was speaking about the Saviour's dying on the cross, while the Indians all around were sobbing. I began to feel serious, and then the tears fell involuntarily. Frequently I wiped my eyes, but still the tears *would flow*. I asked myself, *am I crying too?* Brethren, I was ashamed to exhibit tears; but now [here he raised his hand to heaven] it is not through cowardice that I cry, for I never shed a tear on the battle-field, nor even when my children or my friends lay dead before me. No! I never dropped a tear. I feel to-night very happy and

thankful to know that the Great Spirit did not, while I was in darkness, say, 'I will never bless this Indian.' I feel an ardent love for you all. I love *Jesus*, who has done so much for sinful me." He then sat down. Brother John Sunday now arose, and interpreted what his brother had just said; and at the close of his remarks, he turned to the whites, who had come here from Cobourg, and several other places, and said, "Brothers, that was a *great big mercy* for that *great big man.*"

I might add other cases here, but it is scarcely necessary. Suffice it to say that we enjoyed the services throughout. As I looked around, I recognized some whom I knew, and had often seen before the Gospel reached us, and who had usually spent Christmas in the gutter,— degraded, miserable, and starving. The language of the Psalmist might well have been quoted by each of these poor brethren—"Thou hast raised me up out of the filthiest sink (English translation, *'the miry clay,'*) and hast planted my feet firmly on a rock." Yes, the rock Christ Jesus.

New Year's day was observed in the same religious manner. And I cannot but remark here that it is to be greatly regretted that so many Christians in the States spend this day in gadding about from house to house, and indulging in luxuries to excess. Nay, more; I have been informed that not a few professors entertain their visitors with *firewater* or *devil's spittle* on that day. What a contradiction this would be in the estimation of converted Indians, were they to witness these scenes!

During the winter, the General Council of the Nation was held at the Credit River mission. Chief Joseph Sawyer was elected President of the Council. This noble chief has filled the chair several times since, with great credit. Several petitions, and other important documents were drawn up and signed by the different chiefs, to be presented to the Government of Canada. The whole Council waited on the Governor General, Lord Sydenham, in a body; they presented their petitions. (See Note A, at the end of this chapter.) In reply, we received but little satisfaction; he closed his note by saying, "My children, for the present I bid you all farewell." His Lordship did not even deign to affix his *name* to the note. Since then, nothing has been heard of our papers, and therefore we must conclude that they have been laid *under* the table. But what could be expected of a *"father,"* who could smile in the presence of his *"children,"* and yet stab them in the dark? (See Note B, at the close of the chapter, where the reader will find an extract from his letter to Lord John Russell.) To rebut his

false representations, I would appeal to the Report of the Commissioners on Indian Affairs in Canada; to the missionaries; and to the whole civilised and Christianised population of the Chippewa nation. I can therefore say, without the fear of respectable contradiction, that his assertions have no foundation in truth. A few drunken Indians, it is true, may be found in Canada; and these alone would be willing to call him *Father*.

It was at this General Council that I became acquainted with Captain Howell's family, of Toronto, formerly of England, and after an intimate acquaintance of some six months, I was united in marriage to his daughter Elizabeth. My wife has been a help meet indeed; she has shared my woes, my trials, my privations, and has faithfully laboured to instruct and assist the poor Indians, whenever an opportunity occurred. I often feel astonished when I reflect upon what she has endured, considering that she does not possess much physical strength. I can truly say that she has willingly partaken of the same cup that I have, although that cup has often contained *gall*. I trust that I have not transgressed the bounds of delicacy, in speaking of one who has sacrificed so much in becoming the partner of an Indian missionary. I will simply add, that Mr. and Mrs. Howell, and their daughters Caroline and Elizabeth, were then, and are now, members of the Methodist church.

In the spring which preceded my marriage, I was appointed by my people at Rice Lake to transact some business for them at Toronto. I accordingly left Rice Lake and reached Toronto in April. Just before leaving for Rice Lake, I called to see my cousin, Thomas Kezhig, who was confined to his house by consumption. While on my journey homewards, between Toronto and Port Hope, as I was sleeping on one of the sofas of the steamboat, I had the following singular dream in relation to my cousin above mentioned:—

I found myself in a path on a wide plain, which led towards the south, between two cottages. I was impressed with a belief that it was my duty to proceed to the end of the road, which, from appearances, great multitudes had walked over. On nearing the cottages, I discovered a small gate, attended by a keeper. At first he refused me an entrance, but after much persuasion he permitted me to pass, extorting from me a promise to return as soon as I should reach a certain spot, from which I could see the end of the path. I passed through the gate and travelled over a beautiful rolling country, with groves, flowers, and fruits, on my right and on my left, which delighted my eyes;

while the singing of birds delighted my ears. I walked through several streams which ran smoothly over beds of beautiful pebbles. From one of these streams I drank, and felt much refreshed. In some places I saw the impress of men's feet on the pebbles, which proved that persons had gone before me. Some time after this, I heard several voices conversing about the country to which they were travelling. I ascended a hill, from which I beheld a scene which no language can describe. In front was a large granite rock, in the form of a pyramid; it was exceedingly high; had seats on each side from the bottom to the top; and on these sat a great multitude who had died in the Lord. Here and there was a vacant seat. Some, however, were standing, and all had a pair of wings. Those that were sitting had wings, and seemed ready to fly! On the very summit, and above the rest, there was a spacious seat, or magnificent throne. One sat on this throne who shone like the sun! Over his crowned head was a circle, resembling a rainbow, on which was written, with letters of gold, "This is the King Jesus." What a splendid sight! it dazzled my eyes. Above his head were clouds of angels; these were performing beautiful gyrations. Sometimes they descended so low, that I plainly could see the upper side of their wings, which reflected a brilliant light from the throne. I did not hear them speak, but there was a noise like a mighty rushing wind, occasioned by their wings, which were constantly in motion. There were myriads upon myriads of these winged angels; the very heavens were covered with them. I observed between me and this great rock a river, part of which was as black as jet, and the rest as yellow as gold. It flowed gracefully along the edge of the beautiful green, near the rock. I saw two men plunge into its bosom, and swim. As soon as they reached the spot where the water was black, their clothes fell off of them, and were carried away by the current, while they themselves reached the shore on the opposite side. They now assumed forms too glorious for tongue or pen to describe; even imagination must fail here. They now seemed to rise up out of the river; and as they stood upon its bed, with their long white wings majestically expanded and dripping, they clapped their hands and exclaimed, "Glory to God in the highest; glory and honor to Jesus." They now stepped out of the stream, walked side by side, and ascended to their seats midway up the rock! While they were ascending, the entire multitude cheered and welcomed them. "Glory to God," "Hallelujah," with many other exclamations, were echoed in loud peals throughout the whole region. My eyes wept big burning tears, which overflowed my face. I tried to

join the happy throng in ejaculating *hallelujah*, and made several fruitless attempts to cross the river. I felt as if I were fettered, and fastened to a stake. Presently, I heard the sound of footsteps behind me; I turned around suddenly, and beheld my cousin, Thomas Kezhig, passing along. I addressed him, and said, "Where are you going, cousin?" He replied, "I am going where my *mother* and *sister* have gone; but *you* must return home soon, for you are needed there; you will one day follow us to the skies." I exerted myself to approach him, but in vain. He turned about, ran down the hill to the water, plunged in, and swam like a duck. His clothes now fell off of him, as did those of the two individuals referred to above. I saw him rise; he exclaimed, *"Glory to Jesus!"* Some one exclaimed from the rock, "Thomas Kezhig is come, Thomas Kezhig is come." Immediately two flew from their seats, and presented themselves before him, near the edge of the water. They embraced each other, and clapped their wings, as if filled with joy. O what a happy, happy scene! The immense throng of angelic beings witnessed this sight, and lowered their flight. Those on the rock now stood up at his approach, and flapped their wings. The two who had flown to him led him by the hand to a seat. Every eye was now upon him; and the whole heavens seemed to echo, *"Welcome to thy rest, thou child of affliction."* I recognised in these two his mother and sister, who had died a few years before, with a hope full of glory. I could have given worlds for permission to cross the river. I wept sorely, and felt it incumbent to return, according to my promise to the keeper of the gate. The keeper inquired, "Well, did you see them?" But my heart was too full to give utterance to my thoughts. I now awoke, much agitated, and still weeping. I looked at my watch, and discovered that it was a quarter-past one o'clock, p.m.

In the evening I met one of my step-brothers at Port Hope; he had just arrived. The first words that he uttered were, "Our cousin is no more." I inquired, "When did he die?" He replied, "Today, about one o'clock." "Then," said I, "he is happy in the realms of bliss." The next day, as I stooped over his cold remains, I could still see his glorified spirit as in my dream, welcomed to the land of angels. O! "Let me die the death of the righteous, and let my last end be like his." I loved him tenderly, and had good reason to believe that he also loved me. My readers will, I trust, excuse me for having inflicted upon them this dream. It is even now so vivid in my recollection, and being somewhat curious and peculiar, that I have ventured to give it. It is but a dream, and I wish it to go for what it is worth, and no more.

I left Toronto for the west, on the third of June, and arrived at Buffalo the same evening, just in time to fulfil an engagement. I was to address the Sunday School Missionary Society at the Methodist Episcopal Church. I was obliged to leave Mrs. Copway at Toronto, as she was not quite prepared to depart; but the following day she met me in Buffalo. Here the brethren prevailed on us to stay over the Sabbath. Sabbath morning I preached at Black Rock, and in Buffalo in the evening. What a curious, inquisitive, and teasing people, some of the Yankees are! Yet, they are very friendly withal, for every one seemed to be striving to induce us to go to their homes to take tea and to pass the night. I had been married but a few days, and the following were some of the questions put to me:— "How did you obtain your wife?" "Where were you married?" "Did her father consent?" "How many of your people have married our white women?" These and similar inquiries were constantly made, and were exceedingly annoying. But notwithstanding all this, I could say, "Farewell, *dear friends* of Buffalo; thank you for your kindness, your good wishes, and your prayers. Farewell, Sister Dobson, Brother M., and Brother Vanderpool,"—a *noble*-hearted and whole-souled man.

On the seventh of June we parted with my wife's sister, Caroline, who had come with my wife from Toronto as far as Buffalo. We were soon sailing on Lake Erie. On the eighth we were in Cleveland. Here we were obliged to stop, as the regular boat was engaged to convey persons to the great Whig Convention at Fort Meigs. But we passed a very agreeable time, however, especially with Mr. and Mrs. Peet. On the twelfth, an opportunity offered by which we could go as far as Amherstburg, on our way to Detroit. The steamboat *Milwaukie* stopped at Cleveland on her route upwards, and on board of her we went. Soon we fell in with Rev. John Clark, who was on his way from the General Conference to Chicago, in company with Rev. Mr. Colclazier, of Detroit. It was my design to preach on board, but was prevented on account of the rolling of the boat, which caused much seasickness, and our early arrival at Amherstburg. Here we stayed one week, and passed many happy hours, especially with Sister Scott. From Amherstburg we went to Detroit. On the eighteenth, we started from Detroit for Mackinaw, on board the steamboat *Robert Fulton,* which place we reached on the twentieth; here we remained a few days with B. Chapman, Esq. Here I heard of the death of one of our traders, Lavaque, a pious man, and a particular friend. I preached his funeral sermon, and then his remains were consigned to the grave.

Many wept on this occasion, for he was much beloved. Mrs. Copway was now suffering from chills and fever, which she first contracted at Toronto. On the twenty-third, we took passage on board the steamboat *Fairport*, and arrived at Green Bay early the next morning. Mrs. Copway's indisposition induced me to remain here until she should feel better. Brother Chenoworth, the stationed preacher, was absent, and it devolved on me to fill his pulpit on the Sabbath. We had a most interesting season in waiting on the Lord. Mrs. Copway's fever continued three weeks, and when it was thought that she had recovered, we took land carriage to Prairie Du Chien. But before we had gone many miles, she was again seized with chills and fever, and we were obliged to tarry at the house of a Mr. McCarty. His family were kind, and would not receive any compensation for their trouble. I now proposed to Mrs. C. to return to Green Bay, but she would not consent; saying, that as we had started, it were better to keep on. Every other day she had the fever. O how it distressed me to witness her affliction! We passed through the villages of the Stockbridge and Brother Town Indians. Their lands are good, and it is to be hoped that they will continue to conduct themselves well.

On the seventeenth July, we arrived at Winnebago Lake, where we took dinner with Brother White. After leaving this place, we had to kindle up a fire in the groves several times, in order to cook something for breakfast, and for the rest of the day; there being no settlers within twenty miles. Some men seem to have come to these "diggings" only for the purpose of defrauding travellers out of their goods and money. For every slim and dirty meal we had to pay fifty cents. There is a house between Fort Winnebago and Prairie Du Chien which I can never forget. We had to pay fifty cents for each meal(?); twenty-five cents for lodging in beds swarming with fleas and bugs. Sleep was out of the question; so I spent the hours of the night on the seat of what was called a chair. August twenty-third, we arrived at Prairie Du Chien, after much fatigue, having travelled ten days. Brother Kavanaugh had just arrived from St. Peter's, and had us conveyed to Dubuque in a canoe. Here Mrs. Copway remained, till I returned from the Conference, which was held at Mount Morris. From Dubuque we went to Prairie Du Chien in a steamboat; on the twenty-sixth we were compelled to go in our canoe to St. Peter's, on account of the shallowness of the river. Our company consisted of Brothers Spates, Huddleston, Brown, Jones, Mrs. Copway, her sister, and myself. We encamped, occasionally, on the banks of the Mississippi.

We were more than two weeks travelling 300 miles, to St. Peter's. We had a tent, which we pitched every night. On the twenty-sixth September, we had to mount the bluffs of the Mississippi river; here we found a number of Indian deities, made of stone. Mrs. Copway and her sister tumbled them all down into the river. Their worshippers must have been astounded and mortified when they returned, and discovered that their gods had vanished. On several occasions we were dripping wet. On the ninth of October we arrived at St. Peter's; we here had the happiness and privilege of associating with the Presbyterian missionaries three weeks; they were affectionate and truly kind to us. These were Brothers Garvin, Pond, Denton, and their wives. We had yet to journey nearly 300 miles. After some delay in getting ready, we started in our canoe. On the twenty-seventh of October we went about fifteen miles up the river; on the twenty-eighth, we could proceed no farther on account of the ice. Now what was to be done? If the winter sets in, while we are on our journey, we shall have to suffer much. We therefore concluded to go by land to Elk River mission. On the nineteenth, we hired a Frenchman to convey our things in his cart. It being late when we started, we walked but five miles the first day; we really dreaded the journey. On the thirtieth, while we were crossing the Rice River, the cart was upset; our provisions and clothes were filled with water, and many of our things went floating down the river. I made a fire, and we passed the rest of the day in drying our articles; fortunately, not one of us was in the cart. Mrs. Copway exhibited much patience and fortitude; she reproved us for murmuring, on account of this and other mishaps, and laughed, while our pies and cakes were sailing down the river. On the thirty-first we walked the whole day, and reached Rum River,—called so, because a barrel of rum had been concealed there. It would be too tedious to narrate *all* the circumstances connected with the rest of our journey.

On the sixth of November we arrived at the mission, having travelled, in all, about 2080 miles. The Ojibway Indians had fled from this mission, on account of their enemies, the Sioux, whom they dreaded. Here, then, we had no employment; no one to instruct! We now endured much suffering. I was taken sick with the dysentery, and remained so four months, although, occasionally, I could move about. Brother Huddleston, also, became sick; he was taken on the twenty-fifth of December, and died on the thirtieth, of dysentery. This was truly a time of trial. We buried him near the banks of the Mississippi,

on New Year's day. He had come here to do good; but O how inscrutable are the ways of God! The chief of the Ojibways had now arrived, and addressed us in the following language:—

"Brothers, I am sorry to see you all in such afflicting circumstances. I see that you loved him; and from what little I saw and knew of him, I believe he was a good man. He came here to do us good—to teach our children. You ask me where you shall bury your brother? I will tell you. Bury him on that little hill (pointing to it), so that we may see his grave as we pass up and down the river. I will tell my people to keep the grave in good order, and to respect it. No grass shall be allowed to grow too near it; we will see that it is weeded. Next summer, I will build a heap of stones about it, that all may see and know where the good man lies—he who came to bless us. Tell his father that the Sioux, our enemies, will not molest his remains."

This chief was not a pious man. Three of his warriors now went to the hill, cleared away the snow, and dug the grave according to our directions. We committed his lifeless body to the cold grave in a strange land! I never knew how much I loved him, until he was gone. Filled with tears, sobs, and sighs, Brother Spates performed the last sad office over the remains of our dearly beloved brother, while the rude blast was blowing the snow in every direction. Just before he died, he admonished and entreated us to meet him in heaven, where he assured us he was going. "Blessed are the dead, that die in the Lord."

The chief now invited us to go and reside with him at Rabbit River; and in February we did so, after having travelled three days. During these three days, however, we had often to shovel away the snow, build a fire, and spread the bedding without any tent over it. We awoke one morning, and found the snow two inches deep on the bed clothes. We built a large fire, by which we warmed ourselves and boiled some coffee. Our bread was frozen; but we thawed it, and made a meal. When this was over, off we started. By the way, I ought to have mentioned that I had a pony for Mrs. Copway and her sister, on which they could ride. Through the winter he lived on rushes, and browsed like a deer. The poor fellow had to give out, about two miles before we reached Rabbit River; Mrs. Copway, therefore, had to walk this distance on the ice, which greatly fatigued her. On Saturday night, quite late, we arrived at the shanty of Chief Hole-in-the-Sky. In all our journeyings Mrs. C. was always ready and willing to endure every hardship. She never murmured nor appeared discontented. This often

encouraged me, and afforded us much relief. I record with gratitude that God enabled her and her sister to bear up under the severest trials and hardships. We could have no earthly gain in view; the grace of God alone, therefore, supported us by day and by night, in sickness, in perils, in storms, in fatigues, in despondency, and in solitary places. At Rabbit River we laboured with considerable success; but on account of the war raging between the Sioux and the Ojibways, these two missions, with that at Ottawa Lake, had to be abandoned.

NOTE A.

"1st. The soil at the Credit is generally very poor, and, consequently, the crops are light, and this, in a great measure, discourages our people from becoming good farmers. The situation of the Credit Reserve is better calculated for commercial than agricultural purposes.

"2nd. We have learned, by experience, that living together in a village, while endeavouring to follow farming, is attended with many disadvantages, and loss of time; it is therefore desirable, that all the Indians who wish to become planters should be settled on their own lots.

"3rd. The evil example of many of the white people around our village exposes our people to the temptation of drinking fire-water, and of committing other vices.

"4th. We are of opinion, that, if we go and settle on a good tract of land, many of our young men, who are now spending their time in idleness, would be induced to become industrious, and attend to their farming."

NOTE B.

"GOVERNMENT HOUSE,
"*Kingston, 22nd July,* 1841.

"MY LORD,—I have the honour to acknowledge the receipt of your despatch of the 1st instant, No. 393, on the subject of the Indian Department in Canada. I beg to assure your lordship that I have given the subject my attentive consideration, and I hope to be able to submit for your approval a scheme for the consolidation of the Department. At the same time the matter is attended with great difficulty, arising from the peculiarity of the duties which the officers of the Department have to perform, the extent of country comprised within their jurisdiction, and, above all, from the system pursued with regard to the Indians, which, in my opinion, is of the most mistaken character. All my observation has completely satisfied me, that the direct interference of the Government is only advantageous to the Indians who can still follow their accustomed pursuits, and that if they become settlers they should be compelled to fall into the ranks of the rest of her Majesty's subjects, exercising the same independent control over their own property and their own actions, and subject to the same general laws as other citizens.

"The attempt to combine a system of pupilage with the settlement of these

people in civilised parts of the country, leads only to embarrassment to the Government, expense to the Crown, a waste of the resources of the province, and an injury to the Indians themselves. Thus circumstanced, the Indian loses all the good qualities of his wild state, and acquires nothing but the vices of civilisation. He does not become a good settler, he does not become an agriculturist or a mechanic. He does become a drunkard and a debauchee, and his females and family follow the same course. He occupies valuable land, unprofitably to himself and injuriously to the country. He gives infinite trouble to the Government, and adds nothing either to the wealth, the industry, or the defence of the province.

<div align="right">

"I have, &c.,

(Signed) "SYDENHAM."

</div>

"The Right Hon. Lord J. Russell."

The above is a fair specimen of the treatment we have received, in many cases, from those who ought to have done all they could to raise us to a position of respectability.

The natives are now doing well. They have farms of their own, upon which many of them raise from ten to fifteen hundred bushels of wheat for their families. By their own means they have kept up their schools. Churches, erected by themselves, are everywhere to be seen. We have ministers and school-teachers belonging to our own nation. And yet we have not improved.

I would ask, how much encouragement and assistance in education have we received from our former fathers? Again and again we have asked to be aided in education; if we had asked for whiskey, we could have got it; but anything to raise and benefit us we could not get.

XIII

———Let terror strike slaves mute,
Much danger makes great hearts most resolute.—*M.*

In the spring we were out of provisions, and had to fish for a living for about three weeks. Brother Spates taught school, and cousin Johnson and myself visited the wigwams daily, for the purpose of

singing and praying, and reading the words of God. They always received us kindly; and soon their minds and hearts began to feel serious, and they inclined strongly towards Christianity. It was not long after, that many of them professed to have made their peace with God, and expressed their determination to obey the precepts of Jesus. Here we must acknowledge that God "made us glad according to the days wherein he had afflicted us." We had "not laboured in vain, nor spent our strength for nought," although we had to confess that we were unprofitable servants. While conversing with a chief upon the importance of true religion, he became much troubled, and admitted that his own religion was not so good as the religion of the Bible; "But," said he, "I will embrace your religion when I shall have returned from one more battle with the Sioux; and I will then advise my people to embrace it too." What a struggle this poor fellow had within! His name was *Bah-goo-na-ge-shig* (Hole-in-the-Sky.) He had always been kind to me and mine; in the spring he presented me about eighty pounds of sugar, observing, at the same time, "I have brought this from the Sugar Bush to-day; you will require some for your family, and I cheerfully give it."

Brother Brace and his family now arrived from Prairie Du Chien. What tales of suffering did they communicate! They had travelled six hundred miles in the midst of winter; and were exposed to all winds and weathers. But, thank God, now they were with us! Their clothes were almost in strings, and their children were in rags. Expecting to find enough to live on as soon as they arrived, they brought nothing with them. Thank heaven, we were just enabled to keep them and ourselves from starving.

The Indians desired us to visit several other places, and establish ourselves there. The whole country seemed ripe for the Gospel. It was thought best that Brother Spates and myself should go down to St. Peter's, by water, and obtain provision. We were four days going, and, on our arrival, a war party was just on the eve of departing for our mission, where they intended to murder all the Ojibways they could find. I requested Brother Spates to accompany me back by land, to inform the Indians of the intention of the Sioux. He said, "there would be too much risk in going before the war party." But my wife and sister were there; they, as well as my poor people, might be barbarously murdered. After repeated efforts to get some one to accompany me, but without success, I was determined to go alone. I trusted in the God of battles, and, with his aid, I was confident that I

could prevent these merciless and blood-thirsty warriors from imbruing their hands in the blood of my nation. I was ready for a start; and went to Chief Little Crow's village, to tell him that I was going to the Rabbit River mission. Not thinking that I was in earnest, or had courage enough, he said, "Tell Hole-in-the-Sky, I am coming to get his scalp." This took place three hours before they were ready to march. In the midst of *jeers* and *war-whoops*, I left their mission-house. They did not believe that I intended to go farther than Fort Snelling. As soon as I was out of sight, I began to run as fast as I was able. I called at the Post Office, which was nine miles from the Crow mission, got my papers and letters, and ran about seven miles over the prairie without stopping. I bought a pony on the road, of a Frenchman, and having no saddle, I rode but three miles of the whole distance. I tied my pack on his back, and made him run all the afternoon. In the night, I slept without a fire. I was so anxious to get home that I had no appetite for eating, the first two days. I went at the rate of about seventy-five miles per day, and arrived home at noon, on the fourth day; having walked two hundred and forty miles, forded eight large streams, and crossed the broad Mississippi twice. My coat and pantaloons were in strips. I crossed the Mississippi just in front of our mission-house, and, as soon as possible, I told the chief that the war party were now on their way to our mission, to kill them. I advised him to lead away the women and children, which they did, and the next day they *all* left us. We, that is, my family, myself, and the other missionaries, were now left to the mercy of the Sioux. But they did not come, although they sent spies. Brother Brace, cousin Johnson, and I, now ventured to take our families down to St. Peter's. We left in a large bark canoe, and had only *one loaf* of bread, *two quarts* of beans, and *two quarts* of molasses. Brother Brace was so sick, that we had to lift him in and out of the canoe.

We saw tracks of the war party on our way to St. Peter's. They watched us on the river, as we heard afterwards. We encamped about one mile and a half this side of their watering place, during the night, and did not know that they knew this fact, as will be seen in the sequel. They came and held a council just across the river from our encampment; they could see the light of our fire. The war chiefs agreed that four of the warriors should swim over to us and take us all prisoners. One was to take the canoe to the other side of the river, to bring over the rest of the party. They were to kill me and my cousin Johnson. But the chief said to them, "If you kill these men, the Great

Spirit will be angry, and he will send his white children to kill us and our children."

One of the warriors told the chief that he was a coward, and that he ought to have remained at home. To this the chief replied, "I am no coward; and we will see who are cowards when we come in front of our enemies." Thus they disputed, and even quarrelled, among themselves, till daylight. The same morning we left without breakfast, and on the morning following we were beyond their reach.

We saw where they had raised a number of logs, so that they might lie in ambush. I ought to mention, that we were perfectly ignorant of all their plans and actions, until we arrived at St. Peter's. The chief himself communicated to us what has been stated above, in the presence of his warriors.

This country is, indeed, a dangerous place for the Ojibway missionaries; but not so for the whites, for they never pretend to interfere with them, in any way.

Before Conference, and while I was obliged to be at their mission, for there was no other road for us to go, the Sioux tried to intimidate me by pointing their guns at my breast, and by flourishing their war clubs about my head; they would say, "I wish you had *longer hair*, so that I could take a good hold of it and scalp you." I often went to see them in their tepees (wigwams); this was good policy. They frequently showed me some of the scalps of the Ojibways, and danced the scalping dance. What awful noises they made, as they danced in their fantastic dresses, with their faces painted black. They reminded me much of his Satanic and fiendish majesty, rejoicing over a damned spirit entering hell.

During this summer I accompanied brother Kavanaugh to Sandy Lake mission, at the head of the Mississippi. I returned by the falls of St. Anthony, while Brother Kavanaugh went by the way of Lake Superior, he having business with the American Fur Company. When I arrived, I learned that the elder son of Brother Kavanaugh had been drowned; he fell from a ledge of rocks. Sister Kavanaugh felt, deeply, this mercifully severe dispensation. Brother Kavanaugh now arrived; poor man! he could not speak to me for some time. I met him some distance from his house; he had heard of the circumstance, but had not, as yet, been home. "How unsearchable are God's judgments, and his ways past finding out." Yet, withal, in such dark hours, many a Christian sees parental love. Ah! we may often exclaim, in the language

of good old Jacob, "All these things are against me;" but we may also say, "God orders everything for the good of his own."

That summer we went to Conference, which was held in Platteville. I was then appointed to establish a mission at Fon du Lac, at the head of Lake Superior. Brother James Simpson was appointed school teacher.

We travelled from the Sioux mission up the St. Croix River, crossed over to Burnt-wood River, and thence to Lake Superior. Having provided food, I departed with Mrs. Copway and her sister, John Jacob, Massey, and Brother Simpson, about the fifteenth of September. We were two weeks on the St. Croix River; and part of this time I was so sick as to become delirious. I was just able to walk over the two-mile portage to Burnt-wood River. The other men, therefore, had to carry the large canoe two miles; this was hard, but it was impossible for me to help them. We were now out of provisions. I have been told, by good authority, the following singular fact:—There is but one spring which forms the two rivers—the St. Croix, which runs down to the Mississippi; and the Burnt-wood River, which runs down to Lake Superior.

In going down the Burnt-wood River, our progress was slow. We were out of provisions from Thursday till Sabbath morning, when we arrived at Fon du Lac. On Saturday, Mrs. Copway and her sister had a small piece of bread between them; the rest lived upon *hope*. In the afternoon, we rowed about twenty-eight miles, and on Sabbath morning, just at day-break, we had to start for our station, Fon du Lac; about twelve o'clock we arrived there, and saw John Laundree, the trader, who was celebrated for his hospitality. I shook hands with him; he asked me if I was sick, and said, "You look pale." I told him we were all hungry, and had had nothing to eat but a small piece of bread since Friday evening. "Ah, indeed!" said he, "I will soon have breakfast for you." Mrs. Laundree, after a few minutes, had every thing necessary for our cheer and comfort. While eating, I thought, that whatever might be said of Catholics, this was a truly Christian act, and heaven will not let it pass unnoticed.

In the evening I addressed a company of traders and Indians. I found the Indians in a miserable state; the cause of which I attribute wholly to their intercourse with the traders, the principal part of whom are notoriously wicked and profane. I felt very thankful, however, that we were here; yet I was filled with anxieties; for how should I begin my labours? Brother Simpson and I commenced by

fitting up the old mission-house, formerly occupied by the Rev. Mr. Ely, who had taught many to read and write. The school-house, also, was fitted up, and in it Brother Simpson taught, till the spring. Our prospects seemed to brighten up, and we had good reason to think that the Indians were glad to have us with them; for they sent their children regularly to school, and our religious meetings were well attended. During the winter, several became seriously and religiously affected; and in the spring, a few believed that they had experienced a change of heart. This encouraged us much. I can never forget the happy seasons I enjoyed, in my visits from house to house, and in the woods. I endeavoured to seek out all; and the good Master was gracious to me. I have often travelled about among them on snow shoes, weeping for joy. Often, too, did I sleep alone in the woods, having had to dig away the snow to prepare a place to lie on. Though frequently hungry, faint, and lonely, I enjoyed the presence of the Lord. On one occasion I was sorely tried. I accompanied one of the traders about 180 miles, to purchase cattle for our place. I bought a cow for my own immediate family, and in the spring it was killed and eaten by the Indians. Had they been in want, there might have been some excuse for such an act. We expected her to "come in" in about three weeks, and her milk was to be our chief dependence. It was a cruel piece of work. After having travelled, too, 360 miles for the purpose of obtaining her, and then to be thus deprived, was a hard case truly. Had she lived, many of the children of the Indians would have shared in the milk. When will the poor Indians be instructed in right principles?

From a long experience and close observations among the Sioux and the Ojibways, in regard to the hostile feelings existing between them, I have been brought to the following conclusions:—

1. That Christianity and education alone will check their malevolent and hostile feelings, and thus put an end to their bloody wars. For this end, missionaries must be sent to both nations.

2. That it is useless to send missionaries without suitable interpreters to assist them.

3. That missions should be established in the vicinities of the borders of the neutral grounds of these two powerful and savage nations; because in these places there is but little, if anything, to excite them to revenge.

4. That wherever a mission is once established, it must never be abandoned.

5. That where any Protestant mission is established in any village, no other denomination should establish another in the same place, or interfere in any other way.

6. That missionaries ought to assist each other, whenever they happen to fall in each other's way, or are requested to do so.

7. That missionaries ought not to preach their own peculiar doctrines, to the disadvantage of other denominations; for this not only lessens their own influence, but likewise that of others.

The scenery near the head of Lake Superior is almost as splendid as that of the beautiful Hudson. There is a magnificent fall, about eight miles above the mission. The Indians often kill moose, bears, and deer, in this region. In the spring, summer, and fall, they live on fish. As we had no salt, we were obliged to preserve our fish by hanging them on poles, with their heads downwards, and in this manner they would freeze. When the spring arrived, they began to thaw, and becoming soft, would fall from the poles. Late in the fall, white fish ascend the rapids, and can be scooped up with nets. In the spring, fish of every kind, and in great abundance, ascend these rapids.

On the 9th of April, 1842, it pleased the Lord to bless us with a son. This was our first child—a fine healthy boy. We thanked God for his goodness and mercy in preserving all our lives in the desert, and while surrounded by savages. I committed and commended him to God. May he live to take his station in the missionary field.

Brother Kavanaugh was kind enough to visit us; he returned by the way of Sandy Lake mission. I accompanied him over the first portage; here we knelt down on the green, and worshipped the God of missions. We now parted; but I still hope to see this affectionate brother again, even in this world. But if we shall never meet on earth, I trust we shall in heaven, "where the wicked cease from troubling, and the weary are at rest."

> "Where we shall forget our sorrows and pain,
> And with our Redeemer in glory shall reign;
> Shall sing the anthems resounding on high,
> And bathe in the ocean that never shall dry."

XIV

Farewell!—a word that hath been and must be;
A sound that makes us linger—yet, farewell!—*B.*

We were often delightfully associated with the Presbyterian mission-aries at La Pointe, the Rev. Messrs. Hall and Wheeler, and their amiable families. Their benevolence and Christian courtesy are above any praise that we can render; but we would acknowledge that our hearts overflow with great gratitude whenever we recall them to mind. It was here that I became acquainted with the Rev. Mr. Boutwell. I preached for these beloved brethren several times, and we enjoyed sweet communion, and some thrilling seasons together.

The Council of the Ojibway nation assembled in this place about the first of October. The Government agent, R. Stewart, of Detroit, treated with them for their mineral regions, for which the Government gave them a large amount in money. From this time I shall date the dissipation, misery, and ruin of this part of our nation.

1. Because it induced speculators to visit them yearly, to sell their goods at enormous prices, and their whiskey, which inevitably ruins both body and soul.

2. Because it opens the door for all sorts of unprincipled men and vagabonds, and for the miners, many of whom are no better than pickpockets.

3. Because, in possessing so much money, without any correct views of economy, utility, or prudence, it becomes to them "the root of all evil"—a curse, instead of a blessing.

In these appropriations the American Government have grossly erred. What benefit can the many thousands of dollars, which are paid annually, be to the Indians, if they are not capable of exercising any

judgment in relation to a proper use of money? The fact is that, at the end of every year, they are sunk into deeper degradation. I would now ask, what are millions of money without education? I do not mean that an *equivalent* should not be given for lands ceded to the Government. No; but I do mean that this equivalent should be appropriated in such a way as to produce the greatest benefits and the happiest results. If a certain amount had been given in cash, another amount in cattle and farming utensils, another in clothing, another in houses and school-houses, and the like; and with these, if a few mechanics, farmers, and teachers had been sent among them, the Indians might have become industrious, intelligent, and useful citizens. One-third of each annual payment would be sufficient to educate, and to supply all the wants of their children. It may be supposed by some, that the white people settled near them give them good advice, and urge upon them the propriety and necessity of appropriating their money in the manner just suggested. Yet this is not only *not the case*, but these very whites, at least a large majority of them, are continually laying plans by which they can extort from these unlettered and ignorant Indians whatever they possess. I write not at random, on these matters. I am too well acquainted with them, from painful observation and bitter experience. I have been present at *ten* payments; viz., at Sault St. Marie, Mackinaw, Green Bay, Prairie Du Chien, and St. Peter's. During these payments, quantities of whiskey were brought to the Indians, or else they were seduced to go elsewhere to purchase it. Poor untutored red men! you were deluded, and made drunk by white men, and then, in your hellish and drunken passions, you turned around and imbued your hands in the blood of your own relatives and brethren. And were I to narrate some of the scenes which occurred among the white faces (with black hearts) on these occasions, it would sicken the heart; nay, it would make mad the guilty, and appal the innocent. The very devil himself might shudder.

It was now two years since I left Canada; I received letters from there, from the Rev. Messrs. Stinton, Green, and Jones, requesting me to return home and labour with them. At first I did not deem it advisable to go, because I felt under many obligations to those who had sent me to school for two years, and had rendered me other kind services; and it was not until after repeated solicitations had been made, and money to defray my travelling expenses had been remitted, that I consented. I obtained permission from my superintendent, Rev. J. R. Goodrich, to depart. I left La Pointe, Oct. 10th, in the schooner

"Algonquin," for Sault St. Marie. From there we took a row-boat for Mackinaw, and at M. took a steamboat for Buffalo; we now proceeded onwards, and arrived at Toronto on the 28th of October. My wife's parents and relatives, and very many dear friends, were delighted to see us again, after an absence of two years. We found them all well, and felt grateful to God for another expression of his abundant goodness and mercy. I spent much of my time in narrating the scenes we had witnessed, and a full account of my mission.

In about a month I was sent to Credit River (Mrs. C. remained behind, in her father's family). Here I taught school till Christmas, when I began travelling with Rev. Wm. Ryerson, on a missionary tour towards Montreal. We were absent about threee months, and preached or spoke every day. We collected about a thousand dollars per month. The eloquence and piety of Brother R. seemed to be duly appreciated wherever he went. He is the best platform speaker that I ever heard in the Methodist connexion. I had supposed, however, that he would be dull and monotonous; but this was far, very far from the fact.

Having returned from this tour to Toronto, I was next appointed by the Missionary Society to labour at the Saugeeng mission, in the place of the Rev. Thomas Williams. On this journey my wife accompanied me. The distance was 160 miles, and we reached there on the 12th of April, 1843. On our way, we stopped at Goderich; and from thence we took a canoe about sixty five miles.

I entered upon my duties as a missionary among the Christian Indians. I met with difficulties, for I could obtain nothing without money; and even when a request was made, it was not met by the Society. I could not be convinced that it was my duty to starve, and, therefore, concluded I must leave. My Indian brethren stepped forward at this time, and petitioned Governor Metcalf to afford me a living from the Government. Their request was granted, and I was paid by Government 400 dollars per year, for three years. I should have continued here, but the next year my services were demanded among my relatives at Rice Lake.

In the summer, I took Mrs. Copway to Tornoto, and left her at her father's, while I was absent at Montreal with the Rev. Mr. Jones. Here we waited on the Governor-general, and presented our views, and those of our people, respecting the formation of a Manual Labour School for the benefit of the Indians. The Governor expressed himself as favourably disposed, but was too sick to take an active part in it. But before this, the Canada Conference had appointed Rev. P. Jones

and myself, to visit the missions, and ascertain how much each mission was willing to contribute for this object.* During this fall, Mr. Jones and family left for England.

I returned to Toronto and took my family back to Saugeeng mission. While on our passage, in a schooner, our little son, who was about three years old, fell overboard; we heard him fall into the water. I ran immediately to the side of the vessel, and jumped into the lake. The schooner was sailing quite rapidly, and had passed him about twenty yards. I swam as fast as possible, and saw him sink. When I reached the spot where he sank, I dived down about seven feet, seized hold of him, and brought him to the surface. As the waves were running high, it was with the greatest difficulty that I could keep him above the water, so that he could breathe; and I was compelled at times to let him sink an instant, that I might breathe myself. I heard him cry, which was encouraging, for I was fearful that he was dying. At one time I almost despaired of saving either of our lives. I was about giving up all hope, when I saw the yawl boat near me, and I was told that I was just about sinking, when the captain rescued us from a watery grave. The captain, and all on board, were so frightened, that they lost some time in concluding what to do. Had they luffed at once, and despatched the yawl, two or three minutes might have been saved. But I ought not to complain; our lives were spared, and thanks be to a kind Providence for his timely deliverance. I then gave him up to God, and prayed that he might be preserved, and be devoted to the cause of Christ.

We now resumed our labours at the mission. While at this station there were many hopeful conversions. A remarkable circumstance is, that during the whole three years of my sojourn in this field of labour, I never knew but *one single case* in which fire-water was used. I must not omit noticing here a very faithful teacher in my charge, Jacob Jackson; his influence was of the best kind; he was also a very pleasant and interesting singer. It has been but a few years since these Indians were converted. They now have good farms, dwellings, school-houses, meeting-houses, and a saw-mill. How wonderful are the effects of the Gospel! They also take delight in praying, and in singing the praises of God. Had the American Government adopted the same course towards the La Pointe Indians, that the British Government adopted towards these, the same lasting blessings would have ensued.

*The amount reported from the Indians alone was $2,800.

XV

Eloquence that charms and burns,
Startles, soothes, and wins by turns.—C.

Of late, the General Councils of the Christianised Ojibways have been convened and conducted in the same manner as public and other business meetings are conducted among the whites. The last General Council, which consisted of Ojibways and Ottawas, was held at Saugeeng. The chiefs came from Lakes St. Clair, Huron, Ontario, and Simcoe, and from Rice and Mud Lakes. The object of this convention was to devise plans by which the tract of land now owned by the Saugeeng Indians could be held for the sole benefit of the Ojibway nation; to petition the Government for aid in establishing a Manual Labour School; to ascertain the views and feelings of the chiefs in relation to forming one large settlement among themselves at Owen's Sound, there to live in future; and to attend to other things of minor importance. There were forty-eight chiefs present from Canada West alone. Chief Sawyer took the chair, and the writer had the honour of being Vice-president. Chief John Jones, of Owen Sound, was selected to deliver the opening address, in which he was to give an outline of the subjects to be discussed. The meeting was now called to order; and after singing, and an appropriate prayer by Chief John Sunday, Chief Jones arose; all were silent, and every eye was turned towards him. After rolling his small but piercing black eye over the vast assembly, he spoke as follows:—

"Brothers! You have been called from all parts of Canada, and even from the north of Georgian Bay. You are from your homes, your wives, and your children. We might regret this, were it not for the circumstances that require you here.

"Fellow Chiefs and Brothers, I have pondered with deep solicitude our present condition, and the future welfare of our children, as well as of ourselves. I have studied deeply and anxiously, in order to arrive at a true knowledge of the proper course to be pursued to secure to us and to our descendants, and even to others around us, the greatest amount of peace, health, happiness, and usefulness. The interests of the Ojibways and the Ottawas are near and dear to my heart; for them I have passed many sleepless nights, and have often suffered from an agitated mind. These nations, I am proud to say, are my brothers; many of them are bone of my bone, and for them, if needs be, I could willingly, nay, cheerfully, sacrifice anything. Brothers, you see my heart. [Here the speaker held out a piece of *white paper,* emblematical of a *pure* heart.]

"Fellow Chiefs and Warriors! I have looked over your wigwams throughout Canada, and have arrived at the conclusion that you are in a warm place; your neighbours, the whites, are kindling fires all around you [that is, clearing the lands.] One purpose for which you have been called together, is to devise some plan by which we can live together, and become a happy people, so that our dying fires may not go out [our nation may not become extinct], but may be kindled in one place, which will prove a blessing to our children.

"Brothers! Some of you are living on small parcels of land, and others on islands. We now offer you any portion of the land which we own in this region, that we may, the rest of our days, smoke the pipe of friendship, live and die together, and see our children play and be reared on one spot. We ask no money of you. We love you; and because we love you, and feel for your children, we propose this.

"Brothers! There are many other subjects which we think ought to come under your consideration besides those already stated. But the most important are:—

"1. Whether it would not be better for the whole Ojibway nation to reside on this our territory?

"2. Would it not be well to devise ways and means to establish Manual Labour Schools for the benefit of the nation?

"3. Ought not a petition to be drawn up and presented to our Great Father [the Governor General], for the purpose of fixing upon a definite time for the distribution of the annual 'presents,' and the small annuities of each tribe?

"4. Is it not desirable to petition the Governor General to appoint a resident Indian interpreter, to assist the agent in Tornoto?

"5. As we [the Christian part of our nation] have abandoned our former customs and ceremonies, ought we not to make our own laws, in order to give character and stability to our chiefs, as well as to empower them to treat with the Government under which we live, that they may, from time to time, present all our grievances and other matters to the General Government?

"My Chiefs, Brothers, Warriors! This morning [the speaker now pointed his finger towards heaven] look up and see the blue sky; there are no clouds; the sun is bright and clear. Our fathers taught us that at such assemblies, when the sky was without clouds, the Great Spirit was smiling upon them. May he now preside over us, that we may make a long, smooth, and straight path for our children. It is true. I seldom see you all; but this morning I shake hands with you all in my heart.

"Brothers! This is all I have to say."

On taking his seat, eighty-four-chiefs responded *"Hah!"* an exclamation of great applause.

Several chiefs spoke, and highly approved of what had been proposed, and expressed their gratitude for the kind offer of the lands. It was proposed to petition his Excellency the Governor to grant and secure to the Indians the whole of this territory.

The following was drawn up by John Jones, Jacob Jackson, and David Wa-wa-nosh:—

"The Petition of the Ojibway Chiefs, in General Council assembled, respecting the unceded lands north of Saugeeng and Owen's Sound, June 5th, 1845;

"To our Great Father, LORD METCALF, Governor General of British North America, and Captain General of the same, &c., &c.,

HUMBLY SHEWETH:

"FATHER—Your Petitioners having ceded a great portion of their once extensive territory about Saugeeng and Owen's Sound, and a portion of it having been restored to them since the treaty of 1836, by your Excellency's gracious commands;

"Father—Your Petitioners are very anxious that the reserve (now still known as the Indian Territory) be a perpetual reserve; as a future refuge for a general colonisation of the Ojibway nation, comprising the scattered tribes in Canada West;

"Father—And that these lands may now and for ever be opened to all the tribes; that whenever any tribe is disposed to move, that they may have nothing to fear, but have access of any of the good lands to settle upon.

"Father—You have settled your white children on those lands that once

were our fathers'; we ask now to let us have the only remaining land we have to ourselves, unmolested.

"Father—This is the prayer of your red children; and feeling confident that you will give it every important consideration which it requires, your red children will listen to hear the answer of their Great Father. And they, as in duty bound, will ever pray."

Forty-seven names, besides that of the President, were attached to this petition.

Never was I more delighted than with the appearance of this body. As I sat and looked at them, I contrasted their former (degraded) with their present (elevated) condition. The Gospel, I thought, had done all this. If any one had told me, twenty years ago, that such would be their condition, I should have ridiculed the idea, and set the narrator down for a fool or a maniac. This assembly was not convened for the purpose of devising schemes of murder—plans by which they could kill their enemies—but to adopt measures by which peace, harmony, and love might be secured, and a "smooth and straight path" made for their children. I see nothing at present to hinder them from increasing in knowledge, happiness, and usefulness, except the conduct of the Government agents, many of whom are inimical to our nation, and often prove a curse to her.

Several other papers were drawn up, and signed by the President, by order of the General Council. One of these I must be allowed to give, although it concerns myself:—

"TO ALL TO WHOM IT MAY CONCERN.—In the General Council of the Ojibway nation of Indians. We, the chiefs of the various tribes of the Ojibway Indians, do hereby appoint and authorise our beloved brother, the Rev. George Copway, as our agent for the Manual Labour School, to procure subcriptions for the same, believing that this will be one of the greatest means, if established, of raising our young men to become like our white brothers; to learn industry, economy, and to gain knowledge, that we may become a happy and a prosperous people.

"Signed, by order of the General Council,
"JOSEPH SAWYER, [L.S.]
"President of the General Council of the Ojibway Nation. "*Saugeeng*, July 4, 1845."

I will also give an extract from my letter to the Rev. Mr. Wilkinson, who was then President of the Canada Conference, immediately after the close of the General Council.

[*Extract from Letter Book, Page* 151.]
"SAUGEENG, MISSION, July 14, 1845.
"To the President of the Conference, REV. MR. WILKINSON.

* * * * * *

"The late General Council have appointed me their agent for the Manual Labour School. I shall be happy to receive any instructions you may think proper to give, on my way down (to Montreal), for I am anxious to see this going on.

* * * * *

"I remain, yours, &c.,
"GEORGE COPWAY,
"Missionary at Saugeeng."

The speeches of Jones, Sunday, Taunchey, McKue, D. Sawyer, J. Youngs, and W. Herkimer, were excellent. That of John Sunday, particularly, was uncommonly eloquent. His keen black eyes flashing fire, and his large brawny arms extended, gave great effect to his speech. As a matter of course, there were often differences of opinion, as well as warm discussions, upon various subjects; some would even feel that their views were not fairly treated; still there were no unkind remarks, no calling of hard names, no abuse, no ridicule, no insults, no threats, no intrigues, no blows, and *no challenges to meet on the field* of HONOUR(?). The individual who had the floor was never interrupted; profound attention was given, and a death-like silence was observed. Occasionally, it is true, there was perpetrated a pleasant and innocent *jeu d' esprit*, an example of which I will give.

During a protracted debate, in which Chief John Jones took a very active part, some facts were elicited, and some views were presented, which induced him to change some of his former opinions, and vote on the other side. One of the speakers, at the close of his remarks, referred to this fact, and observed, very good humouredly, "If he wishes to be like a *fish worm without a head*—capable of moving forwards or backwards—let him alone."

I have often been asked the question, "What is the reason that the Indians are diminishing in numbers, in the midst of their white neighbours?" To state all that might be said in replying to this question, would require almost a separate volume. But the following are a few of the principal reasons:—

1. The introduction of King Alcohol among them.

2. The introduction of new diseases, produced by their intercourse with the whites, and by adopting their intemperate habits.

3. Their inability to pursue that course of living, after abandoning their wigwams, which tends to health and old age.

4. Their spirits are broken down, in consequence of seeing that their *race* are becoming homeless, friendless, moneyless, and trodden down by the whites.

5. Their future prospects are gloomy and cheerless—enough to break down the noblest spirits.

There are many other reasons which could be assigned for their diminution; but are not these sufficient of themselves to crush and exterminate even any *white* race, if not protected and defended by friends and wholesome laws? Our people have been driven from their homes, and have been cajoled out of the few sacred spots where the bones of their ancestors and children lie; and where they themselves expected to lie, when released from the trials and troubles of life. Were it possible to reverse the order of things, by placing the whites in the same condition, how long would it be endured? There is not a white man, who deserves the name of *man*, that would not rather die than be deprived of his home, and driven from the graves of his relatives. "Oh shame, where is thy blush?"

With all the wholesome and enlightened laws—with all the advantages and privileges of the glorious Gospel, that shine so richly and brightly all around the white man—the poor ignorant Indians are compelled, at the point of the bayonet, to forsake the sepulchres of those most dear to them, and to retire to a strange land, where there is no inhabitant to welcome them!!! May the day soon dawn, when Justice will take her seat upon the throne.

If I did not think that there were some who are alive to the interests of my people, and often shed a tear for them—if I did not think that I could discover a gleam of light and hope in the future "I should of all men be most miserable." "Surely the bitterness of death" would be "past." I look, then, to the Gospel and to education as my only hope.

I will now state, in a very brief manner, what I think ought to be done, by those whose benevolent feelings lead them to commiserate the condition of the aborigines of America.

1. They should establish missions and high schools wherever the whites have frequent intercourse with them.

2. They should use their influence, as soon as the Indians are well educated, and understand the laws of the land, to have them placed on the same footing as the whites.

3. They should try to procure for them a territorial or district government, so that they may represent their own nation.

4. They should obtain for them deeds of their own lands; and, if qualified according to law, urge their right to vote.

The Indians will be sure to waste and squander whatever they may receive from the American or British government, unless *some*, at least, of the above suggestions shall have been put into practice.

The Council was now dissolved. The President, Chief Sawyer, proceeded to his Excellency the Governor General, and presented the petitions, in the name of the General Council. These petitions, as we learned afterwards, were received with a simple *nod* of the head! O mercy! is this for ever to be our destiny? Common humanity, at least, might have induced his lordship to speak a few consolatory words, if nothing else. Our reception was both discouraging and chilling. When we have a press of our own, we shall, perhaps, be able to plead our own cause. Give us but the *Bible*, and the influence of a *Press*, and we ask no more.

The General Council appointed me to go to Walpole, to present their address to the Walpole Island Indians, entreating them to embrace Christianity. I visited them in July.

XVI

Breathes there a man with soul so dead,
Who never to himself hath said—
This is my own, my native land?—*S.*

As the Ojibway nation are within the bounds of the two Governments—the American and the British—I will give a separate account of each. The number of our nation, according to Drake, in 1842, was thirty thousand; and this is not far from the truth. The best work

upon the Indians, however, is that deservedly popular book, by Col. McKinney, of New York—the *undoubted* friend of the red man.

I will now speak of that part of the nation who occupy places within the bounds of the United States. They inhabit all the northern part of Michigan, or the south shore of Lake Huron; the whole northern part of Wisconsin territory; all the south shore of Lake Superior, for eight hundred miles; the upper part of the Mississippi, and Sandy, Leach, and Red Lakes.

That part of our nation who live in the British possessions, occupy from Gononaque, below Kingston, throughout all western Canada; the north of Lake Huron; the north of Lake Superior; the north of Lake Winnipeg; the north of Red River Lake, about one hundred miles. The whole extent, therefore, occupied is over one thousand nine hundred miles east and west, and from two to three hundred miles north and south.

There are over five thousand living under the British Government, and less than twenty-five thousand under the American Government. There are about five thousand of these who receive religious instruction; missionaries of different denominations being sent from Canada and the United States. The Methodists were the first who preached to the Ojibways, or Massissaugas (as they are frequently called). They commenced at Credit River, in Canada West, in 1824, and at Grape Island in 1827. The conversion of some of the Ojibways commenced during those years. Native teachers were then sent to their brethren in the west, where the influence of Christianity is still felt. There are twenty-three Methodist Missionary Stations; six of which are in the States, and the remainder in Canada. There are four Presbyterian Missions, all of which are in the States; viz., La Pointe, Bad River, Leach Lake, and Red Lake. There are seven Episcopalian Mission Stations, all of which are in Canada, except one, which is at Green Bay. There are two Baptist Mission Stations, one at Sault St. Marie, and the other at Green Bay. The Roman Catholics have their missionaries in nearly all the principal places in the west.

Those who are not under religious instruction, although accessible, are wandering without the Gospel. There is a field in the territory of Wisconsin where missionaries should be sent. There are Indians all around the shores of Lake Superior, who have, from time to time, called for missionaries, and have not yet been supplied. The Hudson Bay Company have, of late, adopted a plan which, in my opinion, does them much credit; they employ missionaries to give instruction

to the Indians and their children in the principles of Christianity. There are persons who once belonged to other nations, who now live in the territory of the Ojibways.

The present state of the Christianised Ojibways is such, that they are fully ripe for greater advancement in religion, literature, and the arts and sciences. Multitudes have left their wigwams, their woods, and the chase, and are now endeavouring to tread in the footsteps of worthy white men. The reasons for all this, are the following:—

1. Their chiefs have seen the necessity of making a "smooth and straight path for their children," by appropriating as much of their means as they could spare.

2. The rising generation are beginning to thirst for learning, and are cultivating a taste for improvement more than ever.

3. Native teachers are now being trained to go to their brethren, and preach to them, in their own language, Christ, and him crucified. By this means the nation must be elevated.

Our prospects as a nation are becoming brighter through missionary efforts. There are many in Wisconsin, and at Lake du Flambeau, who have requested that missionaries be sent along the south shore of Lake Superior. The same may be said of those residing about Winnipeg and Red Lakes. Much of the western part of Red Lake is full of "the habitations of cruelty;" for the Chippewas and Sioux are habitually destroying each other.

I will here give extracts from the Report of the Commissioners, in 1842, to the Provincial Parliament, relative to the Mission Stations; also subjoin the names of the villages, with their condition, and the chiefs of each village, as far as I could ascertain them; which will show their progress, and their present state, and also those who have abandoned the wigwam and the chase, and resorted to farming for a living.

1. CHIPPEWAS ON THE RIVER THAMES.

The Chippewas and Munsees occupy a tract of land, containing about 9000 acres, in the township of Caradoc, within the London district, a distance of about twenty-five miles from the Moravian village. It is only within ten years that the Chippewas have been reclaimed from a wandering life, and settled in their present location. The Munsees have been settled since the year 1800, on land belonging to the Chippewas, with the consent of that tribe. The present number of Chippewas is 378, and of Munsees, 242.

The Chippewas and Munsees are not collected in a village, but live on small farms scattered over their tract. Some of the Chippewas are settled on surveyed

lots of twenty acres each. This tribe occupy seventy-six log-houses, and six wigwams; they possess twenty-five barns. They have 450 acres under cultivation. Their stock consists of thirty oxen, twenty-seven cows, forty-four heifers, eighty-two horses and colts, and 400 swine. Their agricultural implements include nine ploughs, nine harrows, twenty-three scythes and sickles, nineteen ox-chains, a fanning mill, four waggons and carts, seven spades, &c.; they have a blacksmith's forge, and two and a half sets of carpenter's tools.

JOHN RILEY, *Chief.*

2. THE CHIPPEWAS AT AMHERSTBURG.

They all profess Christianity, and several of them are examples of true piety. The majority are Wesleyan Methodists, and the others Roman Catholics. They have no place of worship of their own. They can command the means. The Methodist minister, however, who is stationed in the town of Amherstburg, visits those of his persuasion every Sunday, and, with the aid of an interpreter, preaches, reads, and expounds the Scriptures to them. They also have a general prayer meeting among themselves, once a fortnight, and they meet occasionally more privately for social prayer; some of them maintain family worship. The Roman Catholics attend chapel at Amherstburg, which is about three miles from their settlement.

There is at present no school among them, but they have expressed their desire to establish one, and would gladly avail themselves of instruction for their children. When there was one, the attendance of the scholars was very irregular, but their ability in acquiring knowledge was in no way inferior to that of the white children.

3. CHIPPEWAS OF THE ST. CLAIR.

These Indians are among the first whom Sir John Colborne endeavoured to settle and civilise. Previously to 1830, they were wandering heathen, like their brethren elsewhere, scattered over the western part of the Upper Province; they were drunken and dissipated in their habits, and without either religious or moral restraint. In 1830 and 1831, a number of them were collected on a reserve in the township of Sarnia, near the head of the River St. Clair, and containing 10,280 acres. A number of houses were built for them, and an officer was appointed for their superintendence. Their conversion to Christianity, and their progress in religious knowledge, and in the acquisition of sober, orderly, and industrious habits, have been, under the care of missionaries of the Wesleyan Methodist Society, both rapid and uniform. From the formation of the mission, 221 adults and 239 children have been baptised and admitted into the Methodist community. The total number, up to the year 1839–40, does not appear to have exceeded 350. Since then, their number has increased greatly by immigration, chiefly from the Saginaw Bay, in the State of Michigan, and by the settlement of wandering Indians; and, in 1842, as many as 741 received presents.

The Indians of the River aux Sables have about sixty acres under improvement, and one log house. Those at Kettle Point have twenty acres of improved

land, and two log houses. The land on the Upper Reserve was regularly surveyed and laid out into farms. The chief, with the approval of the superintendent, placed most of the present occupants on these lands; but it is not indispensable that he should be consulted, as the members of the tribe may choose any unoccupied spot. When once in possession they are secure from intrusion, but repeated ill conduct, or drunkenness, would subject them to be expelled from the reserve of the chief.

WA-WA-NOSH,
SALT, } *Chiefs.*

4. CHIPPEWAS AT WALPOLE ISLAND.

These Indians are also known under the name of Chippewas of Chenaille Ecarte. The Chippewas who have long hunted over the waste lands about the Chenaille Ecarte and Bear Creek, are a branch of the same nation which is settled in Sarnia, and share in the same annuity:

The Pottawatamies are recent immigrants from the United States.

The settlement at Walpole Island was commenced at the close of the American war, when Col. M'Kie, called by the Indians "White Elk," collected and placed upon the island, which lies at the junction of the River and Lake St. Clair, the scattered remains of some tribes of Chippewas who had been engaged on the British side. Being left for many years without any interference or assistance on the part of the Government, they became a prey to the profligate whites settled on the frontier, who, by various frauds, and in moments of intoxication, obtained leases and took possession of the most fertile and valuable part of the island.

5. CHIPPEWAS ON THE RIVER CREDIT.

These Indians are the remnant of a tribe which formerly possessed a considerable portion of the Home and Gore Districts, of which, in 1818, they surrendered the greater part, for an annuity of £532 10s, reserving only certain small tracts at the River Credit, and at Sixteen and Twelve Mile Creeks. They were the first tribe converted to Christianity in Upper Canada.

Previous to the year 1823, they were wandering pagans. In that year, Messrs. Peter and John Jones, the sons of a white surveyor and a Massissauga woman, having been converted to Christianity, and admitted members of the Wesleyan Methodist Church, became anxious to redeem their countrymen from their degraded state of heathenism and destitution. They accordingly collected a considerable number together, and, by rote and frequent repetitions, taught the first principles of Christianity to the adults, who were too far advanced in years to learn to read and write. In this manner, the Lord's Prayer, the Creed, and the Commandments, were committed to memory. As soon as the tribes were converted, they perceived the evils attendant on their former state of ignorance and vagrancy. They began to work, which they never had done before; they recognised the advantage of cultivating the soil;

they totally gave up drinking, to which they had been greatly addicted, and became sober, industrious, and consistent Christians.

J. SAWYER, } *Chiefs.*
P. JONES,

J. JONES, *War Chief.*

6. THE CHIPPEWAS OF ALNWICK.

These Indians were converted to Christianity in the years 1826–7. They were then pagans, wandering in the neighbourhood of Bellville, Kingston, and Gananoque, and were known under the name of the Massissaugas of the Bay of Quinte. In those years, between 200 and 300 were received into the Wesleyan Methodist Church, and settled on Grape Island, in the Bay of Quinte, six miles from Bellville, where they commenced planting, and where schools were established by the missionary for their instruction. On this island they resided eleven years, subsisting by agriculture and hunting. Their houses were erected partly by their own labour, and partly at the expense of the Methodist Missionary Society. The number, at length, amounted to twenty-three; besides which, they had a commodious building for religious service and school, another room for an infant school, a hospital, smithery, a shoemaker's shop, and a building for joiners' and cabinet work.

SUNDAY, } *Chiefs.*
SIMPSON,

G. COMEGO, *Ch. & M. Inter.*

7. CHIPPEWAS AT RICE LAKE.

These Indians belong to the same tribe, the Massissaugas, or Chippewas of Rice Lake, who, in 1818, surrendered the greater part of the tract now forming the Newcastle district, for an annuity of £740. They have all been reclaimed from their primitive wandering life, and settled in their present locations within the last ten or twelve years.

The Rice Lake settlement is on the northern side of the lake, and at about twelve miles from Peterborough. The number of Indians is 114. They possess about 1550 acres of land, which are subdivided into 50 acre lots; of this, 1120 acres were granted, in April, 1834, to trustees, "in trust, to hold the same for the benefit of the Indian tribes in the province, and with a view to their conversion and civilisation;" and the remaining 430 have been since purchased with their own funds. They have rather more land cleared than the Indians of Alnwick, about 400 acres; but the cultivation is not so good. The village contains thirty houses, three barns, a school-house, and a chapel with a bell. The head chief of the tribe resides here. For some time these Indians were under the charge of an officer appointed by the Indian Department, who assisted in their settlement; but at present they have no special superintendent.

POUDASH,
COPWAY, } *Chiefs.*
CROW,

8. Chippewas at Mud Lake.

The Mud Lake Indians are settled on a point of land on the Mud or Chemong Lake, sixteen miles north-west of Peterborough. They are ninety-four in number, and possess twenty dwelling houses, with three stables. They occupy a grant of 1600 acres in the township of Smith, made to the New England Company for their benefit, in April, 1837, of which about 200 acres are in cultivation. These Indians were for some time under the management of the late Mr. Scott, agent for the New England Company, and belong to the Wesleyan Methodist Church. A chapel is in the course of erection at the village, where there is already a mission-house and a school.

NOGEE,
IRON, } *Chiefs.*
MCKUE,

9. Chippewas at Balsam Lake.

The Balsam Lake Indians, ninety in number, are at present settled within the township of Bexley, on a point of land jutting out into Lake Balsam, which is the most northerly of the chain of lakes, running northward across the back townships of the district of Newcastle. The reserve, which was granted to them by the Crown, is 1206 acres in extent. Of this they have about 200 acres in cultivation. Their village contains twelve houses, a barn, and a commodious schoolhouse, in which Divine service is performed by a resident Methodist missionary. But within the present year (1843), these Indians having become dissatisfied with the climate and the quality of the land at the Balsam Lake, have purchased 600 acres on the banks of Lake Scugog, to be paid out of their share of their annuity, and are making preparations for removing from their former settlement. Their improvements will be sold for their benefit. Their reason for removing evinces their desire to advance in the pursuit of agriculture.

CRANE, *Chief.*

10. Chippewas of Rama.

These Indians formerly occupied the lands about Lake Simcoe, Holland River, and the unsettled country in the rear of the Home District. General Darling reported of them, in 1828, that they had expressed a strong desire to be admitted to Christianity, and to adopt the habits of civilised life; and that, in these respects, they might be classed with the Massissaugas of the Bay of Quinte and Rice Lake, but were then in a more savage state. In 1830, Lieutenant-governor Sir J. Colborne collected them on a tract of land on the north-west shore of Lake Simcoe, of 9800 acres in extent, where they cleared a road between that lake and Lake Huron. They consisted of three tribes of Chippewas, under Chiefs Yellowhead, Aisance, and Snake, and a brand of Pottawatamies from Drummond Island; their number was about 500, under the care of Mr. Anderson, now the superintendent at Manitoulin, who was appointed to take charge of their settlement and civilisation; they made a rapid

progress. The tribe under the Chief Yellowhead, now settled at Rama, were located at the Narrows on Lake Simcoe; Aisance's tribe, at present residing at Beausoleil, Matchadash Bay, was settled at Coldwater, at the other extremity of the reserve, the distance between them being fourteen miles.

YELLOWHEAD,
NA-NAH-GE-SKUNG, } *Chiefs.*
BIG SHILLINGE,

11. CHIPPEWAS OF BEAUSOLEIL ISLAND, MATCHADASH BAY, LAKE HURON.

This band, under the Chief Aisance, is the same which was settled by Sir John Colborne at Coldwater. Their present village, which is not very distant from the former settlement, was only commenced last year. It contains fourteen houses and a barn; the number of the band is 232. They have about 100 acres under cultivation.

The majority of these Indians are Roman Catholics. They have not, as yet, any place of worship or school. In the former settlement they were occasionally visited by the Roman Catholic priest resident at Penetanguishene.

AISANCE,
JAMES KA-DAH-GE-QUON, } *Chiefs.*

12. CHIPPEWAS OF SNAKE ISLAND, LAKE SIMCOE.

This body of Indians was one of the three bands established at Coldwater and the Narrows, and separated from them on the abandonment of those settlements. They now occupy one of the three islands on Lake Simcoe which were set apart for this tribe many years ago. They are 109 in number, and occupy twelve dwelling-houses. They have also two barns and a school-house, in which their children are instructed by a respectable teacher, and Divine service is performed by a resident missionary of the Methodist persuasion, to which these Indians belong. They have about 150 acres in cultivation, and are improving in habits of industry and agricultural skill. Their missionary, who has been acquainted with them since July, 1839, states that the majority of them are strictly moral in their character, that most of the adults are decidedly pious, and that many of them, for consistency of character, would not suffer by a comparison with white Christians of any denomination.

J. SNAKE, *Chief.*

13. CHIPPEWAS OF SAUGEENG, LAKE HURON.

It was from these Indians, and their brethren, since settled at Owen's Sound, that Sir Francis Head, in 1836, obtained a surrender of the vast tract of land lying north of the London and Gore Districts, and between the Home District and Lake Huron, containing 1,600,000 acres. He reserved, at the same time, for the Indians, the extensive peninsula lying between Lake Huron and

Georgian Bay, north of Owen's Sound, and supposed to contain about 450,000 acres.

J. Metegoub,
Alexander, } *Chiefs*
Ah-yah-bance,

14. Chippewas of Big Bay, in Owen's Sound, Lake Huron.

These Indians were formerly either wanderers in the Saugeeng tract, surrendered to Sir F. Head, or lived in scattered wigwams on the shores of Big Bay. According to the agreement then made with them, it was proposed that they should either repair to Manitoulin, or to that part of their former territory which lies north of Owen's Sound; upon which it was promised "that houses should be built for them, and proper assistance given, to enable them to become civilised, and to cultivate land."

John Jones } *Chiefs.*
Peter,

15. Chippewas and others, in the Township of Bedford.

Within a few years past, some stragglers from the Rice Lake tribe have settled in the township of Bedford, about twenty-five miles north of the town of Kingston; and recently they have been joined by a band of eighty-one Indians from Lower Canada, belonging to the post of the Lake of Two Mountains. As the settlement is of recent formation, and the claim of these Indians upon the attention of the Department of Upper Canada has only been brought forward last year, they have not yet been visited by any officer of the Department, and no account can be given of the settlement. By instructions issued in 1843, they were transferred from the Roll of Lower Canada to that of the Upper Province, and, accordingly, received their presents for the first time in that Province.

My beloved Reader—I am now about closing my narrative, and in doing this there are but a few things to say. Throughout the work I have confined my remarks chiefly to my own nation. But it must not be supposed, on this account, that I am forgetful of my brethren of the other Indian nations. The prayers and benevolent efforts of all Christendom should be directed towards all men every where. The Gospel should be preached to every creature; and the field is the *wide* WORLD.

The Menomenees in Wisconsin, the Winnebagoes and Pottawatamies in Iowa, the warlike nations of the Sacs and Foxes, the Osages, Pawnees, Mandans, Kansas, Creeks, Omahas, Otoes, Delawares, Iowas, and a number of others elsewhere, must perish, as did their brethren in the eastern States, unless the white man send them the

Gospel, and the blessings of education. There is field enough for all denominations to labour in, without interfering with each other. It is too late in the day to assert that the Indians cannot be raised up out of their degraded state, and educated for God and heaven. None need be discouraged since the Ojibways in Western Canada have been converted. No language is adequate to portray the misery, wretchedness, and degradation in which we were, when the word of God was first brought and preached to us.

It is not necessary to detail each and every wrong that my poor people have suffered at the hands of the white man. Enough has already been said, in various parts of the work, to prove that they have been most grossly abused, peeled, and wronged. Nor shall I notice the *personal wrongs* that I myself have received; and from those, too, of whom I had good reason to hope better things. I once thought that there were some things that I could never forgive; but the religion of Jesus, and the law of love, have taught me differently. I *do* forgive them; and may God forgive them and me too.

I have sometimes heard it said that our forefathers were cruel to the forefathers of the whites. But was not this done through ignorance, or in self-defence? Had your fathers adopted the plan of the great philanthropist, William Penn, neither fields, nor clubs, nor waters, would have been crimsoned with each other's blood. The white men have been like the greedy lion, pouncing upon and devouring its prey. They have driven us from our nation, our homes, and possessions; compelled us to seek a refuge in Missouri, among strangers and wild beasts; and will, perhaps, soon compel us to scale the Rocky Mountains; and, for aught I can tell, we may yet be driven to the Pacific Ocean, there to find our graves. My only trust is, that there is a just God. Was it to perpetrate such acts that you have been exalted above all other nations? Providence intended you for a *blessing*, and not a *curse* to us. You have sent your missionaries to Burmah, China, the Sandwich Islands, and to almost every part of the world; and shall the Indians *perish at your own door?*

Is it not well known that the Indians have a generous and magnanimous heart? I feel proud to mention in this connection the names of a Pocahontas, Massasoit, Skenandoah, Logan, Kusic, Pushmataha, Philip, Tecumseh, Osceola, Petalesharro, and thousands of others. Such names are an honour to the world! Let a late Governor of Massachusetts* speak for our fathers, when they first beheld the trembling white man:—

* Edward Everett, Esq.

"Brothers! when our fathers came over the great waters, they were a small band. The red man stood upon the rock by the seaside, and saw our fathers. He might have pushed them into the water and drowned them. But he stretched out his arms to our fathers and said, 'Welcome, white men!' Our fathers were hungry, and the red man gave them corn and venison. Our fathers were cold, and the red man wrapped them up in his blanket. We are now numerous and powerful, but we remember the kindness of the red man to our fathers."

And what have we received since, in return? Is it for the deeds of a Pocahontas, a Massasoit, and a host of others, that we have been plundered and oppressed, and expelled from the hallowed graves of our ancestors? If help cannot be obtained from England and America, where else can we look? Will you, then, lend us a helping hand, and make some amends for past injuries?

It is often said, that the Indians are *revengeful, cruel,* and *ungovernable.* But go to them with nothing but *The* BIBLE *in your hands,* and LOVE *in your hearts,* and you may live with them in perfect safety, share their morsel with them, and, like the celebrated Bartram, return to your homes UNHARMED. They very soon learn to venerate the Bible; as a proof of this, I will give an instance that came under my own eye:—While at the Rabbit River mission, a chief from the west visited me. After reading to him several chapters from the Bible, he said, with much surprise, "Is *this* the book that I hear so much about in *my* country?" I replied, "Yes; and these are the words of *Ke-sha-mon-e-doo*," (the Great Spirit.) "Will you not," said he, "give me one? I wish to show it to my people." I told him, "Not without you first promise that you will take care of it." He promised me that he would. I handed it to him; he took it, and turned it over and over, and then exclaimed, *"Wonderful, wonderful! this is the book of the Great Spirit!"* He then wrapped it up in a silk handkerchief, and the handkerchief in three or four folds of cloth. I heard, afterwards, from the trader, that the book was still kept sacred. O, if my poor brother could but *read* and *understand* that blessed volume, how soon would his dumb idols be "cast down to the moles and to the bats!" Will no one go and tell him and his nation of the boundless, beseeching, bleeding, dying love of a Saviour, and urge upon them the importance of such a preparation of heart as will enable them "to give up their account with joy?" The Great Spirit is no respecter of persons; He has made of one blood all the nations of the earth; He loves all his children alike; and his highest attributes are *love, mercy,* and *justice.* If this be so,—and who dare doubt it?—will He not stretch out his hand and

help them, and avenge their wrongs? "If offences *must* come," let it be recollected that *woe* is denounced against them "from *whom* they come."

I again propose that the territories of the Indians in the British dominions be annexed to that Government, and those in the American dominions to the Federal Union. And, finally, in the language of that excellent, magnanimous, and benevolent friend of the poor children of the forest, Col. Thos. McKinney, I would say,—

"I have already referred, in the commencement of this proposal to annex the Indian territory to our Union, to those good men, who, in the character of missionaries, have kept side by side with the Indians, in so many of their afflictions and migrations. I will again refer to them, and implore them, by all the lost labour of the past, and by the hopes of the future; by the critical condition of the pacific relations that exist between the Indians and us; and by the sacredness of the cause in which they are engaged, to look well and earnestly into this subject, and learn from the past what *must* attend upon their labours in the future, if the change I propose, or some other change equivalent to it, be not brought about. And seeing, as they must see, that the plan I propose, or some other, is indispensable to the success they seek to command, I implore them to take up the subject in all its bearings, and by the instrumentalities which they have at command, manufacture, collect, and embody public opinion, in regard to what may be determined to be done; and by memorial, and personal agencies, bring this opinion to bear upon Congress, with whom alone the power is vested, to redeem, disenthral, and save, and bless, the remnants of this aboriginal race. And I make the same appeal to all the good, of all religious persuasions, both in the Church and out of it, and politicians of all parties, to second this attempt, feeble as I know it to be, to save the Indians, and consolidate and perpetuate peace between them and us, and, by so doing, ward off the terrible retribution which must sooner or later, unless it be averted, fall upon this nation."

XVII

Wise men ne'er sit and wail their loss,
But cheerly seek how to redress their harm.—*S*.

The following address before the Legislature of Pennsylvania will give some idea of the great object I have been endeavoring to bring before the different legislative bodies of the United States. At the close of the address I insert a copy of the resolution which has been passed in the North Carolina Legislature, as a specimen of the desire entertained by many for the success of my cause in America. Many others have passed similar resolutions. I have received letters of commendation from Government and from the mayors of the largest cities, and it is for this great object that I desire the kind aid of the Christian public.

GENTLEMEN,—My limited knowledge of your language will render it somewhat difficult for me to be understood this evening, as I speak a tongue which is not my own—which is not my native language. Permit me, however, to ask your indulgence while I endeavour to present to you the claims of the Indian, and at the same time I solicit you to extend to me, personally, your sympathy, as well as to the cause in which I am engaged. Besides the embarrassments under which I labour at the present moment, I have had for several days past a severe cold, which, in a great degree, incapacitates me from speaking with that ease and freedom that I could wish, in order to lay my heart open to you.

In presenting the claims of my unfortunate race, I cannot resist recurring to the period when the Indian and the white man first commenced their intercourse, three hundred and fifty-six years ago.

The Indian was then an inhabitant of all the eastern countries on which rest the different cities of the Atlantic States. The Indian was the sovereign of the whole country; the mountain echoed with his voice, and all he saw was his. The game of the forest he claimed as his own, the fish of the waters and the course of the rivers were also his. Proudly he then roamed through the country where now stand your farms and your mighty cities. There was then no cloud that the heathen saw portending to danger. The heavens were clear before his eye. He knew no boundaries; he knew no limits to his desire. And when he was found in this country, he had no extent of society, he had no extensive institutions, which have since been established where he then lived. There were no palaces, with their gaudy attendants; but, wherever you now see the mountains of your State, whether in the north, the south, or the west, you may picture to your mind's eye the noble form of the Indian standing on one of their lofty peaks. He made his native mountains his throne, and it was from thence he could see, to a limited extent, his boundless empire.

While the Paleface trembled on Plymouth Rock, shivering there with cold, his billow-tossed limbs were gathered by our fathers, who brought him to their firesides, and introduced him to their people. The Palefaces were then a small nation, but they have since become a great one, and the proud sons of the forest have, one by one, fallen away, like the stars that die at a distance in the skies. In return for our kindness and friendly feeling towards you, we look to you for production, for guardianship, for instruction, as we protected and taught your fathers in the early history of this country. Several years back, with much solicitude, I endeavoured to study the peculiar wants of my poor people, as well as the condition of the emigrants westward; and in order to promote the welfare and interests of both, I attempted, to the best of my ability, to mature a plan which, I think, if carried into effect, will prove highly beneficial and advantageous to both people, the whites as well as the Indians. Gentlemen, I feel assured that when you shall have heard all my remarks on this important and interesting subject, you will not accuse me of selfishness on this occasion, as I have not overlooked your nation in advocating the claims of my own.

In presenting my plan before you this evening, gentlemen, permit me to state, in as few words as possible, what I have to say, as I wish to accomplish my visits to the different State Legislatures now in session, on this errand, with as little delay as possible. On the 31st of

March last, you may remember that a meeting was held in the city of Philadelphia, where I attended for the first time, and broached the subject of civilisation among the Indians in a more extensive and elaborate manner than on the present occasion. I found, however, that it was done at a consumption of a great deal more time and an expenditure of money than I could conveniently afford. I found that the getting up of meetings in cities was a more tardy and inefficient method of obtaining the action of Congress in the matter, than in personally soliciting and enlisting the aid, influence, and action of the legislatures of the several States. I have visited the different States of the Union, presented to them my views in relation to saving the Indians, and, if possible, to get their expressions of approbation of my plan, in order that their resolutions might be addressed to Congress, in the hope that they may set apart a territory in the west, in which all the Indian tribes shall be collected, and there remain unmolested for ever. Gentlemen, I have found this project, as far as I have gone, meet the views of those who have counselled me in the matter.

The object I have in view is to call upon the General Government to grant to the Indians a part of the north western territory, west of the Iowa territory, and between the Nebraska and Minesotta territories, for the use and occupancy of all those Indians who are living there in a scattered condition, where they can enjoy permanent homes, the advantages of education and agricultural instruction, so that, after a time, when they shall have become Christianised and enlightened, they may be incorporated into the Federal Union as a State. Before we can do much good for the Indians, we must, as I have already said, provide them *permanent* homes, and by that means secure to them peace of mind, which is absolutely necessary to ensure their improvement and progress in the arts of civilisation. Much good can be effected in this way; and all the Indian tribes will assemble together, and go to their new and permanent homes, there to live in peace and harmony.

But the Indians, in their present isolated condition, are eternally at war with each other, and every influence is now brought to bear upon them, that is calculated to increase their revengeful feelings toward one another. I do not refer to the civilised, educated, and enlightened portion of the Indians that are now living in different parts of the United States, as, for instance, the Indians of the State of New York, and those in Michigan, and the States of North and South Carolina, as well as Georgia. All these Indians, however, will go to the far west, and there join their brethren and form one family. I repeat, that I do

not mean that the more improved and educated portion of them will remove from their present homes, but only those who are not so advanced in civilisation. Let them remain where they are, and go on improving and enjoying all the blessings of civilisation. I mean that those Indians that are scattered in Michigan, the territory of Iowa, and on the banks of the Mississippi, shall go to one place, and form a great settlement among themselves.

Gentlemen, in advocating this plan in the different States of the Union, I have been asked the question—"Have not the Indians now homes in the west, which the United States have granted them, on the other side of the Mississippi?" Those Indians in Arkansas—the Chickasaws and Creeks, and several other nations have homes there, and the same kind that they had when they were east of the Mississippi river. It is said that their homes have been so secured to them that no one can buy their homes from them. That, gentlemen, is our present version of the acts of the General Government with the Indians; but have they not been violated in bygone ages? Have not the laws which have been secured to this people been violated by those who succeeded to the law-making power? Most assuredly they have. Unfortunately for the Government of the United States, the commissioners appointed by it to select a territory for the Indians, selected the best portions of the west, and the consequence has been that circumstances have rendered it impossible—and unfortunately—for them to hold their lands.

In the first place, their position is such that their land extends all the way from Texas to the North, like a barrier through which emigration must press. There, roads are to be constructed and canals opened through their country. Military roads, too, will be opened for emigrants; and, no sooner do you propose to go and buy one acre of land to open these highways, than the eye of the Indian will be directed with suspicion to their Great Father, and the Indians will be removed from the last acre of land that they hold.

2. The quality of their land is another great inducement to deprive them of it, and they never can hold it. Several months ago, I was conversing on the subject with Mr. Albert Gallatin, of New York, when he remarked, "That is one of the greatest reasons why the Indians can never hold the lands which the United States has ceded to them. The quality is such, that the people living out west will tease the Indian, and also the Government of the United States, that in the end the land will be bought again from the Indians by the Government."

Then, again, the day will come when we will see trouble, as in the State of Georgia.

3. The quantity of the land is so great that they cannot hold it. And what do the Indians want with so much land, when we are attempting to teach them the science of agriculture? For the having so much land begets a feverish anxiety on their part for deer hunting; and, as long as there is a deer on their territory, so long will they let fall every agricultural implement from their hands, and take their guns, to maintain themselves by hunting.

4. They have no means of educating their children, because they are inhabiting so broad an extent of country, that it is impossible for the people of the United States to supply them with schools, and teachers of morality, and the arts and sciences, which are necessary to elevate their condition.

5. They depend upon the proceeds of the sales of their lands, and having a great quantity for sale, they dispose of it, and will reason thus:—"My children will fare no worse than I have fared. I was living yonder; my father sold a portion of the territory which we occupy to the United States, upon the proceeds of which I and my children have lived, and now the United States will buy this land from us. My children will fare the same as I fared, ever since I sold it to the United States.* Therefore, it will not be worth while to have plantations, because they will only be a loss to us; for, no sooner have we our plantations and our farms, than we must be compelled to sell them through necessity." This moving, then, must still go on westwardly, till the last Indian shall stand on the barren peaks of the Rocky Mountains, and gaze on the land which has been taken from him. The kindhearted then will drop a tear for the fate of that race, which was once noble and free as the eagle that soars in the skies.

6. The scarcity of food which must follow, will produce trouble between the Indians and the Government of the United States; for, as long as there is a deer or a buffalo on this side of the Rocky Mountains, no cloud of discord will be over the head of the Indian and the white man. But, no sooner will the last resource of the Indian be gone, than he will nerve himself for the worst, and take up his weapons of warfare. He will feed for a time upon the cattle on the frontier, but no sooner has he killed a bullock or a steer for his subsistence, than the newspapers abroad will proclaim that "the Indians are coming against

*That is, living on their annuities for the time being.

us, and they are killing our cattle by hundreds;" that the whole country is in danger; and soon the soldiers will be on the spot, and the rattling of their fire-arms be heard, giving proof of the destruction of a race that once lived in this country. And when, gentlemen, that day comes, the Indian will die with his weapons of war—for he will not die but at the mouth of the cannon, when desperation has driven him to it. In order to avert this state of things, I have addressed the legislatures of the several States. I love peace—I am for peace.

7. The Indians, in their present distinctive position—in the isolated condition in which they are found—will perpetuate the peculiarities which characterise them as a nation apart from others. The Sioux, the Winnebagoes the Pottawatamies, the Osages, and the rest of the Indians have their several peculiarities; but when you come to throw their interest in the centre, the effect will be to unite the one tribe to the other—an interest which the United States alone is capable of giving and controlling. What, I ask, would be the natural results of such an arrangement, if carried into operation? In the first place, there would be a perceptible improvement in the physical, intellectual and moral condition of the Indians. Their seminaries of learning would be permanent. There is now annually appropriated, by the generosity of the people of the United States, for the purpose of educating the Indians, the sum of 10,000 dollars, and that is so divided in the west, that sometimes two or three dollars of it come to us at the head waters of the Mississippi and the Lake Superior. The money, in short, is so scattered along the banks of the Mississippi river, and the banks of the great northern lakes, as not to be of any perceptible advantage to those for whom it is intended. The small sum of 10,000 dollars, circulated over so extensive a country, and intended to be used in paying teachers to educate the Indians, does little or no good.

Suppose you were to go and sow seed on the ground, putting two grains there, and one here, and another yonder, when the ground was rich to produce fruit; and, in the spring of the year, on going to it, you would find but a very spare crop—a little stick here and another there only—the little birds having had access to the seed at all times, and much of which would be destroyed by disease. This by way of illustration. But, gentlemen, put the Indians on one territory, in a central position, and use the fund now set apart for school purposes, and you will have schools and seminaries of learning that shall reflect credit alike upon the Indians and the Government of the United States, the benefits and good effects of which will be felt for ages to come.

Wherever the Government and the missionaries have succeeded in educating the Indians, they have become an industrious, moral, and well-behaved people. We have learned to read and write. We have tried to become like the white people, but when the Indian sees the deer bounding before him, he will let drop all his implements of husbandry, and follow the chase.

But no sooner have the Indians gone on and made improvements, and our children begun to like to go to the school-houses which have been erected, than we hear the cry of the United States Government, "We want your lands;" and, in going from one place to another, the Indian loses all that he had previously learned. But were they to be placed in a position where they would for ever be free from molestation, then they would profit by the establishment of schools among them, and religion and piety would increase and flourish among that people. The disastrous effects of removing the Indians have been shown on the banks of the Ohio and the Sandusky, and in Georgia and New York; where the Presbyterians laboured hard to make the Indians what they were, twenty-five or thirty years ago. And no sooner did the tree of piety begin to expand its limbs, than comes the request, "We want you to go westward. We want your lands." The Indian reluctantly gives up his land to the American Government, not believing, at first, that they were in earnest; but, when he was convinced of the fact, and his soul being almost teased out of him, and the soldiers having dug up the tree, and taken it to the woods of Arkansas, there to plant it, he surrendered.

We have ever been told that while the eye of philosophy has ever looked on, that, under all favourable circumstances, the Indian would be Indian still. And, I would ask, who, under such circumstances, would improve? We cannot find institutions of learning, even among the whites, cherished though they may be to a greater extent, always patronised according to their worth.

2. When the Indians have a permanent home given, then what they did on their plantations would of course be permanent. When you give them a home, you will find contentment around their firesides; but, if they see a probability of their being removed still farther westward, the Indians will act as they have always done, showing that they have no faith in the Government of the United States.

Yes! when I went to Washington, last April, I saw there a chief from Green Bay, whose name was John Quincy, to whom I opened my heart as to what I intended, if possible, to accomplish. No sooner did

he learn what my object was, than he rose from his seat, and stretching forth his hands—the tears running from his eyes—he said, "I hope the Great Spirit will preserve your life till you accomplish this object; for if the day shall come when the United States shall grant to the Indians a country to the west, I will be the first one to move there, for I am tired of moving about from place to place; for, when we came from the State of New York to Green Bay, we were told that we should not have to remove again; and now, again, Col. Medilly will not settle with us for $7,000, in order that we might sell our lands again, as we did several years ago." The poor man then sat down.

Ah, my dear friends, if there be any one here who calls himself a man, I would ask him if he would not feel for any one placed in such circumstances as these?

3. By circumscribing the domains of the Indians, you will make agriculturists of them. Twenty-five years ago, in Canada, we were all hunters, and it is now seventeen or eighteen years since we became agriculturists. So long as there was a deer to hunt, within a range of eighteen or twenty miles, we did not regard agricultural pursuits; but no sooner was the country cleared and settled, than we became agriculturists. No sooner did they find that they could raise grain in the quantity of 1000 bushels a year, than they were encouraged to labour.

4. The Indians are a social race. They are social among themselves, and were they to be placed in a central position, the intimacy between the several nations would soon become strong, and they would be on the most friendly terms. Their respective nationalities would, before the lapse of many years, be lost, and they would become social and kind towards each other; and thus would be brought about a peaceful state of society, which is necessary in order to their improvement.

5. Contentment would be followed by all its attendant blessings. The missionary societies would have great influence, and one school teacher could be employed in educating hundreds; but, while the Indians are in a separate and isolated condition, they cannot avail themselves of these advantages. So that, in forty or fifty years hence, the condition of the Indians will be greatly ameliorated and improved. I say it is impossible for you, according to your present system, to succeed in converting the whole of the North American Indians.

6. You must convince the Indians that it is for their good and their salvation—that it will be just and right. The Indian is not a stupid being. When he is convinced, by the advice and arguments of some

kind-hearted man, that his home is never to be touched again—that his children are never to be removed, and that the fruit of his labour is never to be blasted as heretofore,—then will he accept it and act upon it.

7. The improvement of which I speak cannot be accomplished in one day, or in one year, or five years. The elements are now ripening in the far west. If the Government of the United States would look to the example of William Penn, and assure the Indians that their new home should be permanent, then they need never fear that one arrow is ever to be directed against it, or the people of the United States. So long as the people follow the example of that kind and good-hearted man, William Penn, towards the Indians of Delaware, when he first came to this country, they never need be at war with the Indian tribes.

8. Emulation would spring up all around them. Some may do well, and thus set an example to those who are not doing well. We do not expect much from the old men, but after they shall have passed away—have ceased to exist—their children will imbibe a different spirit from them. They will be guided and governed by Christianity on the one hand, and education on the other.

9. Your Government expenses would become less. Now you are trying to fortify the whole of the west by means of barracks and garrisons. You have spent thousands upon thousands, and millions upon millions of dollars, for the last forty or fifty years, and what has it been for? Because, it is said, it is necessary to defend the frontier settlements from the encroachments of the Indians. Therefore it is that you have sent your soldiers to your garrisons from Arkansas away down to the north. Now all that we have to ask is, to have but one garrison in the central part of the territory. If there is any bad feeling among the Indians, that will be a check upon them. Instead of incurring so much expense and trouble in undertaking to fortify the entire far west with barracks and garrisons, I would ask the Government to give us four or five hundred soldiers, to go (not as a great many have done, to break down and overawe the Indian spirit, under pretext that they are encroaching upon the white people) to ward off the hard-hearted white men, who disturb the peace of the Indians by selling them liquors—for many of them are worse than the worst kind of Indians I ever did see. (Applause and laughter.)

10. In buying up the country which lies on this side of the Rocky Mountains, I would have given but one price for it—for, according to Col. McKinney's statement, you have given a quarter of a cent per

acre for the land to the Indians, who have afterwards sold it to the Government for half a cent, by having to purchase it so often.

11. The expense of sending agents to reside among the Indians has become a loss on the part of the Government, for we would ask but one or two. You have got ten or fifteen among the Chippewas, and ten or fifteen among other nations, and consequently you have expended thousands of dollars needlessly. And some of these agents do not know the Indian character, and are, therefore, unfit to be agents. We want agents who would keep the door, and all the whites that should come among us would have to come through them. By this means we would ward off a great many wicked men; and when there are any offenders against the laws of the United States, we will hand them over for punishment, and when also there should happen to be any offenders against our own laws, we will punish them. If there is any misunderstanding between the Indians and the agents, then the difficulty can be adjusted between the parties.

12. The expense of transporting the Indians has been great to the Government, but as soon as you give country to the Indians, you will be relieved from the trouble of removing them, for they will go there of themselves.

13. The missionary labours there would become permanent, which has not been the case since their labours have been broken up. And the Indian has always been the sufferer.

14. Gentlemen, in conclusion, I deem it necessary to give the reasons why the Indians have decreased and not improved,—why they have decreased in a vastly greater proportion since the introduction of the white race on this continent, than before. Prior to their landing on these shores, the small pox, and many other virulent and noxious diseases, were unknown among the Indians.

The wars that have raged among themselves. Before the discovery of America, and before the introduction of fire-arms from Europe, the wars among the Indians were not so fatal and destructive as they are now. They have been taught to handle fire-arms with a great deal of skill. The history of Pennsylvania,—the history of the New England States, and the history of the south, all tells in what manner those wars were conducted. Champlain, in 1612, supplied the Indians in the north with firearms, to oppose the Six Nations in that part of Canada, now composing a portion of the State of New York, who at length became so reduced in numbers that they were compelled to give up the contest. And so it was with the Spaniards in the south, who, as

well as the French and English, also furnished arms to the Indians. In all the wars that have been waged in this country among the European powers, the Indian was always asked to show his fearless nature on the battle-field, in behalf of the English, French, Spaniards, and Americans. And when the Indian has received these weapons of war from them, his heart has bled, and he has suffered. Yes! look towards the south. In 1763, the Spaniards were waging war against the French. Look in the State of New York, among that class of people who were of German descent, who encouraged the Indians to war against each other. Look, too, among the people of the north in Canada, where the British Government furnished the Indians with munitions of war, and encouraged them to fight against the North Americans. Sometimes the Indian has been called a savage, because he has been called upon to go and show his bravery in the field.

I ask you, gentlemen, as intelligent men,—men who live in an enlightened age,—which was the most savage, those who knew not the origin of these wars, or those who did? Spirituous liquor has been the great cause of the decrease of the Indians of this country. Disease, war, and famine have alike preyed upon the life of the Indian. But, ah, alcoholic spirits have cut off the existence of those nations who have left the records of their existence upon their rivers and their mountians. I remember well, when I was but a child, that my mother related to me the introduction of liquor on the shores of Lake Superior. Some young men (said she,) were urged to go down to Montreal. They went, and returned late in the year; a council of the nation was called, and one of the men seized a war club and knocked down another. He then fled into the woods, and his brother took the place of the murderer, ordered the men to make two fires, and place a post behind him; then to paint his bare breast black, and put a white spot near the place where he felt his heart beating. And when all these things had been done, twelve warriors came forth with their bows and arrows to shoot him in the breast as soon as he was ready. "Don't shoot me," he said, "till I have sung the death song." When he was ready, he called out to his brother, "I am now ready to die in your stead, and if you can live to endure the idea, that the world shall look upon you as a coward, you will not disgrace the clan to which you belong, by shrinking from that which you merit;" and then he began to sing. The murderer now ran to him, and pushing him aside, pointed to his breast, and made a white spot where he felt his heart beating. He then exclaimed, "I am not a coward—I am not afraid to die—I went to the woods to get

sober, for I would not die drunk." After saying this, he commenced singing the death song, and when he gave the signal that he was ready to die, twelve arrows pierced his heart, and he fell, one of the first victims to alcohol.

> "Ah! brandy, brandy, bane of life,
> Spring of tumult, source of strife;
> Could I but half thy curses tell,
> The wise would wish thee safe in hell."

[Here Mr. Copway read the series of resolutions which had been passed by the legislatures of North Carolina and South Carolina, respectively.]

Mr. C. resumed, saying,—In conclusion, gentlemen, I will say that I have detained you too long. I ask nothing more than what is reasonable, and in asking this of the people of the United States, I feel more confident that my humble petition will be granted by this legislature, at least, on account of Pennsylvania's early history, in connection with the Indians. I am convinced that there has been friendly relations existing between the Indians and the people of Pennsylvania particularly. Oh, when I think of that day when peace reigned between the Indians and William Penn! That was a glorious period, and he was a kind-hearted and humane man.

I have ever venerated the name of William Penn, and whenever I have thought of the tree under which he made his treaty, which never has been broken, I have often thought, if I had only been under the boughs of that old elm tree, I should have been satisfied. I sent to Philadelphia, three or four years ago, to endeavour to procure a little piece of that tree, but I failed to obtain it; and I never succeeded in getting hold of any of it until yesterday. Yesterday I received a card from a lady in Philadelphia, requesting me to call at her house; I did so, and, on entering one of the rooms, I saw a picture of the old tree. After salutation, she said, "There is the tree under which William Penn made his treaty with the Indians. I have understood that you were inquiring for a piece of it, and many have tried to get it from me; and I do not know why I have not parted with it before; and now, it seems to me, is the proper time to part with it. I will give it to you."

And I took it in my hand and pressed it to my bosom. There it is, and I hope, as long as I live and venerate the name of Willaim Penn, that I shall keep it close to where my heart beats, for I revere the memory of that old man. I venerate the very day when he first came

to negotiate with the Indians of this country. For seventy years not a cloud in the heavens portended danger and discord. The Great Spirit even smiled upon the wild Indian and the white man, as they smoked the pipe of peace. Oh, last summer, when I was in the city of Washington, on the 4th of July, I thought to myself, when I saw the people enjoying themselves, and flocking around at the laying of the cornerstone of the monument to the memory of Washington, that if the day came when the Indians shall have peaceable possession of their homes in the west, I would get my people to raise another monument to the memory of George Washington. We will point our children to his noble form, and speak of his exalted character and love of country, in the hope that they may emulate his spirit, and follow his glorious example in all that was great and good.

We trust that the time may come when the Indians of the far west will have it in their power, as it is their inclination, to erect a monument as well to the memory of Gen. Washington as to that of William Penn. The eagle of liberty is stretching forth his wings all over the earth, and the mountains of France and Germany have received him. The isles of the sea are celebrating their songs of liberty, and will not, I ask, the Indian participate in the glorious jubilee? You, gentlemen, have too much partriotism in your hearts—you have too much love in your hearts—to let the Indian die without being lamented.

Many have asked—"Who is that Indian? Where has he come from, and where was he born? And what is he about?" They have asked one another these questions, when I have been endeavouring to explain my views in relation to the salvation of my poor countrymen. Thank heaven, I am an Indian. Yes; were I to be the last to stand on the peaks of the Rocky Mountains, I would still raise my hand to the world as a part of a noble specimen of humanity, the representative of the Indians who once lived in this country. I heard one gentleman say to another— "Who is that?" alluding to myself. "Who is he?" Now, if he is in this hall at the present time, tell him "I am a native American." [Applause and laughter.]

Mr. C., in conclusion, said—I beg this audience—highly intelligent and respectable as it is—to receive my warm acknowledgments for their kind attention this evening; and I pray the Great Spirit that you and I may, while we live, do something for the benefit of the world— that, when we are about to visit the world to come, and the Angel of Death appears to sever our bodies from our souls, that the latter may fly, like an eagle, to mansions in the skies. I trust that the white man

and the Indian may meet where they shall swear eternal friendship before their God.

A few days after I had delivered the foregoing address, a very appropriate resolution was passed by the Pennsylvania Legislature, approving of my plan for saving my poor brethren.

I laid a petition before the Congress of the United States at their last meeting, which will be acted on during the coming session, and I shall never cease to petition the Government until something is done in furtherance of the object I have proposed.

I subjoin a copy of the resolution passed by the Legislature of North Carolina, after I had delivered an address before that body:—

"Whereas, the condition of the various Indian tribes upon the western frontier of the United States appeals to the humanity and justice of the General Government, to devise some plan by which a permanent home may be secured to them; by which their existence as a people may be secured and perpetuated; by which their moral, intellectual, and social condition may be improved, and the blessings of civilisation and civil liberty at length secured to them:

"Be it therefore resolved, &c., that we recommend this subject to the serious consideration of the Congress of the United States, that in the exercise of their wisdom they may mature a plan by which the *Indian Tribes* inhabiting our western frontier territory may be placed more directly under the paternal care of the General Government; by which a specific region of country may be set apart for their permanent abode, secured to them for ever against further encroachment, and undisturbed by the great current of western emigration; by which their moral, intellectual, and social condition may be improved and elevated; by which the blessings of education, civilisation, and Christianity may be imparted to them; by which they may all be brought together and united in one grand confederation, and thus prepared for the enjoyment of civil and religious liberty; and, if found practicable, they may be ultimately admitted into our Federal Union."

Governor Ch. Manly, of this State, transmitted the above resolution to the Congress of the United States.

XVIII

The following letters were originally addressed to the newspapers in Boston. I have been requested to give them in this work, with a few of the notices from the editors of the American papers, to whom I owe a great debt of gratitude for aiding me in all that I have done for my brethren.

LETTER I.

New York.

SIR,—Before leaving these Atlantic cities for the woods in the far distant west, permit me to converse with your readers, some of whom may have seen notices of the addresses and lectures of an Indian chief, in the halls of different legislatures from south to north.

The great object of my efforts has been to awaken an interest in the minds of the people of the Atlantic States, in behalf of that long-neglected race, the aborigines of America. That Government might collect the Indians in one body, in the west, for the purpose of forming them into one State, thus preparing the way for their improvement.

The deep interest I have seen manifested in behalf of the Indians, by the American people of the States through which I have travelled, leads me to believe that the majority of the Palefaces wish the red men well.

The North Carolina Legislature passed a joint resolution after I had addressed them, strongly recommending my plan to the consideration of the American Government; and the resolution was transmitted to Congress.

My next visit was to the Legislature of South Carolina, where I was received in the kindest manner, and had the honour of addressing the members on the fifteenth of last December. At the expiration of a few

days a resolution was passed by the House in my favour, and con-curred in by the Senate.

I then started for the north, remaining for a short time in Charles-ton, where the crowds who attended my lectures denoted the feeling of the people of that city, to whom I am indebted for numerous favours.

I stopped in Wilmington, N.C., and addressed the Virginia Legis-lature, but that body was so pressed with business that no resolution was passed; but I was informed that one will be, at its next session.

My address before the Pennsylvania Legislature was published in full. I greatly esteem the people of that State, for their deep regard for my efforts to educate and elevate the Indian. They are worthily the descendants of William Penn. They have always been *friends* of the Indians, and have stood at their side when all others forsook them and fled. They have taught them to handle the hoe, and taught them to love the Maker of all.

After delivering a course of lectures, by request of the mayor, and other eminent citizens in Philadelphia, I left for New York. This is the Rome of the New World. It takes full one year of close effort to interest the people, and there is but one way in which this can be done—to let the shadow of a mighty dollar appear on the walls of their public halls.

By the advice of friends, I visited your city, in which I found many warm-hearted friends. The kindness bestowed upon an Indian stranger by your worthy governor, by Amos A. Lawrence, Esq., and other influential citizens, can never be forgotten. As my friend H. W. Longfellow has beautifully said:—

> "Friends, my soul with joy remembers!
> How like quivering flames they start,
> When I fan the living embers,
> On the hearthstone of my heart."

What else could I do but love and esteem the American people? I love their Bible and their institutions. I admire their magnanimity and their perseverance. Industry, being guided by their intelligence, causes the sea to do their will, and has opened channels, through which commerce pours its treasures at their feet. The roar of the cannon speaks for its defence, and the flag that waves over it is the charter of its rights.

While revolution after revolution follows in the Old World, and

thrones crumble beneath the giant tread of freedom, our own nation stands firm in the right, and, instead of blood and carnage, diffuses among its inhabitants the principles of education. The struggle in the Old World has but commenced. The fearful struggle between the powers of darkness and the powers of light, between the *lion* of despotism and the *eagle* of freedom.

America! America! I adore thee! Land of intelligence, of industry, and the fruits thereof. I have drunk from thy mountain streams. I have gazed at thy lofty mountains, and floated in my birchen canoe over the calm surface of thy glassy lakes.

> "America, America, heaven's blessings attend thee,
> While we live, we shall cherish and love and defend thee!
> Though the scorner may sneer, and the witless defame thee,
> Our heart swells with gladness whenever we name thee."

My letter is dated in New York. As an Indian, I walk these streets amid the palaces of the white man. The walls, how high—the streets, how hard! All rush by me with arrow-like speed. Silks and rags go side by side in Broadway. Here are the world's extremes. I cannot remain here long. I must away to the western woods and lakes, to the falls of St. Anthony, across the prairies, to the base of the Rocky Mountains. I shall take the fish-hook and pole. When I have been lucky you shall hear from me, and I will send you an invitation to partake of a feast at the foot of the Rocky Mountains.

You will hear from me at Washington, before I leave for the west.

<div align="right">

Yours, &c.

KAH-GE-GA-GAH-BOWH.

</div>

LETTER II.

<div align="right">

Washington, May, 1849.

</div>

SIR,—In my last I told you that I would write from Washington, and now, not knowing how soon I may be off from here, I sit down to talk once again with your numerous readers.

Washington! What a name! The nation's pride, the centre of patriots, and the model of men for centuries to come. The wide world's languages with their dialects have learned to pronounce it. The fame of the man, though silent, will speak to new-born millions. Mothers

whisper this name in the ears of innocency. How appropriate for a newborn republic! Those massive pillars of the Capitol and the White House, and that shaft which is about to be reared to the skies, must wear away before the name will cease to be a motto for nations abroad, and for the two hundred States which must exist, when all this American land is subdued by commerce and art.

Washington is comparatively still to what it generally is. But the same dust that rose in white columns, when I first saw the city three years ago, is still here rising from the Avenue. To-day the north-west winds have been rather uncourteous to aged heads, and garments play rather curious tricks.

The trees on the Avenue look quite green. The song of birds among them is heard, and the tiny homes for a tiny race are being built. The flowers sweeten the air, and children sportfully play with the gold fish in the reservoir, in front of the Capitol. To-day, tired with looking at mud walls, just before sunset I went to Georgetown heights. I passed by people who had the same disagreeable disease with which Yankee-dom is afflicted, namely, "curiosity,"—white men and women, a glorious mixture—you know what I mean. Mouths were opened. "There is that Indian chief," said an urchin, advancing before me. I made at him as though I would *cane* him, and I have not since seen him; for, as he started, he made an effort to squeal, and whirled around a corner as though he would run to the end of the world, and neither stop nor look back. Scare that boy again in like manner, and he would be as white as his neighbours. Poor child, I would not harm a straight hair of your head.

After reaching the top, nearly out of breath, I glanced my eyes over the panoramic view about me. The wind, how bracing—the gentle rustling of the leaves of the trees, how musically delightful! Before me lay the waters of the Potomac, clothed with white sails.

"What is yon dark streak?" inquiries my friend. "It is the bridge, a mile and a quarter long."

The sun began to sink. With what a gorgeous fold it enwraps itself, as the music of creation lulls it to rest. The clouds around it, attending ministers on its departure, on one side appeared as a full blaze; on the other, like giant waves foaming and careering onward. It has sunk behind the trees, and their foliage is in a crimson hue. O, could I have a bower there! Methinks that when I slept I should dream of Eden's pleasant groves!

What a beautiful sight! A Boston poet stood before me like a statue,

gazed, wondered, admired! He said nothing, but his eyes flashed with the fire of his soul. In his silence there was language! Far off on yonder branch sings the mocking bird of the south, and nearer was a robin, both chanting the praise of their Creator. Other birds flew by to their nest. Night creeping over the vale below, I turned away reluctantly from the glorious scene.

Just now I have passed the large building, the Treasury—Uncle Samuel's pocket—in which is held the common cents of the nation.

Good night! My friend has gone ahead of me, and is waiting my arrival in the land of nod.

May 15.—I have just learned a Washington secret, viz., that my friend——is to dine with the Cabinet to-day, or rather that the Cabinet is to dine with him. Mention it to no one. You can whisper it to the ladies, however—they can keep a secret.

The dust! I wish to leave it, and away to the green fields of the west. I am to know to-day whether I am to receive the aid of Government in the prosecution of my plan to concentrate and civilise the Indians of the west. God knows that the Indians deserve aid and instruction from the American people, and they seem desirous to grant it. What the people wish to do, the Government will not hinder them from doing; and, to the credit of the men at the head of national affairs be it said, they seem anxious to recompense the red men for the wrongs of the past.

I must close. The clouds are at this moment gathering in their might, and threaten to flood us with cold water.

I am, yours,

KAH-GE-GA-GAH-BOWH.

LETTER III.

Mount Vernon, May, 1849.

SIR,—To-day, for the first time, I had the good fortune to find time to visit this place; the final resting spot of the greatest of modern men.

Mayor Seaton, of Washington, gave us a note to the present occupant, Mr. Washington; and after a ride of sixteen miles by land, in company with my friend Mr. John S. Adams, of Boston, we came in view of the spot. On our way to the tomb we were obliged to travel a most disagreeable road—ditches, rivulets, narrow passes, tangled

woods, and other evils obstructed our way. We drove up to the gate and "uncle" somebody came hobbling along to open it. In these diggins, habituate yourself in calling every negro you meet, who is half a minute older than yourself, "uncle," and you will pass anywhere.

He opened the gate and we entered; looking upon the old dilapidated brick walls on our right hand, and going up to the door, I delivered my note, and was soon requested to walk into the passage.

"Dah," said a curly-headed urchin, "walk around and see what you can see."

"But where is Mr. Washington?" I inquired.

"He is in dat room dah, sir."

"What, is he sick?"

"No, sair; but you will look round de room and see what you can see."

We strolled about the parlour, sitting-room, and passage, and used all the exertion we could to "see what we could see." We looked about us in vain for some person to conduct us to the tomb. When I asked the coloured boy the location of it, he struck out his long arm in a horizontal position, and pointing to a long brick wall, said "Dah!"

I went to the front of the once elegant mansion, and stood on the brow of a hill, under the branches of a tall tree. The Potomac lay below, and not a ripple was to be seen. The air was sultry and still. O, how still! Two magnolia trees in front of the house were seemingly drooping into decay, but the cool air of the evening was only needed to revive them.

The house was in a very neglected, timeworn condition; the oak trees seemed to flourish better than anything else; and the windows corresponded with other parts of the house, except two of them, which seemed to have more attention bestowed on them than did the others, being adorned with superb curtain hangings.

Seeing no white man, we avaied ourselves of the guidance of an old negro. He began to speak of the greatness of George Washington, and between each word would escape a sigh.

"There," said he, "is the place where massa Washington sleeps."

Here, at the gate, I stood, and when I gazed on the marble coffin which contained his body an indescribable feeling filled my soul, of pleasure and regret. Here rest the remains of a man whose fame is as boundless as the ocean—whose honour towers above the skies—whose

virtues are sung in other lands, and will be a lesson to the children of generations yet to come—a model for heroes, a model for Christians. Here rests the man in whose breast burned the true flame of patriotism; the man whose voice was heard above the din of battle—whose counsels piloted the ship of freedom through tempestuous seas, and who hoisted the stars and stripes, beneath which American commerce now floats in security. It was he who fed the young eagles in their defenceless homes, in their hour of peril, till they became strong, till the hour of peril was past, and they were let loose to bear over the world the charter of freedom which Washington marked out for it. They go from east to west, and soon all shall be free—this earth a paradise, and men and angels one.

Who of all the ambitious Caesars of the Old World could be compared with George Washington? When we speak of Napoleon, the heart is sickened with the thought of blood. But around the memory of Washington, the light of an unclouded sun is seen. The one led on his warriors with an iron sceptre—the other governed them with a smile. Both died. One soothed by the hands of an angel, the other pressed down by the thoughts of the anguish he had caused. The grave of one was where the ocean looked in fury—the grave of the other in quiet, watered by the tears of grateful millions of freemen.

Absorbed with thoughts like these, for the first time my inflexible nature gave way to its *feelings*. I could not help it.

I am sorry that they do not keep it better. It should be a marble castle, in which the angel of light might watch his dust till the morn of the resurrection.

I turned from the tomb, and on the tree there sat a moaning dove. It seemed to be conscious that we came there to weep. Warble on, little bird! When we are blest with a home in paradise, I will feed thee with fruits immortal.

The sun is sinking in a blaze of glory. The skies are of a crimson hue, and the foliage of the tree throws its shadow upon our path. The tame deer are sporting around us, and with many pleasures and regrets we leave.

It is now nearly seven o'clock, p.m., and we have eighteen miles to go; so, for the present, farewell.

KAH-GE-GA-GAH-BOWH.

LETTER IV.

Norfolk, Va., May 29, 1849.

DEAR SIR,—From the date of my letter you will learn that I am still going south, instead of north or west.

Norfolk is now full of alarming rumours. The cholera is here, and people are more religiously inclined than usual. A revival is now in progress in one of the churches, the result of which will, I trust, remain longer than the epidemic; though, doubtless, in some cases it will pass away with the alarm that gave it birth.

This place is favourably situated for commerce, having a good harbour, the best I have ever seen. The land in its vicinity is very good for agricultural purposes, and the principal products are corn, tobacco, and sweet potatoes. Ships are here from all ports. In view are vessels just arrived, others just departing. Hark! you can hear the sailor's song and the rattling of the cordage. Up, up go the sails—one toss of the sailor's hat, one adieu to the landsmen, and they are off. These white sails on the ocean are like lilies on the pond, dotting it wherever commerce has travelled.

There is something sublimely grand in the idea of a frail bark struggling across from continent to continent. Storm raging, winds howling and waves moaning, and thus to be upon the deep, hemmed in by the mighty walls of the ocean!—but I must stop writing about it, for a sensation of sea sickness already creeps over me at the bare thought of it.

It is near ten o'clock, a.m., and curiosity leads me to go over the ferry, to the place where that ship of ships, the *Pennsylvania,* is anchored. Her masts tower above all others, a hundred feet higher than the highest. When I inquired whether I could be conveyed on board, I was told that the cholera was on board, and that one of the four persons who had been attacked by it was dead. So, instead of going on board the ship, I strolled about the navy yard, which exceeds any place of the kind I have ever seen; the row of houses, workshops and ship-houses. What a noisy place. Go it, yet hammers and tongs and saw-mills! There are at present a thousand men at work in this yard. Spike-makers, cable and anchor makers, groups here and groups there, making extensive preparations for war; and nothing is done for peace! I think the day is not far distant when the good reputation of our nation will not be based on the number of its guns or the size of its naval fleet.

Cannons and balls! This is a part of civilisation which I hope my people will never learn. Some time ago the famous warrior Black Hawk was brought from Washington to this yard, to see the preparations which the Government was making for war; more particularly, however, to see the great ship. I am told that he was conducted all over the yard, and no sign of emotion did he manifest until he was led to the great ship. He gazed in wonder at the tall masts, the strong rigging, the steam engine, and the boilers, and asked, "Who made this great canoe?" He was told, and with a shake of the head said, "I should like to see the man that made this big canoe; he must be a great warrior." He inquired who it was that guided it? When he was shown, he could hardly believe that the person had power in his arms to steer such a canoe in a storm.

Strawberries are plenty here, but few persons eat them, supposing them to contain too much cholera. I devoured a pretty good portion of them the other day, and am certain there was none in those I ate. In Portsmouth, I found the streets well limed and *white-washed*. I think the prevailing epidemic will rage here, as the ground is very low, flat, and there is much stagnant water.

The famous Cypress Swamp is not far from here, where the staves are obtained, and in which snakes and alligators abound.

Many runaway slaves are housed in this swamp, and live like bears in the woods, seldom seeing any white people. Some have lived thus for twenty years. They raise their grain in patches, and the region is very large.

The Virginians are very hospitable people. About a year ago, while in Richmond, a request was sent to me to visit Charles city. In about a week afterwards, I made arrangements to go.

When I arrived in the city I did not know it. I alighted, and found about one thousand people who had met to hear the Indian. A church was open. Tall oaks and pines shadowed us, that had maintained their position for at least a hundred years. There was not another house at a less distance than three miles,—and such was Charles city! I thought, if that was a city, we could boast of many cities in the wild woods.

Though the people here are very hospitable, there are two classes of Yankees against whom they hold an inveterate disllike, namely, fanatical abolitionists, and clock pedlers.

Would to God slavery was abolished! but there is too much fire and brimstone in the denunciations of men of misguided zeal. What! crush the Constitution of the United States? It seems like a mole beneath the

earth, crying out, "take down the sun, for it does me no good." If you ask, what shall be done to abolish slavery? I reply, use those means which are in the hands of the people; diffuse sound education; let the ministry of north and south *preach and practise a pure Christianity;* then will the slaves be set free.

The Virginians are not a stubborn people. Many of them have spoken freely to me, and expressed their convictions of the evils of slavery, but they are much like the *Indian* in one particular; they *will not be driven to do a good act.* You may drive an Indian to the very gate of heaven, but he will not enter to enjoy its pleasures; but entwine the thread of love and gentleness with the hand of kindness and you can lead him—yea, a nation too. That spirit which is thus diffused in the act disarms the savage breast of its fires, and thus it is with all men.

I had expected to have been on my way west before this, but the Indian department having no funds at its disposal, I shall be obliged to endeavour to interest the American people during this summer. Having received assurances of kindness from the various departments of Government, I am led to hope that at the next session of Congress I shall secure its aid.

My next will be a notice of the noble deeds of Pocahontas, the daughter of the renowned Powhatan, the pride and glory of the American Indians.

I am, Sir, yours, &c.,
KAH-GE-GA-GAH-BOWH.

LETTER V.

JAMES RIVER—SMITH AND POCAHONTAS.

Chesapeake Bay, July 15, 1849.

DEAR SIR,—The noble river which has its name from the first adventurer in that part of our country now known as Virginia, flows amid scenes of picturesque beauty. It is swollen by a number of smaller streams that empty into it. I never gazed on any object in my life more attentively than I did on that river, when for the first time I passed over its surface. I gazed thoughtfully on either side, and fancied a bold untutored Indian bounding among its shaded coverts, before the Paleface came among his tribe with those elements of sin, which have caused the downfall and almost entire extinction of his race.

Albeit noon, quite a stir was seen among the passengers of the "Curtis Peck," as we passed down the river. Many eyes were directed towards a point on our left, and some one said, "we shall soon see old Jamestown." It was at this place that the first settlement was made by Smith and his comrades, in the year 1607. Virginia can boast of the many sons she has produced to fill the presidential chair of our nation, and of many daughters who signalised themselves by acts of bravery in the struggle for freedom. Of these last, none exceeds, in point of distinterested benevolence, Pocahontas, the daughter of Powhatan, the then ruling chief of that vast area of country. Smith was taken by a party of the warriors of Powhatan, some distance from his own residence, and after being led about from village to village as an object of wonder, escorted by a party of warriors, dressed in the skins of wild beasts, and their heads decorated very fantastically with feathers, was led to Werowocomoco, on the north side of the Fork River, at that time the residence of Powhatan.

Word had previously been sent to the chief that the pale stranger had been taken, and no doubt his pleasure was asked respecting the disposal of him. Smith was taken by a guard to the door of Powahtan's lodge, and he was not mistaken in his supposition that he was to be presented to that renowned prince. Around were the wigwams of the warriors, and he was obliged to withstand the inquisitive gaze of the people. He says, in his narrative, that when he entered the lodge, Powhatan sat on his throne at the upper part of the enclosure, with a majesty he had never before seen in Christian or pagan lands. The lofty and bold demeanor of the prince gave Smith a very favourable opinion of him. His family and friends were around him, and his couch was hung with rich furs.

A consultation was held to decide as to what should be done. Meanwhile, he was treated as a distinguished warrior of their nation. The queen herself brought the water that he used in washing. She placed food before him and desired him to eat, but the anxiety he felt as to his fate prevented him from partaking. It was at length decided that he should die at their hands, as he was at the head of the band of strangers who had come among them, and they knew not but that his intentions were evil.

Preparations for his execution were quickly made—the song and the dance begun. All gazed at the victim with wild intensity. The women brought their young to look at the pale stranger. Young and old pitied

his fate, but, according to the custom of the people, remained silent, and looked on the fulfilment of the decrees of the aged.

The warriors were commanded by Powhatan to bring a stone from the side of the river. All being arranged, the victim was seized by two warriors, and led to the place of execution. Smith showed not the least sign of fear, but calmly laid himself down as if to sleep, upon the spot from which he never expected to rise. The warriors stood with their heavy clubs raised, which, at the beck of Powhatan, would fall upon the bold adventurer. Men, women, and children surrounded the spot, and it was at this time that they sympathised with the ill-fated man.

A little girl was now seen whispering in the ears of Powhatan. Her simple and childlike actions betrayed the feelings of a heart which pitied Smith. She spake earnestly, and held on his arms, as if she would not be denied her request. The chief advanced. One motion from him, and all would be over. A shout pierced the air, and Powhatan gave the word. As soon as given, Pocahontas flew from beside her father, and flung herself between Smith and the uplifted club of the warrior, and gazed with imploring look, and eyes bathed in tears, upon her father. O what a lovely picture!—how godlike! how noble! Hard-hearted must that man be, who could not be moved by such an exhibition. The warrior's arms hung down; the fiery flash of Powhatan's eye disappeared, as he bade his warriors desist. Pocahontas having done her work, ran among the crowd, to escape the gaze of the people. Smith was liberated, and by special favour became an inmate of the chief's lodge.

Pocahontas was but ten or eleven years old when this occurred, and how romantic must have been the scene! Heroic was the deed which has immortalised her name! Reader, she was a savage! And it has been said of her race, that they are without tears—unfeeling, cold, cruel, revengeful: but show me, if you can, in American history a parallel.

A few words more. First, historians have disagreed as to the motive that influenced her in the matter. Some say that Pocahontas loved Smith. I cannot find anything in the history of those times that leads me to suppose that the love she had for him was any greater than that she had for all her fellow-creatures. Smith has been charged with ingratitude, on account of his not reciprocating the love which some have supposed the Indian girl bestowed upon him. I, for one, admire the deed of Pocahontas, and have always regarded Smith as a worthy man in every particular. As a warrior, bold; in his schemes, fearless; in danger, calm; and in misfortune, never despairing. Notwithstanding

all these traits of character, I still must censure his after-conduct. When Pocahontas was in England, he did not notice her, nor even acknowledge her as a benefactor, although by periling her life she had saved his own. Such conduct on his part stamps his character with a foul blot, which his deeds of bravery can never conceal.

Second: her name, which must have been given her after her rescue of Smith, indicates that her nation looked on her with some suspicion—*Pah-ka-on-tis*. In this she suffered wrongfully. Partially disowned by her nation, the neglect she received in England at the hands of Smith was more than her spirit could bear, and, after receiving Christian baptism, she died at Gravesend, England, in the year 1617.

Pocahontas! No marble would long enough endure, to hand down the record of her noble deeds to all who should listen to the story of her heroism. You will not wonder that I admire her character, or think her name merits a place among the great of earth.

I am, yours, &c.,
KAH-GE-GA-GAH-BOWH.

P.S.—I leave soon for the west. You will next hear from me at Niagara; then from the falls of St. Marie—Lake Superior—falls of St. Anthony, and the Rocky Mountains.

THE PLEASURES OF SUMMER TRAVEL IN THE WEST.
(For the Chicago Tribune)

"He sucks intelligence in every clime,
And spreads the honey of his deep research,
At his return—a rich repast for me."

The many sources of recreation and amusement which a traveller finds along his way in the west, are varied and interesting, and seem to me a world of successive glowing scenes. My memory still burns with the heat of excitement, caused by the animating objects of interest with which I have often been surrounded. The wide-spread prairies— the gardens of Nature—the streams of crystal waters which roll their tides over the pebbled course of vales, singing their music to the skies—the bluffs towering on each side of the "Father of the Waters," as it seeks its level in the ocean, far off in the sunny south—the mounds which often, one after the other, in chains, skirt their way through woodlands and then on the prairies—the relics, or rather the

tombstones of by-gone generations now resting in their silence—the waving grass over the rolling prairie by gentle winds, and the thousand wild flowers which often make the very air sweet with their fragrance. O, the west, the west, the mighty west for me!—where groves wave their tops to the sweet air, wholesome, fresh, and pure; and where game roam with the child of the forest, from brook to brook, and quaff wholesome waters as they gush from the side of hills.

During the past season, wandering over the great west, I found much pleasure, perhaps more, where few would feel interested. The same things may not excite in the minds of many, while, from my own nature, and the early associations of childhood, they seem natural.

In ascending the waters of the Mississippi I found many things which gave me pleasure. The towering naked bluffs on the banks are imposingly grand at times. They appear like giant sentinels watching with vigilance the silent waters of the river below. In the morning they seemed to blaze forth in the air, when the sun arose with an unclouded sky.

It was just evening, when the boat, which carried a full freight of merchandise and passengers, neared the "mountain in the water," about ninety miles above the town of Prairie du Chien. We had been puffing and puffing all the day long, and our boat was still heading up stream. On our right was a vast wilderness, and on our left were to be seen the naked peaks of the bluffs, as though in the act of falling on the waters, as they dimly appeared, while the rays of the sun rapidly disappeared, from the waters of the great river. Between these is the noted mountain called the "mountain in the water," because it is surrounded at its base with the waters of the river. When we were nearly ten miles from it we could discover the woods which skirted the edge—the lone pine and cedar trees which deck its brow. The sun no longer reflected on the waters, nor its rays lighted the lilies of the vale; but the mountain in the water assumed one of the grandest scenes I ever beheld. There it was, in full view, clothed in all the princely array of nature. The shadows of the bluffs from the western banks began to creep up to its heights, slowly ascending to its top. All around, in nature's own garb and in nature's own fires, glowed with its splendour. The wild water-fowl in flocks ascended, and in descending lit on the surface of the water, and the surrounding shore was echoing with our boat's hoarse puff, which seemed animated with the pleasing view. The top of the mountain was in a blaze—the red sky of the west reflected in the waters, and the sun's rays began to disrobe

the mountain; "five minutes more," said I, as I held the watch in my hand, "and then the sun will sink;" and as the last rays of the sun disappeared, the shades of night began to creep from the waters below, until they covered the whole from view. The mountain and light reminded me of the death of the virtuous, dying in full hope of immortality, disrobed of their cares, and to slumber in submission to the will of a propitious God.

The next morning, at sunrise, we were just entering the lake called "Lake Pepin." The river here widens, and the bluffs can be seen unobscured on each shore. The pebbly beach is full of cornelians, which are found along its shore. One of those bluffs is noted for being the place where a Sioux damsel, some eighty years ago, made a fatal leap on account of disappointed love.

The numerous things of interest which I found in the Upper Mississippi, I cannot now speak of; but my visit to the Government offices of the territory, and to the American Fur Company, having been satisfactory, as well as to the Indians, whom I had seen, in pursuance of the great object of concentrating the North-west Indian tribes, which everywhere met with favour.

I had two days of hunting to my satisfaction, which will last me until next summer. One was to hunt with the gun; and having secured a brace of pigeons and about a dozen of wild ducks, I returned that day satisfied; but the following, at the crystal waters of St. Croix, was worth all the shooting, when, with my angling rod, I caught over three dozen of the very best speckled trout. My hands twitch at the recollection of that day's sport, I cannot write intelligibly, and will finish in my next the ramble I made in the valley.

I remain,

Yours, &c.,

KAH-GE-GA-GAH-BOWH,

or, G. COPWAY, Ojibway Nation.

Chicago, Ill., Oct. 16th, 1849.

NOTICES OF THE PRESS.

Lecture of Kah-ge-ga-gah-bowh, on the subject of concentrating the Indians of the North-west, upon Territory to be set apart by the General Government.

Last evening, the celebrated Ojibway chief, Kah-ge-ga-gah-bowh, or George Copway, lectured in the City Saloon upon the above subject, to a large and highly-gratified audience. The lecturer com-

menced by referring to the present condition of the Indians—the calamitous effects of the policy pursued towards them by the United States Government—the causes which have heretofore operated to check their progress in civilisation, and to thwart the efforts constantly being made by philanthropists, who have gone among them for that purpose—all going to show that the inevitable destiny of the Indian race is a yet deeper condition of degradation, of ignorance, of barbarism, and final extirpation, unless some scheme be devised for the amelioration of their condition.

Mr. Copway, after having obtained his education, at the hands of some benevolent gentleman of this State, during the years 1838–9, returned to his nation, fired with the noble impulse of expending his energies in labours for the elevation of his people. For years he toiled and planned in this behalf—established schools and missions—instructed his people in the art of agriculture—endeavoured to teach them the true principles of government, and all other things calculated to advance them in civilisation and individual happiness. These labours gave evidence of abundant fruit; but it was only for a day. A stroke of policy on the part of the General Government—the purchase of lands owned by the tribe—their removal to another territory—the influences under which this removal was effected—the duplicity of agents—the cupidity of contractors and traders—the malign influences and corrupting examples daily around and before them—these obliterated all traces of past labours—destroyed in a day the work of years, and laid prostrate the hopes that had animated the hearts of the labourers.

Mr. Copway had thus become fully convinced that, under existing circumstances, the cause of his brethren must ever remain hopeless, unless something be done to place them in a position entirely removed from the causes which have heretofore barred their progress in civilisation. Impressed with this belief, he had devoted much serious reflection to the subject, the result of which is embodied in the following scheme:—

The Indians of the North-west, consisting of about 100,000 souls, to be concentrated upon territory to be set apart to their use in perpetuity, by the Government of the United States one hundred miles north of Council Bluffs, on the east bank of the Missouri river. The territory thus given to be one hundred and fifty miles square. A Government to be at once organised, by the appointment of a Governor (who shall be a white man), Lieut.-Governor, and Secretary of State, by the President of the United States. A Territorial Council to be elected by the different tribes, in proportion to their population,

which council shall pass all laws needful for the government of the whole people, subject to the veto of the Governor. The lands to be distributed, free of cost, to the people, subject to such regulations of transfer and limitation as the council shall establish; one of which, however, must be that it shall never be transferred to white men. Common schools and higher seminaries of learning to be established throughout the territory, a leading branch in all of which shall be the science and practice of agriculture. White residents to be excluded, except such as shall be employed by the United States and Territorial Governments. For the present, the territory to be represented at Washington by Commissioners to be appointed by the council. Enjoying these facilities for civilisation—from the necessity of things becoming confirmed in local habits, and compelled to the pursuits which elevate and refine—having become familiarised with our institutions, and prepared to appreciate, love, and live under them—in process of time the Indian Territory to apply for admission into the Union as a State, and become an integral part of the great confederacy.

Such is a meagre outline of Mr. Copway's plan. The arguments by which he supported it were plausible and forcible. His audience were carried along with him, and by loud and repeated applause testified to the reasonableness and justice of his arguments and conclusions. We regret that our limits prevent us from giving a more complete synopsis of the address, which occupied near two hours in the delivery. Mr. Copway is a forcible speaker—at times witty, convulsing his audience with laughter—now thrilling them with bursts of lofty eloquence, and now convincing them by cogent logic. The perioration of Mr. C.'s speech was touching and impressive in the highest degree. No one that heard it will readily forget it, or easily lose the impressions made by it.

We may add, in conclusion, that whatever may be said in regard to the plausibility of Mr. Copway's scheme, all must admit that this much and more he may in all justice claim from us for his people. He, as representative of those who once owned the entire continent from sea to sea, without a rival to dispute their claims, may well *demand* of us who, by the law of might, have forcibly taken possession of their fair heritage, so small a boon as the one he now craves from the American people.

AN IMPRESSIVE SERMON.

Yesterday afternoon, amidst the celebration of the solemnities of religion that took place in this City of Churches, few perhaps could have produced more interest than the sermon of the Rev. Mr. Copway,

otherwise known as the Indian Chief, Kah-ge-ga-gah-bowh. It was delivered before a large congregation, in the church at the corner of Tillory and Lawrence Streets. The subject of the lecture was principally confined to the influence of Christianity, with all its sublime influences, among the untutored children of the west—the remnants of those who were once possessors of this soil. The advance of the pioneer white man, as he bore his fire-water and the worst passions of the white man among tribes whose habits taught them to be contented with that which nature in all its abundance had produced, were the subjects upon which he dilated. If the people of this country would send such men as William Penn among them, they would be able to reciprocate the kindness of their white brethren. But, alas! on account of the want of schools amidst the Indians, may be caused that subserviency to their customs, that makes them resort again to the blanket and the wigwam. Their training not being attended to according to the persuasion of the Christian religion, he must go back instead of going forward. The things which are best adapted to advance the natives of the west, are not those that have been the best adapted to their customs. Education in a different form is necessary. The doctrine to love one another, by binding the good fellowship of all nations, is the one that should be inculcated to them.

Human nature is the same everywhere, and the same feelings actuate the hearts of the Christian.

The Rev. Gentleman attributed to these, as well as other causes, the interception of the advance of civilisation amongst the children of the west. There are other reasons that he said might be given, that retarded their improvement. The first was the introduction of the disease called the small pox, and others that were disposed among them, which their knowledge of medicine was unable to control.

The second is the introduction of fire-arms from the hands of the French, Spanish, and English, which has thinned their ranks. The bravery of the Indian has caused him to be placed in the front ranks; and soon his tribe became depopulated. The happiness that reigned around the fire-side of the Indian's domestic circle has been dashed to the ground before these influences, and the introduction of intoxicating liquors, that deprave the moral pulsations of the heart, and send him to an untimely grave.

It was this that destroyed the brightest virtues of a noble people. The tide of avarice and thirst of gold runs on and brings to the trader profit, at the expense of demoralisation and death. It causes them to

covet an enormous territory that is not cultivated, because it is so good—that roads and farms and houses should spring up within it, and cities become populated. The natural consequence that will ensue is that resistance will follow, and the boom of the cannon, and the roll of the warrior's gun, will sound the last requiem of a departed race.

The Rev. Gentleman then concluded by stating that such horrors would be averted by selecting a home that would afford them a resting place in the Minesotta territory, on the banks of the Mississippi, until in the course of time they would learn the arts and sciences, and become attached to the place of their concentration.

The above is but a slight sketch of the remarks that were delivered; remarks which lead many to hope that the time may yet come when the aborigines of a new world—which has afforded a resting place to the tribes that were persecuted by the old, when new ideas had dawned upon them, and made them seek these shores to acquire a liberty that was denied them at home—will finally become a portion of civilised humanity, and worthy associates with their pale brethren, both in this world and the next.—*Brooklyn Advertiser.*

KA-GE-GA-GAH-BOWH.

This celebrated chief of the Ojibways, after a laborious tour south, has returned to our city. He is engaged to deliver lectures in Boston and vicinity the coming two weeks. His lectures on the manners and customs of his people are very interseting. The one delivered not long since in this city, upon the "Romance and Poetry of the Indians," was an interesting and beautiful production.

We purpose in this notice, however, to mention only his lectures on temperance, hoping to answer the many queries made to us on this subject by friends from various parts of New England. To this end, we extract from the *Charleston Courier,* a notice of one of his lectures in that city, which comes so near the point, that we give it preference to anything we *(New Englander,* Boston,) can write:—

"A crowded house assembled to listen to Mr. Copway, the Indian chief and orator. He argued the cause of temperance in every variety of manner, insisting mainly, as was to be expected, on its profound and even awful relations to the red nations of the west. Shouting aloud, in clear tones, he exclaimed, with true Indian enthusiasm, in reference to that cause, '*I love it!*' Then, with manner more subdued, he dwelt

on the reasons why he loved it. He demonstrated successively that it was favourable to humanity, favourable to morality, and favourable to religion. With burning indignation he depicted the wrongs that had been inflicted on his brethren by unprincipled traders, who were themselves often but the scum and refuse of civilisation, and the only medium of communication between the Indians and the better class of whites. What, he asked, could be expected from the members of his nation, when goaded, insulted, corrupted, and maddened by these agents of hell? He showed how much these disastrous infuences had been mitigated by the missionaries of Christianity and the Temperance Reform. He then applied the subject to the state and prospects of the cause among the whites. Here he seemed as much at home as the most experienced temperance lecturer of a paler hue.

"A keen observer must have been of our institutions, our social structure, and our prevailing character, whether for good or evil. Much even of his English was singularly idiomatic. Biting satire—pungent anecdote, set off with most expressive Indian gesticulation—strokes of wit and humour—touches of pathos—bursts of vehement declamation, after the manner now of a Forest, or a Cooper, and now of a zealous western preacher—slip-shod conversational talk—most poetical descriptions of nature, fearless statement, off-hand, calm, Indian independence, altogether formed a compound of a rather rare and inimitable nature. And although there might have been a few things for a very fastidious taste to object against, yet on the whole, *he* must have been a querulous man indeed, who came away dissatisfied with his evening's treat, or unimpressed afresh with the inherent beauty, excellence and necessity of the total abstinence cause.

"Dr. Menderhall was the president, and the Rev. Mr. Kendrick the chaplain of the evening."

The Soul of the Indian

Charles Alexander Eastman
(Ohiyesa)

To my wife
Elaine Goodale Eastman
in grateful recognition of her
ever-inspiring companionship
in thought and work
and in love of her most
Indian-like virtues
I dedicate this book

I speak for each no-tongued tree
That, spring by spring, doth nobler be,
And dumbly and most wistfully
His mighty prayerful arms outspreads,
And his big blessing downward sheds.

<div align="right">SIDNEY LANIER</div>

But there's a dome of nobler span,
 A temple given
Thy faith, that bigots dare not ban—
 Its space is heaven!
Its roof star-pictured Nature's ceiling,
Where, trancing the rapt spirit's feeling,
And God Himself to man revealing,
 Th' harmonious spheres
Make music, though unheard their pealing
 By mortal ears!

<div align="right">THOMAS CAMPBELL</div>

God! sing ye meadow streams with gladsome voice!
Ye pine-groves, with your soft and soul-like sounds!
Ye eagles, playmates of the mountain storm!
Ye lightnings, the dread arrows of the clouds!
Ye signs and wonders of the elements,
Utter forth God, and fill the hills with praise! . . .
Earth, with her thousand voices, praises GOD!

<div align="right">COLERIDGE</div>

Foreword

"We also have a religion which was given to our forefathers, and has been handed down to us their children. It teaches us to be thankful, to be united, and to love one another! We never quarrel about religion."

Thus spoke the great Seneca orator, Red Jacket, in his superb reply to Missionary Cram more than a century ago, and I have often heard the same thought expressed by my countrymen.

I have attempted to paint the religious life of the typical American Indian as it was before he knew the white man. I have long wished to do this, because I cannot find that it has ever been seriously, adequately, and sincerely done. The religion of the Indian is the last thing about him that the man of another race will ever understand.

First, the Indian does not speak of these deep matters so long as he believes in them, and when he has ceased to believe he speaks inaccurately and slightingly.

Second, even if he can be induced to speak, the racial and religious prejudice of the other stands in the way of his sympathetic comprehension.

Third, practically all existing studies on this subject have been made during the transition period, when the original beliefs and philosophy of the native American were already undergoing rapid disintegration.

There are to be found here and there superficial accounts of strange customs and ceremonies, of which the symbolism or inner meaning was largely hidden from the observer; and there has been a great deal of material collected in recent years which is without value because it is modern and hybrid, inextricably mixed with Biblical legend and Caucasian philosophy. Some of it has even been invented for commercial purposes. Give a reservation Indian a present, and he will possibly provide you with sacred songs, a mythology, and folk-lore to order!

My little book does not pretend to be a scientific treatise. It is as true as I can make it to my childhood teaching and ancestral ideals, but from the human, not the ethnological standpoint. I have not cared to pile up more dry bones, but to clothe them with flesh and blood. So much as has been written by strangers of our ancient faith and

149

worship treats it chiefly as matter of curiosity. I should like to emphasize its universal quality, its personal appeal!

The first missionaries, good men imbued with the narrowness of their age, branded us as pagans and devil-worshipers, and demanded of us that we abjure our false gods before bowing the knee at their sacred altar. They even told us that we were eternally lost, unless we adopted a tangible symbol and professed a particular form of their hydra-headed faith.

We of the twentieth century know better! We know that all religious aspiration, all sincere worship, can have but one source and one goal. We know that the God of the lettered and the unlettered, of the Greek and the barbarian, is after all the same God; and, like Peter, we perceive that He is no respecter of persons, but that in every nation he that feareth Him and worketh righteousness is acceptable to Him.

CHARLES A. EASTMAN (OHIYESA)

Contents

I

THE GREAT MYSTERY

Solitary Worship • *The Savage Philosopher* • *The Dual Mind* • *Spiritual Gifts* versus *Material Progress* • *The Paradox of "Christian Civilization"*

The original attitude of the American Indian toward the Eternal, the "Great Mystery" that surrounds and embraces us, was as simple as it was exalted. To him it was the supreme conception, bringing with it the fullest measure of joy and satisfaction possible in this life.

The worship of the "Great Mystery" was silent, solitary, free from all self-seeking. It was silent, because all speech is of necessity feeble and imperfect; therefore the souls of my ancestors ascended to God in wordless adoration. It was solitary, because they believed that He is nearer to us in solitude, and there were no priests authorized to come between a man and his Maker. None might exhort or confess or in any way meddle with the religious experience of another. Among us all men were created sons of God and stood erect, as conscious of their divinity. Our faith might not be formulated in creeds, nor forced upon any who were unwilling to receive it; hence there was no preaching, proselytizing, nor persecution, neither were there any scoffers or atheists.

There were no temples or shrines among us save those of nature. Being a natural man, the Indian was intensely poetical. He would deem it sacrilege to build a house for Him who may be met face to face in the mysterious, shadowy aisles of the primeval forest, or on the sunlit bosom of virgin prairies, upon dizzy spires and pinnacles of naked rock, and yonder in the jeweled vault of the night sky! He who enrobes Himself in filmy veils of cloud, there on the rim of the visible world where our Great-Grandfather Sun kindles his evening campfire, He who rides upon the rigorous wind of the north, or breathes forth His spirit upon aromatic southern airs, whose war-canoe is

153

launched upon majestic rivers and inland seas—He needs no lesser cathedral!

That solitary communion with the Unseen which was the highest expression of our religious life is partly described in the word *hambeday*, literally "mysterious feeling," which has been variously translated "fasting" and "dreaming." It may better be interpreted as "consciousness of the divine."

The first *hambeday*, or religious retreat, marked an epoch in the life of the youth, which may be compared to that of confirmation or conversion in Christian experience. Having first prepared himself by means of the purifying vapor-bath, and cast off as far as possible all human or fleshly influences, the young man sought out the noblest height, the most commanding summit in all the surrounding region. Knowing that God sets no value upon material things, he took with him no offerings or sacrifices other than symbolic objects, such as paints and tobacco. Wishing to appear before Him in all humility, he wore no clothing save his moccasins and breech-clout. At the solemn hour of sunrise or sunset he took up his position, overlooking the glories of earth and facing the "Great Mystery," and there he remained, naked, erect, silent, and motionless, exposed to the elements and forces of His arming, for a night and a day to two days and nights, but rarely longer. Sometimes he would chant a hymn without words, or offer the ceremonial "filled pipe." In this holy trance or ecstasy the Indian mystic found his highest happiness and the motive power of his existence.

When he returned to the camp, he must remain at a distance until he had again entered the vapor-bath and prepared himself for intercourse with his fellows. Of the vision or sign vouchsafed to him he did not speak, unless it had included some commission which must be publicly fulfilled. Sometimes an old man, standing upon the brink of eternity, might reveal to a chosen few the oracle of his long-past youth.

The native American has been generally despised by his white conquerors for his poverty and simplicity. They forget, perhaps, that his religion forbade the accumulation of wealth and the enjoyment of luxury. To him, as to other single-minded men in every age and race, from Diogenes to the brothers of Saint Francis, from the Montanists to the Shakers, the love of possessions has appeared a snare, and the burdens of a complex society a source of needless peril and temptation. Furthermore, it was the rule of his life to share the fruits of his skill

and success with his less fortunate brothers. Thus he kept his spirit free from the clog of pride, cupidity, or envy, and carried out, as he believed, the divine decree—a matter profoundly important to him.

It was not, then, wholly from ignorance or improvidence that he failed to establish permanent towns and to develop a material civilization. To the untutored sage, the concentration of population was the prolific mother of all evils, moral no less than physical. He argued that food is good, while surfeit kills; that love is good, but lust destroys; and not less dreaded than the pestilence following upon crowded and unsanitary dwellings was the loss of spiritual power inseparable from too close contact with one's fellow-men. All who have lived much out of doors know that there is a magnetic and nervous force that accumulates in solitude and that is quickly dissipated by life in a crowd; and even his enemies have recognized the fact that for a certain innate power and self-poise, wholly independent of circumstances, the American Indian is unsurpassed among men.

The red man divided mind into two parts,—the spiritual mind and the physical mind. The first is pure spirit, concerned only with the essence of things, and it was this he sought to strengthen by spiritual prayer, during which the body is subdued by fasting and hardship. In this type of prayer there was no beseeching of favor or help. All matters of personal or selfish concern, as success in hunting or warfare, relief from sickness, or the sparing of a beloved life, were definitely relegated to the plane of the lower or material mind, and all ceremonies, charms, or incantations designed to secure a benefit or to avert a danger, were recognized as emanating from the physical self.

The rites of this physical worship, again, were wholly symbolic, and the Indian no more worshiped the Sun than the Christian adores the Cross. The Sun and the Earth, by an obvious parable, holding scarcely more of poetic metaphor than of scientific truth, were in his view the parents of all organic life. From the Sun, as the universal father, proceeds the quickening principle in nature, and in the patient and fruitful womb of our mother, the Earth, are hidden embryos of plants and men. Therefore our reverence and love for them was really an imaginative extension of our love for our immediate parents, and with this sentiment of filial piety was joined a willingness to appeal to them, as to a father, for such good gifts as we may desire. This is the material or physical prayer.

The elements and majestic forces in nature, Lightning, Wind, Water, Fire, and Frost, were regarded with awe as spiritual powers, but always

secondary and intermediate in character. We believed that the spirit pervades all creation and that every creature possesses a soul in some degree, though not necessarily a soul conscious of itself. The tree, the waterfall, the grizzly bear, each is an embodied Force, and as such an object of reverence.

The Indian loved to come into sympathy and spiritual communion with his brothers of the animal kingdom, whose inarticulate souls had for him something of the sinless purity that we attribute to the innocent and irresponsible child. He had faith in their instincts, as in a mysterious wisdom given from above; and while he humbly accepted the supposedly voluntary sacrifice of their bodies to preserve his own, he paid homage to their spirits in prescribed prayers and offerings.

In every religion there is an element of the supernatural, varying with the influence of pure reason over its devotees. The Indian was a logical and clear thinker upon matters within the scope of his understanding, but he had not yet charted the vast field of nature or expressed her wonders in terms of science. With his limited knowledge of cause and effect, he saw miracles on every hand,—the miracle of life in seed and egg, the miracle of death in lightning flash and in the swelling deep! Nothing of the marvelous could astonish him; as that a beast should speak, or the sun stand still. The virgin birth would appear scarcely more miraculous than is the birth of every child that comes into the world, or the miracle of the loaves and fishes excite more wonder than the harvest that springs from a single ear of corn.

Who may condemn his superstition? Surely not the devout Catholic, or even Protestant missionary, who teaches Bible miracles as literal fact! The logical man must either deny all miracles or none, and our American Indian myths and hero stories are perhaps, in themselves, quite as credible as those of the Hebrews of old. If we are of the modern type of mind, that sees in natural law a majesty and grandeur far more impressive than any solitary infraction of it could possibly be, let us not forget that, after all, science has not explained everything. We have still to face the ultimate miracle,—the origin and principle of life! Here is the supreme mystery that is the essence of worship, without which there can be no religion, and in the presence of this mystery our attitude cannot be very unlike that of the natural philosopher, who beholds with awe the Divine in all creation.

It is simple truth that the Indian did not, so long as his native philosophy held sway over his mind, either envy or desire to imitate the splendid achievements of the white man. In his own thought he

rose superior to them! He scorned them, even as a lofty spirit absorbed in its stern task rejects the soft beds, the luxurious food, the pleasure-worshiping dalliance of a rich neighbor. It was clear to him that virtue and happiness are independent of these things, if not incompatible with them.

There was undoubtedly much in primitive Christianity to appeal to this man, and Jesus' hard sayings to the rich and about the rich would have been entirely comprehensible to him. Yet the religion that is preached in our churches and practiced by our congregations, with its element of display and self-aggrandizement, its active proselytism, and its open contempt of all religions but its own, was for a long time extremely repellent. To his simple mind, the professionalism of the pulpit, the paid exhorter, the moneyed church, was an unspiritual and unedifying thing, and it was not until his spirit was broken and his moral and physical constitution undermined by trade, conquest, and strong drink, that Christian missionaries obtained any real hold upon him. Strange as it may seem, it is true that the proud pagan in his secret soul despised the good men who came to convert and to enlighten him!

Nor were its publicity and its Phariseeism the only elements in the alien religion that offended the red man. To him, it appeared shocking and almost incredible that there were among this people who claimed superiority many irreligious, who did not even pretend to profess the national faith. Not only did they not profess it, but they stooped so low as to insult their God with profane and sacrilegious speech! In our own tongue His name was not spoken aloud, even with utmost reverence, much less lightly or irreverently.

More than this, even in those white men who professed religion we found much inconsistency of conduct. They spoke much of spiritual things, while seeking only the material. They bought and sold everything: time, labor, personal independence, the love of woman, and even the ministrations of their holy faith! The lust for money, power, and conquest so characteristic of the Anglo-Saxon race did not escape moral condemnation at the hands of his untutored judge, nor did he fail to contrast this conspicuous trait of the dominant race with the spirit of the meek and lowly Jesus.

He might in time come to recognize that the drunkards and licentious among white men, with whom he too frequently came in contact, were condemned by the white man's religion as well, and must not be held to discredit it. But it was not so easy to overlook or to excuse

national bad faith. When distinguished emissaries from the Father at Washington, some of them ministers of the gospel and even bishops, came to the Indian nations, and pledged to them in solemn treaty the national honor, with prayer and mention of their God; and when such treaties, so made, were promptly and shamelessly broken, is it strange that the action should arouse not only anger, but contempt? The historians of the white race admit that the Indian was never the first to repudiate his oath.

It is my personal belief, after thirty-five years' experience of it, that there is no such thing as "Christian civilization." I believe that Christianity and modern civilization are opposed and irreconcilable, and that the spirit of Christianity and of our ancient religion is essentially the same.

II

THE FAMILY ALTAR

Pre-natal Influence • Early Religious Teaching • The Function of the Aged • Woman, Marriage and the Family • Loyalty, Hospitality, Friendship

The American Indian was an individualist in religion as in war. He had neither a national army nor an organized church. There was no priest to assume responsibility for another's soul. That is, we believed, the supreme duty of the parent, who only was permitted to claim in some degree the priestly office and function, since it is his creative and protecting power which alone approaches the solemn function of Deity.

The Indian was a religious man from his mother's womb. From the

moment of her recognition of the fact of conception to the end of the second year of life, which was the ordinary duration of lactation, it was supposed by us that the mother's spiritual influence counted for most. Her attitude and secret meditations must be such as to instill into the receptive soul of the unborn child the love of the "Great Mystery" and a sense of brotherhood with all creation. Silence and isolation are the rule of life for the expectant mother. She wanders prayerful in the stillness of great woods, or on the bosom of the untrodden prairie, and to her poetic mind the immanent birth of her child prefigures the advent of a master-man—a hero, or the mother of heroes—a thought conceived in the virgin breast of primeval nature, and dreamed out in a hush that is only broken by the sighing of the pine tree or the thrilling orchestra of a distant waterfall.

And when the day of days in her life dawns—the day in which there is to be a new life, the miracle of whose making has been intrusted to her, she seeks no human aid. She has been trained and prepared in body and mind for this her holiest duty, ever since she can remember. The ordeal is best met alone, where no curious or pitying eyes embarrass her; where all nature says to her spirit: " 'Tis love! 'tis love! the fulfilling of life!" When a sacred voice comes to her out of the silence, and a pair of eyes open upon her in the wilderness, she knows with joy that she has borne well her part in the great song of creation!

Presently she returns to the camp, carrying the mysterious, the holy, the dearest bundle! She feels the endearing warmth of it and hears its soft breathing. It is still a part of herself, since both are nourished by the same mouthful, and no look of a lover could be sweeter than its deep, trusting gaze.

She continues her spiritual teaching, at first silently—a mere pointing of the index finger to nature; then in whispered songs, bird-like, at morning and evening. To her and to the child the birds are real people, who live very close to the "Great Mystery"; the murmuring trees breathe His presence; the falling waters chant His praise.

If the child should chance to be fretful, the mother raises her hand. "Hush! hush!" she cautions it tenderly, "the spirits may be disturbed!" She bids it be still and listen—listen to the silver voice of the aspen, or the clashing cymbals of the birch; and at night she points to the heavenly, blazed trail, through nature's galaxy of splendor to nature's God. Silence, love, reverence,—this is the trinity of first lessons; and to these she later adds generosity, courage, and chastity.

In the old days, our mothers were single-eyed to the trust imposed

upon them; and as a noted chief of our people was wont to say: "Men may slay one another, but they can never overcome the woman, for in the quietude of her lap lies the child! You may destroy him once and again, but he issues as often from that same gentle lap—a gift of the Great Good to the race, in which man is only an accomplice!"

This wild mother has not only the experience of her mother and grandmother, and the accepted rules of her people for a guide, but she humbly seeks to learn a lesson from ants, bees, spiders, beavers, and badgers. She studies the family life of the birds, so exquisite in its emotional intensity and its patient devotion, until she seems to feel the universal mother-heart beating in her own breast. In due time the child takes of his own accord the attitude of prayer, and speaks reverently of the Powers. He thinks that he is a blood brother to all living creatures, and the storm wind is to him a messenger of the "Great Mystery."

At the age of about eight years, if he is a boy, she turns him over to his father for more Spartan training. If a girl, she is from this time much under the guardianship of her grandmother, who is considered the most dignified protector for the maiden. Indeed, the distinctive work of both grandparents is that of acquainting the youth with the national traditions and beliefs. It is reserved for them to repeat the time-hallowed tales with dignity and authority, so as to lead him into his inheritance in the stored-up wisdom and experience of the race. The old are dedicated to the service of the young, as their teachers and advisers, and the young in turn regard them with love and reverence.

Our old age was in some respects the happiest period of life. Advancing years brought with them much freedom, not only from the burden of laborious and dangerous tasks, but from those restrictions of custom and etiquette which were religiously observed by all others. No one who is at all acquainted with the Indian in his home can deny that we are a polite people. As a rule, the warrior who inspired the greatest terror in the hearts of his enemies was a man of the most exemplary gentleness, and almost feminine refinement, among his family and friends. A soft, low voice was considered an excellent thing in man, as well as in woman! Indeed, the enforced intimacy of tent life would soon become intolerable, were it not for these instinctive reserves and delicacies, this unfailing respect for the established place and possessions of every other member of the family circle, this habitual quiet, order, and decorum.

Our people, though capable of strong and durable feeling, were not

demonstrative in their affection at any time, least of all in the presence of guests or strangers. Only to the aged, who have journeyed far, and are in a manner exempt from ordinary rules, are permitted some playful familiarities with children and grandchildren, some plain speaking, even to harshness and objurgation, from which the others must rigidly refrain. In short, the old men and women are privileged to say what they please and how they please, without contradiction, while the hardships and bodily infirmities that of necessity fall to their lot are softened so far as may be by universal consideration and attention.

There was no religious ceremony connected with marriage among us, while on the other hand the relation between man and woman was regarded as in itself mysterious and holy. It appears that where marriage is solemnized by the church and blessed by the priest, it may at the same time be surrounded with customs and ideas of a frivolous, superficial, and even prurient character. We believed that two who love should be united in secret, before the public acknowledgment of their union, and should taste their apotheosis alone with nature. The betrothal might or might not be discussed and approved by the parents, but in either case it was customary for the young pair to disappear into the wilderness, there to pass some days or weeks in perfect seclusion and dual solitude, afterward returning to the village as man and wife. An exchange of presents and entertainments between the two families usually followed, but the nuptial blessing was given by the High Priest of God, the most reverend and holy Nature.

The family was not only the social unit, but also the unit of government. The clan is nothing more than a larger family, with its patriarchal chief as the natural head, and the union of several clans by intermarriage and voluntary connection constitutes the tribe. The very name of our tribe, Dakota, means Allied People. The remoter degrees of kinship were fully recognized, and that not as a matter of form only: first cousins were known as brothers and sisters; the name of "cousin" constituted a binding claim, and our rigid morality forbade marriage between cousins in any known degree, or in other words within the clan.

The household proper consisted of a man with one or more wives and their children, all of whom dwelt amicably together, often under one roof, although some men of rank and position provided a separate lodge for each wife. There were, indeed, few plural marriages except among the older and leading men, and plural wives were usually,

though not necessarily, sisters. A marriage might honorably be dissolved for cause, but there was very little infidelity or immorality, either open or secret.

It has been said that the position of woman is the test of civilization, and that of our women was secure. In them was vested our standard of morals and the purity of our blood. The wife did not take the name of her husband nor enter his clan, and the children belonged to the clan of the mother. All of the family property was held by her, descent was traced in the maternal line, and the honor of the house was in her hands. Modesty was her chief adornment; hence the younger women were usually silent and retiring: but a woman who had attained to ripeness of years and wisdom, or who had displayed notable courage in some emergency, was sometimes invited to a seat in the council.

Thus she ruled undisputed within her own domain, and was to us a tower of moral and spiritual strength, until the coming of the border white man, the soldier and trader, who with strong drink overthrew the honor of the man, and through his power over a worthless husband purchased the virtue of his wife or his daughter. When she fell, the whole race fell with her.

Before this calamity came upon us, you could not find anywhere a happier home than that created by the Indian woman. There was nothing of the artificial about her person, and very little disingenuousness in her character. Her early and consistent training, the definiteness of her vocation, and, above all, her profoundly religious attitude gave her a strength and poise that could not be overcome by any ordinary misfortune.

Indian names were either characteristic nicknames given in a playful spirit, deed names, birth names, or such as have a religious and symbolic meaning. It has been said that when a child is born, some accident or unusual appearance determines his name. This is sometimes the case, but is not the rule. A man of forcible character, with a fine war record, usually bears the name of the buffalo or bear, lightning or some dread natural force. Another of more peaceful nature may be called Swift Bird or Blue Sky. A woman's name usually suggested something about the home, often with the adjective "pretty" or "good," and a feminine termination. Names of any dignity or importance must be conferred by the old men, and especially so if they have any spiritual significance; as Sacred Cloud, Mysterious Night, Spirit Woman, and the like. Such a name was sometimes borne

by three generations, but each individual must prove that he is worthy of it.

In the life of the Indian there was only one inevitable duty,—the duty of prayer—the daily recognition of the Unseen and Eternal. His daily devotions were more necessary to him than daily food. He wakes at daybreak, puts on his moccasins and steps down to the water's edge. Here he throws handfuls of clear, cold water into his face, or plunges in bodily. After the bath, he stands erect before the advancing dawn, facing the sun as it dances upon the horizon, and offers his unspoken orison. His mate may precede or follow him in his devotions, but never accompanies him. Each soul must meet the morning sun, the new, sweet earth, and the Great Silence alone!

Whenever, in the course of the daily hunt, the red hunter comes upon a scene that is strikingly beautiful or sublime—a black thundercloud with the rainbow's glowing arch above the mountain; a white waterfall in the heart of a green gorge; a vast prairie tinged with the blood-red of sunset—he pauses for an instant in the attitude of worship. He sees no need for setting apart one day in seven as a holy day, since to him all days are God's.

Every act of his life is, in a very real sense, a religious act. He recognizes the spirit in all creation, and believes that he draws from it spiritual power. His respect for the immortal part of the animal, his brother, often leads him so far as to lay out the body of his game in state and decorate the head with symbolic paint or feathers. Then he stands before it in the prayer attitude, holding up the filled pipe, in token that he has freed with honor the spirit of his brother, whose body his need compelled him to take to sustain his own life.

When food is taken, the woman murmurs a "grace" as she lowers the kettle; an act so softly and unobtrusively performed that one who does not know the custom usually fails to catch the whisper: "Spirit, partake!" As her husband receives the bowl or plate, he likewise murmurs his invocation to the spirit. When he becomes an old man, he loves to make a notable effort to prove his gratitude. He cuts off the choicest morsel of the meat and casts it into the fire—the purest and most ethereal element.

The hospitality of the wigwam is only limited by the institution of war. Yet, if an enemy should honor us with a call, his trust will not be misplaced, and he will go away convinced that he has met with a royal host! Our honor is the guarantee for his safety, so long as he is within the camp.

Friendship is held to be the severest test of character. It is easy, we think, to be loyal to family and clan, whose blood is in our own veins. Love between man and woman is founded on the mating instinct and is not free from desire and self-seeking. But to have a friend, and to be true under any and all trials, is the mark of a man!

The highest type of friendship is the relation of "brother-friend" or "life-and-death friend." This bond is between man and man, is usually formed in early youth, and can only be broken by death. It is the essence of comradeship and fraternal love, without thought of pleasure or gain, but rather for moral support and inspiration. Each is vowed to die for the other, if need be, and nothing is denied the brother-friend, but neither is anything required that is not in accord with the highest conceptions of the Indian mind.

III

CEREMONIAL AND SYMBOLIC WORSHIP

Modern Perversions of Early Religious Rites • The Sun Dance • The Great Medicine Lodge • Totems and Charms • The Vapor-Bath and the Ceremonial of the Pipe

The public religious rites of the Plains Indians are few, and in large part of modern origin, belonging properly to the so-called "transition period." That period must be held to begin with the first insidious effect upon their manners and customs of contact with the dominant race, and many of the tribes were so influenced long before they ceased to lead the nomadic life.

The fur-traders, the "Black Robe" priests, the military, and finally the Protestant missionaries, were the men who began the disintegration of the Indian nations and the overthrow of their religion, seventy-five to a hundred years before they were forced to enter upon reservation life. We have no authentic study of them until well along in the transition period, when whiskey and trade had already debauched their native ideals.

During the era of reconstruction they modified their customs and beliefs continually, creating a singular admixture of Christian with pagan superstitions, and an addition to the old folk-lore of disguised Bible stories under an Indian aspect. Even their music shows the influence of the Catholic chants. Most of the material collected by modern observers is necessarily of this promiscuous character.

It is noteworthy that the first effect of contact with the whites was an increase of cruelty and barbarity, an intensifying of the dark shadows in the picture! In this manner the "Sun Dance" of the Plains Indians, the most important of their public ceremonials, was abused and perverted until it became a horrible exhibition of barbarism, and was eventually prohibited by the Government.

In the old days, when a Sioux warrior found himself in the very jaws of destruction, he might offer a prayer to his father, the Sun, to prolong his life. If rescued from imminent danger, he must acknowledge the divine favor by making a Sun Dance, according to the vow embraced in his prayer, in which he declared that he did not fear torture or death, but asked life only for the sake of those who loved him. Thus the physical ordeal was the fulfillment of a vow, and a sort of atonement for what might otherwise appear to be reprehensible weakness in the face of death. It was in the nature of confession and thank-offering to the "Great Mystery," through the physical parent, the Sun, and did not embrace a prayer for future favors.

The ceremonies usually took place from six months to a year after the making of the vow, in order to admit of suitable preparation; always in midsummer, and before a large and imposing gathering. They naturally included the making of a feast, and the giving away of much savage wealth in honor of the occasion, although these were no essential part of the religious rite.

When the day came to procure the pole, it was brought in by a party of warriors, headed by some party of distinction. The tree selected was six to eight inches in diameter at the base, and twenty to twenty-five feet high. It was chosen and felled with some solemnity,

including the ceremony of the "filled pipe," and was carried in the fashion of a litter, symbolizing the body of the man who made the dance. A solitary teepee was pitched on a level spot at some distance from the village, and the pole raised near at hand with the same ceremony, in the centre of a circular inclosure of freshcut boughs.

Meanwhile, one of the most noted of our old men had carved out of rawhide, or later of wood, two figures, usually those of a man and a buffalo. Sometimes the figure of a bird, supposed to represent the Thunder, was substituted for the buffalo. It was customary to paint the man red and the animal black, and each was suspended from one end of the crossbar which was securely tied some two feet from the top of the pole. I have never been able to determine that this cross had any significance; it was probably nothing more than a dramatic coincidence that surmounted the Sun-Dance pole with the symbol of Christianity.

The paint indicated that the man who was about to give thanks publicly had been potentially dead, but was allowed to live by the mysterious favor and interference of the Giver of Life. The buffalo hung opposite the image of his own body in death, because it was the support of his physical self, and a leading figure in legendary lore. Following the same line of thought, when he emerged from the solitary lodge of preparation, and approached the pole to dance, nude save for his breechclout and moccasins, his hair loosened and daubed with clay, he must drag after him a buffalo skull, representing the grave from which he had escaped.

The dancer was cut or scarified on the chest, sufficient to draw blood and cause pain, the natural accompaniments of his figurative death. He took his position opposite the singers, facing the pole, and dragging the skull by leather thongs which were merely fastened about his shoulders. During a later period, incisions were made in the breast or back, sometimes both, through which wooden skewers were drawn, and secured by lariats to the pole or to the skulls. Thus he danced without intermission for a day and a night, or even longer, ever gazing at the sun in the daytime, and blowing from time to time a sacred whistle made from the bone of a goose's wing.

In recent times, this rite was exaggerated and distorted into a mere ghastly display of physical strength and endurance under torture, almost on a level with the Caucasian institution of the bull-fight, or the yet more modern prize-ring. Moreover, instead of an atonement or thank-offering, it became the accompaniment of a prayer for success

in war, or in a raid upon the horses of the enemy. The number of dancers was increased, and they were made to hang suspended from the pole by their own flesh, which they must break loose before being released. I well remember the comments in our own home upon the passing of this simple but impressive ceremony, and its loss of all meaning and propriety under the demoralizing additions which were some of the fruits of early contact with the white man.

Perhaps the most remarkable organization ever known among American Indians, that of the "Grand Medicine Lodge," was apparently an indirect result of the labors of the early Jesuit missionaries. In it Caucasian ideas are easily recognizable, and it seems reasonable to suppose that its founders desired to establish an order that would successfully resist the encroachments of the "Black Robes." However that may be, it is an unquestionable fact that the only religious leaders of any note who have arisen among the native tribes since the advent of the white man, the "Shawnee Prophet" in 1762, and the half-breed prophet of the "Ghost Dance" in 1890, both founded their claims or prophecies upon the Gospel story. Thus in each case an Indian religious revival or craze, though more or less threatening to the invader, was of distinctively alien origin.

The Medicine Lodge originated among the Algonquin tribe, and extended gradually throughout its branches, finally affecting the Sioux of the Mississippi Valley, and forming a strong bulwark against the work of the pioneer missionaries, who secured, indeed, scarcely any converts until after the outbreak of 1862, when subjection, starvation, and imprisonment turned our broken-hearted people to accept Christianity, which seemed to offer them the only gleam of kindness or hope.

The order was a secret one, and in some respects not unlike the Free Masons, being a union or affiliation of a number of lodges, each with its distinctive songs and medicines. Leadership was in order of seniority in degrees, which could only be obtained by merit, and women were admitted to membership upon equal terms, with the possibility of attaining to the highest honors. No person might become a member unless his moral standing was excellent, all candidates remained on probation for one or two years, and murderers and adulterers were expelled. The commandments promulgated by this order were essentially the same as the Mosaic Ten, so that it exerted a distinct moral influence, in addition to its ostensible object, which was instruction in the secrets of legitimate medicine.

In this society the uses of all curative roots and herbs known to us were taught exhaustively and practiced mainly by the old, the younger members being in training to fill the places of those who passed away. My grandmother was a well-known and successful practitioner, and both my mother and father were members, but did not practice.

A medicine or "mystery feast" was not a public affair, as members only were eligible, and upon these occasions all the "medicine bags" and totems of the various lodges were displayed and their peculiar "medicine songs" were sung. The food was only partaken of by invited guests, and not by the hosts, or lodge making the feast.

The "Grand Medicine Dance" was given on the occasion of initiating those candidates who had finished their probation, a sufficient number of whom were designated to take the places of those who had died since the last meeting. Invitations were sent out in the form of small bundles of tobacco. Two very large teepees were pitched facing one another, a hundred feet apart, half open, and connected by a roofless hall or colonnade of fresh-cut boughs. One of these lodges was for the society giving the dance and the novices, the other was occupied by the "soldiers," whose duty it was to distribute the refreshments, and to keep order among the spectators. They were selected from among the best and bravest warriors of the tribe.

The preparations being complete, and the members of each lodge garbed and painted according to their rituals, they entered the hall separately, in single file, led by their oldest man or "Great Chief." Standing before the "Soldiers' Lodge," facing the setting sun, their chief addressed the "Great Mystery" directly in a few words, after which all extending the right arm horizontally from the shoulder with open palm, sang a short invocation in unison, ending with a deep: "E-ho-ho-ho!" This performance, which was really impressive, was repeated in front of the headquarters lodge, facing the rising sun, after which each lodge took its assigned place, and the songs and dances followed in regular order.

The closing ceremony, which was intensely dramatic in its character, was the initiation of the novices, who had received their final preparation on the night before. They were now led out in front of the headquarters lodge and placed in a kneeling position upon a carpet of rich robes and furs, the men upon the right hand, stripped and painted black, with a round spot of red just over the heart, while the women, dressed in their best, were arranged upon the left. Both sexes wore the hair loose, as if in mourning or expectation of death. An

equal number of grand medicine-men, each of whom was especially appointed to one of the novices, faced them at a distance of half the length of the hall, or perhaps fifty feet.

After silent prayer, each medicine-man in turn addressed himself to his charge, exhorting him to observe all the rules of the order under the eye of the Mysterious One, and instructing him in his duty toward his fellow-man and toward the Ruler of Life. All then assumed an attitude of superb power and dignity, crouching slightly as if about to spring forward in a foot-race, and grasping their medicine bags firmly in both hands. Swinging their arms forward at the same moment, they uttered their guttural "Yo-ho-ho-ho!" in perfect unison and with startling effect. In the midst of a breathless silence, they took a step forward, then another and another, ending a rod or so from the row of kneeling victims, with a mighty swing of the sacred bags that would seem to project all their mystic power into the bodies of the initiates. Instantly they all fell forward, apparently lifeless.

With this thrilling climax, the drums were vigorously pounded and the dance began again with energy. After a few turns had been taken about the prostrate bodies of the new members, covering them with fine robes and other garments which were later to be distributed as gifts, they were permitted to come to life and to join in the final dance. The whole performance was clearly symbolic of death and resurrection.

While I cannot suppose that this elaborate ritual, with its use of public and audible prayer, of public exhortation or sermon, and other Caucasian features, was practiced before comparatively modern times, there is no doubt that it was conscientiously believed in by its members, and for a time regarded with reverence by the people. But at a later period it became still further demoralized and fell under suspicion of witchhcraft.

There is no doubt that the Indian held medicine close to spiritual things, but in this also he had been much misunderstood; in fact, everything that he held sacred is indiscriminately called "medicine," in the sense of mystery or magic. As a doctor, he was originally very adroit and often successful. He employed only healing bark, roots, and leaves with whose properties he was familiar, using them in the form of a distillation or tea and always singly. The stomach or internal bath was a valuable discovery of his, and the vapor or Turkish bath was in general use. He could set a broken bone with fair success, but never practiced surgery in any form. In addition to all this, the

medicine-man possessed much personal magnetism and authority, and in his treatment often sought to reëstablish the equilibrium of the patient through mental or spiritual influences—a sort of primitive psycho-therapy.

The Sioux word for the healing art is "wah-pee-yah," which literally means readjusting or making anew. "Pay-jee-hoo-tah," literally root, means medicine, and "wakan" signifies spirit or mystery. Thus the three ideas, while sometimes associated, were carefully distinguished.

It is important to remember that in the old days the "medicine-man" received no payment for his services, which were of the nature of an honorable function or office. When the idea of payment and barter was introduced among us, and valuable presents or fees began to be demanded for treating the sick, the ensuing greed and rivalry led to many demoralizing practices, and in time to the rise of the modern "conjurer," who is generally a fraud and trickster of the grossest kind. It is fortunate that his day is practically over.

Ever seeking to establish spiritual comradeship with the animal creation, the Indian adopted this or that animal as his "totem," the emblematic device of his society, family, or clan. It is probable that the creature chosen was the traditional ancestress, as we are told that the First Man had many wives among the animal people. The sacred beast, bird, or reptile, represented by its stuffed skin, or by a rude painting, was treated with reverence and carried into battle to insure the guardianship of the spirits. The symbolic attribute of beaver, bear, or tortoise, such as wisdom, cunning, courage, and the like, was supposed to be mysteriously conferred upon the wearer of the badge. The totem or charm used in medicine was ordinarily that of the medicine lodge to which the practitioner belonged, though there were some great men who boasted a special revelation.

There are two ceremonial usages which, so far as I have been able to ascertain, were universal among American Indians, and apparently fundamental. These have already been referred to as the "eneépee," or vapor-bath, and the "chan-dú-hu-pah-yú-za-pee," or ceremonial of the pipe. In our Siouan legends and traditions these two are preëminent, as handed down from the most ancient time and persisting to the last.

In our Creation myth or story of the First Man, the vapor-bath was the magic used by The-one-who-was-First-Created, to give life to the dead bones of his younger brother, who had been slain by the monsters of the deep. Upon the shore of the Great Water he dug two

round holes, over one of which he built a low inclosure of fragrant cedar boughs, and here he gathered together the bones of his brother. In the other pit he made a fire and heated four round stones, which he rolled one by one into the lodge of boughs. Having closed every aperture save one, he sang a mystic chant while he thrust in his arm and sprinkled water upon the stones with a bunch of sage. Immediately steam arose, and as the legend says, "there was an appearance of life." A second time he sprinkled water, and the dry bones rattled together. The third time he seemed to hear soft singing from within the lodge; and the fourth time a voice exclaimed: "Brother, let me out!" (It should be noted that the number four is the magic or sacred number of the Indian.)

This story gives the traditional origin of the "eneépee," which has ever since been deemed essential to the Indian's effort to purify and recreate his spirit. It is used both by the doctor and by his patient. Every man must enter the cleaning bath and take the cold plunge which follows, when preparing for any spiritual crisis, for possible death, or imminent danger.

Not only the "eneépee" itself, but everything used in connection with the mysterious event, the aromatic cedar and sage, the water, and especially the water-worn boulders, are regarded as sacred, or at the least adapted to a spiritual use. For the rock we have a special reverent name—"Tunkan," a contraction of the Sioux word for Grandfather.

The natural boulder enters into many of our solemn ceremonials, such as the "Rain Dance," and the "Feast of Virgins." The lone hunter and warrior reverently holds up his filled pipe to "Tunkan," in solitary commemoration of a miracle which to him is as authentic and holy as the raising of Lazarus to the devout Christian.

There is a legend that the First Man fell sick, and was taught by his Elder Brother the ceremonial use of the pipe, in a prayer to the spirits for ease and relief. This simple ceremony is the commonest daily expression of thanks or "grace," as well as an oath of loyalty and good faith when the warrior goes forth upon some perilous enterprise, and it enters even into his "hambeday," or solitary prayer, ascending as a rising vapor or incense to the Father of Spirits.

In all the war ceremonies and in medicine a special pipe is used, but at home or on the hunt the warrior employs his own. The pulverized weed is mixed with aromatic bark of the red willow, and pressed lightly into the bowl of the long stone pipe. The worshiper lights it gravely and takes a whiff or two; then, standing erect, he holds it

silently toward the Sun, our father, and toward the Earth, our mother. There are modern variations, as holding the pipe to the Four Winds, the Fire, Water, Rock, and other elements or objects of reverence.

There are many religious festivals which are local and special in character, embodying a prayer for success in hunting or warfare, or for rain and bountiful harvests, but these two are the sacraments of our religion. For baptism we substitute the "eneépee," the purification by vapor, and in our holy communion we partake of the soothing incense of tobacco in the stead of bread and wine.

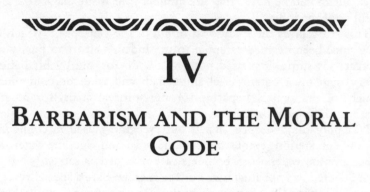

IV

BARBARISM AND THE MORAL CODE

Silence the Corner-Stone of Character • Basic Ideas of Morality • "Give All or Nothing!" Rules of Honorable Warfare • An Indian Conception of Courage

Long before I ever heard of Christ, or saw a white man, I had learned from an untutored woman the essence of morality. With the help of dear Nature herself, she taught me things simple but of mighty import. I knew God. I perceived what goodness is. I saw and loved what is really beautiful. Civilization has not taught me anything better!

As a child, I understood how to give; I have forgotten that grace since I became civilized. I lived the natural life, whereas I now live the artificial. Any pretty pebble was valuable to me then; every growing tree an object of reverence. Now I worship with the white man before a painted landscape whose value is estimated in dollars! Thus the

Indian is reconstructed, as the natural rocks are ground to powder, and made into artificial blocks which may be built into the walls of modern society.

The first American mingled with his pride a singular humility. Spiritual arrogance was foreign to his nature and teaching. He never claimed that the power of articulate speech was proof of superiority over the dumb creation; on the other hand, it is to him a perilous gift. He believes profoundly in silence—the sign of a perfect equilibrium. Silence is the absolute poise or balance of body, mind, and spirit. The man who preserves his selfhood ever calm and unshaken by the storms of existence—not a leaf, as it were, astir on the tree; not a ripple upon the surface of shining pool—his, in the mind of the unlettered sage, is the ideal attitude and conduct of life.

If you ask him: "What is silence?" he will answer: "It is the Great Mystery!" "The holy silence is His voice!" If you ask: "What are the fruits of silence?" he will say: "They are self-control, true courage or endurance, patience, dignity, and reverence. Silence is the corner-stone of character."

"Guard your tongue in youth," said the old chief, Wabashaw, "and in age you may mature a thought that will be of service to your people!"

The moment that man conceived of a perfect body, supple, symmetrical, graceful, and enduring—in that moment he had laid the foundation of a moral life! No man can hope to maintain such a temple of the spirit beyond the period of adolescence, unless he is able to curb his indulgence in the pleasures of the senses. Upon this truth the Indian built a rigid system of physical training, a social and moral code that was the law of his life.

There was aroused in him as a child a high ideal of manly strength and beauty, the attainment of which must depend upon strict temperance in eating and in the sexual relation, together with severe and persistent exercise. He desired to be a worthy link in the generations, and that he might not destroy by his weakness that vigor and purity of blood which had been achieved at the cost of much self-denial by a long line of ancestors.

He was required to fast from time to time for short periods, and to work off his superfluous energy by means of hard running, swimming, and the vapor-bath. The bodily fatigue thus induced, especially when coupled with a reduced diet, is a reliable cure for undue sexual desires.

Personal modesty was early cultivated as a safeguard, together with

a strong self-respect and pride of family and race. This was accomplished in part by keeping the child ever before the public eye, from his birth onward. His entrance into the world, especially in the case of the first-born, was often publicly announced by the herald, accompanied by a distribution of presents to the old and needy. The same thing occurred when he took his first step, when his ears were pierced, and when he shot his first game, so that his childish exploits and progress were known to the whole clan as to a larger family, and he grew into manhood with the saving sense of a reputation to sustain.

The youth was encouraged to enlist early in the public service, and to develop a wholesome ambition for the honors of a leader and feast-maker, which can never be his unless he is truthful and generous, as well as brave, and ever mindful of his personal chastity and honor. There were many ceremonial customs which had a distinct moral influence; the woman was rigidly secluded at certain periods, and the young husband was forbidden to approach his own wife when preparing for war or for any religious event. The public or tribal position of the Indian is entirely dependent upon his private virtue, and he is never permitted to forget that he does not live to himself alone, but to his tribe and his clan. Thus habits of perfect self-control were early established, and there were no unnatural conditions or complex temptations to beset him until he was met and overthrown by a stronger race.

To keep the young men and young women strictly to their honor, there were observed among us, within my own recollection, certain annual ceremonies of a semi-religious nature. One of the most impressive of these was the sacred "Feast of Virgins," which, when given for the first time, was equivalent to the public announcement of a young girl's arrival at a marriageable age. The herald, making the rounds of the teepee village, would publish the feast something after this fashion:

"Pretty Weasel-woman, the daughter of Brave Bear, will kindle her first maidens' fire to-morrow! All ye who have never yielded to the pleading of man, who have not destroyed your innocency, you alone are invited, to proclaim anew before the Sun and the Earth, before your companions and in the sight of the Great Mystery, the chastity and purity of your maidenhood. Come ye, all who have not known man!"

The whole village was at once aroused to the interest of the coming event, which was considered next to the Sun Dance and the Grand Medicine Dance in public importance. It always took place in mid-

summer, when a number of different clans were gathered together for the summer festivities, and was held in the centre of the great circular encampment.

Here two circles were described, one within the other, about a rudely heart-shaped rock which was touched with red paint, and upon either side of the rock there were thrust into the ground a knife and two arrows. The inner circle was for the maidens, and the outer one for their grandmothers or chaperones, who were supposed to have passed the climacteric. Upon the outskirts of the feast there was a great public gathering, in which order was kept by certain warriors of highest reputation. Any man among the spectators might approach and challenge any young woman whom he knew to be unworthy; but if the accuser failed to prove his charge, the warriors were accustomed to punish him severely.

Each girl in turn approached the sacred rock and laid her hand upon it with all solemnity. This was her religious declaration of her virginity, her vow to remain pure until her marriage. If she should ever violate the maidens' oath, then welcome that keen knife and those sharp arrows!

Our maidens were ambitious to attend a number of these feasts before marriage, and it sometimes happened that a girl was compelled to give one, on account of gossip about her conduct. Then it was in the nature of a challenge to the scandalmongers to prove their words! A similar feast was sometimes made by the young men, for whom the rules were even more strict, since no young man might attend this feast who had so much as spoken of love to a maiden. It was considered a high honor among us to have won some distinction in war and the chase, and above all to have been invited to a seat in the council, before one had spoken to any girl save his own sister.

It was our belief that the love of possessions is a weakness to be overcome. Its appeal is to the material part, and if allowed its way it will in time disturb the spiritual balance of the man. Therefore the child must early learn the beauty of generosity. He is taught to give what he prizes most, and that he may taste the happiness of giving, he is made at an early age the family almoner. If a child is inclined to be grasping, or to cling to any of his little possessions, legends are related to him, telling of the contempt and disgrace falling upon the ungenerous and mean man.

Public giving is a part of every important ceremony. It properly belongs to the celebration of birth, marriage, and death, and is

observed whenever it is desired to do special honor to any person or event. Upon such occasions it is common to give to the point of utter impoverishment. The Indian in his simplicity literally gives away all that he has, to relatives, to guests of another tribe or clan, but above all to the poor and the aged, from whom he can hope for no return. Finally, the gift to the "Great Mystery," the religious offering, may be of little value in itself, but to the giver's own thought it should carry the meaning and reward of true sacrifice.

Orphans and the aged are invariably cared for, not only by their next of kin, but by the whole clan. It is the loving parent's pride to have his daughters visit the unfortunate and the helpless, carry them food, comb their hair, and mend their garments. The name "Wenonah," bestowed upon the eldest daughter, distinctly implies all this, and a girl who failed in her charitable duties was held to be unworthy of the name.

The man who is a skillful hunter, and whose wife is alive to her opportunities, makes many feasts, to which he is careful to invite the older men of his clan, recognizing that they have outlived their period of greatest activity, and now love nothing so well as to eat in good company, and to live over the past. The old men, for their part, do their best to requite his liberality with a little speech, in which they are apt to relate the brave and generous deeds of their host's ancestors, finally congratulating him upon being a worthy successor of an honorable line. Thus his reputation is won as a hunter and a feast-maker, and almost as famous in his way as the great warrior is he who has a recognized name and standing as a "man of peace."

The true Indian sets no price upon either his property or his labor. His generosity is only limited by his strength and ability. He regards it as an honor to be selected for a difficult or dangerous service, and would think it shame to ask for any reward, saying rather: "Let him whom I serve express his thanks according to his own bringing up and his sense of honor!"

Nevertheless, he recognizes rights in property. To steal from one of his own tribe would be indeed disgrace, and if discovered, the name of "Wamanon," or Thief, is fixed upon him forever as an unalterable stigma. The only exception to the rule is in the case of food, which is always free to the hungry if there is none by to offer it. Other protection than the moral law there could not be in an Indian community, where there were neither locks nor doors, and everything was open and easy of access to all comers.

The property of the enemy is spoil of war, and it is always allowable to confiscate it if possible. However, in the old days there was not much plunder. Before the coming of the white man, there was in fact little temptation or opportunity to despoil the enemy; but in modern times the practice of "stealing horses" from hostile tribes has become common, and is thought far from dishonorable.

Warfare we regarded as an institution of the "Great Mystery"—an organized tournament or trial of courage and skill, with elaborate rules and "counts" for the coveted honor of the eagle feather. It was held to develop the quality of manliness, and its motive was chivalric or patriotic, but never the desire for territorial aggrandizement or the overthrow of a brother nation. It was common, in early times, for a battle or skirmish to last all day, with great display of daring and horsemanship, but with scarcely more killed and wounded than may be carried from the field during a university game of football.

The slayer of a man in battle was expected to mourn for thirty days, blackening his face and loosening his hair according to the custom. He of course considered it no sin to take the life of an enemy, and this ceremonial mourning was a sign of reverence for the departed spirit. The killing in war of non-combatants, such as women and children, is partly explained by the fact that in savage life the woman without husband or protector is in pitiable case, and it was supposed that the spirit of the warrior would be better content if no widow and orphans were left to suffer want, as well as to weep.

A scalp might originally be taken by the leader of the war party only, and at that period no other mutilation was practiced. It was a small lock not more than three inches square, which was carried only during the thirty days' celebration of a victory, and afterward given religious burial. Wanton cruelties and the more barbarous customs of war were greatly intensified with the coming of the white man, who brought with him fiery liquor and deadly weapons, aroused the Indian's worst passions, provoking in him revenge and cupidity, and even offered bounties for the scalps of innocent men, women, and children.

Murder within the tribe was a grave offense, to be atoned for as the council might decree, and it often happened that the slayer was called upon to pay the penalty with his own life. He made no attempt to escape or to evade justice. That the crime was committed in the depths of the forest or at dead of night, witnessed by no human eye, made no difference to his mind. He was thoroughly convinced that all is known

to the "Great Mystery," and hence did not hesitate to give himself up, to stand his trial by the old and wise men of the victim's clan. His own family and clan might by no means attempt to excuse or to defend him, but his judges took all the known circumstances into consideration, and if it appeared that he slew in self-defense, or that the provocation was severe, he might be set free after a thirty days' period of mourning in solitude. Otherwise the murdered man's next of kin were authorized to take his life; and if they refrained from doing so, as often happened, he remained an outcast from the clan. A willful murder was a rare occurrence before the days of whiskey and drunken rows, for we were not a violent or a quarrelsome people.

It is well remembered that Crow Dog, who killed the Sioux chief, Spotted Tail, in 1881, calmly surrendered himself and was tried and convicted by the courts in South Dakota. After his conviction, he was permitted remarkable liberty in prison, such as perhaps no white man has ever enjoyed when under sentence of death.

The cause of his act was a solemn commission received from his people, nearly thirty years earlier, at the time that Spotted Tail usurped the chieftainship by the aid of the military, whom he had aided. Crow Dog was under a vow to slay the chief, in case he ever betrayed or disgraced the name of the Brule Sioux. There is no doubt that he had committed crimes both public and private, having been guilty of misuse of office as well as of gross offenses against morality; therefore his death was not a matter of personal vengeance but of just retribution.

A few days before Crow Dog was to be executed, he asked permission to visit his home and say farewell to his wife and twin boys, then nine or ten years old. Strange to say, the request was granted, and the condemned man sent home under escort of the deputy sheriff, who remained at the Indian agency, merely telling his prisoner to report there on the following day. When he did not appear at the time set, the sheriff dispatched the Indian police after him. They did not find him, and his wife simply said that Crow Dog had desired to ride alone to the prison, and would reach there on the day appointed. All doubt was removed next day by a telegram from Rapid City, two hundred miles distant, saying: "Crow Dog has just reported here."

The incident drew public attention to the Indian murderer, with the unexpected result that the case was reopened, and Crow Dog acquitted. He still lives, a well-preserved man of about seventy-five years, and is much respected among his own people.

It is said that, in the very early days, lying was a capital offense among us. Believing that the deliberate liar is capable of committing any crime behind the screen of cowardly untruth and double-dealing, the destroyer of mutual confidence was summarily put to death, that the evil might go no further.

Even the worst enemies of the Indian, those who accuse him of treachery, blood-thirstiness, cruelty, and lust, have not denied his courage, but in their minds it is a courage that is ignorant, brutal, and fantastic. His own conception of bravery makes of it a high moral virtue, for to him it consists not so much in aggressive self-assertion as in absolute self-control. The truly brave man, we contend, yields neither to fear nor anger, desire nor agony; he is at all times master of himself; his courage rises to the heights of chivalry, patriotism, and real heroism.

"Let neither cold, hunger, nor pain, nor the fear of them, neither the bristling teeth of danger nor the very jaws of death itself, prevent you from doing a good deed," said an old chief to a scout who was about to seek the buffalo in midwinter for the relief of a starving people. This was his childlike conception of courage.

V

THE UNWRITTEN SCRIPTURES

A Living Book • The Sioux Story of Creation • The First Battle • Another Version of the Flood • Our Animal Ancestry

A missionary once undertook to instruct a group of Indians in the truths of his holy religion. He told them of the creation of the earth in six days, and of the fall of our first parents by eating an apple.

The courteous savages listened attentively, and, after thanking him, one related in his turn a very ancient tradition concerning the origin of the maize. But the missionary plainly showed his disgust and disbelief, indignantly saying:—

"What I delivered to you were sacred truths, but this that you tell me is mere fable and falsehood!"

"My brother," gravely replied the offended Indian, "it seems that you have not been well grounded in the rules of civility. You saw that we, who practice these rules, believed your stories; why, then, do you refuse to credit ours?"

Every religion has its Holy Book, and ours was a mingling of history, poetry, and prophecy, of precept and folk-lore, even such as the modern reader finds within the covers of his Bible. This Bible of ours was our whole literature, a living Book, sowed as precious seed by our wisest sages, and springing anew in the wondering eyes and upon the innocent lips of little children. Upon its hoary wisdom of proverb and fable, its mystic and legendary lore thus sacredly preserved and transmitted from father to son, was based in large part our customs and philosophy.

Naturally magnanimous and open-minded, the red man prefers to believe that the Spirit of God is not breathed into man alone, but that the whole created universe is a sharer in the immortal perfection of its Maker. His imaginative and poetic mind, like that of the Greek, assigns to every mountain, tree, and spring its spirit, nymph, or divinity either beneficent or mischievous. The heroes and demigods of Indian tradition reflect the characteristic trend of his thought, and his attribution of personality and will to the elements, the sun and stars, and all animate or inanimate nature.

In the Sioux story of creation, the great Mysterious One is not brought directly upon the scene or conceived in anthropomorphic fashion, but remains sublimely in the background. The Sun and the Earth, representing the male and female principles, are the main elements in his creation, the other planets being subsidiary. The enkindling warmth of the Sun entered into the bosom of our mother, the Earth, and forthwith she conceived and brought forth life, both vegetable and animal.

Finally there appeared, mysteriously Ish-ná-e-cha-ge, the "First-Born," a being in the likeness of man, yet more than man, who roamed solitary among the animal people and understood their ways and their language. They beheld him with wonder and awe, for they

could do nothing without his knowledge. He had pitched his tent in the centre of the land, and there was no spot impossible for him to penetrate.

At last, like Adam, the "First-Born" of the Sioux became weary of living alone, and formed for himself a companion—not a mate, but a brother—not out of a rib from his side, but from a splinter which he drew from his great toe! This was the Little Boy Man, who was not created full-grown, but as an innocent child, trusting and helpless. His Elder Brother was his teacher throughout every stage of human progress from infancy to manhood, and it is to the rules which he laid down, and his counsels to the Little Boy Man, that we trace many of our most deep-rooted beliefs and most sacred customs.

Foremost among the animal people was Unk-to-mee, the Spider, the original trouble-maker, who noted keenly the growth of the boy in wit and ingenuity, and presently advised the animals to make an end of him, "for," said he, "if you do not, some day he will be the master of us all!" But they all loved the Little Boy Man, because he was so friendly and so playful. Only the monsters of the deep sea listened, and presently took his life, hiding his body in the bottom of the sea. Nevertheless, by the magic power of the First-Born, the body was recovered and was given life again in the sacred vapor-bath, as described in a former chapter.

Once more our first ancestor roamed happily among the animal people, who were in those days a powerful nation. He learned their ways and their language—for they had a common tongue in those days; learned to sing like the birds, to swim like the fishes, and to climb sure-footed over rocks like the mountain sheep. Notwithstanding that he was their good comrade and did them no harm, Unk-to-mee once more sowed dissension among the animals, and messages were sent into all quarters of the earth, sea, and air, that all the tribes might unite to declare war upon the solitary man who was destined to become their master.

After a time the young man discovered the plot, and came home very sorrowful. He loved his animal friends, and was grieved that they should combine against him. Besides, he was naked and unarmed. But his Elder Brother armed him with a bow and flint-headed arrows, a stone war-club and a spear. He likewise tossed a pebble four times into the air, and each time it became a cliff or wall of rock about the teepee.

"Now," said he, "it is time to fight and to assert your supremacy,

for it is they who have brought the trouble upon you, and not you upon them!"

Night and day the Little Boy Man remained upon the watch for his enemies from the top of the wall, and at last he beheld the prairies black with buffalo herds, and the elk gathering upon the edges of the forest. Bears and wolves were closing in from all directions, and now from the sky the Thunder gave his fearful war-whoop, answered by the wolf's long howl.

The badgers and other burrowers began at once to undermine his rocky fortress, while the climbers undertook to scale its perpendicular walls.

Then for the first time on earth the bow was strung, and hundreds of flint-headed arrows found their mark in the bodies of the animals, while each time that the Boy Man swung his stone war-club, his enemies fell in countless numbers.

Finally the insects, the little people of the air, attacked him in a body, filling his eyes and ears, and tormenting him with their poisoned spears, so that he was in despair. He called for help upon his Elder Brother, who ordered him to strike the rocks with his stone war-club. As soon as he had done so, sparks of fire flew upon the dry grass of the prairie and it burst into flame. A mighty smoke ascended, which drove away the teasing swarms of the insect people, while the flames terrified and scattered the others.

This was the first dividing of the trail between man and the animal people, and when the animals had sued for peace, the treaty provided that they must ever after furnish man with flesh for his food and skins for clothing, though not without effort and danger on his part. The little insects refused to make any concession, and have ever since been the tormentors of man; however, the birds of the air declared that they would punish them for their obstinacy, and this they continue to do unto this day.

Our people have always claimed that the stone arrows which are found so generally throughout the country are the ones that the first man used in his battle with the animals. It is not recorded in our traditions, much less is it within the memory of our old men, that we have ever made or used similar arrow-heads. Some have tried to make use of them for shooting fish under water, but with little success, and they are absolutely useless with the Indian bow which was in use when America was discovered. It is possible that they were made by some pre-historic race who used much longer and stronger bows, and who

were workers in stone, which our people were not. Their stone implements were merely natural boulders or flint chips, fitted with handles of raw-hide or wood, except the pipes, which were carved from a species of stone which is soft when first quarried, and therefore easily worked with the most primitive tools. Practically all the flint arrow-heads that we see in museums and elsewhere were picked up or ploughed up, while some have been dishonestly sold by trafficking Indians and others, embedded in trees and bones.

We had neither devil nor hell in our religion until the white man brought them to us, yet Unk-to-mee, the Spider, was doubtless akin to that old Serpent who tempted mother Eve. He is always characterized as tricky, treacherous, and at the same time affable and charming, being not within the gifts of wit, prophecy, and eloquence. He is an adroit magician, able to assume almost any form at will, and impervious to any amount of ridicule and insult. Here we have, it appears, the elements of the story in Genesis; the primal Eden, the tempter in animal form, and the bringing of sorrow and death upon earth through the elemental sins of envy and jealousy.

The warning conveyed in the story of Unk-to-mee was ever used with success by Indian parents, and especially grandparents, in the instruction of their children. Ish-na-e-cha-ge, on the other hand, was a demigod and mysterious teacher, whose function it was to initiate the first man into his tasks and pleasures here on earth.

After the battle with the animals, there followed a battle with the elements, which in some measure parallels the Old Testament story of the flood. In this case, the purpose seems to have been to destroy the wicked animal people, who were too many and too strong for the lone man.

The legend tells us that when fall came, the First-Born advised his younger brother to make for himself a warm tent of buffalo skins, and to store up much food. No sooner had he done this than it began to snow, and the snow fell steadily during many moons. The Little Boy Man made for himself snow-shoes, and was thus enabled to hunt easily, while the animals fled from him with difficulty. Finally wolves, foxes, and ravens came to his door to beg for food, and he helped them, but many of the fiercer wild animals died of cold and starvation.

One day, when the hungry ones appeared, the snow was higher than the tops of the teepee poles, but the Little Boy Man's fire kept a hole open and clear. Down this hole they peered, and lo! the man had

rubbed ashes on his face by the advice of his Elder Brother, and they both lay silent and motionless on either side of the fire.

Then the fox barked and the raven cawed his signal to the wandering tribes, and they all rejoiced and said: "Now they are both dying or dead, and we shall have no more trouble!" But the sun appeared, and a warm wind melted the snow-banks, so that the land was full of water. The young man and his Teacher made a birch-bark canoe, which floated upon the surface of the flood, while of the animals there were saved only a few, who had found a foothold upon the highest peaks.

The youth had now passed triumphantly through the various ordeals of his manhood. One day his Elder Brother spoke to him and said: "You have now conquered the animal people, and withstood the force of the elements. You have subdued the earth to your will, and still you are alone! It is time to go forth and find a woman whom you can love, and by whose help you may reproduce your kind."

"But how am I to do this?" replied the first man, who was only an inexperienced boy. "I am here alone, as you say, and I know not where to find a woman or a mate!"

"Go forth and seek her," replied the Great Teacher; and forthwith the youth set out on his wanderings in search of a wife. He had no idea how to make love, so that the first courtship was done by the pretty and coquettish maidens of the Bird, Beaver, and Bear tribes. There are some touching and whimsical love stories which the rich imagination of the Indian has woven into this old legend.

It is said, for example, that at his first camp he had built for himself a lodge of green boughs in the midst of the forest, and that there his reverie was interrupted by a voice from the wilderness—a voice that was irresistibly and profoundly sweet. In some mysterious way, the soul of the young man was touched as it had never been before, for this call of exquisite tenderness and allurement was the voice of the eternal woman!

Presently a charming little girl stood timidly at the door of his pine-bough wigwam. She was modestly dressed in gray, with a touch of jet about her pretty face, and she carried a basket of wild cherries which she shyly offered to the young man. So the rover was subdued, and love turned loose upon the world to upbuild and to destroy! When at last she left him, he peeped through the door after her, but saw only a robin, with head turned archly to one side, fluttering away among the trees.

His next camp was beside a clear, running stream, where a plump and industrious maid was busily at work chopping wood. He fell promptly in love with her also, and for some time they lived together in her cosy house by the waterside. After their boy was born, the wanderer wished very much to go back to his Elder Brother and to show him his wife and child. But the beaver-woman refused to go, so at last he went alone for a short visit. When he returned, there was only a trickle of water beside the broken dam, the beautiful home was left desolate, and wife and child were gone forever!

The deserted husband sat alone upon the bank, sleepless and faint with grief, until he was consoled by a comely young woman in glossy black, who took compassion upon his distress and soothed him with food and loving attentions. This was the bear-woman, from whom again he was afterward separated by some mishap. The story goes that he had children by each of his many wives, some of whom resembled their father, and these became the ancestors of the human race, while those who bore the characteristics of their mother returned to her clan. It is also said that such as were abnormal or monstrous in form were forbidden to reproduce their kind, and all love and mating between man and the animal creation was from that time forth strictly prohibited. There are some curious traditions of young men and maidens who transgressed this law unknowingly, being seduced and deceived by a magnificent buck deer, perhaps, or a graceful doe, and whose fall was punished with death.

The animal totems so general among the tribes were said to have descended to them from their great-grandmother's clan, and the legend was often quoted in support of our close friendship with the animal people. I have sometimes wondered why the scientific doctrine of man's descent has not in the same way apparently increased the white man's respect for these our humbler kin.

Of the many later heroes or Hiawathas who appear in this voluminous unwritten book of ours, each introduced an epoch in the long story of man and his environment. There is, for example, the Avenger of the Innocent, who sprang from a clot of blood; the ragged little boy who won fame and a wife by shooting the Red Eagle of fateful omen; and the Star Boy, who was the offspring of a mortal maiden and a Star.

It was this last who fought for man against his strongest enemies, such as Wazeeyah, the Cold or North-Wind. There was a desperate battle between these two, in which first one had the advantage and

then the other, until both were exhausted and declared a truce. While he rested, Star Boy continued to fan himself with his great fan of eagle feathers, and the snow melted so fast that North-Wind was forced to arrange a treaty of peace, by which he was only to control one half the year. So it was that the orderly march of the seasons was established, and every year Star Boy with his fan of eagle feathers sets in motion the warm winds that usher in the spring.

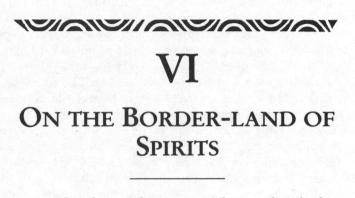

VI

ON THE BORDER-LAND OF SPIRITS

Death and Funeral Customs • The Sacred Lock of Hair • Reincarnation and the Converse of Spirits • Occult and Psychic Powers • The Gift of Prophecy

The attitude of the Indian toward death, the test and background of life, is entirely consistent with his character and philosophy. Death has no terrors for him; he meets it with simplicity and perfect calm, seeking only an honorable end as his last gift to his family and descendants. Therefore he courts death in battle; on the other hand, he would regard it as disgraceful to be killed in a private quarrel. If one be dying at home, it is customary to carry his bed out of doors as the end approaches, that his spirit may pass under the open sky.

Next to this, the matter that concerns him most is the parting with his dear ones, especially if he have any little children who must be left behind to suffer want. His family affections are strong, and he grieves

intensely for the lost, even though he has unbounded faith in a spiritual companionship.

The outward signs of mourning for the dead are far more spontaneous and convincing than is the correct and well-ordered black of civilization. Both men and women among us loosen their hair and cut it according to the degree of relationship or of devotion. Consistent with the idea of sacrificing all personal beauty and adornment, they trim off likewise from the dress its fringes and ornaments, perhaps cut it short, or cut the robe or blanket in two. The men blacken their faces, and widows or bereaved parents sometimes gash their arms and legs till they are covered with blood. Giving themselves up wholly to their grief, they are no longer concerned about any earthly possession, and often give away all that they have to the first comers, even to their beds and their home. Finally, the wailing for the dead is continued night and day to the point of utter voicelessness; a musical, weird, and heart-piercing sound, which has been compared to the "keening" of the Celtic mourner.

The old-time burial of the Plains Indians was upon a scaffold of poles, or a platform among the boughs of a tree—their only means of placing the body out of reach of wild beasts, as they had no implements with which to dig a suitable grave. It was prepared by dressing in the finest clothes, together with some personal possessions and ornaments, wrapped in several robes, and finally in a secure covering of raw hide. As a special mark of respect, the body of a young woman or a warrior was sometimes laid out in state in a new teepee, with the usual household articles and even with a dish of food left beside it, not that they supposed the spirit could use the implements or eat the food, but merely as a last tribute. Then the whole people would break camp and depart to a distance, leaving the dead alone in an honorable solitude.

There was no prescribed ceremony of burial, though the body was carried out with more or less solemnity by selected young men, and sometimes noted warriors were the pall-bearers of a man of distinction. It was usual to choose a prominent hill with a commanding outlook for the last resting-place of our dead. If a man were slain in battle, it was an old custom to place his body against a tree or rock in a sitting position, always facing the enemy, to indicate his undaunted defiance and bravery, even in death.

I recall a touching custom among us, which was designed to keep the memory of the departed near and warm in the bereaved household.

A lock of hair of the beloved dead was wrapped in pretty clothing, such as it was supposed that he or she would like to wear if living. This "spirit bundle," as it was called, was suspended from a tripod, and occupied a certain place in the lodge which was the place of honor. At every meal time, a dish of food was placed under it, and some person of the same sex and age as the one who was gone must afterward be invited in to partake of the food. At the end of a year from the time of death, the relatives made a public feast and gave away the clothing and other gifts, while the lock of hair was interred with appropriate ceremonies.

Certainly the Indian never doubted the immortal nature of the spirit or soul of man, but neither did he care to speculate upon its probable state or condition in a future life. The idea of a "happy hunting-ground" is modern and probably borrowed, or invented by the white man. The primitive Indian was content to believe that the spirit which the "Great Mystery" breathed into man returns to Him who gave it, and that after it is freed from the body, it is everywhere and pervades all nature, yet often lingers near the grave or "spirit bundle" for the consolation of friends, and is able to hear prayers. So much of reverence was due the disembodied spirit, that it was not customary with us even to name the dead aloud.

It is well known that the American Indian had somehow developed occult power, and although in the latter days there have been many impostors, and, allowing for the vanity and weakness of human nature, it is fair to assume that there must have been some even in the old days, yet there are well-attested instances of remarkable prophecies and other mystic practice.

A Sioux prophet predicted the coming of the white man fully fifty years before the event, and even described accurately his garments and weapons. Before the steamboat was invented, another prophet of our race described the "Fire Boat" that would swim upon their mighty river, the Mississippi, and the date of this prophecy is attested by the term used, which is long since obsolete. No doubt, many predictions have been colored to suit the new age, and unquestionably false prophets, fakirs, and conjurers have become the pest of the tribes during the transition period. Nevertheless, even during this period there was here and there a man of the old type who was implicitly believed in to the last.

Notable among these was Tachánk-pee Hó-tank-a, or His War Club Speaks Loud, who foretold a year in advance the details of a great

war-party against the Ojibways. There were to be seven battles, all successful except the last, in which the Sioux were to be taken at a disadvantage and suffer crushing defeat. This was carried out to the letter. Our people surprised and slew many of the Ojibways in their villages, but in turn were followed and cunningly led into an ambush whence but few came out alive. This was only one of his remarkable prophecies.

Another famous "medicine-man" was born on the Rum River about one hundred and fifty years ago, and lived to be over a century old. He was born during a desperate battle with the Ojibways, at a moment when, as it seemed, the band of Sioux engaged were to be annihilated. Therefore the child's grandmother exclaimed: "Since we are all to perish, let him die a warrior's death in the field!" and she placed his cradle under fire, near the spot where his uncle and grandfathers were fighting, for he had no father. But when an old man discovered the new-born child, he commanded the women to take care of him, "for," said he, "we know not how precious the strength of even one warrior may some day become to his nation!"

This child lived to become great among us, as was intimated to the superstitious by the circumstances of his birth. At the age of about seventy-five years, he saved his band from utter destruction at the hands of their ancestral enemies, by suddenly giving warning received in a dream of the approach of a large war-party. The men immediately sent out scouts, and felled trees for a stockade, barely in time to meet and repel the predicted attack. Five years later, he repeated the service, and again saved his people from awful slaughter. There was no confusion of figures or omens, as with lesser medicine-men, but in every incident that is told of him his interpretation of the sign, whatever it was, proved singularly correct.

The father of Little Crow, the chief who led the "Minnesota massacre" of 1862, was another prophet of some note. One of his characteristic prophecies was made only a few years before he died, when he had declared that, although already an old man, he would go once more upon the war-path. At the final war-feast, he declared that three of the enemy would be slain, but he showed great distress and reluctance in foretelling that he would lose two of his own men. Three of the Ojibways were indeed slain as he had said, but in the battle the old war prophet lost both his two sons.

There are many trustworthy men, and men of Christian faith, to vouch for these and similar events occuring as foretold. I cannot

pretend to explain them, but I know that our people possessed remarkable powers of concentration and abstraction, and I sometimes fancy that such nearness to nature as I have described keeps the spirit sensitive to impressions not commonly felt, and in touch with the unseen powers. Some of us seemed to have a peculiar intuition for the locality of a grave, which they explained by saying that they had received a communication from the spirit of the departed. My own grandmother was one of these, and as far back as I can remember, when camping in a strange country, my brother and I would search for and find human bones at the spot she had indicated to us as an ancient burial-place or the spot where a lone warrior had fallen. Of course, the outward signs of burial had been long since obliterated.

The Scotch would certainly have declared that she had the "second sight," for she had other remarkable premonitions or intuitions within my own recollection. I have heard her speak of a peculiar sensation in the breast, by which, as she said, she was advised of anything of importance concerning her absent children. Other native women have claimed a similar monitor, but I never heard of one who could interpret it with such accuracy. We were once camping on Lake Manitoba when we received news that my uncle and his family had been murdered several weeks before, at a fort some two hundred miles distant. While all our clan were wailing and mourning their loss, my grandmother calmly bade them cease, saying that her son was approaching, and that they would see him shortly. Although we had no other reason to doubt the ill tidings, it is a fact that my uncle came into camp two days after his reported death.

At another time, when I was fourteen years old, we had just left Fort Ellis on the Assiniboine River, and my youngest uncle had selected a fine spot for our night camp. It was already after sundown, but my grandmother became unaccountably nervous, and positively refused to pitch her tent. So we reluctantly went on down the river, and camped after dark at a secluded place. The next day we learned that a family who were following close behind had stopped at the place first selected by my uncle, but were surprised in the night by a roving war-party, and massacred to a man. This incident made a great impression upon our people.

Many of the Indians believed that one may be born more than once, and there were some who claimed to have full knowledge of a former incarnation. There were also those who held converse with a "twin spirit," who had been born into another tribe or race. There was a

well-known Sioux war-prophet who lived in the middle of the last century, so that he is still remembered by the old men of his band. After he had reached middle age, he declared that he had a spirit brother among the Ojibways, the ancestral enemies of the Sioux. He even named the band to which his brother belonged, and said that he also was a war-prophet among his people.

Upon one of their hunts along the border between the two tribes, the Sioux leader one evening called his warriors together, and solemnly declared to them that they were about to meet a like band of Ojibway hunters, led by his spirit twin. Since this was to be their first meeting since they were born as strangers, he earnestly begged the young men to resist the temptation to join battle with their tribal foes.

"You will know him at once," the prophet said to them, "for he will not only look like me in face and form, but he will display the same totem, and even sing my war songs!"

They sent out scouts, who soon returned with news of the approaching party. Then the leading men started with their peace-pipe for the Ojibway camp, and when they were near at hand they fired three distinct volleys, a signal of their desire for a peaceful meeting.

The response came in like manner, and they entered the camp, with the peace-pipe in the hands of the prophet.

Lo, the stranger prophet advanced to meet them, and the people were greatly struck with the resemblance between the two men, who met and embraced one another with unusual fervor.

It was quickly agreed by both parties that they should camp together for several days, and one evening the Sioux made a "warriors' feast" to which they invited many of the Ojibways. The prophet asked his twin brother to sing one of his sacred songs, and behold! it was the very song that he himself was wont to sing. This proved to the warriors beyond doubt or cavil the claims of their seer.

American Indian Stories

Zitkala-Ša
(Gertrude Bonnin)

Foreword

Zitkala-Ša: The Evolution of a Writer
By Dexter Fisher

The nineteenth century marked a period of dramatic upheaval for many American Indian tribes, who, in the wake of America's great expansion westward, found themselves dispossessed of their ancestral lands, depleted in numbers, and confined to reservations. Fearful that their oral traditions would disappear forever as the tribal community became more and more fragmented under the demoralizing conditions of reservation life, some American Indians began to write down the legends and folktales of their tribes, as well as their personal narratives, in an effort to preserve their history and culture for posterity. Writing became a means not only to perpetuate tradition in the face of cultural disintegration but also a chance for Native Americans to tell their side of the story to a wider audience. By the end of the nineteenth century, a written literature based on tribal oral traditions was beginning to emerge that would reach fruition in the 1960s and 1970s in the works of contemporary American Indians.

Zitkala-Ša, a Sioux of the Yankton band, is one of the early Indian writers who attempted to make the transition from written to oral form and to bridge the gap between tradition and assimilation. Born in 1876, Zitkala-Ša published most of her work at the turn of the century. Her collection of traditional Sioux tales, *Old Indian Legends*, appeared in 1901, and the autobiographical essays that were to be collected later in *American Indian Stories* (1921) were initially published in *Harpers* and the *Atlantic Monthly* in 1900 and 1901.

American Indian Stories is an important collection because it represents one of the first attempts by a Native American woman to write her own story without the aid of an editor, an interpreter, or an ethnographer. In *American Indian Stories*, Zitkala-Ša presents carefully and, at times, sentimentally, the pain and difficulty of growing up Indian in a white man's world.

"Impressions of an Indian Childhood," "The School Days of an Indian Girl," and "An Indian Teacher among Indians"—the autobio-

graphical sketches included in *American Indian Stories*—serve as
emblems of the experience of many Indians living in transition between
two worlds—the remembered past and the alien present, tradition and
change.

Struggling to find her own voice in her literature, Zitkala-Ša is also
conscious of her role in preserving her culture for a wider audience,
as she notes in a letter to Carlos Montezuma dated 20 February 1901:

> As for my plans—I do not mean to give up my literary work—but while
> the old people last I want to get from them their treasured ideas of life.
> This I can do by living among them. Thus I mean to divide my time
> between teaching and getting story material.[1]

Later on that spring, she writes again to Montezuma from the Yankton
Agency where she has gone to stay with her mother for a time, saying,

> This place is full of material for stories but I am so uncertain . . . I am
> quite well and hope I may soon find a good writing mood—to do justice
> to the abandoned material around me.
>
> (June 1901)

Zitkala-Ša had every right to feel nervous about her mission to become
the literary counterpart of the oral storytellers of her tribe because she
felt compelled to live up to the critical expectations of her white
audience. She had already become the darling of a small literary coterie
in Boston whose members were enthusiastic about the autobiographi-
cal sketches and short stories she had begun to place in *Harper's* and
the *Atlantic Monthly* the year before. Ginn and Company had given
her a contract for *Old Indian Legends*, which would appear in the fall
of 1901, and were anxiously awaiting material for a second book that
would be, in their words, "a fine series of Indian legends, the greatest
that the world has ever known." And in its April issue of 1900,
Harper's Bazaar had included her in a column entitled "Persons Who
Interest Us":

> A young Indian girl, who is attracting much attention in Eastern cities on
> account of her beauty and many talents, is Zitkala-Ša, . . . Zitkala-Ša is of
> the Sioux tribe of Dakota and until her ninth year was a veritable little
> savage, running wild over the prairie and speaking no language but her
> own . . . She has also published lately a series of articles in a leading
> magazine . . . which display a rare command of English and much artistic
> feeling. (p. 330)

Also an accomplished violinist, Zitkala-Ša had studied at the New England Conservatory of Music and appeared both as a soloist and an orator with the Carlisle Indian Band to the critical acclaim of the *New York Musical Courier*, which hailed her as "charmingly artistic and graceful." The *Brooklyn Times* described her recitation of Hiawatha in glowing terms and called her a "picture to be remembered." Indeed, as early as 1898, she had been singled out of a group of Sioux visiting New York by Joseph T. Keiley, who made a number of photographic portraits of her that would be exhibited over the next few years in New York and abroad and eventually would become part of Alfred Stieglitz's collection. Clearly, it would seem, Zitkala-Ša had arrived.

But into what world? To her mother and the traditional Sioux on the reservation where she had grown up, she was highly suspect because, in their minds, she had abandoned, even betrayed, the Indian way of life by getting an education in the white man's world. To those at the Carlisle Indian School where she had taught from 1898–99, on the other hand, she was an anathema because she insisted on remaining "Indian," writing embarrassing articles such as "Why I Am a Pagan" that flew in the face of the assimilationist thrust of their education. A particularly bitter review of one of her stories appears in the 12 April 1901 edition of *The Red Man and Helper*, Carlisle's newspaper, with this prefatory note:

> All that Zitkalasa has in the way of literary ability and culture she owes to the good people, who, from time to time, have taken her into their homes and hearts and given her aid. Yet not a word of gratitude or allusion to such kindness on the part of her friends has ever escaped her in any line of anything she has written for the public. By this course she injures herself and harms the educational work in progress for the race from which she sprang. In a list of educated Indians whom we have in mind, some of whom have reached higher altitudes in literary and professional lines than Zitkalasa, we know of no other case of such pronounced morbidness.

The reviewer goes on to pronounce the story in question, "The Soft-Hearted Sioux," morally bad. And why so? Because it challenges the very core of educational policy at Carlisle. A fictional account of the inadequacy of off-reservation schools to prepare Indians to live within their own cultures, the story is told in the first person by a young Sioux who describes the conflict he experienced in being unable to fulfill his father's desire that he become a warrior and huntsman because he has spent nine years at a missionary school and "hunted

for the soft heart of Christ, and prayed for the huntsman who chased
the buffalo on the plains."

Despite its sentimentality, the story raises the fundamental question
of survival that was to confront all Indians educated off the reserva-
tion. What price assimilation?

For Zitkala-Ša, the conflict between tradition and acculturation was
to plague her throughout her life. Born as Gertrude Simmons on the
Yankton Reservation in South Dakota in 1876, she spent her first eight
years of life on the reservation with her mother in a seemingly idyllic
state of harmony, as she describes in "Impressions of an Indian
Childhood," published in the *Atlantic Monthly* in 1900:

> I was a wild little girl of seven. Loosely clad in a slip of brown buckskin,
> and light footed with a pair of soft moccasins on my feet, I was as free as
> the wind that blew my hair, and no less spirited than a bounding deer.
> These were my mother's pride—my wild freedom and over flowing spirit.

Educated in the traditions of the Sioux, she listened to the legends at
night and learned to imitate her mother's bead work during the day.
Though her mother had been married to three different white men
and had lived at times off the reservation, she never learned to speak
English and retained always the Sioux way of life. When Gertrude's
father, a man named Felker, deserted the family before his daughter's
birth, the mother decided to return to the Yankton agency to live. She
also determined to give Gertrude the name of her second husband,
Simmons.[2] Gertrude christened herself Zitkala-Ša, Red Bird, when she
had a falling out with her sister-in-law. She writes of the event in a
letter to Montezuma:

> I have a half-brother whose name is Simmons. Once my father scolded my
> brother, and my mother took such offense from it—that eventually it
> resulted in a parting—so as I grew I was called by my brother's name
> Simmons. I bore it a long time till my brother's wife—angry with me
> because I insisted upon getting an education—said I had deserted home
> and I might give up my brother's name "Simmons" too. Well, you can
> guess how queer I felt—away from my own people—homeless—penni-
> less—and even without a name! Then I chose to make a name for myself—
> and I guess I have made "Zitkala-Sa" known—for even Italy writes it in
> her language.
>
> (June 1901)

In creating her own name and essentially her own oral history, Zitkala-
Ša is asserting at one and the same time her independence and her

cultural ties. As Zitkala-Ša, she will try to recreate the spirit of her tribe in her collection of legends, though she is never able to return to Yankton permanently.

Against her mother's wishes and under the seductive pressure of the missionaries, she first leaves Yankton at age eight to study at White's Manual Institute in Wabash, Indiana. Though White's was run by the Quakers, it adhered to the policy of the Bureau of Indian Affairs that Indian children would more rapidly assimilate into American society if they were kept away from the reservation for long periods of time. Three years passed before Gertrude Simmons returned home at age eleven.

The cultural clashes experienced at the school during the painful time she was learning English and trying to accommodate to American customs seemed insignificant in comparison to the alienation she felt upon returning to her mother's house, where she stayed for the next four years. She writes:

> During this time I seemed to hang in the heart of chaos, beyond the touch or voice of human aid. My brother, being almost ten years my senior, did not quite understand my feelings. My mother had never gone inside of a school house and so she was not capable of comforting her daughter who could read and write. Even nature seemed to have no place for me. I was neither a wee girl nor a tall one; neither a wild Indian nor a tame one. This deplorable situation was the effect of my brief course in the East. . . .[3]

Headstrong and independent, Gertrude Simmons tried to convince herself and her mother that the bit of education she had received made it impossible for her to fit comfortably back into the traditional customs of her tribe, and she returned to complete her education at White's and to study two years at Earlham College in Richmond, Indiana. This was the beginning of a schism with her mother that would only widen over the years, culminating in a bitter contest over her mother's right to a patent in fee for her land allotment.[4]

While at Earlham from 1895 to 1897, Gertrude Simmons distinguishes herself as an orator and poet, publishing essays and highly formal poems in the school's newspaper and winning several debating honors. It is during this period that her literary talents begin to take shape, and as she becomes more and more fluent in English, language becomes the tool for articulating the tension she is to experience throughout her life between her heritage with its imperative of tradition and the inevitable pressure of acculturation. In her early essays,

despite their stiff formality, the pattern of ambivalence is already there, as she alternates between a controlled rage over the mistreatment of Indians and a desire to convince America of the Indian's humanity. Her impulse is toward the cutting edge of truth as she defends the Indians' right to feel revenge in one of her essays:

> What if he fought? His forests were felled; his game frightened away; his streams of finny shoals usurped. He loved his family and would defend them. He loved the fair land of which he was rightful owner. He loved the inheritance of his fathers, their traditions, their groves; he held them a priceless legacy to be sacredly kept. He loved his native land. Do you wonder still that in his breast he should brood revenge, when ruthlessly driven from the temples where he worshipped? Do you wonder still that he sulked in forest gloom to avenge the desolation of his home? Is patriotism a virtue only in Saxon hearts? Is there no charity to cover his crouching form as he stealthily opposed his relentless foe?[5]

Yet, ever mindful of her white audience and of her own position between two alien worlds, she consents to the wisdom of learning the "White Man's ways." In the same essay, she writes:

> We come from mountain fastnesses, from cheerless plains, from far-off low-wooded streams, seeking the "White Man's ways." Seeking your skill in industry and in art, seeking labor and honest independence, seeking the treasures of knowledge and wisdom, seeking to comprehend the spirit of your laws and the genius of your noble institutions, seeking by a new birthright to unite with yours our claim to a common country, seeking the Sovereign's crown that we may stand side by side with you in ascribing royal honor to our nation's flag. America, I love thee. "Thy people shall be my people and thy God my God." (179)

Zitkala-Ša won second place in the Indiana State Oratorical Contest of 1896 for the essay from which these two excerpts were taken. The victory was important to her because she had been humiliated all evening long by a large white banner bearing a derogatory image of her with the word "squaw" on it. But her triumph was short-lived because ever present in the back of her mind was her "mother far away on the Western plains, and she was holding a charge against [her]." Though she would spend her life working for the rights of Indians and would become one of the most vocal spokespersons of the Pan-Indian movement in the 1920s and 1930s, Zitkala-Ša was never reconciled with her mother. She spent her life in balance between two worlds, using the language of one to translate the needs of another. She was in

a truly liminal position, always on the threshold of two worlds but never fully entering either.

In 1900, Zitkala-Ša published three autobiographical essays in the January, February, and March issues of the *Atlantic Monthly*: "Impressions of an Indian Childhood," "The School Days of an Indian Girl," and "An Indian Teacher among Indians." In December of 1902, the *Atlantic Monthly* published her essay, "Why I Am a Pagan." During this same period, she published two short stories, "The Trial Path" and "The Soft-Hearted Sioux," respectively in the March and October 1901 issues of *Harper's Magazine*. "A Warrior's Daughter," another short story, appeared in a 1902 issue of *Everybody's Magazine*. These essays and stories were later published in 1921 in a collection entitled *American Indian Stories* by Hayworth Press of Washington, D.C. *Old Indian Legends*, published by Ginn and Co. of Boston, appeared in 1901. With the exception of some scattered poems and short stories that appeared in various Indian rights magazines, as well as the Carlisle Indian School newspaper, these two books constitute Zitkala-Ša's published literary output. Within a brief three-year period, her career as a creative writer blossomed for a moment and then declined.

The decline of her "literary" career coincided directly with her marriage on May 10, 1902, to Raymond T. Bonnin, also a Sioux, with whom she moved to the Uintah and Ouray reservation in Utah, where they lived for the next fourteen years and had one son, Raymond O. Bonnin, born in 1903. As the wife of a government employee for the Bureau of Indian Affairs, Zitkala-Ša became Mrs. Gertrude Bonnin, working in various capacities among the Utah Indians, organizing community activities for the women such as sewing classes and lunch programs, teaching for a period, and even starting a band among the children.

Her creative impulse was not dormant for long, however, and during this period she also collaborated quite intensely with William Hanson on the composition of "Sun Dance," an Indian opera that premiered in 1913 in Vernal, Utah. The opera was so successful among both Indians and whites that it was performed numerous times by the original company and then by Brigham Young University. In 1937, "Sun Dance" was selected by the New York Light Opera Guild as the American opera for the year and was performed in New York City. Edward Ellsworth Hipsher defines the reason for the success of the opera in *American Opera and Its Composers:*

The opera does not depict the Indian in the dime novel fashion familiar in the stage and screen. It is a sympathetic portrayal of the real Indian in a conscientious attempt to delineate the manners, the customs, the dress, the religious ideals, the superstitions, the songs, the games, the ceremonials— in short, the life of a noble people too little understood.[6]

Zitkala-Ša contributed substantially to the composition of the opera by telling Hanson the rituals surrounding the Sun Dance in minute detail and sharing with him numerous tales and legends that are woven into the opera's story. She also played tribal songs for him upon her violin which he then transcribed in order to keep both the music and the content of the opera as authentic as possible.

In 1916, the Bonnins moved to Washington, D.C., because Gertrude had been elected secretary of the Society of the American Indian, the organization with whom she had corresponded since its inception at Ohio State University in 1911. Founded and governed exclusively by Indians, the SAI provided a collective forum for Indians who sought to redress the multitude of inequities they had suffered. Under the auspices of the SAI, Bonnin launched her life's work in Indian reform, lecturing and campaigning across the country for Indian citizenship, employment of Indians in the Bureau of Indian Affairs, equitable settlement of tribal land claims, and stabilization of laws relating to Indians. Her temporary post as editor from 1918 to 1919 of the Society's publication, the *American Indian Magazine,* gave her the opportunity to reach an even wider audience in print and her editorials ranged from reports on annual meetings to testimonies to the loyal patriotism of American Indians who had volunteered to fight for America in World War I.[7]

In 1920 the SAI dissolved, and the Bonnins turned their energies to other arenas. Raymond Bonnin went to work as a law clerk in a Washington office, and Gertrude concentrated her efforts in work with the General Federation of Women's Clubs, convincing the Federation to establish an Indian Welfare Committee in 1921. With the support of the Federation, Bonnin continued her reform work, ever pressing for Indian citizenship, as well as for improvements in education and health care and the preservation of Indian culture. One concrete result of the collective efforts of Bonnin and the Federation was an investigation into government treatment of certain Oklahoma tribes, which led to the formation of the Meriam Commission and the subsequent appointment by President Hoover in 1928 of members of the Indian Rights Association to the top two positions in the Bureau

of Indian Affairs. The results of the Oklahoma investigation in which Bonnin participated were published in 1924 in a monograph entitled *Oklahoma's Poor Rich Indians: An Orgy of Graft and Exploitation of the Five Civilized Tribes—Legalized Robbery.*[8] That same year, American Indians were finally granted U.S. citizenship.

Her apprenticeship at an end, Gertrude Bonnin was fully prepared, then, in 1926 to found her own political organization, the National Council of American Indians, of which she was the single president until her death in 1938. The organization, as described in *Indian Truth*, was designed to "create increased interest in behalf of the Indians, and secure for them added recognition of their personal and property rights.[9] And in *The Indian's Friend*, it was termed a "non-partisan, non-sectarian organization carrying on an Information Service for untrained Indian citizen voters and helping them to organize themselves in assemblies for discussion."[10]

Here was the perfect opportunity for a woman who had suffered intensely her alienation from her own family and who yet disdained to curry favor from the white world. Armed with her oratorical skills, learned—not without pain—twenty years earlier and refined through her work with the SAI and the Federation, and her literary ability, she would work as an independent reformer on behalf of suppressed Indians across the country and represent their problems, with the help of legal advice from her husband, to the Bureau of Indian Affairs in whose world she now moved with familiar ease. She became known to Indians and government officials alike as a persuasive public speaker and an effective, if relentless, mediator. She had, at last, found the way to use her education and skills of expression to aid her people, not to be an object of suspicion to them, and in doing so, she became the champion of the underdog Indian and a scourge to irresponsible Indian agents.

In the National Archives, Record Group No. 75 contains the Central Files for 1907–1939 of the Bureau of Indian Affairs, within which are literally hundreds of pages of correspondence from and about Gertrude Bonnin. Without question, the Bonnins' motives were not always altruistic as they did earn their living through the legal advice they rendered, and they did campaign among Indians aggressively for the issues and candidates they believed in. More often than not, though, their angriest critics were inept or corrupt Indian agents and their staunchest supporters those reservation Indians whose lives

had been demoralized by poverty and neglect and who had thought it impossible that their voices would ever be heard.

Controversial to the end, Gertrude Bonnin remained an enigma—a curious blend of civilized romanticism and aggressive individualism. Her own image of herself eventually evolved into an admixture of myth and fact, so that by the time of her death in 1938, she believed, and it was erroneously stated in three obituaries, that she was the granddaughter of Sitting Bull, though the Yankton tribal rolls indicated that her own mother was older than Sitting Bull.[11]

In one biographical sketch, Bonnin is described thus:

> The literature of Indian reform gives much attention to the maladjustments suffered by white-educated Indians who returned to their own people. Less well known is the role of these educated Indians in pressing for "progressive" reforms both on and off the reservation. Gertrude Simmons Bonnin was an Indian progressive; her career indicates both the achievements and frustrations attendant upon that role.[12]

Her career also exemplifies the tremendous difficulty confronting minority people who would become writers but who are constantly under pressure from their own groups to use literature toward sociopolitical ends. For American Indian writers, this dilemma has been further compounded by the heritage of an oral tradition that has its own aesthetic imperatives. It is not surprising at all that Zitkala-Ša subsumed her creative energy into a life work of progressive reform for Indians. The wonder is that she wrote at all and in so doing became one of the first Indians to bring to the attention of a white audience the traditions of a tribe as well as the personal sensibilities of one of its members. It would be false to say that Zitkala-Ša launched an American Indian literary tradition, but it is possible, in examining the cameo of her life and literature, to say that she struggled toward a vision of wholeness in which the conflicting parts of her existence could be reconciled. That she did not fully succeed is evident in her work, which is a model of ambivalences, of oscillations between two diametrically opposed worlds, but is also a model of retrieved possibilities, a creative, human endeavor that stands at the beginning of many such endeavors eventually to culminate in the finely crafted work of contemporary American Indian writers.

NOTES AND REFERENCES

1. Carlos Montezuma was a Yavapai who became quite famous as one of the first Indians to become a doctor. Based in Chicago, he was a national

spokesman for Indian rights throughout his life. He and Zitkala-Ša were engaged to be married for a brief period and exchanged numerous letters which have been included in the Carlos Montezuma papers presently in the Division of Archives and Manuscripts of the State Historical Society of Wisconsin. The correspondence quoted here is taken from Microfilm 151, Reel No. 1, of the Carlos Montezuma Papers.

2. The family history of Ellen Simmons' three marriages and her subsequent return to the Yankton Agency may be found in Record No. 10-1622-09—Yankton 312 of Record Group No. 75, National Archives, Washington, D.C.

Other biographical information on Zitkala-Ša exists in several places under her married name, Gertrude Bonnin: *Who's Who in the Nation's Capital,* ed. Stanley H. Williamson (Washington, D.C., 1927/34/35); Marion Gridley, *American Indian Women* (New York, 1974). Gridley, however, is inaccurate on the date of birth of Zitkala-Ša and several details of her education. *Great North American Indians—Profiles in Life and Leadership,* ed. Frederick J. Dockstader (New York, 1977). Dockstader falsely claims that Zitkala-Ša's father was John Haysting Simmons, who had died long before Ellen Simmons married her third husband. *Indians of Today,* ed. Marion Gridley (Crawfordsville, Indiana, 1936). The best brief account of Zitkala-Ša's life may be found in *Notable American Women—1607–1950—A Biographical dictionary,* ed. Edward T. James (Cambridge, Mass., 1971).

Zitkala-Ša is listed as Gertie Simmons Bonnin, No. 209, on the Indian Census Roll taken in 1930 at the Yankton Reservation. According to that Census, she would have been born in 1873, was only one quarter Sioux, and was eight years older than her husband, Raymond T. Bonnin. The latter may be true, but the rest of my research, including the headstone on her grave at Arlington Cemetery, indicates that she was born in 1876 and was one half Sioux because her mother was a full blood and her father was white. Her ID number for allotment, annuity and identification is AL-594-609.

3. "The School Days of an Indian Girl" in *American Indian Stories* (Glorieta, New Mexico, 1976; repr. of the 1921 edition published by Hayworth Publishing House, Washington, D.C.), p. 69. Subsequent references will be taken from this edition. This particular autobiographical essay first appeared in the February 1900 issue of the *Atlantic Monthly.*

4. For further information on the dispute between Zitkala-Ša and her mother, see the following files in Record Group No. 75 at the National Archives: 10 1622-09, 1966-10, 1995-10, 2637-10, 3212-10, 9008-10, 7783-10, 41629-10, Yankton Agency. Apparently, when Ellen Simmons applied for a patent in fee, she had the full support of her son by her first marriage, Peter St. Pierre. David Simmons, a half brother, and Zitkala-Ša protested the sale of the land because, according to the superintendent of the Agency, they would receive none of the profits from the sale. Various tribesmen, as well as BIA officials, were called in to testify on the character of the individuals concerned. It is clear from reading all the documents that the conflict was a classic case of the old order versus the new, reservation Indians imbued with tradition versus non-reservation Indians committed to reform.

5. "Side by Side," *The Earlhamite,* 2 (March 16, 1896): 178.

6. Philadelphia: Theo. Presser Col, 1927, p. 247. All of the information on the opera itself, including reviews, the story, performances, cast, etc., may be found in the papers of William Hanson, MSS 299, Brigham Young University.

7. For an excellent history of the Pan-Indian movement and the activities of the society of American Indians, see Hazel Hertzberg, *The Search for an American Indian Identity—Modern Pan Indian Movements* (Syracuse, New York, 1971).

8. A report by Gertrude Bonnin, Charles H. Fabens, Matthew K. Sniffen (Philadelphia: Office of the Indian Rights Association, 1924; Indian Rights Association Publication, 2nd Series, No. 127).

9. *Indian Truth*, 3, no. 3 (March, 1926): 3.

10. *The Indians Friend*, 61, no. 4 (July, 1929): 7.

11. The *New York Times*, the *Washington Daily News* and the *Washington Star* all listed Bonnin as the granddaughter of Sitting Bull. Bonnin died on 26 January 1938; services were held for her at the Church of the Latter Day Saints, and she was buried in Arlington Cemetery (she was eligible because of her husband's honorable service in the U.S. Army during World War I). Bonnin's tombstone reads: "Gertrude Simmons Bonnin—'Zitkala Sa' of the Sioux Indians—1876–1938."

12. *Notable American Women—1607–1950—A Biographical Dictionary*, ed. Edward T. James (Cambridge, Mass.: The Belknap Press of Harvard University Press, 1971), p. 200.

Contents

IMPRESSIONS OF AN INDIAN CHILDHOOD

I

MY MOTHER

A wigwam of weather-stained canvas stood at the base of some irregularly ascending hills. A footpath wound its way gently down the sloping land till it reached the broad river bottom; creeping through the long swamp grasses that bent over it on either side, it came out on the edge of the Missouri.

Here, morning, noon, and evening, my mother came to draw water from the muddy stream for our household use. Always, when my mother started for the river, I stopped my play to run along with her. She was only of medium height. Often she was sad and silent, at which times her full arched lips were compressed into hard and bitter lines, and shadows fell under her black eyes. Then I clung to her hand and begged to know what made the tears fall.

"Hush; my little daughter must never talk about my tears"; and smiling through them, she patted my head and said, "Now let me see how fast you can run today." Whereupon I tore away at my highest possible speed, with my long black hair blowing in the breeze.

I was a wild little girl of seven. Loosely clad in a slip of brown buckskin, and light-footed with a pair of soft moccasins on my feet, I was as free as the wind that blew my hair, and no less spirited than a bounding deer. These were my mother's pride,—my wild freedom and overflowing spirits. She taught me no fear save that of intruding myself upon others.

Having gone many paces ahead I stopped, panting for breath, and laughing with glee as my mother watched my every movement. I was not wholly conscious of myself, but was more keenly alive to the fire within. It was as if I were the activity, and my hands and feet were only experiments for my spirit to work upon.

Returning from the river, I tugged beside my mother, with my hand upon the bucket I believed I was carrying. One time, on such a return, I remember a bit of conversation we had. My grown-up cousin, Warca-

209

Ziwin (Sunflower), who was then seventeen, always went to the river alone for water for her mother. Their wigwam was not far from ours; and I saw her daily going to and from the river. I admired my cousin greatly. So I said: "Mother, when I am tall as my cousin Warca-Ziwin, you shall not have to come for water. I will do it for you."

With a strange tremor in her voice which I could not understand, she answered, "If the paleface does not take away from us the river we drink."

"Mother, who is this bad paleface?" I asked.

"My little daughter, he is a sham,—a sickly sham! The bronzed Dakota is the only real man."

I looked up into my mother's face while she spoke; and seeing her bite her lips, I knew she was unhappy. This aroused revenge in my small soul. Stamping my foot on the earth, I cried aloud, "I hate the paleface that makes my mother cry!"

Setting the pail of water on the ground, my mother stooped, and stretching her left hand out on the level with my eyes, she placed her other arm about me; she pointed to the hill where my uncle and my only sister lay buried.

"There is what the paleface has done! Since then your father too has been buried in a hill nearer the rising sun. We were once very happy. But the paleface has stolen our lands and driven us hither. Having defrauded us of our land, the paleface forced us away.

"Well, it happened on the day we moved camp that your sister and uncle were both very sick. Many others were ailing, but there seemed to be no help. We traveled many days and nights; not in the grand, happy way that we moved camp when I was a little girl, but we were driven, my child, driven like a herd of buffalo. With every step, your sister, who was not as large as you are now, shrieked with the painful jar until she was hoarse with crying. She grew more and more feverish. Her little hands and cheeks were burning hot. Her little lips were parched and dry, but she would not drink the water I gave her. Then I discovered that her throat was swollen and red. My poor child, how I cried with her because the Great Spirit had forgotten us!

"At last, when we reached this western country, on the first weary night your sister died. And soon your uncle died also, leaving a widow and an orphan daughter, your cousin Warca-Ziwin. Both your sister and uncle might have been happy with us today, had it not been for the heartless paleface."

My mother was silent the rest of the way to our wigwam. Though I

saw no tears in her eyes, I knew that was because I was with her. She seldom wept before me.

II
THE LEGENDS

During the summer days my mother built her fire in the shadow of our wigwam.

In the early morning our simple breakfast was spread upon the grass west of our tepee. At the farthest point of the shade my mother sat beside her fire, toasting a savory piece of dried meat. Near her, I sat upon my feet, eating my dried meat with unleavened bread, and drinking strong black coffee.

The morning meal was our quiet hour, when we two were entirely alone. At noon, several who chanced to be passing by stopped to rest, and to share our luncheon with us, for they were sure of our hospitality.

My uncle, whose death my mother ever lamented, was one of our nation's bravest warriors. His name was on the lips of old men when talking of the proud feats of valor; and it was mentioned by younger men, too, in connection with deeds of gallantry. Old women praised him for his kindness toward them; young women held him up as an ideal to their sweethearts. Every one loved him, and my mother worshiped his memory. Thus it happened that even strangers were sure of welcome in our lodge, if they but asked a favor in my uncle's name.

Though I heard many strange experiences related by these wayfarers, I loved best the evening meal, for that was the time old legends were told. I was always glad when the sun hung low in the west, for then my mother sent me to invite the neighboring old men and women to eat supper with us. Running all the way to the wigwams, I halted shyly at the entrances. Sometimes I stood long moments without saying a word. It was not any fear that made me so dumb when out upon such a happy errand; nor was it that I wished to withhold the invitation, for it was all I could do to observe this very proper silence. But it was a sensing of the atmosphere, to assure myself that I should not hinder other plans. My mother used to say to me, as I was almost bounding away for the old people: "Wait a moment before you invite any one. If other plans are being discussed, do not interfere, but go elsewhere."

The old folks knew the meaning of my pauses; and often they coaxed my confidence by asking, "What do you seek, little grand-daughter?"

"My mother says you are to come to our tepee this evening," I instantly exploded, and breathed the freer afterwards.

"Yes, yes, gladly, gladly I shall come!" each replied. Rising at once and carrying their blankets across one shoulder, they flocked leisurely from their various wigwams toward our dwelling.

My mission done, I ran back, skipping and jumping with delight. All out of breath, I told my mother almost the exact words of the answers to my invitation. Frequently she asked, "What were they doing when you entered their tepee?" This taught me to remember all I saw at a single glance. Often I told my mother my impressions without being questioned.

While in the neighboring wigwams sometimes an old Indian woman asked me, "What is your mother doing?" Unless my mother had cautioned me not to tell, I generally answered her questions without reserve.

At the arrival of our guests I sat close to my mother, and did not leave her side without first asking her consent. I ate my supper in quiet, listening patiently to the talk of the old people, wishing all the time that they would begin the stories I loved best. At last, when I could not wait any longer, I whispered in my mother's ear, "Ask them to tell an Iktomi story, mother."

Soothing my impatience, my mother said aloud, "My little daughter is anxious to hear your legends." By this time all were through eating, and the evening was fast deepening into twilight.

As each in turn began to tell a legend, I pillowed my head in my mother's lap; and lying flat upon my back, I watched the stars as they peeped down upon me, one by one. The increasing interest of the tale aroused me, and I sat up eagerly listening to every word. The old women made funny remarks, and laughed so heartily that I could not help joining them.

The distant howling of a pack of wolves or the hooting of an owl in the river bottom frightened me, and I nestled into my mother's lap. She added some dry sticks to the open fire, and the bright flames leaped up into the faces of the old folks as they sat around in a great circle.

On such an evening, I remember the glare of the fire shone on a tattooed star upon the brow of the old warrior who was telling a story. I

watched him curiously as he made his unconscious gestures. The blue star upon his bronzed forehead was a puzzle to me. Looking about, I saw two parallel lines on the chin of one of the old women. The rest had none. I examined my mother's face, but found no sign there.

After the warrior's story was finished, I asked the old woman the meaning of the blue lines on her chin, looking all the while out of the corners of my eyes at the warrior with the star on his forehead. I was a little afraid that he would rebuke me for my boldness.

Here the old woman began: "Why, my grandchild, they are signs,— secret signs I dare not tell you. I shall, however, tell you a wonderful story about a woman who had a cross tattooed upon each of her cheeks."

It was a long story of a woman whose magic power lay hidden behind the marks upon her face. I fell asleep before the story was completed.

Ever after that night I felt suspicious of tattooed people. Wherever I saw one I glanced furtively at the mark and round about it, wondering what terrible magic power was covered there.

It was rarely that such a fearful story as this one was told by the camp fire. Its impression was so acute that the picture still remains vividly clear and pronounced.

III

THE BEADWORK

Soon after breakfast mother sometimes began her beadwork. On a bright, clear day, she pulled out the wooden pegs that pinned the skirt of our wigwam to the ground, and rolled the canvas part way up on its frame of slender poles. Then the cool morning breezes swept freely through our dwelling, now and then wafting the perfume of sweet grasses from newly burnt prairie.

Untying the long tasseled strings that bound a small brown buckskin bag, my mother spread upon a mat beside her bunches of colored beads, just as an artist arranges the paints upon his pallette. On a lapboard she smoothed out a double sheet of soft white buckskin; and drawing from a beaded case that hung on the left of her wide belt a long, narrow blade, she trimmed the buckskin into shape. Often she worked upon small moccasins for her small daughter. Then I became intensely interested in her designing. With a proud, beaming face, I

watched her work. In imagination, I saw myself walking in a new pair of snugly fitting moccasins. I felt the envious eyes of my playmates upon the pretty red beads decorating my feet.

Close beside my mother I sat on a rug, with a scrap of buckskin in one hand and an awl in the other. This was the beginning of my practical observation lessons in the art of beadwork. From a skein of finely twisted threads of silvery sinews my mother pulled out a single one. With an awl she pierced the buckskin, and skillfully threaded it with the white sinew. Picking up the tiny beads one by one, she strung them with the point of her thread, always twisting it carefully after every stitch.

It took many trials before I learned how to knot my sinew thread on the point of my finger, as I saw her do. Then the next difficulty was in keeping my thread stiffly twisted, so that I could easily string my beads upon it. My mother required of me original designs for my lessons in beading. At first I frequently ensnared many a sunny hour into working a long design. Soon I learned from self-inflicted punishment to refrain from drawing complex patterns, for I had to finish whatever I began.

After some experience I usually drew easy and simple crosses and squares. These were some of the set forms. My original designs were not always symmetrical nor sufficiently characteristic, two faults with which my mother had little patience. The quietness of her oversight made me feel strongly responsible and dependent upon my own judgment. She treated me as a dignified little individual as long as I was on my good behavior; and how humiliated I was when some boldness of mine drew forth a rebuke from her!

In the choice of colors she left me to my own taste. I was pleased with an outline of yellow upon a background of dark blue, or a combination of red and myrtle-green. There was another of red and bluish-gray that was more conventionally used. When I became a little familiar with designing and the various pleasing combinations of color, a harder lesson was given me. It was the sewing on, instead of beads, some tinted porcupine quills, moistened and flattened between the nails of the thumb and forefinger. My mother cut off the prickly ends and burned them at once in the centre fire. These sharp points were poisonous, and worked into the flesh wherever they lodged. For this reason, my mother said, I should not do much alone in quills until I was as tall as my cousin Warca-Ziwin.

Always after these confining lessons I was wild with surplus spirits,

and found joyous relief in running loose in the open again. Many a summer afternoon a party of four or five of my playmates roamed over the hills with me. We each carried a light sharpened rod about four feet long, with which we pried up certain sweet roots. When we had eaten all the choice roots we chanced upon, we shouldered our rods and strayed off into patches of a stalky plant under whose yellow blossoms we found little crystal drops of gum. Drop by drop we gathered this nature's rock-candy, until each of us could boast of a lump the size of a small bird's egg. Soon satiated with its woody flavor, we tossed away our gum, to return again to the sweet roots.

I remember well how we used to exchange our necklaces, beaded belts, and sometimes even our moccasins. We pretended to offer them as gifts to one another. We delighted in impersonating our own mothers. We talked of things we had heard them say in their conversations. We imitated their various manners, even to the inflection of their voices. In the lap of the prairie we seated ourselves upon our feet, and leaning our painted cheeks in the palms of our hands, we rested our elbows on our knees, and bent forward as old women were most accustomed to do.

While one was telling of some heroic deed recently done by a near relative, the rest of us listened attentively, and exclaimed in undertones, "Han! han!" (yes! yes!) whenever the speaker paused for breath, or sometimes for our sympathy. As the discourse became more thrilling, according to our ideas, we raised our voices in these interjections. In these impersonations our parents were led to say only those things that were in common favor.

No matter how exciting a tale we might be rehearsing, the mere shifting of a cloud shadow in the landscape near by was sufficient to change our impulses; and soon we were all chasing the great shadows that played among the hills. We shouted and whooped in the chase; laughing and calling to one another, we were like little sportive nymphs on that Dakota sea of rolling green.

On one occasion I forgot the cloud shadow in a strange notion to catch up with my own shadow. Standing straight and still, I began to glide after it, putting out one foot cautiously. When, with the greatest care, I set my foot in advance of myself, my shadow crept onward too. Then again I tried it; this time with the other foot. Still again my shadow escaped me. I began to run; and away flew my shadow, always just a step beyond me. Faster and faster I ran, setting my teeth and clenching my fists, determined to overtake my own fleet shadow. But

ever swifter it glided before me, while I was growing breathless and hot. Slackening my speed, I was greatly vexed that my shadow should check its pace also. Daring it to the utmost, as I thought, I sat down upon a rock imbedded in the hillside.

So! my shadow had the impudence to sit down beside me!

Now my comrades caught up with me, and began to ask why I was running away so fast.

"Oh, I was chasing my shadow! Didn't you ever do that?" I inquired, surprised that they should not understand.

They planted their moccasined feet firmly upon my shadow to stay it, and I arose. Again my shadow slipped away, and moved as often as I did. Then we gave up trying to catch my shadow.

Before this peculiar experience I have no distinct memory of having recognized any vital bond between myself and my own shadow. I never gave it an afterthought.

Returning our borrowed belts and trinkets, we rambled homeward. That evening, as on other evenings, I went to sleep over my legends.

IV
THE COFFEE-MAKING

One summer afternoon my mother left me alone in our wigwam while she went across the way to my aunt's dwelling.

I did not much like to stay alone in our tepee for I feared a tall, broad-shouldered crazy man, some forty years old, who walked loose among the hills. Wiyaka-Napbina (Wearer of a Feather Necklace) was harmless, and whenever he came into a wigwam he was driven there by extreme hunger. He went nude except for the half of a red blanket he girdled around his waist. In one tawny arm he used to carry a heavy bunch of wild sunflowers that he gathered in his aimless ramblings. His black hair was matted by the winds, and scorched into a dry red by the constant summer sun. As he took great strides, placing one brown bare foot directly in front of the other, he swung his long lean arm to and fro.

Frequently he paused in his walk and gazed far backward, shading his eyes with his hand. He was under the belief that an evil spirit was haunting his steps. This was what my mother told me once, when I sneered at such a silly big man. I was brave when my mother was near by, and Wiyaka-Napbina walking farther and farther away.

"Pity the man, my child. I knew him when he was a brave and handsome youth. He was overtaken by a malicious spirit among the hills, one day, when he went hither and thither after his ponies. Since then he can not stay away from the hills," she said.

I felt so sorry for the man in his misfortune that I prayed to the Great Spirit to restore him. But though I pitied him at a distance, I was still afraid of him when he appeared near our wigwam.

Thus, when my mother left me by myself that afternoon I sat in a fearful mood within our tepee. I recalled all I had ever heard about Wiyaka-Napbina; and I tried to assure myself that though he might pass near by, he would not come to our wigwam because there was no little girl around our grounds.

Just then, from without a hand lifted the canvas covering of the entrance; the shadow of a man fell within the wigwam, and a large roughly moccasined foot was planted inside.

For a moment I did not dare to breathe or stir, for I thought that could be no other than Wiyaka-Napbina. The next instant I sighed aloud in relief. It was an old grandfather who had often told me Iktomi legends.

"Where is your mother, my little grandchild?" were his first words.

"My mother is soon coming back from my aunt's tepee," I replied.

"Then I shall wait awhile for her return," he said, crossing his feet and seating himself upon a mat.

At once I began to play the part of a generous hostess. I turned to my mother's coffeepot.

Lifting the lid, I found nothing but coffee grounds in the bottom. I set the pot on a heap of cold ashes in the centre, and filled it half full of warm Missouri River water. During this performance I felt conscious of being watched. Then breaking off a small piece of our unleavened bread, I placed it in a bowl. Turning soon to the coffeepot, which would never have boiled on a dead fire had I waited forever, I poured out a cup of worse than muddy warm water. Carrying the bowl in one hand and cup in the other, I handed the light luncheon to the old warrior. I offered them to him with the air of bestowing generous hospitality.

"How! how!" he said, and placed the dishes on the ground in front of his crossed feet. He nibbled at the bread and sipped from the cup. I sat back against a pole watching him. I was proud to have succeeded so well in serving refreshments to a guest all by myself. Before the old warrior had finished eating, my mother entered. Immediately she

wondered where I had found coffee, for she knew I had never made any, and that she had left the coffeepot empty. Answering the question in my mother's eyes, the warrior remarked, "My granddaughter made coffee on a heap of dead ashes, and served me the moment I came."

They both laughed, and mother said, "Wait a little longer, and I shall build a fire." She meant to make some real coffee. But neither she nor the warrior, whom the law of our custom had compelled to partake of my insipid hospitality, said anything to embarrass me. They treated my best judgment, poor as it was, with the utmost respect. It was not till long years afterward that I learned how ridiculous a thing I had done.

V

THE DEAD MAN'S PLUM BUSH

One autumn afternoon many people came streaming toward the dwelling of our near neighbor. With painted faces, and wearing broad white bosoms of elk's teeth, they hurried down the narrow footpath to Haraka Wambdi's wigwam. Young mothers held their children by the hand, and half pulled them along in their haste. They overtook and passed by the bent old grandmothers who were trudging along with crooked canes toward the center of excitement. Most of the young braves galloped hither on their ponies. Toothless warriors, like the old women, came more slowly, though mounted on lively ponies. They sat proudly erect on their horses. They wore their eagle plumes, and waved their various trophies of former wars.

In front of the wigwam a great fire was built, and several large black kettles of venison were suspended over it. The crowd were seated about it on the grass in a great circle. Behind them some of the braves stood leaning against the necks of their ponies, their tall figures draped in loose robes which were well drawn over their eyes.

Young girls, with their faces glowing like bright red autumn leaves, their glossy braids falling over each ear, sat coquettishly beside their chaperons. It was a custom for young Indian women to invite some older relative to escort them to the public feasts. Though it was not an iron law, it was generally observed.

Haraka Wambdi was a strong young brave, who had just returned from his first battle, a warrior. His near relatives, to celebrate his new

rank, were spreading a feast to which the whole of the Indian village was invited.

Holding my pretty striped blanket in readiness to throw over my shoulders, I grew more and more restless as I watched the gay throng assembling. My mother was busily broiling a wild duck that my aunt had that morning brought over.

"Mother, mother, why do you stop to cook a small meal when we are invited to a feast?" I asked, with a snarl in my voice.

"My child, learn to wait. On our way to the celebration we are going to stop at Chanyu's wigwam. His aged mother-in-law is lying very ill, and I think she would like a taste of this small game."

Having once seen the suffering on the thin, pinched features of this dying woman, I felt a momentary shame that I had not remembered her before.

On our way I ran ahead of my mother and was reaching out my hand to pick some purple plums that grew on a small bush, when I was checked by a low "Sh!" from my mother.

"Why, mother, I want to taste the plums!" I exclaimed, as I dropped my hand to my side in disappointment.

"Never pluck a single plum from this bush, my child, for its roots are wrapped around an Indian's skeleton. A brave is buried here. While he lived he was so fond of playing the game of striped plum seeds that, at his death, his set of plum seeds were buried in his hands. From them sprang up this little bush."

Eyeing the forbidden fruit, I trod lightly on the sacred ground, and dared to speak only in whispers until we had gone many paces from it. After that time I halted in my ramblings whenever I came in sight of the plum bush. I grew sober with awe, and was alert to hear a long-drawn-out whistle rise from the roots of it. Though I had never heard with my own ears this strange whistle of departed spirits, yet I had listened so frequently to hear the old folks describe it that I knew I should recognize it at once.

The lasting impression of that day, as I recall it now, is what my mother told me about the dead man's plum bush.

VI

THE GROUND SQUIRREL

In the busy autumn days my cousin Warca-Ziwin's mother came to our wigwam to help my mother preserve foods for our winter use. I

was very fond of my aunt, because she was not so quiet as my mother. Though she was older, she was more jovial and less reserved. She was slender and remarkably erect. While my mother's hair was heavy and black, my aunt had unusually thin locks.

Ever since I knew her she wore a string of large blue beads around her neck,—beads that were precious because my uncle had given them to her when she was a younger woman. She had a peculiar swing in her gait, caused by a long stride rarely natural to so slight a figure. It was during my aunt's visit with us that my mother forgot her accustomed quietness, often laughing heartily at some of my aunt's witty remarks.

I loved my aunt threefold: for her hearty laughter, for the cheerfulness she caused my mother, and most of all for the times she dried my tears and held me in her lap, when my mother had reproved me.

Early in the cool mornings, just as the yellow rim of the sun rose above the hills, we were up and eating our breakfast. We awoke so early that we saw the sacred hour when a misty smoke hung over a pit surrounded by an impassable sinking mire. This strange smoke appeared every morning, both winter and summer; but most visibly in midwinter it rose immediately above the marshy spot. By the time the full face of the sun appeared above the eastern horizon, the smoke vanished. Even very old men, who had known this country the longest, said that the smoke from this pit had never failed a single day to rise heavenward.

As I frolicked about our dwelling I used to stop suddenly, and with a fearful awe watch the smoking of the unknown fires. While the vapor was visible I was afraid to go very far from our wigwam unless I went with my mother.

From a field in the fertile river bottom my mother and aunt gathered an abundant supply of corn. Near our tepee they spread a large canvas upon the grass, and dried their sweet corn in it. I was left to watch the corn, that nothing should disturb it. I played around it with dolls made of ears of corn. I braided their soft fine silk for hair, and gave them blankets as various as the scraps I found in my mother's workbag.

There was a little stranger with a black-and-yellow-striped coat that used to come to the drying corn. It was a little ground squirrel, who was so fearless of me that he came to one corner of the canvas and carried away as much of the sweet corn as he could hold. I wanted very much to catch him and rub his pretty fur back, but my mother

said he would be so frightened if I caught him that he would bite my fingers. So I was as content as he to keep the corn between us. Every morning he came for more corn. Some evenings I have seen him creeping about our grounds; and when I gave a sudden whoop of recognition he ran quickly out of sight.

When mother had dried all the corn she wished, then she sliced great pumpkins into thin rings; and these she doubled and linked together into long chains. She hung them on a pole that stretched between two forked posts. The wind and sun soon thoroughly dried the chains of pumpkin. Then she packed them away in a case of thick and stiff buckskin.

In the sun and wind she also dried many wild fruits,—cherries, berries, and plums. But chiefest among my early recollections of autumn is that one of the corn drying and the ground squirrel.

I have few memories of winter days at this period of my life, though many of the summer. There is one only which I can recall.

Some missionaries gave me a little bag of marbles. They were all sizes and colors. Among them were some of colored glass. Walking with my mother to the river, on a late winter day, we found great chunks of ice piled all along the bank. The ice on the river was floating in huge pieces. As I stood beside one large block, I noticed for the first time the colors of the rainbow in the crystal ice. Immediately I thought of my glass marbles at home. With my bare fingers I tried to pick out some of the colors, for they seemed so near the surface. But my fingers began to sting with the intense cold, and I had to bite them hard to keep from crying.

From that day on, for many a moon, I believed that glass marbles had river ice inside of them.

VII
THE BIG RED APPLES

The first turning away from the easy, natural flow of my life occurred in an early spring. It was in my eighth year; in the month of March, I afterward learned. At this age I knew but one language, and that was my mother's native tongue.

From some of my playmates I heard that two paleface missionaries were in our village. They were from that class of white men who wore big hats and carried large hearts, they said. Running direct to my

mother, I began to question her why these two strangers were among us. She told me, after I had teased much, that they come to take away Indian boys and girls to the East. My mother did not seem to want me to talk about them. But in a day or two, I gleaned many wonderful stories from my playfellows concerning the strangers.

"Mother, my friend Judéwin is going home with the missionaries. She is going to a more beautiful country than ours; the palefaces told her so!" I said wistfully, wishing in my heart that I too might go.

Mother sat in a chair, and I was hanging on her knee. Within the last two seasons my big brother Dawée had returned from a three years' education in the East, and his coming back influenced my mother to take a farther step from her native way of living. First it was a change from the buffalo skin to the white man's canvas that covered our wigwam. Now she had given up her wigwam of slender poles, to live, a foreigner, in a home of clumsy logs.

"Yes, my child, several others besides Judéwin are going away with the palefaces. Your brother said the missionaries had inquired about his little sister," she said, watching my face very closely.

My heart thumped so hard against my breast, I wondered if she could hear it.

"Did he tell them to take me, mother?" I asked, fearing lest Dawée had forbidden the palefaces to see me, and that my hope of going to the Wonderland would be entirely blighted.

With a sad, slow smile, she answered: "There! I knew you were wishing to go, because Judéwin has filled your ears with the white man's lies. Don't believe a word they say! Their words are sweet, but, my child, their deeds are bitter. You will cry for me, but they will not even soothe you. Stay with me, my little one! Your brother Dawée says that going East, away from your mother, is too hard an experience for his baby sister."

Thus my mother discouraged my curiosity about the lands beyond our eastern horizon; for it was not yet an ambition for Letters that was stirring me. But on the following day the missionaries did come to our very house. I spied them coming up the footpath leading to our cottage. A third man was with them, but he was not my brother Dawée. It was another, a young interpreter, a paleface who had a smattering of the Indian language. I was ready to run out to meet them, but I did not dare to displease my mother. With great glee, I jumped up and down on our ground floor. I begged my mother to

open the door, that they would be sure to come to us. Alas! They came, they saw, and they conquered!

Judéwin had told me of the great tree where grew red, red apples; and how we could reach out our hands and pick all the red apples we could eat. I had never seen apple trees. I had never tasted more than a dozen red apples in my life; and when I heard of the orchards of the East, I was eager to roam among them. The missionaries smiled into my eyes and patted my head. I wondered how mother could say such hard words against him.

"Mother, ask them if little girls may have all the red apples they want, when they go East," I whispered aloud, in my excitement.

The interpreter heard me, and answered: "Yes, little girl, the nice red apples are for those who pick them; and you will have a ride on the iron horse if you go with these good people."

I had never seen a train, and he knew it.

"Mother, I am going East! I like big red apples, and I want to ride on the iron horse! Mother, say yes!" I pleaded.

My mother said nothing. The missionaries waited in silence; and my eyes began to blur with tears, though I struggled to choke them back. The corners of my mouth twitched, and my mother saw me.

"I am not ready to give you any word," she said to them. "Tomorrow I shall send you my answer by my son."

With this they left us. Alone with my mother, I yielded to my tears, and cried aloud, shaking my head so as not to hear what she was saying to me. This was the first time I had ever been so unwilling to give up my own desire that I refused to hearken to my mother's voice.

There was a solemn silence in our home that night. Before I went to bed I begged the Great Spirit to make my mother willing I should go with the missionaries.

The next morning came, and my mother called me to her side. "My daughter, do you still persist in wishing to leave your mother?" she asked.

"Oh, mother, it is not that I wish to leave you, but I want to see the wonderful Eastern land," I answered.

My dear old aunt came to our house that morning, and I heard her say, "Let her try it."

I hoped that, as usual, my aunt was pleading on my side. My brother Dawée came for mother's decision. I dropped my play, and crept close to my aunt.

"Yes, Dawée, my daughter, though she does not understand what it

all means, is anxious to go. She will need an education when she is grown, for then there will be fewer real Dakotas, and many more palefaces. This tearing her away, so young, from her mother is necessary, if I would have her an educated woman. The palefaces, who owe us a large debt for stolen lands, have begun to pay a tardy justice in offering some education to our children. But I know my daughter must suffer keenly in this experiment. For her sake, I dread to tell you my reply to the missionaries. Go, tell them that they may take my little daughter, and that the Great Spirit shall not fail to reward them according to their hearts."

Wrapped in my heavy blanket, I walked with my mother to the carriage that was soon to take us to the iron horse. I was happy. I met my playmates, who were also wearing their best thick blankets. We showed one another our new beaded moccasins, and the width of the belts that girdled our new dresses. Soon we were being drawn rapidly away by the white man's horses. When I saw the lonely figure of my mother vanish in the distance, a sense of regret settled heavily upon me. I felt suddenly weak, as if I might fall limp to the ground. I was in the hands of strangers whom my mother did not fully trust. I no longer felt free to be myself, or to voice my own feelings. The tears trickled down my cheeks, and I buried my face in the folds of my blanket. Now the first step, parting me from my mother, was taken, and all my belated tears availed nothing.

Having driven thirty miles to the ferryboat, we crossed the Missouri in the evening. Then riding again a few miles eastward, we stopped before a massive brick building. I looked at it in amazement, and with a vague misgiving, for in our village I had never seen so large a house. Trembling with fear and distrust of the palefaces, my teeth chattering from the chilly ride, I crept noiselessly in my soft moccasins along the narrow hall, keeping very close to the bare wall. I was as frightened and bewildered as the captured young of a wild creature.

THE SCHOOL DAYS OF AN INDIAN GIRL

I
THE LAND OF RED APPLES

There were eight in our party of bronzed children who were going East with the missionaries. Among us were three young braves, two tall girls, and we three little ones, Judéwin, Thowin, and I.

We had been very impatient to start on our journey to the Red Apple Country, which, we were told, lay a little beyond the great circular horizon of the Western prairie. Under a sky of rosy apples we dreamt of roaming as freely and happily as we had chased the cloud shadows on the Dakota plains. We had anticipated much pleasure from a ride on the iron horse, but the throngs of staring palefaces disturbed and troubled us.

On the train, fair women, with tottering babies on each arm, stopped their haste and scrutinized the children of absent mothers. Large men, with heavy bundles in their hands, halted near by, and riveted their glassy blue eyes upon us.

I sank deep into the corner of my seat, for I resented being watched. Directly in front of me, children who were no larger than I hung themselves upon the backs of their seats, with their bold white faces toward me. Sometimes they took their forefingers out of their mouths and pointed at my moccasined feet. Their mothers, instead of reproving such rude curiosity, looked closely at me, and attracted their children's further notice to my blanket. This embarrassed me, and kept me constantly on the verge of tears.

I sat perfectly still, with my eyes downcast, daring only now and then to shoot long glances around me. Chancing to turn to the window at my side, I was quite breathless upon seeing one familiar object. It was the telegraph pole which strode by at short paces. Very near my mother's dwelling, along the edge of a road thickly bordered with wild sunflowers, some poles like these had been planted by white men. Often I had stopped, on my way down the road, to hold my ear against the pole, and, hearing its low moaning, I used to wonder what

the paleface had done to hurt it. Now I sat watching for each pole that glided by to be the last one.

In this way I had forgotten my uncomfortable surroundings, when I heard one of my comrades call out my name. I saw the missionary standing very near, tossing candies and gums into our midst. This amused us all, and we tried to see who could catch the most of the sweetmeats.

Though we rode several days inside of the iron horse, I do not recall a single thing about our luncheons.

It was night when we reached the school grounds. The lights from the windows of the large buildings fell upon some of the icicled trees that stood beneath them. We were led toward an open door, where the brightness of the lights within flooded out over the heads of the excited palefaces who blocked our way. My body trembled more from fear than from the snow I trod upon.

Entering the house, I stood close against the wall. The strong glaring light in the large whitewashed room dazzled my eyes. The noisy hurrying of hard shoes upon a bare wooden floor increased the whirring in my ears. My only safety seemed to be in keeping next to the wall. As I was wondering in which direction to escape from all this confusion, two warm hands grasped me firmly, and in the same moment I was tossed high in midair. A rosy-cheeked paleface woman caught me in her arms. I was both frightened and insulted by such trifling. I stared into her eyes, wishing her to let me stand on my own feet, but she jumped me up and down with increasing enthusiasm. My mother had never made a plaything of her wee daughter. Remembering this I began to cry aloud.

They misunderstood the cause of my tears, and placed me at a white table loaded with food. There our party were united again. As I did not hush my crying, one of the older ones whispered to me, "Wait until you are alone in the night."

It was very little I could swallow besides my sobs, that evening.

"Oh, I want my mother and my brother Dawée! I want to go to my aunt!" I pleaded; but the ears of the palefaces could not hear me.

From the table we were taken along an upward incline of wooden boxes, which I learned afterward to call a stairway. At the top was a quiet hall, dimly lighted. Many narrow beds were in one straight line down the entire length of the wall. In them lay sleeping brown faces, which peeped just out of the coverings. I was tucked into bed with

one of the tall girls, because she talked to me in my mother tongue and seemed to soothe me.

I had arrived in the wonderful land of rosy skies, but I was not happy, as I had thought I should be. My long travel and the bewildering sights had exhausted me. I fell asleep, heaving deep, tired sobs. My tears were left to dry themselves in streaks, because neither my aunt nor my mother was near to wipe them away.

II

THE CUTTING OF MY LONG HAIR

The first day in the land of apples was a bitter cold one; for the snow still covered the ground, and the trees were bare. A large bell rang for breakfast, its loud metallic voice crashing through the belfry overhead and into our sensitive ears. The annoying clatter of shoes on bare floors gave us no peace. The constant clash of harsh noises, with an undercurrent of many voices murmuring an unknown tongue, made a bedlam within which I was securely tied. And though my spirit tore itself in struggling for its lost freedom, all was useless.

A paleface woman, with white hair, came up after us. We were placed in a line of girls who were marching into the dining room. These were Indian girls, in stiff shoes and closely clinging dresses. The small girls wore sleeved aprons and shingled hair. As I walked noiselessly in my soft moccasins, I felt like sinking to the floor, for my blanket had been stripped from my shoulders. I looked hard at the Indian girls, who seemed not to care that they were even more immodestly dressed than I, in their tightly fitting clothes. While we marched in, the boys entered at an opposite door. I watched for the three young braves who came in our party. I spied them in the rear ranks, looking as uncomfortable as I felt.

A small bell was tapped, and each of the pupils drew a chair from under the table. Supposing this act meant they were to be seated, I pulled out mine and at once slipped into it from one side. But when I turned my head, I saw that I was the only one seated, and all the rest at our table remained standing. Just as I began to rise, looking shyly around to see how chairs were to be used, a second bell was sounded. All were seated at last, and I had to crawl back into my chair again. I heard a man's voice at one end of the hall, and I looked around to see him. But all the others hung their heads over their plates. As I glanced

at the long chain of tables, I caught the eyes of a paleface woman upon me. Immediately I dropped my eyes, wondering why I was so keenly watched by the strange woman. The man ceased his mutterings, and then a third bell was tapped. Every one picked up his knife and fork and began eating. I began crying instead, for by this time I was afraid to venture anything more.

But this eating by formula was not the hardest trial in that first day. Late in the morning, my friend Judéwin gave me a terrible warning. Judéwin knew a few words of English; and she had overheard the paleface woman talk about cutting our long, heavy hair. Our mothers had taught us that only unskilled warriors who were captured had their hair shingled by the enemy. Among our people, short hair was worn by mourners, and shingled hair by cowards!

We discussed our fate some moments, and when Judéwin said, "We have to submit, because they are strong," I rebelled.

"No, I will not submit! I will struggle first!" I answered.

I watched my chance, and when no one noticed I disappeared. I crept up the stairs as quietly as I could in my squeaking shoes,—my moccasins had been exchanged for shoes. Along the hall I passed, without knowing whither I was going. Turning aside to an open door, I found a large room with three white beds in it. The windows were covered with dark green curtains, which made the room very dim. Thankful that no one was there, I directed my steps toward the corner farthest from the door. On my hands and knees I crawled under the bed, and cuddled myself in the dark corner.

From my hiding place I peered out, shuddering with fear whenever I heard footsteps near by. Though in the hall loud voices were calling my name, and I knew that even Judéwin was searching for me, I did not open my mouth to answer. Then the steps were quickened and the voices became excited. The sounds came nearer and nearer. Women and girls entered the room. I held my breath and watched them open closet doors and peep behind large trunks. Some one threw up the curtains, and the room was filled with sudden light. What caused them to stoop and look under the bed I do not know. I remember being dragged out, though I resisted by kicking and scratching wildly. In spite of myself, I was carried downstairs and tied fast in a chair.

I cried aloud, shaking my head all the while until I felt the cold blades of the scissors against my neck, and heard them gnaw off one of my thick braids. Then I lost my spirit. Since the day I was taken from my mother I had suffered extreme indignities. People had stared

at me. I had been tossed about in the air like a wooden puppet. And now my long hair was shingled like a coward's! In my anguish I moaned for my mother, but no one came to comfort me. Not a soul reasoned quietly with me, as my own mother used to do; for now I was only one of many little animals driven by a herder.

III
THE SNOW EPISODE

A short time after our arrival we three Dakotas were playing in the snowdrift. We were all still deaf to the English language, excepting Judéwin, who always heard such puzzling things. One morning we learned through her ears that we were forbidden to fall lengthwise in the snow, as we had been doing, to see our own impressions. However, before many hours we had forgotten the order, and were having great sport in the snow, when a shrill voice called us. Looking up, we saw an imperative hand beckoning us into the house. We shook the snow off ourselves, and started toward the woman as slowly as we dared.

Judéwin said: "Now the paleface is angry with us. She is going to punish us for falling into the snow. If she looks straight into your eyes and talks loudly, you must wait until she stops. Then, after a tiny pause, say, 'No.' " The rest of the way we practiced upon the little word "no."

As it happened, Thowin was summoned to judgment first. The door shut behind her with a click.

Judéwin and I stood silently listening at the keyhole. The paleface woman talked in very severe tones. Her words fell from her lips like crackling embers, and her inflection ran up like the small end of a switch. I understood her voice better than the things she was saying. I was certain we had made her very impatient with us. Judéwin heard enough of the words to realize all too late that she had taught us the wrong reply.

"Oh, poor Thowin!" she gasped, as she put both hands over her ears.

Just then I heard Thowin's tremulous answer, "No."

With an angry exclamation, the woman gave her a hard spanking. Then she stopped to say something. Judéwin said it was this: "Are you going to obey my word the next time?"

Thowin answered again with the only word at her command, "No."

This time the woman meant her blows to smart, for the poor frightened girl shrieked at the top of her voice. In the midst of the whipping the blows ceased abruptly, and the woman asked another question: "Are you going to fall in the snow again?"

Thowin gave her bad password another trial. We heard her say feebly, "No! No!"

With this the woman hid away her half-worn slipper, and led the child out, stroking her black shorn head. Perhaps it occurred to her that brute force is not the solution for such a problem. She did nothing to Judéwin nor to me. She only returned to us our unhappy comrade, and left us alone in the room.

During the first two or three seasons misunderstandings as ridiculous as this one of the snow episode frequently took place, bringing unjustifiable frights and punishments into our little lives.

Within a year I was able to express myself somewhat in broken English. As soon as I comprehended a part of what was said and done, a mischievous spirit of revenge possessed me. One day I was called in from my play for some misconduct. I had disregarded a rule which seemed to me very needlessly binding. I was sent into the kitchen to mash the turnips for dinner. It was noon, and steaming dishes were hastily carried into the dining-room. I hated turnips, and their odor which came from the brown jar was offensive to me. With fire in my heart, I took the wooden tool that the paleface woman held out to me. I stood upon a step, and, grasping the handle with both hands, I bent in hot rage over the turnips. I worked my vengeance upon them. All were so busily occupied that no one noticed me. I saw that the turnips were in a pulp, and that further beating could not improve them; but the order was, "Mash these turnips," and mash them I would! I renewed my energy; and as I sent the masher into the bottom of the jar, I felt a satisfying sensation that the weight of my body had gone into it.

Just here a paleface woman came up to my table. As she looked into the jar, she shoved my hands roughly aside. I stood fearless and angry. She placed her red hands upon the rim of the jar. Then she gave one lift and strode away from the table. But lo! the pulpy contents fell through the crumbled bottom to the floor! She spared me no scolding phrases that I had earned. I did not heed them. I felt triumphant in my revenge, though deep within me I was a wee bit sorry to have broken the jar.

As I sat eating my dinner, and saw that no turnips were served, I

whooped in my heart for having once asserted the rebellion within me.

IV

THE DEVIL

Among the legends the old warriors used to tell me were many stories of evil spirits. But I was taught to fear them no more than those who stalked about in material guise. I never knew there was an insolent chieftain among the bad spirits, who dared to array his forces against the Great Spirit, until I heard this white man's legend from a paleface woman.

Out of a large book she showed me a picture of the white man's devil. I looked in horror upon the strong claws that grew out of his fur-covered fingers. His feet were like his hands. Trailing at his heels was a scaly tail tipped with a serpent's open jaws. His face was a patchwork: he had bearded cheeks, like some I had seen palefaces wear; his nose was an eagle's bill, and his sharp-pointed ears were pricked up like those of a sly fox. Above them a pair of cow's horns curved upward. I trembled with awe, and my heart throbbed in my throat, as I looked at the king of evil spirits. Then I heard the paleface woman say that this terrible creature roamed loose in the world, and that little girls who disobeyed school regulations were to be tortured by him.

That night I dreamt about this evil divinity. Once again I seemed to be in my mother's cottage. An Indian woman had come to visit my mother. On opposite sides of the kitchen stove, which stood in the center of the small house, my mother and her guest were seated in straight-backed chairs. I played with a train of empty spools hitched together on a string. It was night, and the wick burned feebly. Suddenly I heard some one turn our door-knob from without.

My mother and the woman hushed their talk, and both looked toward the door. It opened gradually. I waited behind the stove. The hinges squeaked as the door was slowly, very slowly pushed inward.

Then in rushed the devil! He was tall! He looked exactly like the picture I had seen of him in the white man's papers. He did not speak to my mother, because he did not know the Indian language, but his glittering yellow eyes were fastened upon me. He took long strides around the stove, passing behind the woman's chair. I threw down

my spools, and ran to my mother. He did not fear her, but followed closely after me. Then I ran round and round the stove, crying aloud for help. But my mother and the woman seemed not to know my danger. They sat still, looking quietly upon the devil's chase after me. At last I grew dizzy. My head revolved as on a hidden pivot. My knees became numb, and doubled under my weight like a pair of knife blades without a spring. Beside my mother's chair I fell in a heap. Just as the devil stooped over me with outstretched claws my mother awoke from her quiet indifference, and lifted me on her lap. Whereupon the devil vanished, and I was awake.

On the following morning I took my revenge upon the devil. Stealing into the room where a wall of shelves was filled with books, I drew forth The Stories of the Bible. With a broken slate pencil I carried in my apron pocket, I began by scratching out his wicked eyes. A few moments later, when I was ready to leave the room, there was a ragged hole in the page where the picture of the devil had once been.

V

IRON ROUTINE

A loud-clamoring bell awakened us at half-past six in the cold winter mornings. From happy dreams of Western rolling lands and unlassoed freedom we tumbled out upon chilly bare floors back again into a paleface day. We had short time to jump into our shoes and clothes, and wet our eyes with icy water, before a small hand bell was vigorously rung for roll call.

There were too many drowsy children and too numerous orders for the day to waste a moment in any apology to nature for giving her children such a shock in the early morning. We rushed downstairs, bounding over two high steps at a time, to land in the assembly room.

A paleface woman, with a yellow-covered roll book open on her arm and a gnawed pencil in her hand, appeared at the door. Her small, tired face was coldly lighted with a pair of large gray eyes.

She stood still in a halo of authority, while over the rim of her spectacles her eyes pried nervously about the room. Having glanced at her long list of names and called out the first one, she tossed up her chin and peered through the crystals of her spectacles to make sure of the answer "Here."

Relentlessly her pencil black-marked our daily records if we were not present to respond to our names, and no chum of ours had done it successfully for us. No matter if a dull headache or the painful cough of slow consumption had delayed the absentee, there was only time enough to mark the tardiness. It was next to impossible to leave the iron routine after the civilizing machine had once begun its day's buzzing; and as it was inbred in me to suffer in silence rather than to appeal to the ears of one whose open eyes could not see my pain, I have many times trudged in the day's harness heavy-footed, like a dumb sick brute.

Once I lost a dear classmate. I remember well how she used to mope along at my side, until one morning she could not raise her head from her pillow. At her deathbed I stood weeping, as the paleface woman sat near her moistening the dry lips. Among the folds of the bedclothes I saw the open pages of the white man's Bible. The dying Indian girl talked disconnectedly of Jesus the Christ and the paleface who was cooling her swollen hands and feet.

I grew bitter, and censured the woman for cruel neglect of our physical ills. I despised the pencils that moved automatically, and the one teaspoon which dealt out, from a large bottle, healing to a row of variously ailing Indian children. I blamed the hard-working, well-meaning, ignorant woman who was inculcating in our hearts her superstitious ideas. Though I was sullen in all my little troubles, as soon as I felt better I was ready again to smile upon the cruel woman. Within a week I was again actively testing the chains which tightly bound my individuality like a mummy for burial.

The melancholy of those black days has left so long a shadow that it darkens the path of years that have since gone by. These sad memories rise above those of smoothly grinding school days. Perhaps my Indian nature is the moaning wind which stirs them now for their present record. But, however tempestuous this is within me, it comes out as the low voice of a curiously colored seashell, which is only for those ears that are bent with compassion to hear it.

VI
FOUR STRANGE SUMMERS

After my first three years of school, I roamed again in the Western country through four strange summers.

During this time I seemed to hang in the heart of chaos, beyond the touch or voice of human aid. My brother, being almost ten years my senior, did not quite understand my feelings. My mother had never gone inside of a schoolhouse, and so she was not capable of comforting her daughter who could read and write. Even nature seemed to have no place for me. I was neither a wee girl nor a tall one; neither a wild Indian nor a tame one. This deplorable situation was the effect of my brief course in the East, and the unsatisfactory "teenth" in a girl's years.

It was under these trying conditions that, one bright afternoon, as I sat restless and unhappy in my mother's cabin, I caught the sound of the spirited step of my brother's pony on the road which passed by our dwelling. Soon I heard the wheels of a light buckboard, and Dawée's familiar "Ho!" to his pony. He alighted upon the bare ground in front of our house. Tying his pony to one of the projecting corner logs of the low-roofed cottage, he stepped upon the wooden doorstep.

I met him there with a hurried greeting, and, as I passed by, he looked a quiet "What?" into my eyes.

When he began talking with my mother, I slipped the rope from the pony's bridle. Seizing the reins and bracing my feet against the dashboard, I wheeled around in an instant. The pony was ever ready to try his speed. Looking backward, I saw Dawée waving his hand to me. I turned with the curve in the road and disappeared. I followed the winding road which crawled upward between the bases of little hillocks. Deep water-worn ditches ran parallel on either side. A strong wind blew against my cheeks and fluttered my sleeves. The pony reached the top of the highest hill, and began an even race on the level lands. There was nothing moving within that great circular horizon of the Dakota prairies save the tall grasses, over which the wind blew and rolled off in long, shadowy waves.

Within this vast wigwam of blue and green I rode reckless and insignificant. It satisifed my small consciousness to see the white foam fly from the pony's mouth.

Suddenly, out of the earth a coyote came forth at a swinging trot that was taking the cunning thief toward the hills and the village beyond. Upon the moment's impulse, I gave him a long chase and a wholesome fright. As I turned away to go back to the village, the wolf sank down upon his haunches for rest, for it was a hot summer day; and as I drove slowly homeward, I saw his sharp nose still pointed at me, until I vanished below the margin of the hilltops.

In a little while I came in sight of my mother's house. Dawée stood in the yard, laughing at an old warrior who was pointing his forefinger, and again waving his whole hand, toward the hills. With his blanket drawn over one shoulder, he talked and motioned excitedly. Dawée turned the old man by the shoulder and pointed me out to him.

"Oh, han!" (Oh, yes) the warrior muttered, and went his way. He had climbed the top of his favorite barren hill to survey the surrounding prairies, when he spied my chase after the coyote. His keen eyes recognized the pony and driver. At once uneasy for my safety, he had come running to my mother's cabin to give her warning. I did not appreciate his kindly interest, for there was an unrest gnawing at my heart.

As soon as he went away, I asked Dawée about something else.

"No, my baby sister, I cannot take you with me to the party tonight," he replied. Though I was not far from fifteen, and I felt that before long I should enjoy all the privileges of my tall cousin, Dawée persisted in calling me his baby sister.

That moonlight night, I cried in my mother's presence when I heard the jolly young people pass by our cottage. They were no more young braves in blankets and eagle plumes, nor Indian maids with prettily painted cheeks. They had gone three years to school in the East, and had become civilized. The young men wore the white man's coat and trousers, with bright neckties. The girls wore tight muslin dresses, with ribbons at neck and waist. At these gatherings they talked English. I could speak English almost as well as my brother, but I was not properly dressed to be taken along. I had no hat, no ribbons, and no close-fitting gown. Since my return from school I had thrown away my shoes, and wore again the soft moccasins.

While Dawée was busily preparing to go I controlled my tears. But when I heard him bounding away on his pony, I buried my face in my arms and cried hot tears.

My mother was troubled by my unhappiness. Coming to my side, she offered me the only printed matter we had in our home. It was an Indian Bible, given her some years ago by a missionary. She tried to console me. "Here, my child, are the white man's papers. Read a little from them," she said most piously.

I took it from her hand, for her sake; but my enraged spirit felt more like burning the book, which afforded me no help, and was a perfect delusion to my mother. I did not read it, but laid it unopened on the floor, where I sat on my feet. The dim yellow light of the

braided muslin burning in a small vessel of oil flickered and sizzled in the awful silent storm which followed my rejection of the Bible.

Now my wrath against the fates consumed my tears before they reached my eyes. I sat stony, with a bowed head. My mother threw a shawl over her head and shoulders, and stepped out into the night.

After an uncertain solitude, I was suddenly aroused by a loud cry piercing the night. It was my mother's voice wailing among the barren hills which held the bones of buried warriors. She called aloud for her brothers' spirits to support her in her helpless misery. My fingers grew icy cold, as I realized that my unrestrained tears had betrayed my suffering to her, and she was grieving for me.

Before she returned, though I knew she was on her way, for she had ceased her weeping, I extinguished the light, and leaned my head on the window sill.

Many schemes of running away from my surroundings hovered about in my mind. A few more moons of such a turmoil drove me away to the eastern school. I rode on the white man's iron steed, thinking it would bring me back to my mother in a few winters, when I should be grown tall, and there would be congenial friends awaiting me.

VII
INCURRING MY MOTHER'S DISPLEASURE

In the second journey to the East I had not come without some precautions. I had a secret interview with one of our best medicine men, and when I left his wigwam I carried securely in my sleeve a tiny bunch of magic roots. This possession assured me of friends wherever I should go. So absolutely did I believe in its charms that I wore it through all the school routine for more than a year. Then, before I lost my faith in the dead roots, I lost the little buckskin bag containing all my good luck.

At the close of this second term of three years I was the proud owner of my first diploma. The following autumn I ventured upon a college career against my mother's will.

I had written for her approval, but in her reply I found no encouragement. She called my notice to her neighbors' children, who had completed their education in three years. They had returned to their homes, and were then talking English with the frontier settlers.

Her few words hinted that I had better give up any slow attempt to learn the white man's ways, and be content to roam over the prairies and find my living upon wild roots. I silenced her by deliberate disobedience.

Thus, homeless and heavy-hearted, I began anew my life among strangers.

As I hid myself in my little room in the college dormitory, away from the scornful and yet curious eyes of the students, I pined for sympathy. Often I wept in secret, wishing I had gone West, to be nourished by my mother's love, instead of remaining among a cold race whose hearts were frozen hard with prejudice.

During the fall and winter seasons I scarcely had a real friend, though by that time several of my classmates were courteous to me at a safe distance.

My mother had not yet forgiven my rudeness to her, and I had no moment for letter-writing. By daylight and lamplight, I spun with reeds and thistles, until my hands were tired from their weaving, the magic design which promised me the white man's respect.

At length, in the spring term, I entered an oratorical contest among the various classes. As the day of competition approached, it did not seem possible that the event was so near at hand, but it came. In the chapel the classes assembled together, with their invited guests. The high platform was carpeted, and gayly festooned with college colors. A bright white light illumined the room, and outlined clearly the great polished beams that arched the domed ceiling. The assembled crowds filled the air with pulsating murmurs. When the hour for speaking arrived all were hushed. But on the wall the old clock which pointed out the trying moment ticked calmly on.

One after another I saw and heard the orators. Still, I could not realize that they longed for the favorable decision of the judges as much as I did. Each contestant received a loud burst of applause, and some were cheered heartily. Too soon my turn came, and I paused a moment behind the curtains for a deep breath. After my concluding words, I heard the same applause that the others had called out.

Upon my retreating steps, I was astounded to receive from my fellow-students a large bouquet of roses tied with flowing ribbons. With the lovely flowers I fled from the stage. This friendly token was a rebuke to me for the hard feelings I had borne them.

Later, the decision of the judges awarded me the first place. Then there was a mad uproar in the hall, where my classmates sang and

shouted my name at the top of their lungs; and the disappointed students howled and brayed in fearfully dissonant tin trumpets. In this excitement, happy students rushed forward to offer their congratulations. And I could not conceal a smile when they wished to escort me in a procession to the students' parlor, where all were going to calm themselves. Thanking them for the kind spirit which prompted them to make such a proposition, I walked alone with the night to my own little room.

A few weeks afterward, I appeared as the college representative in another contest. This time the competition was among orators from different colleges in our State. It was held at the State capital, in one of the largest opera houses.

Here again was a strong prejudice against my people. In the evening, as the great audience filled the house, the student bodies began warring among themselves. Fortunately, I was spared witnessing any of the noisy wrangling before the contest began. The slurs against the Indian that stained the lips of our opponents were already burning like a dry fever within my breast.

But after the orations were delivered a deeper burn awaited me. There, before that vast ocean of eyes, some college rowdies threw out a large white flag, with a drawing of a most forlorn Indian girl on it. Under this they had printed in bold black letters words that ridiculed the college which was represented by a "squaw." Such worse than barbarian rudeness embittered me. While we waited for the verdict of the judges, I gleamed fiercely upon the throngs of palefaces. My teeth were hard set, as I saw the white flag still floating insolently in the air.

Then anxiously we watched the man carry toward the stage the envelope containing the final decision.

There were two prizes given, that night, and one of them was mine! The evil spirit laughed within me when the white flag dropped out of sight, and the hands which hurled it hung limp in defeat.

Leaving the crowd as quickly as possible, I was soon in my room. The rest of the night I sat in an armchair and gazed into the crackling fire. I laughed no more in triumph when thus alone. The little taste of victory did not satisfy a hunger in my heart. In my mind I saw my mother far away on the Western plains, and she was holding a charge against me.

An Indian Teacher
Among Indians

I
MY FIRST DAY

Though an illness left me unable to continue my college course, my pride kept me from returning to my mother. Had she known of my worn condition, she would have said the white man's papers were not worth the freedom and health I had lost by them. Such a rebuke from my mother would have been unbearable, and as I felt then it would be far too true to be comfortable.

Since the winter when I had my first dreams about red apples I had been traveling slowly toward the morning horizon. There had been no doubt about the direction in which I wished to go to spend my energies in a work for the Indian race. Thus I had written my mother briefly, saying my plan for the year was to teach in an Eastern Indian school. Sending this message to her in the West, I started at once eastward.

Thus I found myself, tired and hot, in a black veiling of car smoke, as I stood wearily on a street corner of an old-fashioned town, waiting for a car. In a few moments more I should be on the school grounds, where a new work was ready for my inexperienced hands.

Upon entering the school campus, I was surprised at the thickly clustered buildings which made it a quaint little village, much more interesting than the town itself. The large trees among the houses gave the place a cool, refreshing shade, and the grass a deeper green. Within this large court of grass and trees stood a low green pump. The queer boxlike case had a revolving handle on its side, which clanked and creaked constantly.

I made myself known, and was shown to my room,—a small, carpeted room, with ghastly walls and ceiling. The two windows, both on the same side, were curtained with heavy muslin yellowed with age. A clean white bed was in one corner of the room, and opposite it was a square pine table covered with a black woolen blanket.

Without removing my hat from my head, I seated myself in one of

the two stiff-backed chairs that were placed beside the table. For several heart throbs I sat still looking from ceiling to floor, from wall to wall, trying hard to imagine years of contentment there. Even while I was wondering if my exhausted strength would sustain me through this undertaking, I heard a heavy tread stop at my door. Opening it, I met the imposing figure of a stately gray-haired man. With a light straw hat in one hand, and the right hand extended for greeting, he smiled kindly upon me. For some reason I was awed by his wondrous height and his strong square shoulders, which I felt were a finger's length above my head.

I was always slight, and my serious illness in the early spring had made me look rather frail and languid. His quick eye measured my height and breadth. Then he looked into my face. I imagined that a visible shadow flitted across his countenance as he let my hand fall. I knew he was no other than my employer.

"Ah ha! so you are the little Indian girl who created the excitement among the college orators!" he said, more to himself than to me. I thought I heard a subtle note of disappointment in his voice. Looking in from where he stood, with one sweeping glance, he asked if I lacked anything for my room.

After he turned to go, I listened to his step until it grew faint and was lost in the distance. I was aware that my car-smoked appearance had not concealed the lines of pain on my face.

For a short moment my spirit laughed at my ill fortune, and I entertained the idea of exerting myself to make an improvement. But as I tossed my hat off a leaden weakness came over me, and I felt as if years of weariness lay like water-soaked logs upon me. I threw myself upon the bed, and, closing my eyes, forgot my good intention.

II
A TRIP WESTWARD

One sultry month I sat at a desk heaped up with work. Now, as I recall it, I wonder how I could have dared to disregard nature's warning with such recklessness. Fortunately, my inheritance of a marvelous endurance enabled me to bend without breaking.

Though I had gone to and fro, from my room to the office, in an unhappy silence, I was watched by those around me. On an early morning I was summoned to the superintendent's office. For a half-

hour I listened to his words, and when I returned to my room I remembered one sentence above the rest. It was this: "I am going to turn you loose to pasture!" He was sending me West to gather Indian pupils for the school, and this was his way of expressing it.

I needed nourishment, but the midsummer's travel across the continent to search the hot prairies for overconfident parents who would intrust their children to strangers was a lean pasturage. However, I dwelt on the hope of seeing my mother. I tried to reason that a change was a rest. Within a couple of days I started toward my mother's home.

The intense heat and the sticky car smoke that followed my homeward trail did not noticeably restore my vitality. Hour after hour I gazed upon the country which was receding rapidly from me. I noticed the gradual expansion of the horizon as we emerged out of the forests into the plains. The great high buildings, whose towers overlooked the dense woodlands, and whose gigantic clusters formed large cities, diminished, together with the groves, until only little log cabins lay snugly in the bosom of the vast prairie. The cloud shadows which drifted about on the waving yellow of long-dried grasses thrilled me like the meeting of old friends.

At a small station, consisting of a single frame house with a rickety board walk around it, I alighted from the iron horse, just thirty miles from my mother and my brother Dawée. A strong hot wind seemed determined to blow my hat off, and return me to olden days when I roamed bareheaded over the hills. After the puffing engine of my train was gone, I stood on the platform in deep solitude. In the distance I saw the gently rolling land leap up into bare hills. At their bases a broad gray road was winding itself round about them until it came by the station. Among these hills I rode in a light conveyance, with a trusty driver, whose unkempt flaxen hair hung shaggy about his ears and his leather neck of reddish tan. From accident or decay he had lost one of his long front teeth.

Though I call him a paleface, his cheeks were of a brick red. His moist blue eyes, blurred and bloodshot, twitched involuntarily. For a long time he had driven through grass and snow from this solitary station to the Indian village. His weather-stained clothes fitted badly his warped shoulders. He was stooped, and his protruding chin, with its tuft of dry flax, nodded as monotonously as did the head of his faithful beast.

All the morning I looked about me, recognizing old familiar sky

lines of rugged bluffs and round-topped hills. By the roadside I caught glimpses of various plants whose sweet roots were delicacies among my people. When I saw the first cone-shaped wigwam, I could not help uttering an exclamation which caused my driver a sudden jump out of his drowsy nodding.

At noon, as we drove through the eastern edge of the reservation, I grew very impatient and restless. Constantly I wondered what my mother would say upon seeing her little daughter grown tall. I had not written her the day of my arrival, thinking I would surprise her. Crossing a ravine thicketed with low shrubs and plum bushes, we approached a large yellow acre of wild sunflowers. Just beyond this nature's garden we drew near to my mother's cottage. Close by the log cabin stood a little canvas-covered wigwam. The driver stopped in front of the open door, and in a long moment my mother appeared at the threshold.

I had expected her to run out to greet me, but she stood still, all the while staring at the weather-beaten man at my side. At length, when her loftiness became unbearable, I called to her, "Mother, why do you stop?"

This seemed to break the evil moment, and she hastened out to hold my head against her cheek.

"My daughter, what madness possessed you to bring home such a fellow?" she asked, pointing at the driver, who was fumbling in his pockets for change while he held the bill I gave him between his jagged teeth.

"Bring him! Why, no, mother, he has brought me! He is a driver!" I exclaimed.

Upon this revelation, my mother threw her arms about me and apologized for her mistaken inference. We laughed away the momentary hurt. Then she built a brisk fire on the ground in the tepee, and hung a blackened coffeepot on one of the prongs of a forked pole which leaned over the flames. Placing a pan on a heap of red embers, she baked some unleavened bread. This light luncheon she brought into the cabin, and arranged on a table covered with a checkered oilcloth.

My mother had never gone to school, and though she meant always to give up her own customs for such of the white man's ways as pleased her, she made only compromises. Her two windows, directly opposite each other, she curtained with a pink-flowered print. The naked logs were unstained, and rudely carved with the axe so as to fit

into one another. The sod roof was trying to boast of tiny sunflowers, the seeds of which had probably been planted by the constant wind. As I leaned my head against the logs, I discovered the peculiar odor that I could not forget. The rains had soaked the earth and roof so that the smell of damp clay was but the natural breath of such a dwelling.

"Mother, why is not your house cemented? Do you have no interest in a more comfortable shelter?" I asked, when the apparent inconveniences of her home seemed to suggest indifference on her part.

"You forget, my child, that I am now old, and I do not work with beads any more. Your brother Dawée, too, has lost his position, and we are left without means to buy even a morsel of food," she replied.

Dawée was a government clerk in our reservation when I last heard from him. I was surprised upon hearing what my mother said concerning his lack of employment. Seeing the puzzled expression on my face, she continued: "Dawée! Oh, has he not told you that the Great Father at Washington sent a white son to take your brother's pen from him? Since then Dawée has not been able to make use of the education the Eastern school has given him."

I found no words with which to answer satisfactorily. I found no reason with which to cool my inflamed feelings.

Dawée was a whole day's journey off on the prairie, and my mother did not expect him until the next day. We were silent.

When, at length, I raised my head to hear more clearly the moaning of the wind in the corner logs, I noticed the daylight streaming into the dingy room through several places where the logs fitted unevenly. Turning to my mother, I urged her to tell me more about Dawée's trouble, but she only said: "Well, my daughter, this village has been these many winters a refuge for white robbers. The Indian cannot complain to the Great Father in Washington without suffering outrage for it here. Dawée tried to secure justice for our tribe in a small matter, and today you see the folly of it."

Again, though she stopped to hear what I might say, I was silent.

"My child, there is only one source of justice, and I have been praying steadfastly to the Great Spirit to avenge our wrongs," she said, seeing I did not move my lips.

My shattered energy was unable to hold longer any faith, and I cried out desperately: "Mother, don't pray again! The Great Spirit does not care if we live or die! Let us not look for good or justice: then we shall not be disappointed!"

"Sh! my child, do not talk so madly. There is Taku Iyotan Wasaka,[1] to which I pray," she answered, as she stroked my head again as she used to do when I was a smaller child.

III
MY MOTHER'S CURSE UPON WHITE SETTLERS

One black night mother and I sat alone in the dim starlight, in front of our wigwam. We were facing the river, as we talked about the shrinking limits of the village. She told me about the poverty-stricken white settlers, who lived in caves dug in the long ravines of the high hills across the river.

A whole tribe of broad-footed white beggars had rushed hither to make claims on those wild lands. Even as she was telling this I spied a small glimmering light in the bluffs.

"That is a white man's lodge where you see the burning fire," she said. Then, a short distance from it, only a little lower than the first, was another light. As I became accustomed to the night, I saw more and more twinkling lights, here and there, scattered all along the wide black margin of the river.

Still looking toward the distant firelight, my mother continued: "My daughter, beware of the paleface. It was the cruel paleface who caused the death of your sister and your uncle, my brave brother. It is this same paleface who offers in one palm the holy papers, and with the other gives a holy baptism of firewater. He is the hypocrite who reads with one eye, 'Thou shalt not kill,' and with the other gloats upon the sufferings of the Indian race." Then suddenly discovering a new fire in the bluffs, she exclaimed, "Well, well, my daughter, there is the light of another white rascal!"

She sprang to her feet, and, standing firm beside her wigwam, she sent a curse upon those who sat around the hated white man's light. Raising her right arm forcibly into line with her eye, she threw her whole might into her doubled fist as she shot it vehemently at the strangers. Long she held her outstretched fingers toward the settler's lodge, as if an invisible power passed from them to the evil at which she aimed.

[1]An absolute Power.

IV

RETROSPECTION

Leaving my mother, I returned to the school in the East. As months passed over me, I slowly comprehended that the large army of white teachers in Indian schools had a larger missionary creed than I had suspected.

It was one which included self-preservation quite as much as Indian education. When I saw an opium-eater holding a position as teacher of Indians, I did not understand what good was expected, until a Christian in power replied that this pumpkin-colored creature had a feeble mother to support. An inebriate paleface sat stupid in a doctor's chair, while Indian patients carried their ailments to untimely graves, because his fair wife was dependent upon him for her daily food.

I find it hard to count that white man a teacher who tortured an ambitious Indian youth by frequently reminding the brave changeling that he was nothing but a "government pauper."

Though I burned with indignation upon discovering on every side instances no less shameful than those I have mentioned, there was no present help. Even the few rare ones who have worked nobly for my race were powerless to choose workmen like themselves. To be sure, a man was sent from the Great Father to inspect Indian schools, but what he saw was usually the students' sample work *made* for exhibition. I was nettled by this sly cunning of the workmen who hookwinked the Indian's pale Father at Washington.

My illness, which prevented the conclusion of my college course, together with my mother's stories of the encroaching frontier settlers, left me in no mood to strain my eyes in searching for latent good in my white co-workers.

At this stage of my own evolution, I was ready to curse men of small capacity for being the dwarfs their God had made them. In the process of my education I had lost all consciousness of the nature world about me. Thus, when a hidden rage took me to the small white-walled prison which I then called my room, I unknowingly turned away from my one salvation.

Alone in my room, I sat like the petrified Indian woman of whom my mother used to tell me. I wished my heart's burdens would turn me to unfeeling stone. But alive, in my tomb, I was destitute!

For the white man's papers I had given up my faith in the Great Spirit. For these same papers I had forgotten the healing in trees and

brooks. On account of my mother's simple view of life, and my lack of any, I gave her up, also. I made no friends among the race of people I loathed. Like a slender tree, I had been uprooted from my mother, nature, and God. I was shorn of my branches, which had waved in sympathy and love for home and friends. The natural coat of bark which had protected my oversensitive nature was scraped off to the very quick.

Now a cold bare pole I seemed to be, planted in a strange earth. Still, I seemed to hope a day would come when my mute aching head, reared upward to the sky, would flash a zigzag lightning across the heavens. With this dream of vent for a long-pent consciousness, I walked again amid the crowds.

At last, one weary day in the schoolroom, a new idea presented itself to me. It was a new way of solving the problem of my inner self. I liked it. Thus I resigned my position as teacher; and now I am in an Eastern city, following the long course of study I have set for myself. Now, as I look back upon the recent past, I see it from a distance, as a whole. I remember how, from morning till evening, many specimens of civilized peoples visited the Indian school. The city folks with canes and eyeglasses, the countrymen with sunburnt cheeks and clumsy feet, forgot their relative social ranks in an ignorant curiosity. Both sorts of these Christian palefaces were alike astounded at seeing the children of savage warriors so docile and industrious.

As answers to their shallow inquiries they received the students' sample work to look upon. Examining the neatly figured pages, and gazing upon the Indian girls and boys bending over their books, the white visitors walked out of the schoolhouse well satisfied: they were educating the children of the red man! They were paying a liberal fee to the government employees in whose able hands lay the small forest of Indian timber.

In this fashion many have passed idly through the Indian schools during the last decade, afterward to boast of their charity to the North American Indian. But few there are who have paused to question whether real life or long-lasting death lies beneath this semblance of civilization.

THE GREAT SPIRIT

When the spirit swells my breast I love to roam leisurely among the green hills; or sometimes, sitting on the brink of the murmuring Missouri, I marvel at the great blue overhead. With half-closed eyes I watch the huge cloud shadows in their noiseless play upon the high bluffs opposite me, while into my ear ripple the sweet, soft cadences of the river's song. Folded hands lie in my lap, for the time forgot. My heart and I lie small upon the earth like a grain of throbbing sand. Drifting clouds and tinkling waters, together with the warmth of a genial summer day, bespeak with eloquence the loving Mystery round about us. During the idle while I sat upon the sunny river brink, I grew somewhat, though my response be not so clearly manifest as in the green grass fringing the edge of the high bluff back of me.

At length retracing the uncertain footpath scaling the precipitous embankment, I seek the level lands where grow the wild prairie flowers. And they, the lovely little folk, soothe my soul with their perfumed breath.

Their quaint round faces of varied hue convince the heart which leaps with glad surprise that they, too, are living symbols of omnipotent thought. With a child's eager eye I drink in the myriad star shapes wrought in luxuriant color upon the green. Beautiful is the spiritual essence they embody.

I leave them nodding in the breeze, but take along with me their impress upon my heart. I pause to rest me upon a rock embedded on the side of a foothill facing the low river bottom. Here the Stone-Boy, of whom the American aborigine tells, frolics about, shooting his baby arrows and shouting aloud with glee at the tiny shafts of lightning that flash from the flying arrow-beaks. What an ideal warrior he became, baffling the siege of the pests of all the land till he triumphed over their united attack. And here he lay,—Inyan our great-great-grandfather, older than the hill he rested on, older than the race of men who love to tell of his wonderful career.

Interwoven with the thread of this Indian legend of the rock, I fain would trace a subtle knowledge of the native folk which enabled them to recognize a kinship to any and all parts of this vast universe. By the leading of an ancient trail I move toward the Indian village.

With the strong, happy sense that both great and small are so surely enfolded in His magnitude that, without a miss, each has his allotted individual ground of opportunities, I am buoyant with good nature.

Yellow Breast, swaying upon the slender stem of a wild sunflower, warbles a sweet assurance of this as I pass near by. Breaking off the clear crystal song, he turns his wee head from side to side eyeing me wisely as slowly I plod with moccasined feet. Then again he yields himself to his song of joy. Flit, flit hither and yon, he fills the summer sky with his swift, sweet melody. And truly does it seem his vigorous freedom lies more in his little spirit than in his wing.

With these thoughts I reach the log cabin whither I am strongly drawn by the tie of a child to an aged mother. Out bounds my four-footed friend to meet me, frisking about my path with unmistakable delight. Chän is a black shaggy dog, "a thoroughbred little mongrel" of whom I am very fond. Chän seems to understand many words in Sioux, and will go to her mat even when I whisper the word, though generally I think she is guided by the tone of the voice. Often she tries to imitate the sliding inflection and long-drawn-out voice to the amusement of our guests, but her articulation is quite beyond my ear. In both my hands I hold her shaggy head and gaze into her large brown eyes. At once the dilated pupils contract into tiny black dots, as if the rougish spirit within would evade my questioning.

Finally resuming the chair at my desk I feel in keen sympathy with my fellow-creatures, for I seem to see clearly again that all are akin. The racial lines, which once were bitterly real, now serve nothing more than marking out a living mosaic of human beings. And even here men of the same color are like the ivory keys of one instrument where each resembles all the rest, yet varies from them in pitch and quality of voice. And those creatures who are for a time mere echoes of another's note are not unlike the fable of the thin sick man whose distorted shadow, dressed like a real creature, came to the old master to make him follow as a shadow. Thus with a compassion for all echoes in human guise, I greet the solemn-faced "native preacher" whom I find awaiting me. I listen with respect for God's creature, though he mouth most strangely the jangling phrases of a bigoted creed.

As our tribe is one large family, where every person is related to all the others, he addressed me:—

"Cousin, I came from the morning church service to talk with you."

"Yes?" I said interrogatively, as he paused for some word from me.

Shifting uneasily about in the straight-backed chair he sat upon, he began: "Every holy day (Sunday) I look about our little God's house, and not seeing you there, I am disappointed. This is why I come today. Cousin, as I watch you from afar, I see no unbecoming behavior and hear only good reports of you, which all the more burns me with the wish that you were a church member. Cousin, I was taught long years ago by kind missionaries to read the holy book. These godly men taught me also the folly of our old beliefs.

"There is one God who gives reward or punishment to the race of dead men. In the upper region the Christian dead are gathered in unceasing song and prayer. In the deep pit below, the sinful ones dance in torturing flames.

"Think upon these things, my cousin, and choose now to avoid the after-doom of hell fire!" Then followed a long silence in which he clasped tighter and unclasped again his interlocked fingers.

Like instantaneous lightning flashes came pictures of my own mother's making, for she, too, is now a follower of the new superstition.

"Knocking out the chinking of our log cabin, some evil hand thrust in a burning taper of braided dry grass, but failed of his intent, for the fire died out and the half-burned brand fell inward to the floor. Directly above it, on a shelf, lay the holy book. This is what we found after our return from a several days' visit. Surely some great power is hid in the sacred book!"

Brushing away from my eyes many like pictures, I offered midday meal to the converted Indian sitting wordless and with downcast face. No sooner had he risen from the table with "Cousin, I have relished it," than the church bell rang.

Thither he hurried forth with his afternoon sermon. I watched him as he hastened along, his eyes bent fast upon the dusty road till he disappeared at the end of a quarter of a mile.

The little incident recalled to mind the copy of a missionary paper brought to my notice a few days ago, in which a "Christian" pugilist commented upon a recent article of mine, grossly perverting the spirit of my pen. Still I would not forget that the pale-faced missionary and the hoodooed aborigine are both God's creatures, though small indeed their own conceptions of Infinite Love. A wee child toddling in a wonder world, I prefer to their dogma my excursions into the natural gardens where the voice of the Great Spirit is heard in the twittering

of birds, the rippling of mighty waters, and the sweet breathing of flowers.

Here, in a fleeting quiet, I am awakened by the fluttering robe of the Great Spirit. To my innermost consciousness the phenomenal universe is a royal mantle, vibrating with His divine breath. Caught in its flowing fringes are the spangles and oscillating brilliants of sun, moon, and stars.

THE SOFT-HEARTED SIOUX

Beside the open fire I sat within our tepee. With my red blanket wrapped tightly about my crossed legs, I was thinking of the coming season, my sixteenth winter. On either side of the wigwam were my parents. My father was whistling a tune between his teeth while polishing with his bare hand a red stone pipe he had recently carved. Almost in front of me, beyond the center fire, my old grandmother sat near the entranceway.

She turned her face toward her right and addressed most of her words to my mother. Now and then she spoke to me, but never did she allow her eye to rest upon her daughter's husband, my father. It was only upon rare occasions that my grandmother said anything to him. Thus his ears were open and ready to catch the smallest wish she might express. Sometimes when my grandmother had been saying things which pleased him, my father used to comment upon them. At other times, when he could not approve of what was spoken, he used to work or smoke silently.

On this night my old grandmother began her talk about me. Filling the bowl of her red stone pipe with dry willow bark, she looked across at me.

"My grandchild, you are tall and are no longer a little boy." Narrowing her old eyes, she asked, "My grandchild, when are you going to bring here a handsome young woman?" I stared into the fire rather than meet her gaze. Waiting for my answer, she stooped forward and through the long stem drew a flame into the red stone pipe.

I smiled while my eyes were still fixed upon the bright fire, but I said nothing in reply. Turning to my mother, she offered her the pipe. I glanced at my grandmother. The loose buckskin sleeve fell off at her elbow and showed a wrist covered with silver bracelets. Holding up the fingers of her left hand, she named off the desirable young women of our village.

"Which one, my grandchild, which one?" she questioned.

"Hoh!" I said, pulling at my blanket in confusion. "Not yet!" Here

my mother passed the pipe over the fire to my father. Then she, too, began speaking of what I should do.

"My son, be always active. Do not dislike a long hunt. Learn to provide much buffalo meat and many buckskins before you bring home a wife." Presently my father gave the pipe to my grandmother, and he took his turn in the exhortations.

"Ho, my son, I have been counting in my heart the bravest warriors of our people. There is not one of them who won his title in his sixteenth winter. My son, it is a great thing for some brave of sixteen winters to do."

Not a word had I to give in answer. I knew well the fame of my warrior father. He had earned the right of speaking such words, though even he himself was a brave only at my age. Refusing to smoke my grandmother's pipe because my heart was too much stirred by their words, and sorely troubled with a fear lest I should disappoint them, I arose to go. Drawing my blanket over my shoulders, I said, as I stepped toward the entranceway: "I go to hobble my pony. It is now late in the night."

II

Nine winters' snows had buried deep that night when my old grandmother, together with my father and mother, designed my future with the glow of a camp fire upon it.

Yet I did not grow up the warrior, huntsman, and husband I was to have been. At the mission school I learned it was wrong to kill. Nine winters I hunted for the soft heart of Christ, and prayed for the huntsmen who chased the buffalo on the plains.

In the autumn of the tenth year I was sent back to my tribe to preach Christianity to them. With the white man's Bible in my hand, and the white man's tender heart in my breast, I returned to my own people.

Wearing a foreigner's dress, I walked, a stranger, into my father's village.

Asking my way, for I had not forgotten my native tongue, an old man led me toward the tepee where my father lay. From my old companion I learned that my father had been sick many moons. As we drew near the tepee, I heard the chanting of a medicine-man within it. At once I wished to enter in and drive from my home the sorcerer

of the plains, but the old warrior checked me. "Ho, wait outside until the medicine-man leaves your father," he said. While talking he scanned me from head to feet. Then he retraced his steps toward the heart of the camping-ground.

My father's dwelling was on the outer limits of the round-faced village. With every heart-throb I grew more impatient to enter the wigwam.

While I turned the leaves of my Bible with nervous fingers, the medicine-man came forth from the dwelling and walked hurriedly away. His head and face were closely covered with the loose robe which draped his entire figure.

He was tall and large. His long strides I have never forgot. They seemed to me then the uncanny gait of eternal death. Quickly pocketing my Bible, I went into the tepee.

Upon a mat lay my father, with furrowed face and gray hair. His eyes and cheeks were sunken far into his head. His sallow skin lay thin upon his pinched nose and high cheekbones. Stooping over him, I took his fevered hand. How, Ate?" I greeted him. A light flashed from his listless eyes and his dried lips parted. "My son!" he murmured, in a feeble voice. Then again the wave of joy and recognition receded. He closed his eyes, and his hand dropped from my open palm to the ground.

Looking about, I saw an old woman sitting with bowed head. Shaking hands with her, I recognized my mother. I sat down between my father and mother as I used to do, but I did not feel at home. The place where my old grandmother used to sit was now unoccupied. With my mother I bowed my head. Alike our throats were choked and tears were streaming from our eyes; but far apart in spirit our ideas and faiths separated us. My grief was for the soul unsaved; and I thought my mother wept to see a brave man's body broken by sickness.

Useless was my attempt to change the faith in the medicine-man to that abstract power named God. Then one day I became righteously mad with anger that the medicine-man should thus ensnare my father's soul. And when he came to chant his sacred songs I pointed toward the door and bade him go! The man's eyes glared upon me for an instant. Slowly gathering his robe about him, he turned his back upon the sick man and stepped out of our wigwam. "Ha, ha, ha! my son, I can not live without the medicine-man!" I heard my father cry when the sacred man was gone.

III

On a bright day, when the winged seeds of the prairie-grass were flying hither and thither, I walked solemnly toward the centre of the camping-ground. My heart beat hard and irregularly at my side. Tighter I grasped the sacred book I carried under my arm. Now was the beginning of life's work.

Though I knew it would be hard, I did not once feel that failure was to be my reward. As I stepped unevenly on the rolling ground, I thought of the warriors soon to wash off their war-paints and follow me.

At length I reached the place where the people had assembled to hear me preach. In a large circle men and women sat upon the dry red grass. Within the ring I stood, with the white man's Bible in my hand. I tried to tell them of the soft heart of Christ.

In silence the vast circle of bareheaded warriors sat under an afternoon sun. At last, wiping the wet from my brow, I took my place in the ring. The hush of the assembly filled me with great hope.

I was turning my thoughts upward to the sky in gratitude, when a stir called me to earth again.

A tall, strong man arose. His loose robe hung in folds over his right shoulder. A pair of snapping black eyes fastened themselves like the poisonous fangs of a serpent upon me. He was the medicine-man. A tremor played about my heart and a chill cooled the fire in my veins.

Scornfully he pointed a long forefinger in my direction and asked:

"What loyal son is he who, returning to his father's people, wears a foreigner's dress?" He paused a moment, and then continued: "The dress of that foreigner of whom a story says he bound a native of our land, and heaping dry sticks around him, kindled a fire at his feet!" Waving his hand toward me, he exclaimed, "Here is the traitor to his people!"

I was helpless. Before the eyes of the crowd the cunning magician turned my honest heart into a vile nest of treachery. Alas! the people frowned as they looked upon me.

"Listen!" he went on. "Which one of you who have eyed the young man can see through his bosom and warn the people of the nest of young snakes hatching there? Whose ear was so acute that he caught the hissing of snakes whenever the young man opened his mouth? This one has not only proven false to you, but even to the Great Spirit who made him. He is a fool! Why do you sit here giving ear to a

foolish man who could not defend his people because he fears to kill, who could not bring venison to renew the life of his sick father? With his prayers, let him drive away the enemy! With his soft heart, let him keep off starvation! We shall go elsewhere to dwell upon an untainted ground."

With this he disbanded the people. When the sun lowered in the west and the winds were quiet, the village of cone-shaped tepees was gone. The medicine-man had won the hearts of the people.

Only my father's dwelling was left to mark the fighting-ground.

IV

From a long night at my father's bedside I came out to look upon the morning. The yellow sun hung equally between the snow-covered land and the cloudless blue sky. The light of the new day was cold. The strong breath of winter crusted the snow and fitted crystal shells over the rivers and lakes. As I stood in front of the tepee, thinking of the vast prairies which separated us from our tribe, and wondering if the high sky likewise separated the soft-hearted Son of God from us, the icy blast from the North blew through my hair and skull. My neglected hair had grown long and fell upon my neck.

My father had not risen from his bed since the day the medicine-man led the people away. Though I read from the Bible and prayed beside him upon my knees, my father would not listen. Yet I believed my prayers were not unheeded in heaven.

"Ha, ha, ha! my son," my father groaned upon the first snowfall. "My son, our food is gone. There is no one to bring me meat! My son, your soft heart has unfitted you for everything!" Then covering his face with the buffalo-robe, he said no more. Now while I stood out in that cold winter morning, I was starving. For two days I had not seen any food. But my own cold and hunger did not harass my soul as did the whining cry of the sick old man.

Stepping again into the tepee, I untied my snow-shoes, which were fastened to the tent-poles.

My poor mother, watching by the sick one, and faithfully heaping wood upon the centre fire, spoke to me:

"My son, do not fail again to bring your father meat, or he will starve to death."

"How, Ina," I answered, sorrowfully. From the tepee I started

forth again to hunt food for my aged parents. All day I tracked the white level lands in vain. Nowhere, nowhere were there any other footprints but my own! In the evening of this third fast-day I came back without meat. Only a bundle of sticks for the fire I brought on my back. Dropping the wood outside, I lifted the door-flap and set one foot within the tepee.

There I grew dizzy and numb. My eyes swam in tears. Before me lay my old grayhaired father sobbing like a child. In his horny hands he clutched the buffalo-robe, and with his teeth he was gnawing off the edges. Chewing the dry stiff hair and buffalo-skin, my father's eyes sought my hands. Upon seeing them empty, he cried out:

"My son, your soft heart will let me starve before you bring me meat! Two hills eastward stand a herd of cattle. Yet you will see me die before you bring me food!"

Leaving my mother lying with covered head upon her mat, I rushed out into the night.

With a strange warmth in my heart and swiftness in my feet, I climbed over the first hill, and soon the second one. The moonlight upon the white country showed me a clear path to the white man's cattle. With my hand upon the knife in my belt, I leaned heavily against the fence while counting the herd.

Twenty in all I numbered. From among them I chose the best-fattened creature. Leaping over the fence, I plunged my knife into it.

My long knife was sharp, and my hands, no more fearful and slow, slashed off choice chunks of warm flesh. Bending under the meat I had taken for my starving father, I hurried across the prairie.

Toward home I fairly ran with the life-giving food I carried upon my back. Hardly had I climbed the second hill when I heard sounds coming after me. Faster and faster I ran with my load for my father, but the sounds were gaining upon me. I heard the clicking of snow-shoes and the squeaking of the leather straps at my heels; yet I did not turn to see what pursued me, for I was intent upon reaching my father. Suddenly like thunder an angry voice shouted curses and threats into my ear! A rough hand wrenched my shoulder and took the meat from me! I stopped struggling to run. A deafening whir filled my head. The moon and stars began to move. Now the white prairie was sky, and the stars lay under my feet. Now again they were turning. At last the starry blue rose up into place. The noise in my ears was still. A great quiet filled the air. In my hand I found my long knife dripping with blood. At my feet a man's figure lay prone in

blood-red snow. The horrible scene about me seemed a trick of my senses, for I could not understand it was real. Looking long upon the blood-stained snow, the load of meat for my starving father reached my recognition at last. Quickly I tossed it over my shoulder and started again homeward.

Tired and haunted I reached the door of the wigwam. Carrying the food before me, I entered with it into the tepee.

"Father, here is food!" I cried, as I dropped the meat near my mother. No answer came. Turning about, I beheld my gray-haired father dead! I saw by the unsteady firelight an old gray-haired skeleton lying rigid and stiff.

Out into the open I started, but the snow at my feet became bloody.

V

On the day after my father's death, having led my mother to the camp of the medicine-man, I gave myself up to those who were searching for the murderer of the paleface.

They bound me hand and foot. Here in this cell I was placed four days ago.

The shrieking winter winds have followed me hither. Rattling the bars, they howl unceasingly: "Your soft heart! your soft heart will see me die before you bring me food!" Hark! something is clanking the chain on the door. It is being opened. From the dark night without a black figure crosses the threshold. * * * It is the guard. He comes to warn me of my fate. He tells me that tomorrow I must die. In his stern face I laugh aloud. I do not fear death.

Yet I wonder who shall come to welcome me in the realm of strange sight. Will the loving Jesus grant me pardon and give my soul a soothing sleep? or will my warrior father greet me and receive me as his son? Will my spirit fly upward to a happy heaven? or shall I sink into the bottomless pit, an outcast from a God of infinite love?

Soon, soon I shall know, for now I see the east is growing red. My heart is strong. My face is calm. My eyes are dry and eager for new scenes. My hands hang quietly at my side. Serene and brave, my soul awaits the men to perch me on the gallows for another flight. I go.

THE TRIAL PATH

It was an autumn night on the plain. The smoke-lapels of the cone-shaped tepee flapped gently in the breeze. From the low night sky, with its myriad fire points, a large bright star peeped in at the smoke-hole of the wigwam between its fluttering lapels, down upon two Dakotas talking in the dark. The mellow stream from the star above, a maid of twenty summers, on a bed of sweetgrass, drank in with her wakeful eyes. On the opposite side of the tepee, beyond the centre fireplace, the grandmother spread her rug. Though once she had lain down, the telling of a story has aroused her to a sitting posture.

Her eyes are tight closed. With a thin palm she strokes her wind-shorn hair.

"Yes, my grandchild, the legend says the large bright stars are wise old warriors, and the small dim ones are handsome young braves," she reiterates, in a high, tremulous voice.

"Then this one peeping in at the smoke-hole yonder is my dear old grandfather," muses the young woman, in long-drawn-out words.

Her soft rich voice floats through the darkness within the tepee, over the cold ashes heaped on the centre fire, and passes into the ear of the toothless old woman, who sits dumb in silent reverie. Thence it flies on swifter wing over many winter snows, till at last it cleaves the warm light atmosphere of her grandfather's youth. From there her grandmother made answer:

"Listen! I am young again. It is the day of your grandfather's death. The elder one, I mean, for there were two of them. They were like twins, though they were not brothers. They were friends, inseparable! All things, good and bad, they shared together, save one, which made them mad. In that heated frenzy the younger man slew his most intimate friend. He killed his elder brother, for long had their affection made them kin."

The voice of the old woman broke. Swaying her stooped shoulders to and fro as she sat upon her feet, she muttered vain exclamations beneath her breath. Her eyes, closed tight against the night, beheld behind them the light of bygone days. They saw again a rolling black cloud spread itself over the land. Her ear heard the deep rumbling of a tempest in the west. She bent low a cowering head, while angry

259

thunder-birds shrieked across the sky. "Hejä! heyä!" (No! no!) groaned the toothless grandmother at the fury she had awakened. But the glorious peace afterward, when yellow sunshine made the people glad, now lured her memory onward through the storm.

"How fast, how loud my heart beats as I listen to the messenger's horrible tale!" she ejaculates. "From the fresh grave of the murdered man he hurried to our wigwam. Deliberately crossing his bare shins, he sat down unbidden beside my father, smoking a long-stemmed pipe. He had scarce caught his breath when, panting, he began:

" 'He was an only son, and a much-adored brother.'

"With wild, suspecting eyes he glanced at me as if I were in league with the man-killer, my lover. My father, exhaling sweet-scented smoke, assented—'How.' Then interrupting the 'Eya' on the lips of the round-eyed tale-bearer, he asked, 'My friend, will you smoke?' He took the pipe by its red-stone bowl, and pointed the long slender stem toward the man. 'Yes, yes, my friend,' replied he, and reached out a long brown arm.

"For many heart-throbs he puffed out the blue smoke, which hung like a cloud between us. But even through the smoke-mist I saw his sharp black eyes glittering toward me. I longed to ask what doom awaited the young murderer, but dared not open my lips, lest I burst forth into screams instead. My father plied the question. Returning the pipe, the man replied: 'Oh, the chieftain and his chosen men have had counsel together. They have agreed it is not safe to allow a man-killer loose in our midst. He who kills one of our tribe is an enemy, and must suffer the fate of a foe.'

"My temples throbbed like a pair of hearts!

"While I listened, a crier passed by my father's tepee. Mounted, and swaying with his pony's steps, he proclaimed in a loud voice these words (hark! I hear them now!): "Ho-po! Give ear, all you people. A terrible deed is done. Two friends—ay, brothers in heart—have quarreled together. Now one lies buried on the hill, while the other sits, a dreaded man-killer, within his dwelling." Says our chieftain: "He who kills one of our tribe commits the offense of an enemy. As such he must be tried. Let the father of the dead man choose the mode of torture or taking of life. He has suffered livid pain, and he alone can judge how great the punishment must be to avenge his wrong." It is done.

" 'Come, every one, to witness the judgment of a father upon him who was once his son's best friend. A wild pony is now lassoed. The

man-killer must mount and ride the ranting beast. Stand you all in two parallel lines from the centre tepee of the bereaved family to the wigwam opposite in the great outer ring. Between you, in the wide space, is the given trial-way. From the outer circle the rider must mount and guide his pony toward the centre tepee. If, having gone the entire distance, the man-killer gains the centre tepee still sitting on the pony's back, his life is spared and pardon given. But should he fall, then he himself has chosen death.'

"The crier's words now cease. A lull holds the village breathless. Then hurrying feet tear along, swish, swish, through the tall grass. Sobbing women hasten toward the trialway. The muffled groan of the round camp-ground is unbearable. With my face hid in the folds of my blanket, I run with the crowd toward the open place in the outer circle of our village. In a moment the two long files of solemn-faced people mark the path of the public trial. Ah! I see strong men trying to lead the lassoed pony, pitching and rearing, with white foam flying from his mouth. I choke with pain as I recognize my handsome lover desolately alone, striding with set face toward the lassoed pony. 'Do not fall! Choose life and me!' I cry in my breast, but over my lips I hold my thick blanket.

"In an instant he has leaped astride the frightened beast, and the men have let go their hold. Like an arrow sprung from a strong bow, the pony, with extended nostrils, plunges halfway to the centre tepee. With all his might the rider draws the strong reins in. The pony halts with wooden legs. The rider is thrown forward by force, but does not fall. Now the maddened creature pitches, with flying heels. The line of men and women sways outward. Now it is back in place, safe from the kicking, snorting thing.

"The pony is fierce, with its large black eyes bulging out of their sockets. With humped back and nose to the ground, it leaps into the air. I shut my eyes. I can not see him fall.

"A loud shout goes up from the hoarse throats of men and women. I look. So! The wild horse is conquered. My lover dismounts at the doorway of the centre wigwam. The pony, wet with sweat and shaking with exhaustion, stands like a guilty dog at his master's side. Here at the entranceway of the tepee sit the bereaved father, mother, and sister. The old warrior father rises. Stepping forward two long strides, he grasps the hand of the murderer of his only son. Holding it so the people can see, he cries, with compassionate voice, 'My son!' A murmur of surprise sweeps like a puff of sudden wind along the lines.

"The mother, with swollen eyes, with her hair cut square with her shoulders, now rises. Hurrying to the young man, she takes his right hand. 'My son!' she greets him. But on the second word her voice shook, and she turned away in sobs.

"The young people rivet their eyes upon the young woman. She does not stir. With bowed head, she sits motionless. The old warrior speaks to her. 'Shake hands with the young brave, my little daughter. He was your brother's friend for many years. Now he must be both friend and brother to you.'

"Hereupon the girl rises. Slowly reaching out her slender hand, she cries, with twitching lips, 'My brother!' The trial ends."

"Grandmother!" exploded the girl on the bed of sweet-grass. "Is this true?"

"Tosh!" answered the grandmother, with a warmth in her voice. "It is all true. During the fifteen winters of our wedded life many ponies passed from our hands, but this little winner, Ohiyesa, was a constant member of our family. At length, on that sad day your grandfather died, Ohiyesa was killed at the grave."

Though the various groups of stars which move across the sky, marking the passing of time, told how the night was in its zenith, the old Dakota woman ventured an explanation of the burial ceremony.

"My grandchild, I have scarce ever breathed the sacred knowledge in my heart. Tonight I must tell you one of them. Surely you are old enough to understand.

"Our wise medicine-man said I did well to hasten Ohiyesa after his master. Perchance on the journey along the ghostpath your grandfather will weary, and in his heart wish for his pony. The creature, already bound on the spirit-trail, will be drawn by that subtle wish. Together master and beast will enter the next camp-ground."

The woman ceased her talking. But only the deep breathing of the girl broke the quiet, for now the night wind had lulled itself to sleep.

"Hinnu! hinnu! Asleep! I have been talking in the dark, unheard. I did wish the girl would plant in her heart this sacred tale," muttered she, in a querulous voice.

Nestling into her bed of sweet-scented grass, she dozed away into another dream. Still the guardian star in the night sky beamed compassionately down upon the little tepee on the plain.

A Warrior's Daughter

In the afternoon shadow of a large tepee, with red-painted smoke lapels, sat a warrior father with crossed shins. His head was so poised that his eye swept easily the vast level land to the eastern horizon line.

He was the chieftain's bravest warrior. He had won by heroic deeds the privilege of staking his wigwam within the great circle of tepees.

He was also one of the most generous gift givers to the toothless old people. For this he was entitled to the red-painted smoke lapels on his cone-shaped dwelling. He was proud of his honors. He never wearied of rehearsing nightly his own brave deeds. Though by wigwam fires he prated much of his high rank and widespread fame, his great joy was a wee black-eyed daughter of eight sturdy winters. Thus as he sat upon the soft grass, with his wife at his side, bent over her bead work, he was singing a dance song, and beat lightly the rhythm with his slender hands.

His shrewd eyes softened with pleasure as he watched the easy movements of the small body dancing on the green before him.

Tusee is taking her first dancing lesson. Her tightly-braided hair curves over both brown ears like a pair of crooked little horns which glisten in the summer sun.

With her snugly moccasined feet close together, and a wee hand at her belt to stay the long string of beads which hang from her bare neck, she bends her knees gently to the rhythm of her father's voice.

Now she ventures upon the earnest movement, slightly upward and sidewise, in a circle. At length the song drops into a closing cadence, and the little woman, clad in beaded deerskin, sits down beside the elder one. Like her mother, she sits upon her feet. In a brief moment the warrior repeats the last refrain. Again Tusee springs to her feet and dances to the swing of the few final measures.

Just as the dance was finished, an elderly man, with short, thick hair loose about his square shoulders, rode into their presence from the rear, and leaped lightly from his pony's back. Dropping the rawhide rein to the ground, he tossed himself lazily on the grass. "Hunhe, you have returned soon," said the warrior, while extending a hand to his little daughter.

Quickly the child ran to her father's side and cuddled close to him,

while he tenderly placed a strong arm about her. Both father and child, eyeing the figure on the grass, waited to hear the man's report.

"It is true," began the man, with a stranger's accent. "This is the night of the dance."

"Hunha!" muttered the warrior with some surprise.

Propping himself upon his elbows, the man raised his face. His features were of the Southern type. From an enemy's camp he was taken captive long years ago by Tusee's father. But the unusual qualities of the slave had won the Sioux warrior's heart, and for the last three winters the man had had his freedom. He was made real man again. His hair was allowed to grow. However, he himself had chosen to stay in the warrior's family.

"Hunha!" again ejaculated the warrior father. Then turning to his little daughter, he asked, "Tusee, do you hear that?"

"Yes, father, and I am going to dance tonight!"

With these words she bounded out of his arm and frolicked about in glee. Hereupon the proud mother's voice rang out in a chiding laugh.

"My child, in honor of your first dance your father must give a generous gift. His ponies are wild, and roam beyond the great hill. Pray, what has he fit to offer?" she questioned, the pair of puzzled eyes fixed upon her.

"A pony from the herd, mother, a fleetfooted pony from the herd!" Tusee shouted with sudden inspiration.

Pointing a small forefinger toward the man lying on the grass, she cried, "Uncle, you will go after the pony tomorrow!" And pleased with her solution of the problem, she skipped wildly about. Her childish faith in her elders was not conditioned by a knowledge of human limitations, but thought all things possible to grown-ups.

"Hähob!" exclaimed the mother, with a rising inflection, implying by the expletive that her child's buoyant spirit be not weighted with a denial.

Quickly to the hard request the man replied, "How! I go if Tusee tells me so!"

This delighted the little one, whose black eyes brimmed over with light. Standing in front of the strong man, she clapped her small, brown hands with joy.

"That makes me glad! My heart is good! Go, uncle, and bring a handsome pony!" she cried. In an instant she would have frisked away, but an impulse held her tilting where she stood. In the man's own

tongue, for he had taught her many words and phrases, she exploded, "Thank you, good uncle, thank you!" then tore away from sheer excess of glee.

The proud warrior father, smiling and narrowing his eyes, muttered approval, "Howo! Hechetu!"

Like her mother, Tusee has finely pencilled eyebrows and slightly extended nostrils; but in her sturdiness of form she resembles her father.

A loyal daughter, she sits within her tepee making beaded deerskins for her father, while he longs to stave off her every suitor as all unworthy of his old heart's pride. But Tusee is not alone in her dwelling. Near the entranceway a young brave is half reclining on a mat. In silence he watches the petals of a wild rose growing on the soft buckskin. Quickly the young woman slips the beads on the silvery sinew thread, and works them into the pretty flower design. Finally, in a low, deep voice, the young man begins:

"The sun is far past the zenith. It is now only a man's height above the western edge of land. I hurried hither to tell you tomorrow I join the war party."

He pauses for reply, but the maid's head drops lower over her deerskin, and her lips are more firmly drawn together. He continues:

"Last night in the moonlight I met your warrior father. He seemed to know I had just stepped forth from your tepee. I fear he did not like it, for though I greeted him, he was silent. I halted in his pathway. With what boldness I dared, while my heart was beating hard and fast, I asked him for his only daughter.

"Drawing himself erect to his tallest height, and gathering his loose robe more closely about his proud figure, he flashed a pair of piercing eyes upon me.

" 'Young man,' said he, with a cold, slow voice that chilled me to the marrow of my bones, 'hear me. Naught but an enemy's scalp-lock, plucked fresh with your own hand, will buy Tusee for your wife.' Then he turned on his heel and stalked away."

Tusee thrusts her work aside. With earnest eyes she scans her lover's face.

"My father's heart is really kind. He would know if you are brave and true," murmured the daughter, who wished no ill-will between her two loved ones.

Then rising to go, the youth holds out a right hand. "Grasp my

hand once firmly before I go, Hoye. Pray tell me, will you wait and watch for my return?"

Tusee only nods assent, for mere words are vain.

At early dawn the round camp-ground awakes into song. Men and women sing of bravery and of triumph. They inspire the swelling breasts of the painted warriors mounted on prancing ponies bedecked with the green branches of trees.

Riding slowly around the great ring of cone-shaped tepees, here and there, a loud-singing warrior swears to avenge a former wrong, and thrusts a bare brown arm against the purple east, calling the Great Spirit to hear his vow. All having made the circuit, the singing war party gallops away southward.

Astride their ponies laden with food and deerskins, brave elderly women follow after their warriors. Among the foremost rides a young woman in elaborately beaded buckskin dress. Proudly mounted, she curbs with the single rawhide loop a wild-eyed pony.

It is Tusee on her father's warhorse. Thus the war party of Indian men and their faithful women vanish beyond the southern skyline.

A day's journey brings them very near the enemy's borderland. Nightfall finds a pair of twin tepees nestled in a deep ravine. Within one lounge the painted warriors, smoking their pipes and telling weird stories by the firelight, while in the other watchful women crouch uneasily about their center fire.

By the first gray light in the east the tepees are banished. They are gone. The warriors are in the enemy's camp, breaking dreams with their tomahawks. The women are hid away in secret places in the long thicketed ravine.

The day is far spent, the red sun is low over the west.

At length straggling warriors return, one by one, to the deep hollow. In the twilight they number their men. Three are missing. Of these absent ones two are dead; but the third one, a young man, is a captive to the foe.

"He-he!" lament the warriors, taking food in haste.

In silence each woman, with long strides, hurries to and fro, tying large bundles on her pony's back. Under cover of night the war party must hasten homeward. Motionless, with bowed head, sits a woman in her hiding-place. She grieves for her lover.

In bitterness of spirit she hears the warriors' murmuring words. With set teeth she plans to cheat the hated enemy of their captive. In the meanwhile low signals are given, and the war party, unaware of

Tusee's absence, steal quietly away. The soft thud of pony-hoofs grows fainter and fainter. The gradual hush of the empty ravine whirrs noisily in the ear of the young woman. Alert for any sound of footfalls nigh, she holds her breath to listen. Her right hand rests on a long knife in her belt. Ah, yes, she knows where her pony is hid, but not yet has she need of him. Satisfied that no danger is nigh, she prowls forth from her place of hiding. With a panther's tread and pace she climbs the high ridge beyond the low ravine. From thence she spies the enemy's camp-fires.

Rooted to the barren bluff the slender woman's figure stands on the pinnacle of night, outlined against a starry sky. The cool night breeze wafts to her burning ear snatches of song and drum. With desperate hate she bites her teeth.

Tusee beckons the stars to witness. With impassioned voice and uplifted face she pleads:

"Great Spirit, speed me to my lover's rescue! Give me swift cunning for a weapon this night! All-powerful Spirit, grant me my warrior-father's heart, strong to slay a foe and mighty to save a friend!"

In the midst of the enemy's camp-ground, underneath a temporary dance-house, are men and women in gala-day dress. It is late in the night, but the merry warriors bend and bow their nude, painted bodies before a bright center fire. To the lusty men's voices and the rhythmic throbbing drum, they leap and rebound with feathered headgears waving.

Women with red-painted cheeks and long, braided hair sit in a large half-circle against the willow railing. They, too, join in the singing, and rise to dance with their victorious warriors.

Amid this circular dance arena stands a prisoner bound to a post, haggard with shame and sorrow. He hangs his disheveled head.

He stares with unseeing eyes upon the bare earth at his feet. With jeers and smirking faces the dancers mock the Dakota captive. Rowdy braves and small boys hoot and yell in derision.

Silent among the noisy mob, a tall woman, leaning both elbows on the round willow railing, peers into the lighted arena. The dancing center fire shines bright into her handsome face, intensifying the night in her dark eyes. It breaks into myriad points upon her beaded dress. Unmindful of the surging throng jostling her at either side, she glares in upon the hateful, scoffing men. Suddenly she turns her head. Tittering maids whisper near her ear:

"There! There! See him now, sneering in the captive's face. 'Tis he

who sprang upon the young man and dragged him by his long hair to yonder post. See! He is handsome! How gracefully he dances!"

The silent young woman looks toward the bound captive. She sees a warrior, scarce older than the captive, flourishing a tomahawk in the Dakota's face. A burning rage darts forth from her eyes and brands him for a victim of revenge. Her heart mutters within her breast, "Come, I wish to meet you, vile foe, who captured my lover and tortures him now with a living death."

Here the singers hush their voices, and the dancers scatter to their various resting-places along the willow ring. The victor gives a reluctant last twirl of his tomahawk, then, like the others, he leaves the center ground. With head and shoulders swaying from side to side, he carries a high-pointing chin toward the willow railing. Sitting down upon the ground with crossed legs, he fans himself with an outspread turkey wing.

Now and then he stops his haughty blinking to peep out of the corners of his eyes. He hears some one clearing her throat gently. It is unmistakably for his ear. The wing-fan swings irregularly to and fro. At length he turns a proud face over a bare shoulder and beholds a handsome woman smiling.

"Ah, she would speak to a hero!" thumps his heart wildly.

The singers raise their voices in unison. The music is irresistible. Again lunges the victor into the open arena. Again he leers into the captive's face. At every interval between the songs he returns to his resting-place. Here the young woman awaits him. As he approaches she smiles boldly into his eyes. He is pleased with her face and her smile.

Waving his wing-fan spasmodically in front of his face, he sits with his ears pricked up. He catches a low whisper. A hand taps him lightly on the shoulder. The handsome woman speaks to him in his own tongue. "Come out into the night. I wish to tell you who I am."

He must know what sweet words of praise the handsome woman has for him. With both hands he spreads the meshes of the loosely woven willows, and crawls out unnoticed into the dark.

Before him stands the young woman. Beckoning him with a slender hand, she steps backward, away from the light and the restless throng of onlookers. He follows with impatient strides. She quickens her pace. He lengthens his strides. Then suddenly the woman turns from him and darts away with amazing speed. Clinching his fists and biting

his lower lip, the young man runs after the fleeing woman. In his maddened pursuit he forgets the dance arena.

Beside a cluster of low bushes the woman halts. The young man, panting for breath and plunging headlong forward, whispers loud, "Pray tell me, are you a woman or an evil spirit to lure me away?"

Turning on heels firmly planted in the earth, the woman gives a wild spring forward, like a panther for its prey. In a husky voice she hissed between her teeth, "I am a Dakota woman!"

From her unerring long knife the enemy falls heavily at her feet. The Great Spirit heard Tusee's prayer on the hilltop. He gave her a warrior's strong heart to lessen the foe by one.

A bent old woman's figure, with a bundle like a grandchild slung on her back, walks round and round the dance-house. The wearied onlookers are leaving in twos and threes. The tired dancers creep out of the willow railing, and some go out at the entrance way, till the singers, too, rise from the drum and are trudging drowsily homeward. Within the arena the center fire lies broken in red embers. The night no longer lingers about the willow railing, but, hovering into the dance-house, covers here and there a snoring man whom sleep has overpowered where he sat.

The captive in his tight-binding rawhide ropes hangs in hopeless despair. Close about him the gloom of night is slowly crouching. Yet the last red, crackling embers cast a faint light upon his long black hair, and, shining through the thick mats, caress his wan face with undying hope.

Still about the dance house the old woman prowls. Now the embers are gray with ashes.

The old bent woman appears at the entrance way. With a cautious, groping foot she enters. Whispering between her teeth a lullaby for her sleeping child in her blanket, she searches for something forgotten.

Noisily snored the dreaming men in the darkest parts. As the lisping old woman draws nigh, the captive again opens his eyes.

A forefinger she presses to her lip. The young man arouses himself from his stupor. His senses belie him. Before his wide-open eyes the old bent figure straightens into its youthful stature. Tusee herself is beside him. With a stroke upward and downward she severs the cruel cords with her sharp blade. Dropping her blanket from her shoulders, so that it hangs from her girdled waist like a skirt, she shakes the large bundle into a light shawl for her lover. Quickly she spreads it over his bare back.

"Come!" she whispers, and turns to go; but the young man, numb and helpless, staggers nigh to falling.

The sight of his weakness makes her strong. A mighty power thrills her body. Stooping beneath his outstretched arms grasping at the air for support, Tusee lifts him upon her broad shoulders. With half-running, triumphant steps she carries him away into the open night.

A DREAM OF HER GRANDFATHER

Her grandfather was a Dakota "medicine man." Among the Indians of his day he was widely known for his successful healing work. He was one of the leading men of the tribe and came to Washington, D.C., with one of the first delegations relative to affairs concerning the Indian people and the United States government.

His was the first band of the Great Sioux Nation to make treaties with the government in the hope of bringing about an amicable arrangement between the red and white Americans. The journey to the nation's capital was made almost entirely on pony-back, there being no railroads, and the Sioux delegation was beset with many hardships on the trail. His visit to Washington, in behalf of peace among men, proved to be his last earthly mission. From a sudden illness, he died and was buried here.

When his small granddaughter grew up she learned the white man's tongue, and followed in the footsteps of her grandfather to the very seat of government to carry on his humanitarian work. Though her days were filled with problems for welfare work among her people, she had a strange dream one night during her stay in Washington. The dream was this: Returning from an afternoon out, she found a large cedar chest had been delivered to her home in her absence. She sniffed the sweet perfume of the red wood, which reminded her of the breath of the forest,—and admired the box so neatly made, without trimmings. It looked so clean, strong and durable in its native genuineness. With elation, she took the tag in her hand and read her name aloud. "Who sent me this cedar chest?" she asked, and was told it came from her grandfather.

Wondering what gift it could be her grandfather wished now to confer upon her, wholly disregarding his death years ago, she was all eagerness to open the mystery chest.

She remembered her childhood days and the stories she loved to hear about the unusual powers of her grandfather,—recalled how she, the wee girl, had coveted the medicine bags, beaded and embroidered in porcupine quills, in symbols designed by the great "medicine man,"

271

her grandfather. Well did she remember her merited rebuke that such things were never made for relics. Treasures came in due time to those ready to receive them.

In great expectancy, she lifted the heavy lid of the cedar chest. "Oh!" she exclaimed, with a note of disappointment, seeing no beaded Indian regalia or trinkets. "Why does my grandfather send such a light gift in a heavy, large box?" She was mystified and much perplexed.

The gift was a fantastic thing, of texture far more delicate than a spider's filmy web. It was a vision! A picture of an Indian camp, not painted on canvas nor yet written. It was dream-stuff, suspended in the thin air, filling the inclosure of the cedar wood container. As she looked upon it, the picture grew more and more real, exceeding the proportions of the chest. It was all so illusive a breath might have blown it away; yet there it was, real as life,—a circular camp of white cone-shaped tepees, astir with Indian people. The village crier, with flowing head-dress of eagle plumes, mounted on a prancing white pony, rode within the arena. Indian men, women and children stopped in groups and clusters, while bright painted faces peered out of tepee doors, to listen to the chieftain's crier.

At this point, she, too, heard the full melodious voice. She heard distinctly the Dakota words he proclaimed to the people. "Be glad! Rejoice! Look up, and see the new day dawning! Help is near! Hear me, every one."

She caught the glad tidings and was thrilled with new hope for her people.

THE WIDESPREAD ENIGMA
CONCERNING BLUE-STAR
WOMAN

It was summer on the western plains. Fields of golden sunflowers facing eastward, greeted the rising sun. Blue-Star Woman, with wind-shorn braids of white hair over each ear, sat in the shade of her log hut before an open fire. Lonely but unmolested she dwelt here like the ground squirrel that took its abode nearby,—both through the easy tolerance of the land owner. The Indian woman held a skillet over the burning embers. A large round cake, with long slashes in its center, was baking and crowding the capacity of the frying pan.

In deep abstraction Blue-Star Woman prepared her morning meal. "Who am I?" had become the obsessing riddle of her life. She was no longer a young woman, being in her fifty-third year. In the eyes of the white man's law, it was required of her to give proof of her membership in the Sioux tribe. The unwritten law of heart prompted her naturally to say, "I am a being. I am Blue-Star Woman. A piece of earth is my birthright."

It was taught for reasons now forgot that an Indian should never pronounce his or her name in answer to any inquiry. It was probably a means of protection in the days of black magic. Be this as it may, Blue-Star Woman lived in times when this teaching was disregarded. It gained her nothing, however, to pronounce her name to the government official to whom she applied for her share of tribal land. His persistent question was always, "Who were your parents?"

Blue-Star Woman was left an orphan at a tender age. She did not remember them. They were long gone to the spirit-land,—and she could not understand why they should be recalled to earth on her account. It was another one of the old, old teachings of her race that the names of the dead should not be idly spoken. It had become a sacrilege to mention carelessly the name of any departed one, especially in matters of disputes over worldly possessions. The unfortunate circumstances of her early childhood, together with the lack of written records of a roving people, placed a formidable barrier between her

and her heritage. The fact was events of far greater importance to the tribe than her reincarnation had passed unrecorded in books. The verbal reports of the old-time men and women of the tribe were varied,—some were actually contradictory. Blue-Star Woman was unable to find even a twig of her family tree.

She sharpened one end of a long stick and with it speared the fried bread when it was browned. Heedless of the hot bread's "Tsing!" in a high treble as it was lifted from the fire, she added it to the six others which had preceded it. It had been many a moon since she had had a meal of fried bread, for she was too poor to buy at any one time all the necessary ingredients, particularly the fat in which to fry it. During the breadmaking, the smoke-blackened coffeepot boiled over. The aroma of freshly made coffee smote her nostrils and roused her from the tantalizing memories.

The day before, friendly spirits, the unseen ones, had guided her aimless footsteps to her Indian neighbor's house. No sooner had she entered than she saw on the table some grocery bundles. "Iye-que, fortunate one!" she exclaimed as she took the straight-backed chair offered her. At once the Indian hostess untied the bundles and measured out a cupful of green coffee beans and a pound of lard. She gave them to Blue-Star Woman, saying, "I want to share my good fortune. Take these home with you." Thus it was that Blue-Star Woman had come into unexpected possession of the materials which now contributed richly to her breakfast.

The generosity of her friend had often saved her from starvation. Generosity is said to be a fault of Indian people, but neither the Pilgrim Fathers nor Blue-Star Woman ever held it seriously against them. Blue-Star Woman was even grateful for this gift of food. She was fond of coffee,—that black drink brought hither by those daring voyagers of long ago. The coffee habit was one of the signs of her progress in the white man's civilization, also had she emerged from the tepee into a log hut, another achievement. She had learned to read the primer and to write her name. Little Blue-Star attended school unhindered by a fond mother's fears that a foreign teacher might not spare the rod with her darling.

Blue-Star Woman was her individual name. For untold ages the Indian race had not used family names. A new-born child was given a brand-new name. Blue-Star Woman was proud to write her name for which she would not be required to substitute another's upon her marriage, as is the custom of civilized peoples.

"The times are changed now," she muttered under her breath. "My individual name seems to mean nothing." Looking out into space, she saw the nodding sunflowers, and they acquiesced with her. Their drying leaves reminded her of the near approach of autumn. Then soon, very soon, the ice would freeze along the banks of the muddy river. The day of the first ice was her birthday. She would be fifty-four winters old. How futile had been all these winters to secure her a share in tribal lands. A weary smile flickered across her face as she sat there on the ground like a bronze figure of patience and long-suffering.

The breadmaking was finished. The skillet was set aside to cool. She poured the appetizing coffee into her tin cup. With fried bread and black coffee she regaled herself. Again her mind reverted to her riddle. "The missionary preacher said he could not explain the white man's law to me. He who reads daily from the Holy Bible, which he tells me is God's book cannot understand mere man's laws. This also puzzles me," thought she to herself. "Once a wise leader of our people, addressing a president of this country, said: 'I am a man. You are another. The Great Spirit is our witness!' This is simple and easy to understand, but the times are changed. The white man's laws are strange."

Blue-Star Woman broke off a piece of fried bread between a thumb and forefinger. She ate it hungrily, and sipped from her cup of fragrant coffee. "I do not understand the white man's law. It's like walking in the dark. In this darkness, I am growing fearful of everything."

Oblivious to the world, she had not heard the footfall of two Indian men who now stood before her.

Their short-cropped hair looked blue-black in contrast to the faded civilian clothes they wore. Their white man's shoes were rusty and unpolished. To the unconventional eyes of the old Indian woman, their celluloid collars appeared like shining marks of civilization. Blue-Star Woman looked up from the lap of mother earth without rising. "Hinnu, hinnu!" she ejaculated in undisguised surprise. "Pray, who are these would-be white men?" she inquired.

In one voice and by an assumed relationship the two Indian men addressed her. "Aunt, I shake hands with you." Again Blue-Star Woman remarked, "Oh, indeed! these near white men speak my native tongue and shake hands according to our custom." Did she guess the truth, she would have known they were simply deluded mortals, deceiving others and themselves most of all. Boisterously laughing and making conversation, they each in turn gripped her withered hand.

Like a sudden flurry of wind, tossing loose ends of things, they broke into her quiet morning hour and threw her groping thoughts into greater chaos. Masking their real errand with long-drawn faces, they feigned a concern for her welfare only. "We come to ask how you are living. We heard you were slowly starving to death. We heard you are one of those Indians who have been cheated out of their share in tribal lands by the government officials."

Blue-Star Woman became intensely interested.

"You see we are educated in the white man's ways," they said with protruding chests. One unconsciously thrust his thumbs into the armholes of his ill-fitting coat and strutted about in his pride. "We can help you get your land. We want to help our aunt. All old people like you ought to be helped before the younger ones. The old will die soon, and they may never get the benefit of their land unless some one like us helps them to get their rights, without further delay."

Blue-Star Woman listened attentively.

Motioning to the mats she spread upon the ground, she said: "Be seated, my nephews." She accepted the relationship assumed for the occasion. "I will give you some breakfast." Quickly she set before them a generous helping of fried bread and cups of coffee. Resuming her own meal, she continued, "You are wonderfully kind. It is true, my nephews, that I have grown old trying to secure my share of land. It may not be long till I shall pass under the sod."

The two men responded with "How, how," which meant, "Go on with your story. We are all ears." Blue-Star Woman had not yet detected any particular sharpness about their ears, but by an impulse she looked up into their faces and scrutinized them. They were busily engaged in eating. Their eyes were fast upon the food on the mat in front of their crossed shins. Inwardly she made a passing observation how, like ravenous wolves, her nephews devoured their food. Coyotes in midwinter could not have been more starved. Without comment she offered them the remaining fried cakes, and between them they took it all. She offered the second helping of coffee, which they accepted without hesitancy. Filling their cups, she placed her empty coffeepot on the dead ashes.

To them she rehearsed her many hardships. It had become a habit now to tell her long story of disappointments with all its petty details. It was only another instance of good intentions gone awry. It was a paradox upon a land of property that its path to future glory be stained with the blood of its aborigines. Incongruous as it is, the two

nephews, with their white associates, were glad of a condition so profitable to them. Their solicitation for Blue-Star Woman was not at all altruistic. They thrived in their grafting business. They and their occupation were the by-product of an unwieldly bureaucracy over the nation's wards.

"Dear aunt, you failed to establish the facts of your identity," they told her. Hereupon Blue-Star Woman's countenance fell. It was ever the same old words. It was the old song of the government official she loathed to hear. The next remark restored her courage. "If any one can discover evidence, it's us! I tell you, aunt, we'll fix it all up for you." It was a great relief to the old Indian woman to be thus unburdened of her riddle, with a prospect of possessing land. "There is one thing you will have to do,—that is, to pay us half of your land and money when you get them." Here was a pause, and Blue-Star Woman answered slowly, "Y-e-s," in an uncertain frame of mind.

The shrewd schemers noted her behavior. "Wouldn't you rather have a half of a crust of bread than none at all?" they asked. She was duly impressed with the force of their argument. In her heart she agreed, "A little something to eat is better than nothing!" The two men talked in regular relays. The flow of smooth words was continuous and so much like purring that all the woman's suspicions were put soundly to sleep. "Look here, aunt, you know very well that pairie fire is met with a back-fire." Blue-Star Woman, recalling her experiences in fire-fighting, quickly responded, "Yes, oh, yes."

"In just the same way, we fight crooks with crooks. We have clever white lawyers working with us. They are the back-fire." Then, as if remembering some particular incident, they both laughed aloud and said, "Yes, and sometimes they use us as the back-fire! We trade fifty-fifty."

Blue-Star Woman sat with her chin in the palm of one hand with elbow resting in the other. She rocked herself slightly forward and backward. At length she answered, "Yes, I will pay you half of my share in tribal land and money when I get them. In bygone days, brave young men of the order of the White-Horse-Riders sought out the aged, the poor, the widows and orphans to aid them, but they did their good work without pay. The White-Horse-Riders are gone. The times are changed. I am a poor old Indian woman. I need warm clothing before winter begins to blow its icicles through us. I need fire wood. I need food. As you have said, a little help is better than none."

Hereupon the two pretenders scored another success.

They rose to their feet. They had eaten up all the fried bread and drained the coffeepot. They shook hands with Blue-Star Woman and departed. In the quiet that followed their departure she sat munching her small piece of bread, which, by a lucky chance, she had taken on her plate before the hungry wolves had come. Yet slowly she ate the fragment of fried bread as if to increase it by diligent mastication. A self-condemning sense of guilt disturbed her. In her dire need she had become involved with tricksters. Her nephews laughingly told her, "We use crooks, and crooks use us in the skirmish over Indian lands."

The friendly shade of the house shrank away from her and hid itself under the narrow eaves of the dirt covered roof. She shrugged her shoulders. The sun high in the sky had witnessed the affair and now glared down upon her white head. Gathering upon her arm the mats and cooking utensils, she hobbled into her log hut.

Under the brooding wilderness silence, on the Sioux Indian Reservation, the superintendent summoned together the leading Indian men of the tribe. He read a letter which he had received from headquarters in Washington, D.C. It announced the enrollment of Blue-Star Woman on their tribal roll of members and the approval of allotting land to her.

It came as a great shock to the tribesmen. Without their knowledge and consent their property was given to a strange woman. They protested in vain. The superintendent said, "I received this letter from Washington. I have read it to you for your information. I have fulfilled my duty. I can do no more." With these fateful words he dismissed the assembly.

Heavy hearted, Chief High Flier returned to his dwellng. Smoking his long-stemmed pipe he pondered over the case of Blue-Star Woman. The Indian's guardian had got into a way of usurping autocratic power in disposing of the wards' property. It was growing intolerable. "No doubt this Indian woman is entitled to allotment, but where? Certainly not here," he thought to himself.

Laying down his pipe, he called his little granddaughter from her play. "You are my interpreter and scribe," he said. "Bring your paper and pencil." A letter was written in the child's sprawling hand, and signed by the old chieftain. It read:

"My Friend:
"I make letter to you. My heart is sad. Washington give my tribe's land to a woman called Blue-Star. We do not know her. We were not asked to give

land, but our land is taken from us to give to another Indian. This is not right. Lots of little children of my tribe have no land. Why this strange woman get our land which belongs to our children? Go to Washington and ask if our treaties tell him to give our property away without asking us. Tell him I thought we made good treaties on paper, but now our children cry for food. We are too poor. We cannot give even to our own little children. Washington is very rich. Washington now owns our country. If he wants to help this poor Indian woman, Blue-Star, let him give her some of his land and his money. This is all I will say until you answer me. I shake hands with you with my heart. The Great Spirit hears my words. They are true.

> "Your friend,
> "Chief High Flier.
> "X (his mark)."

The letter was addressed to a prominent American woman. A stamp was carefully placed on the envelope.

Early the next morning, before the dew was off the grass, the chieftain's riding pony was caught from the pasture and brought to his log house. It was saddled and bridled by a younger man, his son with whom he made his home. The old chieftain came out, carrying in one hand his long-stemmed pipe and tobacco pouch. His blanket was loosely girdled about his waist. Tightly holding the saddle horn, he placed a moccasined foot carefully into the stirrup and pulled himself up awkwardly into the saddle, muttering to himself, "Alas, I can no more leap into my saddle. I now must crawl about in my helplessness." He was past eighty years of age, and no longer agile.

He set upon his ten-mile trip to the only post office for hundreds of miles around. In his shirt pocket, he carried the letter destined, in due season, to reach the heart of American people. His pony, grown old in service, jogged along the dusty road. Memories of other days thronged the wayside, and for the lonely rider transformed all the country. Those days were gone when the Indian youths were taught to be truthful,—to be merciful to the poor. Those days were gone when moral cleanliness was a chief virtue; when public feasts were given in honor of the virtuous girls and young men of the tribe. Untold mischief is now possible through these broken ancient laws. The younger generation were not being properly trained in the high virtues. A slowly starving race was growing mad, and the pitifully weak sold their lands for a pot of porridge.

"He, he, he! He, he, he!" he lamented. "Small Voice Woman, my own relative is being represented as the mother of this strange Blue-Star—the papers were made by two young Indian men who have

learned the white man's ways. Why must I be forced to accept the mischief of children? My memory is clear. My reputation for veracity is well known.

Small Voice Woman lived in my house until her death. She had only one child and it was a *boy!"* He held his hand over this thumping heart, and was reminded of the letter in his pocket. "This letter,— what will happen when it reaches my good friend?" he asked himself. The chieftain rubbed his dim eyes and groaned, "If only my good friend knew the folly of turning my letter into the hands of bureaucrats! In face of repeated defeat, I am daring once more to send this one letter." An inner voice said in his ear, "And this one letter will share the same fate of the other letters."

Startled by the unexpected voice, he jerked upon the bridle reins and brought the drowsy pony to a sudden halt. There was no one near. He found himself a mile from the post office, for the cluster of government buildings, where lived the superintendent, were now in plain sight. His thin frame shook with emotion. He could not go there with his letter.

He dismounted from his pony. His quavering voice chanted a bravery song as he gathered dry grasses and the dead stalks of last year's sunflowers. He built a fire, and crying aloud, for his sorrow was greater than he could bear, he cast the letter into the flames. The fire consumed it. He sent his message on the wings of fire and he believed she would get it. He yet trusted that help would come to his people before it was too late. The pony tossed his head in a readiness to go. He knew he was on the return trip and he was glad to travel.

The wind which blew so gently at dawn was now increased into a gale as the sun approached the zenith. The chieftain, on his way home, sensed a coming storm. He looked upward to the sky and around in every direction. Behind him, in the distance, he saw a cloud of dust. He saw several horsemen whipping their ponies and riding at great speed. Occasionally he heard their shouts, as if calling after some one. He slackened his pony's pace and frequently looked over his shoulder to see who the riders were advancing in hot haste upon him. He was growing curious. In a short time the riders surrounded him. On their coats shone brass buttons, and on their hats were gold cords and tassels. They were Indian police.

"Wan!" he exclaimed, finding himself the object of their chase. It was their foolish ilk who had murdered the great leader, Sitting Bull.

"Pray, what is the joke? Why do young men surround an old man quietly riding home?"

"Uncle," said the spokesman, "we are hirelings, as you know. We are sent by the government superintendent to arrest you and take you back with us. The superintendent says you are one of the bad Indians, singing war songs and opposing the government all the time; this morning you were seen trying to set fire to the government agency."

"Hunhunhe!" replied the old chief, placing the palm of his hand over his mouth agape in astonishment. "All this is unbelievable!"

The policeman took hold of the pony's bridle and turned the reluctant little beast around. They led it back with them and the old chieftain sat unresisting in the saddle. High Flier was taken before the superintendent, who charged him with setting fires to destroy government buildings and found him guilty. Thus Chief High Flier was sent to jail. He had already suffered much during his life. He was the voiceless man of America. And now in his old age he was cast into prison. The chagrin of it all, together with his utter helplessness to defend his own or his people's human rights, weighed heavily upon his spirit.

The foul air of the dingy cell nauseated him who loved the open. He sat wearily down upon the tattered mattress, which lay on the rough board floor. He drew his robe closely about his tall figure, holding it partially over his face, his hands covered within the folds. In profound gloom the gray-haired prisoner sat there, without a stir for long hours and knew not when the day ended and night began. He sat buried in his desperation. His eyes were closed, but he could not sleep. Bread and water in tin receptacles set upon the floor beside him untouched. He was not hungry. Venturesome mice crept out upon the floor and scampered in the dim starlight streaming through the iron bars of the cell window. They squeaked as they dared each other to run across his moccasined feet, but the chieftain neither saw nor heard them.

A terrific struggle was waged within his being. He fought as he never fought before. Tenaciously he hung upon hope for the day of salvation—that hope hoary with age. Defying all odds against him, he refused to surrender faith in good people.

Underneath his blanket, wrapped so closely about him, stole a luminous light. Before his stricken consciousness appeared a vision. Lo, his good friend, the American woman to whom he had sent his messages by fire, now stood there a legion! A vast multitude of

women, with uplifted hands, gazed upon a huge stone image. Their upturned faces were eager and very earnest. The stone figure was that of a woman upon the brink of the Great Waters, facing eastward. The myriad living hands remained uplifted till the stone woman began to show signs of life. Very magestically she turned around, and, lo, she smiled upon this great galaxy of American women. She was the Statue of Liberty! It was she, who, though representing human liberty, formerly turned her back upon the American aborigine. Her face was aglow with compassion. Her eyes swept across the outspread continent of America, the home of the red man.

At this moment her torch flamed brighter and whiter till its radiance reached into the obscure and remote places of the land. Her light of liberty penetrated Indian reservations. A loud shout of joy rose up from the Indians of the earth, everywhere!

All too soon the picture was gone. Chief High Flier awoke. He lay prostrate on the floor where during the night he had fallen. He rose and took his seat again upon the mattress. Another day was ushered into his life. In his heart lay the secret vision of hope born in the midnight of his sorrows. It enabled him to serve his jail sentence with a mute dignity which baffled those who saw him.

Finally came the day of his release. There was rejoicing over all the land. The desolate hills that harbored wailing voices nightly now were hushed and still. Only gladness filled the air. A crowd gathered around the jail to greet the chieftain. His son stood at the entrance way, while the guard unlocked the prison door. Serenely quiet, the old Indian chief stepped forth. An unseen stone in his path caused him to stumble slightly, but his son grasped him by the hand and steadied his tottering steps. He led him to a heavy lumber wagon drawn by a small pony team which he had brought to take him home. The people thronged about him—hundreds shook hands with him and went away singing native songs of joy for the safe return to them of their absent one.

Among the happy people came Blue-Star Woman's two nephews. Each shook the chieftain's hand. One of them held out an ink pad saying, "We are glad we were able to get you out of jail. We have great influence with the Indian Bureau in Washington, D.C. When you need help, let us know. Here press your thumb in this pad." His companion took from his pocket a document prepared for the old chief's signature, and held it on the wagon wheel for the thumb mark. The chieftain was taken by surprise. He looked into his son's eyes to know the meaning of these two men. "It is our agreement," he

explained to his old father. "I pledged to pay them half of your land if they got you out of jail."

The old chieftain sighed, but made no comment. Words were vain. He pressed his indelible thumb mark, his signature it was, upon the deed, and drove home with his son.

AMERICA'S INDIAN PROBLEM

The hospitality of the American aborigine, it is told, saved the early settlers from starvation during the first bleak winters. In commemoration of having been so well received, Newport erected "a cross as a sign of English dominion." With sweet words he quieted the suspicions of Chief Powhatan, his friend. He "told him that the arms (of the cross) represented Powhatan and himself, and the middle their united league."

DeSoto and his Spaniards were graciously received by the Indian Princess Cofachiqui in the South. While on a sight-seeing tour they entered the ancestral tombs of those Indians. DeSoto "dipped into the pearls and gave his two joined hands full to each cavalier to make rosaries of, he said, to say prayers for their sins on. We imagine if their prayers were in proportion to their sins they must have spent the most of their time at their devotions."

It was in this fashion that the old world snatched away the fee in the land of the new. It was in this fashion that America was divided between the powers of Europe and the aborigines were dispossessed of their country. The barbaric rule of might from which the paleface had fled hither for refuge caught up with him again, and in the melee the hospitable native suffered "legal disability."

History tells that it was from the English and the Spanish our government inherited its legal victims, the American Indians, whom to this day we hold as wards and not as citizens of their own freedom loving land. A long century of dishonor followed this inheritance of somebody's loot. Now the time is at hand when the American Indian shall have his day in court through the help of the women of America. The stain upon America's fair name is to be removed, and the remnant of the Indian nation, suffering from malnutrition, is to number among the invited invisible guests at your dinner tables.

In this undertaking there must be cooperation of head, heart and hand. We serve both our own government and a voiceless people within our midst. We would open the door of American opportunity to the red man and encourage him to find his rightful peace in our American life. We would remove the barrriers that hinder his normal development.

Wardship is no substitute for American citizenship, therefore we seek his enfranchisement. The many treaties made in good faith with the Indian by our government we would like to see equitably settled. By a constructive program we hope to do away with the "piecemeal legislation" affecting Indians here and there which has proven an exceedingly expensive and disappointing method.

Do you know what *your* Bureau of Indian Affairs, in Washington, D.C., really is? How it is organized and how it deals with wards of the nation? This is our first study. Let us be informed of facts and then we may formulate our opinions. In the remaining space allowed me I shall quote from the report of the Bureau of Municipal Research, in their investigation of the Indian Bureau, published by them in the September issue, 1915, No. 65, "Municipal Research," 261 Broadway, New York City. This report is just as good for our use today as when it was first made, for very little, if any, change has been made in the administration of Indian Affairs since then.

PREFATORY NOTE

"While this report was printed for the information of members of Congress, it was not made a part of the report of the Joint Commission of Congress, at whose request it was prepared, and is not available for distribution."

UNPUBLISHED DIGEST OF STATUTORY AND TREATY PROVISIONS
GOVERNING INDIAN FUNDS

"When in 1913 inquiry was made into the accounting and reporting methods of the Indian Office by the President's Commission on Economy and Efficiency, it was found there was no digest of the provisions of statutes and treaties with Indian tribes governing Indian funds and the trust obligations of the government. Such a digest was therefore prepared. It was not completed, however, until after Congress adjourned March 4, 1913. Then, instead of being published, it found its way into the pigeon-holes in the Interior Department and the Civil Service Commission, where the working papers and unpublished reports of the commission were ordered stored. The digest itself would make a document of about three hundred pages."

Unpublished Outline of Organization

"By order of the President, the commission, in cooperation with various persons assigned to this work, also prepared at great pains a complete analysis of the organization of every department, office and commission of the federal government as of July 1, 1912. This represented a complete picture of the government as a whole in summary outline; it also represented an accurate picture of every administrative bureau, office, and of every operative or field station, and showed in his working relation each of the 500,000 officers and employees in the public service. The report in typewritten form was one of the working documents used in the preparation of the 'budget' submitted by President Taft to Congress in February 1913. The 'budget' was ordered printed by Congress, but the cost thereof was to be charged against the President's appropriation. There was not enough money remaining in this appropriation to warrant the printing of the report on organization. It, therefore, also found repose in a dark closet."

Too Voluminous to Be Made Part of This Series

"Congress alone could make the necessary provision for the publication of these materials; the documents are too voluminous to be printed as a part of this series, even if official permission were granted. It is again suggested, however, that the data might be made readily accessible and available to students by placing in manuscript division of the Library of Congress one copy of the unpublished reports and working papers of the President's Commission on Economy and Efficiency. This action was recommended by the commission, but the only official action taken was to order that the materials be placed under lock and key in the Civil Service Commission."

Need for Special Care in Management

"The need for special care in the management of Indian Affairs lies in the fact that in theory of law the Indian has not the rights of a citizen. He has not even the rights of a foreign resident. The Indian individually does not have access to the courts; he can not individually appeal to the administrative and judicial branches of the public service

for the enforcement of his rights. He himself is considered as a ward of the United States. His property and funds are held in trust. * * * The Indian Office is the agency of the government for administering both the guardianship of the Indian and the trusteeship of his properties."

CONDITIONS ADVERSE TO GOOD ADMINISTRATION

"The legal status of the Indian and his property is the condition which makes it incumbent on the government to assume the obligation of protector. What is of special interest in this inquiry is to note the conditions under which the Indian Office has been required to conduct its business. In no other relation are the agents of the government under conditions more adverse to efficient administration. The influence which make for the infidelity to trusteeship, for subversion of properties and funds, for the violation of physical and moral welfare have been powerful. The opportunities and inducements are much greater than those which have operated with ruinous effect on other branches of public service and on the trustees and officers of our great private corporations. In many instances, the integrity of these have been broken down."

GOVERNMENT MACHINERY INADEQUATE

"* * * Behind the sham protection, which operated largely as a blind to publicity, have been at all times great wealth in the form of Indian funds to be subverted; valuable lands, mines, oil fields, and other natural resources to be despoiled or appropriated to the use of the trader; and large profits to be made by those dealing with trustees who were animated by motives of gain. This has been the situation in which the Indian Service has been for more than a century—the Indian during all this time having his rights and properties to greater or less extent neglected; the guardian, the government, in many instances, passive to conditions which have contributed to his undoing."

OPPORTUNITIES STILL PRESENT

"And still, due to the increasing value of his remaining estate, there is left an inducement to fraud, corruption, and institutional incompe-

tence almost beyond the possibility of comprehension. The properties and funds of the Indians today are estimated at not less than one thousand millions of dollars. There is still a great obligation to be discharged, which must run through many years. The government itself owes many millions of dollars for Indian moneys which it has converted to its own use, and it is of interest to note that it does not know and the officers do not know what is the present condition of the Indian funds in their keeping."

PRIMARY DEFECTS

"* * * The story of the mismanagement of Indian Affairs is only a chapter in the history of the mismanagement of corporate trusts. The Indian has been the victim of the same kind of neglect, the same abortive processes, the same malpractices as have the life insurance policyholders, the bank depositor, the industrial and transportation shareholder. The form of organization of the trusteeship has been one which does not provide for independent audit and supervision. The institutional methods and practices have been such that they do not provide either a fact basis for official judgment or publicity of facts which, if made available, would supply evidence of infidelity. In the operation of this machinery, there has not been the means provided for effective official scrutiny and the public conscience could not be reached."

AMPLE PRECEDENTS TO BE FOLLOWED

"Precedents to be followed are ample. In private corporate trusts that have been mismanaged a basis of appeal has been found only when some favorable circumstance has brought to light conditions so shocking as to cause those people who have possessed political power, as a matter of self-protection, to demand a thorough reorganization and revision of methods. The same motive has lain back of legislation for the Indian. But the motive to political action has been less effective, for the reason that in the past the Indians who have acted in self-protection have either been killed or placed in confinement. All the machinery of government has been set to work to repress rather than to provide adequate means for justly dealing with a large population which had no political rights."—Edict Magazine.

Coyote Stories

Mourning Dove
(Christine Quintasket, Humishuma)

Introduction

By Jay Miller

C*oyote Stories* consumed the final years of Christine Quintasket, who wrote under the name of Mourning Dove (sometimes she used *Humishuma*, the Colville-Okanogan term for "mourning dove").[1] She was an enrolled member of the Colville Reservation of north-central Washington. With little schooling and less exposure to literature, she early determined to become a writer of fiction, particularly western novels. Prior to her efforts, Indian women authors like Pauline Johnson and Zitkala-Ša (Gertrude Simmons Bonin) had devoted themselves to short stories. Earning money as a migrant laborer or housekeeper, Mourning Dove wrote every day. Even on days when she spent ten hours packing apples, she wrote into the night, long after other exhausted workers had gone to sleep.

After drafting her only full novel about 1912, she put it away until, several years later, she met Lucullus Virgil McWhorter, a Yakima Valley businessman sympathetic to Indian causes, and they began to collaborate on a final version.[2] Finished in 1916, *Cogewea* was not published until 1927. During the interim, Mourning Dove was encouraged to record the stories and traditions of her people, the Interior Salish.[3]

Though initially reluctant, Mourning Dove soon warmed to the task of collecting "folklores," as she always called her subject. She had heard stories her entire life from relatives and visiting elders. Once motivated, she deliberately sought out aged members of other communities to hear, and afterward record, their stories. Most nights, she either carefully wrote stories she had heard that evening or reworked legends collected previously. When satisfied, she sent or took bundles of them to Yakima for McWhorter to edit.

To help her with spelling, agreement, and grammar, McWhorter introduced her to Heister Dean Guie, who wrote for the Yakima city newspaper. Beginning as silent editor, Guie became increasingly involved in the project. He and Mourning Dove passed letters to each other through McWhorter, who sometimes had to smooth out diffi-

culties. Guie was after consistency and returned, again and again, to the same points, much to the frustration of Mourning Dove. He asked for the identifications and spellings of animal names in Salishan languages, for the pattern number (Was it three or five?), and for details of dress and ornament. Eventually, he did drawings to illustrate characters, depicting their animal characterizations over their spirit and human aspects. Guie also convinced the others that these stories should be written "for the children of another race to read" (as Mourning Dove said at the end of the Preface).

As she did in the stories, Mourning Dove fashioned an expurgated version of her life for the public. A version of it appears in her Preface, where she dates her birth to 1888 and says her father's father was "a Hudson's Bay Company man, a hardy, adventurous Celt." The reservation censuses and her father's other children, however, deny these claims.

Christine Quintasket was first named on the tribal census of 30 June 1891, where she was listed as eight years old, and she was shown to be the same age on the roll for 1893. Since she was always large for her age, I judge that she was born about 1885. A decade later, she was enrolled briefly as Christine Joseph by her parents in the Sacred Heart/ Colville/Goodwin Mission School at Ward, Washington, near Kettle Falls. She quickly became ill and was taken home by her father. A major portion of her trauma was the result of the school's insistence that she speak only English. Previously she had spoken only Salish, but now she was punished for doing so by the nuns, who, incongruously, were themselves native speakers of French. She enrolled again, successfully, from about 1896 to 1899, when she made her First Communion. In 1900 all native students were transferred to the government school at Fort Spokane.

In 1902 her mother, Lucy Stuikin, died and Christine went home to care for her siblings. After her father, Joseph Quintasket, married Cecilia Williams in 1904, Christine found employment for three years at Fort Shaw Indian School near Great Falls, Montana, where she could attend classes and visit her grandmother, Maria, who was living among the Kootenay at Tobacco Plains. In 1908 she witnessed the roundup of the last wild bison herd in the United States, and, from hints in her writings, seems to have had a religious vision involving a buffalo skull.

At Fort Shaw she met Harold McLeod, married him in 1909, and went to live at Polson. The marriage was rocky, and Christine often

lived away from him. In 1912 she moved to Portland, where she apparently assumed the pen name of Morning Dove, a character in Salishan legends associated with the dawn (new beginnings) and faithfulness, and drafted her novel, partially in reaction to the treatment of Indians in contemporary Western writings.[4]

To gain greater facility with written English, she attended a Calgary business college in 1913–15. The next year, she was the school teacher on the Inkameep Reserve in British Columbia. Her younger sister had married into the chiefly family there and the sisters enjoyed living among their father's Okanagan relatives, just north of the Colville Reservation. While she was teaching, Christine's nights were devoted to revising and finishing her novel, *Cogewea*, with the help of McWhorter, who also urged her to begin collective native stories. She did so, although both she and McWhorter erred in thinking that Salishan legendary history was quickly disappearing.

On 8 September 1919, she married Fred Galler, a Wenatchi, and settled at East Omak on the western edge of the Colville Reservation, when they were not camping in orchards and fields as migrant laborers. Once back on the reservation, she became increasingly involved in native rights, bridging the differences between her people and their white neighbors.

Although many locals were suspicious of her literary efforts, her name was often in the press as a regional celebrity. During a museum visit in December 1921, she learned that the correct ornithological spelling for her pen name was Mourning Dove. She adopted that spelling, with all of its tragic overtones.

She continued to move around the Inland Empire, taking on odd jobs with her husband, collecting folklores, and writing. Her novel was slow to appear, and she was often vexed with the publisher. Still, she persisted. When it did come out in 1927, she became a more public figure, although known only by her pen or married names, despite the fact that most Colvilles knew her as Quintasket.

She joined with other native women to found social and handiwork clubs, and began to speak out about native rights and agency abuses. She also joined with other Colvilles to have the oversized agency staff reduced. An agency farming instructor whose job was threatened attacked Christine's literary aspirations by spreading word that she had not written her novel but had only allowed her pen name to be used as a front for its white author, presumably McWhorter. Greatly

angered, Christine received an apology from this agency farmer, just before he lost his job. Years later, they became neighbors and friends.

Driven more than ever, with fatal consequences for her health, she set out to prove her own abilities and drafted versions of her autobiography. It has now been edited and published[5] after half a century in storage.

She joined with other activists in 1930 to found the Colville Indian Association, seeking payments still outstanding from unresolved land claims. They also became concerned with the alleged misuse of tribal monies. In 1933 she reminded a company leasing land on the reservation that it had not met its commitment to hire tribal members. In May 1935 she became the first woman elected to the Colville Tribal Council.

Her political efforts and her persistent writing took their toll. Christine Galler was taken to a state asylum on 30 July and died there on 8 August 1936 at 10:15 p.m. Much of the time she was delirious, reliving fearsome encounters with the Devil she had first experienced during a bout with influenza in 1918. The cause of death was listed as "exhaustion from manic psychosis," and her occupation was given as housewife and authoress. Her father, Joseph, outlived her. Throughout her life, she had been careful to shield him from her literary audience. Largely, this was to protect his privacy, but, in part, it was also to avoid questions about her claim that Joseph's father had been Irish or Scots. He was always listed as a full blood on the tribal rolls. Both his parents were Okanagans, although his mother also had ties with the Nicola, a tiny Athapaskan-speaking group since assimilated among Salishans. Given the tenor of the times and region, her claims to some white ancestry probably gave her more freedom to move among her neighbors and to appeal to a broader readership.

Thus, despite claims of traditional authenticity, Mourning Dove's legends are not true to Salishan recitations. They have been sanitized, and the portions that she called "ugly" have been removed. Nor are they as casual or spontaneous as they would be in native settings. Fearful for the demise of these stories, Salishans today continue to tell them, albeit in English rather than native languages. Elders will sometimes remind each other of stories and compare notes on distinctive family versions. The best Coyote stories are usually heard at wakes, while family and friends are sitting up all night with the deceased. During the darkest of the night, old ladies will begin to tell

the most outrageous stories, helping to relieve the grief and keep everyone awake.

Stories can only be told when they do not interfere with more vital activities. Thus, they are usually limited to winter evenings. Exceptions are permitted, however, among leading families when they are passing a site mentioned in legend. Then it is very appropriate to relate the story while surrounded by landmarks mentioned in it.

The audience is as fully involved with the recitation as the speaker; they all have roles to play. During public narratives, listeners must periodically respond to indicate they are paying attention and to encourage the storyteller. For the Interior Salish, the usual response was the sound used for the affirmative, which was also the predominant vowel of these dialect chains. Moving up the Columbia River from Vantage, the "ay" chain consisted of the Columbians, Wenatchis (Peskwaws), Entiats, and Chelans; the Methows used a distinctive "ii" but historically were adopting the "ay"; and the Okanogans, Nespelems, Sanpoils, Colviles (Kettle Falls), and Arrow Lakes used the "aa". These tribes, mostly occupying tributaries of the Columbia River from prehistoric times, eventually settled on the Colville Reservation. To the east, the Spokans, Kalispels, and Flatheads (the original Salish) used an "ac" diphthong like that in "bat". Although these features of Salish oral literature are important for understanding the performance aspects of this tradition, they were not considered necessary for the literary presentation intended by Mourning Dove and her editors.

Though concerned with the decorum of these stories, Mourning Dove did include some carry-overs and hints from the traditional contexts, but she carefully avoided calling attention to them. Her treatment of Coyote is particularly cursory, requiring further explication.

Coyote is a complex figure, often baffling to a white audience. He is more anti-hero than hero, more buffoon than champion. He is, for native people, the ultimate negative example, sharing this distinction with other trickster-transformer figures such as Hare in the East, Raven in the Northwest, and Spider in the Plains. Like them, he is Everyone, a native version of the medieval European Everyman, expanded beyond the human species to encompass all of sapient life. His greatest flaw is pride and self-importance. Among the Interior Salish, he is known by two names, although Mourning Dove uses only *Sin-ka-lip*, the most common term. When the stories are told in a

Salishan language, however, Coyote refers to himself as Smyaw, derived from a root meaning "important."⁶

Throughout the Americas, not just among the Salishans, the original inhabitants of the world were indeed people, but they were other-than-human and amorphous. Their essential form was that which later became restricted to the human species, with arms, legs, hands, head, and overall vulnerability. In addition, these primal people also had the attributes of spirits and of species. Sometimes, they are described as shimmering and iridescent. Through tricks of light and shadow, they could change shape and attributes as need or whim arose.

Things remained inchoate during the time of most of the legends. Somehow, these people began to sense that a change was coming because, as so many stories say, "Humans are coming soon." To plan for the arrival of the "new people," a council was held, convened by the leader of that world. It is this council that is the subject of the first story in Mourning Dove's book, albeit in abbreviated version.

For Colville elders of today the fullest account says that all of the people met to decide the names and activities each would assume in the new age. For example, Salmon and Bear agreed to offer their flesh to humans in return for careful treatment and respect. Other people went off in a huff and threatened dire consequences for humans, becoming known as people eaters. It was these renegades and monsters who had to be tamed before humans could settle down.

In the most sacred version, the leader had a pole stacked with rings in front of him. Each ring represented a name and a lifeway. At the very bottom of the pole was the ring intended for Coyote, a ne'er-do-well if there ever was one. As described, Coyote intended to stay up all night and be the first one at the dawn council so as to assume a more exalted position than his actions had hitherto merited. Instead, he fell asleep and his wife, the ever faithful Mole, did not disturb him. After waking, he rushed to the meeting place demanding a great name. The leader was so impressed by Coyote's ability to think for himself, although to selfish ends, that he reversed the pole and put Coyote in charge of finishing up the world.

In some version, when all was set, the leader himself, not his wife as Mourning Dove said, decreed that he would help humans in the future by becoming Sweatlodge, the place for purification, prayer, and petition. He had no head, arms, or legs as Sweatlodge and so Coyote became his substitute.

As he bestowed every one of the names, the leader also gave out

medicine powers. He would point to the center of a person's body, to the heart, which is the seat of thought and emotions.[7] and proclaim what that power would be. Typically, Coyote misunderstood this gesture, assuming that the leader was pointing at his stomach. Thus, by virtue of the creative force granted to his thoughts, Coyote received a special power different from other beings. The representatives of his power lived in Coyote's intestines until he summoned their help. At that moment, they came out and took the form of five feces or, as polite Colvilles say, turds. Coyote called them his younger siblings and asked their advice, which they always gave wisely, although each encounter always ended with Coyote, suddenly brilliant, claiming that their help was superfluous because, after all, he had known what to do all the time. If his younger siblings were slow or reluctant to offer advice, he bullied them into cooperation by threatening to cause a rainstorm which would melt them.

Here, then, is Coyote at his best and worst: a vastly powerful being who relies on feces to get himself out of difficulties. Moreover, all of his activities are filled with the full range of earthy and physiological processes, especially gluttony, lust, and greed. Throughout, he claims more than he is capable of, regardless of the consequences, often death. As a precaution, Sweatlodge gave Fox, Coyote's kinsman, the ability to restore life by stepping over any shred of bone or fur left of Coyote. Traditionally, Fox had to step over him five times, the ancient pattern number, but with the arrival of Jesuit missionaries and the acceptance of Catholicism, modern accounts mention only three times, the Judeo-Christian pattern number. Throughout these stories, Mourning Dove follows the modern usage of three.

Some of Coyote's escapades are included by Mourning Dove, but a few are not because they might offend white sensibilities. In some cases, she turned episodes within a series of adventures into separate stories; a practice allowed within the creativity of the tradition, however. For any story, the only sure way of knowing that it is over is to have Coyote die at the conclusion. Of course, the next tale begins with Fox restoring Coyote's life so that anything can happen.

Although each Salishan family, band, and tribe had its own version of these stories, there were generalized plots for the most important of the sagas. For Coyote, there are series that describe how he made the world the way it is today, pronouncing the "commandment" at the end of each episode to "set the law" about some present condition.

The most famous of these involved Coyote bringing salmon up the

Columbia River and its tributaries.[8] According to most versions, Coyote heard that there were five sisters living near the mouth of the Columbia and keeping wonderful fish in a trap. Coyote wanted to eat these fish, so he went there. Just above the trap, he turned himself into a baby fastened into a cradleboard and floated down the river. The sisters saw him and, having no children of their own, rescued him, although the youngest girl was vocal about her suspicion that the baby was really Coyote. Infused with maternal sentiments, the older sisters paid no attention, alerting the audience to be aware of the youngest-smartest motif so common in Plateau mythology.

Every day the women went out to gather food to eat with their fish and, while they were away, Coyote assumed his usual form and worked on releasing the Salmon. He made five stone bowls and five picks, went down to the trap, and began to dislodge its supports. This went on for some time, with Coyote turning himself back into a baby before the sisters came home each night.

One day, however, the youngest sister could stand it no longer and went back home to test her suspicions. Sure enough, the baby was not there and, looking further, she discovered Coyote dismantling the Salmon trap. Yelling to her sisters that Coyote was stealing their Salmon, she mobilized an attack. Coyote wore a stone bowl like a helmet until it broke under the blows of the sisters; then he put on another. As the last bowl and the last pick broke, the Salmon were released and Coyote led them upriver. Whenever he was hungry, he called a Salmon onto a beach, clubbed it, cooked it, and ate it. By returning the bones to the river, however, the Salmon came back to life and continued upstream.

Coyote, only too typically, soon tired of this easy life and decided to visit the people living in villages at the confluences of tributaries of the Columbia. He entered each village and offered the gift of Salmon in return for a wife while he stayed in the community. The size and number of Salmon sent into local streams were consistent with the beauty of the wife.[9]

Thus, the Colviles at Kettle Falls were most hospitable and received plentiful runs of huge Salmon. The Entiats were less generous, so their river had a brief run of small fish. The Methows were mildly accommodating and gained moderate-sized Salmon. Because the Chelans and Nespelems refused him, their rivers now have waterfalls blocking passage upriver. Furthermore, for every fishery, Coyote also set the techniques and fishing gear to be used. At each locale, what modern

elders call the "proof" of such commandments can be found. Often, these are figures drawn on rock faces depicting the use of spears, traps, nets, or weirs. Understandably, the best procedure to use at that place is also the one decreed by Coyote. For example, the size and color specified for a net matched that of water conditions. The use of a spear or leister allowed for limitations of space and sparseness of the run.

At Kettle Falls, where the salmon were huge until Grand Coulee Dam blocked their return, large basket traps were extremely effective, and the take was shared with anyone who was there at the time of distribution. Failure to share these salmon among one and all violated the local commandment and offended the Salmon people, who would be less likely to return the next year. Hence, complete and total sharing was the rule and practice at the falls.[10]

Nearer Mourning Dove's ancestral home at Piya (Kelly Hill), small salmon went up the Kettle River as far as Cascade Falls. Recently, when biologists tried to introduce landlocked salmon above the falls, they died, and elders remarked that Coyote's commandment forbidding salmon above the falls is still in force.[11]

According to tradition, therefore, each of these stories was localized for all time, a belief known to Mourning Dove only too well, though ignored in print, except in her account of the Hee-Hee Wishing Stone.

Today, various landmarks around the Colville Reservation are explained as the work of Coyote. At Brewster, the domed hill behind the town is known in Salish as Coyote's House, one of many. Steamboat Rock near Grand Coulee Dam is known for the variety of plants growing on its top. These are said to be the result of Coyote stopping there with a basket full of goodies, accidently tipping it over, and angrily commanding that these particular foods stay there. The mesa itself is said by some elders to be the overturned basket. Soap Lake received its greasy consistency when Coyote hid something in its waters and, as one elder put it delicately, "went potty" there so no one could see what was hidden.

Other incidents in the life of Coyote are discussed in the appended commentary on Mourning Dove's versions of each story. While her overall arrangement may seem haphazard, these stories are bracketed between events that were milestones in Coyote's life, Naming Day at its start and the Arrow Trail to the Sky World much later. Afterward, Coyote left the people and moved to the East, some say to a glass-domed house floating in the ocean, from which he will return when he is needed again. Some elders predict a day when Coyote will come

back and smash all of the dams built along the Columbia, washing away environmental pollution and once again bringing the Salmon upriver.

As hope for the future and shaper of the past, Coyote's appeal continues unabated among both natives and scholars. One of the most poignant summaries of his attraction comes from the Chemehuevis, a tribe along the Colorado River,[12] who say with chagrin that, while recognizing the many figures of rectitude in their mythology, nevertheless, "We follow Coyote" because "He embodies *all* the human traits: laziness and patient industry or frantic exertion; foolishness and skillful planning; selfishness and concern for others . . . he is the incomplete and the imperfect . . . Coyote has fun, and it is fun to hear about him and his exploits. What he lacks in dignity he makes up in sheer exuberance." Moreover, Coyote is not hopeless. Among the Chinook of the lower Columbia, there was a tendency for Coyote to develop "from a trickster who is impelled by youthful drives, to a conscience-controlled announcer and transformer."[13]

For almost two decades of help, I would like to thank Colville elders Charles Quintasket, Isabel Friedlander Arcasa, TB Charlie, and Juliann Timentwa. Because a sense of place is such a vital component of understanding these works, it seems significant that Coyote and I reached an understanding at Lithia Park in Ashland, Oregon, while Shakespeare hovered in the wings. I would like to dedicate this reissue of Colville stories to the families of Joseph Quintasket, who exemplify Colville traditions at their best.

NOTES

1. Jay Miller, "Mourning Dove: The Author as Cultural Mediator" in *Being and Becoming Indian: Biographical Studies of North American Frontiers* (Chicago: Dorsey Press, 1989), pp. 160–82; *Mourning Dove: A Salishan Autobiography*, ed. Jay Miller (Lincoln: University of Nebraska Press, 1990).

2. Alice Poindexter (Dexter) Fisher, "The Transportation of Tradition: A Study of Zitkala-Sa and Mourning Dove, Two Transitional American Indian Writers," Ph.D. diss., City College of New York, 1979.

3. Nelson Ault, The Papers of Lucullus Virgil McWhorter (Pullman: Friends of the Washington State University, 1959).

4. Compare Theresa Broderick, *The Brand. A Tale of the Flathead Reservation* (Seattle: The Alice Harriman Book Co., 1909).

5. *Mourning Dove: A Salishan Autobiography*, 1990.

6. Compare Anthony Mattina, *Colville-Okanagan Dictionary* (University of Montana Occasional Papers in Linguistics no. 5. 1987), pp. 105, 303.

7. Jay Miller, "The Matter of the (Thoughtful) Heart: Centrality, Focality, or Overlap," *Journal of Anthropological Research*, 36 (Fall 1980): 338–42.

8. Compare Verne Ray, "Native Villages and Groupings of the Columbia Basin," *Pacific Northwest Quarterly*, 27 (1936): 99–152.

9. Compare *Tales of the Okanagans*, ed. Donald M. Hines (Fairfield, Wash.: Ye Galleon Press, 1976).

10. David H. Chance, "Influences of the Hudson's Bay Company on the Native Cultures of the Colville District," *Northwest Anthropological Research Notes, Memoir* 2 (1973); Christopher J. Turnbull, "Archaeology and Ethnohistory in the Arrow Lakes, Southeastern British Columbia" (Ottawa: National Museum of Man, Mercury Series 65, 1977); Wayne Suttles, "Plateau Pacifism Reconsidered: Ethnography, Ethnology, and Ethnohistory," in *Coast Salish Essays* (Seattle: University of Washington Press, 1987), pp. 282–86.

11. Compare *Tales of the Okanagans*, p. 25.

12. Carobeth Laird, *The Chemehuevis* (Banning, Calif.: Malki Museum Press, 1976), pp. 231–32.

13. Melville Jacobs, *The Content and Style of an Oral Literature: Clackamas Chinook Myths and Tales*, Viking Fund Publications in Anthropology no. 26 (1959).

Foreword

I am glad that Humishuma has written these stories of her people. Since the old Indians in whom these folk-tales are vested are passing away from us, it is good that we bestir ourselves and salvage at least a part of our inheritance. And what a rich store every tribe would have if each had a historian to record its tales!

Story-telling is an ancient profession, and these stories are among our oldest possessions. For many years before the white man ever came to our homeland these legends were told over and over, and handed down from generation to generation. They were our books, our literature, and the memories of the story-tellers were the leaves upon which they were written.

We who lived the days of tribal life before our destruction began remember with gratefulness our story-tellers and the delight and joy and richness which they imparted to our lives. We never tired of their tales, though told countless times. They will, forsooth, never grow old, for they have within them the essence of things that cannot grow old. These legends are of America, as are its mountains, rivers, and forests, and as are its people. They belong!

Story-telling was, and is today, a means of pastime, but the real value of tribal stories lay in the fact that they were closely related to the lives of the people. As history and as literature they became inherited traditions, and they were as wide in their character as the experiences of the people. They told of travels, adventures, and discoveries. In them and through them lived our brave and heroic. There were those that carried lessons and morals for daily guidance. Then, too, there were fairy tales, lovely in their fantasy of thought.

But our legends are passing as the old are passing, and our young are not learning them—which is a part of our destruction. This is sad, especially as the public seems to be becoming somewhat aware of the significance of these tales.

So, in writing the legends of her tribespeople, Humishuma is fulfilling a duty to her forefathers, and at the same time she is performing a service to posterity.

These stories are valuable. They will continue to grow more valuable as the years go by, for through the few snatches of recorded song and

story the spirit of the Indian will live and breathe, and, though the figure of the American Indian passes forever from the stage of life, the spirit is imperishable.

CHIEF STANDING BEAR.

Preface

The Animal People were here first—before there were any real people.

Coyote was the most important because, after he was put to work by the Spirit Chief, he did more than any of the others to make the world a good place in which to live. There were times, however, when Coyote was not busy for the Spirit Chief. Then he amused himself by getting into mischief and stirring up trouble. Frequently he got into trouble himself, and then everybody had a good laugh—everybody but Mole. She was Coyote's wife.

My people call Coyote *Sin-ka-lip'*, which means Imitator. He delighted in mocking and imitating others, or in trying to, and, as he was a great one to play tricks, sometimes he is spoken of as "Trick Person."

Our name for the Animal People is *Chip-chap-tiqulk* (the "k" barely is sounded), and we use the same word for the stories that are told about the Animal People and legendary times. To the younger generations, *chip-chap-tiqulk* are improbable stories; that is a result of the white man's schools. But to the old Indians, *chip-chap-tiqulk* are not at all improbable; they are accounts of what really happened when the world was very young.

My people are the Okanogan[1] and the *Swhy-ayl'-puh* (Colville),

[1]Okanogan—variously spelled *Okanagon, Okinagan, Oknacken, Oakinacken, Okinakane, etc.*—has the native pronunciation *Okan-nock-kane*. Its translation has puzzled more scholarly heads than mine. Some white writers have said that the word means "rendezvous," applying originally to the head of the Okanogan River at Osoyoos Lake, where the various tribes often gathered. But only the last syllable, *gan* (more properly *kane* or *kain*) has been interpreted. Like our words *kan* and *kin*, it means "head," "tip," or "top."

Now, there is a word, *wickan*, that means "seeing," and *wickanakane* means "seeing-the-head (top or tip)." It is quite possible that *okan* is an ancient variation or contraction of *wickan*. Hence, we could have *Okan-nock-kane* interpreted as "Seeing-the-top." The top of what? Of *Chopaka* (Sticking), a snow peak to the west of the Okanogan Valley. That is what some of the older Indians believe, although they are not positive as to the accuracy of the reference.

Chopaka is visible from a long distance. It is an outstanding topographical feature of the tribe's ancient stamping-grounds.

In the beginning the Okanogan may have designated themselves, or been described by other tribes, as "People-living-where-you-can-see-the-top" (of Chopaka), or as "People-seeing-the-top," the phrase becoming shortened to "Seeing-the-top" (*Wickanakane*).

closely related Salishan tribes, and I also have relatives in the *En-koh-tu-me-whoh,* or Nicola, band of the Thompson River Indians in British Columbia. My father's mother was a Nicola, and his father was a Hudson's Bay Company man, a hardy, adventurous Celt. My father, Joseph *Quintasket* (Dark Cloud), was born in the Upper Okanogan community near Kelowna, B. C., but has lived, since a boy, with the Lower Okanogan and the Colville, south of the international boundary. It is with the Lower, or River, Okanogan and the *Swhy-ayl'-puh* on the Colville Reservation in northeastern Washington that I am identified.

The *Swhy-ayl'-puh*—also called *Schu-ayl-pk, Schwelpi* and *Shoyel-pee*—became known as the Colville following the establishment of Fort Colville by the Hudson's Bay Company in 1825–26. The fort, named after Andrew Colville, a London governor of the Company, was built near Kettle Falls in the Columbia River, in the heart of the *Swhy-ayl'-puh* country.

My mother's name was Lucy *Stui'-kin.* She was a *Swhy-ayl'-puh* full-blood. Her grandfather was *See-whelh-ken,* who was head chief of the tribe for many years. His nephew, *Kin-kan-nawh,* whom the white people called Pierre Jerome, was chief when the American government made the tribe give up its home in the Colville Valley in 1872 and move to poorer land on the other side of the Columbia. My mother was born at Kettle Falls—the "Big Falls" of these legends—and she and father were married in a log church at that location. The church was built by Indians who had accepted the teachings of the missionaries.

I was born in a canoe on the Kootenai River, near Bonner's Ferry, Idaho, in the Moon of the Leaves (April), 1888. My parents were traveling with a packtrain, which my uncle, Louie *Stui'-kin,* operated between Walla Walla, Washington and Fort Steele, B. C. during the mining rush that year. My mother and grandmother were being ferried across the river when I arrived. The Indian who was paddling their canoe stripped off his shirt and handed it to grandmother, who wrapped me up in it.

It used to be the custom for story-tellers to go from village to village and relate *chip-chap-tiqulk* to the children. How gladly were those

This explanation I have not seen in print, have never seen it advanced by any of the white people who have investigated. I cannot claim that it is correct, but I consider it as logical and as near the truth, if not nearer, as other guesses that have been submitted.

MOURNING DOVE.

tribal historians welcomed by busy mothers, and how glad were the boys and girls when one came to visit!

Vividly I recall old *S'whist-kane* (Lost-Head), also known as Old Narciss, and how, in the course of a narrative, he would jump up and mimic his characters, speaking or singing in a strong or weak voice, just as the Animal Persons were supposed to have done. And he would dance around the fire in the tule-mat covered lodge until the pines rang with the gleeful shouts of the smallest listeners. We thought of this as all fun and play, hardly aware that the tale-telling and impersonations were a part of our primitive education.

Another favorite was Broken Nose Abraham. He was old and crippled. He came to our village usually on a white horse, riding double with his blind wife, who held the reins and guided the horse at his direction. It always thrilled us to see Broken Nose ride into camp; he had a stock of such fascinating stories. Broken Nose could not dance for us. He could not even walk without the support of his two canes. But he sang exciting war songs, and we liked to sing with him.

Some of the women were noted story-tellers, but they never made it a business to go from village to village to tell them. We children would go to them. I particularly remember *Ka-at-qhu* (Big Lip), Old Jennie, *Tee-qualt* (Tall), or Long Thresa, and my maternal grandmother, *Soma-how-atqhu* (She-got-her-power-from-the-water). I loved these simple, kindly people, and I think of them often. And in my memory I treasure a picture of my dear mother, who, when I was a very little girl, made the bedtime hours happy for me with the legends she told. She would tell them to me until I fell asleep. Two that are in this collection, "Why Marten's Face Is Wrinkled" and "Why Mosquitoes Bite People," she told over and over again, and I never grew tired of hearing them.

My father always enjoyed telling the old stories, and he does still. He and *Ste-heet-qhu* (Soup), Toma Martin and *Kleen-ment-itqu* are among the few men and women left who can tell *chip-chap-tiqulk*. I thank them for helping me. And I must acknowledge my debt to a blue-eyed "Indian," Lucullus Virgil McWhorter, whom the Yakimas adopted many snows ago and named *He-mēne Kā'wan* (Old Wolf). His heart is warm toward the red people. In him the Indians of the Pacific Northwest have a true friend. But for his insistence and encouragement, these legends would not have been set down by me for the children of another race to read.

<div align="right">MOURNING DOVE.</div>

Contents

I

THE SPIRIT CHIEF NAMES THE ANIMAL PEOPLE

Hah-ah' eel-me'-whem, the great Spirit Chief,[1] called the Animal People together. They came from all parts of the world. Then the Spirit Chief told them there was to be a change, that a new kind of people was coming to live on the earth.

"All of you *Chip-chap-tiqulk*—Animal People—must have names," the Spirit Chief said. "Some of you have names now, some of you haven't. But tomorrow all will have names that shall be kept by you and your descendants forever. In the morning, as the first light of day shows in the sky, come to my lodge and choose your names. The first to come may choose any name that he or she wants. The next person may take any other name. That is the way it will go until all the names are taken. And to each person I will give work to do."

That talk made the Animal People very excited. Each wanted a proud name and the power to rule some tribe or some part of the world, and everyone determined to get up early and hurry to the Spirit Chief's lodge.

Sin-ka-lip'—Coyote—boasted that no one would be ahead of him. He walked among the people and told them that, that he would be the first. Coyote did not like his name; he wanted another. Nobody respected his name, Imitator, but it fitted him. He was called *Sin-ka-lip'* because he liked to imitate people. He thought that he could do anything that other persons did, and he pretended to know everything. He would ask a question, and when the answer was given he would say:

[1]*Hah-ah'*, or *Hwa-hwa'*—Spirit. *Eel-me'-whem*—Chief. While the Okanogan, Colville, and other Salishan stock tribes of the interior paid homage to a great variety of minor "powers" or deities (as many members of the tribes still do), they firmly believed in a Spirit Chief, or Chief Spirit, an all-powerful Man Above. This belief was theirs before they ever heard of Christianity, notwithstanding statements that have been made to the contrary.

313

"I knew that before. I did not have to be told."

Such smart talk did not make friends for Coyote. Nor did he make friends by the foolish things he did and the rude tricks he played on people.

"I shall have my choice of the three biggest names," he boasted. "Those names are: *Kee-lau-naw*, the Mountain Person—Grizzly Bear, who will rule the four-footed people; *Milka-noups*—Eagle,[2] who will rule the birds, and *En-tee-tee-ueh*, the Good Swimmer—Salmon. Salmon will be the chief of all the fish that the New People use for food."

Coyote's twin brother, Fox, who at the next sun took the name *Why-ay'-looh*—Soft Fur, laughed. "Do not be so sure, *Sin-ka-lip'*," said Fox. "Maybe you will have to keep the name you have. People despise that name. No one wants it."

"I am tired of that name," Coyote said in an angry voice. "Let someone else carry it. Let some old person take it—someone who cannot win in war. I am going to be a great warrior. My smart brother, I will make you beg of me when I am called Grizzly Bear, Eagle, or Salmon."

"Your strong words mean nothing," scoffed Fox. "Better go to your *swool'-hu* (tepee) and get some sleep, or you will not wake up in time to choose any name."

Coyote stalked off to his tepee. He told himself that he would not sleep any that night; he would stay wide awake. He entered the lodge, and his three sons called as if with one voice:

"*Le-ee'-oo!*" ("Father!")[3]

They were hungry, but Coyote had brought them nothing to eat. Their mother, who after the naming day was known as *Pul'-laqu-whu*—Mole, the Mound Digger—sat on her foot at one side of the doorway. Mole was a good woman, always loyal to her husband in spite of his mean ways, his mischief-making, and his foolishness. She never was jealous, never talked back, never replied to his words of abuse. She looked up and said:

[2]*Milka-noups*—the "War Eagle," or "Man Eagle" (golden eagle), whose white plumes with black or brown tips are prized for decorative and ceremonial purposes, particularly for war bonnets and other headgear, dance bustles, coup sticks, and shields. The tail feathers of the bald eagle, *Pak-la-kin* (White-headed-bird) are not valued so highly. In the old days the use of eagle feathers was restricted to the men. Except in rare instances, women were not privileged to wear them.

[3]*Le-ee'-oo*. This form of address is employed only by males. A daughter calls her father *Mes-tem*, and her mother *Toom*. A son calls his mother *Se-go-ee*.

"Have you no food for the children? They are starving. I can find no roots to dig."

"*Eh-ha!*" Coyote grunted. "I am no common person to be addressed in that manner. I am going to be a great chief tomorrow. Did you know that? I will have a new name. I will be Grizzly Bear. Then I can devour my enemies with ease. And I shall need you no longer. You are growing too old and homely to be the wife of a great warrior and chief."

Mole said nothing. She turned to her corner of the lodge and collected a few old bones, which she put into a *klek'-chin* (cooking-basket). With two sticks she lifted hot stones from the fire and dropped them into the basket. Soon the water boiled, and there was weak soup for the hungry children.

"Gather plenty of wood for the fire," Coyote ordered. "I am going to sit up all night."

Mole obeyed. Then she and the children went to bed.

Coyote sat watching the fire. Half of the night passed. He got sleepy. His eyes grew heavy. So he picked up two little sticks and braced his eyelids apart. "Now I can stay awake," he thought, but before long he was fast asleep, although his eyes were wide open.

The sun was high in the sky when Coyote awoke. But for Mole he would not have wakened then. Mole called him. She called him after she returned with her name from the Spirit Chief's lodge. Mole loved her husband. She did not want him to have a big name and be a powerful chief. For then, she feared, he would leave her. That was why she did not arouse him at daybreak. Of this she said nothing.

Only half-awake and thinking it was early morning, Coyote jumped at the sound of Mole's voice and ran to the lodge of the Spirit Chief. None of the other *Chip-chap-tiqulk* were there. Coyote laughed. Blinking his sleepy eyes, he walked into the lodge. "I am going to be *Kee-lau-naw*," he announced in a strong voice. "That shall be my name."

"The name Grizzly Bear was taken at dawn," the Spirit Chief answered.

"Then I shall be *Milka-noups*," said Coyote, and his voice was not so loud.

"Eagle flew away at sunup," the other replied.

"Well, I shall be called *En-tee-tee-ueh*," Coyote said in a voice that was not loud at all.

"The name Salmon also has been taken," explained the Spirit Chief.

"All the names except your own have been taken. No one wished to steal your name."

Poor Coyote's knees grew weak. He sank down beside the fire that blazed in the great tepee, and the heart of *Hah-ah' El-me'-whem* was touched.

"*Sin-ka-lip'*," said that Person, "you must keep your name. It is a good name for you. You slept long because I wanted you to be the last one here. I have important work for you, much for you to do before the New People come. You are to be chief of all the tribes.

"Many bad creatures inhabit the earth. They bother and kill people, and the tribes cannot increase as I wish. These *En-alt-na Skil-ten*— People-Devouring Monsters—cannot keep on like that. They must be stopped. It is for you to conquer them. For doing that, for all the good things you do, you will be honored and praised by the people that are here now and that come afterward. But, for the foolish and mean things you do, you will be laughed at and despised. That you cannot help. It is your way.

"To make your work easier, I give you *squastenk'*. It is your own special magic power. No one else ever shall have it. When you are in danger, whenever you need help, call to your power. It will do much for you, and with it you can change yourself into any form, into anything you wish.

"To your twin brother, *Why-ay'-looh*, and to others I have given *shoo'-mesh*.[4] It is strong power. With that power Fox can restore your life should you be killed. You bones may be scattered but, if there is one hair of your body left, Fox can make you live again. Others of the people can do the same with their *shoo'-mesh*. Now, go, *Sin-ka-lip'*! Do well the work laid for your trail!"

Well, Coyote was a chief after all, and he felt good again. After that day his eyes were different. They grew slant from being propped open that night while he sat by his fire. The New People, the Indians, got their slightly slant eyes from Coyote.

After Coyote had gone, the Spirit Chief thought it would be nice for the Animal People and the coming New People to have the benefit

[4]*Shoo'-mesh*. With the exception of Coyote's "power," all "medicine" is spoken of as *shoo'-mesh*, which is regarded as definite aid communicated by the Spirit Chief through various mediums, inanimate objects as well as living creatures. Not infrequently an Indian will seek to test the potency of his medicine over that of another. Some present day medicine-men and medicine-women are reputed to possess magic power strong enough to cause the sickness or even the death of enemies, of anyone incurring their displeasure.

of the spiritual sweat-house. But all of the Animal People had names, and there was no one to take the name of Sweat-house—*Quil'-sten,* the Warmer.[5] So the wife of the Spirit Chief took the name. She wanted the people to have the sweat-house, for she pitied them. She wanted them to have a place to go to purify themselves, a place where they could pray for strength and good luck and strong medicine-

[5]*Quil'-sten*—Sweat-house. A mystic shrine for both temporal and spiritual cleansing, the sweat-house is one of the most venerated institutions. Its use is governed by strict rules, said to have originated with Coyote, the great "law-giver." To break any of the rules is to invite misfortune, if not disaster.

Sweat-houses, or lodges, are mound-shaped, round at the base, three and one-half to four feet high at the center, and four to six feet in diameter, accommodating three to five persons. In some sweat-houses there is room but for one or two bathers.

Willow shoots, service berry or other pliant stems, depending upon the locality and growth available, are planted like interlocking croquet wickets to make the frame. Where these "ribs" cross, they are tied together with strips of bark. There are never less than eight ribs. The frame is covered with swamp tule mats, blankets, or canvas. In primitive times sheets of cottonwood bark, top-dressed with earth, frequently formed the covering. Where a permanent residence is established, the framework is covered with tule mats, top-dressed with three or more inches of soil that is well packed and smoothed. The floor is carpeted with matting, grass, ferns, or fir boughs. The last are regarded as "strong medicine," and always are used if obtainable. They give the bather strength, and they are liked, besides, for their aromatic odor. The Indians rub their bodies with the soft tips of the fir boughs, both for the purpose of deriving power and for the scent imparted.

Just within and at one side of the lodge entrance, a small hole serves as a receptacle for the stones that are heated in a brisk fire a few steps from the structure. The stones, the size of a man's fist, are smooth, unchipped, "dry land" stones—never river-bed rocks. The latter crack and explode too easily when subjected to a combination of intense heat and cold water. By means of stout sticks, the heated stones are carried or rolled from the fire into the sweathouse. Then the entrance is curtained tightly with mat or blanket, and the bather sprinkles cold water on the little pile of stones, creating a dense steam.

To the novice, five minutes spent in the sweltering, midnight blackness of the cramping structure seem an eternity and almost unendurable.

Several "sweats," each followed by a dip in a nearby stream or pool, properly constitute one sweat-bath. The customary period for a single sweat is ten to twenty minutes, although votaries from rival bands or tribes often crouch together in the steam for twice or thrice that time. Thus they display to one another their virility and hardihood. To further show their strength and their contempt for the discomfort of such protracted sweating, they will blow on their arms and chests. The forcing of the breath against the superheated skin produces a painful, burning sensation. Hours, even days, may be spent in "sweat-housing."

The stones used are saved and piled outside the sweat-lodge, where they remain undisturbed. For services rendered they are held in a regard bordering on reverence. An Indian would not think of spitting or stepping on these stones or of "desecrating" them in any way.

Old-time warriors and hunters always "sweat-housed" before starting on their expeditions, and many of the modern, school-educated Indian men and women often resort to the sweat-house to pray for good fortune and health.

power, and where they could fight sickness and get relief from their troubles.

The ribs, the frame poles, of the sweat-house represent the wife of *Hah-ah' Ele-me'-whem*. As she is a spirit, she cannot be seen, but she always is near. Songs to her are sung by the present generation. She hears them. She hears what her people say, and in her heart there is love and pity.

II

FOX AND COYOTE AND WHALE

Fox had a beautiful wife. He was very much in love with her, but she had stopped caring for him. Fox was a great hunter, and every day he brought home food and fine skins for his wife to make into robes and clothing. He did not know that, while he was away hunting, his wife would sit beside the *Swah-netk'-qhu*[1] and sing love songs to the water. Painting her face with bright colors, she would pour out her love thoughts in song.

Coyote came to visit his twin brother, and he soon noticed the strange actions of his sister-in-law. He spoke to Fox. "*Why-ay'-looh*," he said, "I think your wife is in love with somebody else." But Fox could not believe she loved anyone but him. He was blinded by his love for her. Then, one sun, he and Coyote returned from a hunt and she was not in the lodge. So Fox started to look for her. He walked down toward the river and there he saw his wife. She was sitting on the river bank, singing a love song. She did not see Fox. He watched her.

As Fox watched, the water began to rise. Slowly it rose, higher and higher, and soon, out in the middle of the river, appeared a big monster of the fish-kind. The monster was *En-hah-et'-qhu*, the Spirit of the Water—Whale. It swam to the shore. As it touched dry land, it changed into a tall handsome man with long braided hair. This monster-man made love to the wife of Fox.

Sad at heart, Fox turned away. He went to his lodge. He said nothing, but he wondered how he could win back his wife's love. He worried about her as the suns passed. She grew pale and thin. Nothing that Fox could do pleased her. Her thoughts always were with the man who was not a man but a monster. One day when Fox and Coyote came home from hunting, she was gone, and the fire in the

[1]*Swah-netk'-qhu* (also recorded as *Swah-netk'-qha, Swah-netk'-qua, Soin-et'-kwu* and *Schwan-ate'-koo*—the Columbia River).

lodge was cold. Fox called and called. He got no answer. His heart was heavy.

A few suns later Fox looked up the river and saw an odd-shaped canoe coming. It was only half of a canoe. Two Water Maidens were standing in it, rocking it from side to side. They were singing:

> We come for food,
> Food for the Chief's stolen wife.
> The water-food does not suit her.
> That is why we come! We come!

As the Water Maidens approached, Fox and Coyote hid in the tepee. The maidens beached the half-canoe and entered the lodge. They began to pick up dried meat to take to the stolen wife. Coyote and Fox sprang from their hiding places and caught the maidens, and Fox asked about his wife—where she was and how to get to her. The maidens were silent. Then the brothers threatened to kill them unless they answered, and the maidens said:

"To find the person who stole her, you must go over the Big Falls[2] and under the water. His lodge is under the falls, under the water—a dangerous trip for Land People. Every trail is watched. Even if you get there, the mighty Whale chief will kill you. He is bad."

The Water Maidens had told all they knew, so Fox broke their necks. He and Coyote dressed in the maidens' robes and started down the river in the half-canoe. Standing on the sides of the strange craft, they rocked it as they had seen the maidens do, and rode it down the river and over the roaring falls. "Let me do all the talking," Fox warned Coyote. "I know better what to say." Down through the pouring, flashing waters they shot with the half-canoe. The thunder of the falls hurt their ears. And then, suddenly, they were landing at a great encampment of Water People, a strange kind of people to them. All of the people were strange except *Gou-kouh-whay'-na*—Mouse.

[2]Big Falls—Kettle Falls in the Columbia River, two miles below the mouth of Kettle River, in Stevens and Ferry counties, Washington. *Swah-netk'-qhu*, which means "Big Water" and also "Big Waterfalls," is applied by the Okanogan to Kettle Falls, as well as to the river. Early French-Canadian travelers, trappers and traders called the falls *La Chaudiere*, hence "Kettle." The water churning in the pot-holes among the rocks was likened to water boiling in huge kettles or caldrons. The Indians call these pot-holes *klek'-chin* because of their fancied resemblance to the primitive cooking-baskets. For many years prior to the establishment of Fort Colville, and even thereafter, the Indians living in the vicinity of the falls were known as *Les Chaudieres* and as Kettle, Bucket, Caldron, and Pot Indians.

She was there. She knew them and they knew her. Fox jumped ashore. Coyote, following, tripped and touched the water, and Mouse, the Sly One, laughed. "Ha-ha!" said Mouse, "Coyote nearly fell into the water."

"Do not speak," Fox whispered to Mouse. "Say nothing. I will pay you well."

But some of the Water People had heard. "What, *Gou-kouh-whay'-na*, did you say?" they inquired.

"Nothing," Mouse answered. "Nothing of importance. I was just joking."

"Yes, you did say something," said a Water Person. "You said that Coyote nearly fell into the water. You cannot fool me."

Mouse insisted that she had not said that, and the other Water People believed her. They knew she was a fickle person and giddy, and they did not think much of her because she went everywhere to steal. She went everywhere, and that is why she understood all the different languages.

Carrying packs of dried meat and berries they had brought with them, Coyote and Fox made their way to the lodge of Whale, the chief. He and the stolen wife sat side by side in the lodge. The wife was glad to get the meat and berries, her kind of food.

Fox and Coyote kept their robes over their faces until everyone else was asleep. Then, when everything was quiet, Fox slipped up to Whale and cut off the monster's head with a flint knife. At the same time Coyote picked up the stolen wife and ran for the broken canoe. The noise they made awoke the camp, and the people rushed out of their lodges to see Coyote carrying off Fox's wife and Fox close behind, carrying the head of their chief. The people chased them, but the three got into the broken canoe, and Fox quickly put Coyote and the woman into his *shoo'-mesh* pipe. Then Fox pushed the half-canoe into the water and it shot up to the river's surface below the falls. There Fox landed. He took Coyote and his twice-stolen wife out of the medicine-pipe, and the head of the Whale Monster he threw toward the setting sun.

"In the Big Salt Water (ocean) shall Whale Monster stay," said Fox. "No longer shall he live in the smaller waters, in the rivers, where he can make love to the wives of men, where he can lure wives from their husbands."

As Fox and his wife and brother walked up the bank to their tepee, the headless body of Whale Monster turned over and over in the

depths of the river, making the Big Falls of the *Swah-netk'-qhu* more fearful and thunderous, the way they are today, spilling with such force over the great rocks.

The wife of Fox became contented and happy again, glad to be back in her husband's lodge. But since that day Whale Monster was vanquished the Land People and the Water People have not loved each other. Fox made it so.

III

Coyote Fights Some Monsters

Coyote was far from his home by the *Swah-nekt'-qhu*. For many suns he had been traveling toward the sunrise. He had crossed the Rocky Mountains and was in the great plains country. *Sin-kit-zas-caw'-ha*—Horse—lived there. Horse was a dangerous monster, and he was much bigger than is any horse today.

As soon as he saw Coyote, Horse took after him. They ran and ran over the bare plains. Every time that Coyote looked back, Horse was closer. Coyote became scared. "*Squas-tenk'!*" he cried. "Do something for me!"

His power heard. It made three trees. They grew out of the ground straight ahead of him. And just in time, for Horse was about to catch him.

Into the first tree jumped Coyote. He laughed, for he thought he was safe. But his laugh was short; Horse began to cut down the tree with his strong teeth and great hoofs. Horse made the splinters fly. Soon the tree creaked, and then it cracked and groaned, and then—*she-wha-a-am!*—it crashed to the plain, and Coyote went sailing through the air. He hit the ground hard, and Horse thought he had him, but Coyote staggered to his feet and got into the second tree.

Then Horse cut down that tree, and Coyote had another bad fall. Horse almost caught him. But Coyote skipped and dodged and finally got into the third tree. "Now what can I do?" he wondered. He was in a bad fix. Horse began to chop this last tree out from under him.

"Oh, *Sin-kit-zas-caw'-ha*, wait!" Coyote shouted. "I am not ready to die. Before you kill me, let me smoke my pipe—my pipe I like so well."

"You may have one smoke, *Sin-ka-lip'*," said Horse. "That is all. After that I shall kill you."

Puffing on his pipe, Coyote spoke to his medicine. It gave him a

327

whip. Coyote jumped on his enemy's broad back, and struck fiercely with the whip. Horse was taken by surprise. He bawled and bucked; he whirled around and around; he stood on his hind feet and on his front feet; he threw himself; he rolled—tried all his tricks.

Coyote stayed with him, and he kept smacking Horse with the medicine-whip. He whipped Horse until the monster's head was battered and his eyes were swollen shut. After awhile Horse could not buck and fight any more. He was tired out. He begged for mercy. Coyote hopped off his back and looked at him. Horse was changed. He was not big and dangerous now. He was smaller, much smaller. Coyote had beaten him down.

"From this sun you are for people to ride," Coyote said. "Only when first ridden will you buck and be mean. Even old men will be able to sit on you. And old women will use you for carrying their camp things. On you they will put their heavy packs of roots and berries and meat."

He left the horse standing there, and went on. His way led past a cave. It was the home of *Kika-wau'-pa*—Dog who was a big and ferocious monster. Dog rushed out of the cave. Coyote ran. Coyote stumbled, falling into a mole hole, and that made him think of his faithful wife, Mole. Making himself small, he crawled into the hole, and there was Mole herself.

"Make your underground trails," Coyote said. "Make many of your tunnels. Hurry!"

Mole set to work. She dug fast, for Dog was digging to get at her husband. She dug many tunnels, as Coyote had ordered.

Dog soon uncovered Coyote, who then resumed his usual form, and said:

"Wait, *Kika-wau'-pa!* Do not kill me yet. Let me smoke my pipe first."

Dog did not object to that, and Coyote smoked. As he sucked on his pipe, Coyote spoke to his *squas-tenk'*. It gave him an armful of stones. Hitting Dog with a stone, he ran. Dog howled with pain and rage, and set out after him. Dog stumbled over one of Mole's mounded tunnels and fell, and Coyote hit him with another stone. Dog did not know that Mole had been busy changing the ground there, and every time he came to a tunnel he stumbled and fell, and each time he went down Coyote hit him with a stone. That was the way it went, and in a little while Dog was so tired and bruised that he could not take another

step. Then Coyote finished him, and out of the monster's body ran a small dog, its tail between its legs.

"You shall be the most faithful animal the New People will have," said Coyote to the little dog. "Even old men and old women will own you. You will both fear and like your owners. Never must you attack a stranger unless the stranger treats you badly."

Coyote left the little dog. Presently he came to a big *che-yeep'* (tree), which he started to pass around. The tree bent and caught him with its branches. He wriggled and squirmed, but he could not get loose, so he whispered to his medicine. At once a great strength came to Coyote. With a mighty wrench, he tore the tree apart; tore it into two forks, like unfinished canoes, and he was free. Looking around, he noticed on the ground the bleached bones of travelers whom Tree Monster had eaten, and he said:

"After this sun you cannot hurt anyone. No one will fear you. You will provide wood for the New People. Because your limbs are pitchy and so easy to burn, all trees that are forked will be the kind that the old women will go to for firewood. That wood will be easy for them to gather."

From that place Coyote's trail took him into a deep *insis-k-chin* (canyon). As he walked deeper and deeper into it, he felt himself being swallowed. Scared, he tried to turn back. He could not move. He begged not to be eaten. The sound of his voice made Canyon Monster hesitate, and Coyote spoke to his *squas-tenk'*. It placed a long tree on his shoulders. Coyote swung the tree across the mouth of Canyon Monster. Then he laughed—the monster could not hurt him now.

"You no longer are a person-eating monster," Coyote said. "The New People will not be afraid of you. When they are too lazy to walk down your throat, they will walk on trees thrown across your mouth."

Coyote walked away from there and came to a coulee. He started into it. Something bumped and pricked his back. He could not see anything behind him and he ran. But the strange jabbing and bumping did not stop, so he stood still and spoke to his power. It gave him a flint knife. He slashed back over his shoulder. The knife struck something solid, and there was a loud groan and a heavy thud. Then Coyote saw what had been bothering him. On the ground was *Ste-eel'-tza*—Elk.[1] That monster was dead. Its power to stay invisible was gone. Coyote made a small elk from Elk Monster's body.

[1]*Ste-eel'-tza*—"pounded-meat." As the fresh elk meat tends to spoil quickly, most of

"No more shall you abuse people on the trails," he said. "You will fear the New People, and they will use your flesh for food and your skin for robes."

Coyote went on. He saw a cradleboard propped against a tree. Fastened in the cradle was a baby. No one else was in sight, and Coyote wondered where the mother had gone. Hoping he might be paid for showing attention to the little one, Coyote rocked it and sang. He wanted the mother to hear and come. Louder and louder he sang, but nobody came, and the baby began to cry. Thinking it must be hungry, Coyote poked one of his fingers into its mouth. "Do not cry," he said. "Here is *tah tat!*"

Then Coyote had a surprise. The baby was swallowing his hand! He jerked his hand away; the flesh was stripped off clean. Coyote realized that he was holding, not a baby, but a person-eating monster.

"I will find your mother, little *skwas-qu-see* (baby). I will look for her," he said, and he put the baby down and walked away. He slipped into a thicket. There he called softly to his *squas-tenk'*. It handed him a flint knife that was shaped like a finger. The blade was sharp. Coyote returned to Baby Monster and picked it up. Talking nice words, he put the knife-finger in the monster's mouth. He held the knife-finger in his own fingers, and Baby Monster swallowed his whole arm. That was what Coyote wanted. He pulled his arm back, pulled it back quickly, and the sharp knife-finger ripped open the monster's insides. Out tumbled a lot of bones, bones of people the false baby had eaten.

"You cannot do this way any more," said Coyote. "A New People soon will be here. You are not to eat them as you have these others. From now on, babies, when born, will be the most helpless of all creatures. That must be, so you cannot cheat by taking their form."

Weary of fighting monsters, Coyote started for home. "Even babies are monsters in this strange land," he remarked. "I will go back to my own country by the *Swah-netk'-qhu* and rest."

it is "jerked," or dried, or made into pemmican. When half dry, the meat is pounded to break the fibre, which makes it easier to chew.

If made into pemmican, the meat is mixed with grease and service berries. Properly prepared, pemmican will keep for several years.

In the old days, much of this jerked elk meat and elk pemmican was obtained by the Okanogans in trade. It was transported from the source of supply and from camp to camp in rawhide containers, parfleches, which the Indians called *pen'-pen-nox* (folded-at-the-ends).

IV

CHIPMUNK AND OWL-WOMAN

K*ots-se-we-ah*—Chipmunk—was a little girl. She lived with her grandmother in the woods. Chipmunk liked to walk through the woods and pick berries. Some of the berries she ate, and some she put in a little basket that hung at her side. The basket was made from a deer's hoof.

There was one berry bush that the little girl visited every day. She called it her very own. It was a *see'-ah* (service berry) bush.[1] She would climb into it and eat all the berries she could hold. And as she ate them she would count: "One berry ripe! Two berries ripe! Three berries ripe!"

One sun, while in the bush counting and eating berries, Chipmunk heard steps on the ground below. She looked. Standing under the bush was *Snee'-nah*—Owl-woman. On Owl-woman's back was a big basket, and in the basket were many little children that Owl-woman had stolen. Owl-woman traveled from camp to camp, stealing children. Whenever she got hungry she ate one or two of them.

Chipmunk was not frightened very much, for she knew that Owl-woman could not reach her up in the *see'-ah* bush, and Owl-woman knew that too. But Owl-woman was cunning. In her best voice, she said: "*Kots-se-we-ah*, your father wants you."

"I have no father," Chipmunk answered. "He died long ago."

Owl-woman thought for a moment. Then she said: "Your mother wants you. She wants you to come home."

"My mother died many snows ago," Chipmunk replied.

"Your aunt wants you to come home."

"I never had an aunt," and Chipmunk laughed.

"Your uncle is looking for you," lied Owl-woman.

"That is funny," said Chipmunk laughing, some more. "I never had an uncle."

[1]The service berry, *Amelanchier alnifolia*. The fruit resembles the black currant but has a sweeter flavor. The Indians gather large quantities and sun-dry them for winter use. The berries are used also in the making of pemmican.

"Well," Owl-woman sighed, "your grandfather wants you."

"That is strange, for my grandfather died before I was born."

Then Owl-woman said: "Your grandmother wants you at home right away!"

Chipmunk could believe that. She was silent for a little, and then she said:

"I will not come down unless you hide your eyes."

"All right, I will hide my eyes. See I have them covered," and Owl-woman pretended that she had. She placed her claw-hands over them.

"I can see your big eyes blinking behind your fingers," cried Chipmunk. "I shall not come down until you have hidden them entirely."

Owl-woman pretended to hide her eyes entirely, but she left a small space between her fingers—just a little crack to look through.

Chipmunk really thought that the eyes were covered, but she wasn't taking any chance of being fooled. Instead of dropping from branch to branch to the ground, she jumped from the top of the bush. She jumped over Owl-woman's head, and, as she went sailing over, Owl-woman reached for her. Owl-woman's fingers clawed down Chipmunk's back, ripping off long strips of the soft fur, but the little girl got away. Ever since that time the chipmunks have carried the marks of Owl-woman's claws—the marks are the stripes you see on the chipmunk's backs.

Chipmunk ran and ran, and Owl-woman followed as fast as she could.

When Chipmunk reached home, she was trembling and out of breath. She hardly could speak. All she could say was:

"*Sing-naw! Sing-naw!*" ("Owl! Owl!")

The deaf old grandmother misunderstood. "Did you step on a thorn?" she asked.

"*Sing-naw! Sing-naw!*" Chipmunk kept repeating. She was so frightened, it was all she could say.

Only after Chipmunk had said that many times did the grandmother understand. Then she tried to hide the little girl in her bed, but Chipmunk would not keep still there. She ran around under the robes. Anyone could see she was there. So the grandmother took her out of the bed and dropped her into a berry basket. But that wouldn't do, for Chipmunk rattled around in the basket and made a lot of noise. Then the grandmother tried to hide her in a basket of soup, and poor Chipmunk nearly drowned. She and her grandmother were in despair.

They did not know what to do. Then they heard a voice—it came from a tree near the tepee. It was the voice of *Wy-wetz'-kula*, the Tattler—Meadow Lark, who was singing:

> "Two little oyster shells
> Hide her in!"

Quickly the grandmother put Chipmunk between two little oyster shells. And, knowing Meadow Lark was a gossip and a tattler, she took off her necklace and threw it to the singer. She hoped that the present would please Meadow Lark and keep her from telling where Chipmunk was hidden. Meadow Lark put on the necklace and flew away.

Soon Owl-woman came along.

"Where is the child I am hunting?" she said.

The grandmother pretended that she had not seen her grandchild, so Owl-woman began to look around. She looked in the bed, in the berry basket and in the soup. She looked everywhere she could think might be a hiding place. At last she turned to leave, and just then Meadow Lark flew back to the tree near the tepee. Meadow Lark sang:

> "I will tell you, if you pay me.
> I will tell you, if you pay me.
> Where she is! Where she is!"

Owl-woman hurried outside and threw a bright yellow vest to the Tattler, who put it on, and sang:

> "Two little oyster shells,
> Take her out!
> Two little oyster shells,
> Take her out!"

Then Meadow Lark flew away. The necklace she was given for helping Chipmunk and the yellow vest she earned for tattling she wears to this day.

Owl-woman pushed the grandmother aside and snatched Chipmunk out of the oyster shells. With her sharp fingers she cut Chipmunk open and took out her heart and swallowed it.

"*Eh!* Yom-yom! It is good. Little girls' hearts are the best," said Owl-woman, smacking her lips.

Owl-woman went her way, carrying her big basket of children. In a little while the weeping grandmother heard a familiar voice. Meadow Lark was singing again from the tree. Her song was:

"Put a berry in her heart!
Put a berry in her heart!"

Drying her tears, the grandmother put a half-ripe *see'-ah* berry in Chipmunk's breast and sewed up the hole. Then she stepped over Chipmunk three times, and Chipmunk jumped up as alive and as well as ever.

Owl-woman had not walked far when she met Coyote. He knew her—knew how wicked she was. "*Snee'-nah*," he said, "I like to eat children, too. Let us travel together and we will have better luck finding them."

Owl-woman was pleased. She thought that the two of them, traveling together and helping each other, would be stronger than all of the monsters in the world. She smiled. "Yes, that is good," she said. "Let us go together." So they walked along like old friends.

Pretty soon Coyote said: "I am getting hungry. Here is a good place to make a fire. Let us stop here and roast those children you are carrying in the basket."

Owl-woman said she was hungry, too, and she set her big basket on the ground. Coyote persuaded her to let all of the children out so they could do the work of gathering wood for the fire. Coyote bossed them around, talking in a cruel way. That was for Owl-woman's ears—that cruel talk. But to each child he whispered: "Get the wood that has the most pitch and get plenty of solid pitch. Do that if you wish to return to your parents."

Coyote's words made the children work hard. Soon there was a roaring fire.

"This is to be an important feast," Coyote told Owl-woman. "You should paint your face. Paint it with charcoal and rub it with pitch. The pitch will make the charcoal stay on. Your arms should be painted the same way. The children and I will help you fix up."

Coyote's attention flattered Owl-woman. She let him and the children help her to prepare for the feast. They painted her arms with charcoal, and then smeared them with pitch, and she painted her face the same way.

"Now, let us roast the children," she said.

"No, not yet," Coyote advised. "Wait until the wood burns to red coals. That pitch smoke would spoil the taste. But we can do something while we are waiting. We can dance. Let us dance the Sun-dance. While we are having a good time, the children shall gather forked roasting sticks."

"Good, we will dance," said Owl-woman. "But why the forked roasting sticks?"

"Because forked sticks are better than straight ones for roasting children."

Coyote told the children to hurry and gather forked sticks, and he and Owl-woman began to dance. They danced and danced. Owl-woman grew tired. She wanted to stop.

"Do not stop so soon," Coyote urged. "You are a good dancer. I like to see you dance."

Owl-woman believed those sly words. She danced harder and harder, until she staggered. Then, as if in play, Coyote shoved her, and she fell. Coyote laughed, and Owl-woman laughed, and she got up and danced again. Coyote danced beside her. And when she got close to the fire he shoved her right into the flames. He called to the children, and they brought the forked sticks which they and Coyote used to hold Owl-woman in the fire. Covered as she was with pitch, Owl-woman burned like pitchwood.

In that way perished the wicked Owl-woman. Bad persons always must pay for the evil workings of their minds.

V

COYOTE AND THE BUFFALO

No buffalo ever lived in the *Swah-netk'-qhu* country. That was Coyote's fault. If he had not been so foolish and greedy, the people beside the *Swah-netk'-qhu* would not have had to cross the Rockies to hunt the *quas-peet-za* (curled-hairs).[1]

This is the way it happened:

Coyote was traveling over the plains beyond the big mountains. He came to a flat. There he found an old buffalo skull. It was the skull of Buffalo Bull. Coyote always had been afraid of Buffalo Bull. He remembered the many times Bull Buffalo had scared him, and he laughed upon seeing the old skull there on the flat.

"Now I will have some fun," Coyote remarked. "I will have revenge for the times Buffalo made me run."

He picked up the skull and threw it into the air; he kicked it and spat on it; he threw dust in the eye-sockets. He did these things many times, until he grew tired. Then he went his way. Soon he heard a rumbling behind him. He thought it was thunder, and he looked at the sky. The sky was clear. Thinking he must have imagined the sound, he walked on, singing. He heard the rumbling again, only much closer and louder. Turning around, he saw Buffalo Bull pounding along after him, chasing him. His old enemy had come to life!

Coyote ran, faster than he thought he could run, but Buffalo gained steadily. Soon Buffalo was right at his heels. Coyote felt his hot breath.

"Oh, *Squas-tenk'*, help me!" Coyote begged, and his power answered by putting three trees in front of him. They were there in the wink of an eye. Coyote jumped and caught a branch of the first tree and swung out of Buffalo's way. Buffalo rammed the tree hard, and it

[1]*Quas-peet-za* ("curled-hairs" or "curly-haired.") The same word is used for "buffalo robes." The Okanogan and other interior Northwest tribes occasionally hunted buffalo east of the Rockies, and they frequently obtained buffalo robes and dried buffalo meat in trade.

shook as if in a strong wind. Then Buffalo chopped at the trunk with his horns, first with one horn and then the other. He chopped fast, and in a little while over went the tree, and with it went Coyote. But he was up and into the second tree before Buffalo Bull could reach him. Buffalo soon laid that tree low, but he was not quick enough to catch Coyote, who scrambled into the third and last tree.

"Buffalo, my friend, let me talk with you," said Coyote, as his enemy hacked away at the tree's trunk. "Let me smoke my pipe. I like the *kinnikinnick*.[2] Let me smoke. Then I can die more content."

"You may have time for one smoke," grunted Bull Buffalo, resting from his chopping.

Coyote spoke to his medicine-power, and a pipe, loaded and lighted, was given to him. He puffed on it once and held out the pipe to Buffalo Bull.

"No, I will not smoke with you," said that one. "You made fun of my bones. I have enough enemies without you. Young Buffalo is one of them. He killed me and stole all my fine herd."

"My uncle,"[3] said Coyote, "you need new horns. Let me make new horns for you. Then you can kill Young Buffalo. Those old horns are dull and worn."

Bull Buffalo was pleased with that talk. He decided he did not want to kill Coyote. He told Coyote to get down out of the tree and make the new horns. Coyote jumped down and called to his power. It scolded him for getting into trouble, but it gave him a flint knife and a stump of pitchwood. From this stump Coyote carved a pair of fine heavy horns with sharp points. He gave them to Buffalo Bull. All buffalo bulls have worn the same kind of horns since.

Buffalo Bull was very proud of his new horns. He liked their sharpness and weight and their pitch-black color. He tried them out

[2]*Kinnikinnick*—the Bear Berry, *Arctostaphylos Uvaursi*, which grows on high mountain ridges. The thick evergreen leaves are toasted and then crumbled. The modern mixture for pipe smoking is about two-thirds tobacco to one-third *kinnikinnick*. The leaves are toasted either before an open fire, by placing a sprig of the plant in a cleft stick that is stuck in the ground, or in a sweat-house. In the latter case, branches of the shrub are laid on the sweat-house framework, between the frame and the covering, and left for an hour or more—during the course of a sweat-bath. The leaves are browned and dried as effectively by the steam as by dry heat.

[3]"My uncle." Coyote is not claiming actual relationship with Buffalo. He uses the term to curry favor. Indians commonly employ *uncle, cousin, brother, sister, aunt, grandfather* and *grandmother* in addressing persons to whom they are not related. They do this either to express genuine affection or respect, or to cajole and flatter. Cousins and intimate friends regularly are called *brothers* or *sisters*.

on what was left of the pitchwood stump. He made one toss and the stump flew high in the air, and he forgave Coyote for his mischief. They became good friends right there. Coyote said he would go along with Buffalo Bull to find Young Buffalo.

They soon came upon Young Buffalo and the big herd he had won from Buffalo Bull. Young Buffalo laughed when he saw his old enemy, and he walked out to meet him. He did not know, of course, about the new horns. It was not much of a fight, that fight between Young Buffalo and Buffalo Bull. With the fine new horns, Buffalo Bull killed the other easily, and then he took back his herd, all his former wives and their children. He gave Coyote a young cow, the youngest cow, and he said:

"Never kill her, *Sin-ka-lip'!* Take good care of her and she will supply you with meat forever. When you get hungry, just slice off some choice fat with a flint knife. Then rub ashes on the wound and the cut will heal at once."

Coyote promised to remember that, and they parted. Coyote started back to his own country, and the cow followed. For a few suns he ate only the fat when he was hungry. But after awhile he became tired of eating fat, and he began to long for the sweet marrow-bones and the other good parts of the buffalo. He smacked his lips at the thought of having some warm liver.

"Buffalo Bull will never know," Coyote told himself, and he took his young cow down beside a creek and killed her.

As he peeled off the hide, crows and magpies came from all directions. They settled on the carcass and picked at the meat. Coyote tried to chase them away, but there were too many of them. While he was chasing some, others returned and ate the meat. It was not long until they had devoured every bit of the meat.

"Well, I can get some good from the bones and marrow-fat," Coyote remarked, and he built a fire to cook the bones. Then he saw an old woman walking toward him. She came up to the fire.

"*Sin-ka-lip'*," she said, "you are a brave warrior, a great chief. Why should you do woman's work? Let me cook the bones while you rest."

Vain Coyote! He was flattered. He believed she spoke her true mind. He stretched out to rest and he fell asleep. In his sleep he had a bad dream. It awoke him, and he saw the old woman running away with the marrow-fat and the boiled grease. He looked into the cooking-basket. There was not a drop of soup left in it. He chased the old

woman. He would punish her! But she could run, too, and she easily kept ahead of him. Every once in awhile she stopped and held up the marrow-fat and shouted: "*Sin-ka-lip'*, do you want this?"

Finally Coyote gave up trying to catch her. He went back to get the bones. He thought he would boil them again. He found the bones scattered all around, so he gathered them up and put them into the cooking-basket. Needing some more water to boil them in, he went to the creek for it, and when he got back, there were no bones in the basket! In place of the bones was a little pile of tree limbs!

Coyote thought he might be able to get another cow from Buffalo Bull, so he set out to find him. When he came to the herd, he was astonished to see the cow he had killed. She was there with the others! She refused to go with Coyote again, and Buffalo Bull would not give him another cow. Coyote had to return to his own country without a buffalo.

That is why there never have been any buffalo along the *Swah-netk'-qhu*.

VI

WHY THE FLINT-ROCK CANNOT FIGHT BACK

Sto-way'-na—Flint[1]—was rich and powerful. His lodge was toward the sunrise. It was guarded by *Squr-bein*—Crane. He was the watcher. He watched from the top of a lone tree. When anybody approached, Crane would call out and warn Flint, and Flint would come out of his lodge and meet the visitor.

There was an open flat in front of the lodge. Flint met all his visitors there. Warriors and hunters came and bought flint for arrow-points and spear-heads. They paid Flint big prices for the privilege of chipping off the hard stone. Some who needed flint for their weapons were poor and could not buy. These poor persons Flint turned away.

Coyote heard about Flint and, as he wanted some arrow-points, he asked his *squas-tenk'* to help him. *Squas-tenk'* refused.

"Hurry, do what I ask, or I will throw you away and let the rain wash you—wash you cold," said Coyote, and then the power gave him three rocks that were harder than the flint-rock. It also gave him a little dog that had only one ear. But this ear was sharp, like a knife; it was a knife-ear.

Then to his wife, Mole, Coyote said: "Go and make your underground trails in the flat where *Sto-way'-na* lives. When you have finished and see me talking with him, show yourself so we can see you."

Then Coyote set out for Flint's lodge. As he got near it, he had his power make a fog to cover the land, and thick fog spread over everything. Crane, the watcher, up in the lone tree, could not see Coyote. He did not know that Coyote was around.

Coyote climbed the tree and took Crane from his high perch and broke his neck. Crane had no time to cry out. Then Coyote went on

[1]*Sto-way'-na*—literally "hard rock."

to Flint's lodge. He was almost there when Flint's dog, Grizzly Bear, jumped out of the lodge and ran toward him.

Coyote was not scared, and he yelled at Flint: "Stop your grizzly bear dog! Stop him, or my dog will kill him."

That amused Flint, who was looking through the doorway. He saw that Coyote's one-eared dog was very small, hardly a mouthful for Grizzly Bear. Flint came out of his lodge. He was laughing.

"Sin-ka-lip', you better take your dog away. My Grizzly Bear will eat him up."

"No, stop your dog," repeated Coyote. "One-Ear is bad!"

"Hah!" laughed Flint. "No dog can hurt my Grizzly Bear!"

So, without more talk, Coyote sent One-Ear at Grizzly Bear, who opened his mouth wide. The little dog went right ahead and jumped straight into Grizzly Bear's mouth, and kept on going. He went clear through Grizzly Bear. His sharp knife-ear cut Flint's dog wide open.

"See!" Coyote said. "I told you that One-Ear was bad. He can kill anything."

About that time Mole appeared at the far edge of the flat. She was dressed in skins that were painted red, and she looked very handsome.

"My friend," Coyote spoke to Flint, "see that woman over there. Let us run a race. The one who gets to her first shall take her for his wife."

Flint was willing. So they raced. They ran toward Mole. She pretended to be digging *spit-lum* (bitter-root).[2] She had made tunnels all through the flat, and they were a bother to Flint. He kept stepping into them and falling, and every time he fell Coyote would jump over him, and shout: *"Eh! Ha-yea!* My friend, what is wrong?"

Flint was heavy, and slow in picking himself up. Sometimes Coyote jumped over him twice before he could get up. When they got to where Mole was standing, she changed herself into a real mole and skipped into one of her tunnels. Then Coyote began to hit Flint with the *squas-tenk'* rocks. At each blow they scaled off big flakes of flint.

Flint tried to catch Coyote, but every few steps he stumbled into one of Mole's tunnels, and he grew weaker and weaker. Coyote kept striking him with the medicine-rocks. At last all of the monster's body was chipped way. Only the heart was left. Then Flint died.

[2]*Spit-lum* (bitter-root)—*Lewisia rediviva*. A small, slender, white starchy root that may be eaten raw but is preferred cooked. It is cooked by steaming or boiling. Many Indians today like it with cream and sugar, and it is relished when dried and mixed with huckleberries. It also is a favorite and effective remedy for digestive disturbances. The roots are peeled soon after they have been dug, before they have time to dry.

Coyote picked up the heart and threw it across the flat. There it is today. It is a hill standing there. Much flint is found there.[3]

The pieces of Flint's body which were scattered around on the flat were gathered up by Coyote and thrown all over the earth for warriors and hunters to use.

That done, Coyote said: "*Sto-way'-na*, you are a person no more. From this sun you are only dead stone!"

And that is why the flint-rock is senseless and cannot fight back when chipped for arrow-heads. Coyote made it so before the New People came.

[3]This hill, known as "Square Butte," is in Cascade County, Montana, twenty-two miles west and a little south of Great Falls, and about five miles south of the old Fort Shaw Indian School, which Mourning Dove attended for awhile in her girlhood. She frequently went to the butte with picnic parties of Indian children. Fairly flat on top with steep sides, the butte rises some four hundred feet above the surrounding plain, and can be seen from distances of thirty to forty miles in almost any direction. Old Indians say that flint of fine quality was to be found there. Columbia Basin Indians who ventured along the upper reaches of the Missouri River to hunt buffalo were familiar with the landmark. It was observed by the Lewis and Clark expedition on June 13, 1805, the same day on which Captain Lewis found the Great Falls of the Missouri.

The top of the butte is approximately two miles long in a direction of a little northwest of north and south and about one and one-half miles wide, and is used for grazing purposes. It is said that there is only one point of access to the top; it is on the west side.

The butte wears a volcanic cap, the result of a volcanic overflow which occurred when the Mission Range, thirty miles to the south and about fifty miles long, east and west, was thrown up. The cap is pyroxene-porphyry, rather dense and roughly columnar, and rests on a sandstone formation which contains oyster shells and fine specimens of the straight baculite shell, perfectly preserved.

VII

How Turtle Got His Tail

No one could run faster than Rabbit. He had won many races and prizes. He had won Frog's tail from Frog and Bear's tail from Bear. Rabbit's own tail was very long.

One sun, Turtle, who had no tail at all, went to Rabbit and said: "*Spe-pa-lee'-na,* my friend, I would like to race with you. I think I can beat you. I would like to win those tails, yours and the others."

Rabbit laughed, for *Ar-sikh'* was such a slow traveler. Rabbit made fun of him before the people. But Turtle insisted, and Rabbit finally agreed to race with him. "Beating you will be easy," said Rabbit. "When do you want to race?"

"Let us race tomorrow while the morning is young," said Turtle.

The people all gathered the next morning early to watch the strange race between Rabbit, the swift-jumper, and Turtle, the slow-walker. They started, and Rabbit quickly left Turtle far behind.

"No use for me to run all the way now," Rabbit remarked to himself. "I will sit down awhile and wait for that silly *Ar-sikh'*. That will make him feel foolish." So Rabbit stopped to rest. He went to sleep. When he awoke, he was surprised to see Turtle moving slowly along some distance ahead.

"I must have slept long," said Rabbit, and he hopped swiftly after the slow-walker. He passed Turtle and kept on going until, when he looked back, he could not see the other. Then he sat down to wait, and again he fell asleep. While Rabbit slept, Turtle crawled by, and when Rabbit opened his eyes there was Turtle far ahead. But that did not worry Rabbit. He easily overtook the slow one.

That is the way they raced, Rabbit running and resting and going to sleep, and Turtle plodding, plodding without a stop. The race trail was long. It went to a half-way stake and returned to the point of starting. On the home stretch, Rabbit decided to take one last rest. He intended to stay awake, but, in spite of himself, he fell asleep. When he finally awoke he could not see Turtle anywhere.

"He ought to be in sight by now," said Rabbit. "Perhaps he has given up." Then Rabbit rubbed his eyes and looked again. Away off, near the finish-line, he was a speck. It was Turtle. Rabbit was startled. He jumped up and ran. He ran his fastest, but he had slept too long. Turtle crawled over the finish-line first. Rabbit was a few leaps behind. The people laughed and laughed at Rabbit, and he was very much ashamed.

Cutting off his own tail, so that there was only a little stump left, Rabbit gave it to Turtle. He also gave Turtle the other two tails. Turtle first tried on Bear's tail. It was too long and bushy. He threw it aside and tried on Rabbit's own tail. That did not suit him, either, as the fur was thick and fine—the water and mud would make it too heavy. Then Turtle put on Frog's tail.

"That is the tail I need," said Turtle. "Frog's tail matches my color, it hasn't any fur or hair on it, and it is just the right size."

All turtles have tails like that today, while rabbits have scarcely any tail at all.

VIII

WHY SKUNK'S TAIL IS BLACK AND WHITE

Far off in his own country, *Sen-kes-tia*—Skunk—heard about the race between Turtle and Rabbit. As Skunk did not have a tail, he thought he would like to race Turtle for the tails of Rabbit and Bear. He set out for Turtle's country. With him went his friend, *E-whe-whoot'-ken*—Sharp-Claws. That was Badger. They rode a little white horse, and sat double, like warriors on parade.

When they got to where Turtle lived, Skunk asked him to race. Turtle refused. Skunk was very angry, for he had ridden a long way just to make that race, and he raised a big fuss. Now, the people were afraid of Skunk because of his strong odor; it was strong medicine. With it Skunk could kill people, and those persons there were afraid he might kill some of them. They told Turtle he had to race whether he wanted to or not. Then Turtle agreed, but Skunk said:

"I will not race on foot. My friend, *E-whe-whoot'-ken*, and I will ride double on this white horse."

"All right," Turtle replied, because he did not dare to object. "You ride the white horse."

Turtle knew he didn't have a chance in that race. It was over before he could even get a fair start, and he had to give the tails of Rabbit and Bear to Skunk. His own tail was safe. Skunk had no use for it.

Skunk put on both of the tails he had won. He made them into one tail, and that is why all skunks now have bushy black and white tails.

After the race Badger was not ready to go home. He wanted to stay and visit awhile, but Skunk made him get on the little white horse. They started. Pretty soon Badger thought of a trick to make Skunk leave him behind. Badger suddenly fell off the horse. He flopped off to the ground and pretended to be dead. Skunk got off and looked at him. Skunk felt very sad.

"I loved my friend, *E-whe-whoot'-ken*," Skunk cried. "I will not

leave him in this place, so far from home. Rather than go away and leave him, I would eat him. Yes, I will eat him. I will eat him this evening."

Badger was scared. He had not thought of anything like that happening—of being eaten. He did not know what to do. Skunk cried and cried, and after awhile Skunk sang:

> *"I will never leave my friend, E-whe-whoot'-ken.*
> *I will not give up his flesh to anyone;*
> *Not even to an enemy.*
> *Only Whee'-Who—Whistler, the Hoary*
> *Marmot—*
> *Can make me run away and leave him."*

That mention of Whistler, the Hoary Marmot, gave hope to Badger. He knew that Skunk was afraid of Whistler.

Skunk started to walk, carrying Badger in his arms. Badger whistled. It was a low whistle. Skunk jumped and looked around. Then Badger whistled a little louder. Skunk began to run. Badger whistled still louder, and Skunk threw him down and jumped into some thick brush. Skunk crawled deep into the brush to hide. He thought that Whistler was coming. Badger got up and ran, and Skunk did not see him go.

As Badger and Skunk parted as good friends, their friendship never has died.

IX

RATTLESNAKE AND SALMON

The lodge of *En-tee-tee-ueh*—Salmon—was in the cliffs above the Big Falls of the *Swah-netk'-qhu*. Salmon was a great warrior.

Salmon heard of a beautiful girl who lived in the Kalispel country. Many warriors were trying to win her, Salmon heard, and he decided he would win her himself. So he went to her country and made war on the people. He beat them and took away the maiden. He brought her home with him. She loved Salmon from the first. She loved him for his red handsome face.

Many warriors wanted to kill Salmon and take his bride, but they did not know how to get at the pair in the lodge above the roaring falls. But near Salmon's lodge lived *Hah-ah-ooh-lah*[1]—Rattlesnake. He was an old man. He envied Salmon. He decided to kill him. He made war-arrows, singing as he worked. And then, one sun when he had finished the arrows, Rattlesnake strung his bow and stepped outside his bough-covered lodge and sent an arrow into Salmons' head.

Salmon tumbled from his cliff home into the river. His body floated down the river. Salmon's wife cried. The three Wolf brothers had been watching. They saw Salmon die. They took Salmon's wife to their own camp. There she was made to work—to be a slave—and she was watched night and day by the wives of the three brothers. She was unhappy; she felt very bad.

The river carried Salmon's body a long way. Finally it was washed

[1]*Hah-ah-ooh-lah* (also pronounced *Hah-ah-lawh* and *Hwa-bwa-ulah*). Variously translated as: "Evil Spirit of the Earth," "Evil of the Earth," and "Wicked Crawler." Like the other interior Northwest tribes, the Okanogan believe that rattlesnakes have strong magic power, and they treat the reptiles with the utmost respect. Meeting a rattler, an Indian will address it with placating and ingratiating words to "keep on its good side." However much they may detest and dread the rattlesnake, they never talk about him save in a most respectful manner, because, they say, his power enables him to hear what is said, regardless of how far distant he may be from the speaker. And they will not kill a rattlesnake except as a matter of necessity—to save a life or ward off an attack—or for the sake of revenge, if the snake has attacked or injured someone.

upon a sand-bar, to bleach in the sun. Soon only the skull and the backbone remained.

Gou-kouh-whay'-na—Mouse, the Sly One—came there to the sand-bar one day with her sister. They were looking for something to steal. They found what was left of Salmon. Mouse was very sad, for Salmon had been her chief. She went to a camp near-by and stole some salmon oil. With that oil she greased the skull and backbone every sun for many suns. After awhile the flesh began to grow around the bones. Slowly Salmon was restored to life by the oil Mouse rubbed on him. At last he could get up and move around, and after many moons he became strong again. Then he went back to the Big Falls, to his home. As his wife was not there, he went over to Rattlensake's lodge to ask about her. He heard Rattlesnake singing.

"Ta-pin-ee, ex-en-lee-ah!" ("I shot him, and he ran down the cliffs!")[2] And Rattlesnake sang this: "I shot him! He was a chief, but he is a chief no more!"

Salmon walked into Rattlesnake's lodge. Out of the corner of one eye, Rattlesnake saw him, but he did not let on that he saw, and he changed his song. He pretended to be mourning in Salmon's death. Salmon said nothing. He stooped and picked a piece of blazing wood from the fire and touched it to the dry bough lodge covering. He jumped outside, and the flames leaped up. Rattlesnake was trapped. He could not get out; he was burned to death. From one of Rattlesnake's eyes crawled a small snake. It was Rattlesnake's mystery-power.

"Always shall you crawl on your belly," Salmon told the little rattlesnake. "That is my revenge."

Then Salmon started in search of his wife. He found her in the camp of the three Wolf brothers. Two of the brothers he killed, and he told the third, the youngest, to get out of that country. He told him to go into the timber country and never come back. Wolf went. He was the first of the timber wolves. That is how the race of timber wolves originated.

Salmon and his wife did not return to their lodge in the cliffs. He took her into the water below the Big Falls, where they would be safe from the enemies they had among the Land People.

The arrow-point that Rattlesnake shot into Salmon's head stayed in his head. All salmon have arrow-points like that in their heads today.

[2]The dialect here is not Okanogan. It is supposed to be Rattlesnake's own language.

X

COYOTE MEETS WIND AND SOME OTHERS

Coyote wanted to travel, to see some new country, so he took Mole and the children to the lodge of his friend, Badger. He asked Badger to care for them, and Badger said he would.

"I am going to hunt for enemies, *E-whe-whoot'-ken*, my friend," said Coyote. "I am going where there is great danger. Here is a little sack that belongs to me. Hang it on a tepee pole. If it should fall from the pole, you will know that I am dead. If it stays where you hang it, I am alive."

Badger hung the sack on a tepee pole, and Coyote started. He traveled for some time without meeting any enemies or getting into trouble. Then, one sun, he heard someone singing at the top of a high cliff. He went that way. He saw a sweat-house by the edge of the cliff. Inside was the singer. Hanging on a branch of a tree by the sweat-house was a suit of very fine buck-skin clothes. Coyote liked that suit. He wanted it. He walked up to the sweat-house.

"I would like to sweat with you," he called, and the singer, who was *Sin-nee-iut*—Wind, stopped singing.

"I have used up all the water," he answered. "If you want to sweat-house you will have to get water down at the bottom of this cliff."

"I will get some water," Coyote said, and he picked up a water-basket and went down to the base of the cliff and filled it with water. He carried it back to Wind's sweat-lodge. "I have the water. I will pass it in to you," and he lifted the door-flap as if to hand the basket in to Wind. But, as Wind reached for the basket, Coyote threw all of the water on the hot stones in the sweat-house. That made such a steam that Wind was scalded to death.

Coyote laughed and put on the fine buckskin clothing, which was decorated with nice shell ornaments. Quite pleased with himself, Coyote walked away. Pretty soon he wished there was a gentle breeze

to blow the shells and make them rattle. Right away his wish brought a soft breeze that tinkled the shells. Then Coyote wished for a stronger wind, and a strong wind came. It blew harder and harder, until it lifted Coyote off his feet and spun him through the air. His wishing had brought *Sin-nee-iut* back to life.

The wind carried Coyote to the top of the cliffs that watch over the Big Falls of the *Swah-netk'-qhu.* There he grasped a little bush that grew out of the cliff. The bush was *Spet-zen'*—Hemp—and her sister. The Hemp sisters stripped Coyote of his stolen clothes, and they held him down under the edge of the cliff. Wind came along presently, looking for Coyote. "Where is *Sin-ka-lip'*?" he asked.

"He fell into the falls and was drowned," answered Hemp, and Wind believed her. He put on his clothes and went away. Then the sisters pulled Coyote up beside them. He was glad to be saved, and he said, "Now, what can I do to help you?"

"We barely exist," said Hemp. "All the time we suffer from thirst. We have to live on the little moisture that sprays up from the falls. It is not enough. We need water."

"I will give you water," said Coyote, and he walked off a few steps and threw water on the rocks around Hemp and her sister. Then, out of the cliff trickled some water. You will notice today that hemp grows only where the ground is wet.

Coyote left the Hemp sisters and walked until he came to a large encampment by a lake. Yelling that enemies were coming, he ran into the camp like he was being chased. The people were scared. They grabbed their weapons and made their canoes ready for war. Then Coyote talked to his *squas-tenk'*. He had it put all of the people to sleep. Coyote collected their weapons and food, which he loaded into one canoe. Then he broke all the other canoes and paddled out on the lake.

When the people awoke they hurried to make new weapons and new canoes. They knew who had tricked them. They started after Coyote. Seeing them coming, he caused a heavy fog with his medicine-power. The fog settled close to the water and all over the lake. None of the people could see into the fog—none but *Swa-lah'-kin*—Frog-woman. The fog did not bother her. She took the lead and guided others. Not knowing that Frog-woman could follow through the fog, Coyote thought he was safe. He paddled his canoe to shore and went to sleep on the beach. There the people found and killed him.

Many moons later, *Sui-ah'*—Cougar—traveled through that coun-

try. He traveled high up along the mountain sides. As he came close to the death-place of Coyote, he became thirsty and went down to the lake. There he found what was left of Coyote. He collected the remains and stepped over Coyote three times, and Coyote returned to life.

"*Eh-ahe! Kes-sap tee-seh-eet!*" ("Eh! Long time sleep!") said Coyote, stretching and yawning.

"You have not been sleeping," corrected Cougar. "You were dead. You were killed by the Arrow Lakes people."

"May I go along with you, Big Teeth?" asked Coyote.

"Well, I prefer to travel alone," said Cougar, "but you may come with me, if you will promise to keep out of mischief."

Coyote said he would keep out of trouble, so they set out together. That night they camped on a mountain top. Cougar brought out a small bag of food. Coyote thought it would not be enough for the both of them. He was hungry—he was always hungry. Cougar read his thoughts.

"There is plenty here for the two of us," he said. "Eat all you want." So Coyote ate heartily. When he and Cougar had finished, he was surprised to see that the bag was as full of food as at first. Cougar told Coyote to throw the scraps away. Coyote did not want to do that. He thought that was wasteful. But Cougar insisted, and he threw away the scraps. Then they slept.

In the morning Cougar brought out another bag—a deer-bladder full of food—and, when they were through eating, the bladder was still full. That day, from the top of a mountain, Cougar pointed out his lodge.

"I must go home now to my children, as they are hungry," he said. "I will give you a bow and two arrows," and he gave them to Coyote. "This first arrow is to kill deer. Shoot it through a divide in a hill and you will kill a deer. This other arrow is for birds. Do not get them mixed. Do not shoot a bird with the deer-arrow and do not shoot a deer with the bird-arrow. If you use them wrong, you will lose the arrows."

After Cougar left him, Coyote tried his new arrows. He shot the deer-arrow through a divide and killed a deer. He ate the deer. Then he shot a pheasant with the bird-arrow, and he ate the pheasant. He saw another pheasant. He shot it with the deer-arrow, but it did not fall. It sat, with the arrow sticking through it. So he shot the bird-arrow, and the pheasant flew off with both arrows. It sailed down the mountain and out of sight. Coyote hated to lose those arrows, so he

tried to follow the pheasant. He came to a tepee. He went in. By the fire sat *Char'-tups*—Fisher. The two lost arrows were there. Fisher had them.

"Long Tail," said Coyote, "I came to get those arrows."

"The arrows belonged to my older brother, *Sui-ah'*," answered Fisher. "I have found them and I will keep them. But I will give you two of my own arrows. They are like the others, and the rule is the same. Do not mix them when you shoot."

Coyote took Fisher's arrows and went away feeling good. But he soon forgot the rule for the arrows. He mixed them, shooting the wrong one first, and a pheasant flew off with both arrows. Following the pheasant, Coyote came to the lodge of *Pip-qus*—Marten, who had the lost arrows in his hand.

"No, I cannot give you these arrows," explained Marten. "They belonged to my older brother, Fisher. I found them, and I will keep them, but I will give you two of my own arrows. They are used the same way, by the same rule."

Marten gave Coyote two arrows, but it was not long before foolish Coyote forgot the rule and shot the wrong one and then the other, and both arrows were lost. He hunted for them until he grew tired. Then he decided to go home.

When he reached his tepee, he stopped outside to listen. He heard Badger crying. He crept close and peeked through the doorway, and his youngest son shouted:

"*Le-ee'-oo!*" ("Father!")

"Your father is dead," Badger said to the boy. "He never will come back."

"No!" the boy answered. "I see my father now! Look—at the doorway." He pointed. Then Badger saw Coyote peeking.

"You were dead," said Badger. "The little sack fell from the pole many moons ago."

"I was tired," Coyote replied. "I slept by the water. The Arrow Lakes people followed me. They found me sleeping. They killed me. Big Teeth found my bones and helped me back to life."

Coyote was glad to be home again, and Mole and the children were glad, too. So was Badger.

XI

WHY GARTERSNAKE WEARS
A GREEN BLANKET

Suck-z'-cum—Thunder-bird—used to fly from the Warmland (South) once every snow to devour the most beautiful of the maidens. He always wanted a maiden as soon as he appeared—at his first rolling among the clouds. He would not stand for any delay. He came at the blooming of the woods-flowers, and then there was wailing in the villages—sorrow for the girl who must give herself to the monster. This maiden, chosen by the tribes because of her great beauty, would have to walk out and meet the monster, and be eaten. Then *Thing-that-hits* would not harm the other people. That was the custom. No one ever thought of trying to change it, of defying the terrible Thunder-bird.

It happened one spring that the girl who was loved by little *Sku-qua-wel'-hau*—Gartersnake—was chosen to be the sacrifice to Thunder-bird. That made Gartersnake very sad. He had no wish to live without her, so he decided to go with her when she went to meet the monster.

Thunder-bird could be seen high in the clouds when the maiden started toward the sacrifice-place. Putting on his best war-shirt, Gartersnake followed her. She looked around and saw him. She begged him to go back, to leave her. She did not want him to be killed, too. But Gartersnake hurried his steps and caught up with her.

"Oh, go back! Go back to our people," she said. "You cannot stand before the awful *Suck-z'-cum*. Let me die alone."

"No! If you must die, I will die with you," answered Gartersnake, and he kept by her side.

Soon they heard the noise of the monster's wings. The maiden cried, and Gartersnake felt weak, but he tried not to show his fear. Thunder-bird roared over them. His great wings shook the air and made the sky dark. He swooped low and from his mouth came a stream of fire. Gartersnake spat back.

"This person must be powerful," said Thunder-bird to himself. "He spits fire as I do." Then, thinking to discover his small enemy's weakness, Thunder-bird asked: "What do you fear? Of what are you afraid?"

"Nothing! There is nothing I fear," replied Gartersnake. "And you cannot hurt me. Nothing can hurt me. If you feel like fighting me, I will show you how to spit real fire. My fire-spit is worse than yours."

Thunder-bird believed those words, for none of the people ever had dared to talk to him like that. Only the frightened, wailing maidens ever had come to meet him. But he hoped to scare the other, and he spat a fearful streak of fire. Gartersnake then spat a stream of sizzling fire that flashed right in the monster's face. Thunder-bird couldn't stand that. He turned and fled, heading for the Warm-land. Spitting his hardest, Gartersnake ran after him, and not until he was sure that the monster really was beaten did Gartersnake stop chasing him. Then he shouted:

"A New People are coming to the world. From this day you will not come down out of the sky to eat people. You may roam the sky, but you shall make only rumblings and crashings in the storm."

Suck-z'-cum never returned to eat any more maidens or to destroy the tribes. But sometimes he clashes his wings and spits his fire through the clouds.

For his bravery the people gave Gartersnake a pretty green blanket with stripes on it. *Sku-qua-wel'-hau*, the Ground Twister, still wears that blanket.[1]

[1] *Sku-qua-wel'-hau*. Modified to *Chewelah*, this name has been applied to a small town and a creek in Stevens County, Washington. The townsite formerly abounded with gartersnakes.

XII

Coyote Quarrels With Mole

Coyote and his wife, Mole, and their children were living by themselves, away from the winter encampment of the people. The other people did not want Coyote around, he was so lazy and tricky. Coyote and his family were poor that winter. They had only a little food, and that was supplied by the faithful Mole. Each day she would go out and gather herbs and moss and dried and shriveled *sko-qeeu* (rose-hips).[1] She did that to keep the five children from starving. And she carried all the wood and water, while Coyote loafed and practised his war songs.

One sun, as Mole was chopping a rotten stump for firewood, a little fawn jumped out of the stump. The deer family had put it there. The deer felt sorry for Mole. They wanted her to have the fawn for food.

Mole dropped her axe and caught the little deer. She told her oldest boy to run and tell his father to come with a knife and cut the fawn's throat.

"Tell your father to hurry," said Mole, "because I cannot hold this fawn long. My strength will give out."

The boy ran fast to the tepee. He told Coyote what Mole had said.

"Go back to your mother and tell her to hold the fawn while I get my bow and arrows ready," Coyote ordered, and the boy ran back to his mother with the message.

Coyote ran out of the lodge and got a piece of dogwood, from which he made a bow. Then he ran to a service berry bush, where he cut two arrows. Then he ran back to his lodge to finish making his weapons. Taking feathers from his war bonnet, he feathered the arrows and, as he had no sinew for a bowstring, he tore the strings off his moccasins and made a string. Then he was ready to shoot the fawn.

All the while Mole was having a hard time holding the fawn. It struggled and kicked and fought to get away, and Mole's strength was leaving her. Her arms ached. She called to Coyote to hurry. He ran

[1]The fruit of the wild rose, *Rosa gymnocarpa*.

out of the lodge and tramped down the snow so he could kneel and shoot. He told Mole to let loose of the fawn so he could shoot it. Mole let go and Coyote shot his arrow, but the little deer fell just then and the arrow missed it. With his second and last arrow Coyote shot again as the fawn leaped up, and again Coyote missed. The fawn escaped into the woods.

Mole was disgusted and angry. She went back to the tepee. There she discovered that Coyote had eaten all the rose-hips, all the food that was left, while he was making his weapons. When Coyote came in, Mole spoke to him about that. They quarreled, and Coyote stabbed her with his flint knife. Mole ran out. Coyote followed. He meant to kill her. Mole changed herself into a real Mole as Coyote stabbed again. He stabbed the earth, and Mole quickly untied her little pouch of *tul-meen* (red facial paint) and put some of the paint on the point of the knife. Drawing the knife out of the ground, Coyote saw the red paint and thought it was blood. He was satisfied that his wife must be dead from that last blow.

Coyote soon found that he could not take care of his children without Mole's help. They could not live as they had before, so Coyote told the four oldest children to visit their "uncle," King-fisher—*Z-reece'*, who was a good hunter and had plenty of food in his lodge. The four boys started for Kingfisher's home, and Coyote took his youngest and favorite son and went traveling. The youngest boy's name was *Top'-kan*.

They traveled many suns without getting much to eat. They were hungry when they came to a large prairie, where a woman dressed in red-painted buckskin was digging *spit-lum* (bitterroot). Seeing her digging reminded Coyote of his wife, and he wished that Mole were alive to dig roots for him to eat. He took *Top'-kan* off his back, where the little boy rode much of the time to keep from tiring, and told him to wait. Then Coyote went toward the strange woman.

"Tell me a story, tell me news, good woman," said Coyote upon getting near to the digger. But the woman did not take any notice of him. She kept on digging roots and cleaning them as she put them in her basket, which was strapped to her side.

Not so easily discouraged, Coyote walked closer, saying: "Tell me news. I am a traveler from a distant country."

"I will tell you a story," said the woman, and she turned angrily to Coyote. "Coyote deserted his children and killed his wife!"

Then Coyote recognized the woman as his own wife, Mole. She had

followed him to watch over little *Top'-kan*, but Coyote had not known that. Grabbing his knife, Coyote ran at his wife. He meant to kill her, but she changed into a real mole and went underground and got away.

Coyote returned to *Top'-kan*. He picked the boy up, put him on his back, and resumed his journey. He sought new lands where his tricks and mischief-making were not known.

XIII

How Coyote Happened to Make the Black Moss Food

Coyote and *Top'-kan* were traveling. Wherever the trail was rough, little *Top'-kan* rode on his father's back. They came to the lodge of *En-ze'-chen*—Wolf, an old man. He was busy skinning a beaver. After watching old Blood-Curdling Call for awhile, Coyote asked: *"En-ze'-chen*, how do you kill the *stun'-whu* (beaver)?"[1]

"It is at the beaver dam," answered Wolf. "I sit on the dam, with one leg in the water. As a beaver passes over my leg, I strike hard with a big stick. The *stun'-whu* cannot live after a blow like that."

"Ha-ha-eah!" Coyote laughed. "That is my way of killing the *stun'-whu!"*

Old Wolf said nothing. He knew that *Sin-ka-lip'*, the Imitator, had never killed beavers in that way. He suspected that Coyote soon would be in trouble.

Coyote took a heavy stick and went down to the beaver dam and sat with one leg in the water, as Wolf instructed. The beavers saw him. One of them said:

"Look! There is *Sin-ka-lip'!* He is trying to trick someone. Let us walk over his leg, and see what he does."

Two young beavers swam up to the dam. They climbed over Coyote's leg, and he struck hard with the heavy stick. He missed the beavers—they were too quick for him—but he hit his leg a terrific whack. He howled and danced with pain and rage, and then he tore into the beaver dam and threw the sticks and mud right and left. In a little while there was no dam there. He found the two beavers that had fooled him. They appeared to be dead.

"They will make good eating," he remarked, and he carried the beavers to where *Top'-kan* was playing. "You can wear these as ear

[1] *Stun'-whu*—the old-time name for beaver. The modern name, applied since the advent of the fur traders, is *skal-weet-za*, which means "money fur."

ornaments while I am getting wood for a fire," Coyote told his son, and he tied the beavers to the little boy's ears, one to each ear.

As soon as Coyote was busy gathering wood, the beavers jumped up and ran, dragging *Top'-kan* behind them. They ran down the bank to the place where the dam had been. There they squirmed into different holes. That stretched *Top'-kan's* ears in opposite directions. *Top'-kan* yelled, for the stretching hurt.

Hearing the cries of his son, Coyote ran to help him. He found poor *Top'-kan* braced between the holes and unable to move. There was nothing to do but to cut the thongs that held the beavers, which Coyote did. The beavers got away. Ever since that time the ears of coyotes have stood long and pointed.

No beaver to roast, Coyote and *Top'-kan* started traveling again. They went along until they came to a large lake. Resting in the water were many *si-mil'-ka-meen* (white swans). Coyote wanted one of those swans to eat, so he swam out into the lake. He kept under water, but the swans were not fooled. They knew he was there.

"Here comes *Sin-ka-lip'!*" they said. "See his tail floating! Let him catch a couple of us, and we will see what he will do."

So two of the younger swans allowed Coyote to catch them. He carried them to shore. They pretended to be dead. He tied them fast to *Top'-kan*. Then he climbed a pine tree to get the pitch-top, where *Kwil-kin*[2]—Porcupine—had gnawed. He wanted the pitch-top for fire-kindling.

Just as he got to the top of the tree, Coyote heard his son crying. He looked down and saw the swans flapping their wings. They were starting to fly. Coyote jumped, but his long hair braid caught on a branch of the pine tree and did not come loose. Coyote swung there, helpless. He could not untangle his hair.

The swans flew past the tree, past Coyote, and up into the sky. Dangling beneath them, tied to them by the thongs, was little *Top'-kan*. When the swans were high in the air they cut the thongs, and *Top'-kan* fell to the ground and was killed. Then Coyote took his flint knife and chopped off his hair braid, and dropped to the earth. He looked up at his hair hanging from the branch.

"You shall not be wasted, my valuable hair. After this you shall be gathered by the people. The old women will make you into food," he said.

[2]*Kwil-kin*—Pine-bough Head.

That was Coyote's ruling near the Beginning. That is why his hair, the long black timber-hair, hangs from trees in the mountains. It is called *squil-lip*. It is the black moss that the people cook in pit-ovens.[3]

Top'-kan did not stay dead. Coyote restored him to life by stepping over his body three times. Then they returned to their own country.

[3]This "black moss" is a pendulous lichen, a species of *Usnea*. It grows on trees and bushes in the mountains. From a short distance it looks very much like unkempt black or dark hair. Palatable and nutritious when cooked, it is considered a delicacy by the Indians.

The moss is cooked in pits that are eighteen inches to four feet deep and three to six feet in diameter, according to the quantity to be prepared. Rectangular pit-ovens sometimes are made, but they are uncommon.

Stones heated in a roaring fire are rolled into the pit, flooring it completely. They are covered with a thick carpet of clean green grass or leaves, and green twigs. Then there is a layer of camas roots, and on this is placed a compact heap of the black moss. This is covered with green grass or leaves. Tule-reed matting is spread over this, and the pit is mounded with about six inches of firmly packed soil. Nowadays, canvas or gunny-sacking frequently takes the place of the reed matting.

At the beginning of the "filling-up" process, one or more thick sticks are planted in the pit. They are withdrawn after the dirt is piled on, leaving open shafts down to the bed of hot stones. Cold water is poured down the shafts, and the orifices are plugged to seal in the steam that is generated. A hot fire of logs is built on the pit-oven and maintained for about forty-eight hours. On the third or fourth day, after the ashes have cooled, the oven is opened and the food taken out.

The moss has melted and run together, forming a thick jelly-like substance bluish-black in color. It is cooled and then is sliced and eaten. Or, it may be dried and stored for future use, in which event it has to be heated or boiled before being served, and resembles molasses. Dried, it becomes hard and keeps indefinitely.

Many of the Indians today like to sweeten the freshly cooked moss with sugar.

The camas roots steamed with the moss are black when removed from the oven, and are deemed a delicious "side dish."

This method of cooking, called by the Okanogans *sil-kip-em* (cooking-in-the-ground), often is used for meats and for camas roots without the black moss ingredient. Some of the women cook apples with the black moss.

XIV

WHY SPIDER HAS SUCH LONG LEGS

T*u-pel*—Spider, the Spinner—was a handsome warrior and good hunter. He lived with his grandmother, *Spu-wel'-kin*—Topknot, Woodpecker. Because he always brought home plenty of game, the maidens of the nearby villages all wanted to marry him. They would visit his lodge, hoping to win him.

Spider had a smoke-test for the maidens. When one came to see him, Spider would send his grandmother outside to close the smoke-flue. She would lap the ear-flaps so that the smoke could not get out. That would make the smoke thick in the lodge, and it would be hard to breathe in there.

Spider thought that he did not want a wife who could not stay in the smoke as long as he could, and he could stay in it a long time. Many maidens had tried the smoke-test and failed. But spider always was nice to them. He would send them home with big packs of meat.

Stun'-whu—Beaver—had a very pretty daughter. She wanted to win Spider. She spoke to her father—asked his help. Beaver's medicine was strong. He gave his power to his daughter and told her how to use it. Then he sent her to Spider's lodge.

Spider liked the girl right away. He wanted her to be his wife. He did not care if she could not stand his smoke-test. Sending his grandmother out to close the smoke-flue, Spider pretended to make a smoky fire. But there was only a little smoke, and it was not the eye-stinging kind.

Beaver's daughter laughed. She sat on a spread robe and laughed at the smoke that Spider made, but she said nothing to Spider. With Beaver's medicine she called the blackest smoke, pitch smoke. It filled the lodge.

For most of that sun Beaver-girl and Spider sat in the lodge, on opposite sides of the fire. Spider's eyes finally became smoke-sick,

and the pitch-smoke choked him. He spoke to Beaver-girl. She made no answer. Spider tried to think. That was hard, for the smoke blinded him, and his whole head ached. His own medicine could not help him. It was weak against the powerful *shoo'-mesh* of Beaver.

Spider wondered if the girl was still in the lodge. He spoke. No answer. He spoke again and again, many times, calling loudly through the smoke-darkness. Maybe the maiden was dead! Maybe the black smoke had killed her!

Spider felt his way around the fire. His foot struck the girl. She laughed. That made Spider ashamed. A woman was beating him in a trial of strength. He kicked Beaver-girl hard. He kicked her three times, and that made her very angry. She caught hold of one of Spider's legs, and she pulled and pulled, stretching the leg out, making it long. Then she pulled his other legs the same way. Spider could not stop her.

Well, when Woodpecker at last uncovered the smoke-flue and turned back the door-flap she saw a strange-looking grandson standing in the swirl of the outrushing smoke. He no longer was handsome. His body was small and his legs were very long and ugly.

Spu-wel'-kin was sorry for him. She knew that the maidens would not try to win him any more. So she ruled that Beaver-girl become his wife. Beaver's daughter was willing; she knew that *Tu-pel* always would provide plenty of game. And Spider was glad. He liked Beaver-girl even though she had treated him so roughly and spoiled his fine looks, and he forgave her for pulling him all out of shape—for making his legs so long.

XV

WHY BADGER IS SO HUMBLE

One time *Why-ay'-looh*—Fox—and Coyote were living in the same lodge. The hunting was poor, and they became very hungry. They hunted hard every sun but did not find any game. At last Fox decided to leave that country and hunt somewhere else, but *Sin-ka-lip'* did not feel like going. So Fox left and Coyote stayed.

Coyote had nothing to eat but insects and leaves, although in a large camp not far away there was plenty of good food. Coyote knew it was useless to ask for food there, as those people hated him. But he intended to get some of that food. He began to scheme. The hungrier he grew the harder he schemed. Finally he had a plan.

Now, in that camp where the food was plentiful lived *E-whe-whoot'-ken*—Badger. He was a handsome person, was Sharp Claws, and he was a proud warrior and a good hunter. Much of the meat he killed he gave to poor persons. He was such a good hunter that many of the old people wanted him for a son-in-law. But Badger did not wish to marry any of the maidens in that village. He thought that sometime he would find a better wife in a far country.

One sun when Badger's four sisters went to the river to take their bath they came upon a pretty woman. She was sitting on the bank, painting her face with many colors. The sisters liked her appearance. They invited her to their lodge. They hoped that their proud brother would like her and make her his wife.

When Badger returned from hunting he was pleased to find the new woman in his lodge. He asked her to sit by his side, to sit in the place that was given to a wife. The woman smiled and said: "I am willing to be your wife, but first I must take some dried meat to my aged parents. Your sisters must go with me and help carry the meat."

Badger agreed to that, and the next sun the pretty woman and the sisters of Badger carried big packs of dried meat to the lodge that the woman said was the home of her aged parents. There the woman told them: "Wait outside while I take the meat in to my parents. They do not like to meet strangers."

The sisters waited outside while the meat was carried into the tepee, and they could hear talking, as if two or three persons were talking. Then, after all the meat was stored away in the lodge, the door-flap was thrown back and out stepped Coyote. He had been the pretty woman. He laughed over the joke he had played on Badger and the sisters.

The sisters were very angry, but they were unable to punish Coyote. They went home. They told Badger of the trick. He was angry and ashamed. It hurt his pride to be fooled in that way. He and his sisters did not want the people to find out, but somehow the people learned of what had happened.

A few suns later Badger wanted to take a sweat-bath. He went to the sweat-house. Some people were there. As he walked up, he heard someone say: "The proud, the handsome Badger is coming. He would not take a woman of his own tribe. He liked Coyote better! We do not want to sweat-house with him."

Those words shamed Badger. He turned from the sweat-house and went to look for Coyote. He found Coyote and chased him out of the country. Then he came home. He was proud no longer. He humbled himself before all the people and took from among them a wife. And he has been humble ever since, has *E-whe-whoot'-ken*.

XVI

COYOTE JUGGLES HIS EYES

As he was walking through the timber one morning, Coyote heard someone say: "I throw you up and you come down in!"

Coyote thought that was strange talk. It made him curious. He wanted to learn who was saying that, and why. He followed the sound of the voice, and he came upon little *Zst-skaka'-na*—Chickadee—who was throwing his eyes into the air and catching them in his eye-sockets. When he saw Coyote peering at him from behind a tree, Chickadee ran. He was afraid of Coyote.

"That is my way, not yours," Coyote yelled after him.

Now, it wasn't Coyote's way at all, but Coyote thought he could juggle his eyes just as easily as Chickadee juggled his, so he tried. He took out his eyes and tossed them up and repeated the words used by the little boy: "I throw you up and you come down in!" His eyes plopped back where they belonged. That was fun. He juggled the eyes again and again.

Two ravens happened to fly that way. They saw what Coyote was doing, and one of them said: "*Sin-ka-lip'* is mocking someone. Let us steal his eyes and take them to the Sun-dance. Perhaps then we can find out his medicine-power."

"Yes, we will do that," agreed the other raven. "We may learn something."

As Coyote tossed his eyes the next time, the ravens swooped, swift as arrows from a strong bow. One of them snatched one eye and the other raven caught the other eye.

"Quoh! Quoh! Quoh!" they laughed, and flew away to the Sun-dance camp.

Oh, but Coyote was mad! He was crazy with rage. When he could hear the ravens laughing no longer, he started in the direction they had gone. He hoped somehow to catch them and get back his eyes. He bumped into trees and bushes, fell into holes and gullies, and banged against boulders. He soon was bruised all over, but he kept on

going, stumbling along. He became thirsty, and he kept asking the trees and bushes what kind they were, so that he could learn when he was getting close to water. The trees and bushes answered politely, giving their names. After awhile he found he was among the mountain bushes, and he knew he was near water. He came soon to a little stream and satisfied his thirst. Then he went on and presently he was in the pine timber. He heard someone laughing. It was *Kok'-qhi Ski'-kaka*—Bluebird. She was with her sister, *Kwas'-kay*—Bluejay.

"Look, sister," said Bluebird. "There is *Sin-ka-lip'* pretending to be blind. Isn't he funny?"

"Do not mind *Sin-ka-lip'*," advised Bluejay. "Do not pay any attention to him. He is full of mean tricks. He is bad."

Coyote purposely bumped into a tree and rolled over and over toward the voices. That made little Bluebird stop her laughing. She felt just a little bit afraid.

"Come, little girl," Coyote called. "Come and see the pretty star that I see!"

Bluebird naturally was very curious, and she wanted to see that pretty star, but she hung back, and her sister warned her again not to pay attention to Coyote. But Coyote used coaxing words; told her how bright the star looked.

"Where is the star?" asked Bluebird, hopping a few steps toward Coyote.

"I cannot show you while you are so far away," he replied. "See, where I am pointing my finger!"

Bluebird hopped close, and Coyote made one quick bound and caught her. He yanked out her eyes and threw them into the air, saying:

"I throw you up and you come down in!" and the eyes fell into his eye-sockets.

Coyote could see again, and his heart was glad. "When did you ever see a star in the sunlight?" he asked Bluebird, and then ran off through the timber.

Bluebird cried, and Bluejay scolded her for being so foolish as to trust Coyote. Bluejay took two of the berries she had just picked and put them into her sister's eye-sockets, and Bluebird could see as well as before. But, as the berries were small, her new eyes were small, too. That is why Bluebird has such berrylike eyes.

While his new eyes were better than none at all, Coyote was not satisfied. They were too little. They did not fit very well into his slant

sockets. So he kept on hunting for the ravens and the Sun-dance camp. One day he came to a small tepee. He heard someone inside pounding rocks together. He went in and saw an old woman pounding meat and berries in a stone mortar. The old woman was *Su-see-wass*—Pheasant. Coyote asked her if she lived alone.

"No," she said, "I have two granddaughters. They are away at the Sun-dance. The people there are dancing with Coyote's eyes."

"Aren't you afraid to be here alone?" Coyote asked. "Isn't there anything that you fear?"

"I am afraid of nothing but the *stet'-chee-hunt* (stinging-bush)," she said.

Laughing to himself, Coyote went out to find a stinging-bush. In a swamp not far away he found several bushes of that kind. He broke off one of those nettle bushes and carried it back to the tepee. Seeing it, Pheasant cried:

"Do not touch me with the *stet'-chee-hunt!* Do not touch me! It will kill me!"

But Coyote had no mercy in his heart, no pity. He whipped poor Pheasant with the stinging-bush until she died. Then, with his flint knife, he skinned her, and dressed himself in her skin. He looked almost exactly like the old woman. He hid her body and began to pound meat in the stone mortar. He was doing that when the granddaughters came home. They were laughing. They told how they had danced over Coyote's eyes. They did not recognize Coyote in their grandmother's skin, but Coyote knew them. One was little Bluebird and the other was Bluejay. Coyote smiled. "Take me with you to the Sun-dance, granddaughters," he said in his best old-woman's voice.

The sisters looked at each other in surprise, and Bluejay answered: "Why, you did not want to go with us when the morning was young."

"Grandmother, how strange you talk!" said Bluebird.

"That is because I burned my mouth with hot soup," said Coyote.

"And, Grandmother, how odd your eyes look!" Bluejay exclaimed. "One eye is longer than the other!"

"My grandchild, I hurt that eye with my cane," explained Coyote.

The sisters did not find anything else wrong with their grandmother, and the next morning the three of them started for the Sun-dance camp. The sisters had to carry their supposed grandmother. They took turns. They had gone part way when Coyote made himself an awkward burden and almost caused Bluejay to fall. That made Bluejay angry, and she threw Coyote to the ground. Bluebird then picked him

up and carried him. As they reached the edge of the Sun-dance camp, Coyote again made himself an awkward burden, and Bluebird let him fall. Many of the people in the camp saw that happen. They thought the sisters were cruel, and the women scolded Bluebird and Bluejay for treating such an old person so badly.

Some of the people came over and lifted Coyote to his feet and helped him into the Sun-dance lodge. There the people were dancing over Coyote's eyes, and the medicine-men were passing the eyes to one another and holding the eyes up high for everyone to see. After a little Coyote asked to hold the eyes, and they were handed to him.

He ran out of the lodge, threw his eyes into the air, and said: "I throw you up and you come down in!"

His eyes returned to their places, and Coyote ran to the top of a hill.

There he looked back and shouted: "Where are the maidens who had Coyote for a grandmother?"

Bluejay and Bluebird were full of shame. They went home, carrying Pheasant's skin, which Coyote had thrown aside. They searched and found their grandmother's body and put it back in the skin, and Pheasant's life was restored. She told them how Coyote had killed her with the stinging-bush.

XVII

WHY MARTEN'S FACE IS WRINKLED

The face of *Pip-qus*—Marten—has not always been wrinkled and homely. Long ago it was smooth and handsome. That was before Marten disobeyed his older brother, *Char'-tups*, Long Tail—Fisher. Before that time, too, Marten would eat only birds and squirrels. Fisher liked venison and fat.

In their country was a mountain that Fisher told Marten not to go near. Fisher told him never to go there, but he gave no reason. Marten could not understand why he should not go to that place; he often noticed his brother setting out in that direction. He did not know that Fisher went to visit a pretty young woman.

For a long time Marten obeyed his brother. Then, one sun, he forgot his brother's words. He was trying to catch some birds. They flitted on ahead of him, going toward the mountain. After awhile he came to the foot of the mountain. He saw a bluejay sitting in a tree. He shot the bluejay with an arrow, and the bluejay fell down through the smoke-hole of a lodge.

Marten walked into the lodge to get the bird. Beside the fire was a pretty young woman. She prepared food for her visitor. She gave him dried venison and berries mixed with fat. Marten never ate that kind of food. The sight and the smell of the dried venison and the fatty berries made him feel sick. He pushed the food away. That insulted the young woman. The food was the best she had.

"You shot my comb, my bluejay," she said, "and now you refuse to eat my food."

She grabbed Marten by the hair and pitched him into the fire, and rubbed his smooth handsome face in the hot ashes until he yelled with pain. Then she threw him out of the lodge.

Marten's face was burned all over. He was almost killed. For some time he lay on the ground. When some of his strength came back, he

got up and sneaked home. He did not want to be seen, he was so full of shame. He hid between the coverings of the lodge,[1] and there he was when his brother returned from hunting.

As he was accustomed to do, Fisher called Marten to catch his load of fresh meat. Marten did not answer. Long Tail called again. Then Marten mocked his brother, which made Fisher angry. He found Marten and pulled him from his hiding place. Fisher intended to punish him, but he changed his mind upon seeing how terribly Marten's face was burned, and he took some grease and rubbed it on the burns.

After a few suns Marten grew very hungry. He would not eat the meat that his brother brought home, and he was not able to hunt for his kind of food. In a few more suns he was so weak and thin that he had to eat something or die. He licked a few drops of grease from his face. It was the venison grease that Fisher had put on the burns. Marten was surprised. The grease tasted good. After that he ate venison and liked it. He still likes such food.

Marten's face finally healed, but the deep burns left many wrinkles, and that is why he is called *Pip-qus*—Wrinkled Face.

The young woman who was the cause of those changes became Fisher's wife.

[1]The lodge coverings here referred to were layers of lapped tule mats. They were quite effective in keeping out the weather. Tanned deer skins also were used for tepee coverings in primitive times, but rarely were buffalo hides available, as among the tribes nearer to and in the buffalo country.

XVIII

CRAWFISH AND GRIZZLY BEAR

Kee-lau-naw—Grizzly Bear—lived in a big forest. He would not let anybody hunt there. People who went there to hunt never came back. Grizzly Bear ate them.

Because they could not get any of the game in Grizzly Bear's forest, the people began to starve. They danced and prayed, asking their powers to help them. One sun the prayers of *Jĭ'-hah*—Crawfish— were answered. He received strong medicine. Then he started for Grizzly Bear's forest.

Owl, who was Grizzly Bear's lookout, saw Crawfish coming. Owl hooted to warn Grizzly Bear, who rushed out of his lodge, roaring his war cry. Crawfish pretended not to see him, and that hurt Grizzly Bear's pride, and he roared louder and gnashed his teeth. But Crawfish paid no attention.

Grizzly Bear rushed back into his lodge and changed his summer teeth for his new, sharp winter teeth. Out he came again. He thought that Crawfish surely would be scared now, for the winter teeth made him look very fierce. But Crawfish still paid no attention. Grizzly Bear went back to his lodge and put on his sharpest claws, and he hurried out, waving his big arms and showing the sharp claws.[1] But Crawfish acted as if he didn't know such a person as Grizzly Bear was around. Crawfish just kept walking along.

Grizzly Bear was used to being treated with respect. He could not understand why Crawfish was not afraid, and he was boiling with rage. He decided to finish Crawfish without more delay. He charged. One quick, strong hug, and there would be no more Crawfish—so thought Grizzly Bear. But just as he expected to grab Crawfish, that person lifted his two red fingers and pinched Grizzly Bear, pinched him hard.

Holding his enemy tight, Crawfish drew him close, pulled him right

[1]The grizzly bear was supposed to go into winter quarters with teeth and claws dulled from usage, and to emerge in the spring with them renewed in sharpness.

up to his sharp red nose. Grizzly Bear was badly scared. He believed he was about to be eaten. He was so frightened that he spit froth and foam into the face of Crawfish. That disgusted Crawfish, but he did not let go. He pinched all the harder, and Grizzly Bear cried in pain and begged for mercy.

"*Kee-lau-naw,*" said Crawfish, "you will have to leave these woods. You will have to go away and leave these woods for the hunters. You must go high in the mountains and make your home. There, away from the people, you can harm them no longer, and you are not to bother people unless they attack you. Start now for the highest mountains. Do not come back! Go! Hurry away from here!"

Grizzly Bear agreed to go. He ran until he found himself in some low mountains. There he stopped and looked around. He could see nobody following him, and he said to himself: "*Jĭ'-hah,* you think you can make me live in the high mountains. I shall not go. I am going home." And he turned and headed for his forest. He was in a hurry to get back. He ran. He started to run between two big red trees. That is, he thought they were trees. But they were the fingers of Crawfish, and they closed around him. They lifted him up and carried him to the place he had reached when he decided to return home.

Grizzly Bear spit in the face of Crawfish again, but that only caused Crawfish to pinch the harder. Then Grizzly Bear begged to be free. He promised to do as Crawfish told him, so Crawfish let him go.

Up hill and down, and up again, ran Grizzly Bear, until he had traveled a long way. He stopped to rest, leaning against a tree, and he looked back over his trail. He saw no one coming, and he changed his mind about going further into the mountains. His temper was sour and he whispered to himself: "*Jĭ'-hah* cannot make me do that. He cannot keep me from my old home. I am going back where I always have lived."

He had barely finished those words when he felt the supposed tree against which he was leaning lift him off the ground. Two big red fingers tightened about his middle. The fingers of Crawfish held him fast. Surprised and badly frightened, Grizzly Bear thought his enemy would show no mercy now. He kicked and groaned, and then he pretended to be half-dead from the squeezing, but Crawfish would not let go.

Then Grizzly Bear cried: "Do not kill me! I will never return to the forest. I will go to the highest mountains, and stay there." This he said five times, and Crawfish let him go.

Crawfish warned: "If you do come back, I will catch you and kill you. This is your last chance. Do not ever come back to the lower country. From this sun your lodge must be in the highest mountains, up where the mists are thickest, where the snows are deepest. A New People are coming to the world. You shall not starve them by keeping all the game to yourself. Go and do not look back!"

Grizzly Bear was glad to get away. He ran, and he did not look back. He did not stop running until he was in the highest range of mountains. There he has made his home ever since.

Crawfish returned to his own country. The people there were glad. Now they could hunt and get plenty of food and plenty of skins.

Since the time that Crawfish whipped Grizzly Bear there have been fewer times of famine.

XIX

COYOTE AND WOOD-TICK

Tired and hungry, Coyote sat in his hunting-camp tepee. Game was scarce, and he had not found any deer for a long time. "I wish I had some deer meat," he said, and he heard something fall at the doorway of the tepee. He got up and looked. *Eh-ahe!* On the ground was a pack of venison! That made Coyote feel good. He quickly kindled a fire and cooked a big meal. He filled his belly and had a good sleep. Next morning he was up and out hunting before Sun's light reached into the woods.

"I will find a deer today," thought Coyote. "That pack of meat at my doorway last night shows that there are deer in this country."

But he did not see a deer all day. By night he was very hungry again and very tired. Resting on his robes in the tepee, he wished aloud for more venison, and another pack of it came bouncing through the doorway. Coyote looked out to see who had brought the meat, but there was no one in sight.

"Now, who answers my wishes so promptly?" he asked himself. "I must find out tomorrow night."

He hunted all the next day without success, and that night, instead of lying on his robe to rest, he crouched just inside the door-flap. Then he wished for deer meat. *Eh-ahe!* There it was—right at his feet—a pack of venison that would last him half-a-moon. Jumping through the doorway, he saw a woman disappearing in the woods. At last he knew—his neighbor. He could not mistake her. He recognized her flat shiny head. She was *Kuk-chil'-ken*—Wood-tick. She had no husband.

In his mean, ungrateful way, Coyote yelled: "You shiny-head! You flat-headed woman! I thought a maiden worth having was favoring me."

Wood-tick no longer was a young woman, and that insult made her very angry. She was used to being treated with respect, for she was the ruler of all the deer. She did not answer Coyote; she did not even look around. She went on as if she had not heard him.

Coyote returned to his camp and ate some of the venison she had given him. That bundle of venison lasted many suns, but it could not last forever. When the last scrap was gone, Coyote wished for more, but no pack of venison fell at his doorway. He wished many times and in a very loud voice. No meat came. Then he realized that *Kuk-chil'-ken* must still be very angry.

"I will make up with her," Coyote remarked, and he walked over to her lodge. Wood-tick would not look at him when he entered. She turned her back and would not answer his greeting. Coyote saw that he could not make up with her, so he grabbed her by the neck and threw her to the ground. He pounded her head with a rock, making her head even flatter than before.

"That's what you get for being stubborn," said Coyote, and he tossed Wood-tick's body to one side.

Wood-tick's tepee was full of meat, so Coyote stayed there and ate all he could hold. In the morning he put on Wood-tick's robes and went outside to call the deer, as she had done every morning.

He used her words: *"Kat-ch-lhn, s'scooly-whn!"*[1] ("Run, deer!")

The deer came. They ran out of the woods, one after the other, in a long line. They ran straight to the lodge. Coyote held up a part of the lodge-covering, as Wood-tick always had done, and the deer went right on through the tepee. Following Wood-tick's custom, Coyote shot the last deer in the line—the largest buck. That was the rule.

Each morning after that Coyote called the deer and shot the largest buck. He did that for a long time, and he had plenty to eat. But after awhile he grew tired of buck meat and wanted a young deer for a change. So he shot a fawn. That scared the other deer; they knew something was wrong.

"That person is not our mistress!" they said. "The eyes are not hers. They are too slant. That must be *Sin-ka-lip'!*"

The deer scattered and vanished in the woods. At the same time all the dried venison that was stored in the lodge came to life and followed the main herd. On their way out of the tepee, the venison-deer picked up Wood-tick's body and carried it on their backs, and Wood-tick came to life, too. Coyote's fine buckskin clothes peeled off him and went along after the venison-deer, and the whole herd kept on going until it reached the mountains, where the deer have remained ever since.

[1]*S'scooly-whn*—This is supposed to be in Wood-tick's dialect. *Kat-ch-lhn* is Okanogan for "run."

As soon as Coyote could collect his senses, he hurried to save what scraps of meat there might be left. He found a little. This he gathered and hid. Some he put behind logs, some in brushy places and some in the ground. But, a little later, when he went to the hiding-places, he had another surprise. Behind the logs, where he had hidden meat and bones, there was nothing but dried bark and dead tree limbs, and in the ground caches he found only stones! Naked and hungry, Coyote went home. Mole, his wife, made new clothes for him.

Old Maid Wood-tick rules the deer to this day. That is why there are wood-ticks on the backs of all the deer.

XX

WHY MOSQUITOES BITE PEOPLE

There were five brothers. The smallest was *Se-lux*—Mosquito. He was lazy and greedy—greedy for blood. When his brothers killed game, they always gave him blood for his share. He never cooked it. He liked it uncooked.

Each night the brothers made Mosquito go to their sweat-house to seek *shoo'-mesh*, as he was the only one of the five who had not received medicine-power. One night he heard voices whispering as he walked toward the sweat-house, and he was afraid. He ran and told his brothers. They called him a coward and whipped him. Then they made him go to the sweat-house to spend the night. Mosquito crawled in there and cried himself to sleep.

Late in the night Mosquito was awakened by shouts and cries, the cries of his brothers. Enemies were killing them in their lodge. Soon the enemy people came to the sweat-house to kill little Mosquito. They jabbed their spears into the sweat-house. Mosquito daubed red paint on the spearpoints. Believing the red paint was the blood of the boy, the enemies went away.

Next morning, after Sun trailed high, Mosquito sneaked out of the sweat-lodge and went to his brothers' tepee. There he found them. They were dead.

Mosquito felt very sad. He cried and cried. After awhile he walked down to the river and made a canoe. Then he floated in it down the river, and he cried all the time. He sang his song for the dead. He stuttered when he talked or sang; he could not help it. The song he sang was:

"*O-O-O! La-la! Co-pah-pool-ee-la kecht-kah!*" ("O-O-Oh! La-la! The-They kil-killed m-my brothers!")

He floated a long way down the river. He came to a big camp. The people saw him, and they shouted: "Come ashore and eat chokecherries," but Mosquito did not stop. He floated on in his canoe and same his mournful song.

He came to a second encampment. The people there shouted: "Come here, come here, *Se-lux!* Come and eat *ollalees* (berries)."

"O-Oh! N-No!" Mosquito answered, in his stuttering voice, and he floated on down the river. He came to a third encampment. Many people were there.

"There comes *Se-lux,*" they said. "He likes blood."

Some of the people called to him to come and eat. Mosquito refused, and he was floating on by when they told him they could give him some uncooked blood. At that, he turned his canoe and paddled to shore. He tied the canoe fast, so it could not drift away, and went to the feast. While he was eating, filling himself with blood in his greedy way, some of the people shoved his canoe out on the river. The current carried it away. Then they told him that the canoe was gone.

Mosquito did not want to lose the canoe. He ran. He could not run fast—his stomach was too full. In his haste, he tripped and fell on a stick, which pierced his stomach and let out all the blood. From the wound flew a little fly. It alighted on a cottonwood tree.

"O-Oh! The-They kil-killed m-my brothers!" it sang.

The people heard the song. They spoke to the little fly: "When the future generations come, you will sing your song for the dead, and you will live on the blood of men—on the blood of people," they said. "That shall be your revenge for the death of your brothers."

XXI

THE GODS OF THE SUN
AND THE MOON

Mole was lonely. Coyote was away on one of his long trips. Mole would not have felt so lonesome if all her children had been with her. But there were only two left with her at home. The others had grown up and gone separate ways, as families do. The two that were left were boys. They were little.

Every sun Mole became more lonely. One day she saw a rock of odd shape. She liked it. She pretended it was Coyote; she made love to it. After it she named the older of her two small boys. She named him *Stee-qu'-lot*—Heated-Rock-Child. The rock was warmed by the sun. On another day, while digging roots she found a root that was white. It pleased her. As her smallest son's skin was light in color, she named him after the root. She named him *Swee'-elt*—White Root.

The moons passed and Coyote did not return. The boys grew. *Swee'-elt* told his mother that he could hear whispers coming up from the ground, and he asked her the reason.

"You are named after the roots," Mole explained. "The roots are your relatives. They call to you."

Stee-qu'-lot said that he could hear the rocks whispering to him, whispering sounds of friendship, and his mother told him that the rocks were his relatives.

Coyote finally came home. He found his sons grown to fine big boys, and he was glad. He was sorry that he had stayed away so long. He took the boys to himself to train. Every morning he got them up and made them swim in the cold river; he taught them to pray for strong medicine-powers. He was preparing them to meet hardships, to become good warriors. They became strong in body and spirit, and Mole was proud of them. *Swee'-elt* was handsome and white of skin, while *Stee-qu'-lot* was red of skin and strong and long of limb. He was a good hunter.

401

Coyote heard there was to be a big council in another country to decide on who should be the gods of *Kya'-len-whu*—the Sun—and *Skuk'-ach Kya'-len-whu*, the Night Sun—Moon. Coyote told his sons about the council. They wanted to go. They killed game, enough to last their parents while they were at the council. As they were leaving, Coyote suddenly decided to go with them. That left poor Mole all alone.

When Coyote and his sons reached the council they found the people worried. The people said they had not found anyone suited to take charge of either Sun or Moon. Many of the people had sought those honors, traveling in the Sun-lodge or the Moon-lodge across the sky, but all had failed. They either were too hot or too cold or too bright or too dim.

"I will be the Sun-god," declared Coyote, and the people allowed him to try. He took the Sun-lodge across the sky. But he watched everything that the people did. Seeing people in secret love, he yelled down to them, much to their embarrassment. He told on those who were hiding. The people were glad when that day was over. They lost no time in taking Coyote from the Sun-lodge. Then they asked Coyote's sons to try, but the sons refused. They wanted to remain on the earth.

Now, among those at the council was *Swa-lah'-kin*—Frog-woman. She was old and ugly, but she was in love with *Swee'-elt*, the white-skinned. Her special medicine was the rain. She caused a big rain to fall, and everything got sopping wet; the people were soaked to the skin and could not get dry, as all their fires were put out. All the fires but Frog-woman's were killed. Everybody shivered with cold—everybody but Frog-woman.

Swee'-elt did not know that Frog-woman's heart was soft toward him. He suggested to his brother that they go to her lodge and get dry by her bright fire. *Stee-qu'-lot* did not want to go. Knowing that Frog-woman loved his brother, he warned *Swee'-elt*; he told him to keep away—told him she was bad and powerful. But *Swee'-elt* became so cold that he went to her lodge by himself. Frog-woman was dressing a deer skin by the fire. Her lodge was warm and dry. *Swee'-elt* was glad he had come.

Looking up at him, Frog-woman said: "My husband! Take your place on the honored robe of your lodge."

Startled, *Swee'-elt* did not cross to the robe. Instead, he sat down near the entrance. He knew he should leave, but he did want to get

warm. Frog-woman coaxed him to move to the husband-robe, but he shook his head and stayed by the doorway. Seeing that her coaxing was of no use, Frog-woman became angry. Suddenly, she changed herself into a real frog and jumped—smack!—at the young man's smooth white face. She struck his cheek and clung there. "Now," said Frog-woman, "you cannot leave me. Not if you go to the edge of the world will you ever get another wife!"

Swee'-elt tried to take Frog-woman off his cheek. He tugged and scraped in vain. All the people came and tried to take her off. Nothing could budge Frog-woman. The people even tried to cut her off and to burn her loose from his cheek, but she did not move. At last *Swee'-elt* gave up hope. Ashamed of his appearance, he decided what to do. He said to the people: "I will take charge of the Moon-lodge. I will go with it across the sky."

Stee-qu'-lot wished to be near his unhappy brother, so he said: "I will take charge of the Sun-lodge. I will take it across the sky."

In his Moon-lodge, *Swee'-elt* travels by night. That is because he is ashamed of his ugly wife. He hates her. She still clings to his cheek. Sometimes you can see her when the nights are clear. And if a frog is killed and laid on its back or held belly toward the sky, you will see a cloud-blanket spread over the Sun or the Moon. The brother-gods always hide their faces from frogs placed in that way. Perhaps they think that the frogs are trying to make love to them.

Because he is of the heated-rock, *Stee-qu'-lot* is well suited to sit in the Sun-lodge. *Swee'-elt*, being related to the white roots in the cool ground, is suited to stay in the Moon-lodge. His white face gives the Moon its light. That dark spot on his face is the hated Frog-woman. Moonlight is cool, because *Swee'-elt* was of the root-growing earth. His descendants are the white-skinned people. The descendants of *Stee-qu'-lot* are the red-skinned people.

When *Swee'-elt* left the council-camp to sit in the Moon-lodge he said: "In the future handsome warriors will marry homely women, and pretty women sometimes will marry homely men."

What *Swee'-elt* said is true to this day. He made it so from the Beginning.

XXII

PORCUPINE LEARNS THE SUN DANCE

The *Khaka'-malh*—Fly-people—had the *Swen-qhum* (Sun-dance) first. The Sun-dance was theirs. It was their medicine. Many people wanted to learn the Sun-dance, to discover the power of the Flies, and many went to the Flies' village to learn the dance. But none ever returned. They were eaten by the crawlers that hatched from the eggs of the Flies. The *Khaka'-malh* kept their secret well.

One time Coyote went to the dance. As he danced, he became covered with eggs. Crawlers hatched from the eggs and ate him—ate most of him. What was left the Flies threw outside their camp. There the remains were found by Fox, who stepped over them three times. That restored Coyote to life.

Then Coyote went in search of someone to help him learn the secret of the Sun-dance. He met *Kwil-kin*—Porcupine, a brave man. He asked Porcupine to go back with him to the Fly village, and Pine-bough Head went. When they got to the camp, Coyote told Porcupine to go and dance while he watched. So Porcupine went on in and danced with the Flies. They laid eggs all over him. But the eggs did not bother Porcupine. Every little while he would shake himself hard, and the creepers that had crawled from the eggs would be killed on his sharp quills.

The Flies laid more and more eggs on Porcupine, and he kept on shaking himself and killing the crawlers; he was too much for the Flies. He killed all of them, too, except a very few small ones. These he permitted to live.

"Hereafter, Flies will not kill anybody," Porcupine told the little Flies. "There shall be no more big Flies to kill people. After this, only that which is dead shall be the egg-laying place of the Flies."

That was how the Flies lost the secret of their Sun-dance and their medicine-power. Because of Porcupine it no longer was a secret. The New People, when they came, were able to learn the Sun-dance.

XXIII

EN-AM-TUES—THE WISHING STONE

There were three brothers, all great warriors. They lived in the Okanogan country. "*Choo'-pahk*—Sticking—was the oldest; the second brother was *Scra'-kan*—Cooper—and the youngest was *Nak-ka'-tuya.*—Cut-up.

Among the Kalispel people lived a maiden named *Scoo'-malt*—Virgin. Her father was chief of the Kalispels.

One sun *Scoo'-malt* filled a basket with camas roots and started for the Okanogan country. She hoped to please the handsome, coppery *Scra'-kan* and become his wife. Upon reaching the summit of the range overlooking the Okanogan Valley from the east, she stopped to make herself beautiful. She combed and braided her long black hair and painted her face with red earth paint.

In their dreams the three brothers saw *Scoo'-malt* coming, and they went to meet her. Each asked her to marry him, and then the younger brothers fought. *Nak-ka'-tuya* slashed the shoulders off *Scra'-kan*, while Scra'-ken knocked *Nak-ka'-tuya* down and kicked him into a long heap, flat on the ground.

Coyote came along as the brothers were fighting, and he laughed at seeing them fighting so hard over the Kalispel maiden. He thought it was a good joke, but his glee angered the girl, and she spoke sharply to him. Her words, in turn, angered Coyote. He would show the maiden that she could not talk that way to him. With the help of his great medicine-power he moved the brothers back to where they had been when they started to meet *Scoo'-malt*, and he changed them into mountains. Then he made *Scoo'-malt* helpless by turning her lower body into stone.

Taking her basketful of *et-quah* (camas), *Scoo'-malt* threw it back to her people, to the Kalispel country, so that none would grow in the land of the Okanogans, and she transformed the rest of herself into stone, to remain there in sight of her stone lovers forever.

Coyote was amused. To the stone maiden, he said: "Because you are a stranger in this place, you will help the coming generations by giving them good luck, but they will have to pay you to make their wishes happen." Then he turned to the mountains that had been warriors, and said: "*Choo'-pahk*, because you are proud and would not take part in the fight, you will stand with your head high and stately. You, *Scra'-kan*, because a virgin of another land came to court you, will be loved always by the women for your handsome coppery body. The women will like pieces of it for decorating their arms and hands. *Nak-ka'-tuya*, because you were beaten and kicked to the ground, you will lie in shame as a mountain ridge for other generations to see."

That is why *Choo'-pahk* (Mt. Chopaka) looks so proud and fine. *Scra'-kan*, nearby, to the north and west, stands without shoulders, a sharp-pointed peak (in British Columbia). Across the valley of the *Similkameen* River lies *Nak-ka'-tuya* (Mt. Richter, B. C.).

The maiden still sits on the summit where she stopped that day long ago to comb her hair and paint her face with the red earth paint. The people call her *En-am-tues*—Sitting-on-the-summit. The place where she sits is *Mock-tsin*—Knoll-between-a-divide. There the people have gone for many generations to ask for good luck and to pay for their asking with gifts so that their wishes would come true.[1]

[1]*En-am-tues* is known to the whites as the *Tee-hee-hee* stone. *Tee-hee-hee*, which is not an Okanogan word, may be a comparatively modern corruption of the verb meaning "to wish" in the Chinook jargon, the old-time trade language of the Northwest. Derived from the pure Chinook *tikekh*, "to wish" in the jargon is given variously as: *t'keh, te-ke, tik-eh, tik-eigh, tak-eigh, tick-ey, tikky,* and so forth.

The "wishing stone," or Camas-woman, as it frequently is called, is one of many wishing stations or shrines in the Northwest where the Indians made offerings. To pass Camas-woman without depositing a gift was said to bring sorrow and ill-luck. In return for even the smallest gift, the older generations of Indians believed she would grant any wish that might be asked. The sick supplicated for health, the poor for worldly goods, the ambitious for success in war, the chase, love, and other undertakings.

After the Indians' contact with the fur-traders, coin entered largely into the gifts, and the white men, learning of the Camas-woman's influence, robbed her of all her wealth.

When the Colville Reservation was thrown open to settlement in 1900, a prospector dynamited the shrine to see if it concealed anything of value.

The stone, originally about five feet in height, is now a pile of its shattered parts. After it was blasted, some of the Indians gathered up the fragments and heaped them to a height of six or seven feet. Mourning Dove remembers when the stone was intact.

En-am-tues, situated on a divide overlooking the Okanogan Valley from the east, is seven miles west and south of Molson, Washington. One of the main cross-country trails passed by it, but there are no modern roads in the vicinity.

The camas which the maiden threw back to her people is the "black camas" that grows on Camas Prairie near Calispell Lake, Pend Oreille County, Washington. Kalispel Indians who dig the root receive as high as a dollar a gallon for it from people of their own and other tribes. The Kalispel country always has been noted for its rich camas grounds.

The name, *Scra'-kan,* applied to one of the brother-mountains, is a modern Okanogan word that originally was used to designate the copper kettles traded to the Indians by the fur companies. Before the coming of the whites, gold nuggets and copper were made into bracelets, the pieces strung together. An ornament of this kind was called *skel-ear-qu-nekst',* which means "circle-around-the-wrist," and this word was the only one by which either of the metals was known.

XXIV

CHICKADEE MAKES A *SHOO'-MESH* BOW

Chickadee wanted to cross the river where Elk had his trail. Elk crossed the river at the same place each sun. Chickadee waited for him there. When Elk came, Chickadee said: *"Ste-eel'-tza,* my grandfather. Take me across on your back."

Now, Elk was not Chickadee's grandfather, but Chickadee wanted to please Elk and gain his favor. Elk agreed to carry the little boy across the river. He took Chickadee on his back and waded into the water. With his flint knife, Chickadee began to cut the back of Elk's neck.

"Zst-skada'-na, what are you doing?" asked Elk.

And Chickadee answered: "Grandfather, I am only scratching your neck."

Elk went on. Soon he thought that Chickadee was scratching too hard, and again he asked what the boy was doing.

"Grandfather, I am only scratching your neck," said Chickadee, but all the time he was cutting, cutting with his flint knife. Just as Elk reached the shore, Chickadee made a last cut and Elk fell dead with a broken neck. Chickadee was glad. He wanted one of Elk's ribs for a bow. Such a bow would have strong *shoo'-mesh.* He skinned Elk with his knife. As he finished taking off the hide, Mother Wolf walked up. She had hidden her two children close by in their cradle that was hung on a tree. Mother Wolf looked greedily at the elk meat.

"Go and get your little cousins," she said. "I left them on a tree by the trail."

Chickadee knew that she wanted to steal the meat, but he did not let on that he knew. He ran along the trail and found the children, but he did not take them to their mother. He carried them in the opposite direction, running far with them. Then he hurried back to Mother Wolf.

"I could not find your babies," he said.

"Why, they are on a tree close by the trail," said Mother Wolf, who thought that Chickadee could not find them. "Look again for them," and Chickadee ran to where he had left the children and carried them still farther away. He hurried back to Mother Wolf.

"No, I cannot find your babies," he said.

Mother Wolf sent him once more. As soon as he was gone she started cutting the elk meat into small pieces. By the time Chickadee returned, the meat was all cut up. Chickadee did not have the children, of course, so Mother Wolf finally had to look for them.

"Do not eat any of the meat until I come back," she told Chickadee. "Wait, and we will eat together," and she started down the trail. It took her a long time to find her children.

Chickadee began to carry the meat away as soon as Mother Wolf was out of sight. He took it to a high cliff, to a ledge halfway up the wall of the cliff. He made several trips, and he finished carrying all the meat there just before Mother Wolf returned with her children. She followed Chickadee's tracks to the foot of the cliff, and then she looked up and saw him sitting on the ledge and roasting the meat over a fire.

"*Zst-skaka'-na*, throw down a mouthful of meat for your little cousins," said Mother Wolf.

"Open their mouths. I will throw down a mouthful to each," answered Chickadee.

Mother Wolf opened the mouths of the little wolves, and into their mouths Chickadee dropped two hot stones that he had wrapped in fat. They swallowed the hot stones and were killed. Mother Wolf was not watching them. She was looking up at Chickadee, hoping he would throw her some meat.

"Now open your mouth, Mother Wolf," he instructed, and when her jaws were wide open Chickadee dropped a big rock, red hot and wrapped in fat. It slid down Mother Wolf's throat, and she fell over, dead.

Chickadee now dried the remainder of his meat in peace, and from one of Elk's ribs he made a bow. It had strong power.

XXV

COYOTE AND CHICKADEE

While roaming the hills one sun, looking for food, Coyote met Chickadee, who was carrying his elk-rib *shoo'-mesh* bow. Chickadee was very proud of his bow and the short stubby arrows that it used. Coyote thought he would like to have that bow, so he made fun of it.

"That bow is no good, *Zst-skaka'-na*," he said. "And such short, fat arrows. They cannot fly far—cannot kill anything. People will laugh at you for carrying such poor weapons. You had better throw them away."

"My bow and arrows may look poor and queer, but I like them," answered Chickadee. "And you think they cannot shoot far. I will show you. Go to the top of that ridge and walk slowly along it. Go there, and I will show you."

"I will go, silly *Zst-skaka'-na*," Coyote said. "That bow cannot put an arrow half way to the top of the ridge," and he started off. He was laughing.

Coyote felt gay. He trotted along, thinking about many foolish things, and by the time he reached the top of the ridge he had forgotten why he was there. He sang as he walked along the top of the ridge. He was enjoying the bright sunlight and the sweet smell of the air. All at once he heard a noise like that of a strange wind, and he stopped to listen.

"*Eh-ahe!*" he said. "That must be the spirits of other snows whispering to me." The words were but out of his mouth when one of Chickadee's arrows was in his ribs. It killed him.

Chickadee went after the arrow. He pulled it out, but he did not keep it. "*Caw!* I do not want that arrow. It smells bad," and he threw it away. He went on from there. He was going to a big council, a council of all the Animal People.

A few suns later Fox came upon the body of his twin brother. He knew that Coyote had been into mischief. He stepped over the body three times, and that brought Coyote to life.

"*Eh-ahe!* I have slept long, *Why-ay'-looh.*" Coyote yawned. "I was resting on this ridge."

"Yes, how long you have slept, *Sin-ka-lip'!* If I had not walked over your trail, you would have slept forever. You should know better than to contend with the little boy. His bow is powerful, and his arrows travel as the lightning. They reach the life, no matter the distance. My heart is sad with your mischief."

"Where did *Zst-skaka'-na* go?"

"He is on his way to the big council. The people are talking of making a trail to the Upper World Land," and with these words Fox left Coyote.

Coyote picked up the arrow that had killed him, and started after Chickadee. He followed fast on the trail, and in a few suns he caught up with Chickadee, who was quite surprised and not at all glad to see him.

"We shall gamble for the bow and the arrows," Coyote spoke. "We will throw arrows at a mark, not using the bow. The winner will take the weapons."

Chickadee had no wish to gamble, but Coyote coaxed and coaxed, and finally Chickadee said "All right." Chickadee thought he would win easily. But Coyote asked his *squas-tenk'* for help, and it moved Chickadee's eye from the mark when the boy threw an arrow, Chickadee could not hit the mark, and Coyote hit it every time, winning the stout bow and the powerful arrows. Then they gambled some more, and Chickadee lost his fine clothes of feathers, his weasel skins, and shell beads, even his hair ornaments—everything—and he was naked.

Coyote dressed in Chickadee's clothes and went his way. He took the bow and the arrows. He would go to the council camp of the Animal People and help them build a trail to the Upper World Land, he said to himself. He was in fine humor. He threw his head from side to side to make the wampum rattle on his hair braids. He laughed at the picture of poor Chickadee, naked by the trail.

Pretty soon Coyote came to a small tepee. He heard children quarreling inside. He went in. No one was to be seen. By the fire were some red *kinnikinnick* berries. Coyote stepped outside the tepee and threw a stone along the ground. It made a noise like his walking on the trail. Then he peeked through the door-flap, and he saw a swarm of little children come out from beneath a bed of skin robes. The

children began to quarrel again, over the best way to roast the red berries.

Coyote stepped back into the lodge. The children dove for their hiding place. All but one slipped under the skin robes. That one Coyote caught.

"Let me show you how to roast the berries," Coyote said. "Come out. I will not hurt you."

The children believed him. They came out. Coyote told them to bring all of the berries to him. He dug a hole in the coals of the fire, and, when the boys and girls started to hand the berries to him, he grabbed the children, too. Only one child got away and hid where Coyote could not find him. Coyote shoved the others into the coals to roast along with the berries. There he left them. As soon as Coyote had gone, the child that had escaped hurried to dig his brothers and sisters out of the coals, but they were dead.

Then Mother and Father *Se-qua'-quelt*—Prairie Chicken—came to the tepee. It was their home. They brought big packs of bugs and berries for their children. When they saw what had happened they sat down and cried. Chickadee was coming down the trail. He heard the crying. He went into the tepee to see if he could help. He felt sorry for the parents. He called to his mystery-power; he asked it to help him. Then he sprinkled ashes on the bodies of the children and stepped over them three times, and the little boys and girls came back to life. And they were as well and happy as if nothing had happened to them.

The parents wanted to pay Chickadee. He told them how Coyote had tricked him and taken his fine weapons and his good clothes. Right away Mother and Father Prairie Chicken guessed who had killed their children. They flew out of the tepee and followed Coyote's trail. Soon they caught up with him. They flew on by and to a high cliff above the river. There they hid and waited.

Singing, Coyote walked along. He felt good. But he was not to feel good very long, for, when he reached the edge of the cliff, Father Prairie Chicken flew at his face, and Mother Prairie Chicken darted between his legs. Blinded by the one and tripped by the other, Coyote lost his balance and pitched off the cliff. As he fell, the parents swooped after him and stripped off Chickadee's clothes and snatched away the medicine-bow and arrows, which they took to Chickadee, who started again for the council.

As he fell, spinning over and over, Coyote called to his *squas-tenk'*. "*Pess-pess qu-lupe!*" ("Come, come out!") he begged. "What shall I

make myself into? A leaf?" Immediately he became a leaf, and the wind carried him high in the air and whirled him around and around until he was dizzy. He did not like that, so he said, "What now shall I make myself into—a pine needle?"

He became a pine needle and began to fall. Faster and faster he fell. He was almost to the river when he grew frightened and changed into cottonwood dust. Up again he was taken by the wind, wa-a-a-y up! The wind puffed him so high that he hardly could breathe. He did not like that. Once more he wished himself into a pine needle, and he fell, faster and faster, toward the river. Just above the water he wanted to slow up. He wanted to be a leaf again, but in his excitement he made a mistake. He wished himself into a *speks'-hene-men*, a pounding-rock (pestle), and he plunged—*ker-glump!*—to the bottom of the river.

There, on the bottom of the river, Coyote was helpless. He could not move, and he could not change into something else. His power was no good to him under water. After awhile he became hungry, and he was sitting like a rock, which he was, when along came *Enshap'-men-itqu*—Water-Bug.

"Take me to dry land," Coyote begged.

"I cannot drag you," Water-Bug answered. "You are much too heavy. I could not even budge you."

"Get all your relations," Coyote urged. "All of you working together can drag me out of this place. I will pay you well for your work."

So Water-Bug got all of his relatives to come and they pulled and tugged and pushed Coyote to dry land, and then he changed himself from a rock to his regular form. His heart was glad, and he gave all of the water-bugs hard coats of many colors, so that they could hide among the sharp river rocks. From that sun the water-bugs have had an easier life in their rock houses.

After he paid the water-bugs for their work, Coyote started once more for the council camp of the Animal People.

XXVI

The Arrow-Trail

Coyote was the last to arrive at the council camp of the Animal People. All the others were there. *Milka-noups*—Eagle, the strongest flier, had scouted to the Upper World Land and told of what he had seen there. A fine country, he said, full of wonders.

Eagle's talk made all the people eager to get up to that country high in the sky, where the best of the berries were thick on the bushes and hunting was easy—without the killing—and food of all kinds was plentiful.

The smartest persons from all over the world talked and schemed, trying to think of a way to reach the land in the sky. They talked and talked for many suns. Finally, someone suggested the shooting of arrows to make a trail through the sky. That thought was good, the council agreed. So the warriors and hunters tried to make an arrow trail. They shot arrow after arrow, but none of their bows were strong enough. All the arrows dropped back to earth. All tried and failed— all but little Chickadee. Being small and modest, he waited until everyone else had tried. Then he strung his elk-rib *shoo'-mesh* bow. Everybody looked at him in surprise. They couldn't believe he really intended to shoot.

Chickadee said nothing, but he drew his bow as far as it would bend, and loosed a short stubby arrow, which flashed up out of sight and did not fall back. Then the little boy sent a second arrow after the first, and it did not come back. Then he shot a third and a fourth and a fifth and many, many more with his wonderful medicine-bow. Each arrow stuck into the one ahead of it, and the first arrow stuck into the Upper World Land. They made a long, straight ladder from the earth up to the mysterious country far above.

One by one, the people climbed up the ladder of arrows. The last to start was *Kee-lau-naw*—Grizzly Bear—who had been busy collecting food to take along. She was not satisfied with a little; she wanted to take a big pack of food. She had gathered wild rhubarb, skunk

cabbage, and other plants she liked to eat. All that food made such a big pack that she hardly could swing it on her back. By the time Grizzly Bear began to climb, the others were in the Upper World Land. The arrow-trail creaked and groaned under the great weight of Grizzly Bear and the heavy pack of food. The higher she climbed, the more the ladder creaked. The strain on it became too much, and all at once there was a thunder-like crash, and the trail pulled loose from the Upper World Land. Down came the arrows, and down came Grizzly Bear. The fall did not kill her, but it gave her bad shaking-up, and she was sore and lame for a long time.

Grizzly Bear's accident was not known to the others. They did not know their trail was destroyed. After their hard climb, they rested and congratulated themselves on reaching such a wonderful country. They were pleased to see so much food. It seemed to be everywhere.

Off in the distance they saw a big camp. They started toward it. They did not notice a scout that was watching them. The scout was a wise bird. He flew to the camp and told the people that enemies were coming, and the headmen of the village shouted: "The Lower Earth People have come to make war. Let us get ready for them."

So, when the Animal People got close to the camp they saw that the Upper World Land People were armed for war. That made them afraid. They did not want to fight in that strange country. They wanted peace. They sent Beaver, their wisest person, to talk and make peace. Beaver took a water-trail, where he was more at home. The trail led close to the camp, where Beaver heard a warrior say: "What shall we do with *Stun'-whu*, the wisest of the earth people? He is coming along the water-trail. He is near."

That scared Beaver. He did not wait to hear more. He swam back as fast as he could. Then the people sent *Eut-la-who*—Raven—to talk peace. He flew low over the camp, but he did not alight, for he heard someone say: "What shall we do with *Eut-la-who*—Shiny Back? He is not liked even by his own people. Who will pierce him with an arrow?"

Well, Raven left in a hurry. One after another, the Animal People approached the camp to make peace, but the other people would have nothing to do with them. At last the Animal People gave up hope. The food that had appeared to be so plentiful was guarded by their enemies, and, as the suns passed, they became thin from hunger. They began to long for their old homes on earth. With sad hearts they turned back to the place where they thought the arrow-trail was

fastened. *Eh-ahe!* It was gone! The only way down to earth was to jump, and it was a long, long jump. It was so far below that none could tell the color of the water or the color of the land.

Some jumped for what they thought was water, and some at what they guessed was land. *Qhu-quak*—Sucker—jumped at what looked like a patch of blue. It was water, but she missed it! She struck on the rocky bank of a river. And later, when high water came, Sucker's body was washed down the river. That restored her to life. But she was not the same as before. The fall to the rocky river bank broke all her bones—smashed them into splinters. That is why there are so many little bones in all suckers today. It is those splinter-like bones that make suckers hard to eat, that give them the name "choking-fish."

Sten-ten'-ywa, the Web-winged—Bat—was so excited when he jumped that he forgot to use his wings. He traveled to earth so fast that he was flattened right out when he hit the ground. He still can travel fast, but he is very ugly looking. He used to be handsome.

Coyote got down safely. First he turned himself into a pine needle, which fell fast. Then he became a leaf and floated gently to the ground. Then he resumed his own form.

After that time the Animal People were content to stay on earth, where they belonged. The breaking of their arrow-trail was the will of the Spirit Chief. He did not want the Animal People bothering the people of the Upper World Land again.

XXVII

COYOTE IMITATES BEAR AND KINGFISHER

One time during the moons of snow, Coyote and Mole and their children were out of food. They were almost starved. Their nearest neighbors, *Skemhuist'*, the Claw-Grabber—Bear,[1] and *Z-reece'*—Kingfisher—had plenty to eat. Bear and Kingfisher always had plenty. Coyote knew this. He said to his wife: *"Pul'-laqu-whu*, I am going over the ridge and see your brother,[2] *Skem-huist'*. He may give me something for us to eat."

Coyote went to Bear's lodge. Bear and his wife had no children. Coyote noticed that they had nothing in their lodge but some bedding and a *klek'-chin* (cooking-basket). There were no signs of food, which made Coyote wonder. For awhile he sat in silence. Then he yawned. Bear knew what that meant. It was a hunger yawn.

Bear turned to his wife and said: "Put the rock in the fire and bring water in the basket. Your brother is hungry."

Bear's wife placed a rock in the fire and went after water. Coyote wondered where the food was to come from, and he yawned again. Bear's wife returned with the cooking-basket nearly full of water. Bear took his flint knife and cut a piece of buckskin from his wife's robe. He pressed the piece into a lump, and, when the rock in the fire was red-hot, he dropped the rock and the lump of buckskin into the cooking-basket. Then he rubbed ashes on his wife's robe, and the robe became whole again. It did not show where it had been cut.

As soon as the water in the basket boiled, Bear emptied a bag of pebbles into it. Coyote thought he wouldn't care for such food—buckskin and pebbles! But when the basket was placed before him, he tasted the food and quickly changed his mind; for the buckskin had become fine, tender meat, and the pebbles were juicy huckleberries!

[1]*Skem-huist*, the Claw-Grabber—the black or brown bear.
[2]Brother—Bear is not Mole's brother. Coyote speaks the word in its flattering sense. He employs it with like meaning in his later reference to Kingfisher.

Coyote ate all of the soup and the huckleberries and some of the meat, but he saved most of the meat for Mole and the children. "Let me carry this meat home in your cooking-basket," he said to Bear.

"All right," Bear answered. "You can send it back by one of your children." But Coyote insisted that Bear come for the basket, that he should come and visit him. Bear did not want to, but Coyote kept insisting until Bear said, "I will come for the basket."

The next sun Bear walked to Coyote's lodge. Seeing him coming down the ridge, Coyote had Mole hide all of their rose-hips that they had been eating for lack of better food. The rosehips were famine food, eaten only in times of starving. Coyote also had Mole clean up the tepee so it would look like Bear's lodge, and beside the fire he had her leave only a cooking-basket, two sticks and a stone.

Looking in, Bear asked for his basket. He did not intend to go inside, but Coyote urged him to enter and sit down. Being polite, Bear did. Then Coyote told Mole to heat the stone in the fire and get a basket of water. Mole obeyed. When the stone was hot, Coyote took out his flint knife and cut a large piece of buckskin from Mole's robe—the only robe she owned. He pressed the piece into a lump, as he had seen Bear do, and he told Mole to put it and the hot stone in the cooking-basket. Using the two sticks as tongs, Mole lifted the stone from the fire and dropped it in the water along with the lump of buckskin. As Bear had done to his wife's robe, Coyote rubbed ashes on Mole's spoiled robe, but it did not become whole again. It remained as he had cut it. Mole felt bad. Then Coyote poured pebbles from a bag into the boiling water. Soon all sat up to eat, but only tough buckskin and hard pebbles were taken from the basket. Coyote said nothing. He was ashamed. After awhile Bear spoke. "*Sin-ka-lip'*," he said, "this is my way, not yours. You cannot do what I can, and I do not try to imitate people as you do."

Then Bear rubbed ashes on Mole's robe and it was as good as ever. Bear picked up his own cooking-basket and went home. Pretty soon Coyote looked into his cooking-basket. What he saw made him grunt with surprise. Instead of buckskin and pebbles, there was plenty of good meat and huckleberries. He laughed.

For many suns Coyote and Mole and their children lived on the meat and the berries that Bear had made for them with his magic power. When all of that food was eaten and they were hungry once more, Coyote said:

"*Pul'-laqu-whu*, I am going to see your brother, *Z-reece'*. Maybe

he will give us something to eat," and he went to Kingfisher's tepee. Invited in, he entered and sat down. He saw nothing to eat in there. He yawned. Kingfisher knew what that meant, and he spoke to the older of his two children. "My son," he said, "go and bring me three willows."

Boy Kingfisher went out. He returned soon with three willow sticks, which Kingfisher took and heated over the fire. When they were hot, he twisted them to make them strong and tied them to his belt. Then he flew to the top of the lodge and from there to the river, where he dove through a hole in the ice. He came up with the willow sticks strung with fish. These were for his neighbor, Coyote. Kingfisher's wife cooked the fish. Coyote ate his fill, but some were left for him to take to Mole and the children. "May I carry these fish home in your cooking-basket?" he asked.

"Yes, take the basket," said Kingfisher. "Send it back by one of your children."

"No, I want you to visit me," Coyote replied. "You come over tomorrow and get the basket."

Kingfisher had no wish to visit Coyote, but Coyote coaxed him and at last he agreed, and the next sun he walked to Coyote's lodge.

"My son," said Coyote to the eldest of his sons, as Kingfisher sat down, "go and bring me three willows."

"What do you want them for?" Boy Coyote asked. "How will you use them?"

"You must know why I want three willows," Coyote scolded. "You always have brought them to me."

Boy Coyote said nothing more. He went out and got three willow sticks, and his father heated them over the fire and twisted them, as he had seen Kingfisher do. He tied the sticks to his belt and tried to fly to the top of the lodge; he had a hard time climbing there without breaking down the whole tepee. From the lodge-top he jumped for a hole in the river ice. He missed the hole and smashed on the ice and was killed.

Kingfisher had been watching from the doorway and smiling to himself. He walked over to where Coyote lay. Taking the willow sticks from Coyote's belt, he tied them to his own belt and dove through the hole in the ice. When he came up he had the willow sticks heavy with fish. These he placed beside Coyote and stepped over him three times. That brought Coyote back to life.

Then Kingfisher said: "This is my way, not yours, *Sin-ka-lip'*. I do not try to imitate others, as you do."

Kingfisher took his basket and went home, and Coyote went back to his tepee. He carried the fish that Kingfisher had caught. He gave them to Mole to cook.

"See! We have plenty to eat now," Coyote laughed. "We have plenty for my imitating Bear and Kingfisher. That is why I imitated them!"

NOTES ON THE STORIES

Mourning Dove called her collection *Okanogan Sweat House*, in homage to the leader of the Animal Spirit People living before Coyote started his transformations. As a living oral literature, these stories have no set form. Their telling depends on narrative skill, audience, and circumstances. Among elders, they are aesthetic treasures in measured verse, yet when told to children, they are abbreviated. The merit of a story rests on the completeness and sensitive patterning of its text, texture, and context. At its fullest, a story is also localized in place and time, ending with an edict about how conditions got to be as they are now.

Other examples of Salishan Plateau stories, legends, tales, and sagas have been published,[1] but these lack details of texture, context, and performance. Mourning Dove's story drafts have also been published,[2] devoid of commentary or insight. These drafts, along with letters, reside in the McWhorter Collection.[3]

Recent scholarship has emphasized the importance of language, performance, and creativity for understanding oral literature. Linguists interested in the dramatic patterning of the text have contributed much, along with accurate representations for the names of mythic characters.[4]

I. Spirit Chief Names the Animal People

A more esoteric version of Naming Day is given in the Introduction, with fuller explanations of the special nature of Coyote's power. This naming properly leads off this collection since it remains the chartering saga for many of the Interior Salishan tribes to this day. Belief in the Chief Above, while since influenced by Christianity, was indeed aboriginal in the Plateau and other regions of the Americas.[5] The origin of Sweatlodge from the wife of the Spirit Chief is a unique feature of this account and has not been satisfactorily explained. Mourning Dove may have intended a feminist stance, or she may have been influenced by Flathead belief in Sweatlodge as Grandmother.

Creation was not an issue among the Salishans. As with many other oral traditions, they simply accepted that the world had always existed,

although variously modified by Coyote and others. Today, due to Biblical influence, the creation of the world has been described. James Teit collected origin stories from the Okanagans, explaining the creation of Earth Woman, Sky, and Underworld through the efforts of Chief Above. Among these three planes, "All are connected by a pole or tree which passes through the middle of each."[6] In another recent version, the connecting axis is an apple tree, a wry comment on the role of Colvilles in the current Washington State apple industry.

Similarly, human arrival is simply accepted. Among the Methows, however, humans were created by Coyote from slices cut from a monster Beaver who rampaged along the Columbia River.

II. Fox and Coyote and Whale

In a similar story, the monster is a giant Otter who lived in the Columbia near Orondo, Washington. Other monsters represented sturgeon, which are indeed enormous in the Columbia. Throughout the Northwest, Mouse is known as a polyglot, a symbolic consequence of the ability of mice to live everywhere, from homes to fields.

III. Coyote Fights Some Monsters

This is a typical series of adventures, told separately or in mixed order, depending on constraints of time and place. Each episode ends with the commandment issued by Coyote establishing the conditions as they are now known to humans. The horse was, however, an historic import to the Plateau, greatly facilitating bison hunting on the Plains.

IV. Chipmunk and Owl

This remains a well-known story, and a likely inspiration for the relations between the grandmother and heroine in Mourning Dove's novel, whose title is taken from the Okanogan word for Chipmunk. Children are still urged to behave by threats of a visit from Sneena.[7] A character type known as Basket Ogress, Sneena was the prototype for the present species of Great Horned Owl. Missing from this version is the usual explanation that Sneena's lower jaw was ripped off and thrown into the water, where it turned into the species of waterfowl

known as coots, which swim together in the distinctive parabolic pattern of a jawbone.

V. Coyote and the Buffalo

The concern with modesty by Mourning Dove and her editors is exemplified by this story. According to all other accounts, Coyote took his revenge by urinating in addition to spitting, kicking, and insulting the bison skull. Missing from this version is the explanation that Coyote stuck his cane into the last tree to hold it steady and thus supplied heartwood to future trees. It was just this heartwood that Coyote later used to make stronger, sharper horns for the old bull.

VI. Why Flint-Rock Cannot Fight Back

In this version, hints remain of the nature of Coyote's medicine powers. When they refuse to help him, he threatens them with a downpour. The native audience would realize what disastrous consequences rain would have for feces and so understand their reconsideration and aid. The color of the dress worn by Mole to attract Flint was described by Charles Quintasket, Mourning Dove's half-brother, as the color of a boiled crayfish shell.

VII. How Turtle Got His Tail

This story represents a native retelling of the Aesop fable about the Hare and the tortoise. Since meeting whites, Colvilles and others have been hearing European stories, making them their own[8] and using them to explain features of their own experience.

VIII. Why Skunk's Tail Is Black and White

In oral literature, Skunk is an extremely dangerous, but also hilarious, character. In this version he is atypically portrayed because, as Mourning Dove often said, if she wrote Skunk stories as they traditionally were told, the authorities would "put her in jail." To appreciate her remark, such a Skunk story has been added after these notes.

IX. Rattlesnake and Salmon

While Mourning Dove placed this story at Kettle Falls and among the Kalispel, the Methows locate it further down the Columbia River.

They say that the chief at Pateros arranged a contest whose winner would marry his daughter. Salmon won over five (or, more recently, three) Wolf brothers, who sought revenge. Rattlesnake took their side and killed Salmon with an arrow, while the Wolf brothers made off with the wife. Salmon floated downriver, revived in the ocean (without the aid of Mouse), and returned to revenge himself on the Wolves and Snake. Though curiously ignored in this variant, Salmon's widow was the first Mourning Dove. Every Spring, until prevented by the dams, mourning doves calling along the banks of the river signaled to the Salishans that the salmon had returned. A token arrowpoint remains in the head of each salmon, a proof of the shot from a craggy island in the Columbia, now partially submerged behind Rocky Reach Dam, marking the petrified home of Rattlesnake.

X. Coyote Meets Wind and Some Others

Although the Hemp sisters appear here as minor characters, plants are important in the oral tradition.[9] At Naming Day, Bitterroot was the first plant to speak, offering to be the first food of spring. Modesty prevented Mourning Dove from explaining that Coyote created the obscuring fog by ejaculating.

XI. Why Gartersnake Wears a Green Blanket

A European account of St. George and the Dragon was probably the inspiration for this version, but it builds upon a widespread Native American belief in the eternal antagonism between Sky and Water, Thunderbird and Seamonster.

XII. Coyote Quarrels with Mole

This is a segment of a series showing Coyote at his worst. He was too lazy and slow to feed his family, and Mole, for once, objected before fleeing for her life. He was left with five sons to care for, and they all were soon starving. While he killed and ate the older ones, he spared the youngest child, Topqn.[10]

XIII. How Coyote Happened to Make Black Moss Food

Coyote and his son continued on, tried to take beaver or swan, but were bested. The Animal People knew that Coyote had wronged his

family, so they were not sympathetic to his hunger. In the process, the son's ears were stretched, so all coyotes now have long ears. The moss that was created from his hair is still a favorite food of Colvilles, who have devised ways of baking it in stove ovens instead of the traditional pit ovens (described in footnote 3, p. 374).

XIV. Why Spider Has Such Long Legs

Spider was punished for his vanity, although he contributed to the public welfare. Beaver's daughter thrived because she was encased in deerskin that acted as a fresh air chamber.

XV. Why Badger Is So Humble

In Salishan folklore, Badger is consummately slow and clumsy. His brief moment of glory ends in humiliation. In other regions, the character refusing marriage is a haughty girl, who usually falls for a handsome man who was a Snake. In this version, the pretty woman was Coyote, a further example of his versatility.

XVI. Coyote Juggles His Eyes

This story is well known throughout the Plateau. The Yakima Coyote (Speelyi) used a flower (still known as Coyote's eyes) as a substitute until he could retrieve his own sight. Among the Colvilles, the bird whose eyes were stolen and replaced with huckleberries is the rufus-sided Towee, which has tiny red eyes. Traditionally, when the Bird sisters attempted to carry the disguised Coyote on their backs, they kept throwing him down not because he made himself an awkward burden but because he was attempting to fondle and penetrate them.

XVII. Why Marten's Face Is Wrinkled

Marten comes off as totally inept. He did not know how to eat venison and grease, he disobeyed his older brother, and he violated the laws of hospitality by refusing the girl's offered food.

XVIII. Crawfish and Grizzly Bear

Because people had danced and prayed, Crayfish, otherwise insignificant, was empowered to best Grizzly Bear. Because bears led

summer and winter lives, they had two sets of teeth, which, along with hide and claws, they wore over their human form. It is interesting that Grizzly stayed in the highest mountains because of a promise, not an edict.

XIX. Coyote and Wood-tick

The role of Wood-tick as deer warden emphasizes the need for a cautious respect of nature, where even the most minuscule can have great power. In another modern story, Wood-tick and Ant were riding a wagon that turned over, giving Wood-tick a flat, shiny head. Grieving, Ant kept tightening her belt so that all ants now have tiny waists.

XX. Why Mosquitoes Bite People

Unlike other stories, this one uses the traditional number, five. In other versions, mosquitoes were created from the ashes of a cremated blood-sucking monster.

XXI. The Gods of Sun and Moon

This story picks up the lives of Mole and Coyote after they separated, correctly noting that Mole "made love" to the rock and root, begetting Warm Red Rock and White Root as replacements for the sons whom Coyote had eaten. After Coyote and Mole were reconciled, they heard about the council to select the Sun and Moon. According to the usual version, the brothers went downriver to the meeting. Along the way, they had to contend with the doglike Monster who lived at Ribbon Cliff on the west side of the Columbia. Fatally wounded, the monster ran around spewing blood, leaving the dark bands which give that rock its English name.

At the council, all of the other contenders had been rejected. For example, Crane was so long that his beak was beginning to set before his toes had left the ground. Coyote called out all that he saw from the sky, mostly illicit relations. As the brothers prepared to try, Frog brought on the rain and lured them into her house. There, as described, White Root refused her offer of marriage and the insulted Frog jumped onto his face and remained there. The final outcome was

that Red Rock became the Sun and White Root became the Moon, even now marked by the dark patch of Frog Woman.

Mourning Dove made reference to this story in her novel: "if you place a frog on its back . . . she will look up at the sun and flirt with him . . . He hates her so badly," he will cause it to rain.[11]

XXII. Porcupine Learns the Sun-Dance

Despite its familiar name, the Plateau tribes did not have the Sun Dance traditionally, although tribes along the border with the Plains adopted it historically along with the horse and other features made stereotypical of all Indians by Hollywood films.

XXIII. En-am-tues—The Wishing Stone

Though blasted apart, the fragments of the Hee-hee-stone are well known and even appear on a popular postcard. Needless to say, Colvilles regard her as a local girl rather than one of Kalispel origin. Similar stories are told of other mountains in the region. Along the coast, Mounts Rainier, Adams, and Baker were once a husband and two wives who separated after a dispute.

XXIV. Chickadee Makes a Shoo-Mesh Bow

Colvilles are very fond of tiny Chickadee and his powerful elk-rib bow, using him as a reminder that great things can come in tiny packages.

XXV. Coyote and Chickadee

Though unexplained, the ending of this story is premised on the commandment of Story II that the Land People and the Water People have become forever separated. Thus, Coyote had to convince the Waterbugs to roll him out of the river; otherwise he could not summon his own help. His powers would have dissolved in the water.

XXVI. The Arrow Trail

Better known as the Arrow Chain, this is a widespread story that is often used to bring down the curtain on the Mythic Age. Supposedly,

people went to the Sky World to get fire. In modern tellings, Mrs. Grizzly Bear broke the chain because she tried to take up everything she owned: her food, pots, pans, and microwave oven. Those who did make it up, had to jump down, as described. Suckers (a variety of fish) are indeed bony, and Bats wrinkled. Within Washington State, this episode is also used to explain why there are only harmless snakes west of the Cascade Mountains, while rattlesnakes occur east of them. Elders say that all snakes used to be everywhere, but, jumping from the sky, rattlers landed in the sagebrush country and gartersnakes among the evergreens.

XXVII. Coyote Imitates Bear and Kingfisher

The theme of this story is better known as Bungling Host. By ending with it, Mourning Dove reminds us that Coyote survived the visit to the sky and many other adventures. He lives on, having learned how important it is to "be yourself," and affirmation of the value of different lifeways.

NOTES

1. Charles Hill-Tout, *The Natives of British North America I: The Far West, the Home of the Salish and Dene* (London: Archibald Constable and Co., 1907); Hill-Tout, "Report on the Ethnology of the Okanakan of British Columbia, an Interior Division of the Salish Stock," *Journal of the Royal Anthropological Institute*, 41 (1911): 130–61; Marian K. Gould on Okanagon and Sanpoil tales in Franz Boas, *Folk-Tales of Salishan and Sahaptin Tribes*, Memoirs of the American Folklore Society, Vol. 11 (1971), pp. 98–118; James A. Teit on Okanagon tales in Boas, pp. 65–97; Verne Ray, "Sanpoil Folk Tales," *Journal of American Folklore*, 46 (1933): 129–87; *Coyote and the Colville*, ed. Eileen Yanan (Omak, Wash.: St. Mary's Mission, 1971); Harry Robinson, *Write It on Your Heart. The Epic World of an Okanagan Storyteller*. Compiled and edited by Wendy Wickwire (Vancouver, British Columbia: Talon Books, 1989).

2. *Tales of the Okanogans*, ed. Donald M. Hines (Fairfield, Wash.: Ye Galleon Press, 1976).

3. Nelson Ault, The Papers of Lucullus Virgil McWhorter, Pullman: Friends of the Washington State University Library, 1959.

4. Anthony Mattina, *Colville-Okanagan Dictionary*, University of Montana Occasional Papers in Linguistice no. 5.

5. Jay Miller, "High-Minded High Gods in North America," *Anthropos* 75 (1980): 916–19.

6. Boas, p. 84.

7. Compare *Tales of the Okanogans*, p. 103.

8. Compare Mattina, *The Golden Woman: The Colville Narrative of Peter J. Seymour* (Tucson: University of Arizona Press, 1985).

9. Nancy Turner, Randy Bouchard, and Dorothy Kennedy, *Ethnobotany of the Okanagan-Colville Indians of British Columbia and Washington*, Occasional Paper 21, 1980, British Columbia Provincial Museum, Victoria.

10. Compare *Tales of the Okanogans*, p. 86.

11. Mourning Dove, *Cogewea, The Half Blood. A Depiction of the Great Montana Cattle Range* (1927; reprint, Lincoln: University of Nebraska Press, 1981), p. 159.

Black Elk Speaks

AS TOLD THROUGH
John G. Neihardt

What is good in this book
is given back
to the six grandfathers
and
to the great men of my people
—Black Elk

Contents

Acknowledgments

The Publisher is grateful to Hilda Neihardt Petri for permission to use manuscripts and photographs belonging to the John G. Neihardt Trust as well as for her assistance and encouragement throughout the preparation of this volume. We also wish to thank Liz Otradovsky, who located photographs and slides and made the copies of them and of the handwritten draft pages of *Black Elk Speaks*; and Raymond DeMallic, associate professor of Anthropology, Indiana University, for suggesting and commenting on the material included in Appendix III.

Introduction

Vine Deloria, Jr.

The twentieth century has produced a world of conflicting visions, intense emotions, and unpredictable events, and the opportunities for grasping the substance of life have faded as the pace of activity has increased. Electronic media shuffle us through a myriad of experiences which would have baffled earlier generations and seem to produce in us a strange isolation from the reality of human history. Our heroes fade into mere personality, are consumed and forgotten, and we avidly seek more avenues to express our humanity. Reflection is the most difficult of all our activities because we are no longer able to establish relative priorities from the multitude of sensations that engulf us. Times such as these seem to illuminate the classic expressions of eternal truths and great wisdom comes to stand out in the crowd of ordinary maxims.

How fortunate it was that in the 1930s as the nation was roaring into a new form of industrialism a Nebraska poet named Neihardt traveled northward to the reservation of the Oglala Sioux in search of materials for his classic epic work on the history of the West. That their conversations and companionship should produce a religious classic, perhaps the only religious classic of this century, is a testimony indeed to the continuing strength of our species. *Black Elk Speaks* was originally published in 1932, when people still believed that progress and the assembly line were identical and that the Depression was but a temporary interlude in an inevitable march toward the millennium. Its eloquent message was lost in the confusion of the times. It was not rejected, but it was hardly received with the veneration it now enjoys. The reception, in fact, reflected one of those overly romantic but simplistic views which suggests that all religions have some validity if they prevent us from acts of bestiality and even the most primitive expressions of religious truth are an effort to connect with the larger reality of Western civilization.

Black Elk Speaks did not follow other contemporary works into oblivion. Throughout the thirties, forties, and fifties it drew a steady

and devoted readership and served as a reliable expression of the substance that undergirded Plains Indian religious beliefs. Outside the Northern Plains, the Sioux tribe, and the western mind set, there were few people who knew the book or listened to its message. But crises mounted and, as we understood the implications of future shock, the silent spring, and the greening of America, people began to search for a universal expression of the larger, more cosmic truths which industrialism and progress had ignored and overwhelmed. In the 1960s interest began to focus on Indians and some of the spiritual realities they seemed to represent. Regardless of the other literature in the field, the scholarly dissertations with inflections and nuances, *Black Elk Speaks* clearly dominated the literature dealing with Indian religions.

Today the book is familiar reading for millions of people, some of whom have no clear conception of Black Elk's tribe, the Oglala Sioux, and others of whom do not, as a rule, even like Indians. The spiritual framework of the pipe ceremonies and the story of Black Elk's life and vision are well known, and speculations on the nature and substance of Plains Indian religion use the book as the criterion by which other books and interpretive essays are to be judged. If any great religious classic has emerged in this century or on this continent, it must certainly be judged in the company of *Black Elk Speaks* and withstand the criticism which such a comparison would inevitably invite.

The most important aspect of the book, however, is not its effect on the non-Indian populace who wished to learn something of the beliefs of the Plains Indians but upon the contemporary generation of young Indians who have been aggressively searching for roots of their own in the structure of universal reality. To them the book has become a North American bible of all tribes. They look to it for spiritual guidance, for sociological identity, for political insight, and for affirmation of the continuing substance of Indian tribal life, now being badly eroded by the same electronic media which are dissolving other American communities.

Black Elk shared his visions with John Neihardt because he wished to pass along to future generations some of the reality of Oglala life and, one suspects, to share the burden of visions that remained unfulfilled with a compatible spirit. Black Elk might have been greatly surprised at the popularity of the book today. He could not help but be pleased by it. If the old camp circle, the sacred hoop of the Lakota, and the old days have been rudely shattered by the machines of a

scientific era, and if they can be no more in the traditional sense, the universality of the images and dreams must testify to the emergence of a new sacred hoop, a new circle of intense community among Indians far outdistancing the grandeur of former times. So important has this book become that one cannot today attend a meeting on Indian religion and hear a series of Indian speakers without recalling the exact parts of the book that lie behind contemporary efforts to inspire and clarify those beliefs that are "truly Indian."

As successful as the book is, the future appears unlimited in contrast with its present achievements. We have not yet seen that generation of theologians who always attend the birth of great religious traditions. The present generation of Indian college students may well be harbingers of this era. Christianity and Buddhism both took half a millennium to adequately express in theological and philosophical frameworks the vision of universal substance which their founders promulgated and lived. Neihardt's *Black Elk Speaks* and *When the Tree Flowered*, and *The Sacred Pipe* by Joseph Epes Brown, the basic works of the Black Elk theological tradition, now bid fair to become the canon or at least the central core of a North American Indian theological canon which will someday challenge the Eastern and Western traditions as a way of looking at the world. Certainly in Black Elk's visions we have a natural relationship to the rest of the cosmos devoid of the trial-court paradigm but incorporating the theme of sacrifice so important to all religions in a consistent and comprehensible way.

Present debates center on the question of Neihardt's literary intrusions into Black Elk's system of beliefs and some scholars have said that the book reflects more of Neihardt than it does of Black Elk. It is, admittedly, difficult to discover if we are talking with Black Elk or John Neihardt, whether the vision is to be interpreted differently, and whether or not the positive emphasis which the book projects is not the optimism of two poets lost in the modern world and transforming drabness into an idealized world. Can it matter? The very nature of great religious teachings is that they encompass everyone who understands them and personalities become indistinguishable from the transcendent truth that is expressed. So let it be with *Black Elk Speaks*. That it speaks to us with simple and compelling language about an aspect of human experience and encourages us to emphasize the best that dwells within us is sufficient. Black Elk and John Neihardt would probably nod affirmatively to that statement and continue their conversation. It is good. It is enough.

Preface

It was during August, 1930, that I first met Black Elk. I was then working on *The Song of the Messiah*, which now stands as the fifth and final narrative poem in my *Cycle of the West*. This *Song* is concerned with what white men have called the "Messiah craze"—the great Messianic dream that came to the desperate Indians in the middle 80's of the 19th century and ended with the massacre at Wounded Knee, South Dakota, on December 29, 1890.

With my son, Sigurd, I had gone to Pine Ridge Reservation for the purpose of finding some old medicine man who had been active in the Messiah Movement and who might somehow be induced to talk to me about the deeper spiritual significance of the matter. I had known many of the Oglala Sioux for some years, and had good friends among the old "longhairs." It was not information that was lacking for my purpose. I had the facts, both from the records and from old men who had lived through that time, sharing the great hope and the tragic disillusionment. What I needed for my purpose was something to be experienced through intimate contact, rather than to be received through telling. (Those of my readers who may be familiar with my *Song of the Messiah* will know what is meant.)

Mr. W. B. Courtright, then Field Agent-in-Charge at Pine Ridge Agency, was a "fan" of mine, being especially well acquainted with my *Song of the Indian Wars*, and through him I learned of an old Sioux by the name of Black Elk, who lived among the barren hills some twenty miles east of the Agency near the combination store and post office called Manderson. Black Elk was a "kind of a preacher," I was told—that is to say, a *wichasha wakon* (holy man, priest)—and he had been of some importance in the Messiah affair. Also, he was second cousin to Crazy Horse, the principal hero of my *Song of the Indian Wars*, and had known the great chieftain well.

So my son and I drove over to Manderson to try our luck with the old man. Flying Hawk, an interpreter with whom I was slightly acquainted, was living there, and he was willing to go with us to see Black Elk at his home about two miles west of Manderson. On the way over, Flying Hawk remarked that he was afraid the old man would not talk to me. I asked why, adding that I had known Indians

447

for many years and they had always talked to me. "Well," he said, "there's something peculiar about this old man. Last week a lady came up from Lincoln, Nebraska, to see him. She wanted to write an article on Crazy Horse, who was the old man's second cousin. I took her over, but the old man wouldn't talk. He is almost blind, and, after he had squinted at her awhile he said, 'I can see that you are a nice-looking woman, and I can feel that you are good; but I do not care to talk to you about these things.' Maybe he will talk to you, but I doubt it."

I myself began to doubt, for, in the first place, I was aware that the knowledge of a holy man was regarded as sacred. Nevertheless I was eager to meet the old man, if for no other reason than that he knew Crazy Horse; and, being a man, I might have better luck than did the lady mentioned.

It was a dead-end road that led through the treeless, yellow hills to Black Elk's home—a one-room log cabin with weeds growing out of the dirt roof. Two old "long-hairs," who lived in similar cabins in sight of the road, mounted ponies and followed us, curious to know what might be going on yonder. Little else but weather ever happened in that country—other than the sun and moon and stars going over—and there was little for the old men to do but wait for yesterday.

When we arrived, Black Elk was standing outside a shade made of pine boughs. It was noon. When we left, after sunset, Flying Hawk said, "That was kind of funny, the way the old man seemed to know you were coming!" My son remarked that he had the same impression; and when I had known the great old man for some years I was quite prepared to believe that he did know, for he certainly had supernormal powers.

Shaking hands with Black Elk, I told him that I was well acquainted with the Omaha Indians and with many of the Sioux; that I had come to get acquainted with him and have a little talk about old times.

"Ah-h-h!" he said, indicating that my suggestion was satisfactory. I was well stocked with packages of cigarettes, and I passed these around, giving special attention to our two uninvited guests, who had squatted near their ponies at a respectful distance with their backs to us, not wishing to intrude but none the less eager to share in the meeting. Then we sat down on the ground, smoking and waiting in silence.

Black Elk, with his near-blind stare fixed on the ground, seemed to have forgotten us. I was about to break the silence by way of getting

something started, when the old man looked up to Flying Hawk, the interpreter, and said (speaking Sioux, for he knew no English): "As I sit here, I can feel in this man beside me a strong desire to know the things of the Other World. He has been sent to learn what I know, and I will teach him."

He was silent again for some minutes; then he spoke to his little grandson, who sat near us, and the boy ran up to the log cabin at the top of the hill. Presently he returned with a sacred ornament which, I learned later, had belonged to Black Elk's father (who also was a holy man) and had been used for many years by both father and son in their sacred ceremonies. It consists of a leather star tinged with blue, and from the center of the star hangs a strip of hide from the breast of a buffalo, together with a feather from the wing of an eagle. The ornament is suspended from a leather loop to be placed about the neck. Holding the star before us, Black Elk said: "Here you see the Morning Star. Who sees the Morning Star shall see more, for he shall be wise." Then lifting the eagle feather, he said. "This means Wakon Tonka (the Great Mysterious One); and it also means that our thoughts should rise high as the eagles do." Then, lifting the strip of buffalo hide, he said: "This means all the good things of this world—food and shelter." Handing the ornament to me, he said: "My friend, I wish you all these things. Put it around your neck."

I thanked the old man and did as he directed. Thereafter we all smoked in silence for awhile, Black Elk with bowed head, staring at the ground.

Finally, the old man began talking about a vision that had come to him in his youth. It was his power-vision, as I learned later, and his fragmentary references to it were evidently intended only to arouse my curiosity, for he could not speak freely about a matter so sacred before the assembled company. It was like half seeing, half sensing a strange and beautiful landscape by brief flashes of sheet lightning.

Often I broke the old man's prolonged silences by referring to the old times before the evil days began and the white men possessed the land. I recalled great battles, high moments in Sioux history, and he would respond politely; but it was increasingly clear that his real interest was in "the things of the Other World."

The sun was near to setting when Black Elk said: "There is so much to teach you. What I know was given to me for men and it is true and it is beautiful. Soon I shall be under the grass and it will be lost. You were sent to save it, and you must come back so that I can teach you."

And I said: "I will come back, Black Elk. When do you want me?" He replied, "In the spring when the grass is so high" (indicating the breadth of a hand).

That winter I corresponded with Black Elk through his son, Ben, who had attended Carlisle for a year or two, and thus arrangements were made for an extended visit the following spring.[1]

During early May, 1931, in company with my eldest daughter, Enid, who had been my secretary for several years, and my second daughter, Hilda, I returned to Black Elk's home that he might relate his life-story to me in fulfillment of a duty that he felt incumbent upon him. His chief purpose was to "save his Great Vision for men."

Great preparations had been made for our coming. Many small pine trees, brought from a considerable distance, were set up around the log cabin, and a sacred tepee, painted with spiritual symbols, had been erected for our dwelling.

The talks began each day shortly after breakfast and often continued until late at night. There were occasional brief intervals of rest when the old man, without comment or apology, would lie down with his head on his arm and fall asleep almost immediately. In a few minutes he would waken, evidently greatly refreshed, and continue his narrative as though there had been no interruption. Most of the time old "long-hair" friends of Black Elk, some much older than he, were present, occasionally supplementing his narrative with their own memories.

Black Elk's son, Ben, acted as interpreter throughout the visit, and my daughter, Enid, a skilled stenographer, kept a faithful record of the narrative and the conversations.[2] Her voluminous stenographic notes, together with her transcript thereof, are preserved among my papers in the Western Historical MSS Collections of the University of Missouri.

Columbia, Mo. John G. Neihardt
Dec. 1, 1960.

[1]See Appendix I.
[2]See Appendix III.

I

The Offering of the Pipe

Black Elk Speaks:

My friend, I am going to tell you the story of my life, as you wish; and if it were only the story of my life I think I would not tell it; for what is one man that he should make much of his winters, even when they bend him like a heavy snow? So many other men have lived and shall live that story, to be grass upon the hills.

It is the story of all life that is holy and is good to tell, and of us two-leggeds sharing in it with the four-leggeds and the wings of the air and all green things; for these are children of one mother and their father is one Spirit.

This, then, is not the tale of a great hunter or of a great warrior, or of a great traveler, although I have made much meat in my time and fought for my people both as boy and man, and have gone far and seen strange lands and men. So also have many others done, and better than I. These things I shall remember by the way, and often they may seem to be the very tale itself, as when I was living them in happiness and sorrow. But now that I can see it all as from a lonely hilltop, I know it was the story of a mighty vision given to a man too weak to use it; of a holy tree that should have flourished in a people's heart with flowers and singing birds, and now is withered; and of a people's dream that died in bloody snow.

But if the vision was true and mighty, as I know, it is true and mighty yet; for such things are of the spirit, and it is in the darkness of their eyes that men get lost.

So I know that it is a good thing I am going to do; and because no good thing can be done by any man alone, I will first make an offering and send a voice to the Spirit of the World, that it may help me to be true. See, I fill this sacred pipe with the bark of the red willow; but before we smoke it, you must see how it is made and what it means. These four ribbons hanging here on the stem are the four quarters of the universe. The black one is for the west where the thunder beings

live to send us rain; the white one for the north, whence comes the great white cleansing wind; the red one for the east, whence springs the light and where the morning star lives to give men wisdom; the yellow for the south, whence come the summer and the power to grow.

But these four spirits are only one Spirit after all, and this eagle feather here is for that One, which is like a father, and also it is for the thoughts of men that should rise high as eagles do. Is not the sky a father and the earth a mother, and are not all living things with feet or wings or roots their children? And this hide upon the mouthpiece here, which should be bison hide, is for the earth, from whence we came and at whose breast we suck as babies all our lives, along with all the animals and birds and trees and grasses. And because it means all this, and more than any man can understand, the pipe is holy.

There is a story about the way the pipe first came to us. A very long time ago, they say, two scouts were out looking for bison; and when they came to the top of a high hill and looked north, they saw something coming a long way off, and when it came closer they cried out, "It is a woman!," and it was. Then one of the scouts, being foolish, had bad thoughts and spoke them; but the other said: "That is a sacred woman; throw all bad thoughts away." When she came still closer, they saw that she wore a fine white buckskin dress, that her hair was very long and that she was young and very beautiful. And she knew their thoughts and said in a voice that was like singing: "You do not know me, but if you want to do as you think, you may come." And the foolish one went; but just as he stood before her, there was a white cloud that came and covered them. And the beautiful young woman came out of the cloud, and when it blew away the foolish man was a skeleton covered with worms.

Then the woman spoke to the one who was not foolish: "You shall go home and tell your people that I am coming and that a big tepee shall be built for me in the center of the nation." And the man, who was very much afraid, went quickly and told the people, who did at once as they were told; and there around the big tepee they waited for the sacred woman. And after a while she came, very beautiful and singing, and as she went into the tepee this is what she sang:

> "With visible breath I am walking.
> A voice I am sending as I walk.
> In a sacred manner I am walking.
> With visible tracks I am walking.
> In a sacred manner I walk."

And as she sang, there came from her mouth a white cloud that was good to smell. Then she gave something to the chief, and it was a pipe with a bison calf carved on one side to mean the earth that bears and feeds us, and with twelve eagle feathers hanging from the stem to mean the sky and the twelve moons, and these were tied with a grass that never breaks. "Behold!" she said. "With this you shall multiply and be a good nation. Nothing but good shall come from it. Only the hands of the good shall take care of it and the bad shall not even see it." Then she sang again and went out of the tepee; and as the people watched her going, suddenly it was a white bison galloping away and snorting, and soon it was gone.

This they tell, and whether it happened so or not I do not know; but if you think about it, you can see that it is true.

Now I light the pipe, and after I have offered it to the powers that are one Power, and sent forth a voice to them, we shall smoke together. Offering the mouthpiece first of all to the One above—so—I send a voice:

Hey hey! hey hey! hey hey! hey hey!

Grandfather, Great Spirit, you have been always, and before you no one has been. There is no other one to pray to but you. You yourself, everything that you see, everything has been made by you. The star nations all over the universe you have finished. The four quarters of the earth you have finished. The day, and in that day, everything you have finished. Grandfather, Great Spirit, lean close to the earth that you may hear the voice I send. You towards where the sun goes down, behold me; Thunder Beings, behold me! You where the White Giant lives in power, behold me! You where the sun shines continually, whence come the day-break star and the day, behold me! You where the summer lives, behold me! You in the depths of the heavens, an eagle of power, behold! And you, Mother Earth, the only Mother, you who have shown mercy to your children!

Hear me, four quarters of the world—a relative I am! Give me the strength to walk the soft earth, a relative to all that is! Give me the eyes to see and the strength to understand, that I may be like you. With your power only can I face the winds.

Great Spirit, Great Spirit, my Grandfather, all over the earth the faces of living things are all alike. With tenderness have these come up out of the ground. Look upon these faces of children without number and with children in their arms, that they may face the winds and walk the good road to the day of quiet.

This is my prayer; hear me! The voice I have sent is weak, yet with earnestness I have sent it. Hear me!

It is finished. Hetchetu aloh!

Now, my friend, let us smoke together so that there may be only good between us.

II

EARLY BOYHOOD

I am a Lakota of the Ogalala band. My father's name was Black Elk, and his father before him bore the name, and the father of his father, so that I am the fourth to bear it. He was a medicine man and so were several of his brothers. Also, he and the great Crazy Horse's father were cousins, having the same grandfather. My mother's name was White Cow Sees; her father was called Refuse-to-Go, and her mother, Plenty Eagle Feathers. I can remember my mother's mother and her father. My father's father was killed by the Pawnees when I was too little to know, and his mother, Red Eagle Woman, died soon after.

I was born in the Moon of the Popping Trees (December) on the Little Powder River in the Winter When the Four Crows Were Killed (1863), and I was three years old when my father's right leg was broken in the Battle of the Hundred Slain.[1] From that wound he limped until the day he died, which was about the time when Big Foot's band was butchered on Wounded Knee (1890). He is buried here in these hills.

I can remember that Winter of the Hundred Slain as a man may remember some bad dream he dreamed when he was little, but I can not tell just how much I heard when I was bigger and how much I

[1]The Fetterman Fight, commonly described as a "massacre," in which Captain Fetterman and 81 men were wiped out on Peno Creek near Fort Phil Kearney, December 21, 1866.

understood when I was little. It is like some fearful thing in a fog, for it was a time when everything seemed troubled and afraid.

I had never seen a Wasichu[2] then, and did not know what one looked like; but every one was saying that the Wasichus were coming and that they were going to take our country and rub us all out and that we should all have to die fighting. It was the Wasichus who got rubbed out in that battle, and all the people were talking about it for a long while; but a hundred Wasichus was not much if there were others and others without number where those came from.

I remember once that I asked my grandfather about this. I said: "When the scouts come back from seeing the prairie full of bison somewhere, the people say the Wasichus are coming; and when strange men are coming to kill us all, they say the Wasichus are coming. What does it mean?" And he said, "That they are many."

When I was older, I learned what the fighting was about that winter and the next summer. Up on the Madison Fork the Wasichus had found much of the yellow metal that they worship and that makes them crazy, and they wanted to have a road up through our country to the place where the yellow metal was; but my people did not want the road. It would scare the bison and make them go away, and also it would let the other Wasichus come in like a river. They told us that they wanted only to use a little land, as much as a wagon would take between the wheels; but our people knew better. And when you look about you now, you can see what it was they wanted.

Once we were happy in our own country and we were seldom hungry, for then the two-leggeds and the four-leggeds lived together like relatives, and there was plenty for them and for us. But the Wasichus came, and they have made little islands for us and other little islands for the fourleggeds, and always these islands are becoming smaller, for around them surges the gnawing flood of the Wasichu; and it is dirty with lies and greed.

A long time ago my father told me what his father told me, that there was once a Lakota holy man, called Drinks Water, who dreamed what was to be; and this was long before the coming of the Wasichus. He dreamed that the four-leggeds were going back into the earth and that a strange race had woven a spider's web all around the Lakotas. And he said: "When this happens, you shall live in square gray houses,

[2] A term used to designate the white man, but having no reference to the color of his skin.

in a barren land, and beside those square gray houses you shall starve." They say he went back to Mother Earth soon after he saw this vision, and it was sorrow that killed him. You can look about you now and see that he meant these dirt-roofed houses we are living in, and that all the rest was true. Sometimes dreams are wiser than waking.

And so when the soldiers came and built themselves a town of logs there on the Piney Fork of the Powder, my people knew they meant to have their road and take our country and maybe kill us all when they were strong enough. Crazy Horse was only about 19 years old then, and Red Cloud was still our great chief. In the Moon of the Changing Season (October) he called together all the scattered bands of the Lakota for a big council on the Powder River, and when we went on the warpath against the soldiers, a horseback could ride through our villages from sunrise until the day was above his head, so far did our camp stretch along the valley of the river; for many of our friends, the Shyela[3] and the Blue Clouds,[4] had come to help us fight.

And it was about when the bitten moon was delayed (last quarter) in the Time of the Popping Trees when the hundred were rubbed out. My friend, Fire Thunder here, who is older than I, was in that fight and he can tell you how it was.

Fire Thunder Speaks:

I was 16 years old when this happened, and after the big council on the Powder we had moved over to the Tongue River where we were camping at the mouth of Peno Creek. There were many of us there. Red Cloud was over all of us, but the chief of our band was Big Road. We started out on horseback just about sunrise, riding up the creek toward the soldiers' town on the Piney, for we were going to attack it. The sun was about half way up when we stopped at the place where the Wasichu's road came down a steep, narrow ridge and crossed the creek. It was a good place to fight, so we sent some men ahead to coax the soldiers out. While they were gone, we divided into two parts and hid in the gullies on both sides of the ridge and waited. After a long while we heard a shot up over the hill, and we knew the soldiers were coming. So we held the noses of our ponies that they might not whinny at the soldiers' horses. Soon we saw our men coming back, and some of them were walking and leading their horses, so that the

[3]Cheyennes.
[4]Arapahoes.

soldiers would think they were worn out. Then the men we had sent ahead came running down the road between us, and the soldiers on horseback followed, shooting. When they came to the flat at the bottom of the hill, the fighting began all at once. I had a sorrel horse, and just as I was going to get on him, the soldiers turned around and began to fight their way back up the hill. I had a six-shooter that I had traded for, and also a bow and arrows. When the soldiers started back, I held my sorrel with one hand and began killing them with the six-shooter, for they came close to me. There were many bullets, but there were more arrows—so many that it was like a cloud of grasshoppers all above and around the soldiers; and our people, shooting across, hit each other. The soldiers were falling all the while they were fighting back up the hill, and their horses got loose. Many of our people chased the horses, but I was not after horses; I was after Wasichus. When the soldiers got on top, there were not many of them left and they had no place to hide. They were fighting hard. We were told to crawl up on them, and we did. When we were close, someone yelled: "Let us go! This is a good day to die. Think of the helpless ones at home!" Then we all cried, "Hoka hey!" and rushed at them. I was young then and quick on my feet, and I was one of the first to get in among the soldiers. They got up and fought very hard until not one of them was alive. They had a dog with them, and he started back up the road for the soldiers' town, howling as he ran. He was the only one left. I did not shoot at him because he looked too sweet;[5] but many did shoot, and he died full of arrows. So there was nobody left of the soldiers. Dead men and horses and wounded Indians were scattered all the way up the hill, and their blood was frozen, for a storm had come up and it was very cold and getting colder all the time. We left all the dead lying there, for the ground was solid, and we picked up our wounded and started back, but we lost most of them before we reached our camp at the mouth of the Peno. There was a big blizzard that night; and some of the wounded who did not die on the way, died after we got home. This was the time when Black Elk's father had his leg broken.

Black Elk Continues:

I am quite sure that I remember the time when my father came home with a broken leg that he got from killing so many Wasichus, and it seems that I can remember all about the battle too, but I think

[5]Because of its current colloquial usage as a vapid sentimentalism, the expression may well seem off key in the mouth of the grizzled old warrior.

I could not. It must be the fear that I remember most. All this time I was not allowed to play very far away from our tepee, and my mother would say, "If you are not good the Wasichus will get you."

We must have broken camp at the mouth of the Peno soon after the battle, for I can remember my father lying on a pony drag with bison robes all around him, like a baby, and my mother riding the pony. The snow was deep and it was very cold, and I remember sitting in another pony drag beside my father and mother, all wrapped up in fur. We were going away from where the soldiers were, and I do not know where we went, but it was west.

It was a hungry winter, for the deep snow made it hard to find the elk; and also many of the people went snowblind. We wandered a long time, and some of the bands got lost from each other. Then at last we were camping in the woods beside a creek somewhere, and the hunters came back with meat.

I think it was this same winter when a medicine man, by the name of Creeping, went around among the people curing snowblinds. He would put snow upon their eyes, and after he had sung a certain sacred song that he had heard in a dream, he would blow on the backs of their heads and they would see again, so I have heard. It was about the dragonfly that he sang, for that was where he got his power, they say.

When it was summer again we were camping on the Rosebud, and I did not feel so much afraid, because the Wasichus seemed farther away and there was peace there in the valley and there was plenty of meat. But all the boys from five or six years up were playing war. The little boys would gather together from the different bands of the tribe and fight each other with mud balls that they threw with willow sticks. And the big boys played the game called Throwing-Them-Off-Their-Horses, which is a battle all but the killing; and sometimes they got hurt. The horsebacks from the different bands would line up and charge upon each other, yelling; and when the ponies came together on the run, they would rear and flounder and scream in a big dust, and the riders would seize each other, wrestling until one side had lost all its men, for those who fell upon the ground were counted dead.

When I was older, I, too, often played this game. We were always naked when we played it, just as warriors are when they go into battle if it is not too cold, because they are swifter without clothes. Once I fell off on my back right in the middle of a bed of prickly pears, and it took my mother a long while to pick all the stickers out of me. I was still too little to play war that summer, but I can remember

watching the other boys, and I thought that when we all grew up and were big together, maybe we could kill all the Wasichus or drive them far away from our country.

It was in the Moon When the Cherries Turn Black (August) that all the people were talking again about a battle, and our warriors came back with many wounded. It was The Attacking of the Wagons,[6] and it made me afraid again, for we did not win that battle as we did the other one, and there was much mourning for the dead. Fire Thunder was in that fight too, and he can tell you how it was that day.

Fire Thunder Speaks:

It was very bad. There is a wide flat prairie with hills around it, and in the middle of this the Wasichus had put the boxes of their wagons in a circle, so that they could keep their mules there at night. There were not many Wasichus, but they were lying behind the boxes and they shot faster than they ever shot at us before. We thought it was some new medicine of great power that they had, for they shot so fast that it was like tearing a blanket. Afterwards I learned that it was because they had new guns that they loaded from behind, and this was the first time they used these guns.[7] We came on after sunrise. There were many, many of us, and we meant to ride right over them and rub them out. But our ponies were afraid of the ring of fire the guns of the Wasichus made, and would not go over. Our women were watching us from the hills and we could hear them singing and mourning whenever the shooting stopped. We tried hard, but we could not do it, and there were dead warriors and horses piled all around the boxes and scattered over the plain. Then we left our horses in a gulch and charged on foot, but it was like green grass withering in a fire. So we picked up our wounded and went away. I do not know how many of our people were killed, but there were very many. It was bad.

Black Elk Continues:

I do not remember where we camped that winter but it must have been a time of peace and of plenty to eat.

Standing Bear Speaks:

I am four years older than Black Elk, and he and I have been good friends since boyhood. I know it was on the Powder that we camped where there were many cottonwood trees. Ponies like to eat the bark

[6]The Wagon Box Fight, which took place about six miles west of Fort Phil Kearney on August 2, 1867.

[7]Breech-loading Springfields.

of these trees and it is good for them. That was the winter when High Shirt's mother was killed by a big tree that fell on her tepee. It was a very windy night and there were noises that 'woke me, and then I heard that an old woman had been killed, and it was High Shirt's mother.

Black Elk Continues:

I was four years old then, and I think it must have been the next summer that I first heard the voices. It was a happy summer and nothing was afraid, because in the Moon When the Ponies Shed (May) word came from the Wasichus that there would be peace and that they would not use the road any more and that all the soldiers would go away. The soldiers did go away and their towns were torn down; and in the Moon of Falling Leaves (November), they made a treaty with Red Cloud that said our country would be ours as long as grass should grow and water flow. You can see that it is not the grass and the water that have forgotten.

Maybe it was not this summer when I first heard the voices, but I think it was, because I know it was before I played with bows and arrows or rode a horse, and I was out playing alone when I heard them. It was like somebody calling me, and I thought it was my mother, but there was nobody there. This happened more than once, and always made me afraid, so that I ran home.

It was when I was five years old that my Grandfather made me a bow and some arrows. The grass was young and I was horseback. A thunder storm was coming from where the sun goes down, and just as I was riding into the woods along a creek, there was a kingbird sitting on a limb. This was not a dream, it happened. And I was going to shoot at the kingbird with the bow my Grandfather made, when the bird spoke and said: "The clouds all over are one-sided." Perhaps it meant that all the clouds were looking at me. And then it said: "Listen! A voice is calling you!" Then I looked up at the clouds, and two men were coming there, headfirst like arrows slanting down; and as they came, they sang a sacred song and the thunder was like drumming. I will sing it for you. The song and the drumming were like this:

> "Behold, a sacred voice is calling you;
> All over the sky a sacred voice is calling."

I sat there gazing at them, and they were coming from the place where the giant lives (north). But when they were very close to me,

they wheeled about toward where the sun goes down, and suddenly they were geese. Then they were gone, and the rain came with a big wind and a roaring.

I did not tell this vision to any one. I liked to think about it, but I was afraid to tell it.

III

THE GREAT VISION

W hat happened after that until the summer I was nine years old is not a story. There were winters and summers, and they were good; for the Wasichus had made their iron road[1] along the Platte and traveled there. This had cut the bison herd in two, but those that stayed in our country with us were more than could be counted, and we wandered without trouble in our land.

Now and then the voices would come back when I was out alone, like someone calling me, but what they wanted me to do I did not know. This did not happen very often, and when it did not happen, I forgot about it; for I was growing taller and was riding horses now and could shoot prairie chickens and rabbits with my bow. The boys of my people began very young to learn the ways of men, and no one taught us; we just learned by doing what we saw, and we were warriors at a time when boys now are like girls.

It was the summer when I was nine years old, and our people were moving slowly towards the Rocky Mountains. We camped one evening in a valley beside a little creek just before it ran into the Greasy Grass,[2] and there was a man by the name of Man Hip who liked me and asked me to eat with him in his tepee.

[1]The Union Pacific Railway.
[2]The Little Big Horn River.

While I was eating, a voice came and said: "It is time; now they are calling you." The voice was so loud and clear that I believed it, and I thought I would just go where it wanted me to go. So I got right up and started. As I came out of the tepee, both my thighs began to hurt me, and suddenly it was like waking from a dream, and there wasn't any voice. So I went back into the tepee, but I didn't want to eat. Man Hip looked at me in a strange way and asked me what was wrong. I told him that my legs were hurting me.

The next morning the camp moved again, and I was riding with some boys. We stopped to get a drink from a creek, and when I got off my horse, my legs crumpled under me and I could not walk. So the boys helped me up and put me on my horse; and when we camped again that evening, I was sick. The next day the camp moved on to where the different bands of our people were coming together, and I rode in a pony drag, for I was very sick. Both my legs and both my arms were swollen badly and my face was all puffed up.

When we had camped again, I was lying in our tepee and my mother and father were sitting beside me. I could see out through the opening, and there two men were coming from the clouds, headfirst like arrows slanting down, and I knew they were the same that I had seen before. Each now carried a long spear, and from the points of these a jagged lightning flashed. They came clear down to the ground this time and stood a little way off and looked at me and said: "Hurry! Come! Your Grandfathers are calling you!"

Then they turned and left the ground like arrows slanting upward from the bow. When I got up to follow, my legs did not hurt me any more and I was very light. I went outside the tepee, and yonder where the men with flaming spears were going, a little cloud was coming very fast. It came and stooped and took me and turned back to where it came from, flying fast. And when I looked down I could see my mother and my father yonder, and I felt sorry to be leaving them.

Then there was nothing but the air and the swiftness of the little cloud that bore me and those two men still leading up to where white clouds were piled like mountains on a wide blue plain, and in them thunder beings lived and leaped and flashed.

Now suddenly there was nothing but a world of cloud, and we three were there alone in the middle of a great white plain with snowy hills and mountains staring at us; and it was very still; but there were whispers.

Then the two men spoke together and they said: "Behold him, the being with four legs!"

I looked and saw a bay horse standing there, and he began to speak: "Behold me!" he said, "My life-history you shall see." Then he wheeled about to where the sun goes down, and said: "Behold them! Their history you shall know."

I looked, and there were twelve black horses yonder all abreast with necklaces of bison hoofs, and they were beautiful, but I was frightened, because their manes were lightning and there was thunder in their nostrils.

Then the bay horse wheeled to where the great white giant lives (the north) and said: "Behold!" And yonder there were twelve white horses all abreast. Their manes were flowing like a blizzard wind and from their noses came a roaring, and all about them white geese soared and circled.

Then the bay wheeled round to where the sun shines continually (the east) and bade me look; and there twelve sorrel horses, with necklaces of elk's teeth, stood abreast with eyes that glimmered like the day-break star and manes of morning light.

Then the bay wheeled once again to look upon the place where you are always facing (the south), and yonder stood twelve buckskins all abreast with horns upon their heads and manes that lived and grew like trees and grasses.

And when I had seen all these, the bay horse said: "Your Grandfathers are having a council. These shall take you; so have courage."

Then all the horses went into formation, four abreast—the blacks, the whites, the sorrels, and the buckskins—and stood behind the bay, who turned now to the west and neighed; and yonder suddenly the sky was terrible with a storm of plunging horses in all colors that shook the world with thunder, neighing back.

Now turning to the north the bay horse whinnied, and yonder all the sky roared with a mighty wind of running horses in all colors, neighing back.

And when he whinnied to the east, there too the sky was filled with glowing clouds of manes and tails of horses in all colors singing back. Then to the south he called, and it was crowded with many colored, happy horses, nickering.

Then the bay horse spoke to me again and said: "See how your horses all come dancing!" I looked, and there were horses, horses everywhere—a whole skyful of horses dancing round me.

"Make haste!" the bay horse said; and we walked together side by side, while the blacks, the whites, the sorrels, and the buckskins followed, marching four by four.

I looked about me once again, and suddenly the dancing horses without number changed into animals of every kind and into all the fowls that are, and these fled back to the four quarters of the world from whence the horses came, and vanished.

Then as we walked, there was a heaped up cloud ahead that changed into a tepee, and a rainbow was the open door of it; and through the door I saw six old men sitting in a row.

The two men with the spears now stood beside me, one on either hand, and the horses took their places in their quarters, looking inward, four by four. And the oldest of the Grandfathers spoke with a kind voice and said: "Come right in and do not fear." And as he spoke, all the horses of the four quarters neighed to cheer me. So I went in and stood before the six, and they looked older than men can ever be—old like hills, like stars.

The oldest spoke again: "Your Grandfathers all over the world are having a council, and they have called you here to teach you." His voice was very kind, but I shook all over with fear now, for I knew that these were not old men, but the Powers of the World. And the first was the Power of the West; the second, of the North; the third, of the East; the fourth, of the South; the fifth, of the Sky; the sixth, of the Earth. I knew this, and was afraid, until the first Grandfather spoke again: "Behold them yonder where the sun goes down, the thunder beings! You shall see, and have from them my power; and they shall take you to the high and lonely center of the earth that you may see; even to the place where the sun continually shines, they shall take you there to understand."

And as he spoke of understanding, I looked up and saw the rainbow leap with flames of many colors over me.

Now there was a wooden cup in his hand and it was full of water and in the water was the sky.

"Take this," he said. "It is the power to make live, and it is yours."

Now he had a bow in his hands. "Take this," he said. "It is the power to destroy, and it is yours."

Then he pointed to himself and said: "Look close at him who is your spirit now, for you are his body and his name is Eagle Wing Stretches."

And saying this, he got up very tall and started running toward

where the sun goes down; and suddenly he was a black horse that stopped and turned and looked at me, and the horse was very poor and sick; his ribs stood out.

Then the second Grandfather, he of the North, arose with a herb of power in his hand, and said: "Take this and hurry." I took and held it toward the black horse yonder. He fattened and was happy and came prancing to his place again and was the first Grandfather sitting there.

The second Grandfather, he of the North, spoke again: "Take courage, younger brother," he said; "on earth a nation you shall make live, for yours shall be the power of the white giant's wing, the cleansing wind." Then he got up very tall and started running toward the north; and when he turned toward me, it was a white goose wheeling. I looked about me now, and the horses in the west were thunders and the horses of the north were geese. And the second Grandfather sang two songs that were like this:

> "They are appearing, may you behold!
> They are appearing, may you behold!
> The thunder nation is appearing, behold!
>
> They are appearing, may you behold!
> They are appearing, may you behold!
> The white geese nation is appearing, behold!"

And now it was the third Grandfather who spoke, he of where the sun shines continually. "Take courage, younger brother," he said, "for across the earth they shall take you!" Then he pointed to where the daybreak star was shining, and beneath the star two men were flying. "From them you shall have power," he said, "from them who have awakened all the beings of the earth with roots and legs and wings." And as he said this, he held in his hand a peace pipe which had a spotted eagle outstretched upon the stem; and this eagle seemed alive, for it was poised there, fluttering, and its eyes were looking at me. "With this pipe," the Grandfather said, "you shall walk upon the earth, and whatever sickens there you shall make well." Then he pointed to a man who was bright red all over, the color of good and of plenty, and as he pointed, the red man lay down and rolled and changed into a bison that got up and galloped toward the sorrel horses of the east, and they too turned to bison, fat and many.

And now the fourth Grandfather spoke, he of the place where you are always facing (the south), whence comes the power to grow.

"Younger brother," he said, "with the powers of the four quarters you shall walk, a relative. Behold, the living center of a nation I shall give you, and with it many you shall save." And I saw that he was holding in his hand a bright red stick that was alive, and as I looked it sprouted at the top and sent forth branches, and on the branches many leaves came out and murmured and in the leaves the birds began to sing. And then for just a little while I thought I saw beneath it in the shade the circled villages of people and every living thing with roots or legs or wings, and all were happy. "It shall stand in the center of the nation's circle," said the Grandfather, "a cane to walk with and a people's heart; and by your powers you shall make it blossom."

Then when he had been still a little while to hear the birds sing, he spoke again: "Behold the earth!" So I looked down and saw it lying yonder like a hoop of peoples, and in the center bloomed the holy stick that was a tree, and where it stood there crossed two roads, a red one and a black. "From where the giant lives (the north) to where you always face (the south) the red road goes, the road of good," the Grandfather said, "and on it shall your nation walk. The black road goes from where the thunder beings live (the west) to where the sun continually shines (the east), a fearful road, a road of troubles and of war. On this also you shall walk, and from it you shall have the power to destroy a people's foes. In four ascents you shall walk the earth with power."

I think he meant that I should see four generations, counting me, and now I am seeing the third.

Then he rose very tall and started running toward the south, and was an elk; and as he stood among the buckskins yonder, they too were elks.

Now the fifth Grandfather spoke, the oldest of them all, the Spirit of the Sky. "My boy," he said, "I have sent for you and you have come. My power you shall see!" He stretched his arms and turned into a spotted eagle hovering. "Behold," he said, "all the wings of the air shall come to you, and they and the winds and the stars shall be like relatives. You shall go across the earth with my power." Then the eagle soared above my head and fluttered there; and suddenly the sky was full of friendly wings all coming toward me.

Now I knew the sixth Grandfather was about to speak, he who was the Spirit of the Earth, and I saw that he was very old, but more as men are old. His hair was long and white, his face was all in wrinkles and his eyes were deep and dim. I stared at him, for it seemed I knew

him somehow; and as I stared, he slowly changed, for he was growing backwards into youth, and when he had become a boy, I knew that he was myself with all the years that would be mine at last. When he was old again, he said: "My boy, have courage, for my power shall be yours, and you shall need it, for your nation on the earth will have great troubles. Come."

He rose and tottered out through the rainbow door, and as I followed I was riding on the bay horse who had talked to me at first and led me to that place.

Then the bay horse stopped and faced the black horses of the west, and a voice said: "They have given you the cup of water to make live the greening day, and also the bow and arrow to destroy." The bay neighed, and the twelve black horses came and stood behind me, four abreast.

The bay faced the sorrels of the east, and I saw that they had morning stars upon their foreheads and they were very bright. And the voice said: "They have given you the sacred pipe and the power that is peace, and the good red day." The bay neighed, and the twelve sorrels stood behind me, four abreast.

My horse now faced the buckskins of the south, and a voice said: "They have given you the sacred stick and your nation's hoop, and the yellow day; and in the center of the hoop you shall set the stick and make it grow into a shielding tree, and bloom." The bay neighed, and the twelve buckskins came and stood behind me, four abreast.

Then I knew that there were riders on all the horses there behind me, and a voice said: "Now you shall walk the black road with these; and as you walk, all the nations that have roots or legs or wings shall fear you."

So I started, riding toward the east down the fearful road, and behind me came the horsebacks four abreast—the blacks, the whites, the sorrels, and the buckskins—and far away above the fearful road the daybreak star was rising very dim.

I looked below me where the earth was silent in a sick green light, and saw the hills look up afraid and the grasses on the hills and all the animals; and everywhere about me were the cries of frightened birds and sounds of fleeing wings. I was the chief of all the heavens riding there, and when I looked behind me, all the twelve black horses reared and plunged and thundered and their manes and tails were whirling hail and their nostrils snorted lightning. And when I looked below

again, I saw the slant hail falling and the long, sharp rain, and where we passed, the trees bowed low and all the hills were dim.

Now the earth was bright again as we rode. I could see the hills and valleys and the creeks and rivers passing under. We came above a place where three streams made a big one—a source of mighty waters[3]—and something terrible was there. Flames were rising from the waters and in the flames a blue man lived. The dust was floating all about him in the air, the grass was short and withered, the trees were wilting, two-legged and four-legged beings lay there thin and panting, and wings too weak to fly.

Then the black horse riders shouted "Hoka hey!" and charged down upon the blue man, but were driven back. And the white troop shouted, charging, and was beaten; then the red troop and the yellow.

And when each had failed, they all cried together: "Eagle Wing Stretches, hurry!" And all the world was filled with voices of all kinds that cheered me, so I charged. I had the cup of water in one hand and in the other was the bow that turned into a spear as the bay and I swooped down, and the spear's head was sharp lightning. It stabbed the blue man's heart, and as it struck I could hear the thunder rolling and many voices that cried "Un-hee!," meaning I had killed. The flames died. The trees and grasses were not withered any more and murmured happily together, and every living being cried in gladness with whatever voice it had. Then the four troops of horsemen charged down and struck the dead body of the blue man, counting coup; and suddenly it was only a harmless turtle.

You see, I had been riding with the storm clouds, and had come to earth as rain, and it was drouth that I had killed with the power that the Six Grandfathers gave me. So we were riding on the earth now down along the river flowing full from the source of waters, and soon I saw ahead the circled village of a people in the valley. And a Voice said: "Behold a nation; it is yours. Make haste, Eagle Wing Stretches!"

I entered the village, riding, with the four horse troops behind me— the blacks, the whites, the sorrels, and the buckskins; and the place was filled with moaning and with mourning for the dead. The wind was blowing from the south like fever, and when I looked around I saw that in nearly every tepee the women and the children and the men lay dying with the dead.

So I rode around the circle of the village, looking in upon the sick

[3]Black Elk thinks this was the Three Forks of the Missouri.

and dead, and I felt like crying as I rode. But when I looked behind me, all the women and the children and the men were getting up and coming forth with happy faces.

And a Voice said: "Behold, they have given you the center of the nation's hoop to make it live."

So I rode to the center of the village, with the horse troops in their quarters round about me, and there the people gathered. And the Voice said: "Give them now the flowering stick that they may flourish, and the sacred pipe that they may know the power that is peace, and the wing of the white giant that they may have endurance and face all winds with courage."

So I took the bright red stick and at the center of the nation's hoop I thrust it in the earth. As it touched the earth it leaped mightily in my hand and was a waga chun, the rustling tree,[4] very tall and full of leafy branches and of all birds singing. And beneath it all the animals were mingling with the people like relatives and making happy cries. The women raised their tremolo of joy, and the men shouted all together: "Here we shall raise our children and be as little chickens under the mother sheo's[5] wing."

Then I heard the white wind blowing gently through the tree and singing there, and from the east the sacred pipe came flying on its eagle wings, and stopped before me there beneath the tree, spreading deep peace around it.

Then the daybreak star was rising, and a Voice said: "It shall be a relative to them; and who shall see it, shall see much more, for thence comes wisdom; and those who do not see it shall be dark." And all the people raised their faces to the east, and the star's light fell upon them, and all the dogs barked loudly and the horses whinnied.

Then when the many little voices ceased, the great Voice said: "Behold the circle of the nation's hoop, for it is holy, being endless, and thus all powers shall be one power in the people without end. Now they shall break camp and go forth upon the red road, and your Grandfathers shall walk with them." So the people broke camp and took the good road with the white wing on their faces, and the order of their going was like this:

First, the black horse riders with the cup of water; and the white horse riders with the white wing and the sacred herb; and the sorrel

[4]The cottonwood.
[5]Prairie hen.

riders with the holy pipe; and the buckskins with the flowering stick. And after these the little children and the youths and maidens followed in a band.

Second, came the tribe's four chieftains, and their band was all young men and women.

Third, the nation's four advisers leading men and women neither young nor old.

Fourth, the old men hobbling with their canes and looking to the earth.

Fifth, old women hobbling with their canes and looking to the earth.

Sixth, myself all alone upon the bay with the bow and arrows that the First Grandfather gave me. But I was not the last; for when I looked behind me there were ghosts of people like a trailing fog as far as I could see—grandfathers of grandfathers and grandmothers of grandmothers without number. And over these a great Voice—the Voice that was the South—lived, and I could feel it silent.

And as we went the Voice behind me said: "Behold a good nation walking in a sacred manner in a good land!"

Then I looked up and saw that there were four ascents ahead, and these were generations I should know. Now we were on the first ascent, and all the land was green. And as the long line climbed, all the old men and women raised their hands, palms forward, to the far sky yonder and began to croon a song together, and the sky ahead was filled with clouds of baby faces.

When we came to the end of the first ascent we camped in the sacred circle as before, and in the center stood the holy tree, and still the land about us was all green.

Then we started on the second ascent, marching as before, and still the land was green, but it was getting steeper. And as I looked ahead, the people changed into elks and bison and all four-footed beings and even into fowls, all walking in a sacred manner on the good red road together. And I myself was a spotted eagle soaring over them. But just before we stopped to camp at the end of that ascent, all the marching animals grew restless and afraid that they were not what they had been, and began sending forth voices of trouble, calling to their chiefs. And when they camped at the end of that ascent, I looked down and saw that leaves were falling from the holy tree.

And the Voice said: "Behold your nation, and remember what your

Six Grandfathers gave you, for thenceforth your people walk in difficulties."

Then the people broke camp again, and saw the black road before them towards where the sun goes down, and black clouds coming yonder; and they did not want to go but could not stay. And as they walked the third ascent, all the animals and fowls that were the people ran here and there, for each one seemed to have his own little vision that he followed and his own rules; and all over the universe I could hear the winds at war like wild beasts fighting.[6]

And when we reached the summit of the third ascent and camped, the nation's hoop was broken like a ring of smoke that spreads and scatters and the holy tree seemed dying and all its birds were gone. And when I looked ahead I saw that the fourth ascent would be terrible.

Then when the people were getting ready to begin the fourth ascent, the Voice spoke like some one weeping, and it said: "Look there upon your nation." And when I looked down, the people were all changed back to human, and they were thin, their faces sharp, for they were starving. Their ponies were only hide and bones, and the holy tree was gone.

And as I looked and wept, I saw that there stood on the north side of the starving camp a sacred man who was painted red all over his body, and he held a spear as he walked into the center of the people, and there he lay down and rolled. And when he got up, it was a fat bison standing there, and where the bison stood a sacred herb sprang up right where the tree had been in the center of the nation's hoop. The herb grew and bore four blossoms on a single stem while I was looking—a blue,[7] a white, a scarlet, and a yellow—and the bright rays of these flashed to the heavens.

I know now what this meant, that the bison were the gift of a good spirit and were our strength, but we should lose them, and from the same good spirit we must find another strength. For the people all seemed better when the herb had grown and bloomed, and the horses raised their tails and neighed and pranced around, and I could see a light breeze going from the north among the people like a ghost; and

[6]At this point Black Elk remarked: "I think we are near that place now, and I am afraid something very bad is going to happen all over the world." He cannot read and knows nothing of world affairs.

[7]Blue as well as black may be used to represent the power of the west.

suddenly the flowering tree was there again at the center of the nation's hoop where the four-rayed herb had blossomed.

I was still the spotted eagle floating, and I could see that I was already in the fourth ascent and the people were camping yonder at the top of the third long rise. It was dark and terrible about me, for all the winds of the world were fighting. It was like rapid gun-fire and like whirling smoke, and like women and children wailing and like horses screaming all over the world.

I could see my people yonder running about, setting the smoke-flap poles and fastening down their tepees against the wind, for the storm cloud was coming on them very fast and black, and there were frightened swallows without number fleeing before the cloud.

Then a song of power came to me and I sang it there in the midst of that terrible place where I was. It went like this:

> A good nation I will make live.
> This the nation above has said.
> They have given me the power to make over.

And when I had sung this, a Voice said: "To the four quarters you shall run for help, and nothing shall be strong before you. Behold him!"

Now I was on my bay horse again, because the horse is of the earth, and it was there my power would be used. And as I obeyed the Voice and looked, there was a horse all skin and bones yonder in the west, a faded brownish black. And a Voice there said: "Take this and make him over; and it was the four-rayed herb that I was holding in my hand. So I rode above the poor horse in a circle, and as I did this I could hear the people yonder calling for spirit power, "A-hey! a-hey! a-hey! a-hey!" Then the poor horse neighed and rolled and got up, and he was a big, shiny, black stallion with dapples all over him and his mane about him like a cloud. He was the chief of all the horses; and when he snorted, it was a flash of lightning and his eyes were like the sunset star. He dashed to the west and neighed, and the west was filled with a dust of hoofs, and horses without number, shiny black, came plunging from the dust. Then he dashed toward the north and neighed, and to the east and to the south, and the dust clouds answered, giving forth their plunging horses without number—whites and sorrels and buckskins, fat, shiny, rejoicing in their fleetness and their strength. It was beautiful, but it was also terrible.

Then they all stopped short, rearing, and were standing in a great hoop about their black chief at the center, and were still. And as they stood, four virgins, more beautiful than women of the earth can be, came through the circle, dressed in scarlet, one from each of the four quarters, and stood about the great black stallion in their places; and one held the wooden cup of water, and one the white wing, and one the pipe, and one the nation's hoop. All the universe was silent, listening; and then the great black stallion raised his voice and sang. The song he sang was this:

> "My horses, prancing they are coming.
> My horses, neighing they are coming;
> Prancing, they are coming.
> All over the universe they come.
> They will dance; may you behold them.
>
> (4 times)
> A horse nation, they will dance. May you behold them."
> (4 times)

His voice was not loud, but it went all over the universe and filled it. There was nothing that did not hear, and it was more beautiful than anything can be. It was so beautiful that nothing anywhere could keep from dancing. The virgins danced, and all the circled horses. The leaves on the trees, the grasses on the hills and in the valleys, the waters in the creeks and in the rivers and the lakes, the four legged and the two-legged and the wings of the air—all danced together to the music of the stallion's song.

And when I looked down upon my people yonder, the cloud passed over, blessing them with friendly rain, and stood in the east with a flaming rainbow over it.

Then all the horses went singing back to their places beyond the summit of the fourth ascent, and all things sang along with them as they walked.

And a Voice said: "All over the universe they have finished a day of happiness." And looking down I saw that the whole wide circle of the day was beautiful and green, with all fruits growing and all things kind and happy.

Then a Voice said: "Behold this day, for it is yours to make. Now you shall stand upon the center of the earth to see, for there they are taking you."

I was still on my bay horse, and once more I felt the riders of the

west, the north, the east, the south, behind me in formation, as before, and we were going east. I looked ahead and saw the mountains there with rocks and forests on them, and from the mountains flashed all colors upward to the heavens. Then I was standing on the highest mountain of them all, and round about beneath me was the whole hoop of the world.[8] And while I stood there I saw more than I can tell and I understood more than I saw; for I was seeing in a sacred manner the shapes of all things in the spirit, and the shape of all shapes as they must live together like one being. And I saw that the sacred hoop of my people was one of many hoops that made one circle, wide as daylight and as starlight, and in the center grew one mighty flowering tree to shelter all the children of one mother and one father. And I saw that it was holy.

Then as I stood there, two men were coming from the east, head first like arrows flying, and between them rose the day-break star. They came and gave a herb to me and said: "With this on earth you shall undertake anything and do it." It was the day-break-star herb, the herb of understanding, and they told me to drop it on the earth. I saw it falling far, and when it struck the earth it rooted and grew and flowered, four blossoms on one stem, a blue, a white, a scarlet, and a yellow; and the rays from these streamed upward to the heavens so that all creatures saw it and in no place was there darkness.

Then the Voice said: "Your Six Grandfathers—now you shall go back to them."

I had not noticed how I was dressed until now, and I saw that I was painted red all over, and my joints were painted black, with white stripes between the joints. My bay had lightning stripes all over him, and his mane was cloud. And when I breathed, my breath was lightning.

Now two men were leading me, head first like arrows slanting upward—the two that brought me from the earth. And as I followed on the bay, they turned into four flocks of geese that flew in circles, one above each quarter, sending forth a sacred voice as they flew: Br-r-r-p, br-r-r-p, br-r-r-p, br-r-r-p!

Then I saw ahead the rainbow flaming above the tepee of the Six Grandfathers, built and roofed with cloud and sewed with thongs of lightning; and underneath it were all the wings of the air and under

[8]Black Elk said the mountain he stood upon in his vision was Harney Peak in the Black Hills. "But anywhere is the center of the world," he added.

them the animals and men. All these were rejoicing, and thunder was like happy laughter.

As I rode in through the rainbow door, there were cheering voices from all over the universe, and I saw the Six Grandfathers sitting in a row, with their arms held toward me and their hands, palms out; and behind them in the cloud were faces thronging, without number, of the people yet to be.

"He has triumphed!" cried the six together, making thunder. And as I passed before them there, each gave again the gift that he had given me before—the cup of water and the bow and arrows, the power to make live and to destroy; the white wing of cleansing and the healing herb; the sacred pipe; the flowering stick. And each one spoke in turn from west to south, explaining what he gave as he had done before, and as each one spoke he melted down into the earth and rose again; and as each did this, I felt nearer to the earth.

Then the oldest of them all said: "Grandson, all over the universe you have seen. Now you shall go back with power to the place from whence you came, and it shall happen yonder that hundreds shall be sacred, hundreds shall be flames! Behold!"

I looked below and saw my people there, and all were well and happy except one, and he was lying like the dead—and that one was myself. Then the oldest Grandfather sang, and his song was like this:

> "There is someone lying on earth in a sacred manner.
> There is someone—on earth he lies.
> In a sacred manner I have made him to walk."

Now the tepee, built and roofed with cloud, began to sway back and forth as in a wind, and the flaming rainbow door was growing dimmer. I could hear voices of all kinds crying from outside: "Eagle Wing Stretches is coming forth! Behold him!"

When I went through the door, the face of the day of earth was appearing with the day-break star upon its forehead; and the sun leaped up and looked upon me, and I was going forth alone.

And as I walked alone, I heard the sun singing as it arose, and it sang like this:

> "With visible face I am appearing.
> In a sacred manner I appear.
> For the greening earth a pleasantness I make.
> The center of the nation's hoop I have made
> pleasant.

> With visible face, behold me!
> The four-leggeds and two-leggeds, I have made
> them to walk;
> The wings of the air, I have made them to fly.
> With visible face I appear.
> My day, I have made it holy."

When the singing stopped, I was feeling lost and very lonely. Then a Voice above me said: "Look back!" It was a spotted eagle that was hovering over me and spoke. I looked, and where the flaming rainbow tepee, built and roofed with cloud, had been, I saw only the tall rock mountain at the center of the world.

I was all alone on a broad plain now with my feet upon the earth, alone but for the spotted eagle guarding me. I could see my people's village far ahead, and I walked very fast, for I was homesick now. Then I saw my own tepee, and inside I saw my mother and my father bending over a sick boy that was myself. And as I entered the tepee, some one was saying: "The boy is coming to; you had better give him some water."

Then I was sitting up; and I was sad because my mother and my father didn't seem to know I had been so far away.

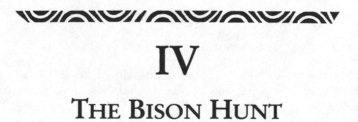

IV

THE BISON HUNT

When I got back to my father and mother and was sitting up there in our tepee, my face was still all puffed and my legs and arms were badly swollen; but I felt good all over and wanted to get right up and run around. My parents would not let me. They told me I had been sick twelve days, lying like dead all the while, and that Whirlwind Chaser, who was Standing Bear's uncle and a medicine man, had brought me back to life. I knew it was the Grandfathers in the Flaming

Rainbow Tepee who had cured me; but I felt afraid to say so. My father gave Whirlwind Chaser the best horse he had for making me well, and many people came to look at me, and there was much talk about the great power of Whirlwind Chaser who had made me well all at once when I was almost the same as dead.

Everybody was glad that I was living; but as I lay there thinking about the wonderful place where I had been and all that I had seen, I was very sad; for it seemed to me that everybody ought to know about it, but I was afraid to tell, because I knew that nobody would believe me, little as I was, for I was only nine years old. Also, as I lay there thinking of my vision, I could see it all again and feel the meaning with a part of me like a strange power glowing in my body; but when the part of me that talks would try to make words for the meaning, it would be like fog and get away from me.

I am sure now that I was then too young to understand it all, and that I only felt it. It was the pictures I remembered and the words that went with them; for nothing I have ever seen with my eyes was so clear and bright as what my vision showed me; and no words that I have ever heard with my ears were like the words I heard. I did not have to remember these things; they have remembered themselves all these years. It was as I grew older that the meanings came clearer and clearer out of the pictures and the words; and even now I know that more was shown to me than I can tell.

That evening of the day when I came back, Whirlwind Chaser, who had got a great name and a good horse for curing me, came over to our tepee. He sat down and looked at me a long time in a strange way, and then he said to my father: "Your boy there is sitting in a sacred manner. I do not know what it is, but there is something special for him to do, for just as I came in I could see a power like a light all through his body."

While he was looking hard at me, I wanted to get up and run away, for I was afraid he might look right into me and see my vision there and tell it wrong, and then maybe all the people would think that I was crazy. For a long while after that, whenever I saw Whirlwind Chaser coming, I would run away and hide for fear he might see into me and tell.

The next morning all the swelling had left my face and legs and arms, and I felt well as ever; but everything around me seemed strange and as though it were far away. I remember that for twelve days after that I wanted to be alone, and it seemed I did not belong to my

people. They were almost like strangers. I would be out alone away from the village and the other boys, and I would look around to the four quarters, thinking of my vision and wishing I could get back there again. I would go home to eat, but I could not make myself eat much; and my father and mother thought that I was sick yet; but I was not. I was only homesick for the place where I had been.

I could not tell what I had seen and heard even to my mother's father, Refuse-To-Go, although before that I used to think that I could tell him anything, for he liked everything a boy could like, and there was no end to the wonderful things he would tell. It was he who made the first bow I ever had, and he always had more arrows ready for me when I had lost all those that he had given me. I loved my father, but Refuse-To-Go was different, and I used to be with him a great deal. This was the first thing I could not tell him.

One day during this time I was out with the bow and arrows my Grandfather had made for me, and as I walked along thinking of my vision, suddenly I felt queer, and for a little while it seemed that the bow and arrows were those that the First Grandfather in the Flaming Rainbow Tepee had given me. Then they were only those that Refuse-To-Go had made, and I felt foolish and tried to make myself think it was all only a dream anyway. So I thought I would forget about it and shoot something. There was a bush and a little bird sitting in it; but just as I was going to shoot, I felt queer again, and remembered that I was to be like a relative with the birds. So I did not shoot. Then I went on down toward a creek, feeling foolish because I had let the little bird go, and when I saw a green frog sitting there, I just shot him right away. But when I picked him up by the legs, I thought: "Now I have killed him," and it made me want to cry.

Standing Bear Speaks:

I remember the time when my friend here was sick. I was four years older than he was. I am a Minneconjou, but our mothers were cousins and we used to play together when our bands were camping in one place. It was at the headwaters of the Greasy Grass (Little Big Horn). Everybody in the village was well, and so was Black Elk. The next thing I heard was that he was dying and just breathing a little. Everybody was excited over it, and they sent for medicine to other bands, but nobody knew what the sickness was. I saw him during this time. He looked dead, and everybody was talking about him. Then he was well all at once, and everybody wondered and talked about it.

I remember too how it was after he got up. Right after that we moved camp to the mouth of Willow Creek, south about two days, and while the village was moving, I rode back to where the smaller boys were in the rear, for I wanted to see my young friend. I said to him: "How, younger brother! You got well after all!" And he said: "How! Yes, I am not sick at all now!" But as we rode along together and talked, he was not like a boy. He was more like an old man. And I can remember his father talking to my father in our tepee while we were eating one evening. He said something like this: "Since my boy was sick, he is not the same boy. He has queer ways and he does not like to be at home. I feel sorry about the way he is, poor boy!"

Then we went on a big hunt and the people did not talk about it any more.

Black Elk Continues:

Yes, we went on a big hunt after we had been at Willow Creek awhile, and it helped me to quit thinking about my vision all the time.

One morning the crier came around the circle of the village calling out that we were going to break camp. The advisers were in the council tepee, and he cried to them: "The advisers, come forth to the center and bring your fires along." It was their duty to save fire for the people, because we had no matches then.

"Now take it down, down!" the crier shouted. And all the people began taking down their tepees, and packing them on pony drags.

Then the crier said: "Many bison, I have heard; many bison, I have heard! Your children, you must take care of them!" He meant to keep the children close while traveling, so that they would not scare the bison.

Then we broke camp and started in formation, the four advisers first, a crier behind them, the chiefs next, and then the people with the loaded pony drags in a long line, and the herd of ponies following. I was riding near the rear with some of the smaller boys, and when the people were going up a long hill, I looked ahead and it made me feel queer again for a little while, because I remembered the nation walking in a sacred manner on the red road in my vision. But this was different, and I forgot about it soon, for something exciting was going to happen, and even the ponies seemed to know.

After we had been traveling awhile, we came to a place where there were many turnips growing, and the crier said: "Take off your loads and let your horses rest. Take your sticks and dig turnips for your-

selves." And while the people were doing this, the advisers sat on a hill nearby and smoked. Then the crier shouted: "Put on your loads!" and soon the village was moving again.

When the sun was high, the advisers found a place to camp where there was wood and also water; and while the women were cooking all around the circle I heard people saying that the scouts were returning, and over the top of a hill I saw three horsebacks coming. They rode to the council tepee in the middle of the village and all the people were going there to hear. I went there too and got up close so that I could look in between the legs of the men. The crier came out of the council tepee and said, speaking to the people for the scouts: "I have protected you; in return you shall give me many gifts." The scouts then sat down before the door of the tepee and one of the advisers filled the sacred pipe with chacun sha sha, the bark of the red willow, and set it on a bison chip in front of him, because the bison was sacred and gave us both food and shelter. Then he lit the pipe, offered it to the four quarters, to the Spirit above and to Mother Earth, and passing it to the scouts he said: "The nation has depended upon you. Whatever you have seen, maybe it is for the good of the people you have seen." The scouts smoked, meaning that they would tell the truth. Then the adviser said: "At what place have you stood and seen the good? Report it to me and I will be glad."

One of the scouts answered: "You know where we started from. We went and reached the top of a hill and there we saw a small herd of bison." He pointed as he spoke.

The adviser said: "Maybe on the other side of that you have seen the good. Report it." The scout answered: "On the other side of that we saw a second and larger herd of bison."

Then the adviser said: "I shall be thankful to you. Tell me all that you have seen out there."

The scout replied: "On the other side of that there was nothing but bison all over the country."

And the adviser said: "Hetchetu aloh!"[1]

Then the crier shouted like singing: "Your knives shall be sharpened, your arrows shall be sharpened. Make ready, make haste; your horses make ready! We shall go forth with arrows. Plenty of meat we shall make!"

Everybody began sharpening knives and arrows and getting the best horses ready for the great making of meat.

[1]"It is so indeed."

Then we started for where the bison were. The soldier band went first, riding twenty abreast, and anybody who dared go ahead of them would get knocked off his horse. They kept order, and everybody had to obey. After them came the hunters, riding five abreast. The people came up in the rear. Then the head man of the advisers went around picking out the best hunters with the fastest horses, and to these he said: "Good young warriors, my relatives, your work I know is good. What you do is good always; so to-day you shall feed the helpless. Perhaps there are some old and feeble people without sons, or some who have little children and no man. You shall help these, and whatever you kill shall be theirs." This was a great honor for young men.

Then when we had come near to where the bison were, the hunters circled around them, and the cry went up, as in a battle, "Hoka hey!" which meant to charge. Then there was a great dust and everybody shouted and all the hunters went in to kill—every man for himself. They were all nearly naked, with their quivers full of arrows hanging on their left sides, and they would ride right up to a bison and shoot him behind the left shoulder. Some of the arrows would go in up to the feathers and sometimes those that struck no bones went right straight through. Everybody was very happy.

Standing Bear Speaks:

I remember that hunt, for before that time I had only killed a calf. I was thirteen years old and supposed to be a man, so I made up my mind I'd get a yearling. One of them went down a draw and I raced after him on my pony. My first shot did not seem to hurt him at all; but my pony kept right after him, and the second arrow went in half way. I think I hit his heart, for he began to wobble as he ran and blood came out of his nose. Hunters cried "Yuhoo!" once when they killed, but this was my first big bison, and I just kept on yelling "Yuhoo!" People must have thought I was killing a whole herd, the way I yelled. When he went down, I got off my horse and began butchering him myself, and I was very happy. All over the flat, as far as I could see, there were men butchering bison now, and the women and the old men who could not hunt were coming up to help. And all the women were making the tremolo of joy for what the warriors had given them. That was in the Moon of Red Cherries (July). It was a great killing.

Black Elk Continues:

I was well enough to go along on my pony, but I was not old enough to hunt. So we little boys scouted around and watched the hunters; and when we would see a bunch of bison coming, we would yell "Yuhoo" like the others, but nobody noticed us.

When the butchering was all over, they hung the meat across the horses' backs and fastened it with strips of fresh bison hide. On the way back to the village all the hunting horses were loaded, and we little boys who could not wait for the feast helped ourselves to all the raw liver we wanted. Nobody got cross when we did this.

During this time, women back at camp were cutting long poles and forked sticks to make drying racks for the meat. When the hunters got home they threw their meat in piles on the leaves of trees.

Then the advisers all went back into the council tepee, and from all directions the people came bringing gifts of meat to them, and the advisers all cried "Hya-a-a-a!," after which they sang for those who had brought them the good gifts. And when they had eaten all they could, the crier shouted to the people: "All come home! It is more than I can eat!" And people from all over the camp came to get a little of the meat that was left over.

The women were all busy cutting the meat into strips and hanging it on the racks to dry. You could see red meat hanging everywhere. The people feasted all night long and danced and sang. Those were happy times.

There was a war game that we little boys played after a big hunt. We went out a little way from the village and built some grass tepees, playing we were enemies and this was our village. We had an adviser, and when it got dark he would order us to go and steal some dried meat from the big people. He would hold a stick up to us and we had to bite off a piece of it. If we bit a big piece we had to get a big piece of meat, and if we bit a little piece, we did not have to get so much. Then we started for the big people's village, crawling on our bellies, and when we got back without getting caught, we would have a big feast and a dance and make kill talks, telling of our brave deeds like warriors. Once, I remember, I had no brave deed to tell. I crawled up to a leaning tree beside a tepee and there was meat hanging on the limbs. I wanted a tongue I saw up there in the moonlight, so I climbed up. But just as I was about to reach it, the man in the tepee yelled "Ye-a-a!" He was saying this to his dog, who was stealing some meat

too, but I thought the man had seen me, and I was so scared I fell out of the tree and ran away crying.

Then we used to have what we called a chapped breast dance. Our adviser would look us over to see whose breast was burned most from not having it covered with the robe we wore; and the boy chosen would lead the dance while we all sang like this:

> "I have a chapped breast.
> My breast is red.
> My breast is yellow."

And we practiced endurance too. Our adviser would put dry sunflower seeds on our wrists. These were lit at the top, and we had to let them burn clear down to the skin. They hurt and made sores, but if we knocked them off or cried Owh!, we would be called women.

V

AT THE SOLDIERS' TOWN

After all the meat was dried, the six bands[1] of our nation that had come together about the time when the great vision came to me, broke camp at the mouth of Willow Creek and scattered in all directions. A small part of our band, the Ogalalas, started south for the Soldiers' Town[2] on Smoky Earth River (the White), for some of our relatives were there and we wanted to see them and have a feast of aguiapi and paezhuta sapa with chahumpi ska in it.[3] All the rest of the Ogalalas stayed in that country with Crazy Horse, who would have nothing to

[1] Ogalalas, Brules, Sans Arcs, Black Kettles, Hunkpapas, Minneconjous.
[2] Fort Robinson.
[3] Aguiapi, "brown all over," bread. Paezhuta sapa, "black medicine," coffee. Chahumpi ska, "white juice of the tree," sugar.

do with the Wasichus. This was late in the Moon When the Cherries are Ripe (July) and we boys had a good time playing. There were not many boys in our small band, and we all played together. I had quit thinking about my vision. The queer feeling had left me and I was not bashful any more; but whenever a thunder storm was coming I felt happy, as though somebody were coming to visit me.

We camped first on Powder River, then on the headwaters of the north fork of Good River (the Cheyenne) where there is a big butte that we called Sits-With-Young-One, because it has a little butte beside it. Then we camped on Driftwood Creek, then on the Plain of Pine Trees, and next on Plum Creek. When we got there, the plums were turning red, but they were not quite ripe yet. My grandfather went out and got some big red ones and they tasted good. When we got to War Bonnet Creek, which is not very far from the Soldiers' Town, my aunt and other relatives were there waiting for us with bread and coffee, and we had a big feast. I was sick all that night, and the next day my parents made me ride on a pony drag, because they were afraid I would surely die this time. But I think it was only too much bread and coffee, and maybe the plums. We camped again at Hips Hill, and by this time most of our people from the Soldiers' Town were among us. The next day about twenty tepees of us went on, and the rest stayed back. We camped with our relatives by White Butte near the Soldiers' Town and stayed there all winter, and we had a good time sliding down hill with sleds made out of bison jaws and ribs tied together with rawhide.

I was ten years old that winter, and that was the first time I ever saw a Wasichu. At first I thought they all looked sick, and I was afraid they might just begin to fight us any time, but I got used to them.

That winter one of our boys climbed the flagpole and chopped it off near the top. This almost made bad trouble, for the soldiers surrounded us with their guns; but Red Cloud, who was living there, stood right in the middle without a weapon and made speeches to the Wasichus and to us. He said the boy who did it must be punished, and he told the Wasichus it was foolish for men to want to shoot grown people because their little boys did foolish things in play; and he asked them if they ever did foolish things for fun when they were boys. So nothing happened after all.

Red Cloud was a great chief, and he was an Ogalala. But at this time he was through with fighting. After the treaty he made with the Wasichus five years before (1868) he never fought again, and he was

living with his band, the Bad Faces, at the Soldiers' Town. Crazy Horse was an Ogalala too, and I think he was the greatest chief of all.

In the Moon of the Red Grass Appearing (April) about thirty tepees of us broke camp and started for the Black Hills to cut tepee poles. We followed down Horse-Head-Cutting Creek to its mouth, and while we were camped there one day I was away from the village alone, when I heard a spotted eagle whistle. I looked up and there he was, hovering over me. The queer feeling came back very strong, and for a little while it seemed that I was in the world of my vision again.

From there we moved on to Buffalo Gap at the foot of the Hills, and my father and I went out alone to look for deer. We climbed up through the timber to the top of a big hill, and it was hard for my father, who was lame from the wound he got in the Battle of the Hundred Slain. When we were on top, my father looked down and said: "There are some yonder. You stay here, and I will go around them." Then the queer feeling came back, and I said without knowing why I said it: "No, father, stay here; for they are bringing them to us." He looked at me hard, and said: "Who is bringing them?" I could not answer; and after he had looked hard at me again, he said: "All right, son." So we lay down there in the grass and waited. They did come to us, and my father got two of them.

While we were butchering and I was eating some liver, I felt sorry that we had killed these animals and thought that we ought to do something in return. So I said: "Father, should we not offer one of these to the wild things?" He looked hard at me again for a while. Then he placed one of the deer with its head to the east, and, facing the west, he raised his hand and cried, "Hey-hey" four times and prayed like this: "Grandfather, the Great Spirit, behold me! To all the wild things that eat flesh, this I have offered that my people may live and the children grow up with plenty."

That was another happy summer, for the big trouble had not come yet. We cut plenty of tepee poles up along the creeks that came down the east side of the Black Hills, and there was all we wanted to eat, for the Hills were like a big food pack for our people. Iron Bull, a little boy my age, and I had great fun fishing. We always made an offering of bait to the fish, saying: "You who are down in the water with wings of red, I offer this to you; so come hither." Then when we caught the first fish, we would put it on a forked stick and kiss it. If we did not do this, we were sure the others would know and stay away. If we caught a little fish, we would kiss it and throw it back, so that it would

not go and frighten the bigger fish. I don't know whether all this helped or not, but we always got plenty of fish, and our parents were proud of us. We tried to catch as many as we could so that people would think much of us.

There was a man by the name of Watanye who was good at spearing fish, and he had very sore lips so that he did not dare to laugh. They were cracked all around his mouth. People would try to make him laugh, but he would just walk away from them. One day he said to me: "Younger brother, I will show you how to spear fish." So we went up the creek, and there was a fish this long (to the elbow) lying in a pool. "Take the spear," Watanye said, "and strike deep, for they are always farther down than they look." I took the spear and thrust with it as hard as I could; but the clear water was much deeper than it seemed. I missed and went over head-first into the cold pool. When I scrambled out, Watanye was all doubled up, hugging his belly, and going "hunh, hunh, hunh!" Blood was running down his chin. He ran away as fast as he could, and for a long while after that, whenever he saw me coming, he would turn and run, so that he would not have to laugh again. Once I hid in a bush until he came along, just to see him run when I jumped out.

I think Watanye liked me a good deal, because he often used to take me out alone to fish or hunt, and he was always teaching me things. Also, he liked to tell me stories, mostly funny ones when he did not have sore lips. I still remember one story he told me about a young Lakota called High Horse, and what a hard time he had getting the girl he wanted. Watanye said the story happened just as he told it, and maybe it did. If it did not, it could have, just as well as not. I will tell that story now.

VI

HIGH HORSE'S COURTING

You know, in the old days, it was not so very easy to get a girl when you wanted to be married. Sometimes it was hard work for a young man and he had to stand a great deal. Say I am a young man and I have seen a young girl who looks so beautiful to me that I feel all sick when I think about her. I can not just go and tell her about it and then get married if she is willing. I have to be a very sneaky fellow to talk to her at all, and after I have managed to talk to her, that is only the beginning.

Probably for a long time I have been feeling sick about a certain girl because I love her so much, but she will not even look at me, and her parents keep a good watch over her. But I keep feeling worse and worse all the time; so maybe I sneak up to her tepee in the dark and wait until she comes out. Maybe I just wait there all night and don't get any sleep at all and she does not come out. Then I feel sicker than ever about her.

Maybe I hide in the brush by a spring where she sometimes goes to get water, and when she comes by, if nobody is looking, then I jump out and hold her and just make her listen to me. If she likes me too, I can tell that from the way she acts, for she is very bashful and maybe will not say a word or even look at me the first time. So I let her go, and then maybe I sneak around until I can see her father alone, and I tell him how many horses I can give him for his beautiful girl, and by now I am feeling so sick that maybe I would give him all the horses in the world if I had them.

Well, this young man I am telling about was called High Horse, and there was a girl in the village who looked so beautiful to him that he was just sick all over from thinking about her so much and he was

getting sicker all the time. The girl was very shy, and her parents thought a great deal of her because they were not young any more and this was the only child they had. So they watched her all day long, and they fixed it so that she would be safe at night too when they were asleep. They thought so much of her that they had made a rawhide bed for her to sleep in, and after they knew that High Horse was sneaking around after her, they took rawhide thongs and tied the girl in bed at night so that nobody could steal her when they were asleep, for they were not sure but that their girl might really want to be stolen.

Well, after High Horse had been sneaking around a good while and hiding and waiting for the girl and getting sicker all the time, he finally caught her alone and made her talk to him. Then he found out that she liked him maybe a little. Of course this did not make him feel well. It made him sicker than ever, but now he felt as brave as a bison bull, and so he went right to her father and said he loved the girl so much that he would give two good horses for her—one of them young and the other one not so very old.

But the old man just waved his hand, meaning for High Horse to go away and quit talking foolishness like that.

High Horse was feeling sicker than ever about it; but there was another young fellow who said he would loan High Horse two ponies and when he got some more horses, why, he could just give them back for the ones he had borrowed.

Then High Horse went back to the old man and said he would give four horses for the girl—two of them young and the other two not hardly old at all. But the old man just waved his hand and would not say anything.

So High Horse sneaked around until he could talk to the girl again, and he asked her to run away with him. He told her he thought he would just fall over and die if she did not. But she said she would not do that; she wanted to be bought like a fine woman. You see she thought a great deal of herself too.

That made High Horse feel so very sick that he could not eat a bite, and he went around with his head hanging down as though he might just fall down and die any time.

Red Deer was another young fellow, and he and High Horse were great comrades, always doing things together. Red Deer saw how High Horse was acting, and he said: "Cousin, what is the matter? Are you sick in the belly? You look as though you were going to die."

Then High Horse told Red Deer how it was, and said he thought he could not stay alive much longer if he could not marry the girl pretty quick.

Red Deer thought awhile about it, and then he said: "Cousin, I have a plan, and if you are man enough to do as I tell you, then everything will be all right. She will not run away with you; her old man will not take four horses; and four horses are all you can get. You must steal her and run away with her. Then afterwhile you can come back and the old man cannot do anything because she will be your woman. Probably she wants you to steal her anyway."

So they planned what High Horse had to do, and he said he loved the girl so much that he was man enough to do anything Red Deer or anybody else could think up

So this is what they did.

That night late they sneaked up to the girl's tepee and waited until it sounded inside as though the old man and the old woman and the girl were sound asleep. Then High Horse crawled under the tepee with a knife. He had to cut the rawhide thongs first, and then Red Deer, who was pulling up the stakes around that side of the tepee, was going to help drag the girl outside and gag her. After that, High Horse could put her across his pony in front of him and hurry out of there and be happy all the rest of his life.

When High Horse had crawled inside, he felt so nervous that he could hear his heart drumming, and it seemed so loud he felt sure it would 'waken the old folks. But it did not, and afterwhile he began cutting the thongs. Every time he cut one it made a pop and nearly scared him to death. But he was getting along all right and all the thongs were cut down as far as the girl's thighs, when he became so nervous that his knife slipped and stuck the girl. She gave a big, loud yell. Then the old folks jumped up and yelled too. By this time High Horse was outside, and he and Red Deer were running away like antelope. The old man and some other people chased the young men but they got away in the dark and nobody knew who it was.

Well, if you ever wanted a beautiful girl you will know how sick High Horse was now. It was very bad the way he felt, and it looked as though he would starve even if he did not drop over dead sometime.

Red Deer kept thinking about this, and after a few days he went to High Horse and said: "Cousin, take courage! I have another plan, and I am sure, if you are man enough, we can steal her this time." And

High Horse said: "I am man enough to do anything anybody can think up, if I can only get that girl."

So this is what they did.

They went away from the village alone, and Red Deer made High Horse strip naked. Then he painted High Horse solid white all over, and after that he painted black stripes all over the white and put black rings around High Horse's eyes. High Horse looked terrible. He looked so terrible that when Red Deer was through painting and took a good look at what he had done, he said it scared even him a little.

"Now," Red Deer said, "if you get caught again, everybody will be so scared they will think you are a bad spirit and will be afraid to chase you."

So when the night was getting old and everybody was sound asleep, they sneaked back to the girl's tepee. High Horse crawled in with his knife, as before, and Red Deer waited outside, ready to drag the girl out and gag her when High Horse had all the thongs cut.

High Horse crept up by the girl's bed and began cutting at the thongs. But he kept thinking, "If they see me they will shoot me because I look so terrible." The girl was restless and kept squirming around in bed, and when a thong was cut, it popped. So High Horse worked very slowly and carefully.

But he must have made some noise, for suddenly the old woman awoke and said to her old man: "Old Man, wake up! There is somebody in this tepee!" But the old man was sleepy and didn't want to be bothered. He said: "Of course there is somebody in this tepee. Go to sleep and don't bother me." Then he snored some more.

But High Horse was so scared by now that he lay very still and as flat to the ground as he could. Now, you see, he had not been sleeping very well for a long time because he was so sick about the girl. And while he was lying there waiting for the old woman to snore, he just forgot everything, even how beautiful the girl was. Red Deer who was lying outside ready to do his part, wondered and wondered what had happened in there, but he did not dare call out to High Horse.

Afterwhile the day began to break and Red Deer had to leave with the two ponies he had staked there for his comrade and girl, or somebody would see him.

So he left.

Now when it was getting light in the tepee, the girl awoke and the first thing she saw was a terrible animal, all white with black stripes on it, lying asleep beside her bed. So she screamed, and then the old

woman screamed and the old man yelled. High Horse jumped up, scared almost to death, and he nearly knocked the tepee down getting out of there.

People were coming running from all over the village with guns and bows and axes, and everybody was yelling.

By now High Horse was running so fast that he hardly touched the ground at all, and he looked so terrible that the people fled from him and let him run. Some braves wanted to shoot at him, but the others said he might be some sacred being and it would bring bad trouble to kill him.

High Horse made for the river that was near, and in among the brush he found a hollow tree and dived into it. Afterwhile some braves came there and he could hear them saying that it was some bad spirit that had come out of the water and gone back in again.

That morning the people were ordered to break camp and move away from there. So they did, while High Horse was hiding in his hollow tree.

Now Red Deer had been watching all this from his own tepee and trying to look as though he were as much surprised and scared as all the others. So when the camp moved, he sneaked back to where he had seen his comrade disappear. When he was down there in the brush, he called, and High Horse answered, because he knew his friend's voice. They washed off the paint from High Horse and sat down on the river bank to talk about their troubles.

High Horse said he never would go back to the village as long as he lived and he did not care what happened to him now. He said he was going to go on the war-path all by himself. Red Deer said: "No, cousin, you are not going on the war-path alone, because I am going with you."

So Red Deer got everything ready, and at night they started out on the war-path all alone. After several days they came to a Crow camp just about sundown, and when it was dark they sneaked up to where the Crow horses were grazing, killed the horse guard, who was not thinking about enemies because he thought all the Lakotas were far away, and drove off about a hundred horses.

They got a big start because all the Crow horses stampeded and it was probably morning before the Crow warriors could catch any horses to ride. Red Deer and High Horse fled with their herd three days and nights before they reached the village of their people. Then they drove the whole herd right into the village and up in front of the

girl's tepee. The old man was there, and High Horse called out to him and asked if he thought maybe that would be enough horses for his girl. The old man did not wave him away that time. It was not the horses that he wanted. What he wanted was a son who was a real man and good for something.

So High Horse got his girl after all, and I think he deserved her.

VII

WASICHUS IN THE HILLS

It was the next summer, when I was 11 years old (1874), that the first sign of a new trouble came to us. Our band had been camping on Split-Toe Creek in the Black Hills, and from there we moved to Spring Creek, then to Rapid Creek where it comes out into the prairie. That evening just before sunset, a big thunder cloud came up from the west, and just before the wind struck, there were clouds of split-tail swallows flying all around above us. It was like a part of my vision, and it made me feel queer. The boys tried to hit the swallows with stones and it hurt me to see them doing this, but I could not tell them. I got a stone and acted as though I were going to throw, but I did not. The swallows seemed holy. Nobody hit one, and when I thought about this I knew that of course they could not.

The next day some of the people were building a sweat tepee for a medicine man by the name of Chips, who was going to perform a ceremony and had to be purified first. They say he was the first man who made a sacred ornament for our great chief, Crazy Horse. While they were heating the stones for the sweat, some boys asked me to go with them to shoot squirrels. We went out, and when I was about to shoot at one, I felt very uneasy all at once. So I sat down, feeling queer, and wondered about it. While I sat there I heard a voice that said: "Go at once! Go home!" I told the boys we must go home

at once, and we all hurried. When we got back, everybody was excited, breaking camp, catching the ponies and loading the drags; and I heard that while Chips was in the sweat tepee a voice had told him that the band must flee at once because something was going to happen there.

It was nearly sundown when we started, and we fled all that night on the back trail toward Spring Creek, then down that creek to the south fork of the Good River. I rode most of the night in a pony drag because I got too sleepy to stay on a horse. We camped at Good River in the morning, but we stayed only long enough to eat. Then we fled again, upstream, all day long until we reached the mouth of Horse Creek. We were going to stay there, but scouts came to us and said that many soldiers had come into the Black Hills; and that was what Chips saw while he was in the sweat tepee. So we hurried on in the night towards Smoky Earth River (the White), and when we got there, I woke up and it was daybreak. We camped a while to eat, and then went up the Smoky Earth, two camps, to Robinson, for we were afraid of the soldiers up there.

Afterward I learned that it was Pahuska[1] who had led his soldiers into the Black Hills that summer to see what he could find. He had no right to go in there, because all that country was ours. Also the Wasichus had made a treaty with Red Cloud (1868) that said it would be ours as long as grass should grow and water flow. Later I learned too that Pahuska had found there much of the yellow metal that makes the Wasichus crazy; and that is what made the bad trouble, just as it did before, when the hundred were rubbed out.

Our people knew there was yellow metal in little chunks up there; but they did not bother with it, because it was not good for anything.

We stayed all winter at the Soldiers' Town, and all the while the bad trouble was coming fast; for in the fall we heard that some Wasichus had come from the Missouri River to dig in the Black Hills for the yellow metal, because Pahuska had told about it with a voice that went everywhere. Later he got rubbed out for doing that.

The people talked about this all winter. Crazy Horse was in the Powder River country and Sitting Bull was somewhere north of the Hills. Our people at the Soldiers' Town thought we ought to get together and do something. Red Cloud's people said that the soldiers had gone in there to keep the diggers out, but we, who were only visiting, did not believe it. We called Red Cloud's people "Hangs-

[1]Long Hair, General Custer.

Around-The-Fort," and our people said they were standing up for the Wasichus, and if we did not do something we should lose the Black Hills.

In the spring when I was twelve years old (1875), more soldiers with many wagons came up from the Soldiers' Town at the mouth of the Laramie River[2] and went into the Hills.

There was much talk all summer, and in the Moon of Making Fat (June) there was a sun dance there at the Soldiers' Town to give the people strength, but not many took part; maybe because everybody was so excited talking about the Black Hills. I remember two men who danced together. One had lost a leg in the Battle of the Hundred Slain and one had lost an eye in the Attacking of the Wagons, so they had only three eyes and three legs between them to dance with. We boys went down to the creek while they were sun dancing and got some elm leaves that we chewed up and threw on the dancers while they were all dressed up and trying to look their best. We even did this to some of the older people, and nobody got angry, because everybody was supposed to be in a good humor and to show their endurance in every kind of way; so they had to stand teasing too. I will tell about a big sun dance later when we come to it.

In the Moon When the Calves Grow Hair (September) there was a big council with the Wasichus on the Smoky Earth River at the mouth of White Clay Creek. I can remember the council, but I did not understand much of it then. Many of the Lakotas were there, also Shyelas and Blue Clouds[3]; but Crazy Horse and Sitting Bull stayed away. In the middle of the circle there was a shade made of canvas. Under this the councilors sat and talked, and all around them there was a crowd of people on foot and horseback. They talked and talked for days, but it was just like wind blowing in the end. I asked my father what they were talking about in there, and he told me that the Grandfather at Washington wanted to lease the Black Hills so that the Wasichus could dig yellow metal, and that the chief of the soldiers had said if we did not do this, the Black Hills would be just like melting snow held in our hands, because the Wasichus would take that country anyway.

It made me sad to hear this. It was such a good place to play and the

[2]Colonel Dodge with 400 men and 75 wagons from Fort Laramie escorted a geological expedition into the Hills that spring and remained until October.

[3]Cheyennes and Arapahoes.

people were always happy in that country. Also I thought of my vision, and of how the spirits took me there to the center of the world.

After the council we heard that creeks of Wasichus were flowing into the Hills and becoming rivers, and that they were already making towns up there. It looked like bad trouble coming, so our band broke camp and started out to join Crazy Horse on Powder River. We camped on Horsehead Creek, then on the War Bonnet after we crossed the old Wasichu's road[4] that made the trouble that time when the hundred were rubbed out. Grass was growing on it. Then we camped at Sage Creek, then on the Beaver, then on Driftwood Creek, and came again to the Plain of Pine Trees at the edge of the Hills.

The nights were sharp now, but the days were clear and still; and while we were camping there I went up into the Hills alone and sat a long while under a tree. I thought maybe my vision would come back and tell me how I could save that country for my people, but I could not see anything clear.

This made me sad, but something happened a few days later that made me feel good. We had gone over to Taking-The-Crow-Horses Creek, where we found many bison and made plenty of meat and tanned many hides for winter. In our band there was a man by the name of Fat, who was always talking about how fast his horse could run. One day while we were camping there I told Fat my pony could run faster than his could, and he laughed at me and said that only crows and coyotes would think my pony was any good. I asked him what he would give me if my pony could beat his, and he said he would give me some black medicine (coffee). So we ran, and I got the black medicine. All the while we were running I thought about the white wing of the wind that the Second Grandfather of my vision gave me; and maybe that power went into my pony's legs.

On Kills-Himself Creek we made more meat and hides and were ready to join Crazy Horse's camp on the Powder. There were some Hang-Around-The-Fort people with us, and when they saw that we were going to join Crazy Horse, they left us and started back to the Soldiers' Town. They were afraid there might be trouble, and they knew Crazy Horse would fight, so they wanted to be safe with the Wasichus. We did not like them very much.

We had no advisers, because we were just a little band, and when we were moving, the boys could ride anywhere. One day while we were

[4]The Bozeman Trail.

heading for Powder River I was riding ahead with Steals Horses, another boy my age, and we saw some footprints of somebody going somewhere. We followed the footprints and there was a knoll beside a creek where a Lakota was lying. We got off and looked at him, and he was dead. His name was Root-of-the-Tail, and he was going over to Tongue River to see his relatives when he died. He was very old and ready to die, so he just lay down and died right there before he saw his relatives again.

Afterwhile we came to the village on Powder River and went into camp at the downstream end. I was anxious to see my cousin, Crazy Horse, again, for now that it began to look like bad trouble coming, everybody talked about him more than ever and he seemed greater than before. Also I was getting older.

Of course I had seen him now and then ever since I could remember, and had heard stories of the brave things he did. I remember the story of how he and his brother were out alone on horseback, and a big band of Crows attacked them, so that they had to run. And while they were riding hard, with all those Crows after them, Crazy Horse heard his brother call out; and when he looked back, his brother's horse was down and the Crows were almost on him. And they told how Crazy Horse charged back right into the Crows and fought them back with only a bow and arrows, then took his brother up behind him and got away. It was his sacred power that made the Crows afraid of him when he charged. And the people told stories of when he was a boy and used to be around with the older Hump all the time. Hump was not young any more at the time, and he was a very great warrior, maybe the greatest we ever had until then. They say people used to wonder at the boy and the old man always being together; but I think Hump knew Crazy Horse would be a great man and wanted to teach him everything.

Crazy Horse's father was my father's cousin, and there were no chiefs in our family before Crazy Horse; but there were holy men; and he became a chief because of the power he got in a vision when he was a boy. When I was a man, my father told me something about that vision. Of course he did not know all of it; but he said that Crazy Horse dreamed and went into the world where there is nothing but the spirits of all things. That is the real world that is behind this one, and everything we see here is something like a shadow from that world. He was on his horse in that world, and the horse and himself on it and the trees and the grass and the stones and everything were

made of spirit, and nothing was hard, and everything seemed to float. His horse was standing still there, and yet it danced around like a horse made only of shadow, and that is how he got his name, which does not mean that his horse was crazy or wild, but that in his vision it danced around in that queer way.

It was this vision that gave him his great power, for when he went into a fight, he had only to think of that world to be in it again, so that he could go through anything and not be hurt. Until he was murdered by the Wasichus at the Soldiers' Town on White River, he was wounded only twice, once by accident and both times by some one of his own people when he was not expecting trouble and was not thinking; never by an enemy. He was fifteen years old when he was wounded by accident; and the other time was when he was a young man and another man was jealous of him because the man's wife liked Crazy Horse.

They used to say too that he carried a sacred stone with him, like one he had seen in some vision, and that when he was in danger, the stone always got very heavy and protected him somehow. That, they used to say, was the reason no horse he ever rode lasted very long. I do not know about this; maybe people only thought it; but it is a fact that he never kept one horse long. They wore out. I think it was only the power of his great vision that made him great.

Now and then he would notice me and speak to me before this; and sometimes he would have the crier call me into his tepee to eat with him. Then he would say things to tease me, but I would not say anything back, because I think I was a little afraid of him. I was not afraid that he would hurt me; I was just afraid. Everybody felt that way about him, for he was a queer man and would go about the village without noticing people or saying anything. In his own tepee he would joke, and when he was on the warpath with a small party, he would joke to make his warriors feel good. But around the village he hardly ever noticed anybody, except little children. All the Lakotas like to dance and sing; but he never joined a dance, and they say nobody ever heard him sing. But everybody liked him, and they would do anything he wanted or go anywhere he said. He was a small man among the Lakotas and he was slender and had a thin face and his eyes looked through things and he always seemed to be thinking hard about something. He never wanted to have many things for himself, and did not have many ponies like a chief. They say that when game was scarce and the people were hungry, he would not eat at all. He was a queer

man. Maybe he was always part way into that world of his vision. He was a very great man, and I think if the Wasichus had not murdered him down there, maybe we should still have the Black Hills and be happy. They could not have killed him in battle. They had to lie to him and murder him. And he was only about thirty years old when he died.

One day after we had camped there on Powder River, I went upstream to see him again, but his tepee was empty and he was gone somewhere, maybe with a war-party against the Crows, for we were close to them now and had to look out for them all the time. Later I did see him. He put his arm across my shoulder and took me into his tepee and we sat down together. I do not remember what he said, but I know he did not say much, and he did not tease me. Maybe he was thinking about the trouble coming.

We did not stay together there very long, but scattered out and camped in different places so that the people and the ponies would all have plenty. Crazy Horse kept his village on Powder River with about a hundred tepees, and our band made camp on the Tongue. We built a corral of poles for the horses at night and herded them all day, because the Crows were great horse-thieves and we had to be careful. The women chopped and stripped cottonwood trees during the day and gave the bark to the horses at night. The horses liked it and it made them sleek and fat.

Beside the mouth of the corral there was a tepee for the horse guard, and one night Crow Nose was staying there and his wife was with him. He had a hole in the tepee so that he could look through. Afterwhile he got very sleepy, so he woke his wife and told her to get up and watch while he had a little rest. By and by she saw something dark moving slowly on the snow out there, so she woke her husband and whispered, "Old man, you'd better get up, for I think I see something." So Crow Nose got up and peeped out and saw a man moving around the corral in the starlight looking for the best horse. Crow Nose told his wife to keep her eye at the hole and let him know when the man was coming out with a horse, and he lay down at the opening of the tepee with the muzzle of his gun sticking out of the flap. By and by they could hear the bar lifted at the mouth of the corral. When his wife touched him, Crow Nose thrust his head outside and saw the man just getting on a horse to ride away. He was black against the sky, so Crow Nose shot him, and the shot woke the whole camp so that many came running with guns and coup sticks. Yellow

Shirt was the first to count coup[5] on the dead Crow, but many followed. A man who has killed an enemy must not touch him, for he has already had the honor of killing. He must let another count coup. When I got there to see, a pile of coup sticks was lying beside the Crow and the women had cut him up with axes and scattered him around. It was horrible. Then the people built a fire right there beside the Crow and we had a kill dance. Men, women, and children danced right in the middle of the night, and they sang songs about Crow Nose who had killed and Yellow Shirt who had counted the first coup.

Then it was daylight, and the crier told us we would move camp to the place where Root-of-the-Tail died. Crow Nose dressed up for war, painted his face black and rode the horse the enemy had tried to steal. When the men paint their faces black, the women all rejoice and make the tremolo, because it means their men are going to kill enemies.

When we camped again, one of Red Cloud's loafers who had started back for the Soldiers' Town because they were afraid there might be trouble, came in and said the Crows had killed all his party but himself, while they were sleeping, and he had escaped because he was out scouting.

During the winter, runners came from the Wasichus and told us we must come into the Soldiers' Town right away or there would be bad trouble. But it was foolish to say that, because it was very cold and many of our people and ponies would have died in the snow. Also, we were in our own country and were doing no harm.

Late in the Moon of the Dark Red Calves (February) there was a big thaw, and our little band started for the Soldiers' Town, but it was very cold again before we got there. Crazy Horse stayed with about a hundred tepees on Powder, and in the middle of the Moon of the Snowblind (March) something bad happened there. It was just day-break. There was a blizzard and it was very cold. The people were sleeping. Suddenly there were many shots and horses galloping through the village. It was the cavalry of the Wasichus, and they were yelling and shooting and riding their horses against the tepees. All the people rushed out and ran, because they were not awake yet and they were frightened. The soldiers killed as many women and children and men as they could while the people were running toward a bluff. Then they set fire to some of the tepees and knocked the others down. But

[5]The act of striking an enemy, dead or alive, with a stick conferred distinction, the first coup naturally counting most.

when the people were on the side of the bluff, Crazy Horse said something, and all the warriors began singing the death song and charged back upon the soldiers; and the soldiers ran, driving many of the people's ponies ahead of them. Crazy Horse followed them all that day with a band of warriors, and that night he took all the stolen ponies away from them, and some of their own horses, and brought them all back to the village.[6]

These people were in their own country and were doing no harm. They only wanted to be let alone. We did not hear of this until quite awhile afterward; but at the Soldiers' Town we heard enough to make us paint our faces black.

VIII

THE FIGHT WITH THREE STARS

We stayed at the Soldiers' Town this time until the grass was good in the Moon When the Ponies Shed (May). Then my father told me we were going back to Crazy Horse and that we were going to have to fight from then on, because there was no other way to keep our country. He said that Red Cloud was a cheap man and wanted to sell the Black Hills to the Wasichus; that Spotted Tail and other chiefs were cheap men too, and that the Hang-Around-the-Fort people were all cheap and would stand up for the Wasichus. My aunt, who was living at the Soldiers' Town, must have felt the way we did, because when we were breaking camp she gave me a six-shooter like the soldiers had, and told me I was a man now. I was thirteen years old and not very big for my age, but I thought I should have to be a man anyway. We boys had practiced endurance, and we were all good riders, and I could shoot straight with either a bow or a gun.

[6]Colonel Reynolds with six companies of cavalry attacked Crazy Horse's village as stated in the early morning of March 16, 1876.

We were a small band, and we started in the night and traveled fast. Before we got to War Bonnet Creek, some Shyelas (Cheyennes) joined us, because their hearts were bad like ours and they were going to the same place. Later I learned that many small bands were doing the same thing and coming together from everywhere.

Just after we camped on the War Bonnet, our scouts saw a wagon train of the Wasichus coming up the old road that caused the trouble before.[1] They had oxen hitched to their wagons and they were part of the river of Wasichus that was running into the Black Hills. They shot at our scouts, and we decided we would attack them. When the war party was getting ready, I made up my mind that, small as I was, I might as well die there, and if I did, maybe I'd be known. I told Jumping Horse, a boy about my age, that I was going along to die, and he said he would too. So we went, and so did Crab and some other boys.

When the Wasichus saw us coming, they put their wagons in a circle and got inside with their oxen. We rode around and around them in a wide circle that kept getting narrower. That is the best way to fight, because it is hard to hit ponies running fast in a circle. And sometimes there would be two circles, one inside the other, going fast in opposite directions, which made us still harder to hit. The cavalry of the Wasichus did not know how to fight. They kept together, and when they came on, you could hardly miss them. We kept apart in the circle. While we were riding around the wagons, we were hanging low on the outside of the ponies and shooting under their necks. This was not easy to do, even when your legs were long, and mine were not yet very long. But I stuck tight and shot with the six-shooter my aunt gave me. Before we started the attack I was afraid, but Big Man told us we were brave boys, and I soon got over being frightened. The Wasichus shot fast at us from behind the wagons, and I could hear bullets whizzing, but they did not hit any of us. I kept thinking of my vision, and maybe that helped. I do not know whether we killed any Wasichus or not. We rode around several times, and once we got close, but there were not many of us and we could not get at the Wasichus behind their wagons; so we went away. This was my first fight. When we were going back to camp, some Shyela warriors told us we were very brave boys, and that we were going to have plenty of fighting.

We were traveling very fast now, for we were in danger and wanted

[1]The Bozeman Trail, closed by the Treaty of 1868.

to get back to Crazy Horse. He had moved over west to the Rosebud River, and the people were gathering there. As we traveled, we met other little bands all going to the same place, until there were a good many of us all mixed up before we got there. Red Cloud's son was with us, but Red Cloud stayed at the Soldiers' Town.

When we came to the ridge on this side of the Rosebud River, we could see the valley full of tepees, and the ponies could not be counted. Many, many people were there—Ogalalas, Hunkpapas, Minneconjous, Sans Arcs, Black Feet, Brules, Santees, and Yanktonais; also many Shyelas and Blue Clouds had come to fight with us. The village was long, and you could not see all the camps with one look. The scouts came out to meet us and bring us in, and everybody rejoiced that we had come. Great men were there: Crazy Horse and Big Road of the Ogalalas; Sitting Bull and Gall and Black Moon and Crow King of the Hunkpapas; Spotted Eagle of the Sans Arcs; the younger Hump and Fast Bull of the Minneconjous; Dull Knife and Ice Bear of the Shyelas; Inkpaduta with the Santees and Yanktonais. Great men were there with all those people and horses. Hetchetu aloh![2]

About the middle of the Moon of Making Fat (June) the whole village moved a little way up the River to a good place for a sun dance. The valley was wide and flat there, and we camped in a great oval with the river flowing through it, and in the center they built the bower of branches in a circle for the dancers, with the opening of it to the east whence comes the light. Scouts were sent out in all directions to guard the sacred place. Sitting Bull, who was the greatest medicine man of the nation at that time, had charge of this dance to purify the people and to give them power and endurance. It was held in the Moon of Fatness because that is the time when the sun is highest and the growing power of the world is strongest. I will tell you how it was done.

First a holy man was sent out all alone to find the waga chun,[3] the holy tree that should stand in the middle of the dancing circle. Nobody dared follow to see what he did or hear the sacred words he would say there. And when he had found the right tree, he would tell the people, and they would come there singing, with flowers all over them. Then when they had gathered about the holy tree, some women who were bearing children would dance around it, because the Spirit of the Sun

[2] It is so indeed.
[3] Rustling tree, cottonwood.

loves all fruitfulness. After that a warrior, who had done some very brave deed that summer, struck the tree, counting coup upon it; and when he had done this, he had to give gifts to those who had least of everything, and the braver he was, the more he gave away.

After this, a band of young maidens came singing, with sharp axes in their hands; and they had to be so good that nobody there could say anything against them, or that any man had ever known them; and it was the duty of any one who knew anything bad about any of them to tell it right before all the people there and prove it. But if anybody lied, it was very bad for him.

The maidens chopped the tree down and trimmed its branches off. Then chiefs, who were the sons of chiefs, carried the sacred tree home, stopping four times on the way, once for each season, giving thanks for each.

Now when the holy tree had been brought home but was not yet set up in the center of the dancing place, mounted warriors gathered around the circle of the village, and at a signal they all charged inward upon the center where the tree would stand, each trying to be the first to touch the sacred place; and whoever was the first could not be killed in war that year. When they all came together in the middle, it was like a battle, with the ponies rearing and screaming in a big dust and the men shouting and wrestling and trying to throw each other off the horses.

After that there was a big feast and plenty for everybody to eat, and a big dance just as though we had won a victory.

The next day the tree was planted in the center by holy men who sang sacred songs and made sacred vows to the Spirit. And the next morning nursing mothers brought their holy little ones to lay them at the bottom of the tree, so that the sons would be brave men and the daughters the mothers of brave men. The holy men pierced the ears of the little ones, and for each piercing the parents gave away a pony to some one who was in need.

The next day the dancing began, and those who were going to take part were ready, for they had been fasting and purifying themselves in the sweat lodges, and praying. First, their bodies were painted by the holy men. Then each would lie down beneath the tree as though he were dead, and the holy men would cut a place in his back or chest, so that a strip of rawhide, fastened to the top of the tree, could be pushed through the flesh and tied. Then the man would get up and

dance to the drums, leaning on the rawhide strip as long as he could stand the pain or until the flesh tore loose.

We smaller boys had a good time during the two days of dancing, for we were allowed to do almost anything to tease the people, and they had to stand it. We would gather sharp spear grass, and when a man came along without a shirt, we would stick him to see if we could make him cry out, for everybody was supposed to endure everything. Also we made pop-guns out of young ash boughs and shot at the men and women to see if we could make them jump; and if they did, everybody laughed at them. The mothers carried water to their holy little ones in bladder bags, and we made little bows and arrows that we could hide under our robes so that we could steal up to the women and shoot holes in the bags. They were supposed to stand anything and not scold us when the water spurted out. We had a good time there.

Right after the sun dance was over, some of our scouts came in from the south, and the crier went around the circle and said: "The scouts have returned and they have reported that soldiers are camping up the river. So, young warriors, take courage and get ready to meet them."

While they were all getting ready, I was getting ready too, because Crazy Horse was going to lead the warriors and I wanted to go with him; but my uncle, who thought a great deal of me, said: "Young nephew, you must not go. Look at the helpless ones. Stay home, and maybe there will be plenty of fighting right here." So the war parties went on without me. Maybe my uncle thought I was too little to do much and might get killed.

Then the crier told us to break camp, and we moved over west towards the Greasy Grass[4] and camped at the head of Spring Creek while the war parties were gone. We learned later that it was Three Stars[5] who fought with our people on the Rosebud that time.[6] He had many walking soldiers and some cavalry, and there were many Crows and Shoshones with him. They were all coming to attack us where we had the sun dance, but Crazy Horse whipped them and they went back to Goose Creek where they had all their wagons. My friend, Iron Hawk, was there that day, and he can tell you how it was.

[4]Little Big Horn.
[5]General Crook.
[6]June 17, 1876.

Iron Hawk Speaks:

I am a Hunkpapa. I was fourteen years old that summer, and I was a big boy. Two war parties went out, a very large one from the south end of the camp, and a small one from the north end. I went with the small one, and there were only about forty of us. The big party got there early in the morning, and when we came, they had been fighting a long while. There is a wide valley there at the bend of the river with some bluffs and hills around it, and it looked as though people were fighting all over that place. There were Crows with the soldiers, and we began fighting with some of them. It looked as though we were getting the best of them. When the soldiers began to advance on the other side of us, and we had to retreat. We were heading for where the big party was, but the soldiers were after us, and the Crows got braver and fought harder because of the soldiers. When we got to the bend, the Crows were right among us, and it was all mixed up fighting there. I don't know whether I killed anybody or not, but I guess I did, for I was scared and fought hard, and the way it was you couldn't keep from killing somebody if you didn't get killed, and I am still alive. There was a Lakota with me by the name of Without-a-Tepee, and a big Crow pulled him right off his horse and he disappeared. Of course, me—I ran for my life, because we could not fight all those Crows and the soldiers too, and I was scared. But I was not running alone. We were all running, with the Crows after us. Then all at once we saw a band of cavalry coming right ahead of us—about thirty of them. I do not know how they got there. Maybe they were returning from a scouting trip. It looked bad for us. Then I heard voices crying in our language: "Take courage! This is a good day to die! Think of the children and the helpless at home!" So we all yelled "Hoka hey!" and charged on the cavalrymen and began shooting them off their horses, for they turned and ran. They were running toward their big party, and I could see many people were fighting over there, but everything was all mixed up, and you could not tell what was happening. It was a pitiful, long-stretched-out battle. They fought all day. Then the Crows were on us from behind, and we turned around and charged back on them. But many soldiers were behind them, coming. So we all had to run, crying "yea-hey" because there were not enough of us. By now I was very scared, and I ran for my life. I came to a rocky place, and my pony stepped between two stones and nearly tore his hoof off. There was a very brave Shyela by the name of Sitting

Eagle. He was a friend of mine and he had been with me in the fight. When I got off my pony to look at his hoof, a single Crow was coming after me. Then I saw my friend, the Shyela, going to meet the Crow. They fought hand-to-hand, and the Crow went down. I wish I had stayed with Sitting Eagle, because then I could have been the first to coup that Crow. But another man did it.

I ran on foot, leading my horse, who was hopping on three legs. Then I saw smoke coming out of a deep gully where there was a creek. I went over to the smoke, and there were three Lakotas who had killed a bison and were having a feast right there while all the fighting was going on over the hill. They invited me, so I sat there and ate, for I was about fourteen years old and I was always hungry. We had to watch out while we ate. One of the men took some clotted blood from the bison and put it in some raw bison hide and fastened it around my pony's hoof so that I could ride.

After we had been eating there a long time, a Lakota came up on his horse with blood and dirt all over his face, and he was angry. He said: "What are you doing here? We're fighting! All you think of is to eat! Why don't you think about the helpless ones at home? Come, make haste! We have got to stand our ground!"

I felt ashamed, so I got on my horse and we started. My horse could go better with his hoof tied up that way. We came to a ridge, and I could see all over the valley of the Rosebud where the fighting was going on. You could not tell who was getting whipped. It looked all mixed up. Some Crows attacked us there and I never got to the big party that was doing the hard fighting, but it was bad enough where I was, except when I was eating. I must have eaten a great deal, for it was evening now. Of course when we got there, they had been fighting a good while already.

We all came away when it was dark, to guard the women and children, and the enemy did not follow us. Of course I thought the Wasichus had whipped us; but I learned it was not so. It was not a finished battle because the night stopped it, but the Wasichus got whipped anyway, and did not attack our village. They went back to their wagons on Goose Creek and stayed there.

Standing Bear Speaks:
I was not in that fight. There were many who were not. The warriors came back in the dark, and everybody was so excited that nobody slept all night.

The next morning, about twenty of us young fellows started out to see where the fight had been. First we saw a dead horse without shoes. Then we saw a dead horse with shoes, and near this one was a soldier full of arrows. We got to where the soldiers had camped after the fight, and there was a place where the ground was fresh and a big fire had been built on it. We started to dig there to see what was hidden. We got down on our hands and knees and dug in the loose ground. After a while we came to a blanket and there was a dead soldier in it, and it was tied around his legs and waist and neck. We pulled him out, and one of the men said: "This is my blanket. I have been looking for this blanket. I will have this blanket." So he took it.

Under that was another dead soldier tied up in a blanket, and then another and another under that. The fourth one was a black Wasichu (Negro). Each time somebody said, "This is my blanket," and took it. I got the fifth one, and the man inside was young, and he had a ring on his finger with a white stone in it that sparkled. I cut off the finger and I had the ring for a long time. One of our men scalped a soldier and started home with the scalp on a stick. When we got on top of the ridge we could see the soldiers of Three Stars retreating toward Goose Creek a long way off. A big dust was rising there. Then we went home.

The village stayed at the head of Spring Creek several days. Then we all broke camp and moved over to the Greasy Grass.

IX

THE RUBBING OUT OF LONG HAIR

Black Elk Continues:

Crazy Horse whipped Three Stars on the Rosebud that day, and I think he could have rubbed the soldiers out there. He could have called

many more warriors from the villages and he could have rubbed the soldiers out at daybreak, for they camped there in the dark after the fight.

He whipped the cavalry of Three Stars when they attacked his village on the Powder that cold morning in the Moon of the Snowblind (March). Then he moved farther west to the Rosebud; and when the soldiers came to kill us there, he whipped them and made them go back. Then he moved farther west to the valley of the Greasy Grass. We were in our own country all the time and we only wanted to be let alone. The soldiers came there to kill us, and many got rubbed out. It was our country and we did not want to have trouble.

We camped there in the valley along the south side of the Greasy Grass before the sun was straight above; and this was, I think, two days before the battle. It was a very big village and you could hardly count the tepees. Farthest up the stream toward the south were the Hunkpapas, and the Ogalalas were next. Then came the Minneconjous, the Sans Arcs, the Blackfeet, the Shyelas; and last, the farthest toward the north, were the Santees and Yanktonais. Along the side towards the east was the Greasy Grass, with some timber along it, and it was running full from the melting of the snow in the Big Horn Mountains. If you stood on a hill you could see the mountains off to the south and west. On the other side of the river, there were bluffs and hills beyond. Some gullies came down through the bluffs. On the westward side of us were lower hills, and there we grazed our ponies and guarded them. There were so many they could not be counted.

There was a man by the name of Rattling Hawk who was shot through the hip in the fight on the Rosebud, and people thought he could not get well. But there was a medicine man by the name of Hairy Chin who cured him.

The day before the battle I had greased myself and was going to swim with some boys, when Hairy Chin called me over to Rattling Hawk's tepee, and told me he wanted me to help him. There were five other boys there, and he needed us for bears in the curing ceremony, because he had his power from a dream of the bear. He painted my body yellow, and my face too, and put a black stripe on either side of my nose from the eyes down. Then he tied my hair up to look like bear's ears, and put some eagle feathers on my head.

While he was doing this, I thought of my vision, and suddenly I seemed to be lifted clear off the ground; and while I was that way, I

knew more things than I could tell, and I felt sure something terrible was going to happen in a short time. I was frightened.

The other boys were painted all red and had real bear's ears on their heads.

Hairy Chin, who wore a real bear skin with the head on it, began to sing a song that went like this:

"At the doorway the sacred herbs are rejoicing."

And while he sang, two girls came in and stood one on either side of the wounded man; one had a cup of water and one some kind of a herb. I tried to see if the cup had all the sky in it, as it was in my vision, but I could not see it. They gave the cup and the herb to Rattling Hawk while Hairy Chin was singing. Then they gave him a red cane, and right away he stood up with it. The girls then started out of the tepee, and the wounded man followed, leaning on the sacred red stick; and we boys, who were the little bears, had to jump around him and make growling noises toward the man. And when we did this, you could see something like feathers of all colors coming out of our mouths. Then Hairy Chin came out on all fours, and he looked just like a bear to me. Then Rattling Hawk began to walk better. He was not able to fight next day, but he got well in a little while.

After the ceremony, we boys went swimming to wash the paint off, and when we got back the people were dancing and having kill talks all over the village, remembering brave deeds done in the fight with Three Stars on the Rosebud.

When it was about sundown we boys had to bring the ponies in close, and when this was done it was dark and the people were still dancing around fires all over the village. We boys went around from one dance to another, until we got too sleepy to stay up any more.

My father 'woke me at daybreak and told me to go with him to take our horses out to graze, and when we were out there he said: "We must have a long rope on one of them, so that it will be easy to catch; then we can get the others. If anything happens, you must bring the horses back as fast as you can, and keep your eyes on the camp."

Several of us boys watched our horses together until the sun was straight above and it was getting very hot. Then we thought we would go swimming, and my cousin said he would stay with our horses till we got back. When I was greasing myself, I did not feel well; I felt queer. It seemed that something terrible was going to happen. But I

went with the boys anyway. Many people were in the water now and many of the women were out west of the village digging turnips. We had been in the water quite a while when my cousin came down there with the horses to give them a drink, for it was very hot now.

Just then we heard the crier shouting in the Hunkpapa camp, which was not very far from us "The chargers are coming! They are charging! The chargers are coming!" Then the crier of the Ogalalas shouted the same words; and we could hear the cry going from camp to camp northward clear to the Santees and Yanktonais.

Everybody was running now to catch the horses. We were lucky to have ours right there just at that time. My older brother had a sorrel, and he rode away fast toward the Hunkpapas. I had a buckskin. My father came running and said: Your brother has gone to the Hunkpapas without his gun. Catch him and give it to him. Then come right back to me." He had my six-shooter too—the one my aunt gave me. I took the guns, jumped on my pony and caught my brother. I could see a big dust rising just beyond the Hunkpapa camp and all the Hunkpapas were running around and yelling, and many were running wet from the river. Then out of the dust came the soldiers on their big horses. They looked big and strong and tall and they were all shooting.[1] My brother took his gun and yelled for me to go back. There was brushy timber just on the other side of the Hunkpapas, and some warriors were gathering there. He made for that place, and I followed him. By now women and children were running in a crowd downstream. I looked back and saw them all running and scattering up a hillside down yonder.

When we got into the timber, a good many Hunkpapas were there already and the soldiers were shooting above us so that leaves were falling from the trees where the bullets struck. By now I could not see what was happening in the village below. It was all dust and cries and thunder; for the women and children were running there, and the warriors were coming on their ponies.

Among us there in the brush and out in the Hunkpapa camp a cry went up: "Take courage! Don't be a woman! The helpless are out of breath!" I think this was when Gall stopped the Hunkpapas, who had been running away, and turned them back.

I stayed there in the woods a little while and thought of my vision. It made me feel stronger, and it seemed that my people were all thunderbeings and that the soldiers would be rubbed out.

[1]This was Reno's detachment attacking from the southern end of the village.

Then another great cry went up out in the dust: "Crazy Horse is coming! Crazy Horse is coming!" Off toward the west and north they were yelling "Hoka hey!" like a big wind roaring, and making the tremolo; and you could hear eagle bone whistles screaming.

The valley went darker with dust and smoke, and there were only shadows and a big noise of many cries and hoofs and guns. On the left of where I was I could hear the shod hoofs of the soldiers' horses going back into the brush and there was shooting everywhere. Then the hoofs came out of the brush, and I came out and was in among men and horses weaving in and out and going upstream, and everybody was yelling, "Hurry! Hurry!" The soldiers were running up stream and we were all mixed there in the twilight and the great noise. I did not see much; but once I saw a Lakota charge at a soldier who stayed behind and fought and was a very brave man.[2] The Lakota took the soldier's horse by the bridle, but the soldier killed him with a six-shooter. I was small and could not crowd in to where the soldiers were, so I did not kill anybody. There were so many ahead of me, and it was all dark and mixed up.

Soon the soldiers were all crowded into the river, and many Lakotas too; and I was in the water awhile. Men and horses were all mixed up and fighting in the water, and it was like hail falling in the river. Then we were out of the river, and people were stripping dead soldiers and putting the clothes on themselves. There was a soldier on the ground and he was still kicking. A Lakota rode up and said to me: "Boy, get off and scalp him." I got off and started to do it. He had short hair and my knife was not very sharp. He ground his teeth. Then I shot him in the forehead and got his scalp.

Many of our warriors were following the soldiers up a hill on the other side of the river. Everybody else was turning back down stream, and on a hill away down yonder above the Santee camp there was a big dust, and our warriors whirling around in and out of it just like swallows, and many guns were going off.[3]

I thought I would show my mother my scalp, so I rode over toward the hill where there was a crowd of women and children. On the way down there I saw a very pretty young woman among a band of warriors about to go up to the battle on the hill, and she was singing like this:

[2]Probably Captain French.
[3]Custer had attacked the camp at the northern end about four miles away.

> "Brothers, now your friends have come!
> Be brave! Be brave!
> Would you see me taken captive?"

When I rode through the Ogalala camp I saw Rattling Hawk sitting up in his tepee with a gun in his hands, and he was all alone there singing a song of regret that went like this:

> "Brothers, what are you doing that I can not do?"

When I got to the women on the hill they were all singing and making the tremolo to cheer the men fighting across the river in the dust on the hill. My mother gave a big tremolo just for me when she saw my first scalp.

I stayed there awhile with my mother and watched the big dust whirling on the hill across the river, and horses were coming out of it with empty saddles.

Standing Bear Speaks:
I am a Minneconjou, and our camp was third from the south. We got up late the morning of the fight. The women went out to dig turnips and two of my uncles went hunting. My grandmother, who was very old and feeble, and one of my uncles and I stayed in a tepee. When the sun was overhead, I went down to the river to swim, and when I came back all I had on was a shirt. My grandmother cooked some meat in the ashes and fed us. While we were eating, my uncle said: "When you have eaten, you must go to the horses right away. Something might happen." An older brother of mine and another man were herding the horses in two bunches on Muskrat Creek down stream below the Santee camp.

Before I finished eating, there was an excitement outside. Then I heard our crier saying that the chargers were coming. When we heard this, my uncle said: "I told you before that something might happen. You'd better go right away and help bring in the horses."

I crossed the Greasy Grass, which was breast deep, and got on top of Black Butte to look. On the other side of the Hunkpapas toward the south, I saw soldiers on horseback spreading out as they came down a slope to the river. They crossed and came on at a trot.[4] I started down the butte, but I was barefoot and there was a big bed of

[4]He saw Reno advancing to the attack about four miles away.

cactus there. I had to go slow, picking my way. A dust cloud was rising up yonder; and then I could see that the Hunkpapas were running, and when I looked over onto the hills toward the south and east I saw other soldiers coming there on horseback.[5] I did not go to the horses. I went down through the cactus as fast as I could and into the village. There were voices all over, and everybody was shouting something and running around. After awhile my older brother came driving our horses, and my uncle said: "Hurry up! We shall go forth!" I caught my gray horse and took my six-shooter and hung my bow and arrows over my shoulder. I had killed a red bird a few days before and I fastened this in my hair. I had made a vow that I would make an offering if this would keep me from getting hurt in the next fight; and it did.

We started and went down stream to the mouth of Muskrat Creek beyond the Santee camp. We were going to meet the second band of soldiers.[6] By the time we got there, they must have been fighting on the hill already, because as we rode up east from the mouth of Muskrat Creek we met a Lakota with blood running out of his mouth and down over his horse's shoulders. His name was Long Elk. There were warriors ahead of us, the "fronters," who are the bravest and have had most practice in war. I was sixteen years old and I was in the rear with the less brave, and we had waited for our horses quite awhile.

Part way up we met another Lakota. He was on foot and he was bleeding and dizzy. He would get up and then he would fall down again. When we got farther up the hill, I could see the soldiers. They were off their horses, holding them by the bridles. They were ready for us and were shooting. Our people were all around the hill on every side by this time. I heard some of our men shouting: "They are gone!" And I saw that many of the soldiers' horses had broken loose and were running away. Everywhere our warriors began yelling: "Hoka hey! Hurry! Hurry!" Then we all went up, and it got dark with dust and smoke. I could see warriors flying all around me like shadows, and the noise of all those hoofs and guns and cries was so loud it seemed quiet in there and the voices seemed to be on top of the cloud. It was like a bad dream. All at once I saw a soldier right beside me, and I leaned over and knocked him down with the butt of the six-shooter. I think I had already shot it empty, but I don't remember

[5]Evidently Custer's detachment, coming to attack at the northern end of the village.
[6]Custer's.

when. The soldier fell off and was under the hoofs. There were so many of us that I think we did not need guns. Just the hoofs would have been enough.

After this we started down the hillside in formation toward the village, and there were dead men and horses scattered along there too. They were all rubbed out.

We were all crazy, and I will tell you something to show how crazy we were. There was a dead Indian lying there on his face, and someone said: "Scalp that Ree!"[7] A man got off and scalped him; and when they turned the dead man over, it was a Shyela—one of our friends. We were all crazy.

We could see the women coming over now in a swarm and they were all making the tremolo. We waited around there awhile, and then we saw soldiers coming on a hill toward the south and east.[8] Everybody began yelling: "Hurry!" And we started for the soldiers. They ran back toward where they came from. One got killed, and many of us got off and couped him. Then we chased all the soldiers back to the hill where they were before.

They had their pack mules and horses on the inside and they had saddles and other things in front of them to hide themselves from bullets, but we surrounded them, and the hill we were on was higher and we could see them plain. We put our horses down under the hills so that they were safe. We all kept shooting at the soldiers and their horses. It was very hot, and there were some soldiers who started down the hill with kettles to get water from the river. They did not get far, and what was left of them went running back up the hill. I heard that some soldiers did get some water later, but I did not see them. Once a Lakota on the other side charged alone right up to the soldiers to show how brave he was, but they killed him, we could not get his body.

By now it was nearly sundown. I had not been feeling hungry because there was the smell of blood everywhere; but now I began to feel hungry anyway. The bravest of the braves got together and talked over what we should do that night. They decided that some of us should go home and eat and bring back something for those who

[7]The Rees were enemies of the Sioux and Custer had Ree scouts with him.

[8]A detachment of Reno's command had set out to help Custer, and the rest of the command followed. They were driven back to the hill to which they had retreated after the disastrous fight in the valley at the southern end of the village.

stayed to watch the soldiers. We could not get at the soldiers, so we were going to starve and dry them out.

I went back home with the others, and it was sundown then. At first I thought they had broken camp, but they had not. They had only gathered all the camps together in one solid village.

I did not go back to the hill with the others that night. We built fires all over the camp, and everybody was excited. I couldn't sleep because when I shut my eyes I could see all those horrible sights again. I think nobody slept.

Next morning early the crier went around and said: "The remainder of the soldiers shall die to-day!" So after we had eaten, we all got ready. This time I was dressed and had my moccasins and leggings on. The day before I had only a shirt. This time I had my saddle too. I was prepared to fight.

We all rode over there, and the party that had watched all night went home. We were scattered all around the soldiers, with our horses under the hill; but it was harder to hit the soldiers now, because they had been digging in the night. The day was very hot, and now and then some soldiers would start crawling down toward the river for a drink. we killed some of these, then the others would run back. Maybe some got water. I do not know. We kept shooting at each other. Once I heard some one cry "Hey-hey!" I crawled over there, and a Lakota had been shot above the eyebrow and he was dead.

After a long while we heard that more soldiers were coming.[9] Then everybody started back home, and there the people were saying: "We will leave this and let it go!"

Then we all broke camp and started for the Big Horn Mountains.

If those soldiers had not come, we would have rubbed them all out on the hill.

Iron Hawk Speaks:

I am a Hunkpapa, and, as I told you before, I was fourteen years old. The sun was overhead and more, but I was eating my first meal that day, because I had been sleeping. While I was eating I heard the crier saying: "The chargers are coming." I jumped up and rushed out to our horses. They were grazing close to camp. I roped one, and the others stampeded, but my older brother had caught his horse already

[9]General Terry was coming up river to the scene of the battle from the mouth of the Little Big Horn.

and headed the others off. When I got on my horse with the rope hitched around his nose, the soldiers were shooting up there and people were running and men and boys were catching their horses that were scared because of the shooting and yelling. I saw little children running up from the river where they had been swimming; and all the women and children were running down the valley.

Our horses stampeded down toward the Minneconjous, but we rounded them up again and brought them back. By now warriors were running toward the soldiers, and getting on the ponies, and many of the Hunkpapas were gathering in the brush and timber near the place where the soldiers had stopped and got off their horses. I rode past a very old man who was shouting: "Boys, take courage! Would you see these little children taken away from me like dogs?"

I went into our tepee and got dressed for war as fast as I could; but I could hear bullets whizzing outside, and I was so shaky that it took me a long time to braid an eagle feather into my hair. Also, I had to hold my pony's rope all the time, and he kept jerking me and trying to get away. While I was doing this, crowds of warriors on horses were roaring by up stream, yelling: "Hoka hey!" Then I rubbed red paint all over my face and took my bow and arrows and got on my horse. I did not have a gun, only a bow and arrows.

When I was on my horse, the fight up stream seemed to be over, because everybody was starting back downstream and yelling: "It's a good day to die!" Soldiers were coming at the other end of the village, and nobody knew how many there were down there.

A man by the name of Little Bear rode up to me on a pinto horse, and he had a very pretty saddle blanket. He said: "Take courage, boy! The earth is all that lasts!" So I rode fast with him and the others downstream, and many of us Hunkpapas gathered on the east side of the river at the foot of a gulch that led back up the hill where the second soldier band[10] was. There was a very brave Shyela with us, and I heard someone say: "He is going!" I looked, and it was this Shyela. He had on a spotted war bonnet and a spotted robe made of some animal's skin and this was fastened with a spotted belt. He was going up the hill alone and we all followed part way. There were soldiers along the ridge up there and they were on foot holding their horses. The Shyela rode right close to them in a circle several times and all the soldiers shot at him. Then he rode back to where we had stopped at

[10]Custer's.

the head of the gulch. He was saying: "Ah, ah!" Someone said: "Shyela friend, what is the matter?" He began undoing his spotted belt, and when he shook it, bullets dropped out. He was very sacred and the soldiers could not hurt him. He was a fine looking man.

We stayed there awhile waiting for something and there was shooting everywhere. Then I heard a voice crying: "Now they are going, they are going!" We looked up and saw the cavalry horses stampeding. These were all gray horses.

I saw Little Bear's horse rear and race up hill toward the soldiers. When he got close, his horse was shot out from under him, and he got up limping because the bullet went through his leg; and he started hobbling back to us with the soldiers shooting at him. His brother-friend, Elk Nation, went up there on his horse and took Little Bear behind him and rode back safe with bullets striking all around him. It was his duty to go to his brother-friend even if he knew he would be killed.

By now a big cry was going up all around the soldiers up there and the warriors were coming from everywhere and it was getting dark with dust and smoke.

We saw soldiers start running down hill right towards us. Nearly all of them were afoot, and I think they were so scared that they didn't know what they were doing. They were making their arms go as though they were running very fast, but they were only walking. Some of them shot their guns in the air. We all yelled "Hoka hey!" and charged toward them, riding all around them in the twilight that had fallen on us.

I met a soldier on horseback, and I let him have it. The arrow went through from side to side under his ribs and it stuck out on both sides. He screamed and took hold of his saddle horn and hung on, wobbling, with his head hanging down. I kept along beside him, and I took my heavy bow and struck him across the back of the neck. He fell from his saddle, and I got off and beat him to death with my bow. I kept on beating him awhile after he was dead, and every time I hit him I said "Hownh!" I was mad, because I was thinking of the women and little children running down there, all scared and out of breath. These Wasichus wanted it, and they came to get it, and we gave it to them. I did not see much more. I saw Brings Plenty kill a soldier with a war club. I saw Red Horn Buffalo fall. There was a Lakota riding along the edge of the gulch, and he was yelling to look out, that there was a

soldier hiding in there. I saw him charge in and kill the soldier and begin slashing him with a knife.

Then we began to go towards the river, and the dust was lifting so that we could see the women and children coming over to us from across the river. The soldiers were all rubbed out there and scattered around.

The women swarmed up the hill and began stripping the soldiers. They were yelling and laughing and singing now. I saw something funny. Two fat old women were stripping a soldier, who was wounded and playing dead. When they had him naked, they began to cut something off that he had, and he jumped up and began fighting with the two fat women. He was swinging one of them around, while the other was trying to stab him with her knife. After awhile, another woman rushed up and shoved her knife into him and he died really dead. It was funny to see the naked Wasichu fighting with the fat women.

By now we saw that our warriors were all charging on some soldiers that had come from the hill up river to help the second band that we had rubbed out. They ran back and we followed, chasing them up on their hill again where they had their pack mules. We could not hurt them much there, because they had been digging to hide themselves and they were lying behind saddles and other things. I was down by the river and I saw some soldiers come down there with buckets. They had no guns, just buckets. Some boys were down there, and they came out of the brush and threw mud and rocks in the soldiers' faces and chased them into the river. I guess they got enough to drink, for they are drinking yet. We killed them in the water.

Afterwhile it was nearly sundown, and I went home with many others to eat, while some others stayed to watch the soldiers on the hill. I hadn't eaten all day, because the trouble started just when I was beginning to eat my first meal.

Black Elk continues:

After I showed my mother my first scalp, I stayed with the women awhile and they were all singing and making the tremolo. We could not see much of the battle for the big dust, but we knew there would be no soldiers left. There were many other boys about my age and younger up there with their mothers and sisters, and they asked me to go over to the battle with them. So we got on our ponies and started. While we were riding down hill toward the river we saw gray horses

with empty saddles stampeding toward the water. We rode over across the Greasy Grass to the mouth of a gulch that led up through the bluff to where the fighting was.

Before we got there, the Wasichus were all down, and most of them were dead, but some of them were still alive and kicking. Many other little boys had come up by this time, and we rode around shooting arrows into the Wasichus. There was one who was squirming around with arrows sticking in him, and I started to take his coat, but a man pushed me away and took the coat for himself. Then I saw something bright hanging on this soldier's belt, and I pulled it out. It was round and bright and yellow and very beautiful and I put it on me for a necklace. At first it ticked inside, and then it did not any more. I wore it around my neck a long time before I found out what it was and how to make it tick again.

Then the women all came over and we went to the top of the hill. Gray horses were lying dead there, and some of them were on top of dead Wasichus and dead Wasichus were on top of them. There were not many of our own dead there, because they had been picked up already; but many of our men were killed and wounded. They shot each other in the dust. I did not see Pahuska,[11] and I think nobody knew which one he was. There was a soldier who was raising his arms and groaning. I shot an arrow into his forehead, and his arms and legs quivered. I saw some Lakotas holding another Lakota up. I went over there, and it was Chase-in-the-Morning's brother, who was called Black Wasichu. He had been shot through the right shoulder downward, and the bullet stopped in his left hip, because he was hanging on the side of his horse when he was hit. They were trying to give him some medicine. He was my cousin, and his father and my father were so angry over this, that they went and butchered a Wasichu and cut him open. The Wasichu was fat, and his meat looked good to eat, but we did not eat any.

There was a little boy, younger than I was, who asked me to scalp a soldier for him. I did, and he ran to show the scalp to his mother. While we were there, most of the warriors chased the other soldiers back to the hill where they had their pack mules. After awhile I got tired looking around. I could smell nothing but blood, and I got sick of it. So I went back home with some others. I was not sorry at all. I was a happy boy. Those Wasichus had come to kill our mothers and

[11]Custer.

fathers and us, and it was our country. When I was in the brush up there by the Hunkpapas, and the first soldiers were shooting, I knew this would happen. I thought that my people were relatives to the thunder beings of my vision, and that the soldiers were very foolish to do this.

Everybody was up all night in the village. Next morning another war party went up to the hill where the other soldiers were, and the men who had been watching there all night came home. My mother and I went along. She rode a mare with a little colt tied beside her and it trotted along with its mother.

We could see the horses and pack mules up there, but the soldiers were dug in. Beneath the hill, right on the west side of the Greasy Grass, were some bullberry bushes, and there was a big boy by the name of Round Fool who was running around the bushes. We boys asked him what he was doing that for, and he said: "There is a Wasichu in that bush." And there was. He had hidden there when the other soldiers ran to the hill-top and he had been there all night. We boys began shooting at him with arrows, and it was like chasing a rabbit. He would crawl from one side to the other while we were running around the bush shooting at him with our bows. Once he yelled "Ow." After awhile we set fire to the grass around the bushes, and he came out running. Some of our warriors killed him.

Once we went up the back of the hill, where some of our men were, and looked over. We could not see the Wasichus, who were lying in their dug-ins, but we saw the horses and pack mules, and many of them were dead. When we came down and crossed the river again, some soldiers shot at us and hit the water. Mother and I galloped back to the camp, and it was about sundown. By then our scouts had reported that more soldiers were coming up stream; so we all broke camp. Before dark we were ready and we started up the Greasy Grass, heading for Wood Louse Creek in the Big Horn Mountains. We fled all night, following the Greasy Grass. My two younger brothers and I rode in a pony-drag, and my mother put some young pups in with us. They were always trying to crawl out and I was always putting them back in, so I didn't sleep much.

By morning we reached a little dry creek and made camp and had a big feast. The meat had spots of fat in it, and I wish I had some of it right now.

When it was full day, we started again and came to Wood Louse Creek at the foot of the mountains, and camped there. A badly

wounded man by the name of Three Bears had fits there, and he would keep saying: "Jeneny, jeneny." I do not know what he meant. He died, and we used to call that place the camp where Jeneny died.

That evening everybody got excited and began shouting: "The soldiers are coming!" I looked, and there they were, riding abreast right toward us. But it was some of our own men dressed in the soldiers' clothes. They were doing this for fun.

The scouts reported that the soldiers had not followed us and that everything was safe now. All over the camp there were big fires and kill dances all night long.

I will sing you some of the kill-songs that our people made up and sang that night. Some of them went like this:

"Long Hair has never returned,
So his woman is crying, crying.
Looking over here, she cries."

* * * * *

"Long Hair, guns I had none.
You brought me many. I thank you!
You make me laugh!"

* * * * *

"Long Hair, horses I had none.
You brought me many. I thank you!
You make me laugh!"

* * * * *

"Long Hair, where he lies nobody knows.
Crying, they seek him.
He lies over here."

* * * * *

"Let go your holy irons (guns).
You are not men enough to do any harm.
Let go your holy irons!"

After awhile I got so tired dancing that I went to sleep on the ground right where I was.

My cousin, Black Wasichu, died that night.

X

WALKING THE BLACK ROAD

We stayed in that country near the Big Horn Mountains for about a moon, maybe a little more. My father told me all the fighting had not done any good, because the Hang-Around-the-Fort people were getting ready to sell the Black Hills to the Wasichu anyway, and that more soldiers were coming to fight us. He said that Three Stars was on Goose Creek and that many other soldiers were up on the Yellowstone, and that these would come together and have us between them.

Some of our people had been leaving us, a few at a time, and going in to live at the agencies the Wasichus had made. But there were many of us left, and so we started with all our ponies to get away from the soldiers.

We traveled in a very long line down the Rosebud and camped where the river flows through between high bluffs. Then we moved on down stream to where we had the big sun dance before the rubbing out of Long Hair. The soldiers had come through that way, and the holy place was all cut up with shod hoofs and made dirty with horse droppings. Then we moved on down stream to a sacred place where there is a big rock bluff right beside the water, and high up on this bluff pictures used to appear, foretelling something important that was going to happen soon. There was a picture on it then, of many soldiers hanging head downward; and the people said it was there before the rubbing out of Long Hair. I do not know; but it was there then, and it did not seem that anybody could get up that high to make a picture.

We moved over to the Tongue River and camped a little while. When

we were there, scouts came in and said that a big fire-boat[1] had come up the Yellowstone with a load of corn for the soldiers' horses, and that it was piled on the other side of the river. Some of our young men went to see, and one of them, Yellow Shirt, got killed by the fireboat's soldiers over there. But the others brought corn home and they gave us some. We parched it, and it was good.

About this time, in the Moon of Black Cherries (August), the scattering of the people began, because by now we learned that the soldiers were coming again. Dull Knife and the Shyelas went over to Willow Creek in the Big Horn Mountains. Many of the Lakotas stole away in small parties and started for the agencies. The rest of us, still a great many, started east, and the soldiers of Three Stars followed us. Our people set fire to the grass behind us as we went, and the smoke back there was wide as the day and the light of the fire was wide as the night. This was to make the soldiers' horses starve.

Then it began to rain, and it kept on raining for days while we traveled east. Our ponies had to work hard in the deep mud, and it must have been bad for the soldiers' horses back there with nothing to eat.

Sitting Bull and Gall with some people left us and started for Grandmother's Land (Canada), and other people were going away from us all the time, but Crazy Horse would not leave the country that was ours.

In the Moon of the Black Calf (September) we were camping near the head of the Grand River when American Horse with many tepees had a fight with the soldiers of Three Stars by the Slim Buttes on Rabbit Creek.[2] They fought hard there in the rain, and the soldiers killed American Horse and chased the women and children out of their homes and took all the papa (dried bison meat) that they had made to feed themselves that winter. Then Crazy Horse went over there with a band of our warriors and chased the soldiers through the rain. They fled southward toward the Black Hills, and many of their horses died in the deep mud. He followed them a long way and made them fight as they fled.

Wherever we went, the soldiers came to kill us, and it was all our own country. It was ours already when the Wasichus made the treaty with Red Cloud, that said it would be ours as long as grass should

[1]Steamboat.
[2]The Battle of Slim Buttes, September 9, 1876.

grow and water flow. That was only eight winters before, and they were chasing us now because we remembered and they forgot.

After that we started west again, and we were not happy anymore, because so many of our people had untied their horses' tails[3] and gone over to the Wasichus. We went back deep into our country, and most of the land was black from the fire, and the bison had gone away. We camped on the Tongue River where there was some cottonwood for the ponies; and a hard winter came on early. It snowed much; game was hard to find, and it was a hungry time for us. Ponies died, and we ate them. They died because the snow froze hard and they could not find the grass that was left in the valleys and there was not enough cottonwood to feed them all. There had been thousands of us together that summer, but there were not two thousand now.

News came to us there in the Moon of the Falling Leaves (November) that the Black Hills had been sold to the Wasichus and also all the country west of the Hills—the country we were in then.[4] I learned when I was older that our people did not want to do this. The Wasichus went to some of the chiefs alone and got them to put their marks on the treaty. Maybe some of them did this when they were crazy from drinking the minne wakan (holy water, whiskey) the Wasichus gave them. I have heard this; I do not know. But only crazy or very foolish men would sell their Mother Earth. Sometimes I think it might have been better if we had stayed together and made them kill us all.

Dull Knife was camping with his band of Shyelas on Willow Creek in the edge of the Big Horn Mountains, and one morning very early near the end of the Moon of Falling Leaves the soldiers came there to kill them.[5] The people were all sleeping. The snow was deep and it was very cold. When the soldiers began shooting into the tepees, the people ran out into the snow, and most of them were naked from their sleeping robes. Men fought in the snow and cold with nothing on them but their cartridge belts, and it was a hard fight, because the warriors thought of the women and children freezing. They could not whip the soldiers, but those who were not killed and did not die from the cold, got away and came to our camp on the Tongue.

I can remember when Dull Knife came with what was left of his

[3]Left the war-path.
[4]The treaty was signed in October, 1876.
[5]Colonel Mackenzie attacked the Cheyenne village as stated on November 26, 1876.

starving and freezing people. They had almost nothing, and some of them had died on the way. Many little babies died. We could give them clothing, but of food we could not give them much, for we were eating ponies when they died. And afterwhile they left us and started for the Soldiers' Town on White River to surrender to the Wasichus; and so we were all alone there in that country that was ours and had been stolen from us.

After that the people noticed that Crazy Horse was queerer than ever. He hardly ever stayed in the camp. People would find him out alone in the cold, and they would ask him to come home with them. He would not come, but sometimes he would tell the people what to do. People wondered if he ate anything at all. Once my father found him out alone like that, and he said to my father: "Uncle, you have noticed me the way I act. But do not worry; there are caves and holes for me to live in, and out here the spirits may help me. I am making plans for the good of my people."

He was always a queer man, but that winter he was queerer than ever. Maybe he had seen that he would soon be dead and was thinking how to help us when he would not be with us any more.

It was a very bad winter for us and we were all sad. Then another trouble came. We had sent out scouts to learn where the soldiers were, and they were camping at the mouth of the Tongue. Early in the Moon of Frost in the Tepee (January), some of our scouts came in and said that the soldiers were coming up the Tongue to fight us, and that they had two wagon guns (cannon) with them.

There was no better place to go, so we got ready to fight them; and I was afraid, because my father told me we had not much ammunition left. We moved the village a little way off up stream, and our warriors were ready on a high bluff when the walking soldiers and their wagons came in the morning.[6] The soldiers built fires and ate their breakfast there in the valley while our people watched them and were hungry. Then they began shooting with the wagon guns that shot twice, because the iron balls went off after they fell. Some of them did not go off, and we boys ran after one of these and got it.

Then the walking soldiers started up the bluff, and it began to snow hard and they fought in the blizzard. We could not stop the soldiers coming up, because we had not much ammunition. The soldiers had

[6]General Miles attacked the village of Crazy Horse on the Tongue River, January 8, 1876.

everything. But our men used spears and guns for clubs when the soldiers got there, and they fought hand to hand awhile, holding the soldiers back until the women could break camp and get away with the children and ponies. We fled in the blizzard southward up the Tongue and over to the Little Powder River. The soldiers followed us awhile, and there was fighting in our rear. We got away, but we lost many things we needed, and when we camped on the Little Powder, we were almost as poor as Dull Knife's people were the day they came to us. It was so cold that the sun made himself fires, and we were eating our starving ponies.

Late in the Moon of the Dark Red Calf (February) or early in the Moon of the Snowblind (March), Spotted Tail, the Brule, with some others, came to us. His sister was Crazy Horse's mother. He was a great chief and a great warrior before he went over to the Wasichus. I saw him and I did not like him. He was fat with Wasichu food and we were lean with famine. My father told me that he came to make his nephew surrender to the soldiers, because our own people had turned against us, and in the spring when the grass was high enough for the horses, many soldiers would come and fight us, and many Shoshones and Crows and even Lakotas and our old friends, the Shyelas, would come against us with the Wasichus. I could not understand this, and I thought much about it. How could men get fat by being bad, and starve by being good? I thought and thought about my vision, and it made me very sad; for I wondered if maybe it was only a queer dream after all.

And then I heard that we would all go into the Soldiers' Town when the grass should appear, and that Crazy Horse had untied his pony's tail and would not fight again.

In the Moon of the Grass Appearing (April) our little band started for the Soldiers' Town ahead of the others, and it was early in the Moon When the Ponies Shed (May) that Crazy Horse came in with the rest of our people and the ponies that were only skin and bones. There were soldiers and Lakota policemen in lines all around him when he surrendered there at the Soldiers' Town. I saw him take off his war bonnet. I was not near enough to hear what he said. He did not talk loud and he said only a few words, and then he sat down.

I was fourteen years old. We had enough to eat now and we boys could play without being afraid of anything. Soldiers watched us, and sometimes my father and mother talked about our people who had

gone to Grandmother's Land with Sitting Bull and Gall, and they wanted to be there. We were camped near Red Cloud's Agency, which was close to the Soldiers' Town. What happened that summer is not a story.

XI

THE KILLING OF CRAZY HORSE

One night early in the Moon When the Calf Grows Hair (September) we broke camp there at Red Cloud Agency without making any noise, and started. My father told me we were going to Spotted Tail's camp, but he did not tell me why until later. We traveled most of the night and then we camped.

But when we were moving again next day, a band of Red Cloud's people overtook us and said there would be bad trouble if we did not come back right away. Some of us turned around then and went back, and soldiers sent the others back a little later; but Crazy Horse went on to his uncle's camp.

After what happened my father told me why Crazy Horse had done this. He was afraid somebody might start trouble down there where all the soldiers were, and the Wasichus had taken our guns away from us, so that we could do nothing if there was bad trouble. The Wasichus had made Spotted Tail head chief of all the Lakotas because he would do what they wanted, and Crazy Horse thought we might be safer there with his uncle. Afterwards, the Hang-Around-the-Fort people said that he was getting ready to tie up his horse's tail again and make war on the Wasichus. How could he do that when we had no guns and could not get any? It was a story the Wasichus told, and their tongues were forked when they told it. Our people believe they did what they did because he was a great man and they could not kill him in battle and he would not make himself over into a Wasichu, as Spotted Tail

and the others did. That summer, my father told me, the Wasichus wanted him to go to Washington with Red Cloud and Spotted Tail and others to see the Great Father there; but he would not go. He told them that he did not need to go looking for his Great Father. He said: "My Father is with me, and there is no Great Father between me and the Great Spirit."

In the evening of the next day after we got back to Red Cloud's Agency, some soldiers came there bringing Crazy Horse with them. He was riding his horse alone a little way ahead. They did not stay there long, but rode on over to the Soldiers' Town, and my father and I went along with many others to see what they were going to do.

When we got over there we could not see Crazy Horse, because there were soldiers and Lakota policemen all around where he was and people crowding outside.

In just a little while I could feel that something very bad was happening in there, and everybody was excited all at once, and you could hear voices buzzing all around. Then I heard a loud cry in our own language, and it said: "Don't touch me! I am Crazy Horse!" And suddenly something went through all the people there like a big wind that strikes many trees all at once. Somebody in there yelled something else, but everybody around me was asking or telling everybody what had happened, and I heard that Crazy Horse was killed, that he was sick, that he was hurt; and I was frightened, because everything felt the way it did that day when we were going up to kill on the Greasy Grass, and it seemed we might all begin fighting right away.

Then everything got quiet, and everybody seemed to be waiting for something. Then the people began to break up and move around, and I heard that Crazy Horse had just taken sick and maybe he would be all right soon.

But it was not long until we all knew what had happened in there, because some of the people saw it happen, and I will tell you how it was.

They told Crazy Horse they would not harm him if he would go to the Soldiers' Town and have a talk with the Wasichu chief there. But they lied. They did not take him to the chief for a talk. They took him to the little prison with iron bars on the windows, for they had planned to get rid of him. And when he saw what they were doing, he turned around and took a knife out of his robe and started out against all those soldiers. Then Little Big Man, who had been his friend and was the one who told us boys that we were brave before my first fight

when we attacked the wagons on War Bonnet Creek, took hold of Crazy Horse from behind and tried to get the knife away. And while they were struggling, a soldier ran a bayonet into Crazy Horse from one side at the back and he fell down and began to die. Then they picked him up and carried him into the soldier chief's office. The soldiers stood all around there and would not let anybody in and made the people go away. My father and I went back to our camp at Red Cloud Agency.

That night I heard mourning somewhere, and then there was more and more mourning, until it was all over the camp.

Crazy Horse was dead. He was brave and good and wise. He never wanted anything but to save his people, and he fought the Wasichus only when they came to kill us in our own country. He was only thirty years old. They could not kill him in battle. They had to lie to him and kill him that way.

I cried all night, and so did my father.

When it was day, Crazy Horse's father and mother brought him over to our camp in a wagon. Then they put him in a box, and I heard that they had to cut him in two because the box was not long enough. They fastened the box on a pony drag and went away alone toward the east and north. I saw the two old people going away alone with their son's body. Nobody followed them. They went all alone, and I can see them going yet. The horse that pulled the pony drag was a buckskin. Crazy Horse's father had a white-faced bay with white hind legs. His mother had a brown mare with a bay colt.

The old people never would tell where they took the body of their son. Nobody knows to-day where he lies, for the old people are dead too. Many have talked about the place, and some have said they knew where it was and would not tell, and many think it is somewhere on Bear Creek in the Badlands. I know one thing, and this is it. The old people came with the body right down Pepper Creek which is just a little way south across the hill from where we are.[1] There were two hunters who were hunting along the creek there and they saw two old people coming with a pony drag, and when they told my father about this, they said a buckskin was pulling the drag that had a box on it; that the old man rode a white-faced bay with white hind legs and the old woman rode a brown mare with a bay colt. These hunters saw the

[1]Black Elk's log cabin is situated about two miles west of Manderson Post Office, Pine Ridge Reservation, South Dakota.

old people coming down Pepper Creek, and later on they saw the old people again on White Horse Creek which is just a little way down Pepper Creek from where they were before. And the hunters said the box was not on the drag any more. So I think that maybe they hid the body somewhere on Pepper Creek over there because the hunters had seen them, and maybe they went back again at night and took the box away into the Badlands. But Crazy Horse might be lying over there just a little way from us right now on Pepper Creek across that hill yonder. I do not know.

It does not matter where his body lies, for it is grass; but where his spirit is, it will be good to be.

XII

GRANDMOTHER'S LAND

At the end of the Moon of Falling Leaves (October), after they had killed Crazy Horse, the Wasichus told us we must move from where we were over to the Missouri River and live there at different agencies they had made for us. One big band started with Red Cloud, and we started with another big band under Spotted Tail. These two bands were about a day's travel apart.

Our people were all sad because Crazy Horse was dead, and now they were going to pen us up in little islands and make us be like Wasichus. So before we had gone very far, some of us broke away and started for the country where we used to be happy. We traveled fast, and the soldiers did not follow us. But when our little band came to the Powder River country, it was not like it used to be, and we were not ready for the winter. So we kept on traveling north, and we went fast, because we wanted to be with our relatives under Sitting Bull and Gall in Grandmother's Land.[1]

[1]Canada.

It was very cold before we reached Clay Creek where our relatives were; but they were glad to see us and took care of us. They had made plenty of meat, for there were many bison in that country; and it was a good winter. The soldiers could not come to kill us there.

I was fifteen years old that winter, and I thought much of my vision and wondered when my duty was to come; for the Grandfathers had shown me my people walking on the black road and how the nation's hoop would be broken and the flowering tree be withered, before I should bring the hoop together with the power that was given me, and make the holy tree to flower in the center and find the red road again. Part of this had happened already, and I wondered when my power would grow, so that the rest might be as I had seen it in my vision. But I could say nothing about this to anyone, because I was only a boy and people would think I was foolish and say: "What can you do if even Sitting Bull can do nothing?"

When the grasses appeared again we went bison hunting, and I was big enough now to hunt with the men. My uncle, Running Horse, and I were out together alone one day. I was riding a bay and leading my roan, which was very fast. My uncle was riding a roan and leading a brown horse. We came to Little River Creek and crossed it, and just then I began feeling queer and I knew something was going to happen. So I said to my uncle: "I have a queer feeling and I think something is going to happen soon. I will watch while you kill a bison and we will make quick work of it and go." He looked at me in a strange way awhile. Then he said "How" and started after a bison. There were several grazing in the valley. I held my horses and watched. When he had killed a fat cow, I went to help him butcher, but I held my horses while I was doing this, for I still had the queer feeling. Then I heard a voice that said: "Go at once and look!" I told Running Horse I would go to the top of the hill and see what was there. So I rode up and I saw two Lakota hunters galloping after a bison across a valley toward some bluffs. Just after they went out of sight behind a bluff, my horse began to prick up his ears and look around and sniff the air. Then I heard some fast shooting over there, then many horses' hoofs. Then I saw a band of about fifty horsebacks coming out from behind the bluff where the two hunters had disappeared. They were Crows, and afterwards we learned that they had killed the two hunters.

So my uncle and I took as much meat as we could and rode fast back to our village and told the others.

This showed that my power was growing, and I was glad.

In the Moon of Making Fat (June), Sitting Bull and Gall had a sun dance at Forest Butte, and afterwards we went hunting again. A man by the name of Iron Tail was with me this time, and we were out alone. I killed a big fat bison cow and we were butchering, when a thunder storm was coming up. Then it began to pour rain, and I heard a voice in the clouds that said: "Make haste! Before the day is out something will happen!"

Of course when I heard this I was excited and told Iron Tail I had heard a voice in the clouds and that we must hurry up and go. We left everything but the fat of the cow, and fled. When we got to the camp of our little band, we were excited and told the people we must flee. So they broke camp and started. We came to Muddy Creek. It was still raining hard and we had trouble getting across because the horses sank in the mud. A part of us got across, but there was an old man with an old woman and a beautiful daughter whose pony-drag got stuck in the middle of the creek. Just then a big band of Crows came charging, and there were so many of them that we could not hold them off and we had to flee, shooting back at them as they came after us.

There was a man called Brave Wolf who did a very great deed there by the ford that day. He was close to the pony-drag of the two old people and the beautiful girl when it got stuck in the mud, so he jumped off his horse, which was a very fast bison-runner, and made the beautiful girl get on. Then he stood there by the two old people and fought until all three were killed. The girl got away on his fast horse. My cousin, Hard-to-Hit, did a brave deed too, and died. He charged back alone at a Crow who was shooting at a Lakota in a bush, and he was killed.

The voice in the clouds had told the truth, and it seemed that my power was growing stronger all the time.

When my cousin, Hard-to-Hit, was killed, it was my duty to protect his wife, so I did; and we got lost from our little party in the dark. It rained all night, and my cousin's wife cried so hard that I had to make her quit for fear some enemy might hear her and find us.

When we reached the big camp in the morning my relatives began mourning for my cousin, Hard-to-Hit. They would put their arms across each other's shoulders and wail. They did this all day long, and I had to do it too. I went around crying, "hownh, hownh," and saying over and over: "My cousin—he thought so much of me and I thought so much of him, and now he is dead. Hownh, hownh." I

liked my cousin well enough, but I did not feel like crying all day. This was what I had to do, and it was hard work.

We stayed on Clay Creek in Grandmother's Land all that summer and the next winter when I was sixteen years old. That was a very cold winter. There were many blizzards, game was hard to find, and afterwhile the papa (dried meat) that we had made in the summer was all eaten. It looked as though we might starve to death if we did not find some game soon, and everybody was downhearted. Little hunting parties went out in different directions, but it is bad hunting in blizzard weather. My father and I started out alone leading our horses in the deep snow. When we got to Little River Creek we made a shelter with our bison robes against a bank of the stream and started a fire. That evening I saw a rabbit in a hollow tree, and when I chopped the tree down there were four rabbits in there. I killed them all, because the snow was so deep they could not get away. My father and I roasted them and we ate all four of them before we went to sleep, because it was hard walking in the snow and we had been empty a good while.

The wind went down that night and it was still and very cold. While I was lying there in a bison robe, a coyote began to howl not far off, and suddenly I knew it was saying something. It was not making words, but it said something plainer than words, and this was it: "Two-legged one, on the big ridge west of you there are bison; but first you shall see two more two-leggeds over there."

My father had dozed off, so I wakened him and said: "Father, I have heard a coyote say that there are bison on the big ridge west of us, and that we shall first see two people over there. Let us get up early."

By this time my father had noticed that I had some kind of queer power, and he believed me. The wind came up again with the daylight, and we could see only a little way ahead when we started west in the morning. Before we came to the ridge, we saw two horses, dim in the blowing snow beside some bushes. They were huddled up with their tails to the wind and their heads hanging low. When we came closer, there was a bison robe shelter in the brush, and in it were an old man and a boy, very cold and hungry and discouraged. They were Lakotas and were glad to see us, but they were feeling weak, because they had been out two days and had seen nothing but snow. We camped there with them in the brush, and then we went up on the ridge afoot. There was much timber up there. We got behind the hill in a sheltered place and waited, but we could see nothing. While we were waiting, we

talked about the people starving at home, and we were all sad. Now and then the snow haze would open up for a little bit and you could see quite a distance, then it would close again. While we were talking about our hungry people, suddenly the snow haze opened a little, and we saw a shaggy bull's head coming out of the blowing snow up the draw that led past us below. Then seven more appeared, and the snow haze came back and shut us in there. They could not see us, and they were drifting with the wind so that they could not smell us.

We four stood up and made vows to the four quarters of the world, saying: "Haho! haho!" Then we got our horses from the brush on the other side of the ridge and came around to the mouth of the draw where the bison would pass as they drifted with the wind.

The two old men were to shoot first and then we two boys would follow the others horseback. Soon we saw the bison coming. The old people crept up and shot, but they were so cold, and maybe excited, that they got only one bison. They cried "Hoka!" and we boys charged after the other bison. The snow was blowing hard in the wind that sucked down the draw, and when we came near them the bison were so excited that they backtracked and charged right past us bellowing. This broke the deep snow for our horses and it was easier to catch them. Suddenly I saw the bison I was chasing go out in a big flurry of snow, and I knew they had plunged into a snow-filled gulch, but it was too late to stop, and my horse plunged right in after them. There we were all together—four bison, my horse and I all floundering and kicking, but I managed to crawl out a little way. I had a repeating rifle that they gave me back at the camp, and I killed the four bison right there, but I had thrown my mittens away and the gun froze to my hands while I was shooting, so that I had to tear the skin to get it loose.

When I went back to the others, the other boy had killed three, so we had eight bison scattered around there in the snow. It was still morning, but it took till nearly dark for my father and the other old man to do the butchering. I could not help, because my hands were frozen. We finally got the meat all piled up in one place, and then we made a camp in a fine shelter behind a big rock with brush all around it and plenty of wood. We had a big fire, and we tied our tanned robes on our horses and fed them plenty of cottonwood bark from the woods by the stream. The raw robes we used for the shelter. Then we had a big feast and we sang and were very happy.

The wind went down and it grew very cold, so we had to keep the

fire going all night. During the night I heard a whimpering outside the shelter, and when I looked, there was a party of porcupines huddled up as close as they thought they dared to be, and they were crying because they were so cold. We did not chase them away, because we felt sorry for them.

We started afoot for camp next day with as much meat loaded on the horses as they could carry. The rest of it we cached by a big tree where it would be easy to find. We traveled all that day very slowly because the snow was deep, and all the while it seemed to be growing colder. At about sundown of the second day we reached camp, and the people were glad to see us with all that meat. Some other men went back later to bring in the meat we had cached.

The morning after we reached home I went out to look for our horses that were in a draw where there was cottonwood, and five of them had frozen to death. The cold was very bad after the wind stopped blowing.

We began to feel homesick for our own country where we used to be happy. The old people talked much about it and the good days before the trouble came. Sometimes I felt like crying when they did that.

XIII

THE COMPELLING FEAR

When the grasses were showing their tender faces again, two families of us started for our own country where we used to be happy. We had only five horses among us, because all the others had died in the cold, and we traveled on foot. It was a very rainy time. After awhile we came to All-Gone-Tree Creek. We came there in the afternoon and camped, and I thought I would take the horses out to eat where the grass was good. But when I had gone only a little way, all of a sudden

the queer feeling came again, and I heard a voice that said: "Be careful and watch! Something you shall see!" The voice was so clear that I looked around to see who was there, and nobody was there. So I staked the horses right there not far from the camp, and sat down to think about it. There was a tall bluff a little way from the camp, and it had two points on it. So I went over there and climbed to one of the tops where there were some big rocks scattered around. I lay down in those rocks and looked all around, but I could see nothing, and I began to wonder if I was only queer in thinking I had heard a voice.

Then I looked over to the other point of the bluff not far away, and there were two men crawling up toward the top on their bellies. I knew they were enemies, and I thought they were Crows; but later I learned that they were Blackfeet. I lay as flat as I could and peeped around a rock at the two men. They were so near that I could have thrown a rock over there, and I thought if I only had my gun I could kill them both. They stopped near the top, and one crawled a little farther and peeped over at our tepees in the valley where the women were having a hard time to get the fires started with wet wood. Then the first one motioned to the second, and they both looked over. I could hear them talking now, and I knew they were planning how to attack us. After a little while they crawled down backwards a short way, then got up and ran downhill and disappeared. When they were gone, I crawled to the other side of the bluff and went down. When I reached the bottom, I sat down and thought of my vision and began to pray to the spirits. I said: "Grandfathers, something may happen to me. But I will depend on the power you have given me. Hear me and help me!" Then I ran over to our tepees and told the people we must flee at once, because I had seen enemies planning to attack.

We were so small a party that we did not dare wait to take our tepees down, so we started right away and traveled very fast. We had to cross All-Gone-Tree Creek and it was bank-full and roaring with the big rains. So two of us boys swam across with rawhide ropes, which the old women fastened around them under their arms, and we pulled them across through the deep water. They nearly drowned before we could drag them out, because the water was swift. Our horses swam across, and we went fast, with the old people on the horses.

As we fled east, a thunder cloud came from the west behind us, and I knew it was coming to protect us. I could hear the thunder beings crying "Hey hey!" to me. The cloud stood over us and did not rain much, but it was full of lightning and of voices.

We had not gone so very far, and it was growing dark, when we heard shooting behind us in the direction of our deserted camp, and we thought the enemies were shooting into the tepees, thinking that we might be in there yet.

It grew very dark, for the thunder cloud with the many voices hung over us, and we traveled fast all night. Then after awhile the cloud broke, and it was daybreak. We camped to eat and sleep.

I knew better than ever now that I really had power, for I had prayed for help from the Grandfathers and they had heard me and sent the thunder beings to hide us and watch over us while we fled.

When we had eaten and slept, we started again and came to a camp of Minneconjous. After that we traveled with our relatives to the mouth of the Poplar River and crossed over the Missouri on a fire-boat that was there. Then after we had hunted awhile, we went to the Soldiers' Town at the mouth of Tongue River and camped there with others of our people who had wandered away from the reservations into our old country.

The soldiers took our guns away from us and most of our horses, leaving us only two horses for every tepee.

There in the Moon of Making Fat we had a sun dance, and after this it seemed I could think of nothing but my vision. I was sixteen years old and more, and I had not yet done anything the Grandfathers wanted me to do, but they had been helping me. I did not know how to do what they wanted me to do.

A terrible time began for me then, and I could not tell anybody, not even my father and mother. I was afraid to see a cloud coming up; and whenever one did, I could hear the thunder beings calling to me: "Behold your Grandfathers! Make haste!" I could understand the birds when they sang, and they were always saying: "It is time! It is time!" The crows in the day and the coyotes at night all called and called to me: "It is time! It is time! It is time!"

Time to do what? I did not know. Whenever I awoke before daybreak and went out of the tepee because I was afraid of the stillness when everyone was sleeping, there were many low voices talking together in the east, and the daybreak star would sing this song in the silence:

> "In a sacred manner you shall walk!
> Your nation shall behold you!"

I could not get along with people now, and I would take my horse and go far out from camp alone and compare everything on the earth and in the sky with my vision. Crows would see me and shout to each other as though they were making fun of me: "Behold him! Behold him!"

When the frosts began I was glad, because there would not be any more thunder storms for a long while, and I was more and more afraid of them all the time, for always there would be the voices crying: "Oo oohey! It is time! It is time!"

The fear was not so great all the while in the winter, but sometimes it was bad. Sometimes the crying of coyotes out in the cold made me so afraid that I would run out of one tepee into another, and I would do this until I was worn out and fell asleep. I wondered if maybe I was only crazy; and my father and mother worried a great deal about me. They said: "It is the strange sickness he had that time when we gave the horse to Whirlwind Chaser for curing him; and he is not cured." I could not tell them what was the matter, for then they would only think I was queerer than ever.

I was seventeen years old that winter.

When the grasses were beginning to show their tender faces again, my father and mother asked an old medicine man by the name of Black Road to come over and see what he could do for me. Black Road was in a tepee all alone with me, and he asked me to tell him if I had seen something that troubled me. By now I was so afraid of being afraid of everything that I told him about my vision, and when I was through he looked long at me and said: "Ah-h-h-h!," meaning that he was much surprised. Then he said to me: "Nephew, I know now what the trouble is! You must do what the bay horse in your vision wanted you to do. You must do your duty and perform this vision for your people upon earth. You must have the horse dance first for the people to see. Then the fear will leave you; but if you do not do this, something very bad will happen to you."

So we began to get ready for the horse dance.

XIV

THE HORSE DANCE

There was a man by the name of Bear Sings, and he was very old and wise. So Black Road asked him to help, and he did.

First they sent a crier around in the morning who told the people to camp in a circle at a certain place a little way up the Tongue from where the soldiers were. They did this, and in the middle of the circle Bear Sings and Black Road set up a sacred tepee of bison hide, and on it they painted pictures from my vision. On the west side they painted a bow and a cup of water; on the north, white geese and the herb; on the east, the daybreak star and the pipe; on the south, the flowering stick and the nation's hoop. Also, they painted horses, elk, and bison. Then over the door of the sacred tepee, they painted the flaming rainbow. It took them all day to do this, and it was beautiful.

They told me I must not eat anything until the horse dance was over, and I had to purify myself in a sweat lodge with sage spread on the floor of it, and afterwards I had to wipe myself dry with sage.

That evening Black Road and Bear Sings told me to come to the painted tepee. We were in there alone, and nobody dared come near us to listen. They asked me if I had heard any songs in my vision, and if I had I must teach the songs to them. So I sang to them all the songs that I had heard in my vision, and it took most of the night to teach these songs to them. While we were in there singing, we could hear low thunder rumbling all over the village outside, and we knew the thunder beings were glad and had come to help us.

My father and mother had been helping too by hunting up all that we should need in the dance. The next morning they had everything ready. There were four black horses to represent the west; four white horses for the north; four sorrels for the east; four buckskins for the

south. For all of these, young riders had been chosen. Also there was a bay horse for me to ride, as in my vision. Four of the most beautiful maidens in the village were ready to take their part, and there were six very old men for the Grandfathers.

Now it was time to paint and dress for the dance. The four maidens and the sixteen horses all faced the sacred tepee. Black Road and Bear Sings then sang a song, and all the others sang along with them, like this:

> "Father, paint the earth on me.
> Father, paint the earth on me.
> Father, paint the earth on me.
> A nation I will make over.
> A two-legged nation I will make holy.
> Father, paint the earth on me."

After that the painting was done.

The four black-horse riders were painted all black with blue lightning stripes down their legs and arms and white hail spots on their hips, and there were blue streaks of lightning on the horses' legs.

The white-horse riders were painted all white with red streaks of lightning on their arms and legs, and on the legs of the horses there were streaks of red lightning, and all the white riders wore plumes of white horse hair on their heads to look like geese.

The riders of the sorrels of the east were painted all red with straight black lines of lightning on their limbs and across their breasts, and there was straight black lightning on the limbs and breasts of the horses too.

The riders of the buckskins of the south were painted all yellow and streaked with black lightning. The horses were black from the knees down, and black lightning streaks were on their upper legs and breasts.

My bay horse had bright red streaks of lightning on his limbs, and on his back a spotted eagle, outstretching, was painted where I sat. I was painted red all over with black lightning on my limbs. I wore a black mask, and across my forehead a single eagle feather hung.

When the horses and the men were painted they looked beautiful; but they looked fearful too.

The men were naked, except for a breech-clout; but the four maidens wore buckskin dresses dyed scarlet, and their faces were scarlet too. Their hair was braided, and they had wreaths of the sweet and cleansing sage, the sacred sage, around their heads, and from the

wreath of each in front a single eagle feather hung. They were very beautiful to see.

All this time I was in the sacred tepee with the Six Grandfathers, and the four sacred virgins were in there too. No one outside was to see me until the dance began.

Right in the middle of the tepee the Grandfathers made a circle in the ground with a little trench, and across this they painted two roads—the red one running north and south, the black one, east and west. On the west side of this they placed a cup of water with a little bow and arrow laid across it; and on the east they painted the daybreak star. Then to the maiden who would represent the north they gave the healing herb to carry and a white goose wing, the cleansing wind. To her of the east they gave the holy pipe. To her of the south they gave the flowering stick; and to her who would represent the west they gave the nation's hoop. Thus the four maidens, good and beautiful, held in their hands the life of the nation.

All I carried was a red stick to represent the sacred arrow, the power of the thunder beings of the west.

We were now ready to begin the dance. The Six Grandfathers began to sing, announcing the riders of the different quarters. First they sang of the black horse riders, like this:

> "They will appear—may you behold them!
> They will appear—may you behold them!
> A horse nation will appear.
> A thunder-being nation will appear.
> They will appear, behold!
> They will appear, behold!"

Then the black riders mounted their horses and stood four abreast facing the place where the sun goes down.

Next the Six Grandfathers sang:

> "They will appear, may you behold them!
> A horse nation will appear, behold!
> A geese nation will appear, may you behold!"

Then the four white horsemen mounted and stood four abreast, facing the place where the White Giant lives.

Next the Six Grandfathers sang:

> "Where the sun shines continually, they will appear!
> A buffalo nation, they will appear, behold!
> A horse nation, they will appear, may you behold!"

Then the red horsemen mounted and stood four abreast facing the east.

Next the Grandfathers sang:

> "Where you are always facing, an elk nation will appear!
> May you behold!
> A horse nation will appear,
> Behold!"

The four yellow riders mounted their buckskins and stood four abreast facing the south.

Now it was time for me to go forth from the sacred tepee, but before I went forth I sang this song to the drums of the Grandfathers:

> "He will appear, may you behold him!
> An eagle for the eagle nation will appear.
> May you behold!"

While I was singing thus in the sacred tepee I could hear my horse snorting and prancing outside. The virgins went forth four abreast and I followed them, mounting my horse and standing behind them facing the west.

Next the Six Grandfathers came forth and stood abreast behind my bay, and they began to sing a rapid, lively song to the drums, like this:

> "They are dancing.
> They are coming to behold you.
> The horse nation of the west is dancing.
> They are coming to behold!"

Then they sang the same of the horses of the north and of the east and of the south. And as they sang of each troop in turn, it wheeled and came and took its place behind the Grandfathers—the blacks, the whites, the sorrels and the buckskins, standing four abreast and facing the west. They came prancing to the lively air of the Grandfathers' song, and they pranced as they stood in line. And all the while my bay was rearing too and prancing to the music of the sacred song.

Now when we were all in line, facing the west, I looked up into a

dark cloud that was coming there and the people all became quiet and the horses quit prancing. And when there was silence but for low thunder yonder, I sent a voice to the spirits of the cloud, holding forth my right hand, thus, palm outward, as I cried four times:

"Hey-a-a-hey! hey-a-a-hey! hey-a-a-hey! hey-a-a-hey!"

Then the Grandfathers behind me sang another sacred song from my vision, the one that goes like this:

> "At the center of the earth, behold a four-legged.
> They have said this to me!"

And as they sang, a strange thing happened. My bay pricked up his ears and raised his tail and pawed the earth, neighing long and loud to where the sun goes down. And the four black horses raised their voices, neighing long and loud, and the whites and the sorrels and the buckskins did the same; and all the other horses in the village neighed, and even those out grazing in the valley and on the hill slopes raised their heads and neighed together. Then suddenly, as I sat there looking at the cloud, I saw my vision yonder once again—the tepee built of cloud and sewed with lightning, the flaming rainbow door and, underneath, the Six Grandfathers sitting, and all the horses thronging in their quarters; and also there was I myself upon my bay before the tepee. I looked about me and could see that what we then were doing was like a shadow cast upon the earth from yonder vision in the heavens, so bright it was and clear. I knew the real was yonder and the darkened dream of it was here.

And as I looked, the Six Grandfathers yonder in the cloud and all the riders of the horses, and even I myself upon the bay up there, all held their hands palms outward toward me, and when they did this, I had to pray, and so I cried:

> "Grandfathers, you behold me!
> Spirits of the World, you behold!
> What you have said to me, I am now performing!
> Hear me and help me!"

Then the vision went out, and the thunder cloud was coming on with lightning on its front and many voices in it, and the split-tail swallows swooped above us in a swarm.

The people of the village ran to fasten down their tepees, while the

black horse riders sang to the drums that rolled like thunder, and this is what they sang:

> "I myself made them fear.
> Myself, I wore an eagle relic.
> I myself made them fear.
> Myself, a lightning power I wore.
> I myself made them fear,
> Made them fear.
> The power of the hail I wore,
> I myself made them fear,
> Made them fear!
> Behold me!"

And as they sang, the hail and rain were falling yonder just a little way from us, and we could see it, but the cloud stood there and flashed and thundered, and only a little sprinkle fell on us. The thunder beings were glad and had come in a great crowd to see the dance.

Now the four virgins held high the sacred relics that they carried, the herb and the white wing, the sacred pipe, the flowering stick, the nation's hoop, offering these to the spirits of the west. Then people who were sick or sad came to the virgins, making scarlet offerings to them, and after they had done this, they all felt better and some were cured of sickness and began to dance for joy.

Now the Grandfathers beat their drums again and the dance began. The four black horsemen, who had stood behind the Grandfathers, went ahead of the virgins, riding toward the west side of the circled village, and all the others followed in their order while the horses pranced and reared.

When the black horse troop had reached the western side, it wheeled around and fell to the rear behind the buckskins, and the white horse band came up and led until it reached the north side of the village. Then these fell back and took the rear behind the blacks, and the sorrels led until they reached the east. Then these fell back behind the whites, and the buckskins led until they reached the south. Then they fell back and took the rear, so that the blacks were leading as before toward the western quarter that was theirs. Each time the leading horse troop reached its quarter, the Six Grandfathers sang of the powers of that quarter, and there my bay faced, pricking up his ears and neighing loud, till all the other horses raised their voices neighing. When I thus faced the north, I sent a voice again and said: "Grand-

father, behold me! What you gave me I have given to the people—the power of the healing herb and the cleansing wind. Thus my nation is made over. Hear and help me!"

And when we reached the east, and after the Grandfathers had sung, I sent a voice: "Grandfather, behold me! My people, with difficulty they walk. Give them wisdom and guide them. Hear and help me!"

Between each quarter, as we marched and danced, we all sang together:

> "A horse nation all over the universe,
> Neighing, they come!
> Prancing, they come!
> May you behold them."

When we had reached the south and the Grandfathers had sung of the power of growing, my horse faced yonder and neighed again, and all the horses raised their voices as before. And then I prayed with hand upraised: "Grandfather, the flowering stick you gave me and the nation's sacred hoop I have given to the people. Hear me, you who have the power to make grow! Guide the people that they may be as blossoms on your holy tree, and make it flourish deep in Mother Earth and make it full of leaves and singing birds."

Then once more the blacks were leading, and as we marched and sang and danced toward the quarter of the west, the black hail cloud, still standing yonder watching, filled with voices crying: "Hey-hey! hey-hey!" They were cheering and rejoicing that my work was being done. And all the people now were happy and rejoicing, sending voices back, "hey-hey, hey-hey"; and all the horses neighed, rejoicing with the spirits and the people. Four times we marched and danced around the circle of the village, singing as we went, the leaders changing at the quarters, the Six Grandfathers singing to the power of each quarter, and to each I sent a voice. And at each quarter, as we stood, somebody who was sick or sad would come with offerings to the virgins—little scarlet bags of the chacun sha sha, the red willow bark. And when the offering was made, the giver would feel better and begin to dance with joy.

And on the second time around, many of the people who had horses joined the dance with them, milling round and round the Six Grandfathers and the virgins as we danced ahead. And more and more got on their horses, milling round us as we went, until there was a whirl

of prancing horses all about us at the end, and all the others danced afoot behind us, and everybody sang what we were singing.

When we reached the quarter of the west the fourth time, we stopped in new formation, facing inward toward the sacred tepee in the center of the village. First stood the virgins, next I stood upon the bay; then came the Six Grandfathers with eight riders on either side of them—the sorrels and the buckskins on their right hand, the blacks and whites upon their left. And when we stood so, the oldest of the Grandfathers, he who was the Spirit of the Sky, cried out: "Let all the people be ready. He shall send a voice four times, and at the last voice you shall go forth and coup the sacred tepee, and who shall coup it first shall have new power!"

All the riders were eager for the charge, and even the horses seemed to understand and were rearing and trying to get away. Then I raised my hand and cried hey-hey four times, and at the fourth the riders all yelled "hoka hey," and charged upon the tepee. My horse plunged inward along with all the others, but many were ahead of me and many couped the tepee before I did.

Then the horses were all rubbed down with sacred sage and led away, and we began going into the tepee to see what might have happened there while we were dancing. The Grandfathers had sprinkled fresh soil on the nation's hoop that they had made in there with the red and black roads across it, and all around this little circle of the nation's hoop we saw the prints of tiny pony hoofs as though the spirit horses had been dancing while we danced.

Now Black Road, who had helped me to perform the dance, took the sacred pipe from the virgin of the east. After filling it with chacun sha sha, the bark of the red willow, he lit and offered it to the Powers of the World, sending a voice thus:

"Grandfathers, you where the sun goes down, you of the sacred wind where the white giant lives, you where the day comes forth and the morning star, you where lives the power to grow, you of the sky and you of the earth, wings of the air and four-leggeds of the world, behold! I, myself, with my horse nation have done what I was to do on earth. To all of you I offer this pipe that my people may live!"

Then he smoked and passed the pipe. It went all over the village until every one had smoked at least a puff.

After the horse dance was over, it seemed that I was above the ground and did not touch it when I walked. I felt very happy, for I could see that my people were all happier. Many crowded around me

and said that they or their relatives who had been feeling sick were well again, and these gave me many gifts. Even the horses seemed to be healthier and happier after the dance.

The fear that was on me so long was gone, and when thunder clouds appeared I was always glad to see them, for they came as relatives now to visit me. Everything seemed good and beautiful now, and kind.

Before this, the medicine men would not talk to me, but now they would come to me to talk about my vision.

From that time on, I always got up very early to see the rising of the daybreak star. People knew that I did this, and many would get up to see it with me, and when it came we said: "Behold the star of understanding!"

XV

THE DOG VISION

We stayed there near the mouth of the Tongue until the end of the Moon of Making Fat (June). Then the soldier chief told us that we could not be in that country because we had sold it and it was not ours any more. We had not sold it; but the soldiers took all the rest of our horses from us and what guns we had and loaded us on a big fireboat that carried us down the Yellowstone and the Missouri to Fort Yates. There they unloaded us, and it was one of the new reservations they had made for the Lakota. Many of Sitting Bull's and Gall's people were there, but Gall and Sitting Bull were still in Grandmother's Land. The soldiers had taken the ponies away from all our people, and they said the Great Father in Washington would pay us for them; but if he ever did I have not heard of it.

I learned that my own band, the Ogalalas, had been taken back to the country where we are now, and I decided that I ought to go there and perform my duty. So in the Moon When the Plums Are Scarlet

(September) I started with three others. We had to go afoot and we had only bows and arrows for weapons.

The Brules had been taken to the place where they are now on Rosebud Creek while I was in Grandmother's Land, and we set out first for where they were, camping seven times on the way.

One evening we crossed Smoky Earth River (the White) and camped on the south side. We camped by a plum thicket, and the plums were ripe. That is all we had to eat. There was a bluff close by, and I went up there alone and sat down with my face to where the sun was setting. It was a clear evening with no wind, and it seemed that everything was listening hard to hear something. While I was looking over there I felt that somebody wanted to talk to me. So I stood up and began to sing the first song of my vision, the one that the two spirits had sung to me.

> "Behold! A sacred voice is calling you!
> All over the sky a sacred voice is calling!"

While I was singing this song, suddenly the two men of my vision were coming again out of the sunset, head first like arrows slanting down. They were pointing at me with their bows. Then they stopped and stood, raising their bows above their heads and looking at me. They said nothing, but I could feel what they wanted. It was that I should do my duty among the Ogalalas with the power they had brought me in the vision. I stood there singing to them, and afterwhile they turned around and went back into the sunset, head first like arrows flying.

When I went back to our little camp by the plum thicket, the others there, who knew of my power and had heard me on the bluff, asked what I had seen up there. I told them I was only singing to some people I knew in the outer world.

I stayed only a little while among the Brules on Rosebud Creek, and then I came on alone to White Clay Creek where the Wasichus were building Pine Ridge Agency for the Ogalalas. Our people called it the Seat of Red Cloud or the Place Where Everything Is Disputed. There I stayed, and that winter in the Moon of Popping Trees I was eighteen years old.[1]

That was a very hard winter, and it was just like one long night, with me lying awake, waiting and waiting and waiting for daybreak.

[1]December, 1881.

For now the thunder beings were like relatives to me and they had gone away when the frost came and would not come back until the grasses showed their tender faces again. Without them I felt lost, and I was alone there among my people. Very few of them had seen the horse dance or knew anything about my vision and the power that it gave me. They seemed heavy, heavy and dark; and they could not know that they were heavy and dark. I could feel them like a great burden upon me; but when I would go all through my vision again, I loved the burden and felt pity for my people.

And now when I look about me upon my people in despair, I feel like crying and I wish and wish my vision could have been given to a man more worthy. I wonder why it came to me, a pitiful old man who can do nothing. Men and women and children I have cured of sickness with the power the vision gave me; but my nation I could not help. If a man or woman or child dies, it does not matter long, for the nation lives on. It was the nation that was dying, and the vision was for the nation; but I have done nothing with it.

When I was still young, I could feel the power all through me, and it seemed that with the whole outer world to help me I could do anything.

I had made a good start to fulfill my duty to the Grandfathers, but I had much more to do; and so the winter was like a long night of waiting for the daybreak.

When the grasses began to show their faces again, I was happy, for I could hear the thunder beings coming in the earth and I could hear them saying: "It is time to do the work of your Grandfathers."

After the long winter of waiting, it was my first duty to go out lamenting. So after the first rain storm I began to get ready.

When going out to lament it is necessary to choose a wise old medicine man, who is quiet and generous, to help. He must fill and offer the pipe to the Six Powers and to the four-leggeds and the wings of the air, and he must go along to watch. There was a good and wise old medicine man by the name of Few Tails, who was glad to help me. First he told me to fast four days, and I could have only water during that time. Then, after he had offered the pipe, I had to purify myself in a sweat lodge, which we made with willow boughs set in the ground and bent down to make a round top. Over this we tied a bison robe. In the middle we put hot stones, and when I was in there, Few Tails poured water on the stones. I sang to the spirits while I was in there being purified. Then the old man rubbed me all over with the sacred

sage. He then braided my hair, and I was naked except that I had a bison robe to wrap around me while lamenting in the night, for although the days were warm, the nights were cold yet. All I carried was the sacred pipe.

It is necessary to go far away from people to lament, so Few Tails and I started from Pine Ridge toward where we are now.[2]

We came to a high hill close to Grass Creek, which is just a little way west from here. There was nobody there but the old man and myself and the sky and the earth. But the place was full of people; for the spirits were there.

The sun was almost setting when we came to the hill, and the old man helped me make the place where I was to stand. We went to the highest point of the hill and made the ground there sacred by spreading sage upon it. Then Few Tails set a flowering stick in the middle of the place, and on the west, the north, the east, and the south sides of it he placed offerings of red willow bark tied into little bundles with scarlet cloth.

Few Tails now told me what I was to do so that the spirits would hear me and make clear my next duty. I was to stand in the middle, crying and praying for understanding. Then I was to advance from the center to the quarter of the west and mourn there awhile. Then I was to back up to the center, and from there approach the quarter of the north, wailing and praying there, and so on all around the circle. This I had to do all night long.

It was time for me to begin lamenting, so Few Tails went away somewhere and left me there all alone on the hill with the spirits and the dying light.

Standing in the center of the sacred place and facing the sunset, I began to cry, and while crying I had to say: "O Great Spirit, accept my offerings! O make me understand!"

As I was crying and saying this, there soared a spotted eagle from the west and whistled shrill and sat upon a pine tree east of me.

I walked backwards to the center, and from there approached the north, crying and saying: "O Great Spirit, accept my offerings and make me understand!" Then a chicken hawk came hovering and stopped upon a bush towards the south.

I walked backwards to the center once again and from there approached the east, crying and asking the Great Spirit to help me

[2]Black Elk's home near Manderson P.O., South Dakota.

understand, and there came a black swallow flying all around me, singing, and stopped upon a bush not far away.

Walking backwards to the center, I advanced upon the south. Until now I had only been trying to weep, but now I really wept, and the tears ran down my face; for as I looked yonder towards the place whence come the life of things, the nation's hoop and the flowering tree, I thought of the days when my relatives, now dead, were living and young, and of Crazy Horse who was our strength and would never come back to help us any more.

I cried very hard, and I thought it might be better if my crying would kill me; then I could be in the outer world where nothing is ever in despair.

And while I was crying, something was coming from the south. It looked like dust far off, but when it came closer, I saw it was a cloud of beautiful butterflies of all colors. They swarmed around me so thick that I could see nothing else.

I walked backwards to the flowering stick again, and the spotted eagle on the pine tree spoke and said: "Behold these! They are your people. They are in great difficulty and you shall help them." Then I could hear all the butterflies that were swarming over me, and they were all making a pitiful, whimpering noise as though they too were weeping.

Then they all arose and flew back into the south.

Now the chicken hawk spoke from its bush and said: "Behold! Your Grandfathers shall come forth and you shall hear them!"

Hearing this, I lifted up my eyes, and there was a big storm coming from the west. It was the thunder being nation, and I could hear the neighing of horses and the sending of great voices.

It was very dark now, and all the roaring west was streaked fearfully with swift fire.

And as I stood there looking, a vision broke out of the shouting blackness torn with fire, and I saw the two men who had come to me first in my great vision. They came head first like arrows slanting earthward from a long flight; and when they neared the ground, I could see a dust rising there and out of the dust the heads of dogs were peeping. Then suddenly I saw that the dust was the swarm of many-colored butterflies hovering all around and over the dogs.

By now the two men were riding sorrel horses, streaked with black lightning, and they charged with bows and arrows down upon the dogs, while the thunder beings cheered for them with roaring voices.

Then suddenly the butterflies changed, and were storm-driven swallows, swooping and whirling in a great cloud behind the charging riders.

The first of these now plunged upon a dog's head and arose with it hanging bloody on his arrow point, while the whole west roared with cheering. The second did the same; and the black west flashed and cheered again. Then as the two arose together, I saw that the dogs' heads had changed to the heads of Wasichus; and as I saw, the vision went out and the storm was close upon me, terrible to see and roaring.

I cried harder than ever now, for I was much afraid. The night was black about me and terrible with swift fire and the sending of great voices and the roaring of the hail. And as I cried, I begged the Grandfathers to pity me and spare me and told them that I knew now what they wanted me to do on earth, and I would do it if I could.

All at once I was not afraid any more, and I thought that if I was killed, probably I might be better off in the other world. So I lay down there in the center of the sacred place and offered the pipe again. Then I drew the bison robe over me and waited. All around me growled and roared the voices, and the hail was like the drums of many giants beating while the giants sang: "Hey-a-hey!"

No hail fell there in the sacred circle where I lay, nor any rain. And when the storm was passed, I raised my robe and listened; and in the stillness I could hear the rain-flood singing in the gulches all around me in the darkness, and far away to eastward there were dying voices calling: "Hey-a-hey!"

The night was old by now, and soon I fell asleep. And as I slept I saw my people sitting sad and troubled all around a sacred tepee, and there were many who were sick. And as I looked on them and wept, a strange light leaped upward from the ground close by—a light of many colors, sparkling, with rays that touched the heavens. Then it was gone, and in the place from whence it sprang a herb was growing and I saw the leaves it had. And as I was looking at the herb so that I might not forget it, there was a voice that 'woke me, and it said: "Make haste! Your people need you!"

I looked and saw the east was just beginning to turn white. Standing up, I faced the young light and began to mourn again and pray. Then the daybreak star came slowly, very beautiful and still; and all around it there were clouds of baby faces smiling at me, the faces of the people not yet born. The stars about them now were beautiful with many colors, and beneath these there were heads of men and women moving

around, and birds were singing somewhere yonder and there were horses nickering and blowing as they do when they are happy, and somewhere deer were whistling and there were bison mooing too. What I could not see of this, I heard.

I think I fell asleep again, for afterwhile I was startled by a voice that said: "Get up, I have come after you!" I looked to see a spirit, but it was the good old man, Few Tails, standing over me. And now the sun was rising.

So we brought the sacred pipe back home and I went into the sweat lodge after offering the pipe to the Six Powers. When I was purified again, some very old men who were good and wise asked me to tell them what I had heard and seen. So after offering and smoking the sacred pipe again, I told it all to them, and they said that I must perform the dog vision on earth to help the people, and because the people were discouraged and sad, I should do this with heyokas, who are sacred fools, doing everything wrong or backwards to make the people laugh. They said they did not know but I would be a great man, because not many men were called to see such visions. I must wait twenty days, they said, and then perform my duty. So I waited.

XVI

HEYOKA CEREMONY

Twenty days passed, and it was time to perform the dog vision with heyokas. But before I tell you how we did it, I will say something about heyokas and the heyoka ceremony, which seems to be very foolish, but is not so.

Only those who have had visions of the thunder beings of the west can act as heyokas. They have sacred power and they share some of this with all the people, but they do it through funny actions. When a vision comes from the thunder beings of the west, it comes with terror

like a thunder storm; but when the storm of vision has passed, the world is greener and happier; for wherever the truth of vision comes upon the world, it is like a rain. The world, you see, is happier after the terror of the storm.

But in the heyoka ceremony, everything is backwards, and it is planned that the people shall be made to feel jolly and happy first, so that it may be easier for the power to come to them. You have noticed that the truth comes into this world with two faces. One is sad with suffering, and the other laughs; but it is the same face, laughing or weeping. When people are already in despair, maybe the laughing face is better for them; and when they feel too good and are too sure of being safe, maybe the weeping face is better for them to see. And so I think that is what the heyoka ceremony is for.

There was a man by the name of Wachpanne (Poor) who took charge of this ceremony for me, because he had acted as a heyoka many times and knew all about it. First he told all the people to gather in a circle on the flat near Pine Ridge, and in the center, near a sacred tepee that was set there, he placed a pot of water which was made to boil by dropping hot stones from a fire into it. First, he had to make an offering of sweet grass to the west. He sat beside the fire with some sweet grass in his hand, and said: "To the Great Spirit's day, to that day grown old and wise, I will make an offering." Then, as he sprinkled the grass upon the fire and the sweet smoke arose, he sang:

> "This I burn as an offering.
> Behold it!
> A sacred praise I am making.
> A sacred praise I am making.
> My nation, behold it in kindness!
> The day of the sun has been my strength.
> The path of the moon shall be my robe.
> A sacred praise I am making.
> A sacred praise I am making."

Then the dog had to be killed quickly and without making any scar, as lightning kills, for it is the power of the lightning that heyokas have.

Over the smoke of the sweet grass a rawhide rope was held to make it sacred. Then two heyokas tied a slip noose in the rope and put this over the neck of the dog. Three times they pulled the rope gently, one at each end of the rope, and the fourth time they jerked it hard, breaking the neck. Then Wachpanne singed the dog and washed it

well, and after that he cut away everything but the head, the spine and the tail. Now walking six steps away from the pot, one for each of the Powers, he turned to the west, offering the head and spine to the thunder beings, then to the north, the east and the south, then to the Spirit above and to Mother Earth.

After this, standing where he was, six steps away, he faced the pot and said: "In a sacred manner I thus boil this dog." Three times he swung it, and the fourth time he threw it so that it fell head first into the boiling water. Then he took the heart of the dog and did with it just what he had done with the head and spine.

During all this time, thirty heyokas, one for each day of a moon, were doing foolish tricks among the people to make them feel jolly. They were all dressed and painted in such funny ways that everybody who saw them had to laugh. One Side and I were fellow clowns. We had our bodies painted red all over and streaked with black lightning. The right sides of our heads were shaved, and the hair on the left side was left hanging long. This looked very funny, but it had a meaning; for when we looked toward where you are always facing (the south) the bare sides of our heads were toward the west, which showed that we were humble before the thunder beings who had given us power. Each of us carried a very long bow, so long that nobody could use it, and it was very crooked too. The arrows that we carried were very long and very crooked, so that it looked crazy to have them. We were riding sorrels with streaks of black lightning all over them, for we were to represent the two men of my dog vision.

Wachpanne now went into the sacred tepee, where he sang about the heyokas:

> "These are sacred,
> These are sacred,
> They have said,
> They have said.
> These are sacred,
> They have said."

Twelve times he sang this, once for each of the moons.

Afterward, while the pot was boiling, One Side and I, sitting on our painted sorrels, faced the west and sang:

> "In a sacred manner they have sent voices.
> Half the universe has sent voices.
> In a sacred manner they have sent voices to you."

Even while we were singing thus, the heyokas were doing foolish things and making laughter. For instance, two heyokas with long crooked bows and arrows painted in a funny way, would come to a little shallow puddle of water. They would act as though they thought it was a wide, deep river that they had to cross; so, making motions, but saying nothing, they would decide to see how deep the river was. Taking their long crooked arrows, they would thrust these into the water, not downwards, but flat-wise just under the surface. This would make the whole arrow wet. Standing the arrows up beside them, they would show that the water was far over their heads in depth, so they would get ready to swim. One would then plunge into the shallow puddle head first, getting his face in the mud and fighting the water wildly as though he were drowning. Then the other one would plunge in to save his comrade, and there would be more funny antics in the water to make the people laugh.

After One Side and I had sung to the west, we faced the pot, where the heart and the head of the dog had been boiling. With sharp pointed arrows, we charged on horseback upon the pot and past it. I had to catch the head upon my arrow and One Side had to catch the heart, for we were representing the two men I had seen in the vision. After we had done this, the heyokas all chased us, trying to get a piece of the meat, and the people rushed to the pot, trying to get a piece of the sacred flesh. Ever so little of it would be good for them, for the power of the west was in it now. It was like giving them medicine to make them happier and stronger.

When the ceremony was over, everybody felt a great deal better, for it had been a day of fun. They were better able now to see the greenness of the world, the wideness of the sacred day, the colors of the earth, and to set these in their minds.

The Six Grandfathers have placed in this world many things, all of which should be happy. Every little thing is sent for something, and in that thing there should be happiness and the power to make happy. Like the grasses showing tender faces to each other, thus we should do, for this was the wish of the Grandfathers of the World.

XVII

THE FIRST CURE

After the heyoka ceremony, I came to live here where I am now between Wounded Knee Creek and Grass Creek. Others came too, and we made these little gray houses of logs that you see, and they are square. It is a bad way to live, for there can be no power in a square.

You have noticed that everything an Indian does is in a circle, and that is because the Power of the World always works in circles, and everything tries to be round. In the old days when we were a strong and happy people, all our power came to us from the sacred hoop of the nation, and so long as the hoop was unbroken, the people flourished. The flowering tree was the living center of the hoop, and the circle of the four quarters nourished it. The east gave peace and light, the south gave warmth, the west gave rain, and the north with its cold and mighty wind gave strength and endurance. This knowledge came to us from the outer world with our religion. Everything the Power of the World does is done in a circle. The sky is round, and I have heard that the earth is round like a ball, and so are all the stars. The wind, in its greatest power, whirls. Birds make their nests in circles, for theirs is the same religion as ours. The sun comes forth and goes down again in a circle. The moon does the same, and both are round. Even the seasons form a great circle in their changing, and always come back again to where they were. The life of a man is a circle from childhood to childhood, and so it is in everything where power moves. Our tepees were round like the nests of birds, and these were always set in a circle, the nation's hoop, a nest of many nests, where the Great Spirit meant for us to hatch our children.

But the Wasichus have put us in these square boxes. Our power is gone and we are dying, for the power is not in us any more. You can

look at our boys and see how it is with us. When we were living by the power of the circle in the way we should, boys were men at twelve or thirteen years of age. But now it takes them very much longer to mature.

Well, it is as it is. We are prisoners of war while we are waiting here. But there is another world.

It was in the Moon of Shedding Ponies (May) when we had the heyoka ceremony. One day in the Moon of Fatness (June), when everything was blooming, I invited One Side to come over and eat with me. I had been thinking about the four-rayed herb that I had now seen twice—the first time in the great vision when I was nine years old, and the second time when I was lamenting on the hill. I knew that I must have this herb for curing, and I thought I could recognize the place where I had seen it growing that night when I lamented.

After One Side and I had eaten, I told him there was a herb I must find, and I wanted him to help me hunt for it. Of course I did not tell him I had seen it in a vision. He was willing to help, so we got on our horses and rode over to Grass Creek. Nobody was living over there. We came to the top of a high hill above the creek, and there we got off our horses and sat down, for I felt that we were close to where I saw the herb growing in my vision of the dog.

We sat there awhile singing together some heyoka songs. Then I began to sing alone a song I had heard in my first great vision:

"In a sacred manner they are sending voices."

After I had sung this song, I looked down towards the west, and yonder at a certain spot beside the creek were crows and magpies, chicken hawks and spotted eagles circling around and around.

Then I knew, and I said to One Side: "Friend, right there is where the herb is growing." He said: "We will go forth and see." So we got on our horses and rode down Grass Creek until we came to a dry gulch, and this we followed up. As we neared the spot the birds all flew away, and it was a place where four or five dry gulches came together. There right on the side of the bank the herb was growing, and I knew it, although I had never seen one like it before, except in my vision.

It had a root about as long as to my elbow, and this was a little

thicker than my thumb. It was flowering in four colors, blue, white, red, and yellow.

We got off our horses, and after I had offered red willow bark to the Six Powers, I made a prayer to the herb, and said to it: "Now we shall go forth to the two-leggeds, but only to the weakest ones, and there shall be happy days among the weak."

It was easy to dig the herb, because it was growing in the edge of the clay gulch. Then we started back with it. When we came to Grass Creek again, we wrapped it in some good sage that was growing there.

Something must have told me to find the herb just then, for the next evening I needed it and could have done nothing without it.

I was eating supper when a man by the name of Cuts-to-Pieces came in, and he was saying: "Hey, hey, hey!" for he was in trouble. I asked him what was the matter, and he said: "I have a boy of mine, and he is very sick and I am afraid he will die soon. He has been sick a long time. They say you have great power from the horse dance and the heyoka ceremony, so maybe you can save him for me. I think so much of him."

I told Cuts-to-Pieces that if he really wanted help, he should go home and bring me back a pipe with an eagle feather on it. While he was gone, I thought about what I had to do; and I was afraid, because I had never cured anybody yet with my power, and I was very sorry for Cuts-to-Pieces. I prayed hard for help. When Cuts-to-Pieces came back with the pipe, I told him to take it around to the left of me, leave it there, and pass out again to the right of me. When he had done this, I sent for One Side to come and help me. Then I took the pipe and went to where the sick little boy was. My father and my mother went with us, and my friend, Standing Bear, was already there.

I first offered the pipe to the Six Powers, then I passed it, and we all smoked. After that I began making a rumbling thunder sound on the drum. You know, when the power of the west comes to the two-leggeds, it comes with rumbling, and when it has passed, everything lifts up its head and is glad and there is greenness. So I made this rumbling sound. Also, the voice of the drum is an offering to the Spirit of the World. Its sound arouses the mind and makes men feel the mystery and power of things.

The sick little boy was on the northeast side of the tepee, and when we entered at the south, we went around from left to right, stopping on the west side when we had made the circle.

You want to know why we always go from left to right like that. I

can tell you something of the reason, but not all. Think of this: Is not the south the source of life, and does not the flowering stick truly come from there? And does not man advance from there toward the setting sun of his life? Then does he not approach the colder north where the white hairs are? And does he not then arrive, if he lives, at the source of light and understanding, which is the east? Then does he not return to where he began, to his second childhood, there to give back his life to all life, and his flesh to the earth whence it came? The more you think about this, the more meaning you will see in it.

As I said, we went into the tepee from left to right, and sat ourselves down on the west side. The sick little boy was on the northeast side, and he looked as though he were only skin and bones. I had the pipe, the drum and the four-rayed herb already, so I asked for a wooden cup, full of water, and an eagle bone whistle, which was for the spotted eagle of my great vision. They placed the cup of water in front of me; and then I had to think awhile, because I had never done this before and I was in doubt.

I understood a little more now, so I gave the eagle bone whistle to One Side and told him how to use it in helping me. Then I filled the pipe with red willow bark, and gave it to the pretty young daughter of Cuts-to-Pieces, telling her to hold it, just as I had seen the virgin of the east holding it in my great vision.

Everything was ready now, so I made low thunder on the drum, keeping time as I sent forth a voice. Four times I cried "Hey-a-a-hey," drumming as I cried to the Spirit of the World, and while I was doing this I could feel the power coming through me from my feet up, and I knew that I could help the sick little boy.

I kept on sending a voice, while I made low thunder on the drum, saying: "My Grandfather, Great Spirit, you are the only one and to no other can any one send voices. You have made everything, they say, and you have made it good and beautiful. The four quarters and the two roads crossing each other, you have made. Also you have set a power where the sun goes down. The two-leggeds on earth are in despair. For them, my Grandfather, I send a voice to you. You have said this to me: The weak shall walk. In vision you have taken me to the center of the world and there you have shown me the power to make over. The water in the cup that you have given me, by its power shall the dying live. The herb that you have shown me, through its power shall the feeble walk upright. From where we are always facing (the south), behold, a virgin shall appear, walking the good red road,

offering the pipe as she walks, and hers also is the power of the flowering tree. From where the Giant lives (the north), you have given me a sacred, cleansing wind, and where this wind passes the weak shall have strength. You have said this to me. To you and to all your powers and to Mother Earth I send a voice for help."

You see, I had never done this before, and I know now that only one power would have been enough. But I was so eager to help the sick little boy that I called on every power there is.

I had been facing the west, of course, while sending a voice. Now I walked to the north and to the east and to the south, stopping there where the source of all life is and where the good red road begins. Standing there I sang thus:

> "In a sacred manner I have made them walk.
> A sacred nation lies low.
> In a sacred manner I have made them walk.
> A sacred two-legged, he lies low.
> In a sacred manner, he shall walk."

While I was singing this I could feel something queer all through my body, something that made me want to cry for all unhappy things, and there were tears on my face.

Now I walked to the quarter of the west, where I lit the pipe, offered it to the powers, and, after I had taken a whiff of smoke, I passed it around.

When I looked at the sick little boy again, he smiled at me, and I could feel that the power was getting stronger.

I next took the cup of water, drank a little of it, and went around to where the sick little boy was. Standing before him, I stamped the earth four times. Then, putting my mouth to the pit of his stomach, I drew through him the cleansing wind of the north. I next chewed some of the herb and put it in the water, afterward blowing some of it on the boy and to the four quarters. The cup with the rest of the water I gave to the virgin, who gave it to the sick little boy to drink. Then I told the virgin to help the boy stand up and to walk around the circle with him, beginning at the south, the source of life. He was very poor and weak, but with the virgin's help he did this.

Then I went away.

Next day Cuts-to-Pieces came and told me that his little boy was feeling better and was sitting up and could eat something again. In

four days he could walk around. He got well and lived to be thirty years old.

Cuts-to-Pieces gave me a good horse for doing this; but of course I would have done it for nothing.

When the people heard about how the little boy was cured, many came to me for help, and I was busy most of the time.

This was in the summer of my nineteenth year (1882), in the Moon of Making Fat.

XVIII

THE POWERS OF THE BISON AND THE ELK

I think I have told you, but if I have not, you must have understood, that a man who has a vision is not able to use the power of it until after he has performed the vision on earth for the people to see. You remember that my great vision came to me when I was only nine years old, and you have seen that I was not much good for anything until after I had performed the horse dance near the mouth of the Tongue River during my eighteenth summer. And if the great fear had not come upon me, as it did, and forced me to do my duty, I might have been less good to the people than some man who had never dreamed at all, even with the memory of so great a vision in me. But the fear came, and if I had not obeyed it, I am sure it would have killed me in a little while.

It was even then only after the heyoka ceremony, in which I performed my dog vision, that I had the power to practice as a medicine man, curing sick people; and many I cured with the power that came through me. Of course it was not I who cured. It was the power from the outer world, and the visions and ceremonies had only

made me like a hole through which the power could come to the two-leggeds. If I thought that I was doing it myself, the hole would close up and no power could come through. Then everything I could do would be foolish. There were other parts of my great vision that I still had to perform before I could use the power that was in those parts. If you think about my great vision again, you will remember how the red man turned into a bison and rolled, and that the people found the good red road after that. If you will read again what is written, you will see how it was.

To use the power of the bison, I had to perform that part of my vision for the people to see. It was during the summer of my first cure that this was done. I carried the pipe to Fox Belly, a wise and good old medicine man, and asked him to help me do this duty. He was glad to help me, but first I had to tell him how it was in that part of my vision. I did not tell him all my vision, only that part. I had never told any one all of it, and even until now nobody ever heard it all. Even my old friend, Standing Bear, and my son here have heard it now for the first time when I have told it to you. Of course there was very much in the vision that even I can not tell when I try hard, because very much of it was not for words. But I have told what can be told.

It has made me very sad to do this at last, and I have lain awake at night worrying and wondering if I was doing right; for I know I have given away my power when I have given away my vision, and maybe I cannot live very long now. But I think I have done right to save the vision in this way, even though I may die sooner because I did it; for I know the meaning of the vision is wise and beautiful and good; and you can see that I am only a pitiful old man after all.

Well, I told Fox Belly all that he needed to know that he might help me. And when he had heard even so little, he said: "My boy, you had a great vision, and I can see that it is your duty to help the people walk the red road in a manner pleasing to the Powers."

This ceremony was not a long one, but it had great meaning, because it made a picture of the relation between the people and the bison, and the power was in the meaning.

First we made a sacred place like a bison wallow at the center of the nation's hoop, and there we set up the sacred tepee. Inside this we made the circle of the four quarters. Across the circle from south to north we painted a red road, and Fox Belly made little bison tracks all along on both sides of it, meaning that the people should walk there with the power and endurance of the bison, facing the great white

cleansing wind of the world. Also, he placed at the north end of the road the cup of water, which is the gift of the west, so that the people, while leaning against the great wind with the endurance of bison, would be going toward the water of life.

I was painted red all over like the man of my vision before he turned into a bison. I wore bison horns, and on the left horn hung a piece of the daybreak-star herb, which bears the four-rayed flower of understanding. On the left side of my body I wore a single eagle feather, which was for my people, hanging on the side of the bison and feeding there.

One Side had come over to help me in this ceremony too. He was painted red all over, and he carried the drum and the pipe, and wherever I went, he followed, as the people follow the bison.

We stood inside the tepee at the south end of the good red road, and Fox Belly sang like this:

> "Revealing this, they walk.
> A sacred herb—revealing it, they walk.
> Revealing this, they walk.
> The sacred life of bison—revealing it, they walk.
> Revealing this, they walk.
> A sacred eagle feather—revealing it, they walk.
> Revealing them, they walk.
> The eagle and the bison—like relatives they walk."

Then, after we had walked the red road, One Side and I went out of the tepee and the people flocked around us, and the sick came with scarlet offerings to be cured. We went all around among the people, acting like bison and making the sounds they make. Then we returned to the tepee, and there the people brought their little children to us, and to each I gave a little of the water of life from the wooden cup, that their feet might know the good red road that leads to health and happiness.

It is from understanding that power comes; and the power in the ceremony was in understanding what it meant; for nothing can live well except in a manner that is suited to the way the sacred Power of the World lives and moves.

After this, I went on curing sick people, and I was busy doing this. I was in doubt no longer. I felt like a man, and I could feel the power with me all the time.

It was during the next summer, when I was in my twentieth year

(1883), that I performed the elk ceremony, as a duty to that part of my great vision. You will remember how the pipe and the bison were in the east and the elk in the south.

This ceremony of the elk was to represent the source of life and the mystery of growing.

I sent a pipe to Running Elk, who was Standing Bear's uncle and a good and wise old man. He came and was willing to help me. We set up a sacred tepee at the center as before. I had to use six elks and four virgins. The elks are of the south, but the power that they represented in my vision is nourished by the four quarters and from the sky and the earth; so there were six of them. The four virgins represented the life of the nation's hoop, which has four quarters; so there were four virgins. Running Elk chose two of the elks, and I, who stood between the Power of the World and the nation's hoop, chose the four others, for my duty was to the life of the hoop on earth. The six elk men wore complete elk hides on their backs and over their heads. Their limbs were painted black from the knee and elbow down, and yellow from there up; for the growing power is rooted in mystery like the night, and reaches lightward. Seeds sprout in the darkness of the ground before they know the summer and the day. In the night of the womb the spirit quickens into flesh. The four virgins wore scarlet dresses, and each had a single eagle feather in her braided hair; for out of the woman the people grows, and the eagle feather again was for the people as in the bison ceremony. The faces of the virgins were painted yellow, the color of the south, the source of life. One had a daybreak star in red upon her forehead. One had a crescent moon in blue, for the power of woman grows with the moon and comes and goes with it. One had the sun upon her forehead; and around the mouth and eyebrows of the fourth a big blue circle was painted to mean the nation's hoop. On the back of each of the elk men was painted the nation's hoop, for upon the backs of men the nation is carried, and in the center of each hoop hung a single eagle feather for the people. They had yellow masks upon their faces, for behind the woman's power of life is hidden the power of man. They all carried flowering sticks cut from the sacred rustling tree (the cottonwood) with leaves left at the top, and the sticks were painted red. The woman is the life of the flowering tree, but the man must feed and care for it. One of the virgins also carried the flowering stick, another carried the pipe which gives peace, a third bore the herb of healing and the fourth held the sacred hoop; for all these powers together are woman's power.

Of course, before any of this was done, those who were to take part were purified in the sweat lodge as always.

We were all inside the sacred tepee, and Running Elk sang this song:

> "Advancing to the quarters,
> Advancing to the quarters,
> They are coming to behold you.
> Advancing to the quarters,
> Advancing to the quarters,
> They are coming to behold you."

Then the elk men all made the elk sound, *unh, unh, unh*. Running Elk then sang again:

> "Singing, I send a voice as I walk.
> Singing, I send a voice as I walk.
> A sacred hoop I wear as I walk."

It was time now to come out of the sacred tepee: first came the virgin with the pipe; next she who bore the flowering stick, then the one who held the herb; and last, the bearer of the nation's hoop. The four virgins stood abreast, facing the west. Then we six elk men came out, snorting and stamping our feet. We stopped abreast, behind the virgins, who now held up the sacred things they carried, offering them to the thunder beings. When they had done this, they walked abreast to the north, while we elk men danced around them in a circle, and there they offered their sacred objects to the great white cleansing wind. In the same way we went to the east and to the south, the virgins making the offering at each place, and we elk men dancing around them in a circle all the while.

From the south, the four virgins turned straight north, following the good red road to the center of the village where the sacred tepee stood, and we elk men followed, dancing around them, for the power of the man encircles and protects the power of the woman.

The four maidens entered the tepee: first, she with the sacred hoop; then she who bore the flowering stick; next, the one who held the cleansing herb; and after her, the bearer of the pipe.

When they had all entered, we elk men followed into the tepee.

This was the ceremony, and as I said before, the power of it was in the understanding of its meaning; for nothing can live well except in a manner suited to the way the Power of the World lives and moves to do its work.

XIX

ACROSS THE BIG WATER

As I told you, it was in the summer of my twentieth year (1883) that I performed the ceremony of the elk. That fall, they say, the last of the bison herds was slaughtered by the Wasichus. I can remember when the bison were so many that they could not be counted, but more and more Wasichus came to kill them until there were only heaps of bones scattered where they used to be. The Wasichus did not kill them to eat; they killed them for the metal that makes them crazy, and they took only the hides to sell. Sometimes they did not even take the hides, only the tongues; and I have heard that fire-boats came down the Missouri River loaded with dried bison tongues. You can see that the men who did this were crazy. Sometimes they did not even take the tongues; they just killed and killed because they liked to do that. When we hunted bison, we killed only what we needed. And when there was nothing left but heaps of bones, the Wasichus came and gathered up even the bones and sold them.

All our people now were settling down in square gray houses, scattered here and there across this hungry land, and around them the Wasichus had drawn a line to keep them in. The nation's hoop was broken, and there was no center any longer for the flowering tree. The people were in despair. They seemed heavy to me, heavy and dark; so heavy that it seemed they could not be lifted; so dark that they could not be made to see any more. Hunger was among us often now, for much of what the Great Father in Washington sent us must have been stolen by Wasichus who were crazy to get money. There were many lies, but we could not eat them. The forked tongue made promises.

I kept on curing the sick for three years more, and many came to me and were made over; but when I thought of my great vision, which

was to save the nation's hoop and make the holy tree to bloom in the center of it, I felt like crying, for the sacred hoop was broken and scattered. The life of the people was in the hoop, and what are many little lives if the life of those lives be gone?

But late in my twenty-third summer (1886), it seemed that there was a little hope. There came to us some Wasichus who wanted a band of Ogalalas for a big show that the other Pahuska[1] had. They told us this show would go across the big water to strange lands, and I thought I ought to go, because I might learn some secret of the Wasichu that would help my people somehow. In my great vision, when I stood at the center of the world, the two men from the east had brought me the daybreak-star herb and they had told me to drop it on the earth; and where it touched the ground it took root and bloomed four-rayed. It was the herb of understanding. Also, where the red man of my vision changed into a bison that rolled, the same herb grew and bloomed when the bison had vanished, and after that the people in my vision found the good red road again. Maybe if I could see the great world of the Wasichu, I could understand how to bring the sacred hoop together and make the tree to bloom again at the center of it.

I looked back on the past and recalled my people's old ways, but they were not living that way any more. They were traveling the black road, everybody for himself and with little rules of his own, as in my vision. I was in despair, and I even thought that if the Wasichus had a better way, then maybe my people should live that way. I know now that this was foolish, but I was young and in despair.

My relatives told me I should stay at home and go on curing people, but I would not listen to them.

The show people sent wagons from Rushville on the iron road to get us, and we were about a hundred men and women. Many of our people followed us half way to the iron road and there we camped and ate together. Afterward we left our people crying there, for we were going very far across the big water.

That evening where the big wagons were waiting for us on the iron road, we had a dance. Then we got into the wagons. When we started, it was dark, and thinking of my home and my people made me very sad. I wanted to get off and run back. But we went roaring all night long, and in the morning we ate at Long Pine. Then we started again and went roaring all day and came to a very big town in the evening.[2]

[1] Long Hair, Buffalo Bill.
[2] Omaha.

Then we roared along all night again and came to a much bigger town.[3] There we stayed all day and all night; and right there I could compare my people's ways with Wasichu ways, and this made me sadder than before. I wished and wished that I had not gone away from home.

Then we went roaring on again, and afterwhile we came to a still bigger town—a very big town.[4] We walked through this town to the place where the show was.[5] Some Pawnees and Omahas were there, and when they saw us they made war-cries and charged, couping us. They were doing this for fun and because they felt glad to see us. I was surprised at the big houses and so many people, and there were bright lights at night, so that you could not see the stars, and some of these lights, I heard, were made with the power of thunder.

We stayed there and made shows for many, many Wasichus all that winter. I liked the part of the show we made, but not the part the Wasichus made. Afterwhile I got used to being there, but I was like a man who had never had a vision. I felt dead and my people seemed lost and I thought I might never find them again. I did not see anything to help my people. I could see that the Wasichus did not care for each other the way our people did before the nation's hoop was broken. They would take everything from each other if they could, and so there were some who had more of everything than they could use, while crowds of people had nothing at all and maybe were starving. They had forgotten that the earth was their mother. This could not be better than the old ways of my people. There was a prisoner's house on an island where the big water came up to the town, and we saw that one day. Men pointed guns at the prisoners and made them move around like animals in a cage. This made me feel very sad, because my people too were penned up in islands, and maybe that was the way the Wasichus were going to treat them.

In the spring it got warmer, but the Wasichus had even the grass penned up. We heard then that we were going to cross the big water to strange lands. Some of our people went home and wanted me to go with them, but I had not seen anything good for my people yet; maybe across the big water there was something to see, so I did not go home, although I was sick and in despair.

[3]Chicago.
[4]New York.
[5]Madison Square Garden.

They put us all on a very big fire-boat, so big that when I first saw, I could hardly believe it; and when it sent forth a voice, I was frightened. There were other big fire-boats sending voices, and little ones too.

Afterwhile I could see nothing but water, water, water, and we did not seem to be going anywhere, just up and down; but we were told that we were going fast. If we were, I thought that we must drop off where the water ended; or maybe we might have to stop where the sky came down to the water. There was nothing but mist where the big town used to be and nothing but water all around.

We were all in despair now and many were feeling so sick that they began to sing their death songs.

When evening came, a big wind was roaring and the water thundered. We had things that were meant to be hung up while we slept in them. This I learned afterward. We did not know what to do with these, so we spread them out on the floor and lay down on them. The floor tipped in every direction, and this got worse and worse, so that we rolled from one side to the other and could not sleep. We were frightened, and now we were all very sick too. At first the Wasichus laughed at us; but very soon we could see that they were frightened too, because they were running around and were very much excited. Our women were crying and even some of the men cried, because it was terrible and they could do nothing. Afterwhile the Wasichus came and gave us things to tie around us so that we could float. I did not put on the one they gave me. I did not want to float. Instead, I dressed for death, putting on my best clothes that I wore in the show, and then I sang my death song. Others dressed for death too, and sang, because if it was the end of our lives and we could do nothing, we wanted to die brave. We could not fight this that was going to kill us, but we could die so that our spirit relatives would not be ashamed of us. It was harder for us because we were all so sick. Everything we had eaten came right up, and then it kept on trying to come up when there was nothing there.

We did not sleep at all, and in the morning the water looked like mountains, but the wind was not so strong. Some of the bison and elk that we had with us for the show died that day, and the Wasichus threw them in the water. When I saw the poor bison thrown over, I felt like crying, because I thought right there they were throwing part of the power of my people away.

After we had been on the fire-boat a long while, we could see many

houses and then many other fire-boats tied close together along the bank. We thought now we could get off very soon, but we could not. There was a little fire-boat that had come through the gate of waters and it stopped beside us, and the people on it looked at everything on our fire-boat before we could get off. We went very slowly nearly all day, I think, and afterwhile we came to where there were many, many houses close together, and more fire-boats than could be counted. These houses were different from what we had seen before. The Wasichus kept us on the fire-boat all night and then they unloaded us, and took us to a place where the show was going to be. The name of this very big town was London. We were on land now, but we still felt dizzy as though we were still on water, and at first it was hard to walk.

We stayed in this place six moons; and many, many people came to see the show.

One day we were told that Majesty was coming. I did not know what that was at first, but I learned afterward. It was Grandmother England (Queen Victoria), who owned Grandmother's Land where we lived awhile after the Wasichus murdered Crazy Horse.

She came to the show in a big shining wagon, and there were soldiers on both sides of her, and many other shining wagons came too. That day other people could not come to the show—just Grandmother England and some people who came with her.

Sometimes we had to shoot in the show, but this time we did not shoot at all. We danced and sang, and I was one of the dancers chosen to do this for the Grandmother, because I was young and limber then and could dance many ways. We stood right in front of Grandmother England. She was little but fat and we liked her, because she was good to us. After we had danced, she spoke to us. She said something like this: "I am sixty-seven years old. All over the world I have seen all kinds of people; but to-day I have seen the best-looking people I know. If you belonged to me, I would not let them take you around in a show like this." She said other good things too, and then she said we must come to see her, because she had come to see us. She shook hands with all of us. Her hand was very little and soft. We gave a big cheer for her, and then the shining wagons came in and she got into one of them and they all went away.

In about a half-moon after that we went to see the Grandmother. They put us in some of those shining wagons and took us to a very beautiful place where there was a very big house with sharp, pointed towers on it. There were many seats built high in a circle, and these

were just full of Wasichus who were all pounding their heels and yelling: "Jubilee! Jubilee! Jubilee!" I never heard what this meant.

They put us together in a certain place at the bottom of the seats. First there appeared a beautiful black wagon with two black horses, and it went all around the show place. I heard that the Grandmother's grandson, a little boy, was in that wagon. Next came a beautiful black wagon with four gray horses. On each of the two right hand horses there was a rider, and a man walked, holding the front left hand horse. I heard that some of Grandmother's relatives were in this wagon. Next came eight buckskin horses, two by two, pulling a shining black wagon. There was a rider on each right hand horse and a man walked, holding the front left hand horse. There were soldiers, with bayonets, facing outward all around this wagon. Now all the people in the seats were roaring and yelling "Jubilee!" and "Victoria!" Then we saw Grandmother England again. She was sitting in the back of the wagon and two women sat in the front, facing her. Her dress was all shining and her hat was all shining and her wagon was all shining and so were the horses. She looked like a fire coming.

Afterward I heard that there was yellow and white metal all over the horses and the wagon.

When she came to where we were, her wagon stopped and she stood up. Then all those people stood up and roared and bowed to her; but she bowed to us. We sent up a great cry and our women made the tremolo. The people in the crowd were so excited that we heard some of them got sick and fell over. Then when it was quiet, we sang a song to the Grandmother.

That was a very happy time.

We liked Grandmother England, because we could see that she was a fine woman, and she was good to us. Maybe if she had been our Grandmother, it would have been better for our people.

XX

THE SPIRIT JOURNEY

Yes, that was a happy time; but it was all over. We went to Manchester and had a show there for several moons.

When the show was going to leave very early next morning, three other young men and myself got lost in Manchester, and the fire-boat went away without us. We could not talk the Wasichu language and we did not know what to do, so we just roamed around. Afterwhile we found two other Lakotas who had been left behind, and one of these could talk English. He said if we went to London we could get money in another show that was there, and then we could go home. We were all sick to go home. So the English-talker got some tickets with the money we all had together, and we went to London on the iron road.

The show was called Mexican Joe. It was a small show, but they gave us a dollar every day for being in it. After we had been in London awhile, Mexican Joe took us to Paris, and we had a show there a long while. There was a Wasichu girl who came to the show very often. She liked me and took me home to see her father and mother. They liked me too and were good to me. I could not talk their language. I made signs, and the girl learned a few Lakota words.

From Paris, we went into Germany and from there to a place where the earth was burning. There was a tall butte, shaped at the top like a tepee, and it was burning up there. I heard that a long time ago a big town and many people disappeared in the earth there.

I was more and more sick to go home all the time now, because it had been two winters since I went away. I could not think of anything else, and afterwhile this made me really sick, but I thought I would have to stay with the show until I could get money enough to go home.

Mexican Joe took us back to Paris, but I could not be in the show because I was so sick now. The girl I told you about took me home to her father and mother, and they made me well. Then one morning I did go home for awhile.

That morning I had on Wasichu clothes and shoes and everything. The only difference was that my hair was long. It was not braided, just hanging back over my shoulders. I was feeling well and we were just sitting down to eat the first meal. This girl-friend of mine was sitting by me, and her mother and father and two sisters were sitting down too.

As we sat there, I looked up at the roof and it seemed to be moving. The house was going around up at the top, and stretching upward as it went around. I could see that we were all rising fast with the whole house, and it was turning around as it 'rose. Then a cloud was coming down as we 'rose, and suddenly I was on it and the other people and the house were falling back away from me.

Then I was alone on this cloud, and it was going fast. I clung to it hard, because I was afraid I might fall off. Far down below I could see houses and towns and green land and streams, and it all looked flat. Then I was right over the big water. I was not afraid any more, because, by now, I knew I was going home. It was dark, and then it was light again, and I could see a big town below me, and I knew it was the one where we first got on the big fire-boat, and that I was in my own country again. I was very happy now. The cloud and I kept on going very fast, and I could see towns and streams and towns and green land. Then I began to recognize the country below me. I saw the Missouri River. Then I saw far off the Black Hills and the center of the world where the spirits had taken me in my great vision.

Then I was right over Pine Ridge, and the cloud stopped. I looked down and could not understand what I saw, because it seemed that nearly all of my people of the different bands were gathered together there in a big camp. I saw my father's and mother's tepee. They were outside, and she was cooking. I wanted to jump off the cloud and be with them, but I was afraid it would kill me. While I was looking down, my mother looked up, and I felt sure she saw me. But just then the cloud started back, going very fast. I was very sad, but I could not get off. There were streams and green land and towns going backward very fast below me. Soon the cloud and I were going right over the very big town again. Then there was only water under me, and the night came without stars; and I was all alone in a black world and I

was crying. But afterwhile some light began to peep in far ahead of me. Then I saw earth beneath me and towns and green land and houses all flying backwards. Soon the cloud stopped over a big town, and a house began coming up toward me, turning around and around as it came. When it touched the cloud, it caught me and began to drop down, turning around and around with me.

It touched the ground, and as it touched I heard the girl's voice, and then other voices of frightened people.

Then I was lying on my back in bed and the girl and her father and her mother and her two sisters and a doctor were looking at me in a queer way, as though they were frightened. The English-talker came from the show and he told me how it was. While I was sitting at breakfast, they said I had looked up and smiled, and then I had fallen like dead out of my chair. I had been dead three days, except that once in awhile I would breathe just a little. Often they said they could not feel my heart at all. They were sure I would soon be really dead, and they were getting ready to buy my coffin.

Maybe if I had not come back to life that time, they would have given me a good coffin; but as it is, I think it will be only a box.

I did not tell the people where I had been, because I knew they could not believe me.

A few days after that, these people heard that Pahuska was in town again. So they took me to where he had his show, and he was glad to see me. He had all his people give me three cheers. Then he asked me if I wanted to be in the show or if I wanted to go home. I told him I was sick to go home. So he said he would fix that. He gave me a ticket and ninety dollars. Then he gave me a big dinner. Pahuska had a strong heart. Afterwhile a policeman came and told me to get my things. He took me to the iron road, and in the morning I was by the big water and they put me on another big fire-boat. We were on the water eight days. I was sick part of the time, but I was not sad, because I was going home.

When the fire-boat was back at the big town in my own country again, I started right away on the iron road.

It was early in the morning when we came to Rushville. There were no Lakotas there at all, but there was a covered wagon with mules starting out for Pine Ridge, so I rode in the wagon.

When I got to Pine Ridge, everything was just as I had seen it from the cloud. All the Lakotas were there, as I had seen them, because that was the year of the treaty (1889) when the Wasichus bought some

more of our land—all that was between the Smoky Earth (the White) and Good River (the Cheyenne). I had been away nearly three years and knew nothing about this foolish thing until then.

My mother's tepee was right where I had seen it when I looked down from the cloud, and other people were camped exactly where I saw them.

My parents were in great joy to see me and my mother cried because she was so happy. I cried too. I was supposed to be a man now, but the tears came out anyway. My mother told me she had dreamed one night in her sleep that I had come back on a cloud, but could not stay. So I told her about my vision.

XXI

THE MESSIAH

There was hunger among my people before I went away across the big water, because the Wasichus did not give us all the food they promised in the Black Hills treaty. They made that treaty themselves; our people did not want it and did not make it. Yet the Wasichus who made it had given us less than half as much as they promised. So the people were hungry before I went away.

But it was worse when I came back. My people looked pitiful. There was a big drouth, and the rivers and creeks seemed to be dying. Nothing would grow that the people had planted, and the Wasichus had been sending less cattle and other food than ever before. The Wasichus had slaughtered all the bison and shut us up in pens. It looked as though we might all starve to death. We could not eat lies, and there was nothing we could do.

And now the Wasichus had made another treaty to take away from us about half the land we had left. Our people did not want this treaty

either, but Three Stars[1] came and made the treaty just the same, because the Wasichus wanted our land between the Smoky Earth and the Good River. So the flood of Wasichus, dirty with bad deeds, gnawed away half of the island that was left to us. When Three Stars came to kill us on the Rosebud, Crazy Horse whipped him and drove him back. But when he came this time without any soldiers, he whipped us and drove us back. We were penned up and could do nothing.

All the time I was away from home across the big water, my power was gone, and I was like a dead man moving around most of the time. I could hardly remember my vision, and when I did remember, it seemed like a dim dream.

Just after I came back, some people asked me to cure a sick person, and I was afraid the power would not come back to me; but it did. So I went on helping the sick, and there were many, for the measles had come among the people who were already weak because of hunger. There were more sick people that winter when the whooping cough came and killed little children who did not have enough to eat.

So it was. Our people were pitiful and in despair.

But early that summer when I came back from across the big water (1889) strange news had come from the west, and the people had been talking and talking about it. They were talking about it when I came home, and that was the first I had heard of it. This news came to the Ogalalas first of all, and I heard that it came to us from the Shoshones and Blue Clouds (Arapahoes). Some believed it and some did not believe. It was hard to believe; and when I first heard of it, I thought it was only foolish talk that somebody had started somewhere. This news said that out yonder in the west at a place near where the great mountains (The Sierras) stand before you come to the big water, there was a sacred man among the Paiutes who had talked to the Great Spirit in a vision, and the Great Spirit had told him how to save the Indian peoples and make the Wasichus disappear and bring back all the bison and the people who were dead and how there would be a new earth. Before I came back, the people had got together to talk about this and they had sent three men, Good Thunder, Brave Bear and Yellow Breast, to see this sacred man with their own eyes and learn if the story about him was true. So these three men had made the long journey west, and in the fall after I came home, they returned to the Ogalalas with wonderful things to tell.

[1]General Crook headed the commission that arranged the treaty of 1889.

There was a big meeting at the head of White Clay Creek, not far from Pine Ridge, when they came back, but I did not go over there to hear, because I did not yet believe. I thought maybe it was only the despair that made people believe, just as a man who is starving may dream of plenty of everything good to eat.

I did not go over to the meeting, but I heard all they had to tell. These three men all said the same thing, and they were good men. They said that they traveled far until they came to a great flat valley[2] near the last great mountains before the big water, and there they saw the Wanekia,[3] who was the son of the Great Spirit, and they talked to him. Wasichus called him Jack Wilson, but his name was Wovoka. He told them that there was another world coming, just like a cloud. It would come in a whirlwind out of the west and would crush out everything on this world, which was old and dying. In that other world there was plenty of meat, just like old times; and in that world all the dead Indians were alive, and all the bison that had ever been killed were roaming around again.

This sacred man gave some sacred red paint and two eagle feathers to Good Thunder. The people must put this paint on their faces and they must dance a ghost dance that the sacred man taught to Good Thunder, Yellow Breast, and Brave Bear. If they did this, they could get on this other world when it came, and the Wasichus would not be able to get on, and so they would disappear. When he gave the two eagle feathers to Good Thunder, the sacred man said: "Receive these eagle feathers and behold them, for my father will cause these to bring your people back to him."

This was all that was heard the whole winter.

When I heard this about the red paint and the eagle feathers and about bringing the people back to the Great Spirit, it made me think hard. I had had a great vision that was to bring the people back into the nation's hoop, and maybe this sacred man had had the same vision and it was going to come true, so that the people would get back on the red road. Maybe I was not meant to do this myself, but if I helped with the power that was given me, the tree might bloom again and the people prosper. This was in my mind all that winter, but I did not know what vision the sacred man out there had seen, and I wished I could talk to him and find out. This was sitting deeper in my mind

[2]Mason Valley, Nevada.
[3]"One Who Makes Live."

every day, and it was a very bad winter, with much hunger and sickness.

My father died in the first part of the winter from the bad sickness that many people had. This made me very sad. Everything good seemed to be going away. My younger brother and sister had died before I came home, and now I was fatherless in this world. But I still had my mother. I was working in a store for the Wasichus so that I could get something for her to eat, and I just kept on working there and thinking about what Good Thunder, Yellow Breast, and Brave Bear had told; but I did not feel sure yet.

During that winter the people wanted to hear some more about this sacred man and the new world coming, so they sent more men out there to learn what they could. Good Thunder and Yellow Breast, with two others, went from Pine Ridge. Some went with them from other agencies, and two of these were Kicking Bear and Short Bull. News came back from these men as they traveled west, and it seemed that everywhere people believed all that we had heard, and more. Letters came back telling us this. I kept on working in the store and helping sick people with my power.

Then it was spring (1890), and I heard that these men had all come back from the west and that they said it was all true. I did not go to this meeting either, but I heard the gossip that was everywhere now, and people said it was really the son of the Great Spirit who was out there; that when he came to the Wasichus a long time ago, they had killed him; but he was coming to the Indians this time, and there would not be any Wasichus in the new world that would come like a cloud in a whirlwind and crush out the old earth that was dying. This they said would happen after one more winter, when the grasses were appearing (1891).

I heard many wonderful things about the Wanekia that these men had seen and heard, and they were good men. He could make animals talk, and once while they were with him he made a spirit vision, and they all saw it. They saw a big water, and beyond it was a beautiful green land where all the Indians that had ever lived and the bison and the other animals were all coming home together. Then the Wanekia, they said, made the vision go out, because it was not yet time for this to happen. After another winter it would happen, when the grasses were appearing.

And once, they said, the Wanekia held out his hat for them to look into; and when they did this, all but one saw there the whole world

and all that was wonderful. But that one could see only the inside of the hat, they said.

Good Thunder himself told me that, with the power of the Wanekia, he had gone to a bison skin tepee; and there his son, who had been dead a long time, was living with his wife, and they had a long talk together.

This was not like my great vision, and I just went on working in the store. I was puzzled and did not know what to think.

Afterwhile I heard that north of Pine Ridge at the head of Cheyenne Creek, Kicking Bear had held the first ghost dance, and that people who danced had seen their dead relatives and talked to them. The next thing I heard was that they were dancing on Wounded Knee Creek just below Manderson.

I did not believe yet, but I wanted to find out things, because all this was sitting more and more strongly in my heart since my father died. Something seemed to tell me to go and see. For awhile I kept from going, but at last I could not any more. So I got on my horse and went to this ghost dance on Wounded Knee Creek below Manderson.

I was surprised, and could hardly believe what I saw; because so much of my vision seemed to be in it. The dancers, both women and men, were holding hands in a big circle, and in the center of the circle they had a tree painted red with most of its branches cut off and some dead leaves on it. This was exactly like the part of my vision where the holy tree was dying, and the circle of the men and women holding hands was like the sacred hoop that should have power to make the tree to bloom again. I saw too that the sacred articles the people had offered were scarlet, as in my vision, and all their faces were painted red. Also, they used the pipe and the eagle feathers. I sat there looking on and feeling sad. It all seemed to be from my great vision somehow and I had done nothing yet to make the tree to bloom.

Then all at once great happiness overcame me, and it all took hold of me right there. This was to remind me to get to work at once and help to bring my people back into the sacred hoop, that they might again walk the red road in a sacred manner pleasing to the Powers of the Universe that are One Power. I remembered how the spirits had taken me to the center of the earth and shown me the good things, and how my people should prosper. I remembered how the Six Grandfathers had told me that through their power I should make my

people live and the holy tree should bloom. I believed my vision was coming true at last, and happiness overcame me.

When I went to the dance, I went only to see and to learn what the people believed; but now I was going to stay and use the power that had been given me. The dance was over for that day, but they would dance again next day, and I would dance with them.

XXII

VISIONS OF THE OTHER WORLD

So I dressed myself in a sacred manner, and before the dance began next morning I went among the people who were standing around the withered tree. Good Thunder, who was a relative of my father and later married my mother, put his arms around me and took me to the sacred tree that had not bloomed, and there he offered up a prayer for me. He said: "Father, Great Spirit, behold this boy! Your ways he shall see!" Then he began to cry.

I thought of my father and my brother and sister who had left us, and I could not keep the tears from running out of my eyes. I raised my face up to keep them back, but they came out just the same. I cried with my whole heart, and while I cried I thought of my people in despair. I thought of my vision, and how it was promised me that my people should have a place in this earth where they could be happy every day. I thought of them on the wrong road now, but maybe they could be brought back into the hoop again and to the good road.

Under the tree that never bloomed I stood and cried because it had withered away. With tears on my face I asked the Great Spirit to give it life and leaves and singing birds, as in my vision.

Then there came a strong shivering all over my body, and I knew that the power was in me.

Good Thunder now took one of my arms, Kicking Bear the other, and we began to dance. The song we sang was like this:

> "Who do you think he is that comes?
> It is one who seeks his mother!"

It was what the dead would sing when entering the other world and looking for their relatives who had gone there before them.

As I danced, with Good Thunder and Kicking Bear holding my arms between them, I had the queer feeling that I knew and I seemed to be lifted clear off the ground. I did not have a vision all that first day. That night I thought about the other world and that the Wanekia himself was with my people there and maybe the holy tree of my vision was really blooming yonder right then, and that it was there my vision had already come true. From the center of the earth I had been shown all good and beautiful things in a great circle of peace, and maybe this land of my vision was where all my people were going, and there they would live and prosper where no Wasichus were or could ever be.

Before we started dancing next day, Kicking Bear offered a prayer, saying: "Father, Great Spirit, behold these people! They shall go forth to-day to see their relatives, and yonder they shall be happy, day after day, and their happiness will not end."

Then we began dancing, and most of the people wailed and cried as they danced, holding hands in a circle; but some of them laughed with happiness. Now and then some one would fall down like dead, and others would go staggering around and panting before they would fall. While they were lying there like dead they were having visions, and we kept on dancing and singing, and many were crying for the old way of living and that the old religion might be with them again.

After awhile I began to feel very queer. First, my legs seemed to be full of ants. I was dancing with my eyes closed, as the others did. Suddenly it seemed that I was swinging off the ground and not touching it any longer. The queer feeling came up from my legs and was in my heart now. It seemed I would glide forward like a swing, and then glide back again in longer and longer swoops. There was no fear with this, just a growing happiness.

I must have fallen down, but I felt as though I had fallen off a swing when it was going forward, and I was floating head first through the air. My arms were stretched out, and all I saw at first was a single eagle

feather right in front of me. Then the feather was a spotted eagle dancing on ahead of me with his wings fluttering, and he was making the shrill whistle that is his. My body did not move at all, but I looked ahead and floated fast toward where I looked.

There was a ridge right in front of me, and I thought I was going to run into it, but I went right over it. On the other side of the ridge I could see a beautiful land where many, many people were camping in a great circle. I could see that they were happy and had plenty. Everywhere there were drying racks full of meat. The air was clear and beautiful with a living light that was everywhere. All around the circle, feeding on the green, green grass, were fat and happy horses; and animals of all kinds were scattered all over the green hills, and singing hunters were returning with their meat.

I floated over the tepees and began to come down feet first at the center of the hoop where I could see a beautiful tree all green and full of flowers. When I touched the ground, two men were coming toward me, and they wore holy shirts made and painted in a certain way. They came to me and said: "It is not yet time to see your father, who is happy. You have work to do. We will give you something that you shall carry back to your people, and with it they shall come to see their loved ones."

I knew it was the way their holy shirts were made that they wanted me to take back. They told me to return at once, and then I was out in the air again, floating fast as before. When I came right over the dancing place, the people were still dancing, but it seemed they were not making any sound. I had hoped to see the withered tree in bloom, but it was dead.

Then I fell back into my body, and as I did this I heard voices all around and above me, and I was sitting on the ground. Many were crowding around, asking me what vision I had seen. I told them just what I had seen, and what I brought back was the memory of the holy shirts the two men wore.

That evening some of us got together at Big Road's tepee and decided to use the ghost shirts I had seen. So the next day I made ghost shirts all day long and painted them in the sacred manner of my vision. As I made these shirts, I thought how in my vision everything was like old times and the tree was flowering, but when I came back the tree was dead. And I thought that if this world would do as the vision teaches, the tree could bloom here too.

I made the first shirt for Afraid-of-Hawk and the second for the son of Big Road.

In the evening I made a sacred stick like that I had seen in my first vision and painted it red with the sacred paint of the Wanekia. On the top of it I tied one eagle feather, and this I carried in the dance after that, wearing the holy shirt as I had seen it.

Because of my vision and the power they knew I had, I was asked to lead the dance next morning. We all stood in a straight line, facing the west, and I prayed: "Father, Great Spirit, behold me! The nation that I have is in despair. The new earth you promised you have shown me. Let my nation also behold it."

After the prayer we stood with our right hands raised to the west, and we all began to weep, and right there, as they wept, some of them fainted before the dance began.

As we were dancing I had the same queer feeling I had before, as though my feet were off the earth and swinging. Kicking Bear and Good Thunder were holding my arms. Afterwhile it seemed they let go of me, and once more I floated head first, face down, with arms extended, and the spotted eagle was dancing there ahead of me again, and I could hear his shrill whistle and his scream.

I saw the ridge again, and as I neared it there was a deep, rumbling sound, and out of it there leaped a flame. But I glided right over it. There were six villages ahead of me in the beautiful land that was all clear and green in living light. Over these in turn I glided, coming down on the south side of the sixth village. And as I touched the ground, twelve men were coming towards me, and they said: "Our Father, the two-legged chief, you shall see!"

Then they led me to the center of the circle where once more I saw the holy tree all full of leaves and blooming.

But that was not all I saw. Against the tree there was a man standing with arms held wide in front of him. I looked hard at him, and I could not tell what people he came from. He was not a Wasichu and he was not an Indian. His hair was long and hanging loose, and on the left side of his head he wore an eagle feather. His body was strong and good to see, and it was painted red. I tried to recognize him, but I could not make him out. He was a very fine-looking man. While I was staring hard at him, his body began to change and became very beautiful with all colors of light, and around him there was light. He spoke like singing: "My life is such that all earthly beings and growing

things belong to me. Your father, the Great Spirit, has said this. You too must say this."

Then he went out like a light in a wind.

The twelve men who were there spoke: "Behold them! Your nation's life shall be such!"

I saw again how beautiful the day was—the sky all blue and full of yellow light above the greening earth. And I saw that all the people were beautiful and young. There were no old ones there, nor children either—just people of about one age, and beautiful.

Then there were twelve women who stood in front of me and spoke: "Behold them! Their way of life you shall take back to earth." When they had spoken, I heard singing in the west, and I learned the song I heard.

Then one of the twelve men took two sticks, one painted white and one red, and, thrusting them in the ground, he said: "Take these! You shall depend upon them. Make haste!"

I started to walk, and it seemed as though a strong wind went under me and picked me up. I was in the air, with outstretched arms, and floating fast. There was a fearful dark river that I had to go over, and I was afraid. It rushed and roared and was full of angry foam. Then I looked down and saw many men and women who were trying to cross the dark and fearful river, but they could not. Weeping, they looked up to me and cried: "Help us!" But I could not stop gliding, for it was as though a great wind were under me.

Then I saw my earthly people again at the dancing place, and fell back into my body lying there. And I was sitting up, and people were crowding around me to ask what vision I had seen.

I told my vision through songs, and the older men explained them to the others. I sang a song, the words of which were those the Wanekia spoke under the flowering tree, and the air of it was that which I heard in the West after the twelve women had spoken. I sang it four times, and the fourth time all the people began to weep together because the Wasichus had taken the beautiful world away from us.

I thought and thought about this vision. The six villages seemed to represent the Six Grandfathers that I had seen long ago in the Flaming Rainbow Tepee, and I had gone to the sixth village, which was for the Sixth Grandfather, the Spirit of the Earth, because I was to stand for him in the world. I wondered if the Wanekia might be the red man of my great vision, who turned into a bison, and then into the four-rayed herb, the daybreak-star herb of understanding. I thought the twelve men and twelve women were for the moons of the year.

XXIII

BAD TROUBLE COMING

While these things were happening, the summer (1890) was getting old. I did not then know all that was going on at other places, but some things I heard, and much more I heard later.

When Good Thunder and Kicking Bear came back in the spring from seeing the Wanekia, the Wasichus at Pine Ridge put them in prison awhile, and then let them go. This showed the Wasichus were afraid of something. In the Moon of Black Cherries (August) many people were dancing at No Water's Camp on Clay Creek, and the agent came and told them to stop dancing. They would not stop, and they said they would fight for their religion if they had to do it. The agent went away, and they kept on dancing. They called him Young-Man-Afraid-of-Lakotas.

Later, I heard that the Brules were dancing over east of us; and then I heard that Big Foot's people were dancing on the Good River reservation; also that Kicking Bear had gone to Sitting Bull's camp on Grand River, and that the people were dancing there too. Word came to us that the Indians were beginning to dance everywhere.

The people were hungry and in despair, and many believed in the good new world that was coming. The Wasichus gave us less than half the beef cattle they promised us in the treaty, and these cattle were very poor. For a while our people would not take the cattle, because there were so few of them and they were so poor. But afterwhile they had to take them or starve to death. So we got more lies than cattle, and we could not eat lies. When the agent told the people to quit dancing, their hearts were bad.

From the dancing on Wounded Knee I went over to the Brules, who were camping on Cut Meat Creek at this time, and I took with me six

shirts like those I had seen the twelve men wearing in my vision, and six dresses like the twelve women wore. I gave these to the Brules and they made others for themselves.

We danced there, and another vision came to me. I saw a Flaming Rainbow, like the one I had seen in my first great vision. Below the rainbow was a tepee made of cloud. Over me there was a spotted eagle soaring, and he said to me: "Remember this." That was all I saw and heard.

I have thought much about this since, and I have thought that this was where I made my great mistake. I had had a very great vision, and I should have depended only upon that to guide me to the good. But I followed the lesser visions that had come to me while dancing on Wounded Knee Creek. The vision of the Flaming Rainbow was to warn me, maybe; and I did not understand. I did not depend upon the great vision as I should have done; I depended upon the two sticks that I had seen in the lesser vision. It is hard to follow one great vision in this world of darkness and of many changing shadows. Among those shadows men get lost.

When I came back from the Brules, the weather was getting cold. Many of the Brules came along when I came back, and joined the Ogalalas in the dancing on Wounded Knee. We heard that there were soldiers at Pine Ridge and that others were coming all the time. Then one morning we heard that the soldiers were marching toward us, so we broke camp and moved west to Grass Creek. From there we went to White Clay and camped awhile and danced.

There came to us Fire Thunder, Red Wound and Young American Horse with a message from the soldiers that this matter of the ghost dance must be looked into, and that there should be rulings over it; and that they did not mean to take the dance away from us. But could we believe anything the Wasichus ever said to us? They spoke with forked tongues.

We moved in closer to Pine Ridge and camped. Many soldiers were there now, and what were they there for?

There was a big meeting with the agent, but I did not go to hear. He made a ruling that we could dance three days every moon, and the rest of the time we should go and make a living for ourselves somehow. He did not say how we could do that. But the people agreed to this.

The next day, while I was sitting in a tepee with Good Thunder, a policeman came to us and said: "I was not sent here, but I came for

your good to tell you what I have heard—that they are going to arrest you two."

Good Thunder thought we ought to go to the Brules, who had a big camp on Wounded Knee below Manderson. So that evening we saddled and started. We came through Pepper Creek and White Horse Creek to Wounded Knee and followed it down to the Brule camp. They were glad to see us.

In the morning the crier went around and called a meeting. I spoke to the Brules, and this is what I said: "My relatives, there is a certain thing that we have done. From that certain sacred thing, we have had visions. In those visions we have seen, and also we have heard, that our relatives who have gone before us are in the Other World that has been revealed to us, and that we too shall go there. They are right now with the Wanekia. If the Wasichus want to fight us, let them do it. Have in your minds a strong desire, and take courage. We must depend upon the departed ones who are in the new world that is coming."

More Brules came there from Porcupine and Medicine Root creeks, and we all broke camp, moving down the Wounded Knee to Smoky Earth River (the White). There a Black Robe (Catholic Priest) came and tried to coax us to return. Our people told him that Wasichu promises were no good; that everything they had promised was a lie. Only a few Ogalalas turned back with the Black Robe. He was a good man and he was badly wounded that winter in the butchering of Big Foot's band. He was a very good man, and not like the other Wasichus.[1]

From Smoky Earth River we moved to High Pockets' place southwest of the Top of the Badlands.[2] While we were there, American Horse and Fast Thunder came to us. They were both chiefs, and they came to bring us in to Pine Ridge. We had to obey. The Brules would not obey and tried to keep us from going. They struck us, and there was quite a struggle for a while; but we went anyway, because we had to go. Kicking Bear stayed with the Brules that time, but he came in to Pine Ridge a little later. A very few of the Brules went along with us.

We camped on White River, then on White Clay, then on Cheyenne Creek north of Pine Ridge. Most of the Ogalalas were camping near there too.

It was about this time that bad news came to us from the north. We

[1]This was Father Craft.
[2]Cuny Table, a high plateau in the midst of the Badlands.

heard that some policemen from Standing Rock had gone to arrest Sitting Bull on Grand River, and that he would not let them take him; so there was a fight, and they killed him.

It was now near the end of the Moon of Popping Trees, and I was twenty-seven years old (December, 1890). We heard that Big Foot was coming down from the Badlands with nearly four hundred people. Some of these were from Sitting Bull's band. They had run away when Sitting Bull was killed, and joined Big Foot on Good River. There were only about a hundred warriors in this band, and all the others were women and children and some old men. They were all starving and freezing, and Big Foot was so sick that they had to bring him along in a pony drag.[3] They had all run away to hide in the Badlands, and they were coming in now because they were starving and freezing. When they crossed Smoky Earth River, they followed up Medicine Root Creek to its head. Soldiers were over there looking for them. The soldiers had everything and were not freezing and starving. Near Porcupine Butte the soldiers came up to the Big Foots, and they surrendered and went along with the soldiers to Wounded Knee Creek where the Brenan store is now.

It was in the evening when we heard that the Big Foots were camped over there with the soldiers, about fifteen miles by the old road from where we were. It was the next morning (December 29, 1890) that something terrible happened.

XXIV

THE BUTCHERING AT WOUNDED KNEE

That evening before it happened, I went in to Pine Ridge and heard these things, and while I was there, soldiers started for where the Big Foots were. These made about five hundred soldiers that were there

[3] He was very ill with pneumonia.

next morning. When I saw them starting I felt that something terrible was going to happen. That night I could hardly sleep at all. I walked around most of the night.

In the morning I went out after my horses, and while I was out I heard shooting off toward the east, and I knew from the sound that it must be wagon-guns (cannon) going off. The sounds went right through my body, and I felt that something terrible would happen.

When I reached camp with the horses, a man rode up to me and said: "Hey-hey-hey! The people that are coming are fired on! I know it!"

I saddled up my buckskin and put on my sacred shirt. It was one I had made to be worn by no one but myself. It had a spotted eagle outstretched on the back of it, and the daybreak star was on the left shoulder, because when facing south that shoulder is toward the east. Across the breast, from the left shoulder to the right hip, was the flaming rainbow, and there was another rainbow around the neck, like a necklace, with a star at the bottom. At each shoulder, elbow, and wrist was an eagle feather; and over the whole shirt were red streaks of lightning. You will see that this was from my great vision, and you will know how it protected me that day.

I painted my face all red, and in my hair I put one eagle feather for the One Above.

It did not take me long to get ready, for I could still hear the shooting over there.

I started out alone on the old road that ran across the hills to Wounded Knee. I had no gun. I carried only the sacred bow of the west that I had seen in my great vision. I had gone only a little way when a band of young men came galloping after me. The first two who came up were Loves War and Iron Wasichu. I asked what they were going to do, and they said they were just going to see where the shooting was. Then others were coming up, and some older men.

We rode fast, and there were about twenty of us now. The shooting was getting louder. A horseback from over there came galloping very fast toward us, and he said: "Hey-hey-hey! They have murdered them!" Then he whipped his horse and rode away faster toward Pine Ridge.

In a little while we had come to the top of the ridge where, looking to the east, you can see for the first time the monument and the burying ground on the little hill where the church is. That is where the terrible thing started. Just south of the burying ground on the

little hill a deep dry gulch runs about east and west, very crooked, and it rises westward to nearly the top of the ridge where we were. It had no name, but the Wasichus sometimes call it Battle Creek now. We stopped on the ridge not far from the head of the dry gulch. Wagon guns were still going off over there on the little hill, and they were going off again where they hit along the gulch. There was much shooting down yonder, and there were many cries, and we could see cavalrymen scattered over the hills ahead of us. Cavalrymen were riding along the gulch and shooting into it, where the women and children were running away and trying to hide in the gullies and the stunted pines.

A little way ahead of us, just below the head of the dry gulch, there were some women and children who were huddled under a clay bank, and some cavalrymen were there pointing guns at them.

We stopped back behind the ridge, and I said to the others: "Take courage. These are our relatives. We will try to get them back." Then we all sang a song which went like this:

> "A thunder being nation I am, I have said.
> A thunder being nation I am, I have said.
> You shall live.
> You shall live.
> You shall live.
> You shall live."

Then I rode over the ridge and the others after me, and we were crying: "Take courage! It is time to fight!" The soldiers who were guarding our relatives shot at us and then ran away fast, and some more cavalrymen on the other side of the gulch did too. We got our relatives and sent them across the ridge to the northwest where they would be safe.

I had no gun, and when we were charging, I just held the sacred bow out in front of me with my right hand. The bullets did not hit us at all.

We found a little baby lying all alone near the head of the gulch. I could not pick her up just then, but I got her later and some of my people adopted her. I just wrapped her up tighter in a shawl that was around her and left her there. It was a safe place, and I had other work to do.

The soldiers had run eastward over the hills where there were some more soldiers, and they were off their horses and lying down. I told

the others to stay back, and I charged upon them holding the sacred bow out toward them with my right hand. They all shot at me, and I could hear bullets all around me, but I ran my horse right close to them, and then swung around. Some soldiers across the gulch began shooting at me too, but I got back to the others and was not hurt at all.

By now many other Lakotas, who had heard the shooting, were coming up from Pine Ridge, and we all charged on the soldiers. They ran eastward toward where the trouble began. We followed down along the dry gulch, and what we saw was terrible. Dead and wounded women and children and little babies were scattered all along there where they had been trying to run away. The soldiers had followed along the gulch, as they ran, and murdered them in there. Sometimes they were in heaps because they had huddled together, and some were scattered all along. Sometimes bunches of them had been killed and torn to pieces where the wagon guns hit them. I saw a little baby trying to suck its mother, but she was bloody and dead.

There were two little boys at one place in this gulch. They had guns and they had been killing soldiers all by themselves. We could see the soldiers they had killed. The boys were all alone there, and they were not hurt. These were very brave little boys.

When we drove the soldiers back, they dug themselves in, and we were not enough people to drive them out from there. In the evening they marched off up Wounded Knee Creek, and then we saw all that they had done there.

Men and women and children were heaped and scattered all over the flat at the bottom of the little hill where the soldiers had their wagon-guns, and westward up the dry gulch all the way to the high ridge, the dead women and children and babies were scattered.

When I saw this I wished that I had died too, but I was not sorry for the women and children. It was better for them to be happy in the other world, and I wanted to be there too. But before I went there I wanted to have revenge. I thought there might be a day, and we should have revenge.

After the soldiers marched away, I heard from my friend, Dog Chief, how the trouble started, and he was right there by Yellow Bird when it happened. This is the way it was:

In the morning the soldiers began to take all the guns away from the Big Foots, who were camped in the flat below the little hill where the

monument and burying ground are now. The people had stacked most of their guns, and even their knives, by the tepee where Big Foot was lying sick. Soldiers were on the little hill and all around, and there were soldiers across the dry gulch to the south and over east along Wounded Knee Creek too. The people were nearly surrounded, and the wagon-guns were pointing at them.

Some had not yet given up their guns, and so the soldiers were searching all the tepees, throwing things around and poking into everything. There was a man called Yellow Bird, and he and another man were standing in front of the tepee where Big Foot was lying sick. They had white sheets around and over them, with eyeholes to look through, and they had guns under these. An officer came to search them. He took the other man's gun, and then started to take Yellow Bird's. But Yellow Bird would not let go. He wrestled with the officer, and while they were wrestling, the gun went off and killed the officer. Wasichus and some others have said he meant to do this, but Dog Chief was standing right there, and he told me it was not so. As soon as the gun went off, Dog Chief told me, an officer shot and killed Big Foot who was lying sick inside the tepee.

Then suddenly nobody knew what was happening, except that the soldiers were all shooting and the wagon-guns began going off right in among the people.

Many were shot down right there. The women and children ran into the gulch and up west, dropping all the time, for the soldiers shot them as they ran. There were only about a hundred warriors and there were nearly five hundred soldiers. The warriors rushed to where they had piled their guns and knives. They fought soldiers with only their hands until they got their guns.

Dog Chief saw Yellow Bird run into a tepee with his gun, and from there he killed soldiers until the tepee caught fire. Then he died full of bullets.

It was a good winter day when all this happened. The sun was shining. But after the soldiers marched away from their dirty work, a heavy snow began to fall. The wind came up in the night. There was a big blizzard, and it grew very cold. The snow drifted deep in the crooked gulch, and it was one long grave of butchered women and children and babies, who had never done any harm and were only trying to run away.

XXV

THE END OF THE DREAM

After the soldiers marched away, Red Crow and I started back toward Pine Ridge together, and I took the little baby that I told you about. Red Crow had one too.

We were going back to Pine Ridge, because we thought there was peace back home; but it was not so. While we were gone, there was a fight around the Agency, and our people had all gone away. They had gone away so fast that they left all the tepees standing.

It was nearly dark when we passed north of Pine Ridge where the hospital is now, and some soldiers shot at us, but did not hit us. We rode into the camp, and it was all empty. We were very hungry because we had not eaten anything since early morning, so we peeped into the tepees until we saw where there was a pot with papa (dried meat) cooked in it. We sat down in there and began to eat. While we were doing this, the soldiers shot at the tepee, and a bullet struck right between Red Crow and me. It threw dust in the soup, but we kept right on eating until we had our fill. Then we took the babies and got on our horses and rode away. If that bullet had only killed me, then I could have died with papa in my mouth.

The people had fled down Clay Creek, and we followed their trail. It was dark now, and late in the night we came to where they were camped without any tepees. They were just sitting by little fires, and the snow was beginning to blow. We rode in among them and I heard my mother's voice. She was singing a death song for me, because she felt sure I had died over there. She was so glad to see me that she cried and cried.

Women who had milk fed the little babies that Red Crow and I brought with us.

I think nobody but the little children slept any that night. The snow blew and we had no tepees.

When it was getting light, a war party went out and I went along; but this time I took a gun with me. When I started out the day before to Wounded Knee, I took only my sacred bow, which was not made to shoot with; because I was a little in doubt about the Wanekia religion at that time, and I did not really want to kill anybody because of it.

But I did not feel like that any more. After what I had seen over there, I wanted revenge; I wanted to kill.

We crossed White Clay Creek and followed it up, keeping on the west side. Soon we could hear many guns going off. So we struck west, following a ridge to where the fight was. It was close to the Mission, and there are many bullets in the Mission yet.

From this ridge we could see that the Lakotas were on both sides of the creek and were shooting at soldiers who were coming down the creek. As we looked down, we saw a little ravine, and across this was a big hill. We crossed and rode up the hillside.

They were fighting right there, and a Lakota cried to me: "Black Elk, this is the kind of a day in which to do something great!" I answered: "How!"[1]

Then I got off my horse and rubbed earth on myself, to show the Powers that I was nothing without their help. Then I took my rifle, got on my horse and galloped up to the top of the hill. Right below me the soldiers were shooting, and my people called out to me not to go down there; that there were some good shots among the soldiers and I should get killed for nothing.

But I remembered my great vision, the part where the geese of the north appeared. I depended upon their power. Stretching out my arms with my gun in the right hand, like a goose soaring when it flies low to turn in a change of weather, I made the sound the geese make— br-r-r-p, br-r-r-p, br-r-r-p; and, doing this, I charged. The soldiers saw, and began shooting fast at me. I kept right on with my buckskin running, shot in their faces when I was near, then swung wide and rode back up the hill.

All this time the bullets were buzzing around me and I was not touched. I was not even afraid. It was like being in a dream about shooting. But just as I had reached the very top of the hill, suddenly

[1] Signifying assent.

it was like waking up, and I was afraid. I dropped my arms and quit making the goose cry. Just as I did this, I felt something strike my belt as though some one had hit me there with the back of an ax. I nearly fell out of my saddle, but I managed to hold on, and rode over the hill.

An old man by the name of Protector was there, and he ran up and held me, for now I was falling off my horse. I will show you where the bullet struck me sidewise across the belly here (showing a long deep scar on the abdomen). My insides were coming out. Protector tore up a blanket in strips and bound it around me so that my insides would stay in. By now I was crazy to kill, and I said to Protector: "Help me on my horse! Let me go over there. It is a good day to die, so I will go over there!" But Protector said: "No, young nephew! You must not die to-day. That would be foolish. Your people need you. There may be a better day to die." He lifted me into my saddle and led my horse away down hill. Then I began to feel very sick.

By now it looked as though the soldiers would be wiped out, and the Lakotas were fighting harder; but I heard that, after I left, the black Wasichu soldiers came, and the Lakotas had to retreat.

There were many of our children in the Mission, and the sisters and priests were taking care of them. I heard there were sisters and priests right in the battle helping wounded people and praying.

There was a man by the name of Little Soldier who took charge of me and brought me to where our people were camped. While we were over at the Mission Fight, they had fled to the O-ona-gazhee[2] and were camped on top of it where the women and children would be safe from soldiers. Old Hollow Horn was there. He was a very powerful bear medicine man, and he came over to heal my wound. In three days I could walk, but I kept a piece of blanket tied around my belly.

It was now nearly the middle of the Moon of Frost in the Tepee (January). We heard that soldiers were on Smoky Earth River and were coming to attack us in the O-ona-gazhee. They were near Black Feather's place. So a party of about sixty of us started on the war-path to find them. My mother tried to keep me at home, because, although I could walk and ride a horse, my wound was not all healed yet. But I would not stay; for, after what I had seen at Wounded Knee, I wanted a chance to kill soldiers.

[2]Sheltering place, an elevated plateau in the Badlands, with precipitous sides, and inaccessible save by one narrow neck of land easily defended.

We rode down Grass Creek to Smoky Earth, and crossed, riding down stream. Soon from the top of a little hill we saw wagons and cavalry guarding them. The soldiers were making a corral of their wagons and getting ready to fight. We got off our horses and went behind some hills to a little knoll, where we crept up to look at the camp. Some soldiers were bringing harnessed horses down to a little creek to water, and I said to the others: "If you will stay here and shoot at the soldiers, I will charge over there and get some good horses." They knew of my power, so they did this, and I charged on my buckskin while the others kept shooting. I got seven of the horses; but when I started back with these, all the soldiers saw me and began shooting. They killed two of my horses, but I brought five back safe and was not hit. When I was out of range, I caught up a fine bald-faced bay and turned my buckskin loose. Then I drove the others back to our party.

By now more cavalry were coming up the river, a big bunch of them, and there was some hard fighting for a while, because there were not enough of us. We were fighting and retreating, and all at once I saw Red Willow on foot running. He called to me: "Cousin, my horse is killed!" So I caught up a soldier's horse that was dragging a rope and brought it to Red Willow while the soldiers were shooting fast at me. Just then, for a little while, I was a wanekia[3] myself. In this fight Long Bear and another man, whose name I have forgotten, were badly wounded; but we saved them and carried them along with us. The soldiers did not follow us far into the Badlands, and when it was night we rode back with our wounded to the O-ona-gazhee.

We wanted a much bigger war-party so that we could meet the soldiers and get revenge. But this was hard, because the people were not all of the same mind, and they were hungry and cold. We had a meeting there, and were all ready to go out with more warriors, when Afraid-of-His-Horses came over from Pine Ridge to make peace with Red Cloud, who was with us there.

Our party wanted to go out and fight anyway, but Red Cloud made a speech to us something like this: "Brothers, this is a very hard winter. The women and children are starving and freezing. If this were summer, I would say to keep on fighting to the end. But we cannot do this. We must think of the women and children and that it is very bad for them. So we must make peace, and I will see that nobody is hurt by the soldiers."

[3]A "make-live," savior.

The people agreed to this, for it was true. So we broke camp next day and went down from the O-ona-gazhee to Pine Ridge, and many, many Lakotas were already there. Also, there were many, many soldiers. They stood in two lines with their guns held in front of them as we went through to where we camped.

And so it was all over.

I did not know then how much was ended. When I look back now from this high hill of my old age, I can still see the butchered women and children lying heaped and scattered all along the crooked gulch as plain as when I saw them with eyes still young. And I can see that something else died there in the bloody mud, and was buried in the blizzard. A people's dream died there. It was a beautiful dream.

And I, to whom so great a vision was given in my youth,—you see me now a pitiful old man who has done nothing, for the nation's hoop is broken and scattered. There is no center any longer, and the sacred tree is dead.

AUTHOR'S POSTSCRIPT

After the conclusion of the narrative, Black Elk and our party were sitting at the north edge of Cuny Table, looking off across the Badlands ("the beauty and the strangeness of the earth," as the old man expressed it). Pointing at Harney Peak that loomed black above the far sky-rim, Black Elk said: "There, when I was young, the spirits took me in my vision to the center of the earth and showed me all the good things in the sacred hoop of the world. I wish I could stand up there in the flesh before I die, for there is something I want to say to the Six Grandfathers."

So the trip to Harney Peak was arranged, and a few days later we were there. On the way up to the summit, Black Elk remarked to his son, Ben: "Something should happen to-day. If I have any power left, the thunder beings of the west should hear me when I send a voice, and there should be at least a little thunder and a little rain." What happened is, of course, related to Wasichu readers as being merely a more or less striking coincidence. It was a bright and cloudless day, and after we had reached the summit the sky was perfectly clear. It was a season of drouth, one of the worst in the memory of the old men. The sky remained clear until about the conclusion of the ceremony.

"Right over there," said Black Elk, indicating a point of rock, "is where I stood in my vision, but the hoop of the world about me was different, for what I saw was in the spirit."

Having dressed and painted himself as he was in his great vision, he faced the west, holding the sacred pipe before him in his right hand. Then he sent forth a voice; and a thin, pathetic voice it seemed in that vast space around us:

"Hey-a-a-hey! Hey-a-a-hey! Hey-a-a-hey! Hey-a-a-hey! Grandfather, Great Spirit, once more behold me on earth and lean to hear my feeble voice. You lived first, and you are older than all need, older than all prayer. All things belong to you—the two-leggeds, the four-leggeds, the wings of the air and all green things that live. You have set the powers of the four quarters to cross each other. The good road and the road of difficulties you have made to cross; and where they

cross, the place is holy. Day in and day out, forever, you are the life of things.

"Therefore I am sending a voice, Great Spirit, my Grandfather, forgetting nothing you have made, the stars of the universe and the grasses of the earth.

"You have said to me, when I was still young and could hope, that in difficulty I should send a voice four times, once for each quarter of the earth, and you would hear me.

"To-day I send a voice for a people in despair.

"You have given me a sacred pipe, and through this I should make my offering. You see it now.

"From the west, you have given me the cup of living water and the sacred bow, the power to make live and to destroy. You have given me a sacred wind and the herb from where the white giant lives —the cleansing power and the healing. The daybreak star and the pipe, you have given from the east; and from the south, the nation's sacred hoop and the tree that was to bloom. To the center of the world you have taken me and showed the goodness and the beauty and the strangeness of the greening earth, the only mother—and there the spirit shapes of things, as they should be, you have shown to me and I have seen. At the center of this sacred hoop you have said that I should make the tree to bloom.

"With tears running, O Great Spirit, Great Spirit, my Grandfather—with running tears I must say now that the tree has never bloomed. A pitiful old man, you see me here, and I have fallen away and have done nothing. Here at the center of the world, where you took me when I was young and taught me; here, old, I stand, and the tree is withered, Grandfather, my Grandfather!

"Again, and maybe the last time on this earth, I recall the great vision you sent me. It may be that some little root of the sacred tree still lives. Nourish it then, that it may leaf and bloom and fill with singing birds. Hear me, not for myself, but for my people; I am old. Hear me that they may once more go back into the sacred hoop and find the good red road, the shielding tree!"

We who listened now noted that thin clouds had gathered about us. A scant chill rain began to fall and there was low, muttering thunder without lightning. With tears running down his cheeks, the old man raised his voice to a thin high wail, and chanted: "In sorrow I am

sending a feeble voice, O Six Powers of the World. Hear me in my sorrow, for I may never call again. O make my people live!"

For some minutes the old man stood silent, with face uplifted, weeping in the drizzling rain.

In a little while the sky was clear again.

APPENDIX I

Transcript of stenographic notes for a letter written by John G. Neihardt to Nick Black Elk, 6 November 1930

Nick Black Elk
Oglala, South Dakota

Dear Friend,

Your letter of November 3 has just reached me, and I am very happy to hear from you! I wondered why I did not hear from you. But I was sure that you would write to me, for I felt when we parted at your home in Manderson that we were friends and that you would not fail me. I see now why you did not write sooner.

I am glad to know that you are willing to make the picture story of the Messiah and of Wounded Knee for me. You say if I will send you $7 for the material, you can go ahead on this work, and I am sending you the money with this letter, so that you can get started. You did not tell me how much you will want for your work. Please do. I think that fawn skin will be even better for the picture than rawhide.

Now I have something to tell you that I hope and believe will interest you as much as it does me. After talking with you four and a half hours and thinking over many things you told me, I feel that the whole story of your life ought to be written truthfully by somebody with the right feeling and understanding of your people and of their great history. My idea is to come back to the reservation next spring, probably in April, and have a number of meetings with you and your old friends among the Oglalas who have shared the great history of your race, during the past half century or more.

I would want you to tell the story of your life beginning at the beginning and going straight through to Wounded Knee. I would have my daughter, who is a shorthand writer, take down everything you would say, and I would want your friends to talk any time about, and share in, the different things that you would tell about. This would make a complete story of your people since your childhood.

So, you see, this book would be not only the story of your life, but

the story of the life of your people. The fact that you have been both a warrior and a medicine man would be of great help in writing the book, because both religion and war are of great importance in history. The book that I sent you at Manderson [*The Song of the Indian Wars*] is a poem dealing only with the wars between the Sioux and white men and does not tell everything that ought to be told. This book about you would be written in prose, and I would use as much of your language in it as possible. My publisher is eager to have me do this, for I have told him all about it.

I would, of course, expect to pay you well for all the time that you would give me. It would probably be necessary for us to have eight or ten meetings. Does this plan seem a good one to you, and if it seems good to you, will you not be willing to help me make it successful? I do feel that so much is known by you Indians that our white people do not know and should know, that I am very eager to write this book if you will help me. Write and tell me how much you think you should be paid for each meeting, and there should be from six to ten meetings. And tell me if you think you could get three or four of the fine old men that you know to meet with us and talk about old times while you are telling your story to me.

This is not a money-making scheme for me. I can make money much faster and easier in other ways. I want to do this book because I want to tell the things that you and your friends know, and I can promise you that it will be an honest and a loving book.

I often look at the beautiful ornaments you gave me, and I am very proud of them. And also when I look at them, I think of what they tell me, and that makes them more beautiful still.

With every kind thought for you and your family.

Your friend,

John G. Neihardt

APPENDIX II
A NEIHARDT-BLACK ELK
PORTFOLIO

The photograph overleaf of Black Elk and Elk is used with the permission of the Smithsonian Institution. All the following photographs are reproduced by permission of the John G. Neihardt Trust. They may not be used in any manner without the written permission of the John G. Neihardt Trust, Hilda N. Petri, Trustee.

Smithsonian Institution, National Anthropological Archives

Black Elk and Elk as they appeared when touring Europe with Buffalo Bill's Wild West.

Enid Neihardt, Nick Black Elk, Ben Black Elk, Standing Bear, and John G. Neihardt

John G. Neihardt in the study in his home in Branson, Missouri, during the early 1930s

Black Elk with his drum and Standing Bear with Black Elk's pipe; in the foreground a Chief Joseph blanket. Photograph taken by John G. Neihardt during the interviews for *Black Elk Speaks*

Black Elk at a feast given by John G. Neihardt in May 1931.
Photograph taken by the author

Standing Bear at the same feast. Photograph taken by the author

Hilda Neihardt, Black Elk, Chase in the Morning, and John G. Neihardt ready for the hoop and spear game. Photograph taken in May 1931 in front of Black Elk's home

Black Elk and Neihardt at the Sioux Victory celebration at Pine Ridge in September 1945

John G. Neihardt with Black Elk's drum in the library of Sky-
rim, his home in Columbia, Missouri, 1958 or 1959

APPENDIX III
THE ORIGIN OF THE PEACE PIPE

During the Black Elk interviews, as John Neihardt has described in the Preface, "a faithful record of the narrative and conversations" was kept by his daughter Enid, a skilled stenographer, and a transcript of her notes lay before him when he wrote *Black Elk Speaks*. To illustrate concretely how Neihardt interpreted the spirit of Black Elk's narrative, this Appendix presents the transcript of Black Elk's oral account of the origin of the peace pipe for comparison with the corresponding passages in Neihardt's handwritten draft. (For comparison with the printed version, see page 456, line 15, through page 457, line 13.)

A comparison of the transcript and the draft reveals that Neihardt suppressed unnecessary details, altered awkward expressions, and introduced a tone of reverence and solemnity, transmuting the oral narrative into literature. For the general reader the omitted details clutter up the story, making it harder to follow; but for anthropologists, folklorists, and students of religion some of these details are significant. For example, from the beginning of the story the woman is seen to be carrying something, and when she arrives at the camp she first places this bundle down facing east. A dozen or so of these specific details which do not appear in the story can be found in the transcript.

The Transcript

ORIGINATION OF PEACE PIPE.

The Indians were in camp and they had a meeting to send scouts out to kill buffalo. The scouts were on top of a hill and as they looked to the north in the distance something was appearing. They were going on, but they wanted to find out what it was and they kept looking and finally it came closer; then they found out it was a woman. Then one of the men said: "That is a woman coming." One of them had bad thoughts of her and one of them said: "This is a sacred woman, throw all bad thots aside." She came up the hill where they were. She was

very beautiful, her long hair hanging down and she had on a beautiful buckskin coat. She put down what she was carrying and covered it up with sage. She knew what they had in their minds. She said: "Probably you do not know me, but if you want to do as you think, come." So the one said to the other, "That is what I told you, but you wouldn't listen to me." So one of the men went and just as he faced her, there was a cloud that came and covered them. The beautiful woman walked out of the cloud and stood there. Then the cloud blew off and the man was nothing but a skeleton with worms eating on it. That is what happened to him for being bad. She turned to the other one and said, "You shall go home and tell thy nation that I am coming. Therefore in the center of thy nation they shall build a big teepee and there I will come." So this man left at once and he was very scared, for his friend was a skeleton. He told the tribe what had happened and they all got excited and right away they prepared a place for her to come. They built a teepee right in the center and she was now in it. She put what she was carrying facing the East. All the people gathered right there. She sang a song as she entered the teepee:

> "With visible breath I am walking.
> A voice I am sending as I walk.
> In a sacred manner I am walking.
> With visible tracks I am walking.
> In a sacred manner I am walking."

Then she presented the pipe to the chief. It was an ordinary pipe but there was a calf carved in one side and there were twelve eagle feathers tied on with a grass that never breaks. She said: "Behold this, for you shall multiply with this and a good nation thou shalt be. You shall get nothing but good from this pipe, so I want it to be in the hands of a good man and the good shall have the privilege of seeing it, but the bad shall not have the privilege of seeing it." This pipe is still in the possession of the Sioux. The first man who kept it was a man by the name of High Hollow Horn. The pipe is handed down from son to son.

She taught them to "keep spirits" and if a man's son dies, the man keeps a piece of his son's hair. This woman was really a white buffalo. Thus the respect for the white buffalo. She told them that when there was no food they should offer this pipe to the Great Spirit and they would know from this pipe when they were going to have trouble. The pipe gets long at certain times and this means hard times. When it

gets short the times are good. After she went back she sang another song. As she went out of the teepee everyone saw a white buffalo kicking up his hind legs and leaving in a hurry snorting as it went.

The Handwritten Draft

There is a story about the way the pipe first came to us. A very long time ago, they say, two scouts were out looking for bison; and when they came to the top of a high hill and looked north they saw something coming a long way off, and when it came closer they cried out, "It is a woman!", and it was. Then one of the scouts, being foolish, had bad thoughts & spoke them; but the other said: "That is a sacred woman; throw all bad thoughts away."

When she came still closer, they saw that she wore a fine white buckskin dress, that her hair was very long and that she was young & very beautiful. And she knew their thoughts and said in a voice that was like singing: "You do not know me, but if you want to do as you think, you may come." And the foolish one went, but just as he stood before her, there was a white cloud that came & covered them. And the beautiful young woman came out of the white cloud, and when it blew away the foolish man was a skeleton covered with worms. Then the woman spoke to the one who was not foolish: "You shall go home & tell your people that I am coming & that a big tepee shall be built for me in the center of the nation." And the man who was very much afraid went quickly and told the people, who did at once as they were told; & there around the big tepee they waited for the sacred woman. And after a while she came, very beautiful & singing, and as she went into the tepee this is what she sang:

> "With visible breath I am walking.
> A voice I am sending as I walk.
> In a sacred manner I am walking.
> With visible tracks I am walking.
> In a sacred manner I am walking."

And as she sang there came from her mouth a white cloud that was sweet to smell.

Then she gave something to the chief, and it was a pipe with a bison calf carved on one side to mean the earth that bears & feeds us, and with twelve eagle feathers hanging from the stem to mean the sky and the twelve moons, and these were tied with a grass that never breaks.

"Behold!" she said. "With this you shall multiply & be a good nation. Nothing but good shall come from it. Only the hands of the good shall take care of it & the bad shall not even see it." Then she sang again & went out of the tepee, and as the people watched her going, suddenly it was a white bison galloping away & snorting, and soon it was gone.

This they tell, and whether it happened so or not I do not know; but if you think about it, you can see that it is true.

5a

away the foolish man was a skeleton
and the worms covered with worms.
Then the woman spoke to the one
who was not foolish: "You shall
go home & tell your people that
I am coming & that a big tepee
shall be built for me in the
center of the nation" and the
man who was very much afraid
went quickly and told the
people, and who they did at once as they were cold,
& there around the big tepee
they waited for the sacred woman
and after a while she came,
very beautiful & and
as the went into the tepee this
is what she sang,

"With visible breath I am walking.
A voice I am sending as I walk.
In a sacred manner I am walking.
With visible tracks I am walking.
In a sacred manner I am walking."
And as the sang a little cloud
came there came from her
mouth a white cloud that was sweet
to smell.

6 a

Then she gave something to the chief
and it was a pipe with a bison
calf carved on one side to mean the earth
that bears & feeds us, and with twelve eagle feathers
hanging from the stem to mean the sky and the twelve moons &
and these painted with a ⊕ grass that
never breaks. "Behold!" she
said, "With this you shall
multiply & be a good nation.
for nothing but good shall
come from it. Only the hands
of the good shall take care of
it & the bad shall not even
see it." Then she sang
again & went out of the tepee,
and as the people watched
her going, suddenly she
was a white bison
galloping away & snorting, and
soon it was gone ⊕
This they tell, and whether
it happened so or not, I do
not know, but if you think
about it, you can see that
it is true.

(back to bottom of page 4)

Further Reading

George Copway

George Copway also published *The Traditional History and Characteristic Sketches of the Ojibway Nation* (1850) and *Running Sketches of Men and Places, in England, France, Germany, Belgium, and Scotland* (1851). The best single account of his life is Donald B. Smith's "The Life of George Copway or Kah-ge-ga-gah-bowh (1818–1869)—and a Review of His Writings," *Journal of Canadian Studies* (23:3) 1988, 5–38.

Charles Eastman

Several of Charles Eastman's works remain in print, including *Indian Boyhood* (1902), *From the Deep Woods to Civilization* (1916), and *Wigwam Evenings* (1909). For an account of his life and writings, see Raymond Wilson's *Ohiyesa: Charles Eastman, Santee Sioux* (Urbana: University of Illinois Press, 1983).

Zitkala-Ša

Originally published in 1901, Zitkala-Šä's *Old Indian Legends* is available from the University of Nebraska Press.

Mourning Dove

Mourning Dove's 1927 novel, *Cogewea*, has been reprinted by the University of Nebraska Press. Jay Miller collected Mourning Dove's autobiographical materials and edited them into a coherent work, *Mourning Dove: A Salishan Autobiography* (Lincoln: University of Nebraska Press, 1990).

Black Elk

The transcripts of the interviews for *Black Elk Speaks* have been preserved. They are published in Raymond J. DeMallie's *The Sixth*

Grandfather: Black Elk's Teachings Given to John G. Neihardt (Lincoln: The University of Nebraska Press, 1984). DeMallie's introduction provides a comprehensive account of Black Elk's life and his ties to Neihardt. Two other books contain Black Elk materials. Neihardt's *When the Tree Flowered* (2nd edition, Lincoln: University of Nebraska Press, 19) includes material from the 1944 interviews. *The Sacred Pipe: Black Elk's Account of the Seven Rites of the Oglala Sioux*, recorded and edited by Joseph Epes Brown (Norman: University of Oklahoma Press, 1953), is based on interviews Brown conducted with Black Elk in the late 1940s.

Anthologies

John Bierhorst's *Four Masterworks of American Indian Literature* (Tucson: University of Arizona Press, 1984) provides in accessible English four of the earliest American Indian literary works: the Aztec *Quetzalcoatl*, the Iroquois *Ritual of Condolence, Cuceb* (a Maya prophecy), and *The Night Chant* of the Navajo.

Alan R. Velie's *American Indian Literature: An Anthology*, revised edition (Norman: University of Oklahoma Press, 1991) is widely used as a college textbook. So is Paula Gunn Allen's *Spider Woman's Granddaughters: Traditional Tales and Contemporary Writing by Native American Women* (Boston: Beacon Press, 1989), a highly praised and highly charged anthology.

Anthologies of American Indian poetry abound. Joseph Bruchac's *Songs from This Earth on Turtle's Back* (Greenfield Center, N.Y.: Greenfield Review Literary Center, 1983) and A. Grove Day's *The Sky Clears* (Lincoln: University of Nebraska Press, 1951) are two of the best.

Critical Studies

The single best survey of American Indian literature is A. LaVonne Brown Ruoff's *American Indian Literatures: An Introduction, Bibliographic Review, and Selected Bibliography* (New York: Modern Language Association, 1990). In turn, Ruoff recommends Andrew Wiget's *Native American Literature* (Boston: Twayne, 1985) as "the best overview of American Indian oral and written literatures." Paula Gunn Allen's *Studies in American Indian Literature: Critical Essays and Course Designs* (New York: Modern Language Association, 1983)

and Brian Swann and Arnold Krupat's *Recovering the Word: Essays on Native American Literature* (Berkeley: University of California Press, 1987) are excellent points of entry for students and scholars.

Kenneth Lincoln's *Native American Renaissance* (Berkeley: University of California Press, 1983) is a sympathetic introduction to twentieth-century American Indian literature. Paula Gunn Allen's *The Sacred Hoop: Recovering the Feminine in American Indian Traditions* (Boston: Beacon Press, 1986) provides much needed relief from the stiff stereotypes of Indian women promoted by popular culture. In *Other Destinies: Understanding the American Indian Novel* (Norman, Oklahoma: University of Oklahoma Press, 1992), Louis Owens shows what current literary critical approaches can contribute to appreciation of American Indian fiction. Arnold Krupat's books have been lightning rods for arguments about the history and interpretation of American Indian literature. His *For Those Who Come After: A Study of Native American Autobiography* (Berkeley: University of California Press, 1985) is fierce and informative.

Research Centers

The Smithsonian Institution in Washington, D.C., and the Darcy McNickle Center at the Newberry Library in Chicago are the nation's two premier repositories of research materials by and about American Indians.

Daniel F. Littlefield, Jr., and James W. Parins currently direct the Native American Archives at the University of Arkansas at Little Rock. They are painstakingly recovering the history of American Indian literature.

The American Indian Studies Research Institute at Indiana University, codirected by Raymond J. DeMallie and Douglas R. Parks is particularly devoted to anthropological research. Their contributions to the recovery and appreciation of American Indian oral literature cannot be overpraised.

The University of California has important research centers at Berkeley and UCLA, both distinguished for interdisciplinary work. Now at Berkeley, Anishinaabe author Gerald Vizenor has published much of importance—poems, autobiography, critical studies, and novels. He edits the American Indian Literature and Critical Studies series for the University of Oklahoma Press.